W9-BUP-262

Special Offer to Buyers of

Patent, Trademark, and Copyright Laws
2003 Edition

Receive 20% Off Related Titles

Qty	Code	Title	List Price	Discount Price
____	1378	Patent, Trademark, and Copyright Laws, '03 Ed.	$115.00	$ 92.00
____	1340	Legal Protection of Digital Information	$155.00	$124.00
____	1354	Patent, Trademark, and Copyright Regulations	$195.00	$156.00
____	1313	Trademark Dilution: Federal, State, and International Law	$275.00	$220.00
____	1381	Patents and the Federal Circuit, 6th Ed.	$425.00	$340.00
____	9326	Patent Prosecution: Practice and Procedure Before the U.S. Patent Office	$375.00	$300.00
____	9339	Electronic and Software Patents: Law and Practice	$415.00	$332.00
____	1129	Drafting Patent License Agreements, 4th Ed.	$125.00	$100.00
____	1240	Patent Law and Practice, 3rd Ed.	$ 95.00	$ 76.00
____	1342	International Patent Litigation: A Country-by-Country Analysis	$340.00	$272.00
____	9328	Computer and Intellectual Property Crime: Federal and State Law	$315.00	$252.00
____	9332	Patent Litigation Strategies Handbook	$245.00	$196.00
____	9356	Intellectual Property Law in Cyberspace	$245.00	$196.00
____	9225	Biotechnology and the Federal Circuit	$215.00	$172.00

If you are not completely satisfied with your order, simply return it with your invoice within 30 days for full cancellation of all charges. *If a method other than UPS Ground is requested for shipping (overnight, etc.), BNA Books will not refund shipping costs.*

SHIP AND BILL TO:

Name: _____

Organization: _____

Address: _____

City/State/Zip: _____

Telephone: _____ E-mail: _____

☐ Bill me. Each invoice includes the cost of books, your state's sales tax, and actual shipping/handling charges.
☐ Charge to my ☐ VISA ☐ MC ☐ AMEX

  Card #: _____ Expiration: _____

  Cardholder: _____

  Signature: _____

Foreign orders will be shipped via international courier. Customers are responsible for any applicable customs duty or tax.

In a Rush? Call our Order Department now at 1-800-960-1220 or fax to (732) 346-1624.

Overnight delivery is available on orders received before 10 a.m. E.S.T. for an additional fee.

Priority Code: PTR3DD

Order on free 30-day review.

NO POSTAGE
NECESSARY IF
MAILED IN THE
UNITED STATES

BUSINESS REPLY MAIL

FIRST-CLASS MAIL   PERMIT NO. 10089   WASHINGTON, DC

POSTAGE WILL BE PAID BY ADDRESSEE

BNA BOOKS, A DIVISION OF
THE BUREAU OF NATIONAL AFFAIRS, INC.
PO BOX 7814
EDISON NJ 08818-9856

PATENT
TRADEMARK
AND COPYRIGHT
LAWS

2003 Edition

Intellectual Property Titles from BNA Books

Biotechnology and the Federal Circuit
by Kenneth J. Burchfiel

*Computer and Intellectual Property
Crime: Federal and State Law*
by A. Hugh Scott

Copyright Law and Practice
by William F. Patry

Drafting Patent License Agreements
by Brian G. Brunsvold
and Dennis P. O'Reilley

*Electronic and Software Patents:
Law and Practice*
Steven W. Lundberg
and Stephen C. Durant,
Editors-in-Chief

*Intellectual Property Law
in Cyberspace*
by G. Peter Albert, Jr.
and Michael Best & Friedrich LLC

Intent-to-Use Trademark Practice
by Phillip H. Smith

*International Patent Litigation:
A Country-by-Country Analysis*
Edited by Michael N. Meller

*International Treaties on
Intellectual Property*
Edited by Marshall A. Leaffer

*Introduction to Intellectual
Property Law*
by Donald A. Gregory,
Charles W. Saber,
and Jon D. Grossman

Legal Protection of Digital Information
by Lee A. Hollaar

*McCarthy's Desk Encyclopedia of
Intellectual Property*
by J. Thomas McCarthy

Patents and the Federal Circuit
by Robert L. Harmon

Patent Law and Practice
by Herbert F. Schwartz

Patent Law Index
by Christopher M. Pickett

Patent Litigation Strategies Handbook
Barry L. Grossman and
Gary M. Hoffman,
Editors-in-Chief

*Patent Prosecution: Practice and
Procedure Before the
U.S. Patent Office*
by Irah H. Donner

*Patent, Trademark, and
Copyright Laws*
Edited by Jeffrey M. Samuels

*Patent, Trademark, and
Copyright Regulations*
Edited by James D. Crowne

*Products Comparison Manual
for Trademark Users*
by Francis M. Pinckney

*Trademark Dilution: Federal, State and
International Law*
by David S. Welkowitz

*Trade Secrets Protection
and Exploitation*
by Jerry Cohen
and Alan S. Gutterman

*For details on these titles visit the BNA Books home page on the Internet
at **www.bnabooks.com** or call **1-800-960-1220** to request a catalog.
All BNA books are available on a 30-day free examination basis.*

PATENT
TRADEMARK
AND COPYRIGHT
LAWS

2003 Edition

Current through February 10, 2003

Edited by
Jeffrey M. Samuels

**David L. Brennan Professor of Law and Director,
Center for Intellectual Property Law and Technology
University of Akron School of Law, Akron Ohio**

formerly
**Assistant Commissioner for Trademarks
U.S. Patent and Trademark Office**

and
Managing Editor
BNA's Patent, Trademark, and Copyright Journal

The Bureau of National Affairs, Inc., Washington, D.C.

Copyright © 1985, 1987, 1989, 1991–2003
The Bureau of National Affairs, Inc.

All rights reserved. No copyright claimed in government or public domain material. However, BNA does claim copyright in the compilation, selection, coordination, and/or arrangement of such material. Authorization to photocopy items for internal or personal use, or the internal or personal use of specific clients, is granted by BNA Books for libraries and other users registered with the Copyright Clearance Center (CCC) Transactional Reporting Service, provided that $1.00 per page is paid directly to CCC, 222 Rosewood Dr. Danvers, MA 01923. 1-57018-378-3/03/$0+$1.00.

1231 25th St., NW, Washington, D.C. 20037-1197

Library of Congress Catalog Number: 84-644547
International Standard Book Number: 1-57018-378-3
International Standard Serial Number: 0741-1219
Printed in the United States of America

Published by BNA Books

Summary Contents

Preface

Patent, Trademark, and Copyright Laws includes Title 35 (Patents), Title 17 (Copyrights), and Chapters 22 and 63 of Title 15 (Trademarks and Technology Innovation) of the United States Code. It also includes miscellaneous sections of the United States Code and other laws relating to intellectual property.

This 2003 edition is updated to reflect all statutory changes through February 10, 2003, including all changes enacted during the Second Session of the 107th Congress. These changes include the "Patent and Trademark Office Authorization Act of 2002," which, among other things, amends provisions of the patent law relating to reexamination and inter partes reexamination proceedings; the "Intellectual Property and High Technology Technical Amendments Act of 2002," which amends Section 102(e) of the Patent Act and makes certain technical amendments to the Patent Act; the "Technology, Education, and Copyright Authorization Act of 2002," which amends the Copyright Act relating to performances and displays of copyrighted works for educational uses; the "Madrid Protocol Implementation Act," which adds a new Title XII to the Lanham Act; and the "Small Webcaster Settlement Act of 2002," which amends Section 114 of the Copyright Act with respect to payment by webcasters for online streaming of copyrighted music.

More specifically, the following public laws are included in this edition:

Pub. L. 107-273 (signed into law on November 2, 2002), Title III of which amends the Patent Act in several significant respects, including reexamination practice and procedure and Section 102(e); amends the Trademark Act to implement the provisions of the Madrid Protocol; and amends the Copyright Act regarding educational uses of copyrighted works; and

Pub. L. 107-321 (signed into law on December 4, 2002), which amends Section 114 of the Copyright Act regarding the payment by webcasters for online streaming of copyrighted music.

Jeffrey M. Samuels
Akron, Ohio
February 2003

Detailed Contents

UNITED STATES CODE

TITLE 35—PATENTS

PART I—UNITED STATES PATENT AND TRADEMARK OFFICE

CHAPTER 1—ESTABLISHMENT, OFFICERS AND EMPLOYEES, FUNCTIONS

CHAPTER 2—PROCEEDINGS IN THE PATENT AND TRADEMARK OFFICE

PART II—PATENTABILITY OF INVENTIONS AND GRANT OF PATENTS

CHAPTER 12—EXAMINATION OF APPLICATION

CHAPTER 13—REVIEW OF PATENT AND TRADEMARK OFFICE DECISION

CHAPTER 14—ISSUE OF PATENT

PART III—PATENTS AND PROTECTION OF
PATENT RIGHTS

CHAPTER 25—AMENDMENT AND CORRECTION OF PATENTS

CHAPTER 26—OWNERSHIP AND ASSIGNMENT

CHAPTER 27—GOVERNMENT INTERESTS IN PATENTS

CHAPTER 28—INFRINGEMENT OF PATENTS

CHAPTER 29—REMEDIES FOR INFRINGEMENT OF PATENT,
AND OTHER ACTIONS

CHAPTER 30—PRIOR ART CITATIONS TO OFFICE AND
EX PARTE REEXAMINATION OF PATENTS

PART IV—PATENT COOPERATION TREATY

Chapter 35—Definitions

Chapter 36—International Stage

CHAPTER 37—NATIONAL STAGE

Detailed Contents

UNITED STATES CODE

TITLE 15, CHAPTER 22—TRADEMARKS

SUBCHAPTER II—THE SUPPLEMENTAL REGISTER

SUBCHAPTER III—GENERAL PROVISIONS

UNCODIFIED LANHAM ACT PROVISIONS

TITLE XII—THE MADRID PROTOCOL

Detailed Contents

UNITED STATES CODE

TITLE 15, CHAPTER 63—TECHNOLOGY INNOVATION

Detailed Contents
UNITED STATES CODE
TITLE 17—COPYRIGHTS

CHAPTER 2—COPYRIGHT OWNERSHIP AND TRANSFER

CHAPTER 3—DURATION OF COPYRIGHT

CHAPTER 4—COPYRIGHT NOTICE, DEPOSIT, AND REGISTRATION

CHAPTER 5—COPYRIGHT INFRINGEMENT AND REMEDIES

CHAPTER 6—MANUFACTURING REQUIREMENTS AND IMPORTATION

CHAPTER 7—COPYRIGHT OFFICE

CHAPTER 8—COPYRIGHT ARBITRATION ROYALTY PANELS

OTHER STATUTES

Note.—Some sections, or portions of sections, or other titles of the United States Code, of the District of Columbia Code, and of the Canal Zone Code, relating to patents, trademarks, copyrights, trade secrets, or to the Patent and Trademark Office and the Copyright Office, are reprinted or noted here for convenience. This collection does not purport to be complete.

FINDING LIST BY U.S.C. SECTION

The Constitutional Provisions

ART. 1, SEC. 8, CL. 3. The Congress shall have power . . . To regulate commerce with foreign nations, and among the several states, and with the Indian tribes.

ART. 1, SEC. 8, CL. 8. The Congress shall have power . . . To promote the progress of science and useful arts, by securing for limited times to authors and inventors the exclusive right to their respective writings and discoveries.

POPULAR NAMES OF SELECTED STATUTES

Economic Espionage Act of 1996
   Pub. L. 104-294; Oct. 11, 1996; 18 U.S.C. § 1831 et seq.
Fairness in Music Licensing Act of 1998
   Pub. L. 105-298; Oct. 27, 1998; 17 U.S.C. §§ 110,512.
Federal Trademark Dilution Act of 1995
   Pub. L. 104-98; Jan. 15, 1996; 15 U.S.C. §§ 1125, 1127
First Inventor Defense Act of 1999
   Pub. L. 106-113; Nov. 29, 1999; 35 U.S.C. § 273
Intellectual Property and High Technology Technical Amendments
   Pub. L. 107-273; Nov. 2, 2002; 35 U.S.C. § 1, et. seq.
Inventors' Rights Act of 1999
   Pub. L. 106-113; Nov. 29, 1999; 35 U.S.C. § 297
Madrid Protocol Implementation Act
   Pub. L. 107-273; Nov. 2, 2002; 15 U.S.C., Title XII
National Technology Transfer and Advancement Act
   Pub. L. 104-113; Mar. 7, 1996; 15 U.S.C. § 3701 et seq.
No Electronic Theft Act
   Pub. L. 105-147; Dec. 16, 1997; 17 U.S.C. § 506, 18 U.S.C. §§ 2319, 2319A, 2320
North American Free Trade Agreement Implementation Act
   Pub. L. 103-182; Dec. 8, 1993; 35 U.S.C. § 102, 15 U.S.C. §§ 1052(e), (f), 17
   U.S.C. § 104A
Online Copyright Infringement Liability Limitation Act
   Pub. L. 105-304; Oct. 28, 1998; 17 U.S.C. § 512
Optional Inter Partes Reexamination Procedure Act
   Pub. L. 106-113; Nov. 29, 1999, 35 U.S.C. §§ 311-318
Patent Act of 1952
   ch. 950, 66 Stat. 792; July 19, 1952; 35 U.S.C. § 1 et seq.
Patent and Trademark Office Efficiency Act
   Pub. L. 106-113; Nov. 29, 1999; 35 U.S.C. § 1 et seq.
Patent Law Amendments Act of 1984
   Pub. L. 98-622; Nov. 8, 1984; 35 U.S.C. § 1 et seq.
Patent Law Foreign Filing Amendments Act of 1988
   Pub. L. 100-418, Title IX, Subtitle B, § 9101; Aug. 23, 1988; 35 U.S.C. § 184 et
   seq.
Plant Patent Amendments Act of 1998
   Pub. L. 105-289; Oct. 27, 1998; 35 U.S.C. § 6 3 .
Process Patent Amendments Act of 1988
   Pub. L. 100-418; Title IX, Subtitle A, Aug. 23, 1988; 35 U.S.C. §§ 271, 287

Satellite Home Viewer Act of 1988
    Pub. L. 100-667; Title II, Nov. 16, 1988; 17 U.S.C. § 119
Satellite Home Viewer Act of 1994
    Pub. L. 103-369; Oct. 18, 1994; 17 U.S.C. § 119
Satellite Home Viewer Improvement Act of 1999
    Pub. L. 106-113; Nov. 29, 1999; 17 U.S.C. §§ 119, 122.
Semiconductor Chip Protection Act of 1984
    Pub. L. 98-620; Title III, Nov. 8, 1984; 17 U.S.C. § 901
Semiconductor International Protection Extension Act of 1991
    Pub. L. 102-64; June 28, 1991; 17 U.S.C. § 901
Small Webcaster Settlement Act of 2002
    Pub. L. 107-321, Dec. 4, 2002, 17 U.S.C. § 1 1 4
Sonny Bono Copyright Term Extension Act
    Pub. L. 105-298; Oct. 27, 1998; 17 U.S.C. § 1 0 1   e t .   s e q .
Stevenson-Wydler Technology Innovation Act of 1980
    Pub. L. 96-480; Oct. 21, 1980; 15 U.S.C. § 3701 et. seq.
Technology, Education, and Copyright Harmonization Act of 2002
    Pub. L. 107-273, Nov. 2, 2002; 17 U.S.C. § 1 1 0
Technology Transfer Commercialization Act of 2000
    Pub. L. 106-404; Nov. 1, 2000; 35 U.S.C. § 2 0 0 et. seq.
Trademark (Lanham) Act of 1946
    ch. 540, 60 Stat. 427; July 5, 1946; 15 U.S.C. § 1051 et seq.
Trademark Amendments Act of 1999
    Pub. L. 106-43; Aug. 5, 1999; 15 U.S.C. § § 1052, 1122, 1125
Trademark Clarification Act of 1984
    Pub. L. 98-620; Title I, Nov. 8, 1984; 15 U.S.C. § 1064
Trademark Counterfeiting Act of 1984
    Pub. L. 98-473, Title II, ch. XV, Oct. 12, 1984, 18 U.S.C. § 2320
Trademark Law Treaty Implementation Act
    Pub. L. 105-298, Oct. 27, 1998; 15 U.S.C. § 1051 et. seq.
Trademark Law Revision Act of 1988
    Pub. L. 100-667; Title 1, Nov. 16, 1988; 15 U.S.C. § 1051 et seq.
Trademark Remedy Clarification Act
    Pub. L. 102-542; Oct. 27, 1992; 15 U.S.C. § 1122
Uruguay Round Agreements Act
    Pub. L. 103-465; Dec. 8, 1994; 35 U.S.C. §§ 104, 111, 154, 271, 15 U.S.C.
    §§ 1052(a), 1127, 17 U.S.C. §§ 104A, 1101 et seq.

Vessel Hull Design Protection Act
  Pub. L. 105-304; Oct. 28, 1998; 17 U.S.C. §§ 1301-1332.
WIPO Copyright and Performances and Phonograms Treaties Implementation Act of 1998
  Pub. L. 105-304; Oct. 28, 1998; 17 U.S.C. §§ 1201-1205.
Work Made For Hire and Copyright Corrections Act of 2000
  Pub. L. 106-379; Oct. 27, 2000; 17 U.S.C. §101 et. seq.

Part 1

PATENTS

UNITED STATES CODE

TITLE 35 — PATENTS

PART I — UNITED STATES PATENT AND TRADEMARK OFFICE

PART II — PATENTABILITY OF INVENTIONS AND GRANT OF PATENTS

PART III — PATENTS AND PROTECTION OF PATENT RIGHTS

PART IV — PATENT COOPERATION TREATY

UNITED STATES CODE

TITLE 35—PATENTS

PART I—UNITED STATES PATENT AND TRADEMARK OFFICE

CHAPTER 1—ESTABLISHMENT, OFFICERS AND EMPLOYEES, FUNCTIONS

§ 1   Establishment

(a) *Establishment.*—The United States Patent and Trademark Office is established as an agency of the United States, within the Department of Commerce. In carrying out its functions, the United States Patent and Trademark Office shall be subject to the policy direction of the Secretary of Commerce, but otherwise shall retain responsibility for decisions regarding the management and administration of its operations and shall exercise independent control of its budget allocations and expenditures, personnel decisions and processes, procurements, and other administrative and management functions in accordance with this title and applicable provisions of law. Those operations designed to grant and issue patents and those operations which are designed to facilitate the registration of trademarks shall be treated as separate operating units within the Office.

(b) *Offices.*—The United States Patent and Trademark Office shall maintain its principal office in the metropolitan Washington, D.C., area, for the service of process and papers and for the purpose of carrying out its functions. The United States Patent and Trademark Office shall be deemed, for purposes of venue in civil actions, to be a resident of the district in which its principal office is located, except where jurisdiction is otherwise provided by law. The United States Patent and Trademark Office may establish satellite offices in such other places in the United States as it considers necessary and appropriate in the conduct of its business.

(c) *Reference.*—For purposes of this title, the United States Patent and Trademark Office shall also be referred to as the "Office" and the "Patent and Trademark Office".

(July 19, 1952, ch. 950, §1, 66 Stat. 792; Jan. 2, 1975, Pub. L. 93-596, §1, 88 Stat. 1949; Nov. 29, 1999, Pub. L. 106-113, §4711, 113 Stat. 1501A-572.)

§ 2   Powers and duties

(a) *In general.*—The United States Patent and Trademark Office, subject to the policy direction of the Secretary of Commerce—

(1) shall be responsible for the granting and issuing of patents and the registration of trademarks; and

(2) shall be responsible for disseminating to the public information with respect to patents and trademarks.

(b) *Specific powers.*—The Office—

(1) shall adopt and use a seal of the Office, which shall be judicially noticed and with which letters patent, certificates of trademark registrations, and papers issued by the Office shall be authenticated;

(2) may establish regulations, not inconsistent with law, which—

(A) shall govern the conduct of proceedings in the Office;

(B) shall be made in accordance with section 553 of title 5;

(C) shall facilitate and expedite the processing of patent applications, particularly those which can be filed, stored, processed, searched, and retrieved electronically, subject to the provisions of section 122 relating to the confidential status of applications;

(D) may govern the recognition and conduct of agents, attorneys, or other persons representing applicants or other parties before the Office, and may require them, before being recognized as representatives of applicants or other persons, to show that they are of good moral character and reputation and are possessed of the necessary qualifications to render to applicants or other persons valuable service, advice, and assistance in the presentation or prosecution of their applications or other business before the Office;

(E) shall recognize the public interest in continuing to safeguard broad access to the United States patent system through the reduced fee structure for small entities under section 41(h)(1) of this title; and

(F) provide for the development of a performance-based process that includes quantitative and qualitative measures and standards for evaluating cost-effectiveness and is consistent with the principles of impartiality and competitiveness;

(3) may acquire, construct, purchase, lease, hold, manage, operate, improve, alter, and renovate any real, personal, or mixed property, or any interest therein, as it considers necessary to carry out its functions;

(4)(A) may make such purchases, contracts for the construction, maintenance, or management and operation of facilities, and contracts for supplies or services, without regard to the provisions of the Federal Property and Administrative Services Act of 1949 (40 U.S.C. 471 et seq.), the Public Buildings Act (40 U.S.C. 601 et seq.), and the Stewart B. McKinney Homeless Assistance Act (42 U.S.C. 11301 et seq.); and

(B) may enter into and perform such purchases and contracts for printing services, including the process of composition, plate-making, presswork, silk screen processes, binding, microform, and the products of such processes, as it considers necessary to carry out the functions of the Office, without regard to sections 501 through 517 and 1101 through 1123 of title 44;

(5) may use, with their consent, services, equipment, personnel, and facilities of other departments, agencies, and instrumentalities of the Federal Government, on a reimbursable basis, and cooperate with such other departments, agencies, and instrumentalities in the establishment and use of services, equipment, and facilities of the Office;

(6) may, when the Director determines that it is practicable, efficient, and cost-effective to do so, use, with the consent of the United States and the agency, instrumentality, Patent and Trademark Office, or international organization concerned, the services, records, facilities, or personnel of any State or local government agency or instrumentality or foreign patent and trademark office or international organization to perform functions on its behalf;

(7) may retain and use all of its revenues and receipts, including revenues from the sale, lease, or disposal of any real, personal, or mixed property, or any interest therein, of the Office;

(8) shall advise the President, through the Secretary of Commerce, on national and certain international intellectual property policy issues;

(9) shall advise Federal departments and agencies on matters of intellectual property policy in the United States and intellectual property protection in other countries;

(10) shall provide guidance, as appropriate, with respect to proposals by agencies to assist foreign governments and international intergovernmental organizations on matters of intellectual property protection;

(11) may conduct programs, studies, or exchanges of items or services regarding domestic and international intellectual property law and the effectiveness of intellectual property protection domestically and throughout the world;

(12)(A) shall advise the Secretary of Commerce on programs and studies relating to intellectual property policy that are conducted, or authorized to be conducted, cooperatively with foreign intellectual property offices and international intergovernmental organizations; and

(B) may conduct programs and studies described in subparagraph (A); and

(13)(A) in coordination with the Department of State, may conduct programs and studies cooperatively with foreign intellectual property offices and international intergovernmental organizations; and

(B) with the concurrence of the Secretary of State, may authorize the transfer of not to exceed $100,000 in any year to the Department of State for the purpose of making special payments to international intergovernmental organizations for studies and programs for advancing international cooperation concerning patents, trademarks, and other matters.

(c) *Clarification of specific powers.*—(1) The special payments under subsection (b)(13)(B) shall be in addition to any other payments or contributions to international organizations described in subsection (b)(13)(B) and shall not be subject to any limitations imposed by law on the amounts of such other payments or contributions by the United States Government.

(2) Nothing in subsection (b) shall derogate from the duties of the Secretary of State or from the duties of the United States Trade Representative as set forth in section 141 of the Trade Act of 1974 (19 U.S.C. 2171).

(3) Nothing in subsection (b) shall derogate from the duties and functions of the Register of Copyrights or otherwise alter current authorities relating to copyright matters.

(4) In exercising the Director's powers under paragraphs (3) and (4)(A) of subsection (b), the Director shall consult with the Administrator of General Services.

(5) In exercising the Director's powers and duties under this section, the Director shall consult with the Register of Copyrights on all copyright and related matters.

(d) *Construction.*—Nothing in this section shall be construed to nullify, void, cancel, or interrupt any pending request-for-proposal let or contract issued by the General Services Administration for the specific purpose of relocating or leasing space to the United States Patent and Trademark Office.

(July 19, 1952, ch. 950, §1, 66 Stat. 792; Jan. 2, 1975, Pub. L. 93-596, §1, 88 Stat. 1949; Nov. 29, 1999, Pub. L. 106-113, §4712, 113 Stat. 1501A-572; Nov. 2, 2002, Pub. L. 107-273, §13206, 116 Stat. 1904.)

§ 3 Officers and employees

(a) Under Secretary and Director—

(1) *In general.*—The powers and duties of the United States Patent and Trademark Office shall be vested in an Under Secretary of Commerce for Intellectual Property and Director of the United States Patent and Trademark Office (in this title referred to as the "Director"), who shall be a citizen of the United States and who shall be appointed by the President, by and with the advice and consent of the Senate. The Director shall be a person who has a professional background and experience in patent or trademark law.

(2) *Duties.*—

(A) *In general.*—The Director shall be responsible for providing policy direction and management supervision for the Office and for the issuance of patents and the registration of trademarks. The Director shall perform these duties in a fair, impartial, and equitable manner.

(B) *Consulting with the Public Advisory Committees.*—The Director shall consult with the Patent Public Advisory Committee established in section 5 on a regular basis on matters relating to the patent operations of the Office, shall consult with the Trademark Public Advisory Committee established in section 5 on a regular basis on matters relating to the trademark operations of the Office, and shall consult with the respective Public Advisory

Committee before submitting budgetary proposals to the Office of Management and Budget or changing or proposing to change patent or trademark user fees or patent or trademark regulations which are subject to the requirement to provide notice and opportunity for public comment under section 553 of title 5, as the case may be.

(3) *Oath.*—The Director shall, before taking office, take an oath to discharge faithfully the duties of the Office.

(4) *Removal.*—The Director may be removed from office by the President. The President shall provide notification of any such removal to both Houses of Congress.

(b) Officers and Employees of the Office—

(1) *Deputy Under Secretary and Deputy Director.*—The Secretary of Commerce, upon nomination by the Director, shall appoint a Deputy Under Secretary of Commerce for Intellectual Property and Deputy Director of the United States Patent and Trademark Office who shall be vested with the authority to act in the capacity of the Director in the event of the absence or incapacity of the Director. The Deputy Director shall be a citizen of the United States who has a professional background and experience in patent or trademark law.

(2) *Commissioners.*—

(A) *Appointment and duties.*—The Secretary of Commerce shall appoint a Commissioner for Patents and a Commissioner for Trademarks, without regard to chapter 33, 51, or 53 of title 5. The Commissioner for Patents shall be a citizen of the United States with demonstrated management ability and professional background and experience in patent law and serve for a term of 5 years. The Commissioner for Trademarks shall be a citizen of the United States with demonstrated management ability and professional background and experience in trademark law and serve for a term of 5 years. The Commissioner for Patents and the Commissioner for Trademarks shall serve as the chief operating officers for the operations of the Office relating to patents and trademarks, respectively, and shall be responsible for the management and direction of all aspects of the activities of the Office that affect the administration of patent and trademark operations, respectively. The Secretary may reappoint a Commissioner to subsequent terms of 5 years as long as the performance of the Commissioner as set forth in the performance agreement in subparagraph (B) is satisfactory.

(B) *Salary and performance agreement.*—The Commissioners shall be paid an annual rate of basic pay not to exceed the maximum rate of basic pay for the Senior Executive Service established under section 5382 of title 5, including any applicable locality-based comparability payment that may be authorized under section 5304(h)(2)(C) of title 5. The compensation of the Commissioners shall be considered, for purposes of section 207(c)(2)(A) of title 18, to be the equivalent of that described under clause (ii) of section 207(c)(2)(A) of title 18. In addition, the Commissioners may receive a bonus in an amount of up to, but not in excess of, 50 percent of the Commissioners' annual rate of basic pay, based upon an evaluation by the Secretary of Commerce, acting through the Director, of the Commissioners' performance as defined in an annual performance agreement between the Commissioners and the Secretary. The annual performance agreements shall incorporate measurable organization and individual goals in key operational areas as delineated in an annual performance plan agreed to by the Commissioners and the Secretary. Payment of a bonus under this subparagraph may be made to the Commissioners only to the extent that such payment does not cause the Commissioners' total aggregate compensation in a calendar year to equal or exceed the amount of the salary of the Vice President under section 104 of title 3.

(C) *Removal.*—The Commissioners may be removed from office by the Secretary for misconduct or nonsatisfactory performance under the performance agreement described in subparagraph (B), without regard to the provisions of title 5. The Secretary shall provide notification of any such removal to both Houses of Congress.

(3) *Other officers and employees.*—The Director shall—

(A) appoint such officers, employees (including attorneys), and agents of the Office as the Director considers necessary to carry out the functions of the Office; and

(B) define the title, authority, and duties of such officers and employees and delegate to them such of the powers vested in the Office as the Director may determine.

The Office shall not be subject to any administratively or statutorily imposed limitation on positions or personnel, and no positions or personnel of the Office shall be taken into account for purposes of applying any such limitation.

(4) *Training of examiners.*—The Office shall submit to the Congress a proposal to provide an incentive program to retain as employees patent and trademark examiners of the primary examiner grade or higher who are eligible for retirement, for the sole purpose of training patent and trademark examiners.

(5) *National security positions.*—The Director, in consultation with the Director of the Office of Personnel Management, shall maintain a program for identifying national security positions and providing for appropriate security clearances, in order to maintain the secrecy of certain inventions, as described in section 181, and to prevent disclosure of sensitive and strategic information in the interest of national security.

(c) *Continued applicability of Title 5.*—Officers and employees of the Office shall be subject to the provisions of title 5 relating to Federal employees.

(d) *Adoption of existing labor agreements.*—The Office shall adopt all labor agreements which are in effect, as of the day before the effective date of the Patent and Trademark Office Efficiency Act, with respect to such Office (as then in effect).

(e) *Carryover of personnel.*—

(1) *From PTO.*—Effective as of the effective date of the Patent and Trademark Office Efficiency Act, all officers and employees of the Patent and Trademark Office on the day before such effective date

shall become officers and employees of the Office, without a break in service.

(2) *Other personnel.*—Any individual who, on the day before the effective date of the Patent and Trademark Office Efficiency Act, is an officer or employee of the Department of Commerce (other than an officer or employee under paragraph (1)) shall be transferred to the Office, as necessary to carry out the purposes of this Act, if—

(A) such individual serves in a position for which a major function is the performance of work reimbursed by the Patent and Trademark Office, as determined by the Secretary of Commerce;

(B) such individual serves in a position that performed work in support of the Patent and Trademark Office during at least half of the incumbent's work time, as determined by the Secretary of Commerce; or

(C) such transfer would be in the interest of the Office, as determined by the Secretary of Commerce in consultation with the Director.

Any transfer under this paragraph shall be effective as of the same effective date as referred to in paragraph (1), and shall be made without a break in service.

(f) *Transition provisions.*—

(1) *Interim appointment of Director.*—On or after the effective date of the Patent and Trademark Office Efficiency Act, the President shall appoint an individual to serve as the Director until the date on which a Director qualifies under subsection (a). The President shall not make more than one such appointment under this subsection.

(2) *Continuation in office of certain officers.*—(A) The individual serving as the Assistant Commissioner for Patents on the day before the effective date of the Patent and Trademark Office Efficiency Act may serve as the Commissioner for Patents until the date on which a Commissioner for Patents is appointed under subsection (b).

(B) The individual serving as the Assistant Commissioner for Trademarks on the day before the effective date of the Patent and Trademark Office Efficiency Act may serve as the Commissioner for

Trademarks until the date on which a Commissioner for Trademarks is appointed under subsection (b).

(July 19, 1952, ch. 950, §1, 66 Stat. 792; Sept. 6, 1958, Pub. L. 85-933, §1, 72 Stat. 1793; Sept. 23, 1959, Pub. L. 86-370, §1(a), 73 Stat. 650; Aug. 14, 1964, Pub. L. 88-426, §305(26), 78 Stat. 425; Jan. 2, 1975, Pub. L. 93-596, §1, 88 Stat. 1949; Jan. 2, 1975, Pub. L. 93-601, §1, 88 Stat. 1956; Aug. 27, 1982, Pub. L. 97-247, §4, 96 Stat. 319; Oct. 15, 1982, Pub. L. 97-366, §4, 96 Stat. 1760; Nov. 8, 1984, Pub. L. 98-622, §405, 98 Stat. 3392; Oct. 28, 1998, Pub. L. 105-304, §401(a), 112 Stat. 2887; Aug. 5, 1999, Pub. L. 106-44, §2(c), 113 Stat. 223; Nov. 29, 1999, Pub. L. 106-113, §4713, 113 Stat. 1501A-575; Nov. 2, 2002, Pub. L. 107-273, §13206, 116 Stat. 1904.)

§ 4   Restrictions on officers and employees as to interest in patents

Officers and employees of the Patent and Trademark Office shall be incapable, during the period of their appointments and for one year thereafter, of applying for a patent and of acquiring, directly or indirectly, except by inheritance or bequest, any patent or any right or interest in any patent, issued or to be issued by the Office. In patents applied for thereafter they shall not be entitled to any priority date earlier than one year after the termination of their appointment.

(July 19, 1952, ch. 950, §1, 66 Stat. 793; Jan. 2, 1975, Pub. L. 93-596, §1, 88 Stat. 1949.)

§ 5   Patent and Trademark Office Public Advisory Committees

(a) *Establishment of Public Advisory Committees.—*

(1) *Appointment.*—The United States Patent and Trademark Office shall have a Patent Public Advisory Committee and a Trademark Public Advisory Committee, each of which shall have nine voting members who shall be appointed by the Secretary of Commerce and serve at the pleasure of the Secretary of Commerce. Members of each Public Advisory Committee shall be appointed for a term of 3 years, except that of the members first appointed, three shall be appointed for a term of 1 year, and three shall be appointed for a term of 2 years. In making appointments to each Committee, the Secretary of Commerce shall consider the risk of loss of competitive advantage in international commerce or other harm to United States companies as a result of such appointments.

(2) *Chair.*—The Secretary shall designate a chair of each Advisory Committee, whose term as chair shall be for 3 years.

(3) *Timing of appointments.*—Initial appointments to each Advisory Committee shall be made within 3 months after the effective date of the Patent and Trademark Office Efficiency Act. Vacancies shall be filled within 3 months after they occur.

(b) *Basis for appointments.*—Members of each Advisory Committee—

(1) shall be citizens of the United States who shall be chosen so as to represent the interests of diverse users of the United States Patent and Trademark Office with respect to patents, in the case of the Patent Public Advisory Committee, and with respect to trademarks, in the case of the Trademark Public Advisory Committee;

(2) shall include members who represent small and large entity applicants located in the United States in proportion to the number of applications filed by such applicants, but in no case shall members who represent small entity patent applicants, including small business concerns, independent inventors, and nonprofit organizations, constitute less than 25 percent of the members of the Patent Public Advisory Committee, and such members shall include at least one independent inventor; and

(3) shall include individuals with substantial background and achievement in finance, management, labor relations, science, technology, and office automation.

In addition to the voting members, each Advisory Committee shall include a representative of each labor organization recognized by the United States Patent and Trademark Office. Such representatives shall be nonvoting members of the Advisory Committee to which they are appointed.

(c) *Meetings.*—Each Advisory Committee shall meet at the call of the chair to consider an agenda set by the chair.

(d) *Duties.*—Each Advisory Committee shall—

(1) review the policies, goals, performance, budget, and user fees of the United States Patent and Trademark Office with respect to patents, in the case of the Patent Public Advisory Committee, and with

respect to Trademarks, in the case of the Trademark Public Advisory Committee, and advise the Director on these matters;

(2) within 60 days after the end of each fiscal year—

(A) prepare an annual report on the matters referred to in paragraph (1);

(B) transmit the report to the Secretary of Commerce, the President, and the Committees on the Judiciary of the Senate and the House of Representatives; and

(C) publish the report in the Official Gazette of the United States Patent and Trademark Office.

(e) *Compensation.*—Each member of each Advisory Committee shall be compensated for each day (including travel time) during which such member is attending meetings or conferences of that Advisory Committee or otherwise engaged in the business of that Advisory Committee, at the rate which is the daily equivalent of the annual rate of basic pay in effect for level III of the Executive Schedule under section 5314 of title 5. While away from such member's home or regular place of business such member shall be allowed travel expenses, including per diem in lieu of subsistence, as authorized by section 5703 of title 5.

(f) *Access to information.*—Members of each Advisory Committee shall be provided access to records and information in the United States Patent and Trademark Office, except for personnel or other privileged information and information concerning patent applications required to be kept in confidence by section 122.

(g) *Applicability of certain ethics laws.*—Members of each Advisory Committee shall be special Government employees within the meaning of section 202 of title 18.

(h) *Inapplicability of Federal Advisory Committee Act.*—The Federal Advisory Committee Act (5 U.S.C. App.) shall not apply to each Advisory Committee.

(i) *Open meetings.*—The meetings of each Advisory Committee shall be open to the public, except that each Advisory Committee may by majority vote meet in executive session when considering personnel, privileged, or other confidential information.

(j) *Inapplicability of Patent Prohibition.*—Section 4 shall not apply to voting members of the Advisory Committees.

(Nov. 29, 1999, Pub. L. 106-113, §4714, 113 Stat. 1501A-578; Nov. 2, 2002, Pub. L. 107-273, §§13203, 13206, 116 Stat. 1902, 1904.)

§ 6 Board of Patent Appeals and Interferences

(a) *Establishment and composition.*—There shall be in the United States Patent and Trademark Office a Board of Patent Appeals and Interferences. The Director, the Deputy Commissioner,* the Commissioner for Patents, the Commissioner for Trademarks, and the administrative patent judges shall constitute the Board. The administrative patent judges shall be persons of competent legal knowledge and scientific ability who are appointed by the Director.

(b) *Duties.*—The Board of Patent Appeals and Interferences shall, on written appeal of an applicant, review adverse decisions of examiners upon applications for patents and shall determine priority and patentability of invention in interferences declared under section 135(a). Each appeal and interference shall be heard by at least three members of the Board, who shall be designated by the Director. Only the Board of Patent Appeals and Interferences may grant rehearings.

(July 19, 1952, ch. 950, §1, 66 Stat. 793; Sept. 6, 1958, Pub. L. 85-933, §2, 72 Stat. 1793; Sept. 23, 1959, Pub. L. 86-370, §1(b), 73 Stat. 650; Jan. 2, 1975, Pub. L. 93-596, §1, 88 Stat. 1949; Jan. 2, 1975, Pub. L. 93-601, §2, 88 Stat. 1956; Nov. 8, 1984, Pub. L. 98-622, §201(a), 98 Stat. 3386; Nov. 29, 1999, Pub. L. 106-113, §4717, 113 Stat. 1501A-580; Nov. 2, 2002, Pub. L. 107-273, §13203, 116 Stat. 1902.)

§ 7 Library

The Director shall maintain a library of scientific and other works and periodicals, both foreign and domestic, in the Patent and Trademark office to aid the officers in the discharge of their duties.

---

* *Ed. Note:* Section 13203(a) of Pub. L. 107-273 provides for inserting "the Deputy Commissioner". Presumably, however, the term "the Deputy Director" was intended. See 35 U.S.C. §3(b)(1).

(July 19, 1952, ch. 950, §1, 66 Stat. 793; Jan. 2, 1975, Pub. L. 93-596, §1, 88 Stat. 1949; Nov. 29, 1999, Pub. L. 106-113, §4717, 113 Stat. 1501A-582.)

§ 8 Classification of patents

The Director may revise and maintain the classification by subject matter of United States letters patent, and such other patents and printed publications as may be necessary or practicable, for the purpose of determining with readiness and accuracy the novelty of inventions for which applications for patent are filed.

(July 19, 1952, ch. 950, §1, 66 Stat. 784; Nov. 29, 1999, Pub. L. 106-113, §4717, 113 Stat. 1501A-582.)

§ 9 Certified copies of records

The Director may furnish certified copies of specifications and drawings of patents issued by the Patent and Trademark Office, and of other records available either to the public or to the person applying therefor.

(July 19, 1952, ch. 950, §1, 66 Stat. 794; Jan. 2, 1975, Pub. L. 93-596, §1, 88 Stat. 1949; Nov. 29, 1999, Pub. L. 106-113, §4717, 113 Stat. 1501A-582.)

§ 10 Publications

(a) The Director may publish in printed, typewritten, or electronic form, the following:

1. Patents and published applications for patents, including specifications and drawings, together with copies of the same. The Patent and Trademark Office may print the headings of the drawings for patents for the purpose of photolithography.

2. Certificates of trademark registrations, including statements and drawings, together with copies of the same.

3. The Official Gazette of the United States Patent and Trademark Office.

4. Annual indexes of patents and patentees, and of trademarks and registrants.

5. Annual volumes of decisions in patent and trademark cases.

6. Pamphlet copies of the patent laws and rules of practice, laws and rules relating to trademarks, and circulars or other publications relating to the business of the Office.

(b) The Director may exchange any of the publications specified in items 3, 4, 5, and 6 of subsection (a) of this section for publications desirable for the use of the Patent and Trademark Office.

(July 19, 1952, ch. 950, §1, 66 Stat. 794; Jan. 2, 1975, Pub. L. 93-596, §1, 88 Stat. 1949; Nov. 29, 1999, Pub. L. 106-113, §§4507, 4717, 4804, 113 Stat. 1501A-565, 580, 589; Nov. 2, 2002, Pub. L. 107-273, §13205, 116 Stat. 1902.)

§ 11 Exchange of copies of patents and applications with foreign countries

The Director may exchange copies of specifications and drawings of United States patents and published applications for patents for those of foreign countries. The Director shall not enter into an agreement to provide such copies of specifications and drawings of United States patents and applications to a foreign country, other than a NAFTA country or a WTO member country, without the express authorization of the Secretary of Commerce. For purposes of this section, the terms `NAFTA country' and `WTO member country' have the meanings given those terms in section 104(b).

(July 19, 1952, ch. 950, §1, 66 Stat. 794; Nov. 29, 1999, Pub. L. 106-113, §§4507, 4717, 4808, 113 Stat. 1501A-565, 580, 589; Nov. 2, 2002, Pub. L. 107-273, §13205, 116 Stat. 1902.)

§ 12 Copies of patents and applications for public libraries

The Director may supply copies of specifications and drawings of patents in printed or electronic form and published applications for patents to public libraries in the United States which shall maintain such copies for the use of the public, at the rate for each year's issue established for this purpose in section 41(d) of this title.

(July 19, 1952, ch. 950, §1, 66 Stat. 794; Aug. 27, 1982, Pub. L. 97-247, §15, 96 Stat. 321; Nov. 29, 1999, Pub. L. 106-113, §§4507, 4717, 4804, 113 Stat. 1501A-565, 580, 589; Nov. 2, 2002, Pub. L. 107-273, §13205, 116 Stat. 1902.)

§ 13 Annual report to Congress

The Director shall report to the Congress, not later than 180 days after the end of each fiscal year, the moneys received and expended by the Office, the purposes for which the moneys were spent, the quality and quantity of the work of the Office, the nature of training provided to examiners, the evaluation of the Commissioner of Patents and the Commissioner of Trademarks by the Secretary of Commerce, the compensation of the Commissioners, and other information relating to the Office.

(July 19, 1952, ch. 950, §1, 66 Stat. 794, Pub. L. 106-113, §§4717, 4718, 113 Stat. 1501A-581.)

CHAPTER 2—PROCEEDINGS IN THE PATENT AND TRADEMARK OFFICE

SEC.

§ 21 Filing date and day for taking action

(a) The Director may by rule prescribe that any paper or fee required to be filed in the Patent and Trademark Office will be considered filed in the Office on the date on which it was deposited with the United States Postal Service or would have been deposited with the United States Postal Service but for postal service interruptions or emergencies designated by the Director.

(b) When the day, or the last day, for taking any action or paying any fee in the United States Patent and Trademark Office falls on Saturday, Sunday, or a federal holiday within the District of Columbia, the action may be taken, or the fee paid, on the next succeeding secular or business day.

(July 19, 1952, ch. 950, §1, 66 Stat. 794; Jan. 2, 1975, Pub. L. 93-596, §1, 88 Stat. 1949; Aug. 27, 1982, Pub. L. 97-247, §12, 96 Stat. 321; Nov. 2, 2002, Pub. L. 107-273, §13206, 116 Stat. 1904.)

§ 22   Printing of papers filed

The Director may require papers filed in the Patent and Trademark Office to be printed, typewritten, or on an electronic medium.

(July 19, 1952, ch. 950, §1, 66 Stat. 795; Jan. 2, 1975, Pub. L. 93-596, §1, 88 Stat. 1949; Nov. 29, 1999, Pub. L. 106-113, §4804, 113 Stat. 1501A-589.)

§ 23   Testimony in Patent and Trademark Office cases

The Director may establish rules for taking affidavits and depositions required in cases in the Patent and Trademark Office. Any officer authorized by law to take depositions to be used in the courts of the United States, or of the State where he resides, may take such affidavits and depositions.

(July 19, 1952, ch. 950, §1, 66 Stat. 795; Jan. 2, 1975, Pub. L. 93-596, §1, 88 Stat. 1949.)

§ 24   Subpoenas, witnesses

The clerk of any United States court for the district wherein testimony is to be taken for use in any contested case in the Patent and Trademark Office, shall, upon the application of any party thereto, issue a subpoena for any witness residing or being within such district, commanding him to appear and testify before an officer in such district authorized to take depositions and affidavits, at the time and place stated in the subpoena. The provisions of the Federal Rules of Civil Procedure relating to the attendance of witnesses and to the production of documents and things shall apply to contested cases in the Patent and Trademark Office.

Every witness subpoenaed and in attendance shall be allowed the fees and traveling expenses allowed to witnesses attending the United States district courts.

A judge of a court whose clerk issued a subpoena may enforce obedience to the process or punish disobedience as in other like cases, on proof that a witness, served with such subpoena, neglected or refused to appear or to testify. No witness shall be deemed guilty of contempt for disobeying such subpoena unless his fees and traveling expenses in going to, and returning from, and one day's attendance at the place of examination, are paid or tendered him at the time of the service of the subpoena; nor for refusing to disclose any secret matter except upon appropriate order of the court which issued the subpoena.

(July 19, 1952, ch. 950, §1, 66 Stat. 795; Jan. 2, 1975, Pub. L. 93-596, §1, 88 Stat. 1949.)

§ 25   Declaration in lieu of oath

(a) The Director may by rule prescribe that any document to be filed in the Patent and Trademark Office and which is required by any law, rule, or other regulation to be under oath may be subscribed to by a written declaration in such form as the Director may prescribe, such declaration to be in lieu of the oath otherwise required.

(b) Whenever such written declaration is used, the document must warn the declarant that willful false statements and the like are punishable by fine or imprisonment, or both (18 U.S.C. 1001).

(Mar. 26, 1964, Pub. L. 88-292, §1, 78 Stat. 171; Jan. 2, 1975, Pub. L. 93-596, §1, 88 Stat. 1949.)

Note: 18 U.S.C. §1001 provides: "Whoever in any matter within the jurisdiction of any department or agency of the United States knowingly and willfully falsifies, conceals or covers up by any trick, scheme, or device a material fact, or makes any false, fictitious or fraudulent statements or representations, or makes or uses any false writing or document knowing the same to contain any false, fictitious or fraudulent statement or entry, shall be fined not more than $10,000 or imprisoned not more than five years, or both." (June 25, 1948, 62 Stat. 749)

§ 26   Effect of defective execution

Any document to be filed in the Patent and Trademark Office and which is required by any law, rule, or other regulation to be executed in a specified manner may be provisionally accepted by the Director despite a defective execution, provided a properly executed document is submitted within such time as may be prescribed.

(Mar. 26, 1964, Pub. L. 88-292, §1, 78 Stat. 171; Jan. 2, 1975, Pub. L. 93-596, §1, 88 Stat. 1949.)

CHAPTER 3—PRACTICE BEFORE PATENT AND TRADEMARK OFFICE

§ 32   Suspension or exclusion from practice

The Director may, after notice and opportunity for a hearing, suspend or exclude, either generally or in any particular case, from further practice before the Patent and Trademark Office, any person, agent, or attorney shown to be incompetent or disreputable, or guilty of gross misconduct, or who does not comply with the regulations established under section 2(b)(2)(D) of this title, or who shall, by word, circular, letter, or advertising, with intent to defraud in any manner, deceive, mislead, or threaten any applicant or prospective applicant, or other person having immediate or prospective business before the Office. The reasons for any such suspension or exclusion shall be duly recorded. The Director shall have the discretion to designate any attorney who is an officer or employee of the United States Patent and Trademark Office to conduct the hearing required by this section. The United States District Court for the District of Columbia, under such conditions and upon such proceedings as it by its rules determines, may review the action of the Director upon the petition of the person so refused recognition or so suspended or excluded.

(July 19, 1952, ch. 950, §1, 66 Stat. 795; Jan. 2, 1975, Pub. L. 93-596, §1, 88 Stat. 1949; Nov. 29, 1999, Pub. L. 106-113, §§4715, 4719, 113 Stat. 1501A-580, 581.)

§ 33   Unauthorized representation as practitioner

Whoever, not being recognized to practice before the Patent and Trademark Office, holds himself out or permits himself to be held out as so recognized, or as being qualified to prepare or prosecute applications for patent, shall be fined not more than $1,000 for each offense.

(July 19, 1952, ch. 950, §1, 66 Stat. 796; Jan. 2, 1975, Pub. L. 93-596, §1, 88 Stat. 1949.)

CHAPTER 4—PATENT FEES; FUNDING; SEARCH SYSTEMS

§ 41   Patent fees*; patent and trademark search systems

(a) The Director shall charge the following fees:

(1) (A) On filing each application for an original patent, except in design or plant cases, $690 [$750].

(B) In addition, on filing or on presentation at any other time, $78 [$84] for each claim in independent form which is in excess of 3, $18 for each claim (whether independent or dependent) which is in excess of 20, and $260 [$280] for each application containing a multiple dependent claim.

(C) On filing each provisional application for an original patent, $150 [$160].

(2) For issuing each original or reissue patent, except in design or plant cases, $1,210 [$1,300].

(3) In design and plant cases—

(A) on filing each design application, $310 [$330];

(B) on filing each plant application, $480 [$520];

(C) on issuing each design patent, $430 [$470]; and

(D) on issuing each plant patent, $580 [$630].

(4) (A) On filing each application for the reissue of a patent, $690 [$750].

(B) In addition, on filing or on presentation at any other time, $78 [$84] for each claim in independent form which is in excess of the number of independent claims of the original patent, and $18 for each claim (whether independent or dependent) which is in excess of 20 and also in excess of the number of claims of the original patent.

(5) On filing each disclaimer, $110 .

(6) (A) On filing an appeal from the examiner to the Board of Patent Appeals and Interferences, $300 [$320].

---

* *Ed. Note:* The dollar amounts in brackets reflect the fees in effect on January 3, 2003, as revised. See 67 Fed. Reg. 70847.

(B) In addition, on filing a brief in support of the appeal, $300 [$320], and on requesting an oral hearing in the appeal before the Board of Patent Appeals and Interferences, $260 [$280].

(7) On filing each petition for the revival of an unintentionally abandoned application for a patent, for the unintentionally delayed payment of the fee for issuing each patent, or for an unintentionally delayed response by the patent owner in any reexamination proceeding, $1,210 [$1,300], unless the petition is filed under section 133 or 151 of this title, in which case the fee shall be $110.

(8) For petitions for 1-month extensions of time to take actions required by the Director in an application—

(A) On filing a first petition, $110;

(B) on filing a second petition, $270 [$300]; and

(C) on filing a third petition or subsequent petition, $490 [$520].

(9) Basic national fee for an international application where the Patent and Trademark Office was the International Preliminary Examining Authority and the International Searching Authority, $670 [$720].

(10) Basic national fee for an international application where the Patent and Trademark Office was the International Searching Authority but not the International Preliminary Examining Authority, $690 [$750].

(11) Basic national fee for an international application where the Patent and Trademark Office was neither the International Searching Authority nor the International Preliminary Examining Authority, $970 [$1,060].

(12) Basic national fee for an international application where the international preliminary examination fee has been paid to the Patent and Trademark Office, and the international preliminary examination report states that the provisions of Article 33 (2), (3), and (4) of the Patent Cooperation Treaty have been satisfied for all claims in the application entering the national stage, $96 [$100].

(13) For filing or later presentation of each independent claim in the national stage of an international application in excess of 3, $78 [$84].

(14) For filing or later presentation of each claim (whether independent or dependent) in a national stage of an international application in excess of 20, $18.

(15) For each national stage of an international application containing a multiple dependent claim, $260 [$280].

For the purpose of computing fees, a multiple dependent claim as referred to in section 112 of this title or any claim depending therefrom shall be considered as separate dependent claims in accordance with the number of claims to which reference is made. Errors in payment of the additional fees may be rectified in accordance with regulations of the Director.

(b) The Director shall charge the following fees for maintaining in force all patents based on applications filed on or after December 12, 1980:

(1) 3 years and 6 months after grant, $830 [$890].

(2) 7 years and 6 months after grant, $1,900 [$2,050].

(3) 11 years and 6 months after grant, $2,910 [$3,150].

Unless payment of the applicable maintenance fee is received in the Patent and Trademark Office on or before the date the fee is due or within a grace period of 6 months thereafter, the patent will expire as of the end of such grace period. The Director may require the payment of a surcharge as a condition of accepting within such 6-month grace period the payment of an applicable maintenance fee. No fee may be established for maintaining a design or plant patent in force.

(c) (1) The Director may accept the payment of any maintenance fee required by subsection (b) of this section which is made within twenty-four months after the six-month grace period if the delay is shown to the satisfaction of the Director to have been unintentional, or at any time after the six-month grace period if the delay is shown to the satisfaction of the Director to have been unavoidable. The Director may require the payment of a surcharge as a condition of accepting payment of any maintenance fee after the six-month grace period. If the Director accepts payment of a maintenance fee after the six-month grace period, the patent shall be considered as not having expired at the end of the grace period.

(2) A patent, the term of which has been maintained as a result of the acceptance of a payment of a maintenance fee under this subsection,

shall not abridge or affect the right of any person or that person's successors in business who made, purchased, offered to sell, or used anything protected by the patent within the United States, or imported anything protected by the patent into the United States after the 6-month grace period but prior to the acceptance of a maintenance fee under this subsection, to continue the use of, to offer for sale, or to sell to others to be used, offered for sale, or sold, the specific thing so made, purchased, offered for sale, used, or imported. The court before which such matter is in question may provide for the continued manufacture, use, offer for sale, or sale of the thing made, purchased, offered for sale, or used within the United States, or imported into the United States, as specified, or for the manufacture, use, offer for sale, or sale in the United States of which substantial preparation was made after the 6-month grace period but before the acceptance of a maintenance fee under this subsection, and the court may also provide for the continued practice of any process that is practiced, or for the practice of which substantial preparation was made, after the 6-month grace period but before the acceptance of a maintenance fee under this subsection, to the extent and under such terms as the court deems equitable for the protection of investments made or business commenced after the 6-month grace period but before the acceptance of a maintenance fee under this subsection.

(d) The Director shall establish fees for all other processing, services, or materials relating to patents not specified in this section to recover the estimated average cost to the Office of such processing, services, or materials, except that the Director shall charge the following fees for the following services:

(1) For recording a document affecting title, $40 per property.

(2) For each photocopy, $.25 per page.

(3) For each black and white copy of a patent, $3.

The yearly fee for providing a library specified in section 13 of this title with uncertified printed copies of the specifications and drawings for all patents in that year shall be $50.

(e) The Director may waive the payment of any fee for any service or material related to patents in connection with an occasional or incidental request made by a department or agency of the Government, or any officer thereof. The Director may provide any applicant issued a notice under section 132 of this title with a copy of the specifications and drawings for all patents referred to in that notice without charge.

(f) The fees established in subsections (a) and (b) of this section may be adjusted by the Director on October 1, 1992, and every year thereafter, to reflect any fluctuations occurring during the previous 12 months in the Consumer Price Index, as determined by the Secretary of Labor. Changes of less than 1 per centum may be ignored.

(g) No fee established by the Director under this section shall take effect until at least 30 days after notice of the fee has been published in the Federal Register and in the Official Gazette of the Patent and Trademark Office.

(h) (1) Fees charged under subsection (a) or (b) shall be reduced by 50 percent with respect to their application to any small business concern as defined under section 3 of the Small Business Act, and to any independent inventor or nonprofit organization as defined in regulations issued by the Director.

(2) With respect to its application to any entity described in paragraph (1), any surcharge or fee charged under subsection (c) or (d) shall not be higher than the surcharge or fee required of any other entity under the same or substantially similar circumstances.

(i) (1) The Director shall maintain, for use by the public, paper, microform, or electronic collections of United States patents, foreign patent documents, and United States trademark registrations arranged to permit search for and retrieval of information. The Director may not impose fees directly for the use of such collections, or for the use of the public patent or trademark search rooms or libraries.

(2) The Director shall provide for the full deployment of the automated search systems of the Patent and Trademark Office so that such systems are available for use by the public, and shall assure full access by the public to, and dissemination of, patent and trademark information, using a variety of automated methods, including electronic bulletin boards and remote access by users to mass storage and retrieval systems.

35 U.S.C. § 41

(3) The Director may establish reasonable fees for access by the public to the automated search systems of the Patent and Trademark Office. If such fees are established, a limited amount of free access shall be made available to users of the systems for purposes of education and training. The Director may waive the payment by an individual of fees authorized by this subsection upon a showing of need or hardship, and if such a waiver is in the public interest.

(4) The Director shall submit to the Congress an annual report on the automated search systems of the Patent and Trademark Office and the access by the public to such systems. The Director shall also publish such report in the Federal Register. The Director shall provide an opportunity for the submission of comments by interested persons on each such report.

(July 19, 1952, ch. 950, §1, 66 Stat. 796; July 24, 1965, Pub. L. 89-83, §§1-2, 79 Stat. 259; Jan. 2, 1975, Pub. L. 93-596, §1, 88 Stat. 1949; Nov. 14, 1975, Pub. L. 94-131, §3, 89 Stat. 690; Dec. 12, 1980, Pub. L. 96-517, §2, 94 Stat. 3017; Aug. 27, 1982, Pub. L. 97-247, §3, 96 Stat. 317; Sept. 8, 1982, Pub. L. 97-256, §101, 96 Stat. 816; Nov. 8, 1984, Pub. L. 98-622, §204, 98 Stat. 3388; Nov. 6, 1986, Pub. L. 99-607, §1, 100 Stat. 3470; Dec. 10, 1991, Pub. L. 102-204, §5, 105 Stat. 1637-39; Oct. 23, 1992, Pub. L. 102-444, §1, 106 Stat. 2245; Dec. 8, 1994, Pub. L. 103-465, §§532, 533, 108 Stat. 4983, 4988; Nov. 10, 1998, Pub. L. 105-358, §3, 112 Stat. 3272; Nov. 29, 1999, Pub. L. 106-113, §§4202, 4605(a), 4732, 4804, 113 Stat. 1501A-554, 570, 581, 589.)

§ 42   Patent and Trademark Office funding

(a) All fees for services performed by or materials furnished by the Patent and Trademark Office will be payable to the Director.

(b) All fees paid to the Director and all appropriations for defraying the costs of the activities of the Patent and Trademark Office will be credited to the Patent and Trademark Office Appropriation Account in the Treasury of the United States.

(c) To the extent and in the amounts provided in advance in appropriations Acts, fees authorized in this title or any other Act to be charged or established by the Director shall be collected by and shall be available to the Director to carry out the activities of the Patent and Trademark Office. All fees available to the Director under section 31 of the Trademark Act of 1946 shall be used only for the processing of trademark registrations and for other activities, services, and materials relating to trademarks and to cover a proportionate share of the administrative costs of the Patent and Trademark Office.

(d) The Director may refund any fee paid by mistake or any amount paid in excess of that required.

(e) The Secretary of Commerce shall, on the day each year on which the President submits the annual budget to the Congress, provide to the Committees on the Judiciary of the Senate and the House of Representatives—

(1) a list of patent and trademark fee collections by the Patent and Trademark Office during the preceding fiscal year;

(2) a list of activities of the Patent and Trademark Office during the preceding fiscal year which were supported by patent fee expenditures, trademark fee expenditures, and appropriations;

(3) budget plans for significant programs, projects, and activities of the Office, including out-year funding estimates;

(4) any proposed disposition of surplus fees by the Office; and

(5) such other information as the committees consider necessary.

(July 19, 1952, ch. 950, §1, 66 Stat. 796; Nov. 14, 1975, Pub. L. 94-131, §4, 89 Stat. 690; Dec. 12, 1980, Pub. L. 96-517, §3, 94 Stat. 3018; Aug. 27, 1982, Pub. L. 97-247, §3, 96 Stat. 319; Sept. 13, 1982, Pub. L. 97-258, §3, 96 Stat. 1065; Dec. 10, 1991, Pub. L. 102-204, §§4-5, 105 Stat. 1637, 1640; Nov. 10, 1998, Pub. L. 105-358, §4, 112 Stat. 3274; Nov. 29, 1999, Pub. L. 106-113, §4205, 113 Stat. 1501A-555.)

PART II—PATENTABILITY OF INVENTIONS AND GRANT OF PATENTS

CHAPTER 10—PATENTABILITY OF INVENTIONS

§ 100   Definitions

When used in this title unless the context otherwise indicates—

(a) The term "invention" means invention or discovery.

(b) The term "process" means process, art or method, and includes a new use of a known process, machine, manufacture, composition of matter, or material.

(c) The terms "United States" and "this country" mean the United States of America, its territories and possessions.

(d) The word "patentee" includes not only the patentee to whom the patent was issued but also the successors in title to the patentee.

(e) The term "third-party requester" means a person requesting ex parte reexamination under section 302 or inter partes reexamination under section 311 who is not the patent owner.

(July 19, 1952, ch. 950, §1, 66 Stat. 797; Nov. 29, 1999, Pub. L. 106-113, §4603, 113 Stat. 1501A-567.)

§ 101   Inventions patentable

Whoever invents or discovers any new and useful process, machine, manufacture, or composition of matter, or any new and useful improvement thereof, may obtain a patent therefor, subject to the conditions and requirements of this title.

(July 19, 1952, ch. 950, §1, 66 Stat. 797.)

§ 102   Conditions for patentability; novelty and loss of right to patent

A person shall be entitled to a patent unless—

(a) the invention was known or used by others in this country, or patented or described in a printed publication in this or a foreign country, before the invention thereof by the applicant for patent, or

(b) the invention was patented or described in a printed publication in this or a foreign country or in public use or on sale in this country, more than one year prior to the date of the application for patent in the United States, or

(c) he has abandoned the invention, or

(d) the invention was first patented or caused to be patented, or was the subject of an inventor's certificate, by the applicant or his legal representatives or assigns in a foreign country prior to the date of the application for patent in this country on an application for patent or inventor's certificate filed more than twelve months before the filing of the application in the United States, or

(e)* the invention was described in (1) an application for patent, published under section 122(b), by another filed in the United States before the invention by the applicant for patent or (2) a patent granted on an application for patent by another filed in the United States before the invention by the applicant for patent, except that an international application filed under the treaty defined in section 351(a) shall have the effects for the purposes of this subsection of an application filed in the United States only if the international application designated the United States and was published under Article 21(2) of such treaty in the English language; or

(f) he did not himself invent the subject matter sought to be patented, or

---

* *Ed. Note:* Pursuant to sec. 13205 of Pub. L. 107-273, this version of 35 U.S.C. §102(e) shall be effective as of November 29, 2000 and shall apply to all patents and all patent applications pending on or filed after November 29, 2000. Patents resulting from an international application filed before November 29, 2000 and applications published pursuant to section 122(b) or Article 21(2) of the treaty defined in section 351(a) resulting from an international application filed before November 29, 2000 shall not be effective as prior art as of the filing date of the international application; however, such patents shall be effective as prior art in accordance with section 102(e) in effect on November 28, 2000.

35 U.S.C. § 102

(g) (1) during the course of an interference conducted under section 135 or section 291, another inventor involved therein establishes, to the extent permitted in section 104, that before such person's invention thereof the invention was made by such other inventor and not abandoned, suppressed, or concealed, or (2) before such person's invention thereof, the invention was made in this country by another inventor who had not abandoned, suppressed, or concealed it. In determining priority of invention under this subsection, there shall be considered not only the respective dates of conception and reduction to practice of the invention, but also the reasonable diligence of one who was first to conceive and last to reduce to practice, from a time prior to conception by the other.

(July 19, 1952, ch. 950, §1, 66 Stat. 797; July 28, 1972, Pub. L. 92-358, §2, 86 Stat. 502; Nov. 14, 1975, Pub. L. 94-131, §5, 89 Stat. 691; Nov. 29, 1999, Pub. L. 106-113, §§4505, 4806, 113 Stat. 1501A-565, 590; Nov. 2, 2002, Pub. L. 107-273, §13205, 116 Stat. 1902.)

§ 103   Conditions for patentability; nonobvious subject matter

(a) A patent may not be obtained though the invention is not identically disclosed or described as set forth in section 102 of this title, if the differences between the subject matter sought to be patented and the prior art are such that the subject matter as a whole would have been obvious at the time the invention was made to a person having ordinary skill in the art to which said subject matter pertains. Patentability shall not be negatived by the manner in which the invention was made.

(b) (1) Notwithstanding subsection (a), and upon timely election by the applicant for patent to proceed under this subsection, a biotechnological process using or resulting in a composition of matter that is novel under section 102 and nonobvious under subsection (a) of this section shall be considered nonobvious if—

   (A) claims to the process and the composition of matter are contained in either the same application for patent or in separate applications having the same effective filing date; and

(B) the composition of matter, and the process at the time it was invented, were owned by the same person or subject to an obligation of assignment to the same person.

(2) A patent issued on a process under paragraph (1)—

(A) shall also contain the claims to the composition of matter used in or made by that process, or

(B) shall, if such composition of matter is claimed in another patent, be set to expire on the same date as such other patent, notwithstanding section 154.

(3) For purposes of paragraph (1), the term "biotechnological process" means—

(A) a process of genetically altering or otherwise inducing a single—or multi-celled organism to—

(i) express an exogenous nucleotide sequence,

(ii) inhibit, eliminate, augment, or alter expression of an endogenous nucleotide sequence, or

(iii) express a specific physiological characteristic not naturally associated with said organism;

(B) cell fusion procedures yielding a cell line that expresses a specific protein, such as a monoclonal antibody; and

(C) a method of using a product produced by a process defined by subparagraph (A) or (B), or a combination of subparagraphs (A) and (B).

(c) Subject matter developed by another person, which qualifies as prior art only under one or more of subsections (e), (f), and (g) of section 102 of this title, shall not preclude patentability under this section where the subject matter and the claimed invention were, at the time the invention was made, owned by the same person or subject to an obligation of assignment to the same person.

(July 19, 1952, ch. 950, §1, 66 Stat. 798; Nov. 8, 1984, Pub. L. 98-622, §103, 98 Stat. 3384; Nov. 1, 1995, Pub. L. 104-41, §1, 109 Stat. 351; Nov. 29, 1999, Pub. L. 106-113, §4807, 113 Stat. 1501A-591.)

35 U.S.C. § 103

§ 104 (old)   Invention made abroad*

(a) *In general.*—In proceedings in the Patent and Trademark Office, in the courts, and before any other competent authority, an applicant for a patent, or a patentee, may not establish a date of invention by reference to knowledge or use thereof, or other activity with respect thereto, in a foreign country other than a NAFTA country, except as provided in sections 119 and 365 of this title. Where an invention was made by a person, civil or military, while domiciled in the United States or a NAFTA country and serving in any other country in connection with operations by or on behalf of the United States or a NAFTA country, the person shall be entitled to the same rights of priority in the United States with respect to such invention as if such invention had been made in the United States or a NAFTA country. To the extent that any information in a NAFTA country concerning knowledge, use, or other activity relevant to proving or disproving a date of invention has not been made available for use in a proceeding in the Office, a court, or any other competent authority to the same extent as such information could be made available in the United States, the Director, court, or such other authority shall draw appropriate inferences, or take other action permitted by statute, rule, or regulation, in favor of the party that requested the information in the proceeding.

(b) *Definition.*—As used in this section, the term "NAFTA country" has the meaning given that term in section 2(4) of the North American Free Trade Agreement Implementation Act.

(July 19, 1952, ch. 950, §1, 66 Stat. 798; Jan. 2, 1975, Pub. L. 93-596, §1, 88 Stat. 1949; Nov. 14, 1975, Pub. L. 94-131, §6, 89 Stat. 691; Nov. 8, 1984, Pub. L. 98-622, §403, 98 Stat. 3392; Dec. 8, 1993, Pub. L. 103-182, §331, 107 Stat. 2113.)

---

* *Ed. Note:* Pursuant to §335 of Pub. L. 103-182, this version of §104 applied to all patent applications filed on or after Dec. 8, 1993; provided that an applicant for a patent or patentee could not establish a date of invention by reference to knowledge or use thereof, or other activity with respect thereto, in a NAFTA country, except as provided in 35 U.S.C. §§119 & 365, that is earlier than Dec. 8, 1993.

However, the GATT implementation legislation in December 1994, Pub. L. 103-465, amended §104 again with respect to patent applications filed on or after Jan. 1, 1996. *See* "Sec. 104 (new)," *infra.*

35 U.S.C. § 104 (old)

§ 104 (new)   Invention made abroad*

(a) *In general.*—

(1) *Proceedings.*—In proceedings in the Patent and Trademark Office, in the courts, and before any other competent authority, an applicant for a patent, or a patentee, may not establish a date of invention by reference to knowledge or use thereof, or other activity with respect thereto, in a foreign country other than a NAFTA country or a WTO member country, except as provided in sections 119 and 365 of this title.

(2) *Rights.*—If an invention was made by a person, civil or military—

(A) while domiciled in the United States, and serving in any other country in connection with operations by or on behalf of the United States,

(B) while domiciled in a NAFTA country and serving in another country in connection with operations by or on behalf of that NAFTA country, or

(C) while domiciled in a WTO member country and serving in another country in connection with operations by or on behalf of that WTO member country,

that person shall be entitled to the same rights of priority in the United States with respect to such invention as if such invention had been made in the United States, that NAFTA country, or that WTO member country, as the case may be.

(3) *Use of information.*—To the extent that any information in a NAFTA country or a WTO member country concerning knowledge, use, or other activity relevant to proving or disproving a date of invention has not been made available for use in a proceeding in the Patent and Trademark Office, a court, or any other competent au-

---

* *Ed. Note:* Pursuant to §531(b) of Public Law 103-465, in general, the amendment made to 35 U.S.C. §104 shall apply to all patent applications filed on or after Jan. 1, 1996. An applicant for a patent, or patentee, may not establish a date of invention for purposes of title 35, U.S.C., that is earlier than Jan. 1, 1996 by reference to knowledge or use, or other activity, in a World Trade Organization member country, except as provided in 35 U.S.C. §§119 & 365. A "NAFTA country" means Canada or Mexico, for such time as NAFTA remains in force and is applicable. A "WTO member country" means a state with respect to which the U.S. applies the WTO Agreement.

35 U.S.C. § 104 (new)

thority to the same extent as such information could be made available in the United States, the Director, court or such other authority shall draw appropriate inferences, or take other action permitted by statute, rule, or regulation, in favor of the party that requested the information in the proceeding.

(b) *Definitions.*—As used in this section—

(1) the term "NAFTA country" has the meaning given that term in section 2(4) of the North American Free Trade Agreement Implementation Act; and

(2) the term "WTO member country" has the meaning given that term in section 2(10) of the Uruguay Round Agreements Act.

(July 19, 1952, ch. 950, §1, 66 Stat. 798; Jan. 2, 1975, Pub. L. 93-596, §1, 88 Stat. 1949; Nov. 14, 1975, Pub. L. 94-131, §6, 89 Stat. 691; Nov. 8, 1984, Pub. L. 98-622, §403, 98 Stat. 3392; Dec. 8, 1993, Pub. L. 103-182, §331, 107 Stat. 2113; Dec. 8, 1994, Pub. L. 103-465, §531, 108 Stat. 4982.)

§ 105   Inventions in outer space

(a) Any invention made, used or sold in outer space on a space object or component thereof under the jurisdiction or control of the United States shall be considered to be made, used or sold within the United States for the purposes of this title, except with respect to any space object or component thereof that is specifically identified and otherwise provided for by an international agreement to which the United States is a party, or with respect to any space object or component thereof that is carried on the registry of a foreign state in accordance with the Convention on Registration of Objects Launched into Outer Space.

(b) Any invention made, used or sold in outer space on a space object or component thereof that is carried on the registry of a foreign state in accordance with the Convention on Registration of Objects Launched into Outer Space, shall be considered to be made, used or sold within the United States for the purposes of this title if specifically so agreed in an international agreement between the United States and the state of registry.

(Nov. 15, 1990, Pub. L. 101-580, §1, 104 Stat. 2863.)

CHAPTER 11—APPLICATION FOR PATENT

§ 111   Application

(a) *In General.*—

(1) *Written application.*—An application for patent shall be made, or authorized to be made, by the inventor, except as otherwise provided in this title, in writing to the Director.

(2) *Contents.*—Such application shall include—

(A) a specification as prescribed by section 112 of this title;

(B) a drawing as prescribed by section 113 of this title; and

(C) an oath by the applicant as prescribed by section 115 of this title.

(3) *Fee and oath.*—The application must be accompanied by the fee required by law. The fee and oath may be submitted after the specification and any required drawing are submitted, within such period and under such conditions, including the payment of a surcharge, as may be prescribed by the Director.

(4) *Failure to submit.*—Upon failure to submit the fee and oath within such prescribed period, the application shall be regarded as abandoned, unless it is shown to the satisfaction of the Director that the delay in submitting the fee and oath was unavoidable or unintentional. The filing date of an application shall be the date on which

the specification and any required drawing are received in the Patent and Trademark Office.

(b) *Provisional Application.**—

(1) *Authorization.*—A provisional application for patent shall be made or authorized to be made by the inventor, except as otherwise provided in this title, in writing to the Director. Such application shall include—

(A) a specification as prescribed by the first paragraph of section 112 of this title; and

(B) a drawing as prescribed by section 113 of this title.

(2) *Claim.*—A claim, as required by the second through fifth paragraphs of section 112, shall not be required in a provisional application.

(3) *Fee.*—

(A) The application must be accompanied by the fee required by law.

(B) The fee may be submitted after the specification and any required drawing are submitted, within such period and under such conditions, including the payment of a surcharge, as may be prescribed by the Director.

(C) Upon failure to submit the fee within such prescribed period, the application shall be regarded as abandoned, unless it is shown to the satisfaction of the Director that the delay in submitting the fee was unavoidable or unintentional.

(4) *Filing date.*—The filing date of a provisional application shall be the date on which the specification and any required drawing are received in the Patent and Trademark Office.

(5) *Abandonment.*—Notwithstanding the absence of a claim, upon timely request and as prescribed by the Director, a provisional application may be treated as an application filed under subsection (a). Subject to section 119(e)(3) of this title, if no such request is made, the

---

* *Ed. Note:* Pursuant to §534(b) of Pub. L. 103-465, this provision took effect June 8, 1995, and applies to all patent applications filed in the United States on or after that date.

35 U.S.C. § 111

provisional application shall be regarded as abandoned 12 months after the filing date of such application and shall not be subject to revival after such 12-month period.

(6) *Other basis for provisional application.*—Subject to all the conditions in this subsection and section 119(e) of this title, and as prescribed by the Director, an application for patent filed under subsection (a) may be treated as a provisional application for patent.

(7) *No right of priority or benefit of earliest filing date.*—A provisional application shall not be entitled to the right of priority of any other application under section 119 or 365(a) of this title or to the benefit of an earlier filing date in the United States under section 120, 121, or 365(c) of this title.

(8) *Applicable provisions.*—The provisions of this title relating to applications for patent shall apply to provisional applications for patent, except as otherwise provided, and except that provisional applications for patent shall not be subject to sections 115, 131, 135, and 157 of this title.

(July 19, 1952, ch. 950, §1, 66 Stat. 798; Aug. 27, 1982, Pub. L. 97-247, §5, 96 Stat. 319; Dec. 8, 1994, Pub. L. 103-465, §532, 108 Stat. 4983; Nov. 29, 1999, Pub. L. 106-113, §4801, 113 Stat. 1501A-588.)

§ 112   Specification

The specification shall contain a written description of the invention, and of the manner and process of making and using it, in such full, clear, concise, and exact terms as to enable any person skilled in the art to which it pertains, or with which it is most nearly connected, to make and use the same, and shall set forth the best mode contemplated by the inventor of carrying out his invention.

The specification shall conclude with one or more claims particularly pointing out and distinctly claiming the subject matter which the applicant regards as his invention.

A claim may be written in independent or, if the nature of the case admits, in dependent or multiple dependent form.

Subject to the following paragraph, a claim in dependent form shall contain a reference to a claim previously set forth and then specify a further limitation of the subject matter claimed. A claim in dependent form shall be construed to incorporate by reference all the limitations of the claim to which it refers.

A claim in multiple dependent form shall contain a reference, in the alternative only, to more than one claim previously set forth and then specify a further limitation of the subject matter claimed. A multiple dependent claim shall not serve as a basis for any other multiple dependent claim. A multiple dependent claim shall be construed to incorporate by reference all the limitations of the particular claim in relation to which it is being considered.

An element in a claim for a combination may be expressed as a means or step for performing a specified function without the recital of structure, material, or acts in support thereof, and such claim shall be construed to cover the corresponding structure, material, or acts described in the specification and equivalents thereof.

(July 19, 1952, ch. 950, §1, 66 Stat. 798; July 24, 1965, Pub. L. 89-83, §9, 79 Stat. 261; Nov. 14, 1975, Pub. L. 94-131, §7, 89 Stat. 691.)

§ 113   Drawings

The applicant shall furnish a drawing where necessary for the understanding of the subject matter sought to be patented. When the nature of such subject matter admits of illustration by a drawing and the applicant has not furnished such a drawing, the Director may require its submission within a time period of not less than two months from the sending of a notice thereof. Drawings submitted after the filing date of the application may not be used (i) to overcome any insufficiency of the specification due to lack of an enabling disclosure or otherwise inadequate disclosure therein, or (ii) to supplement the original disclosure thereof for the purpose of interpretation of the scope of any claim.

(July 19, 1952, ch. 950, §1, 66 Stat. 799; Nov. 14, 1975, Pub. L. 94-131, §8, 89 Stat. 691.)

§ 114   Models, specimens

The Director may require the applicant to furnish a model of convenient size to exhibit advantageously the several parts of his invention.

When the invention relates to a composition of matter, the Director may require the applicant to furnish specimens or ingredients for the purpose of inspection or experiment.

(July 19, 1952, ch. 950, §1, 66 Stat. 799.)

§ 115   Oath of applicant

The applicant shall make oath that he believes himself to be the original and first inventor of the process, machine, manufacture, or composition of matter, or improvement thereof, for which he solicits a patent; and shall state of what country he is a citizen. Such oath may be made before any person within the United States authorized by law to administer oaths, or, when made in a foreign country, before any diplomatic or consular officer of the United States authorized to administer oaths, or before any officer having an official seal and authorized to administer oaths in the foreign country in which the applicant may be, whose authority is proved by certificate of a diplomatic or consular officer of the United States, or apostille of an official designated by a foreign country which, by treaty or convention, accords like effect to apostilles of designated officials in the United States, and such oath shall be valid if it complies with the laws of the state or country where made. When the application is made as provided in this title by a person other than the inventor, the oath may be so varied in form that it can be made by him. For purposes of this section, a consular officer shall include any United States citizen serving overseas, authorized to perform notarial functions pursuant to section 1750 of the Revised Statutes, as amended (22 U.S.C. 4221).

(July 19, 1952, ch. 950, §1, 66 Stat. 799; Aug. 27, 1982, Pub. L. 97-247, §14, 96 Stat. 321; Oct. 21, 1998, Pub. L. 105-277, §2222. 112 Stat. 2681-818.)

§ 116   Inventors

When an invention is made by two or more persons jointly, they shall apply for patent jointly and each make the required oath, except as otherwise provided in this title. Inventors may apply for a patent jointly even though (1) they did not physically work together or at the same time, (2) each did not make the same type or amount of contribution, or (3) each did not make a contribution to the subject matter of every claim of the patent.

35 U.S.C. § 116

If a joint inventor refuses to join in an application for patent or cannot be found or reached after diligent effort, the application may be made by the other inventor on behalf of himself and the omitted inventor. The Director, on proof of the pertinent facts and after such notice to the omitted inventor as he prescribes, may grant a patent to the inventor making the application, subject to the same rights which the omitted inventor would have had if he had been joined. The omitted inventor may subsequently join in the application.

Whenever through error a person is named in an application for patent as the inventor, or through an error an inventor is not named in an application, and such error arose without any deceptive intention on his part, the Director may permit the application to be amended accordingly, under such terms as he prescribes.

(July 19, 1952, ch. 950, §1, 66 Stat. 799; Aug. 27, 1982, Pub. L. 97-247, §6, 96 Stat. 320; Nov. 8, 1984, Pub. L. 98-622, §104, 98 Stat. 3384.)

§ 117   Death or incapacity of inventor

Legal representatives of deceased inventors and of those under legal incapacity may make application for patent upon compliance with the requirements and on the same terms and conditions applicable to the inventor.

(July 19, 1952, ch. 950, §1, 66 Stat. 799.)

§ 118   Filing by other than inventor

Whenever an inventor refuses to execute an application for patent, or cannot be found or reached after diligent effort, a person to whom the inventor has assigned or agreed in writing to assign the invention or who otherwise shows sufficient proprietary interest in the matter justifying such action, may make application for patent on behalf of and as agent for the inventor on proof of the pertinent facts and a showing that such action is necessary to preserve the rights of the parties or to prevent irreparable damage; and the Director may grant a patent to such inventor upon such notice to him as the Director deems sufficient, and on compliance with such regulations as he prescribes.

(July 19, 1952, ch. 950, §1, 66 Stat. 799.)

§ 119 Benefit of earlier filing date; right of priority

(a) An application for patent for an invention filed in this country by any person who has, or whose legal representatives or assigns have, previously regularly filed an application for a patent for the same invention in a foreign country which affords similar privileges in the case of applications filed in the United States or to citizens of the United States, or in a WTO member country, shall have the same effect as the same application would have if filed in this country on the date on which the application for patent for the same invention was first filed in such foreign country, if the application in this country is filed within twelve months from the earliest date on which such foreign application was filed; but no patent shall be granted on any application for patent for an invention which had been patented or described in a printed publication in any country more than one year before the date of the actual filing of the application in this country, or which had been in public use or on sale in this country more than one year prior to such filing.

(b)(1) No application for patent shall be entitled to this right of priority unless a claim is filed in the Patent and Trademark Office, identifying the foreign application by specifying the application number on that foreign application, the intellectual property authority or country in or for which the application was filed, and the date of filing the application, at such time during the pendency of the application as required by the Director.

(2) The Director may consider the failure of the applicant to file a timely claim for priority as a waiver of any such claim. The Director may establish procedures, including the payment of a surcharge, to accept an unintentionally delayed claim under this section.

(3) The Director may require a certified copy of the original foreign application, specification, and drawings upon which it is based, a translation if not in the English language, and such other information as the Director considers necessary. Any such certification shall be made by the foreign intellectual property authority in which the foreign application was filed and show the date of the application and of the filing of the specification and other papers.

35 U.S.C. § 119

(c) In like manner and subject to the same conditions and requirements, the right provided in this section may be based upon a subsequent regularly filed application in the same foreign country instead of the first filed foreign application, provided that any foreign application filed prior to such subsequent application has been withdrawn, abandoned, or otherwise disposed of, without having been laid open to public inspection and without leaving any rights outstanding, and has not served, nor thereafter shall serve, as a basis for claiming a right of priority.

(d) Applications for inventors' certificates filed in a foreign country in which applicants have a right to apply, at their discretion, either for a patent or for an inventor's certificate shall be treated in this country in the same manner and have the same effect for purpose of the right of priority under this section as applications for patents, subject to the same conditions and requirements of this section as apply to applications for patents, provided such applicants are entitled to the benefits of the Stockholm Revision of the Paris Convention at the time of such filing.

(e) (1) * An application for patent filed under section 111(a) or section 363 of this title for an invention disclosed in the manner provided by the first paragraph of section 112 of this title in a provisional application filed under section 111(b) of this title, by an inventor or inventors named in the provisional application, shall have the same effect, as to such invention, as though filed on the date of the provisional application filed under section 111(b) of this title, if the application for patent filed under section 111(a) or section 363 of this title is filed not later than 12 months after the date on which the provisional application was filed and if it contains or is amended to contain a specific reference to the provisional application. *No application shall be entitled to the benefit of an earlier filed provisional application under this subsection unless an amendment containing the specific reference to the earlier filed provisional application is submitted at such time during the pendency of the application as required by the Director. The Director may consider*

---

* Ed. Note: Pursuant to §4508 of Pub. L. 106-113, the italicized material will take effect one year after the Nov. 29, 1999 date of enactment and shall apply to all applications filed under §111 on or after that date and all applications complying with §371 that resulted from international applications filed on or after that date.

the failure to submit such an amendment within that time period as a waiver of any benefit under this subsection. The Director may establish procedures, including the payment of a surcharge, to accept an unintentionally delayed submission of an amendment under this subsection during the pendency of the application.

(2) A provisional application filed under section 111(b) of this title may not be relied upon in any proceeding in the Patent and Trademark Office unless the fee set forth in subparagraph (A) or (C) of section 41(a)(1) of this title has been paid.

(3) If the day that is 12 months after the filing date of a provisional application falls on a Saturday, Sunday, or Federal holiday within the District of Columbia, the period of pendency of the provisional application shall be extended to the next succeeding secular or business day.

(f) Applications for plant breeder's rights filed in a WTO member country (or in a foreign UPOV Contracting Party) shall have the same effect for the purpose of the right of priority under subsections (a) through (c) of this section as applications for patents, subject to the same conditions and requirements of this section as apply to applications for patents.

(g) As used in this section—

(1) the term "WTO member country" has the same meaning as the term is defined in section 104(b)(2) of this title; and

(2) the term "UPOV Contracting Party" means a member of the International Convention for the Protection of New Varieties of Plants.

(July 19, 1952, ch. 950, §1, 66 Stat. 800; Oct. 3, 1961, Pub. L. 87-333, §1, 75 Stat. 748; July 28, 1972, Pub. L. 92-358, §1, 86 Stat. 502; Jan. 2, 1975, Pub. L. 93-596, §1, 88 Stat. 1949; Dec. 8, 1994, Pub. L. 103-465, §532, 108 Stat. 4983; Nov. 29, 1999, Pub. L. 106-113, §§4503, 4801, 4802, 113 Stat. 1501A-563, 588, 589.)

35 U.S.C. § 119

§ 120*   Benefit of earlier filing date in the United States

An application for patent for an invention disclosed in the manner provided by the first paragraph of section 112 of this title in an application previously filed in the United States, or as provided by section 363 of this title, which is filed by an inventor or inventors named in the previously filed application shall have the same effect, as to such invention, as though filed on the date of the prior application, if filed before the patenting or abandonment of or termination of proceedings on the first application or on an application similarly entitled to the benefit of the filing date of the first application and if it contains or is amended to contain a specific reference to the earlier filed application. *No application shall be entitled to the benefit of an earlier filed application under this section unless an amendment containing the specific reference to the earlier filed application is submitted at such time during the pendency of the application as required by the Director. The Director may consider the failure to submit such an amendment within that time period as a waiver of any benefit under this section. The Director may establish procedures, including the payment of a surcharge, to accept an unintentionally delayed submission of an amendment under this section.*

(July 19, 1952, ch. 950, §1, 66 Stat. 800; Nov. 14, 1975, Pub. L. 94-131, §9, 89 Stat. 691; Nov. 8, 1984, Pub. L. 98-622, §104, 98 Stat. 3385; Nov. 29, 1999, Pub. L. 106-113, §4503, 113 Stat. 1501A-563.)

§ 121   Divisional applications

If two or more independent and distinct inventions are claimed in one application, the Director may require the application to be restricted to one of the inventions. If the other invention is made the subject of a divisional application which complies with the requirements of section 120 of this title it shall be entitled to the benefit of the filing date of the original application. A patent issuing on an application with respect to which a requirement for restriction under this section has been made, or on an application filed as a result of such a requirement, shall not be used as a reference either in the Patent and Trademark Office or in the courts against a divisional application or against the original application

---

* *Ed. Note:* Pursuant to §4508 of Pub. L. 106-113, the italicized material will take effect one year after the Nov. 29, 1999 date of enactment and shall apply to all applications filed under §111 on or after that date and all applications complying with §371 that resulted from international applications filed on or after that date.

35 U.S.C. § 120

or any patent issued on either of them, if the divisional application is filed before the issuance of the patent on the other application. If a divisional application is directed solely to subject matter described and claimed in the original application as filed, the Director may dispense with signing and execution by the inventor. The validity of a patent shall not be questioned for failure of the Director to require the application to be restricted to one invention.

(July 19, 1952, ch. 950, §1, 66 Stat. 800; Jan. 2, 1975, Pub. L. 93-596, §1, 88 Stat. 1949.)

§ 122 Confidential status of applications; publication of patent applications

(a) *Confidentiality.*—Except as provided in subsection (b), applications for patents shall be kept in confidence by the Patent and Trademark Office and no information concerning the same given without authority of the applicant or owner unless necessary to carry out the provisions of an Act of Congress or in such special circumstances as may be determined by the Director.

(b) *Publication.*—

(1) *In general.*—(A) Subject to paragraph (2), each application for a patent shall be published, in accordance with procedures determined by the Director, promptly after the expiration of a period of 18 months from the earliest filing date for which a benefit is sought under this title. At the request of the applicant, an application may be published earlier than the end of such 18-month period.

(B) No information concerning published patent applications shall be made available to the public except as the Director determines.

(C) Notwithstanding any other provision of law, a determination by the Director to release or not to release information concerning a published patent application shall be final and nonreviewable.

(2) *Exceptions.*—(A) An application shall not be published if that application is—

(i) no longer pending;

(ii) subject to a secrecy order under section 181 of this title;

(iii) a provisional application filed under section 111(b) of this title; or

(iv) an application for a design patent filed under chapter 16 of this title.

(B)(i) If an applicant makes a request upon filing, certifying that the invention disclosed in the application has not and will not be the subject of an application filed in another country, or under a multilateral international agreement, that requires publication of applications 18 months after filing, the application shall not be published as provided in paragraph (1).

(ii) An applicant may rescind a request made under clause (i) at any time.

(iii) An applicant who has made a request under clause (i) but who subsequently files, in a foreign country or under a multilateral international agreement specified in clause (i), an application directed to the invention disclosed in the application filed in the Patent and Trademark Office, shall notify the Director of such filing not later than 45 days after the date of the filing of such foreign or international application. A failure of the applicant to provide such notice within the prescribed period shall result in the application being regarded as abandoned, unless it is shown to the satisfaction of the Director that the delay in submitting the notice was unintentional.

(iv) If an applicant rescinds a request made under clause (i) or notifies the Director that an application was filed in a foreign country or under a multilateral international agreement specified in clause (i), the application shall be published in accordance with the provisions of paragraph (1) on or as soon as is practical after the date that is specified in clause (i).

(v) If an applicant has filed applications in one or more foreign countries, directly or through a multilateral international agreement, and such foreign filed applications corresponding to an application filed in the Patent and Trademark Office or the description of the invention in such foreign filed applications is less extensive than the application or description of the invention in the application filed in the Patent and Trademark Office, the applicant may submit a redacted copy of the application filed in the Patent and Trademark Office eliminating any part or description of the invention in such application that is not also contained in any of the corresponding applications filed in a foreign country. The Director may only publish the redacted copy of the application unless the redacted copy of the application is not received within 16 months after the earliest effective filing date for which a benefit is sought under this title. The provisions of section 154(d) shall not apply to a claim if the description of the invention published in the redacted application filed under this clause with respect to the claim does not enable a person skilled in the art to make and use the subject matter of the claim.

(c) *Protest and pre-issuance opposition.*—The Director shall establish appropriate procedures to ensure that no protest or other form of pre-issuance opposition to the grant of a patent on an application may be initiated after publication of the application without the express written consent of the applicant.

(d) *National security.*—No application for patent shall be published under subsection (b)(1) if the publication or disclosure of such invention would be detrimental to the national security. The Director shall establish appropriate procedures to ensure that such applications are promptly identified and the secrecy of such inventions is maintained in accordance with chapter 17 of this title.

(July 19, 1952, ch. 950, §1, 66 Stat. 801; Jan. 2, 1975, Pub. L. 93-596, §1, 88 Stat. 1949; Nov. 29, 1999, Pub. L. 106-113, §4502, 113 Stat. 1501A-561.)

CHAPTER 12—EXAMINATION OF APPLICATION

§ 131   Examination of application

The Director shall cause an examination to be made of the application and the alleged new invention; and if on such examination it appears that the applicant is entitled to a patent under the law, the Director shall issue a patent therefor.

(July 19, 1952, ch. 950, §1, 66 Stat. 801.)

§ 132   Notice of rejection; reexamination

(a) Whenever, on examination, any claim for a patent is rejected, or any objection or requirement made, the Director shall notify the applicant thereof, stating the reasons for such rejection, or objection or requirement, together with such information and references as may be useful in judging of the propriety of continuing the prosecution of his application; and if after receiving such notice, the applicant persists in his claim for a patent, with or without amendment, the application shall be reexamined. No amendment shall introduce new matter into the disclosure of the invention.

(b)* The Director shall prescribe regulations to provide for the continued examination of applications for patent at the request of the applicant. The Director may establish appropriate fees for such continued examination and shall provide a 50 percent reduction in such fees for small entities that qualify for reduced fees under section 41(h)(1) of this title.

(July 19, 1952, ch. 950, §1, 66 Stat. 801; Nov. 29, 1999, Pub. L. 106-113, §4403, 113 Stat. 1501A-568.)

---

* *Ed. Note:* Pursuant to §4405 of Pub. L. 106-113, this provision will take effect on May 29, 2000 and shall apply to all applications filed under §111(a) on or after June 8, 1995, and all applications complying with §371 that resulted from international applications filed on or after June 8, 1995, and does not apply to applications for design patents.

35 U.S.C. § 131

§ 133   Time for prosecuting application

Upon failure of the applicant to prosecute the application within six months after any action therein, of which notice has been given or mailed to the applicant, or within such shorter time, not less than thirty days, as fixed by the Director in such action, the application shall be regarded as abandoned by the parties thereto, unless it be shown to the satisfaction of the Director that such delay was unavoidable.

(July 19, 1952, ch. 950, §1, 66 Stat. 801.)

§ 134   Appeal to the Board of Patent Appeals and Interferences

(a) *Patent applicant.*—An applicant for a patent, any of whose claims has been twice rejected, may appeal from the decision of the primary examiner to the Board of Patent Appeals and Interferences, having once paid the fee for such appeal.

(b) *Patent owner.*—A patent owner in any reexamination proceeding may appeal from the final rejection of any claim by the primary examiner to the Board of Patent Appeals and Interferences, having once paid the fee for such appeal.

(c) *Third-party.*—A third-party requester in an inter partes proceeding may appeal to the Board of Patent Appeals and Interferences from the final decision of the primary examiner favorable to the patentability of any original or proposed amended or new claim of a patent, having once paid the fee for such appeal.

(July 19, 1952, ch. 950, §1, 66 Stat. 801; Nov. 8, 1984, Pub. L. 98-622, §204, 98 Stat. 3388; Nov. 29, 1999, Pub. L. 106-113, §4605(b), 113 Stat. 1501A-570; Nov. 2, 2002, Pub. L. 107-273, §§13106, 13202, 116 Stat. 1901.)

§ 135   Interferences

(a) Whenever an application is made for a patent which, in the opinion of the Director, would interfere with any pending application, or with any unexpired patent, an interference may be declared and the Director shall give notice of such declaration to the applicants, or applicant and patentee, as the case may be. The Board of Patent Appeals and Interferences shall determine questions of priority of the inventions and may determine questions of patentability. Any final decision, if adverse to the claim of an applicant, shall constitute the final refusal by the Patent and Trademark Office of the claims involved, and the Director may issue a patent to the applicant who is adjudged the prior inventor. A final judgment adverse to a patentee from which no appeal or other review has been or can be taken or had shall constitute cancellation of the claims involved in the patent, and notice of such cancellation shall be endorsed on copies of the patent distributed after such cancellation by the Patent and Trademark Office.

(b) (1) A claim which is the same as, or for the same or substantially the same subject matter as, a claim of an issued patent may not be made in any application unless such a claim is made prior to one year from the date on which the patent was granted.

(2)* A claim which is the same as, or for the same or substantially the same subject matter as, a claim of an application published under section 122(b) of this title may be made in an application filed after the application is published only if the claim is made before 1 year after the date on which the application is published.

(c) Any agreement or understanding between parties to an interference, including any collateral agreements referred to therein, made in connection with or in contemplation of the termination of the interference, shall be in writing and a true copy thereof filed in the Patent and Trademark Office before the termination of the interference as between the said parties to the agreement or understanding. If any party filing the same so requests, the copy shall be kept separate from the file of the interference, and made available only to Government agencies on written request, or to any person on a showing of good cause. Failure to file the copy of such agreement or understanding shall render permanently unenforceable such agreement or understanding and any patent of such parties involved in the interference or any patent subsequently issued on any application of such parties so involved. The Director may, however, on a showing of good cause for failure to file within the time prescribed, permit the filing of the agreement or understanding during the

---

* *Ed. Note:* Pursuant to §4508 of Pub. L. 106-113, this provision will take effect on Nov. 29, 2000 and shall apply to all applications filed under §111(a) on or after that date, and all applications complying with §371 that resulted from international applications filed on or after that date.

35 U.S.C. § 135

six-month period subsequent to the termination of the interference as between the parties to the agreement or understanding.

The Director shall give notice to the parties or their attorneys of record, a reasonable time prior to said termination, of the filing requirement of this section. If the Director gives such notice at a later time, irrespective of the right to file such agreement or understanding within the six-month period on a showing of good cause, the parties may file such agreement or understanding within sixty days of the receipt of such notice.

Any discretionary action of the Director under this subsection shall be reviewable under section 10 of the Administrative Procedure Act.

(d) Parties to a patent interference, within such time as may be specified by the Director by regulation, may determine such contest or any aspect thereof by arbitration. Such arbitration shall be governed by the provisions of title 9 to the extent such title is not inconsistent with this section. The parties shall give notice of any arbitration award to the Director, and such award shall, as between the parties to the arbitration, be dispositive of the issues to which it relates. The arbitration award shall be unenforceable until such notice is given. Nothing in this subsection shall preclude the Director from determining patentability of the invention involved in the interference.

(July 19, 1952, ch. 950, §1, 66 Stat. 801; Oct. 15, 1962, Pub. L. 87-831, 76 Stat. 958; Jan. 2, 1975, Pub. L. 93-596, §1, 88 Stat. 1949; Nov. 8, 1984, Pub. L. 98-622, §§105 and 202, 98 Stat. 3385–86; Nov. 29, 1999, Pub. L. 106-113, §4507, 113 Stat. 1501A-565.)

CHAPTER 13—REVIEW OF PATENT AND TRADEMARK OFFICE DECISION

§ 141   Appeal to Court of Appeals for the Federal Circuit

An applicant dissatisfied with the decision in an appeal to the Board of Patent Appeals and Interferences under section 134 of this title may appeal the decision to the United States Court of Appeals for the Federal Circuit. By filing such an appeal the applicant waives his or her right to proceed under section 145 of this title. A patent owner, or a third-party requester in an inter partes reexamination proceeding, who is in any reexamination proceeding dissatisfied with the final decision in an appeal to the Board of Patent Appeals and Interferences under section 134 may appeal the decision only to the United States Court of Appeals for the Federal Circuit. A party to an interference dissatisfied with the decision of the Board of Patent Appeals and Interferences on the interference may appeal the decision to the United States Court of Appeals for the Federal Circuit, but such appeal shall be dismissed if any adverse party to such interference, within twenty days after the appellant has filed notice of appeal in accordance with section 142 of this title, files notice with the Director that the party elects to have all further proceedings conducted as provided in section 146 of this title. If the appellant does not, within thirty days after the filing of such notice by the adverse party, file a civil action under section 146, the decision appealed from shall govern the further proceedings in the case.

(July 19, 1952, ch. 950, §1, 66 Stat. 802; Apr. 2, 1982, Pub. L. 97-164, §163, 96 Stat. 49-50; Nov. 8, 1984, Pub. L. 98-622, §203, 98 Stat. 3387; Nov. 29, 1999, Pub. L. 106-113, §4605, 113 Stat. 1501A-570; Nov. 2, 2002, Pub. L. 107-273, §13106, 116 Stat. 1900.)

§ 142   Notice of appeal

When an appeal is taken to the United States Court of Appeals for the Federal Circuit, the appellant shall file in the Patent and Trademark Office a written notice of appeal directed to the Director, within such time after the date of the decision from which the appeal is taken as the Director prescribes, but in no case less than 60 days after that date.

(July 19, 1952, ch. 950, §1, 66 Stat. 802; Jan. 2, 1975, Pub. L. 93-596, §1, 88 Stat. 1949; Apr. 2, 1982, Pub. L. 97-164, §163, 96 Stat. 49; Nov. 8, 1984, Pub. L. 98-620, §414, 98 Stat. 3363.)

§ 143   Proceedings on appeal

With respect to an appeal described in section 142 of this title, the Director shall transmit to the United States Court of Appeals for the Federal Circuit a certified list of the documents comprising the record in the Patent and Trademark Office. The court may request that the Director forward the original or certified copies of such documents during pendency of the appeal. In an ex parte case or any reexamination case, the Director shall submit to the court in writing the grounds for the decision of the Patent and Trademark Office, addressing all the issues involved in the appeal. The court shall, before hearing an appeal, give notice of the time and place of the hearing to the Director and the parties in the appeal.

(July 19, 1952, ch. 950, §1, 66 Stat. 802; Jan. 2, 1975, Pub. L. 93-596, §1, 88 Stat. 1949; Apr. 2, 1982, Pub. L. 97-164, §163, 96 Stat. 49; Nov. 8, 1984, Pub. L. 98-620, §414, 98 Stat. 3363; Nov. 29, 1999, Pub. L. 106-113, §4605, 113 Stat. 1501A-570; Nov. 2, 2002, Pub. L. 107-273, §13202, 116 Stat. 1901.)

§ 144 Decision on appeal

The United States Court of Appeals for the Federal Circuit shall review the decision from which an appeal is taken on the record before the Patent and Trademark Office. Upon its determination the court shall issue to the Director its mandate and opinion, which shall be entered of record in the Patent and Trademark Office and shall govern the further proceedings in the case.

(July 19, 1952, ch. 950, §1, 66 Stat. 802; Jan. 2, 1975, Pub. L. 93-596, §1, 88 Stat. 1949; Apr. 2, 1982, Pub. L. 97-164, §163, 96 Stat. 49; Nov. 8, 1984, Pub. L. 98-620, §414, 98 Stat. 3363.)

§ 145 Civil action to obtain patent

An applicant dissatisfied with the decision of the Board of Patent Appeals and Interferences in an appeal under section 134(a) of this title may, unless appeal has been taken to the United States Court of Appeals for the Federal Circuit, have remedy by civil action against the Director in the United States District Court for the District of Columbia if commenced within such time after such decision, not less than sixty days, as the Director appoints. The court may adjudge that such applicant is entitled to receive a patent for his invention, as specified in any of his claims involved in the decision of the Board of Patent Appeals and Interferences, as the facts in the case may appear and such adjudication shall authorize the Director to issue such patent on compliance with the requirements of law. All the expenses of the proceedings shall be paid by the applicant.

(July 19, 1952, ch. 950, §1, 66 Stat. 803; Apr. 2, 1982, Pub. L. 97-164, §163, 96 Stat. 49; Nov. 8, 1984, Pub. L. 98-622, §203, 98 Stat. 3387; Nov. 29, 1999, Pub. L. 106-113, §4605, 113 Stat. 1501A-570.)

§ 146   Civil action in case of interference

Any party to an interference dissatisfied with the decision of the Board of Patent Appeals and Interferences on the interference, may have remedy by civil action, if commenced within such time after such decision, not less than sixty days, as the Director appoints or as provided in section 141 of this title, unless he has appealed to the United States Court of Appeals for the Federal Circuit, and such appeal is pending or has been decided. In such suits the record in the Patent and Trademark Office shall be admitted on motion of either party upon the terms and conditions as to costs, expenses, and the further cross-examination of the witnesses as the court imposes, without prejudice to the right of the parties to take further testimony. The testimony and exhibits of the record in the Patent and Trademark Office when admitted shall have the same effect as if originally taken and produced in the suit.

Such suit may be instituted against the party in interest as shown by the records of the Patent and Trademark Office at the time of the decision complained of, but any party in interest may become a party to the action. If there be adverse parties residing in a plurality of districts not embraced within the same state, or an adverse party residing in a foreign country, the United States District Court for the District of Columbia shall have jurisdiction and may issue summons against the adverse parties directed to the marshal of any district in which any adverse party resides. Summons against adverse parties residing in foreign countries may be served by publication or otherwise as the court directs. The Director shall not be a necessary party but he shall be notified of the filing of the suit by the clerk of the court in which it is filed and shall have the right to intervene. Judgment of the court in favor of the right of an applicant to a patent shall authorize the Director to issue such patent on the filing in the Patent and Trademark Office of a certified copy of the judgment and on compliance with the requirements of law. (July 19, 1952, ch. 950, §1, 66 Stat. 803; Jan. 2, 1975, Pub. L. 93-596, §1, 88 Stat. 1949; Apr. 2, 1982, Pub. L. 97-164, §163, 96 Stat. 49; Nov. 8, 1984, Pub. L. 98-622, §203, 98 Stat. 3387.)

CHAPTER 14—ISSUE OF PATENT

§ 151   Issue of patent

If it appears that applicant is entitled to a patent under law, a written notice of allowance of the application shall be given or mailed to the applicant. The notice shall specify a sum, constituting the issue fee or a portion thereof, which shall be paid within three months thereafter.

Upon payment of this sum the patent shall issue, but if payment is not timely made, the application shall be regarded as abandoned.

Any remaining balance of the issue fee shall be paid within three months from the sending of a notice thereof and, if not paid, the patent shall lapse at the termination of this three-month period. In calculating the amount of a remaining balance, charges for a page or less may be disregarded.

If any payment required by this section is not timely made, but is submitted with the fee for delayed payment and the delay in payment is shown to have been unavoidable, it may be accepted by the Director as though no abandonment or lapse had ever occurred.

(July 19, 1952, ch. 950, §1, 66 Stat. 803; July 24, 1965, Pub. L. 89-83, §§4 and 6, 79 Stat. 260-61; Jan. 2, 1975, Pub. L. 93-601, §3, 88 Stat. 1956.)

§ 152   Issue of patent to assignee

Patents may be granted to the assignee of the inventor of record in the Patent and Trademark Office, upon the application made and the specification sworn to by the inventor, except as otherwise provided in this title.

(July 19, 1952, ch. 950, §1, 66 Stat. 804; Jan. 2, 1975, Pub. L. 93-596, §1, 88 Stat. 1949.)

35 U.S.C. § 152

§ 153   How issued

Patents shall be issued in the name of the United States of America, under the seal of the Patent and Trademark Office, and shall be signed by the Director or have his signature placed thereon and shall be recorded in the Patent and Trademark Office.

(July 19, 1952, ch. 950, §1, 66 Stat. 804; Jan. 2, 1975, Pub. L. 93-596, §1, 88 Stat. 1949; Nov. 2, 2002, Pub. L. 107-273, §13203, 116 Stat. 1902.)

§ 154   Contents and term of patent;* provisional rights

(a) *In general.*—

(1) *Contents.*—Every patent shall contain a short title of the invention and a grant to the patentee, his heirs or assigns, of the right to exclude others from making, using, offering for sale, or selling the invention throughout the United States or importing the invention into the United States, and, if the invention is a process, of the right to exclude others from using, offering for sale or selling throughout the United States, or importing into the United States, products made by that process, referring to the specification for the particulars thereof.

(2) *Term.*—Subject to the payment of fees under this title, such grant shall be for a term beginning on the date on which the patent issues and ending 20 years from the date on which the application for the patent was filed in the United States or, if the application contains a specific reference to an earlier filed application or applications under section 120, 121, or 365(c) of this title, from the date on which the earliest such application was filed.

(3) *Priority.*—Priority under section 119, 365(a), or 365(b) of this title shall not be taken into account in determining the term of a patent.

(4) *Specification and drawing.*—A copy of the specification and drawing shall be annexed to the patent and be a part of such patent.

---

* *Ed. Note:* Pursuant to §534 of Pub. L. 103-465, the term of a patent granted on an application filed on or after June 8, 1995, and that contains a specific reference to an earlier application filed under section 120, 121, or 365(c) of title 35, U.S.C., shall be measured from the filing date of the earliest filed application.

35 U.S.C. § 153

(b) *Adjustment of patent term.*—*

　(1) *Patent term guarantees.*—

　　(A) *Guarantee of prompt Patent and Trademark Office responses.*— Subject to the limitations under paragraph (2), if the issue of an original patent is delayed due to the failure of the Patent and Trademark Office to—

　　　(i) provide at least one of the notifications under section 132 of this title or a notice of allowance under section 151 of this title not later than 14 months after—

　　　　(I) the date on which an application was filed under section 111(a) of this title; or

　　　　(II) the date on which an international application fulfilled the requirements of section 371 of this title;

　　　(ii) respond to a reply under section 132, or to an appeal taken under section 134, within 4 months after the date on which the reply was filed or the appeal was taken;

　　　(iii) act on an application within 4 months after the date of a decision by the Board of Patent Appeals and Interferences under section 134 or 135 or a decision by a Federal court under section 141, 145, or 146 in a case in which allowable claims remain in the application; or

　　　(iv) issue a patent within 4 months after the date on which the issue fee was paid under section 151 and all outstanding requirements were satisfied,

　　the term of the patent shall be extended 1 day for each day after the end of the period specified in clause (i), (ii), (iii), or (iv), as the case may be, until the action described in such clause is taken.

　　(B) *Guarantee of no more than 3-year application pendency.*—Subject to the limitations under paragraph (2), if the issue of an original patent is delayed due to the failure of the United States Patent and Trademark Office to issue a patent within 3 years after the actual filing date of the application in the United States, not including—

---

* *Ed. Note:* Pursuant to §4405 of Pub. L. 106-113, the provisions of §154(b) take effect on May 29, 2000, and, except for a design patent application, apply to all applications filed on or after that date.

35 U.S.C. § 154

(i) any time consumed by continued examination of the application requested by the applicant under section 132(b);

(ii) any time consumed by a proceeding under section 135(a), any time consumed by the imposition of an order under section 181, or any time consumed by appellate review by the Board of Patent Appeals and Interferences or by a Federal court; or

(iii) any delay in the processing of the application by the United States Patent and Trademark Office requested by the applicant except as permitted by paragraph (3)(C),

the term of the patent shall be extended 1 day for each day after the end of that 3-year period until the patent is issued.

(C) *Guarantee or adjustments for delays due to interferences, secrecy orders, and appeals.*—Subject to the limitations under paragraph (2), if the issue of an original patent is delayed due to—

(i) a proceeding under section 135(a);

(ii) the imposition of an order under section 181; or

(iii) appellate review by the Board of Patent Appeals and Interferences or by a Federal court in a case in which the patent was issued under a decision in the review reversing an adverse determination of patentability,

the term of the patent shall be extended 1 day for each day of the pendency of the proceeding, order, or review, as the case may be.

(2) *Limitations.*—

(A) *In general.*—To the extent that periods of delay attributable to grounds specified in paragraph (1) overlap, the period of any adjustment granted under this subsection shall not exceed the actual number of days the issuance of the patent was delayed.

(B) *Disclaimed term.*—No patent the term of which has been disclaimed beyond a specified date may be adjusted under this section beyond the expiration date specified in the disclaimer.

(C) *Reduction of period of adjustment.*—

(i) The period of adjustment of the term of a patent under paragraph (1) shall be reduced by a period equal to the period of time during which the applicant failed to engage in reasonable efforts to conclude prosecution of the application.

(ii) With respect to adjustments to patent term made under the authority of paragraph (1)(B), an applicant shall be deemed to have failed to engage in reasonable efforts to conclude processing or examination of an application for the cumulative total of any periods of time in excess of 3 months that are taken to respond to a notice from the Office making any rejection, objection, argument, or other request, measuring such 3-month period from the date the notice was given or mailed to the applicant.

(iii) The Director shall prescribe regulations establishing the circumstances that constitute a failure of an applicant to engage in reasonable efforts to conclude processing or examination of an application.

(3) *Procedures for patent term adjustment determination.—*

(A) The Director shall prescribe regulations establishing procedures for the application for and determination of patent term adjustments under this subsection.

(B) Under the procedures established under subparagraph (A), the Director shall—

(i) make a determination of the period of any patent term adjustment under this subsection, and shall transmit a notice of that determination with the written notice of allowance of the application under section 151; and

(ii) provide the applicant one opportunity to request reconsideration of any patent term adjustment determination made by the Director.

(C) The Director shall reinstate all or part of the cumulative period of time of an adjustment under paragraph (2)(C) if the applicant, prior to the issuance of the patent, makes a showing that, in spite of all due care, the applicant was unable to respond within the 3-month period, but in no case shall more than three additional months for each such response beyond the original 3-month period be reinstated.

35 U.S.C. § 154

(D) The Director shall proceed to grant the patent after completion of the Director's determination of a patent term adjustment under the procedures established under this subsection, notwithstanding any appeal taken by the applicant of such determination.

(4) *Appeal of patent term adjustment determination.*—

(A) An applicant dissatisfied with a determination made by the Director under paragraph (3) shall have remedy by a civil action against the Director filed in the United States District Court for the District of Columbia within 180 days after the grant of the patent. Chapter 7 of title 5 shall apply to such action. Any final judgment resulting in a change to the period of adjustment of the patent term shall be served on the Director, and the Director shall thereafter alter the term of the patent to reflect such change.

(B) The determination of a patent term adjustment under this subsection shall not be subject to appeal or challenge by a third party prior to the grant of the patent.

(c) *Continuation.*—

(1) *Determination.*—The term of a patent that is in force on or that results from an application filed before the date that is 6 months after the date of the enactment of the Uruguay Round Agreements Act* shall be the greater of the 20-year term as provided in subsection (a), or 17 years from grant, subject to any terminal disclaimers.

(2) *Remedies.*—The remedies of sections 283, 284, and 285 of this title shall not apply to acts which—

(A) were commenced or for which substantial investment was made before the date that is 6 months after the date of the enactment of the Uruguay Round Agreements Act; and

(B) became infringing by reason of paragraph (1).

(3) *Remuneration.*—The acts referred to in paragraph (2) may be continued only upon the payment of an equitable remuneration to the patentee that is determined in an action brought under chapter 28

---

* *Ed. Note:* The Uruguay Round Agreements Act was enacted on December 8, 1994.

35 U.S.C. § 154

and chapter 29 (other than those provisions excluded by paragraph (2)) of this title.

(d) *Provisional rights.**—

(1) *In general.*—In addition to other rights provided by this section, a patent shall include the right to obtain a reasonable royalty from any person who, during the period beginning on the date of publication of the application for such patent under section 122(b), or in the case of an international application filed under the treaty defined in section 351(a) designating the United States under Article 21(2)(a) of such treaty, the date of publication of the application, and ending on the date the patent is issued—

(A)(i) makes, uses, offers for sale, or sells in the United States the invention as claimed in the published patent application or imports such an invention into the United States; or

(ii) if the invention as claimed in the published patent application is a process, uses, offers for sale, or sells in the United States or imports into the United States products made by that process as claimed in the published patent application; and

(B) had actual notice of the published patent application and, in a case in which the right arising under this paragraph is based upon an international application designating the United States that is published in a language other than English, had a translation of the international application into the English language.

(2) *Right based on substantially identical inventions.*—The right under paragraph (1) to obtain a reasonable royalty shall not be available under this subsection unless the invention as claimed in the patent is substantially identical to the invention as claimed in the published patent application.

(3) *Time limitation on obtaining a reasonable royalty.*—The right under paragraph (1) to obtain a reasonable royalty shall be available only in an action brought not later than 6 years after the patent is issued.

---

* *Ed. Note:* Pursuant to §4508 of Pub. L. 106-113, §154(d) took effect one year after the Nov. 29, 1999 date of enactment and applies to all applications filed under §111 on or after that date and all applications complying with §371 that resulted from international applications filed on or after that date.

35 U.S.C. § 154

The right under paragraph (1) to obtain a reasonable royalty shall not be affected by the duration of the period described in paragraph (1).

(4) *Requirements for international applications.*—

(A) *Effective date.*—The right under paragraph (1) to obtain a reasonable royalty based upon the publication under the treaty defined in section 351(a) of an international application designating the United States shall commence on the date of publication under the treaty of the international application, or, if the publication under the treaty of the international application is in a language other than English, on the date on which the Patent and Trademark Office receives a translation of the publication in the English language.

(B) *Copies.*—The Director may require the applicant to provide a copy of the international application and a translation thereof.

(July 19, 1952, ch. 950, §1, 66 Stat. 804; July 24, 1965, Pub. L. 89-83, §5, 79 Stat. 261; Dec. 12, 1980, Pub. L. 96-517, §4, 94 Stat. 3018; Aug. 23, 1988, Pub. L. 100-418, §9002, 102 Stat. 1563; Dec. 8, 1994, Pub. L. 103-465, §532, 108 Stat. 4983; Oct. 11, 1996, Pub. L. 104-295, Title V91, 110 Stat. 3529; Nov. 29, 1999, Pub. L. 106-113, §§4402, 4504, 113 Stat. 1501A-557, 564; Nov. 2, 2002, Pub. L. 107-273, §§13204, 13206, 116 Stat. 1904.)

§ 155   Patent term extension

Notwithstanding the provisions of section 154, the term of a patent which encompasses within its scope a composition of matter or a process for using such composition shall be extended if such composition or process has been subjected to a regulatory review by the Federal Food and Drug Administration pursuant to the Federal Food, Drug and Cosmetic Act leading to the publication of regulation permitting the interstate distribution and sale of such composition or process and for which there has thereafter been a stay of regulation of approval imposed pursuant to Section 409 of the Federal Food, Drug and Cosmetic Act which stay was in effect on January 1, 1981, by a length of time to be measured from the date such stay of regulation of approval was imposed until such proceedings are finally resolved and commercial marketing permitted. The patentee, his heirs, successors or assigns shall notify the Director within ninety days of the date of enactment of this section or the date the stay of regulation of approval has been removed, whichever is later, of the number of the patent to be extended and the date the stay was imposed and the date commercial marketing was permitted. On receipt of such notice, the Director shall promptly issue to the owner of record of the patent a certificate of extension, under seal, stating the fact and length of the extension and identifying the composition of matter or process for using such composition to which such extension is applicable. Such certificate shall be recorded in the official file of each patent extended and such certificate shall be considered as part of the original patent, and an appropriate notice shall be published in the Official Gazette of the Patent and Trademark Office.

(Jan. 4, 1983, Pub. L. 97-414, §11, 96 Stat. 2065; Nov. 29, 1999, Pub. L. 106-113, §4732, 113 Stat. 1501A-581.)

§ 155A   Patent term restoration

(a) Notwithstanding section 154 of this title, the term of each of the following patents shall be extended in accordance with this section:

(1) Any patent which encompasses within its scope a composition of matter which is a new drug product, if during the regulatory review of the product by the Federal Food and Drug Administration—

(A) the Federal Food and Drug Administration notified the patentee, by letter dated February 20, 1976, that such product's new drug application was not approvable under section 505(b)(1) of the Federal Food, Drug and Cosmetic Act;

(B) in 1977 the patentee submitted to the Federal Food and Drug Administration the results of a health effects test to evaluate the carcinogenic potential of such product;

(C) the Federal Food and Drug Administration approved, by letter dated December 18, 1979, the new drug application for such product; and

(D) the Federal Food and Drug Administration approved, by letter dated May 26, 1981, a supplementary application covering the facility for the production of such product.

(2) Any patent which encompasses within its scope a process for using the composition of matter described in paragraph (1).

(b) The term of any patent described in subsection (a) shall be extended for a period equal to the period beginning February 20, 1976, and ending May 26, 1981, and such patent shall have the effect as if originally issued with such extended term.

(c) The patentee of any patent described in subsection (a) of this section shall, within ninety days after the date of enactment of this section, notify the Director of the number of any patent so extended. On receipt of such notice, the Director shall confirm such extension by placing a notice thereof in the official file of such patent and publishing an appropriate notice of such extension in the Official Gazette of the Patent and Trademark Office.

(Added Oct. 13, 1983, Pub. L. 98-127, §4, 97 Stat. 832; Nov. 29, 1999, Pub. L. 106-113, §4732, 113 Stat. 1501A-581.)

§ 156   Extension of patent term

(a) The term of a patent which claims a product, a method of using a product, or a method of manufacturing a product shall be extended in accordance with this section from the original expiration date of the patent, which shall include any patent term adjustment granted under section 154(b), if—

   (1) the term of the patent has not expired before an application is submitted under subsection (d)(1) for its extension;

   (2) the term of the patent has never been extended under subsection (e)(1) of this section;

   (3) an application for extension is submitted by the owner of record of the patent or its agent and in accordance with the requirements of paragraphs (1) through (4) of subsection (d);

   (4) the product has been subject to a regulatory review period before its commercial marketing or use;

   (5) (A) except as provided in subparagraph (B) or (C), the permission for the commercial marketing or use of the product after such regulatory review period is the first permitted commercial marketing or use of the product under the provision of law under which such regulatory review period occurred;

(B) in the case of a patent which claims a method of manufacturing the product which primarily uses recombinant DNA technology in the manufacture of the product, the permission for the commercial marketing or use of the product after such regulatory review period is the first permitted commercial marketing or use of a product manufactured under the process claimed in the patent; or

(C) for purposes of subparagraph (A), in the case of a patent which—

(i) claims a new animal drug or a veterinary biological product which (I) is not covered by the claims in any other patent which has been extended, and (II) has received permission for the commercial marketing or use in non-food-producing animals and in food-producing animals, and

(ii) was not extended on the basis of the regulatory review period for use in non-food-producing animals,

the permission for the commercial marketing or use of the drug or product after the regulatory review period for use in food-producing animals is the first permitted commercial marketing or use of the drug or product for administration to a food-producing animal.

The product referred to in paragraphs (4) and (5) is hereinafter in this section referred to as the "approved product".

(b) Except as provided in subsection (d)(5)(F), the rights derived from any patent the term of which is extended under this section shall during the period during which the term of the patent is extended—

(1) in the case of a patent which claims a product, be limited to any use approved for the product—

(A) before the expiration of the term of the patent—

(i) under the provision of law under which the applicable regulatory review occurred, or

(ii) under the provision of law under which any regulatory review described in paragraph (1), (4), or (5) of subsection (g) occurred, and

(B) on or after the expiration of the regulatory review period upon which the extension of the patent was based;

(2) in the case of a patent which claims a method of using a product, be limited to any use claimed by the patent and approved for the product—

(A) before the expiration of the term of the patent—

(i) under any provision of law under which an applicable regulatory review occurred, and

(ii) under the provision of law under which any regulatory review described in paragraph (1), (4), or (5) of subsection (g) occurred, and

(B) on or after the expiration of the regulatory review period upon which the extension of the patent was based; and

(3) in the case of a patent which claims a method of manufacturing a product, be limited to the method of manufacturing as used to make—

(A) the approved product, or

(B) the product if it has been subject to a regulatory review period described in paragraph (1), (4), or (5) of subsection (g).

As used in this subsection, the term "product" includes an approved product.

(c) The term of a patent eligible for extension under subsection (a) shall be extended by the time equal to the regulatory review period for the approved product which period occurs after the date the patent is issued, except that—

(1) each period of the regulatory review period shall be reduced by any period determined under subsection (d)(2)(B) during which the applicant for the patent extension did not act with due diligence during such period of the regulatory review period;

(2) after any reduction required by paragraph (1), the period of extension shall include only one-half of the time remaining in the periods described in paragraphs (1)(B)(i), (2)(B)(i), (3)(B)(i), (4)(B)(i), and (5)(B)(i) of subsection (g);

35 U.S.C. § 156

(3) if the period remaining in the term of a patent after the date of the approval of the approved product under the provision of law under which such regulatory review occurred when added to the regulatory review period as revised under paragraphs (1) and (2) exceeds fourteen years, the period of extension shall be reduced so that the total of both such periods does not exceed fourteen years; and

(4) in no event shall more than one patent be extended under subsection (e)(1) for the same regulatory review period for any product.

(d) (1) To obtain an extension of the term of a patent under this section, the owner of record of the patent or its agent shall submit an application to the Director. Except as provided in paragraph (5), such an application may only be submitted within the sixty-day period beginning on the date the product received permission under the provision of law under which the applicable regulatory review period occurred for commercial marketing or use. The application shall contain—

(A) the identity of the approved product and the Federal statute under which regulatory review occurred;

(B) the identity of the patent for which an extension is being sought and the identity of each claim of such patent which claims the approved product or a method of using or manufacturing the approved product;

(C) information to enable the Director to determine under subsections (a) and (b) the eligibility of a patent for extension and the rights that will be derived from the extension and information to enable the Director and the Secretary of Health and Human Services or the Secretary of Agriculture to determine the period of the extension under subsection (g);

(D) a brief description of the activities undertaken by the applicant during the applicable regulatory review period with respect to the approved product and the significant dates applicable to such activities; and

(E) such patent or other information as the Director may require.

(2) (A) Within 60 days of the submittal of an application for extension of the term of a patent under paragraph (1), the Director shall notify—

> (i) the Secretary of Agriculture if the patent claims a drug product or a method of using or manufacturing a drug product and the drug product is subject to the Virus-Serum-Toxin Act, and

> (ii) the Secretary of Health and Human Services if the patent claims any other drug product, a medical device, or a food additive or color additive or a method of using or manufacturing such a product, device, or additive and if the product, device, and additive are subject to the Federal Food, Drug, and Cosmetic Act,

of the extension application and shall submit to the Secretary who is so notified a copy of the application. Not later than 30 days after the receipt of an application from the Director, the Secretary receiving the application shall review the dates contained in the application pursuant to paragraph (1)(C) and determine the applicable regulatory review period, shall notify the Director of the determination, and shall publish in the Federal Register a notice of such determination.

(B) (i) If a petition is submitted to the Secretary making the determination under subparagraph (A), not later than 180 days after the publication of the determination under subparagraph (A), upon which it may reasonably be determined that the applicant did not act with due diligence during the applicable regulatory review period, the Secretary making the determination shall, in accordance with regulations promulgated by such Secretary, determine if the applicant acted with due diligence during the applicable regulatory review period. The Secretary making the determination shall make such determination not later than 90 days after the receipt of such a petition. For a drug product, device, or additive subject to the Federal Food, Drug, and Cosmetic Act or the Public Health Service Act, the Secretary may not delegate the authority to make the determination prescribed by this clause to an office below the Office of the Director of Food and Drugs. For a product subject to the Virus-Serum-Toxin Act, the Secretary of Agriculture may not delegate the authority to make the determination prescribed by this clause to an office below the Office of the Assistant Secretary for Marketing and Inspection Services.

(ii) The Secretary making a determination under clause (i) shall notify the Director of the determination and shall publish in the Federal Register a notice of such determination together with the factual and legal basis for such determination. Any interested person may request, within the 60-day period beginning on the publication of a determination, the Secretary making the determination to hold an informal hearing on the determination. If such a request is made within such period, such Secretary shall hold such hearing not later than 30 days after the date of the request, or at the request of the person making the request, not later than 60 days after such date. The Secretary who is holding the hearing shall provide notice of the hearing to the owner of the patent involved and to any interested person and provide the owner and any interested person an opportunity to participate in the hearing. Within 30 days after the completion of the hearing, such Secretary shall affirm or revise the determination which was the subject of the hearing and shall notify the Director of any revision of the determination and shall publish any such revision in the Federal Register.

(3) For the purposes of paragraph (2)(B), the term "due diligence" means that degree of attention, continuous directed effort, and timeliness as may reasonably be expected from, and are ordinarily exercised by, a person during a regulatory review period.

(4) An application for the extension of the term of a patent is subject to the disclosure requirements prescribed by the Director.

(5) (A) If the owner of record of the patent or its agent reasonably expects that the applicable regulatory review period described in paragraph (1)(B)(ii), (2)(B)(ii), (3)(B)(ii), (4)(B)(ii), or (5)(B)(ii) of subsection (g) that began for a product that is the subject of such

patent may extend beyond the expiration of the patent term in effect, the owner or its agent may submit an application to the Director for an interim extension during the period beginning 6 months, and ending 15 days, before such term is due to expire. The application shall contain—

(i) the identity of the product subject to regulatory review and the Federal statute under which such review is occurring;

(ii) the identity of the patent for which interim extension is being sought and the identity of each claim of such patent which claims the product under regulatory review or a method of using or manufacturing the product;

(iii) information to enable the Director to determine under subsection (a)(1), (2) and (3) the eligibility of a patent for extension;

(iv) a brief description of the activities undertaken by the applicant during the applicable regulatory review period to date with respect to the product under review and the significant dates applicable to such activities; and

(v) such patent or other information as the Director may require.

(B) If the Director determines that, except for permission to market or use the product commercially, the patent would be eligible for an extension of the patent term under this section, the Director shall publish in the Federal Register a notice of such determination, including the identity of the product under regulatory review, and shall issue to the applicant a certificate of interim extension for a period of not more than 1 year.

(C) The owner of record of a patent, or its agent, for which an interim extension has been granted under subparagraph (B), may apply for not more than 4 subsequent interim extensions under this paragraph, except that, in the case of a patent subject to subsection (g)(6)(C), the owner of record of the patent, or its agent, may apply for only 1 subsequent interim extension under this paragraph. Each such subsequent application shall be made during the period beginning 60 days before, and ending 30 days before, the expiration of the preceding interim extension.

(D) Each certificate of interim extension under this paragraph shall be recorded in the official file of the patent and shall be considered part of the original patent.

(E) Any interim extension granted under this paragraph shall terminate at the end of the 60-day period beginning on the date on which the product involved receives permission for commercial marketing or use, except that, if within that 60-day period the applicant notifies the Director of such permission and submits any additional information under paragraph (1) of this subsection not previously contained in the application for interim extension, the patent shall be further extended, in accordance with the provisions of this section—

> (i) for not to exceed 5 years from the date of expiration of the original patent term; or

> (ii) if the patent is subject to subsection (g)(6)(C), from the date on which the product involved receives approval for commercial marketing or use.

(F) The rights derived from any patent the term of which is extended under this paragraph shall, during the period of interim extension—

> (i) in the case of a patent which claims a product, be limited to any use then under regulatory review;

> (ii) in the case of a patent which claims a method of using a product, be limited to any use claimed by the patent then under regulatory review; and

> (iii) in the case of a patent which claims a method of manufacturing a product, be limited to the method of manufacturing as used to make the product then under regulatory review.

(e) (1) A determination that a patent is eligible for extension may be made by the Director solely on the basis of the representations contained in the application for the extension. If the Director determines that a patent is eligible for extension under subsection (a) and that the requirements of paragraphs (1) through (4) of subsection (d) have been complied with, the Director shall issue to the applicant for the extension of the term of the patent a certificate of extension, under seal, for the period prescribed by subsection (c). Such certificate shall be recorded in the official file of the patent and shall be considered as part of the original patent.

(2) If the term of a patent for which an application has been submitted under subsection (d)(1) would expire before a certificate of extension is issued or denied under paragraph (1) respecting the application, the Director shall extend, until such determination is made, the term of the patent for periods of up to one year if he determines that the patent is eligible for extension.

(f) For purposes of this section:

(1) The term "product" means:

(A) A drug product.

(B) Any medical device, food additive, or color additive subject to regulation under the Federal Food, Drug, and Cosmetic Act.

(2) The term "drug product" means the active ingredient of—

(A) a new drug, antibiotic drug, or human biological product (as those terms are used in the Federal Food, Drug, and Cosmetic Act and the Public Health Service Act), or

(B) a new animal drug or veterinary biological product (as those terms are used in the Federal Food, Drug, and Cosmetic Act and the Virus-Serum-Toxin Act) which is not primarily manufactured using recombinant DNA, recombinant RNA, hybridoma technology, or other processes involving site specific genetic manipulation techniques,

including any salt or ester of the active ingredient, as a single entity or in combination with another active ingredient.

(3) The term "major health or environmental effects test" means a test which is reasonably related to the evaluation of the health or environmental effects of a product, which requires at least six months to conduct, and the data from which is submitted to receive permission for commercial marketing or use. Periods of analysis or evalua-

tion of test results are not to be included in determining if the conduct of a test required at least six months.

(4) (A) Any reference to section 351 is a reference to section 351 of the Public Health Service Act.

(B) Any reference to section 503, 505, 512, or 515 is a reference to section 503, 505, 512, or 515 of the Federal Food, Drug, and Cosmetic Act.

(C) Any reference to the Virus-Serum-Toxin Act is a reference to the Act of March 4, 1913 (21 U.S.C. 151-158).

(5) The term "informal hearing" has the meaning prescribed for such term by section 201(y) of the Federal Food, Drug, and Cosmetic Act.

(6) The term "patent" means a patent issued by the United States Patent and Trademark Office.

(7) The term "date of enactment" as used in this section means September 24, 1984, for a human drug product, a medical device, food additive, or color additive.

(8) The term "date of enactment" as used in this section means the date of enactment of the Generic Animal Drug and Patent Term Restoration Act for an animal drug or a veterinary biological product.

(g) For purposes of this section, the term "regulatory review period" has the following meanings:

(1) (A) In the case of a product which is a new drug, antibiotic drug, or human biological product, the term means the period described in subparagraph (B) to which the limitation described in paragraph (6) applies.

(B) The regulatory review period for a new drug, antibiotic drug, or human biological product is the sum of—

(i) the period beginning on the date an exemption under subsection (i) of section 505 or subsection (d) of section 507 became effective for the approved product and ending on the date an application was initially submitted for such drug product under section 351, 505, or 507, and

(ii) the period beginning on the date the application was initially submitted for the approved product under section 351, subsection (b) of section 505, or section 507 and ending on the date such application was approved under such section.

(2) (A) In the case of a product which is a food additive or color additive, the term means the period described in subparagraph (B) to which the limitation described in paragraph (6) applies.

(B) The regulatory review period for a food or color additive is the sum of—

(i) the period beginning on the date a major health or environmental effects test on the additive was initiated and ending on the date a petition was initially submitted with respect to the product under the Federal Food, Drug, and Cosmetic Act requesting the issuance of a regulation for use of the product, and

(ii) the period beginning on the date a petition was initially submitted with respect to the product under the Federal Food, Drug, and Cosmetic Act requesting the issuance of a regulation for use of the product, and ending on the date such regulation became effective or, if objections were filed to such regulation, ending on the date such objections were resolved and commercial marketing was permitted or, if commercial marketing was permitted and later revoked pending further proceedings as a result of such objections, ending on the date such proceedings were finally resolved and commercial marketing was permitted.

(3) (A) In the case of a product which is a medical device, the term means the period described in subparagraph (B) to which the limitation described in paragraph (6) applies.

(B) The regulatory review period for a medical device is the sum of—

(i) the period beginning on the date a clinical investigation on humans involving the device was begun and ending on the date an application was initially submitted with respect to the device under section 515, and

(ii) the period beginning on the date an application was initially submitted with respect to the device under section 515 and ending on the date such application was approved under such Act or the period beginning on the date a notice of completion of a product development protocol was initially submitted under section 515(f)(5) and ending on the date the protocol was declared completed under section 515(f)(6).

(4) (A) In the case of a product which is a new animal drug, the term means the period described in subparagraph (B) to which the limitation described in paragraph (6) applies.

(B) The regulatory review period for a new animal drug product is the sum of—

(i) the period beginning on the earlier of the date a major health or environmental effects test on the drug was initiated or the date an exemption under subsection (j) of section 512 became effective for the approved new animal drug product and ending on the date an application was initially submitted for such animal drug product under section 512, and

(ii) the period beginning on the date the application was initially submitted for the approved animal drug product under subsection (b) of section 512 and ending on the date such application was approved under such section.

(5) (A) In the case of a product which is a veterinary biological product, the term means the period described in subparagraph (B) to which the limitation described in paragraph (6) applies.

(B) The regulatory period for a veterinary biological product is the sum of—

(i) the period beginning on the date the authority to prepare an experimental biological product under the Virus-Serum-Toxin Act became effective and ending on the date an application for a license was submitted under the Virus-Serum-Toxin Act, and

(ii) the period beginning on the date an application for a license was initially submitted for approval under the Virus-Serum-Toxin Act and ending on the date such license was issued.

(6) A period determined under any of the preceding paragraphs is subject to the following limitations:

(A) If the patent involved was issued after the date of the enactment of this section, the period of extension determined on the basis of the regulatory review period determined under any such paragraph may not exceed five years.

(B) If the patent involved was issued before the date of the enactment of this section and—

(i) no request for an exemption described in paragraph (1)(B) or (4)(B) was submitted and no request for the authority described in paragraph (5)(B) was submitted,

(ii) no major health or environmental effects test described in paragraph (2)(B) or (4)(B) was initiated and no petition for a regulation or application for registration described in such paragraph was submitted, or

(iii) no clinical investigation described in paragraph (3) was begun or product development protocol described in such paragraph was submitted,

before such date for the approved product the period of extension determined on the basis of the regulatory review period determined under any such paragraph may not exceed five years.

(C) If the patent involved was issued before the date of the enactment of this section and if an action described in subparagraph (B) was taken before the date of enactment of this section with respect to the approved product and the commercial marketing or use of the product has not been approved before such date, the period of extension determined on the basis of the regulatory review period determined under such paragraph may not exceed two years or in the case of an approved product which is a new animal drug or veterinary biological product (as those terms are used in the Federal Food, Drug, and Cosmetic Act or the Virus-Serum-Toxin Act), three years.

(h) The Director may establish such fees as the Director determines appropriate to cover the costs to the Office of receiving and acting upon applications under this section.

35 U.S.C. § 156

(Sept. 24, 1984, Pub. L., 98-417, §201, 98 Stat. 1598-1602; Nov. 16, 1988, Pub. L. 100-670, §201, 102 Stat. 3984-3988; Dec. 3, 1993, Pub. L. 103-179, §§5-6, 107 Stat. 2040; Dec. 8, 1994, Pub. L. 103-465, §532, 108 Stat. 4983; Nov. 21, 1997, Pub. L. 105-115, §125, 111 Stat. 2326; Nov. 29, 1999, Pub. L. 106-113, §4404, 113 Stat. 1501A-560; Nov. 2, 2002, Pub. L. 107-273, §13206, 116 Stat.1904.)

§ 157   Statutory invention registration

(a) Notwithstanding any other provision of this title, the Director is authorized to publish a statutory invention registration containing the specification and drawings of a regularly filed application for a patent without examination if the applicant—

(1) meets the requirements of section 112 of this title;

(2) has complied with the requirements for printing, as set forth in regulations of the Director;

(3) waives the right to receive a patent on the invention within such period as may be prescribed by the Director; and

(4) pays application, publication and other processing fees established by the Director.

If an interference is declared with respect to such an application, a statutory invention registration may not be published unless the issue of priority of invention is finally determined in favor of the applicant.

(b) The waiver under subsection (a)(3) of this section by an applicant shall take effect upon publication of the statutory invention registration.

(c) A statutory invention registration published pursuant to this section shall have all of the attributes specified for patents in this title except those specified in section 183 and sections 271 through 289 of this title. A statutory invention registration shall not have any of the attributes specified for patents in any other provision of law other than this title. A statutory invention registration published pursuant to this section shall give appropriate notice to the public, pursuant to regulations which the Director shall issue, of the preceding provisions of this subsection. The invention with respect to which a statutory invention certificate is published is not a patented invention for purposes of section 292 of this title.

(d) The Director shall report to the Congress annually on the use of statutory invention registrations. Such report shall include an assessment of the degree to which agencies of the federal government are making use of the statutory invention registration system, the degree to which it aids the management of federally developed technology, and an assessment of the cost savings to the Federal Government of the use of such procedures.

(Nov. 8, 1984, Pub. L. 98-622, §102, 98 Stat. 3383; Nov. 29, 1999, Pub. L. 106-113, §4732, 113 Stat. 1501A-581.)

CHAPTER 15—PLANT PATENTS

§ 161   Patents for plants

Whoever invents or discovers and asexually reproduces any distinct and new variety of plant, including cultivated sports, mutants, hybrids, and newly found seedlings, other than a tuber propagated plant or a plant found in an uncultivated state, may obtain a patent therefor, subject to the conditions and requirements of this title.

The provisions of this title relating to patents for inventions shall apply to patents for plants, except as otherwise provided.

(July 19, 1952, ch. 950, §1, 66 Stat. 804; Sept. 3, 1954, ch. 1259, 68 Stat. 1190.)

§ 162   Description, claim

No plant patent shall be declared invalid for noncompliance with section 112 of this title if the description is as complete as is reasonably possible.

The claim in the specification shall be in formal terms to the plant shown and described.

(July 19, 1952, ch. 950, §1, 66 Stat. 804.)

35 U.S.C. § 161

§ 163   Grant

In the case of a plant patent, the grant shall include the right to exclude others from asexually reproducing the plant, and from using, offering for sale, or selling the plant so reproduced, or any of its parts, throughout the United States, or from importing the plant so reproduced, or any parts thereof, into the United States.

(July 19, 1952, ch. 950, §1, 66 Stat. 804; Oct. 27, 1998, §3, 112 Stat. 2781.)

§ 164   Assistance of Department of Agriculture

The President may by Executive order direct the Secretary of Agriculture, in accordance with the requests of the Director, for the purpose of carrying into effect the provisions of this title with respect to plants (1) to furnish available information of the Department of Agriculture, (2) to conduct through the appropriate bureau or division of the Department research upon special problems, or (3) to detail to the Director officers and employees of the Department.

(July 19, 1952, ch. 950, §1, 66 Stat. 804.)

CHAPTER 16—DESIGNS

SEC.

§ 171   Patents for designs

Whoever invents any new, original and ornamental design for an article of manufacture may obtain a patent therefor, subject to the conditions and requirements of this title.

The provisions of this title relating to patents for inventions shall apply to patents for designs, except as otherwise provided.

(July 19, 1952, ch. 950, §1, 66 Stat. 805.)

§ 172   Right of priority

The right of priority provided for by subsections (a) through (d) of section 119 of this title and the time specified in section 102(d) shall be six months in the case of designs. The right of priority provided for by section 119(e) of this title shall not apply to designs.

(July 19, 1952, ch. 950, §1, 66 Stat. 805; Dec. 8, 1994, Pub. L. 103-465, §532, 108 Stat. 4983.)

§ 173   Term of design patent

Patents for designs shall be granted for the term of fourteen years from the date of grant.

(July 19, 1952, ch. 950, §1, 66 Stat. 805; Aug. 27, 1982, Pub. L. 97-247, §16, 96 Stat. 321; Dec. 8, 1994, Pub. L. 103-465, §532, 108 Stat. 4983.)

CHAPTER 17—SECRECY OF CERTAIN INVENTIONS AND FILING APPLICATIONS IN FOREIGN COUNTRY

SEC.

§ 181 Secrecy of certain inventions and withholding of patent

Whenever publication or disclosure by the publication of an application or by the grant of a patent on an invention in which the Government has a property interest might, in the opinion of the head of the interested Government agency, be detrimental to the national security, the Commissioner of Patents upon being so notified shall order that the invention be kept secret and shall withhold the publication of the application or the grant of a patent therefor under the conditions set forth hereinafter.

Whenever the publication or disclosure of an invention by the publication of an application or by the granting of a patent, in which the Government does not have a property interest, might, in the opinion of the Commissioner of Patents, be detrimental to the national security, he shall make the application for patent in which such invention is disclosed available for inspection to the Atomic Energy Commission, the Secretary of Defense, and the chief officer of any other department or agency of the Government designated by the President as a defense agency of the United States.

Each individual to whom the application is disclosed shall sign a dated acknowledgment thereof, which acknowledgment shall be entered in the file of the application. If, in the opinion of the Atomic Energy Commission, the Secretary of a Defense Department, or the chief officer of another department or agency so designated, the publication or disclosure of the invention by the publication of the application or by the granting of a patent therefor would be detrimental to the national security, the Atomic Energy Commission, the Secretary of a Defense Department, or such other chief officer shall notify the Commissioner of Patents and the Commissioner of Patents shall order that the invention be kept secret and shall withhold the publication of the application or the grant of a patent for such period as the national interest requires, and notify the applicant thereof. Upon proper showing by the head of the department or agency who caused the secrecy order to be issued that the examination of the application might jeopardize the national interest, the Commissioner of Patents shall thereupon maintain the application in a sealed condition and notify the applicant thereof. The owner of an application which has been placed under a secrecy order shall have a right to appeal from the order to the Secretary of Commerce under rules prescribed by him.

An invention shall not be ordered kept secret and the publication of an application or the grant of a patent withheld for a period of more than one year. The Commissioner of Patents shall renew the order at the end thereof, or at the end of any renewal period, for additional periods of one year upon notification by the head of the department or the chief officer of the agency who caused the order to be issued that an affirmative determination has been made that the national interest continues so to require. An order in effect, or issued, during a time when the United States is at war, shall remain in effect for the duration of hostilities and one year following cessation of hostilities. An order in effect, or issued, during a national emergency declared by the President shall remain in effect for the duration of the national emergency and six months thereafter. The Commissioner of Patents may rescind any order upon notification by the heads of the departments and the chief officers of the agencies who caused the order to be issued that the publication or disclosure of the invention is no longer deemed detrimental to the national security.

(July 19, 1952, ch. 950, §1, 66 Stat. 805; Nov. 29, 1999, Pub. L. 106-113, §4507, 113 Stat. 1501A-565).

§ 182   Abandonment of invention for unauthorized disclosure

The invention disclosed in an application for patent subject to an order made pursuant to section 181 of this title may be held abandoned upon its being established by the Commissioner of Patents that in violation of said order the invention has been published or disclosed or that an application for a patent therefor has been filed in a foreign country by the inventor, his successors, assigns, or legal representatives, or anyone in privity with him or them, without the consent of the Commissioner of Patents. The abandonment shall be held to have occurred as of the time of violation. The consent of the Commissioner of Patents shall not be given without the concurrence of the heads of the departments and the chief officers of the agencies who caused the order to be issued. A holding of abandonment shall constitute forfeiture by the applicant, his successors, assigns, or legal representatives, or anyone in privity with him or them, of all claims against the United States based upon such invention.

(July 19, 1952, ch. 950, §1, 66 Stat. 806.)

§ 183   Right to compensation

An applicant, his successors, assigns, or legal representatives, whose patent is withheld as herein provided, shall have the right, beginning at the date the applicant is notified that, except for such order, his application is otherwise in condition for allowance, or February 1, 1952, whichever is later, and ending six years after a patent is issued thereon, to apply to the head of any department or agency who caused the order to be issued for compensation for the damage caused by the order of secrecy and/or for the use of the invention by the Government, resulting from his disclosure. The right to compensation for use shall begin on the date of the first use of the invention by the Government. The head of the department or agency is authorized, upon the presentation of a claim, to enter into an agreement with the applicant, his successors, assigns, or legal representatives, in full settlement for the damage and/or use. This settlement agreement shall be conclusive for all purposes notwithstanding any other provision of law to the contrary. If full settlement of the claim cannot be effected, the head of the department or agency may award and pay to such applicant, his successors, assigns, or legal representatives, a sum not exceeding 75 per centum of the sum which the head of the department or agency considers just compensation for the damage and/or use. A claimant may bring suit against the United States in the United States Claims Court* or in the District Court of the United States for the district in which such claimant is a resident for an amount which when added to the award shall constitute just compensation for the damage and/or use of the invention by the Government. The owner of any patent issued upon an application that was subject to a secrecy order issued pursuant to section 181 of this title, who did not apply for compensation as above provided, shall have the right, after the date of issuance of such patent, to bring suit in the United States Claims Court for just compensation for the damage caused by reason of the order of secrecy and/or use by the Government of the invention resulting from his disclosure. The right to compensation for use shall begin on the date of the first use of the invention by the Government. In a suit under the provisions of this section the United States may avail itself of all defenses it may plead in an action under section 1498 of title 28. This section shall not confer a right of action on anyone or his successors, assigns, or legal representatives who, while in the full-time employment or service of the United States, discovered, invented, or developed the invention on which the claim is based.

(July 19, 1952, ch. 950, §1, 66 Stat. 806; Apr. 2, 1982, Pub. L. 97-164, §160, 96 Stat. 48.)

---

* *Ed. Note:* Pursuant to the Court of Federal Claims Technical and Procedural Improvements Act of 1992, §902(b)(2), Pub. L. 102-572, 106 Stat. 4516, statutory references to the U.S. Claims Court are deemed to refer to the U.S. Court of Federal Claims.

35 U.S.C. § 183

§ 184   Filing of application in foreign country

Except when authorized by a license obtained from the Commissioner of Patents a person shall not file or cause or authorize to be filed in any foreign country prior to six months after filing in the United states an application for patent or for the registration of a utility model, industrial design, or model in respect of an invention made in this country. A license shall not be granted with respect to an invention subject to an order issued by the Commissioner of Patents pursuant to section 181 of this title without the concurrence of the head of the departments and the chief officers of the agencies who caused the order to be issued. The license may be granted retroactively where an application has been filed abroad through error and without deceptive intent and the application does not disclose an invention within the scope of section 181 of this title.

The term "application" when used in this chapter includes applications and any modifications, amendments, or supplements thereto, or divisions thereof.

The scope of a license shall permit subsequent modifications, amendments, and supplements containing additional subject matter if the application upon which the request for the license is based is not, or was not, required to be made available for inspection under section 181 of this title and if such modifications, amendments, and supplements do not change the general nature of the invention in a manner which would require such application to be made available for inspection under such section 181. In any case in which a license is not, or was not, required in order to file an application in any foreign country, such subsequent modifications, amendments, and supplements may be made, without a license, to the application filed in the foreign country if the United States application was not required to be made available for inspection under section 181 and if such modifications, amendments, and supplements do not, or did not, change the general nature of the invention in a manner which would require the United States application to have been made available for inspection under such section 181.

(July 19, 1952, ch. 950, §1, 66 Stat. 807; Aug. 23, 1988, Pub. L. 100-418, §9101, 102 Stat. 1567-68.)

35 U.S.C. § 184

§ 185   Patent barred for filing without license

Notwithstanding any other provisions of law any person, and his successors, assigns, or legal representatives, shall not receive a United States patent for an invention if that person, or his successors, assigns, or legal representatives shall, without procuring the license prescribed in section 184 of this title, have made, or consented to or assisted another's making, application in a foreign country for a patent or for the registration of a utility model, industrial design, or model in respect of the invention. A United States patent issued to such person, his successors, assigns, or legal representatives shall be invalid, unless the failure to procure such license was through error and without deceptive intent, and the patent does not disclose subject matter within the scope of section 181 of this title.

(July 19, 1952, ch. 950, §1, 66 Stat. 807; Aug. 23, 1988, Pub. L. 100-418, §9101, 102 Stat. 1568; Nov. 2, 2002, Pub. L. 107-273, §13206, 116 Stat. 1904.)

§ 186   Penalty

Whoever, during the period or periods of time an invention has been ordered to be kept secret and the grant of a patent thereon withheld pursuant to section 181 of this title, shall, with knowledge of such order and without due authorization, willfully publish or disclose or authorize or cause to be published or disclosed the invention, or material information with respect thereto, or whoever willfully, in violation of the provisions of section 184 of this title, shall file or cause or authorize to be filed in any foreign country an application for patent or for the registration of a utility model, industrial design, or model in respect of any invention made in the United States, shall, upon conviction, be fined not more than $10,000 or imprisoned for not more than two years, or both.

(July 19, 1952, ch. 950, §1, 66 Stat. 807; Aug. 23, 1988, Pub. L. 100-418, §9101, 102 Stat. 1568.)

§ 187   Nonapplicability to certain persons

The prohibitions and penalties of this chapter shall not apply to any officer or agent of the United States acting within the scope of his authority, nor to any person acting upon his written instructions or permission.

(July 19, 1952, ch. 950, §1, 66 Stat. 808.)

§ 188 Rules and regulations, delegation of power

The Atomic Energy Commission, the Secretary of a defense department, the chief officer of any other department or agency of the Government designated by the President as a defense agency of the United States, and the Secretary of Commerce, may separately issue rules and regulations to enable the respective department or agency to carry out the provisions of this chapter, and may delegate any power conferred by this chapter.

(July 19, 1952, ch. 950, §1, 66 Stat. 808.)

CHAPTER 18—PATENT RIGHTS IN INVENTIONS MADE WITH
FEDERAL ASSISTANCE

§ 200 Policy and objective

It is the policy and objective of the Congress to use the patent system to promote the utilization of inventions arising from federally supported research or development; to encourage maximum participation of small business firms in federally supported research and development efforts; to promote collaboration between commercial concerns and nonprofit organizations, including universities; to ensure that inventions made by nonprofit organizations and small business firms are used in a manner to promote free competition and enterprise without unduly encumbering future research and discovery; to promote the commercialization and public availability of inventions made in the United States by United States industry and labor; to ensure that the Government obtains sufficient rights in federally supported inventions to meet the needs of the Government and protect the public against nonuse or unreasonable use of inventions; and to minimize the costs of administering policies in this area.

(Dec. 12, 1980, Pub. L. 96-517, §6, 94 Stat. 3019; Nov. 1, 2000, Pub. L. 106-404, §5, 114 Stat. 1745.)

§ 201   Definitions

As used in this chapter—

(a) The term "Federal agency" means any executive agency as defined in section 105 of title 5, and the military departments as defined by section 102 of title 5.

(b) The term "funding agreement" means any contract, grant, or cooperative agreement entered into between any Federal agency, other than the Tennessee Valley Authority, and any contractor for the performance of experimental, developmental, or research work funded in whole or in part by the Federal Government. Such term includes any assignment, substitution of parties, or subcontract of any type entered into for the performance of experimental, developmental, or research work under a funding agreement as herein defined.

(c) The term "contractor" means any person, small business firm, or nonprofit organization that is a party to a funding agreement.

(d) The term "invention" means any invention or discovery which is or may be patentable or otherwise protectable under this title or any novel variety of plant which is or may be protectable under the Plant Variety Protection Act (7 U.S.C. 2321 et seq.).

(e) The term "subject invention" means any invention of the contractor conceived or first actually reduced to practice in the performance of work under a funding agreement: *Provided,* That in the case of a variety of plant, the date of determination (as defined in section 41(d) of the

Plant Variety Protection Act (7 U.S.C. 2401(d)) must also occur during the period of contract performance.

(f) The term "practical application" means to manufacture in the case of a composition or product, to practice in the case of a process or method, or to operate in the case of a machine or system; and, in each case, under such conditions as to establish that the invention is being utilized and that its benefits are to the extent permitted by law or Government regulations available to the public on reasonable terms.

(g) The term "made" when used in relation to any invention means the conception or first actual reduction to practice of such invention.

(h) The term "small business firm" means a small business concern as defined at section 2 of Pub. L. 85-536 (15 U.S.C. 632) and implementing regulations of the Administrator of the Small Business Administration.

(i) The term "nonprofit organization" means universities and other institutions of higher education or an organization of the type described in section 501(c)(3) of the Internal Revenue Code of 1954 (26 U.S.C. 501(c)) and exempt from taxation under section 501(a) of the Internal Revenue Code (26 U.S.C. 501(a)) or any nonprofit scientific or educational organization qualified under a State nonprofit organization statute.

(Dec. 12, 1980, Pub. L. 96-517, §6, 94 Stat. 3019; Nov. 8, 1984, Pub. L. 98-620, §501, 98 Stat. 3364; Nov. 2, 2002, Pub. L. 107-273, §13206, 116 Stat. 1904.)

§ 202   Disposition of rights

(a) Each nonprofit organization or small business firm may, within a reasonable time after disclosure as required by paragraph (c)(1) of this section, elect to retain title to any subject invention: *Provided, however,* That a funding agreement may provide otherwise (i) when the contractor is not located in the United States or does not have a place of business located in the United States or is subject to the control of a foreign government, (ii) in exceptional circumstances when it is determined by the agency that restriction or elimination of the right to retain title to any subject invention will better promote the policy and objectives of this chapter, (iii) when it is determined by a Government authority which is authorized by statute or Executive order to conduct foreign intelligence or counter-intelligence activities that the restriction or elimination of the right to retain title to any subject invention is necessary to protect the security of such activities or (iv) when the funding agreement includes the operation of a Government-owned, contractor-operated facility of the Department of Energy primarily dedicated to that Department's naval nuclear propulsion or weapons related programs and all funding agreement limitations under this subparagraph on the contractor's right to elect title to a subject invention are limited to inventions occurring under the above two programs of the Department of Energy. The rights of the nonprofit organization or small business firm shall be subject to the provisions of paragraph (c) of this section and the other provisions of this chapter.

(b) (1) The rights of the Government under subsection (a) shall not be exercised by a Federal agency unless it first determines that at least one of the conditions identified in clauses (i) through (iv) of subsection (a) exists. Except in the case of subsection (a)(iii), the agency shall file with the Secretary of Commerce, within thirty days after the award of the applicable funding agreement, a copy of such determination. In the case of a determination under subsection (a)(ii), the statement shall include an analysis justifying the determination. In the case of determinations applicable to funding agreements with small business firms, copies shall also be sent to the Chief Counsel for Advocacy of the Small Business Administration. If the Secretary of Commerce believes that any individual determination or pattern of determinations is contrary to the policies and objectives of this chapter or otherwise not in conformance with this chapter, the Secretary shall so advise the head of the agency concerned and the Administrator of the Office of Federal Procurement Policy, and recommend corrective actions.

(2) Whenever the Administrator of the Office of Federal Procurement Policy has determined that one or more Federal agencies are utilizing the authority of clause (i) or (ii) of subsection (a) of this section in a manner that is contrary to the policies and objectives of this chapter the Administrator is authorized to issue regulations describ-

35 U.S.C. § 202

ing classes of situations in which agencies may not exercise the authorities of those clauses.

(3) At least once every five years, the Comptroller General shall transmit a report to the Committees on the Judiciary of the Senate and House of Representatives on the manner in which this chapter is being implemented by the agencies and on such other aspects of Government patent policies and practices with respect to federally funded inventions as the Comptroller General believes appropriate.

(4) If the contractor believes that a determination is contrary to the policies and objectives of this chapter or constitutes an abuse of discretion by the agency, the determination shall be subject to the section 203(b).

(c) Each funding agreement with a small business firm or nonprofit organization shall contain appropriate provisions to effectuate the following:

(1) That the contractor disclose each subject invention to the Federal agency within a reasonable time after it becomes known to contractor personnel responsible for the administration of patent matters, and that the Federal Government may receive title to any subject invention not disclosed to it within such time.

(2) That the contractor make a written election within two years after disclosure to the Federal agency (or such additional time as may be approved by the Federal agency) whether the contractor will retain title to a subject invention: *Provided,* That in any case where publication, on sale, or public use, has initiated the one year statutory period in which valid patent protection can still be obtained in the United States, the period for election may be shortened by the Federal agency to a date that is not more than sixty days prior to the end of the statutory period: *And provided further,* That the Federal Government may receive title to any subject invention in which the contractor does not elect to retain rights or fails to elect rights within such times.

(3) That a contractor electing rights in a subject invention agrees to file a patent application prior to any statutory bar date that may occur under this title due to publication, on sale, or public use, and shall thereafter file corresponding patent applications in other countries in which it wishes to retain title within reasonable times, and that the

Federal Government may receive title to any subject inventions in the United States or other countries in which the contractor has not filed patent applications on the subject invention within such times.

(4) With respect to any invention in which the contractor elects rights, the Federal agency shall have a nonexclusive, nontransferable, irrevocable, paid-up license to practice or have practiced for or on behalf of the United States any subject invention throughout the world: *Provided,* That the funding agreement may provide for such additional rights, including the right to assign or have assigned foreign patent rights in the subject invention, as are determined by the agency as necessary for meeting the obligations of the United States under any treaty, international agreement, arrangement of cooperation, memorandum of understanding, or similar arrangement, including military agreements relating to weapons development and production.

(5) The right of the Federal agency to require periodic reporting on the utilization or efforts at obtaining utilization that are being made by the contractor or his licensees or assignees: *Provided,* That any such information, as well as any information on utilization or efforts at obtaining utilization obtained as part of a proceeding under section 203 of this chapter shall be treated by the Federal agency as commercial and financial information obtained from a person and privileged and confidential and not subject to disclosure under section 552 of title 5.

(6) An obligation on the part of the contractor, in the event a United States patent application is filed by or on its behalf or by any assignee of the contractor, to include within the specification of such application and any patent issuing thereon, a statement specifying that the invention was made with Government support and that the Government has certain rights in the invention.

(7) In the case of a nonprofit organization, (A) a prohibition upon the assignment of rights to a subject invention in the United States without the approval of the Federal agency, except where such assignment is made to an organization which has as one of its primary functions the management of inventions (provided that such assignee shall be subject to the same provisions as the contractor); (B) a requirement that the contractor share royalties with the inventor; (C)

except with respect to a funding agreement for the operation of a Government-owned-contractor-operated facility, a requirement that the balance of any royalties or income earned by the contractor with respect to subject inventions, after payment of expenses (including payments to inventors) incidental to the administration of subject inventions, be utilized for the support of scientific research or education; (D) a requirement that, except where it proves infeasible after a reasonable inquiry in the licensing of subject inventions shall be given to small business firms; and (E) with respect to a funding agreement for the operation of a Government-owned-contractor-operated facility, requirements (i) that after payment of patenting costs, licensing costs, payments to inventors, and other expenses incidental to the administration of subject inventions, 100 percent of the balance of any royalties or income earned and retained by the contractor during any fiscal year up to an amount equal to 5 percent of the annual budget of the facility, shall be used by the contractor for scientific research, development, and education consistent with the research and development mission and objectives of the facility, including activities that increase the licensing potential of other inventions of the facility; provided that if said balance exceeds 5 percent of the annual budget of the facility, that 75 percent of such excess shall be paid to the Treasury of the United States and the remaining 25 percent shall be used for the same purposes as described above in this clause (D); and (ii) that, to the extent it provides the most effective technology transfer, the licensing of subject inventions shall be administered by contractor employees on location at the facility.

(8) The requirements of sections 203 and 204 of this chapter.

(d) If a contractor does not elect to retain title to a subject invention in cases subject to this section, the Federal agency may consider and after consultation with the contractor grant requests for retention of rights by the inventor subject to the provisions of this Act and regulations promulgated hereunder.

(e) In any case when a Federal employee is a coinventor of any invention made with a nonprofit organization, a small business firm, or a non-Federal inventor, the Federal agency employing such coinventor may, for the purpose of consolidating rights in the invention and if it finds that it would expedite the development of the invention—

(1) license or assign whatever rights it may acquire in the subject invention to the nonprofit organization, small business firm, or non-Federal inventor in accordance with the provisions of this chapter; or

(2) acquire any rights in the subject invention from the nonprofit organization, small business firm, or non-Federal inventor, but only to the extent the party from whom the rights are acquired voluntarily enters into the transaction and no other transaction under this chapter is conditioned on such acquisition.

(f) (1) No funding agreement with a small business firm or nonprofit organization shall contain a provision allowing a Federal agency to require the licensing to third parties of inventions owned by the contractor that are not subject inventions unless such provision has been approved by the head of the agency and a written justification has been signed by the head of the agency. Any such provision shall clearly state whether the licensing may be required in connection with the practice of a subject invention, a specifically identified work object, or both. The head of the agency may not delegate the authority to approve provisions or sign justifications required by this paragraph.

(2) A Federal agency shall not require the licensing of third parties under any such provision unless the head of the agency determines that the use of the invention by others is necessary for the practice of a subject invention or for the use of a work object of the funding agreement and that such action is necessary to achieve the practical application of the subject invention or work object. Any such determination shall be on the record after an opportunity for an agency hearing. Any action commenced for judicial review of such determination shall be brought within sixty days after notification of such determination.

(Dec. 12, 1980, Pub. L. 96-517, §6, 94 Stat. 3020; Nov. 8, 1984, Pub. L. 98-620, §501, 98 Stat. 3364-66; Dec. 10, 1991, Pub. L. 102-204, §10, 105 Stat. 1641; Nov. 29, 1999, Pub. L. 106-113, §4732, 113 Stat. 1501A-581; Nov.1, 2000, Pub. L. 106-404, §6(1), 114 Stat. 1745; Nov. 2, 2002, Pub. L. 107-273, §13206, 116 Stat. 1904.)

35 U.S.C. § 202

§ 203   March-in rights

(a) With respect to any subject invention in which a small business firm or nonprofit organization has acquired title under this chapter, the Federal agency under whose funding agreement the subject invention was made shall have the right, in accordance with such procedures as are provided in regulations promulgated hereunder to require the contractor, an assignee or exclusive licensee of a subject invention to grant a nonexclusive, partially exclusive, or exclusive license in any field of use to a responsible applicant or applicants, upon terms that are reasonable under the circumstances, and if the contractor, assignee, or exclusive licensee refuses such request, to grant such a license itself, if the Federal agency determines that such—

(1) action is necessary because the contractor or assignee has not taken, or is not expected to take within a reasonable time, effective steps to achieve practical application of the subject invention in such field of use;

(2) action is necessary to alleviate health or safety needs which are not reasonably satisfied by the contractor, assignee, or their licensees;

(3) action is necessary to meet requirements for public use specified by Federal regulations and such requirements are not reasonably satisfied by the contractor, assignee, or licensees; or

(4) action is necessary because the agreement required by section 204 has not been obtained or waived or because a licensee of the exclusive right to use or sell any subject invention in the United States is in breach of its agreement obtained pursuant to section 204.

(b) A determination pursuant to this section or section 202(b)(4) shall not be subject to the Contract Disputes Act (41 U.S.C. §601 et seq.). An administrative appeals procedure shall be established by regulations promulgated in accordance with section 206. Additionally, any contractor, inventor, assignee, or exclusive licensee adversely affected by a determination under this section may, at any time within sixty days after the determination is issued, file a petition in the United States Claims

Court,* which shall have jurisdiction to determine the appeal on the record and to affirm, reverse, remand or modify as appropriate, the determination of the Federal agency. In cases described in paragraphs (1) and (3) of subsection (a), the agency's determination shall be held in abeyance pending the exhaustion of appeals or petitions filed under the preceding sentence.

(Dec. 12, 1980, Pub. L. 96-517, §6, 94 Stat. 3022; Nov. 8, 1984, Pub. L. 98-620, §501, 98 Stat. 3367; Nov. 2, 2002, Pub. L. 107-273, §13206, 116 Stat. 1904.)

§ 204   Preference for United States industry

Notwithstanding any other provision of this chapter, no small business firm or nonprofit organization which receives title to any subject invention and no assignee of any such small business firm or nonprofit organization shall grant to any person the exclusive right to use or sell any subject invention in the United States unless such person agrees that any products embodying the subject invention or produced through the use of the subject invention will be manufactured substantially in the United States. However, in individual cases, the requirement for such an agreement may be waived by the Federal agency under whose funding agreement the invention was made upon a showing by the small business firm, nonprofit organization, or assignee that reasonable but unsuccessful efforts have been made to grant licenses on similar terms to potential licensees that would be likely to manufacture substantially in the United States or that under the circumstances domestic manufacture is not commercially feasible.

(Dec. 12, 1980, Pub. L. 96-517, §6, 94 Stat. 3023.)

§ 205   Confidentiality

Federal agencies are authorized to withhold from disclosure to the public information disclosing any invention in which the Federal Government owns or may own a right, title, or interest (including a nonexclusive license) for a reasonable time in order for a patent application to be filed. Furthermore, Federal agencies shall not be required to release cop-

---

* *Ed. Note:* Pursuant to the Court of Federal Claims Technical and Procedural Improvements Act of 1992, §902(b)(2), Pub. L. 102-572, 106 Stat. 4516, statutory references to the U.S. Claims Court are deemed to refer to the U.S. Court of Federal Claims.

ies of any document which is part of an application for patent filed with the United States Patent and Trademark Office or with any foreign patent office.

(Dec. 12, 1980, Pub. L. 96-517, §6, 94 Stat. 3023.)

§ 206 Uniform clauses and regulations

The Secretary of Commerce may issue regulations which may be made applicable to Federal agencies implementing the provisions of sections 202 through 204 of this chapter and shall establish standard funding agreement provisions required under this chapter. The regulations and the standard funding agreement shall be subject to public comment before their issuance.

(Dec. 12, 1980, Pub. L. 96-517, §6, 94 Stat. 3023; Nov. 8, 1984, Pub. L. 98-620, §501, 98 Stat. 3367.)

§ 207 Domestic and foreign protection of federally owned inventions

(a) Each Federal agency is authorized to—

(1) apply for, obtain, and maintain patents or other forms of protection in the United States and in foreign countries on inventions in which the Federal Government owns a right, title, or interest;

(2) grant nonexclusive, exclusive, or partially exclusive licenses under federally owned inventions, royalty-free or for royalties or other consideration, and on such terms and conditions, including the grant to the licensee of the right of enforcement pursuant to the provisions of chapter 29 of this title as determined appropriate in the public interest;

(3) undertake all other suitable and necessary steps to protect and administer rights to federally owned inventions on behalf of the Federal Government either directly or through contract, including acquiring rights for and administering royalties to the Federal Government in any invention, but only to the extent the party from whom the rights are acquired voluntarily enters into the transaction, to facilitate the licensing of a federally owned invention; and

(4) transfer custody and administration, in whole or in part, to another Federal agency, of the right, title, or interest in any federally owned invention.

(b) For the purpose of assuring the effective management of Government-owned inventions, the Secretary of Commerce is authorized to—

(1) assist Federal agency efforts to promote the licensing and utilization of Government-owned inventions;

(2) assist Federal agencies in seeking protection and maintaining inventions in foreign countries, including the payment of fees and costs connected therewith; and

(3) consult with and advise Federal agencies as to areas of science and technology research and development with potential for commercial utilization.

(Dec. 12, 1980, Pub. L. 96-517, §6, 94 Stat. 3023; Nov. 8, 1984, Pub. L. 98-620, §501, 98 Stat. 3367; Nov. 1, 2000, Pub. L. 106-404, §6(2), 114 Stat. 1745.)

§ 208   Regulations governing Federal licensing

The Secretary of Commerce is authorized to promulgate regulations specifying the terms and conditions upon which any federally owned invention, other than inventions owned by the Tennessee Valley Authority, may be licensed on a nonexclusive, partially exclusive, or exclusive basis.

(Dec. 12, 1980, Pub. L. 96-517, §6, 94 Stat. 3024; Nov. 8, 1984, Pub. L. 98-620, §501, 98 Stat. 3367.)

§ 209   Licensing federally owned inventions

(a) *Authority.*—A Federal agency may grant an exclusive or partially exclusive license on a federally owned invention under section 207(a)(2) only if—

(1) granting the license is a reasonable and necessary incentive to—

(A) call forth the investment capital and expenditures needed to bring the invention to practical application; or

(B) otherwise promote the invention's utilization by the public;

(2) the Federal agency finds that the public will be served by the granting of the license, as indicated by the applicant's intentions, plans, and ability to bring the invention to practical application or otherwise promote the invention's utilization by the public, and that the proposed scope of exclusivity is not greater than reasonably necessary to provide the incentive for bringing the invention to practical application, as proposed by the applicant, or otherwise to promote the invention's utilization by the public;

(3) the applicant makes a commitment to achieve practical application of the invention within a reasonable time, which time may be extended by the agency upon the applicant's request and the applicant's demonstration that the refusal of such extension would be unreasonable;

(4) granting the license will not tend to substantially lessen competition or create or maintain a violation of the Federal antitrust laws; and

(5) in the case of an invention covered by a foreign patent application or patent, the interests of the Federal Government or United States industry in foreign commerce will be enhanced.

(b) *Manufacture in United States.*—A Federal agency shall normally grant a license under section 207(a)(2) to use or sell any federally owned invention in the United States only to a licensee who agrees that any products embodying the invention or produced through the use of the invention will be manufactured substantially in the United States.

(c) *Small business.*—First preference for the granting of any exclusive or partially exclusive licenses under section 207(a)(2) shall be given to small business firms having equal or greater likelihood as other applicants to bring the invention to practical application within a reasonable time.

(d) *Terms and conditions.*—Any licenses granted under section 207(a)(2) shall contain such terms and conditions as the granting agency considers appropriate, and shall include provisions—

(1) retaining a nontransferrable, irrevocable, paid-up license for any Federal agency to practice the invention or have the invention prac-

ticed throughout the world by or on behalf of the Government of the United States;

(2) requiring periodic reporting on utilization of the invention, and utilization efforts, by the licensee, but only to the extent necessary to enable the Federal agency to determine whether the terms of the license are being complied with, except that any such report shall be treated by the Federal agency as commercial and financial information obtained from a person and privileged and confidential and not subject to disclosure under section 552 of title 5; and

(3) empowering the Federal agency to terminate the license in whole or in part if the agency determines that—

(A) the licensee is not executing its commitment to achieve practical application of the invention, including commitments contained in any plan submitted in support of its request for a license, and the licensee cannot otherwise demonstrate to the satisfaction of the Federal agency that it has taken, or can be expected to take within a reasonable time, effective steps to achieve practical application of the invention;

(B) the licensee is in breach of an agreement described in subsection (b);

(C) termination is necessary to meet requirements for public use specified by Federal regulations issued after the date of the license, and such requirements are not reasonably satisfied by the licensee; or

(D) the licensee has been found by a court of competent jurisdiction to have violated the Federal antitrust laws in connection with its performance under the license agreement.

(e) *Public notice.*—No exclusive or partially exclusive license may be granted under section 207(a)(2) unless public notice of the intention to grant an exclusive or partially exclusive license on a federally owned invention has been provided in an appropriate manner at least 15 days before the license is granted, and the Federal agency has considered all comments received before the end of the comment period in response to that public notice. This subsection shall not apply to the licensing of inventions made under a cooperative research and development

35 U.S.C. § 209

agreement entered into under section 12 of the Stevenson-Wydler Technology Innovation Act of 1980 (15 U.S.C. 3710a).

(f) *Plan.*—No Federal agency shall grant any license under a patent or patent application on a federally owned invention unless the person requesting the license has supplied the agency with a plan for development or marketing of the invention, except that any such plan shall be treated by the Federal agency as commercial and financial information obtained from a person and privileged and confidential and not subject to disclosure under section 552 of title 5.

(Dec. 12, 1980, Pub. L. 96-517, §6, 94 Stat. 3024; Nov. 1, 2000, Pub. L. 106-404, §4, 114 Stat. 1743; Nov. 2, 2002, Pub. L. 107-273, §13206, 116 Stat. 1904.)

§ 210   Precedence of chapter

(a) This chapter shall take precedence over any other Act which would require a disposition of rights in subject inventions of small business firms or nonprofit organizations contractors in a manner that is inconsistent with this chapter, including but not necessarily limited to the following:

(1) section 10(a) of the Act of June 29, 1935, as added by title I of the Act of August 14, 1946 (7 U.S.C. 427i(a); 60 Stat. 1085);

(2) section 205(a) of the Act of August 14, 1946 (7 U.S.C. 1624(a); 60 Stat. 1090);

(3) section 501(c) of the Federal Mine Safety and Health Act of 1977 (30 U.S.C. 951(c); 83 Stat. 742);

(4) section 106(c) of the National Traffic and Motor Vehicle Safety Act of 1966 (15 U.S.C. 1395(c); 80 Stat. 721);

(5) section 12 of the National Science Foundation Act of 1950 (42 U.S.C. 1871(a); 82 Stat. 360);

(6) section 152 of the Atomic Energy Act of 1954 (42 U.S.C. 2182; 68 Stat. 943);

(7) section 305 of the National Aeronautics and Space Act of 1958 (42 U.S.C. 2457);

(8) section 6 of the Coal Research Development Act of 1960 (30 U.S.C. 666; 74 Stat. 337);

(9) section 4 of the Helium Act Amendments of 1960 (50 U.S.C. 167b; 74 Stat. 920);

(10) section 32 of the Arms Control and Disarmament Act of 1961 (22 U.S.C. 2572; 75 Stat. 634);

(11) section 9 of the Federal Nonnuclear Energy Research and Development Act of 1974 (42 U.S.C. 5908; 88 Stat. 1878);

(12) section 5(d) of the Consumer Product Safety Act (15 U.S.C. 2054(d); 86 Stat. 1211);

(13) section 3 of the Act of April 5, 1944 (30 U.S.C. 323; 58 Stat. 191);

(14) section 8001(c)(3) of the Solid Waste Disposal Act (42 U.S.C. 6981(c); 90 Stat. 2829);

(15) section 219 of the Foreign Assistance Act of 1961 (22 U.S.C. 2179; 83 Stat. 806);

(16) section 427(b) of the Federal Mine Health and Safety Act of 1977 (30 U.S.C. 937(b); 86 Stat. 155);

(17) section 306(d) of the Surface Mining and Reclamation Act of 1977 (30 U.S.C. 1226(d); 91 Stat. 455);

(18) section 21(d) of the Federal Fire Prevention and Control Act of 1974 (15 U.S.C. 2218(d); 88 Stat. 1548);

(19) section 6(b) of the Solar Photovoltaic Energy Research Development and Demonstration Act of 1978 (42 U.S.C. 5585(b); 92 Stat. 2516);

(20) section 12 of the Native Latex Commercialization and Economic Development Act of 1978 (7 U.S.C. 178j; 92 Stat. 2533); and

(21) section 408 of the Water Resources and Development Act of 1978 (42 U.S.C. 7879; 92 Stat. 1360).

The Act creating this chapter shall be construed to take precedence over any future Act unless that Act specifically cites this Act and provides that it shall take precedence over this Act.

(b) Nothing in this chapter is intended to alter the effect of the laws cited in paragraph (a) of this section or any other laws with respect to

35 U.S.C. § 210

the disposition of rights in inventions made in the performance of funding agreements with persons other than nonprofit organizations or small business firms.

(c) Nothing in this chapter is intended to limit the authority of agencies to agree to the disposition of rights in inventions made in the performance of work under funding agreements with persons other than nonprofit organizations or small business firms in accordance with the Statement of Government Patent Policy issued on February 18, 1983, agency regulations, or other applicable regulations or to otherwise limit the authority of agencies to allow such persons to retain ownership of inventions, except that all funding agreements, including those with other than small business firms and nonprofit organizations, shall include the requirements established in section 202(c)(4) and section 203 of this title. Any disposition of rights in inventions made in accordance with the Statement or implementing regulations, including any disposition occurring before enactment of this section, are hereby authorized.

(d) Nothing in this chapter shall be construed to require the disclosure of intelligence sources or methods or to otherwise affect the authority granted to the Director of Central Intelligence by statute or Executive order for the protection of intelligence sources or methods.

(e) The provisions of the Stevenson-Wydler Technology Innovation Act of 1980 shall take precedence over the provisions of this chapter to the extent that they permit or require a disposition of rights in subject inventions which is inconsistent with this chapter.

(Dec. 12, 1980, Pub. L. 96-517, §6, 94 Stat. 3026-3027; Nov. 8, 1984, Pub. L. 98-620, §501, 98 Stat. 3367; Oct. 20, 1986, Pub. L. 99-502, §9, 100 Stat. 1796; Mar. 7, 1996, Pub. L. 104-113, §7, 110 Stat. 779; Nov. 13, 1998, Pub. L. 105-393, §220(c), 112 Stat. 3625; Nov. 2, 2002, Pub. L. 107-273, §13206, 116 Stat. 1904.)

§ 211   Relationship to antitrust laws

Nothing in this chapter shall be deemed to convey to any person immunity from civil or criminal liability, or to create any defenses to actions, under any antitrust law.

(Dec. 12, 1980, Pub. L. 96-517, §6, 94 Stat. 3027).

§ 212　Disposition of rights in educational awards

No scholarship, fellowship, training grant, or other funding agreement made by a Federal agency primarily to an awardee for educational purposes will contain any provision giving the Federal agency any rights to inventions made by the awardee.

(Nov. 8, 1984, Pub. L. 98-620, §501, 98 Stat. 3368.)

PART III—PATENTS AND PROTECTION OF PATENT RIGHTS

CHAPTER 25—AMENDMENT AND CORRECTION OF PATENTS

§ 251　Reissue of defective patents

Whenever any patent is, through error without any deceptive intention, deemed wholly or partly inoperative or invalid, by reason of a defective specification or drawing, or by reason of the patentee claiming more or less than he had a right to claim in the patent, the Director shall, on the surrender of such patent and the payment of the fee required by law, reissue the patent for the invention disclosed in the original patent, and in accordance with a new and amended application, for the unexpired part of the term of the original patent. No new matter shall be introduced into the application for reissue.

35 U.S.C. § 251

The Director may issue several reissued patents for distinct and separate parts of the thing patented, upon demand of the applicant, and upon payment of the required fee for a reissue for each of such reissued patents.

The provisions of this title relating to applications for patent shall be applicable to applications for reissue of a patent, except that application for reissue may be made and sworn to by the assignee of the entire interest if the application does not seek to enlarge the scope of the claims of the original patent.

No reissued patent shall be granted enlarging the scope of the claims of the original patent unless applied for within two years from the grant of the original patent.

(July 19, 1952, ch. 950, §1, 66 Stat. 808.)

§ 252   Effect of reissue

The surrender of the original patent shall take effect upon the issue of the reissued patent, and every reissued patent shall have the same effect and operation in law, on the trial of actions for causes thereafter arising, as if the same had been originally granted in such amended form, but in so far as the claims of the original and reissued patents are substantially identical, such surrender shall not affect any action then pending nor abate any cause of action then existing, and the reissued patent, to the extent that its claims are substantially identical with the original patent, shall constitute a continuation thereof and have effect continuously from the date of the original patent.

A reissued patent shall not abridge or affect the right of any person or that person's successors in business who, prior to the grant of a reissue, made, purchased, offered to sell, or used within the United States, or imported into the United States, anything patented by the reissued patent, to continue the use of, to offer to sell, or to sell to others to be used, offered for sale, or sold, the specific thing so made, purchased, offered for sale, used, or imported unless the making, using, offering for sale, or selling of such thing infringes a valid claim of the reissued patent which was in the original patent. The court before which such matter is in question may provide for the continued manufacture, use, offer for sale, or sale of the thing made, purchased, offered for sale, used, or imported as specified, or for the manufacture, use, offer for sale, or sale in the United States of which substantial preparation was made before the grant of the reissue, and the court may also provide for the continued practice of any process patented by the reissue that is practiced, or for the practice of which substantial preparation was made, before the grant of the reissue, to the extent and under such terms as the court deems equitable for the protection of investments made or business commenced before the grant of the reissue.

(July 19, 1952, ch. 950, §1, 66 Stat. 808; Dec. 8, 1994, Pub. L. 103-465, §533, 108 Stat. 4988; Nov. 29, 1999, Pub. L. 106-113, §4507, 113 Stat. 1501A-565.)

§ 253   Disclaimer

Whenever, without any deceptive intention, a claim of a patent is invalid the remaining claims shall not thereby be rendered invalid. A patentee, whether of the whole or any sectional interest therein, may, on payment of the fee required by law, make disclaimer of any complete claim, stating therein the extent of his interest in such patent. Such disclaimer shall be in writing, and recorded in the Patent and Trademark Office; and it shall thereafter be considered as part of the original patent to the extent of the interest possessed by the disclaimant and by those claiming under him.

In like manner any patentee or applicant may disclaim or dedicate to the public the entire term, or any terminal part of the term, of the patent granted or to be granted.

(July 19, 1952, ch. 950, §1, 66 Stat. 809; Jan. 2, 1975, Pub. L. 93-596, §1, 88 Stat. 1949.)

§ 254   Certificate of correction of Patent and Trademark Office
    mistake

Whenever a mistake in a patent, incurred through the fault of the Patent and Trademark Office, is clearly disclosed by the records of the Office, the Director may issue a certificate of correction stating the fact and nature of such mistake, under seal, without charge, to be recorded in the records of patents. A printed copy thereof shall be attached to each printed copy of the patent, and such certificate shall be considered as part of the original patent. Every such patent, together with such certificate, shall have the same effect and operation in law on the trial of actions for causes thereafter arising as if the same had been originally issued in such corrected form. The Director may issue a corrected patent without charge in lieu of and with like effect as a certificate of correction.

(July 19, 1952, ch. 950, §1, 66 Stat. 809; Jan. 2, 1975, Pub. L. 93-596, §1, 88 Stat. 1949.)

§ 255   Certificate of correction of applicant's mistake

Whenever a mistake of a clerical or typographical nature, or of minor character, which was not the fault of the Patent and Trademark Office, appears in a patent and a showing has been made that such mistake occurred in good faith, the Director may, upon payment of the required fee, issue a certificate of correction, if the correction does not involve such changes in the patent as would constitute new matter or would require reexamination. Such patent, together with the certificate, shall have the same effect and operation in law on the trial of actions for causes thereafter arising as if the same had been originally issued in such corrected form.

(July 19, 1952, ch. 950, §1, 66 Stat. 809; Jan. 2, 1975, Pub. L. 93-596, §1, 88 Stat. 1949.)

§ 256   Correction of named inventor

Whenever through error a person is named in an issued patent as the inventor, or through error an inventor is not named in an issued patent and such error arose without any deceptive intention on his part, the Director may, on application of all the parties and assignees, with proof of the facts and such other requirements as may be imposed, issue a certificate correcting such error.

The error of omitting inventors or naming persons who are not inventors shall not invalidate the patent in which such error occurred if it can be corrected as provided in this section. The court before which such matter is called in question may order correction of the patent on notice and hearing of all parties concerned and the Director shall issue a certificate accordingly.

(July 19, 1952, ch. 950, §1, 66 Stat. 810; Aug. 27, 1982, Pub. L. 97-247, §6, 96 Stat. 320.)

CHAPTER 26—OWNERSHIP AND ASSIGNMENT

§ 261   Ownership; assignment

Subject to the provisions of this title, patents shall have the attributes of personal property.

Applications for patent, patents, or any interest therein, shall be assignable in law by an instrument in writing. The applicant, patentee, or his assigns or legal representatives may in like manner grant and convey an exclusive right under his application for patent, or patents, to the whole or any specified part of the United States.

A certificate of acknowledgment under the hand and official seal of a person authorized to administer oaths within the United States, or, in a foreign country, of a diplomatic or consular officer of the United States or an officer authorized to administer oaths whose authority is proved by a certificate of a diplomatic or consular officer of the United States, or apostille of an official designated by a foreign country which, by treaty or convention, accords like effect to apostilles of designated officials in the United States, shall be prima facie evidence of the execution of an assignment, grant or conveyance of a patent or application for patent.

An assignment, grant or conveyance shall be void as against any subsequent purchaser or mortgagee for a valuable consideration, without notice, unless it is recorded in the Patent and Trademark Office within three months from its date or prior to the date of such subsequent purchase or mortgage.

(July 19, 1952, ch. 950, §1, 66 Stat. 810; Jan. 2, 1975, Pub. L. 93-596, §1, 88 Stat. 1949; Aug. 27, 1982, Pub. L. 97-247, §14, 96 Stat. 321.)

§ 262   Joint owners

In the absence of any agreement to the contrary, each of the joint owners of a patent may make, use, offer to sell, or sell the patented invention within the United States, or import the patented invention into the United States without the consent of and without accounting to the other owners.

(July 19, 1952, ch. 950, §1, 66 Stat. 810; Dec. 8, 1994, Pub. L. 103-465, §533, 108 Stat. 4988.)

CHAPTER 27—GOVERNMENT INTERESTS IN PATENTS

§ 266   [Repealed] (July 24, 1965, Pub. L. 89-83, § 8, 79 Stat. 261.)

§ 267   Time for taking action in Government applications

Notwithstanding the provisions of sections 133 and 151 of this title, the Director may extend the time for taking any action to three years, when an application has become the property of the United States and the head of the appropriate department or agency of the Government has certified to the Director that the invention disclosed therein is important to the armament or defense of the United States.

(July 19, 1952, ch. 950, §1, 66 Stat. 811.)

CHAPTER 28—INFRINGEMENT OF PATENTS

§ 271   Infringement of patent*

(a) Except as otherwise provided in this title, whoever without authority makes, uses, offers to sell, or sells any patented invention, within the United States or imports into the United States any patented invention during the term of the patent therefor, infringes the patent.

(b) Whoever actively induces infringement of a patent shall be liable as an infringer.

(c) Whoever offers to sell or sells within the United States or imports into the United States a component of a patented machine, manufac-

---

* Ed. Note: Pub. L. 103-465, §533(a), which expanded the definition of infringement to include offers to sell patented inventions and importation into the U.S., became effective as of Jan. 1, 1996.

ture, combination or composition, or a material or apparatus for use in practicing a patented process, constituting a material part of the invention, knowing the same to be especially made or especially adapted for use in an infringement of such patent, and not a staple article or commodity of commerce suitable for substantial noninfringing use, shall be liable as a contributory infringer.

(d) No patent owner otherwise entitled to relief for infringement or contributory infringement of a patent shall be denied relief or deemed guilty of misuse or illegal extension of the patent right by reason of his having done one or more of the following: (1) derived revenue from acts which if performed by another without his consent would constitute contributory infringement of the patent; (2) licensed or authorized another to perform acts which if performed without his consent would constitute contributory infringement of the patent; (3) sought to enforce his patent rights against infringement or contributory infringement; (4) refused to license or use any rights to the patent; or (5) conditioned the license of any rights to the patent or the sale of the patented product on the acquisition of a license to rights in another patent or purchase of a separate product, unless, in view of the circumstances, the patent owner has market power in the relevant market for the patent or patented product on which the license or sale is conditioned.

(e) (1) It shall not be an act of infringement to make, use, offer to sell, or sell within the United States or import into the United States a patented invention (other than a new animal drug or veterinary biological product (as those terms are used in the Federal Food, Drug, and Cosmetic Act and the Act of March 4, 1913) which is primarily manufactured using recombinant DNA, recombinant RNA, hybridoma technology, or other processes involving site specific genetic manipulation techniques) solely for uses reasonably related to the development and submission of information under a Federal law which regulates the manufacture, use, or sale of drugs or veterinary biological products.

(2) It shall be an act of infringement to submit—

(A) an application under section 505(j) of the Federal Food, Drug, and Cosmetic Act or described in section 505(b)(2) of such Act for a drug claimed in a patent or the use of which is claimed in a patent, or

(B) an application under section 512 of such Act or under the Act of March 4, 1913 (21 U.S.C. 151-158) for a drug or veterinary biological product which is not primarily manufactured using recombinant DNA, recombinant RNA, hybridoma technology, or other processes involving site specific genetic manipulation techniques and which is claimed in a patent or the use of which is claimed in a patent,

if the purpose of such submission is to obtain approval under such Act to engage in the commercial manufacture, use, or sale of a drug or veterinary biological product claimed in a patent or the use of which is claimed in a patent before the expiration of such patent.

(3) In any action for patent infringement brought under this section, no injunctive or other relief may be granted which would prohibit the making, using, offering to sell, or selling within the United States or importing into the United States of a patented invention under paragraph (1).

(4) For an act of infringement described in paragraph (2)—

(A) the court shall order the effective date of any approval of the drug or veterinary biological product involved in the infringement to be a date which is not earlier than the date of the expiration of the patent which has been infringed,

(B) injunctive relief may be granted against an infringer to prevent the commercial manufacture, use, offer to sell, or sale within the United States or importation into the United States of an approved drug or veterinary biological product, and

(C) damages or other monetary relief may be awarded against an infringer only if there has been commercial manufacture, use, offer to sell, or sale within the United States or importation into the United States of an approved drug or veterinary biological product.

The remedies prescribed by subparagraphs (A), (B), and (C) are the only remedies which may be granted by a court for an act of infringement described in paragraph (2), except that a court may award attorney fees under section 285.

(f) (1) Whoever without authority supplies or causes to be supplied in or from the United States all or a substantial portion of the components of a patented invention, where such components are uncombined in whole or in part, in such manner as to actively induce the combination of such components outside of the United States in a manner that would infringe the patent if such combination occurred within the United States, shall be liable as an infringer.

(2) Whoever without authority supplies or causes to be supplied in or from the United States any component of a patented invention that is especially made or especially adapted for use in the invention and not a staple article or commodity of commerce suitable for substantial noninfringing use, where such component is uncombined in whole or in part, knowing that such component is so made or adapted and intending that such component will be combined outside of the United States in a manner that would infringe the patent if such combination occurred within the United States, shall be liable as an infringer.

(g) Whoever without authority imports into the United States or offers to sell, sells, or uses within the United States a product which is made by a process patented in the United States shall be liable as an infringer, if the importation, offer to sell, sale, or use of the product occurs during the term of such process patent. In an action for infringement of a process patent, no remedy may be granted for infringement on account of the noncommercial use or retail sale of a product unless there is no adequate remedy under this title for infringement on account of the importation or other use, offer to sell, or sale of that product. A product which is made by a patented process will, for purposes of this title, not be considered to be so made after—

(1) it is materially changed by subsequent processes; or

(2) it becomes a trivial and nonessential component of another product.

(h) As used in this section, the term "whoever" includes any State, any instrumentality of a State, and any officer or employee of a State or in-

35 U.S.C. § 271

strumentality of a State acting in his official capacity. Any State, and any such instrumentality, officer, or employee, shall be subject to the provisions of this title in the same manner and to the same extent as any nongovernmental entity.

(i) As used in this section, an "offer for sale" or an "offer to sell" by a person other than the patentee, or any designee of the patentee, is that in which the sale will occur before the expiration of the term of the patent.

(July 19, 1952, ch. 950, §1, 66 Stat. 811; Sept. 24, 1984, Pub. L. 98-417, §202, 98 Stat. 1603; Nov. 8, 1984, Pub. L. 98-622, §101, 98 Stat. 3383; Aug. 23, 1988, Pub. L. 100-418, §9003, 102 Stat. 1563-64; Nov. 16, 1988, Pub. L. 100-670, §201, 102 Stat. 3988-3989; Nov. 19, 1988, Pub. L. 100-703, §201, 102 Stat. 4676; Oct. 28, 1992, Pub. L. 102-560, §2, 106 Stat. 4230; Dec. 8, 1994, Pub. L. 103-465, §533, 108 Stat. 4988.)

§ 272   Temporary presence in the United States

The use of any invention in any vessel, aircraft or vehicle of any country which affords similar privileges to vessels, aircraft or vehicles of the United States, entering the United States temporarily or accidentally, shall not constitute infringement of any patent, if the invention is used exclusively for the needs of the vessel, aircraft or vehicle and is not offered for sale or sold in or used for the manufacture of anything to be sold in or exported from the United States.

(July 19, 1952, ch. 950, §1, 66 Stat. 812; Dec. 8, 1994, Pub. L. 103-465, §533, 108 Stat. 4989.)

§ 273   Defense to infringement based on earlier inventor

(a) *Definitions.*—For purposes of this section—

(1) the terms "commercially used" and "commercial use" mean use of a method in the United States, so long as such use is in connection with an internal commercial use or an actual arm's-length sale or other arm's-length commercial transfer of a useful end result, whether or not the subject matter at issue is accessible to or otherwise known to the public, except that the subject matter for which commercial marketing or use is subject to a premarketing regulatory review period during which the safety or efficacy of the subject matter is established, including any period specified in section 156(g),

shall be deemed "commercially used" and in "commercial use" during such regulatory review period;

(2) in the case of activities performed by a nonprofit research laboratory, or nonprofit entity such as a university, research center, or hospital, a use for which the public is the intended beneficiary shall be considered to be a use described in paragraph (1), except that the use—

(A) may be asserted as a defense under this section only for continued use by and in the laboratory or nonprofit entity; and

(B) may not be asserted as a defense with respect to any subsequent commercialization or use outside such laboratory or nonprofit entity;

(3) the term "method" means a method of doing or conducting business; and

(4) the "effective filing date" of a patent is the earlier of the actual filing date of the application for the patent or the filing date of any earlier United States, foreign, or international application to which the subject matter at issue is entitled under section 119, 120, or 365 of this title.

(b) *Defense to infringement.—*

(1) *In general.*—It shall be a defense to an action for infringement under section 271 of this title with respect to any subject matter that would otherwise infringe one or more claims for a method in the patent being asserted against a person, if such person had, acting in good faith, actually reduced the subject matter to practice at least 1 year before the effective filing date of such patent, and commercially used the subject matter before the effective filing date of such patent.

(2) *Exhaustion of right.*—The sale or other disposition of a useful end product produced by a patented method, by a person entitled to assert a defense under this section with respect to that useful end result shall exhaust the patent owner's rights under the patent to the extent such rights would have been exhausted had such sale or other disposition been made by the patent owner.

35 U.S.C. § 273

(3) *Limitations and qualifications of defense.*—The defense to infringement under this section is subject to the following:

(A) *Patent.*—A person may not assert the defense under this section unless the invention for which the defense is asserted is for a method.

(B) *Derivation.*—A person may not assert the defense under this section if the subject matter on which the defense is based was derived from the patentee or persons in privity with the patentee.

(C) *Not a general license.*—The defense asserted by a person under this section is not a general license under all claims of the patent at issue, but extends only to the specific subject matter claimed in the patent with respect to which the person can assert a defense under this chapter, except that the defense shall also extend to variations in the quantity or volume of use of the claimed subject matter, and to improvements in the claimed subject matter that do not infringe additional specifically claimed subject matter of the patent.

(4) *Burden of proof.*—A person asserting the defense under this section shall have the burden of establishing the defense by clear and convincing evidence.

(5) *Abandonment of use.*—A person who has abandoned commercial use of subject matter may not rely on activities performed before the date of such abandonment in establishing a defense under this section with respect to actions taken after the date of such abandonment.

(6) *Personal defense.*—The defense under this section may be asserted only by the person who performed the acts necessary to establish the defense and, except for any transfer to the patent owner, the right to assert the defense shall not be licensed or assigned or transferred to another person except as an ancillary and subordinate part of a good faith assignment or transfer for other reasons of the entire enterprise or line of business to which the defense relates.

(7) *Limitation on sites.*—A defense under this section, when acquired as part of a good faith assignment or transfer of an entire enterprise

or line of business to which the defense relates, may only be asserted for uses at sites where the subject matter that would otherwise infringe one or more of the claims is in use before the later of the effective filing date of the patent or the date of the assignment or transfer of such enterprise or line of business.

(8) *Unsuccessful assertion of defense.*—If the defense under this section is pleaded by a person who is found to infringe the patent and who subsequently fails to demonstrate a reasonable basis for asserting the defense, the court shall find the case exceptional for the purpose of awarding attorney fees under section 285 of this title.

(9) *Invalidity.*—A patent shall not be deemed to be invalid under section 102 or 103 of this title solely because a defense is raised or established under this section.

(Nov. 29, 1999, Pub. L. 106-113, §4302, 113 Stat. 1501A-555).

CHAPTER 29—REMEDIES FOR INFRINGEMENT OF PATENT, AND OTHER ACTIONS

§ 281   Remedy for infringement of patent

A patentee shall have remedy by civil action for infringement of his patent.

(July 19, 1952, ch. 950, §1, 66 Stat. 812.)

§ 282   Presumption of validity; defenses

A patent shall be presumed valid. Each claim of a patent (whether in independent, dependent, or multiple dependent form) shall be presumed valid independently of the validity of other claims; dependent or multiple dependent claims shall be presumed valid even though dependent upon an invalid claim. Notwithstanding the preceding sentence, if a claim to a composition of matter is held invalid and that claim was the basis of a determination of nonobviousness under section 103(b)(1), the process shall no longer be considered nonobvious solely on the basis of section 103(b)(1). The burden of establishing invalidity of a patent or any claim thereof shall rest on the party asserting such invalidity.

The following shall be defenses in any action involving the validity or infringement of a patent and shall be pleaded:

(1) Noninfringement, absence of liability for infringement or unenforceability,

(2) Invalidity of the patent or any claim in suit on any ground specified in part II of this title as a condition for patentability,

(3) Invalidity of the patent or any claim in suit for failure to comply with any requirement of sections 112 or 251 of this title,

(4) Any other fact or act made a defense by this title.

In actions involving the validity or infringement of a patent the party asserting invalidity or noninfringement shall give notice in the pleadings or otherwise in writing to the adverse party at least thirty days before the trial, of the country, number, date, and name of the patentee of any patent, the title, date, and page numbers of any publication to be relied upon as anticipation of the patent in suit or, except in actions in the United States Claims Court,* as showing the state of the art, and the name and address of any person who may be relied upon as the prior inventor or as having prior knowledge of or as having previously used or offered for sale the invention of the patent in suit. In the absence of such notice proof of the said matters may not be made at the trial except on such terms as the court requires.

Invalidity of the extension of a patent term or any portion thereof under section 154(b) or 156 of this title because of the material failure—

(1) by the applicant for the extension, or

(2) by the Director,

to comply with the requirements of such section shall be a defense in any action involving the infringement of a patent during the period of the extension of its term and shall be pleaded. A due diligence determination under section 156(d)(2) is not subject to review in such an action.

(July 19, 1952, ch. 950, §1, 66 Stat. 812; July 24, 1965, Pub. L. 89-83, §10, 79 Stat. 261; Nov. 14, 1975, Pub. L. 94-131, §10, 89 Stat. 692; Apr. 2, 1982, Pub. L. 97-164, §161, 96 Stat. 49; Sept. 24, 1984, Pub. L. 98-417, §203, 98 Stat. 1603; Nov. 1, 1995, Pub. L. 104-41, §2, 109 Stat. 352; Nov. 29, 1999, Pub. L. 106-113, §4402, 113 Stat. 1501A-557.)

§ 283   Injunction

The several courts having jurisdiction of cases under this title may grant injunctions in accordance with the principles of equity to prevent the violation of any right secured by patent, on such terms as the court deems reasonable.

(July 19, 1952, ch. 950, §1, 66 Stat. 812.)

§ 284   Damages

Upon finding for the claimant the court shall award the claimant damages adequate to compensate for the infringement, but in no event less than a reasonable royalty for the use made of the invention by the infringer, together with interest and costs as fixed by the court.

---

* *Ed. Note:* Pursuant to the Court of Federal Claims Technical and Procedural Improvements Act of 1992, §902(b)(2), Pub. L. 102-572, 106 Stat. 4516, statutory references to the U.S. Claims Court are deemed to refer to the U.S. Court of Federal Claims.

When the damages are not found by a jury, the court shall assess them. In either event the court may increase the damages up to three times the amount found or assessed. Increased damages under this paragraph shall not apply to provisional rights under section 154(d) of this title.

The court may receive expert testimony as an aid to the determination of damages or of what royalty would be reasonable under the circumstances.

(July 19, 1952, ch. 950, §1, 66 Stat. 813; Nov. 29, 1999, Pub. L. 106-113, §4507, 113 Stat. 1501A-565.)

§ 285   Attorney fees

The court in exceptional cases may award reasonable attorney fees to the prevailing party.

(July 19, 1952, ch. 950, §1, 66 Stat. 813.)

§ 286   Time limitation on damages

Except as otherwise provided by law, no recovery shall be had for any infringement committed more than six years prior to the filing of the complaint or counterclaim for infringement in the action.

In the case of claims against the United States Government for use of a patented invention, the period before bringing suit, up to six years, between the date of receipt of a written claim for compensation by the department or agency of the Government having authority to settle such claim, and the date of mailing by the Government of a notice to the claimant that his claim has been denied shall not be counted as part of the period referred to in the preceding paragraph.

(July 19, 1952, ch. 950, §1, 66 Stat. 813.)

§ 287   Limitation on damages and other remedies; marking and notice

(a) Patentees, and persons making, offering for sale, or selling within the United States any patented article for or under them or importing any patented article into the United States, may give notice to the public that the same is patented, either by fixing thereon the word "patent" or the abbreviation "pat.", together with the number of the patent, or when, from the character of the article, this can not be done, by fixing to it, or to the package wherein one or more of them is contained, a label containing a like notice. In the event of failure so to mark, no damages shall be recovered by the patentee in any action for infringement, except on proof that the infringer was notified of the infringement and continued to infringe thereafter, in which event damages may be recovered only for infringement occurring after such notice. Filing of an action for infringement shall constitute such notice.

(b) (1) An infringer under section 271(g) shall be subject to all the provisions of this title relating to damages and injunctions except to the extent those remedies are modified by this subsection or section 9006 of the Process Patent Amendments Act of 1988. The modifications of remedies provided in this subsection shall not be available to any person who—

(A) practiced the patented process;

(B) owns or controls, or is owned or controlled by, the person who practiced the patented process; or

(C) had knowledge before the infringement that a patented process was used to make the product the importation, use, offer for sale, or sale of which constitutes the infringement.

(2) No remedies for infringement under section 271(g) of this title shall be available with respect to any product in the possession of, or in transit to, the person subject to liability under such section before that person had notice of infringement with respect to that product. The person subject to liability shall bear the burden of proving any such possession or transit.

(3) (A) In making a determination with respect to the remedy in an action brought for infringement under section 271(g), the court shall consider—

(i) the good faith demonstrated by the defendant with respect to a request for disclosure,

(ii) the good faith demonstrated by the plaintiff with respect to a request for disclosure, and

(iii) the need to restore the exclusive rights secured by the patent.

35 U.S.C. § 287

(B) For purposes of subparagraph (A), the following are evidence of good faith:

(i) a request for disclosure made by the defendant;

(ii) a response within a reasonable time by the person receiving the request for disclosure; and

(iii) the submission of the response by the defendant to the manufacturer, or if the manufacturer is not known, to the supplier, of the product to be purchased by the defendant, together with a request for a written statement that the process claimed in any patent disclosed in the response is not used to produce such product.

The failure to perform any acts described in the preceding sentence is evidence of absence of good faith unless there are mitigating circumstances. Mitigating circumstances include the case in which, due to the nature of the product, the number of sources for the product, or like commercial circumstances, a request for disclosure is not necessary or practicable to avoid infringement.

(4) (A) For purposes of this subsection, a "request for disclosure" means a written request made to a person then engaged in the manufacture of a product to identify all process patents owned by or licensed to that person, as of the time of the request, that the person then reasonably believes could be asserted to be infringed under section 271(g) if that product were imported into, or sold, offered for sale, or used in, the United States by an unauthorized person. A request for disclosure is further limited to a request—

(i) which is made by a person regularly engaged in the United States in the sale of the same type of products as those manufactured by the person to whom the request is directed, or which includes facts showing that the person making the request plans to engage in the sale of such products in the United States;

(ii) which is made by such person before the person's first importation, use, offer for sale, or sale of units of the product produced by an infringing process and before the person had notice of infringement with respect to the product; and

(iii) which includes a representation by the person making the request that such person will promptly submit the patents identified pursuant to the request to the manufacturer, or if the manufacturer is not known, to the supplier, of the product to be purchased by the person making the request, and will request from that manufacturer or supplier a written statement that none of the processes claimed in those patents is used in the manufacture of the product.

(B) In the case of a request for disclosure received by a person to whom a patent is licensed, that person shall either identify the patent or promptly notify the licensor of the request for disclosure.

(C) A person who has marked, in the manner prescribed by subsection (a), the number of the process patent on all products made by the patented process which have been offered for sale or sold by that person in the United States, or imported by the person into the United States, before a request for disclosure is received is not required to respond to the request for disclosure. For purposes of the preceding sentence, the term "all products" does not include products made before the effective date of the Process Patent Amendments Act of 1988.

(5) (A) For purposes of this subsection, notice of infringement means actual knowledge, or receipt by a person of a written notification, or a combination thereof, of information sufficient to persuade a reasonable person that it is likely that a product was made by a process patented in the United States.

(B) A written notification from the patent holder charging a person with infringement shall specify the patented process alleged to have been used and the reasons for a good faith belief that such process was used. The patent holder shall include in the notification such information as is reasonably necessary to explain fairly the patent holder's belief, except that the patent holder is not required to disclose any trade secret information.

(C) A person who receives a written notification described in subparagraph (B) or a written response to a request for disclosure described in paragraph (4) shall be deemed to have notice of infringement with respect to any patent referred to in such written notification or response unless that person, absent mitigating circumstances—

(i) promptly transmits the written notification or response to the manufacturer or, if the manufacturer is not known, to the supplier, of the product purchased or to be purchased by that person; and

(ii) receives a written statement from the manufacturer or supplier which on its face sets forth a well grounded factual basis for a belief that the identified patents are not infringed.

(D) For purposes of this subsection, a person who obtains a product made by a process patented in the United States in a quantity which is abnormally large in relation to the volume of business of such person or an efficient inventory level shall be rebuttably presumed to have actual knowledge that the product was made by such patented process.

(6) A person who receives a response to a request for disclosure under this subsection shall pay to the person to whom the request was made a reasonable fee to cover actual costs incurred in complying with the request, which may not exceed the cost of a commercially available automated patent search of the matter involved, but in no case more than $500.

(c) (1) With respect to a medical practitioner's performance, of a medical activity that constitutes an infringement under section 271 (a) or (b) of this title, the provisions of sections 281, 283, 284, and 285 of this title shall not apply against the medical practitioner or against a related health care entity with respect to such medical activity.

(2) For the purposes of this subsection:

(A) the term "medical activity" means the performance of a medical or surgical procedure on a body, but shall not include (i) the use of a patented machine, manufacture, or composition of matter in violation of such patent, (ii) the practice of a patented use of a composition of matter in violation of such patent, or (iii) the practice of a process in violation of a biotechnology patent.

(B) the term "medical practitioner" means any natural person who is licensed by a State to provide the medical activity described in subsection (c)(1) or who is acting under the direction of such person in the performance of the medical activity.

(C) the term "related health care entity" shall mean an entity with which a medical practitioner has a professional affiliation under which the medical practitioner performs the medical activity, including but not limited to nursing home, hospital, university, medical school, health maintenance organization, group medical practice, or a medical clinic.

(D) the term "professional affiliation" shall mean staff privileges, medical staff membership, employment or contractual relationship, partnership or ownership interest, academic appointment, or other affiliation under which a medical practitioner provides the medical activity on behalf of, or in association with, the health care entity.

(E) the term "body" shall mean a human body, organ or cadaver, or a nonhuman animal used in medical research or instruction directly relating to the treatment of humans.

(F) the term "patented use of a composition of matter" does not include a claim for a method of performing a medical or surgical procedure on a body that recites the use of a composition of matter where the use of that composition of matter does not directly contribute to achievement of the objective of the claimed method.

(G) the term "State" shall mean any state or territory of the United States, the District of Columbia, and the Commonwealth of Puerto Rico.

(3) This subsection does not apply to the activities of any person, or employee or agent of such person (regardless of whether such person is a tax exempt organization under section 501(c) of the Internal Revenue Code), who is engaged in the commercial development, manufacture, sale, importation, or distribution of a machine, manufacture, or composition of matter or the provision of pharmacy or clinical laboratory services (other than clinical laboratory services provided in a physician's office), where such activities are:

(A) directly related to the commercial development, manufacture, sale, importation, or distribution of a machine, manufacture, or composition of matter or the provision of pharmacy or clinical laboratory services (other than clinical laboratory services provided in a physician's office), and

(B) regulated under the Federal Food, Drug, and Cosmetic Act, the Public Health Service Act, or the Clinical Laboratories Improvement Act.

(4) This subsection shall not apply to any patent issued based on an application the earliest effective filing date of which is prior to September 30, 1996.

(July 19, 1952, ch. 950, §1, 66 Stat. 813; Aug. 23, 1988, Pub. L. 100-418, §9004, 102 Stat. 1564-66; Dec. 8, 1994, Pub. L. 103-465, §533, 108 Stat. 4988; Sept. 30, 1996, Pub. L. 104-208, §616, 110 Stat. 3009-67; Nov. 29, 1999, Pub. L. 106-113, §4803, 113 Stat. 1501A-589.)

§ 288   Action for infringement of a patent containing an invalid claim

Whenever, without deceptive intention, a claim of a patent is invalid, an action may be maintained for the infringement of a claim of the patent which may be valid. The patentee shall recover no costs unless a disclaimer of the invalid claim has been entered at the Patent and Trademark Office before the commencement of the suit.

(July 19, 1952, ch. 950, §1, 66 Stat. 813; Jan. 2, 1975, Pub. L. 93-596, §1, 88 Stat. 1949.)

§ 289   Additional remedy for infringement of design patent

Whoever during the term of a patent for a design, without license of the owner, (1) applies the patented design, or any colorable imitation thereof, to any article of manufacture for the purpose of sale, or (2) sells or exposes for sale any article of manufacture to which such design or colorable imitation has been applied shall be liable to the owner to the extent of his total profit, but not less than $250, recoverable in any United States district court having jurisdiction of the parties.

Nothing in this section shall prevent, lessen, or impeach any other remedy which an owner of an infringed patent has under the provisions of this title, but he shall not twice recover the profit made from the infringement.

(July 19, 1952, ch. 950, §1, 66 Stat. 813.)

§ 290 Notice of patent suits

The clerks of the courts of the United States, within one month after the filing of an action under this title shall give notice thereof in writing to the Director, setting forth so far as known the names and addresses of the parties, name of the inventor, and the designated number of the patent upon which the action has been brought. If any other patent is subsequently included in the action he shall give like notice thereof. Within one month after the decision is rendered or a judgment issued the clerk of the court shall give notice thereof to the Director. The Director shall, on receipt of such notices, enter the same in the file of such patent.

(July 19, 1952, ch. 950, §1, 66 Stat. 814.)

§ 291 Interfering patents

The owner of an interfering patent may have relief against the owner of another by civil action, and the court may adjudge the question of the validity of any of the interfering patents, in whole or in part. The provisions of the second paragraph of section 146 of this title shall apply to actions brought under this section.

(July 19, 1952, ch. 950, §1, 66 Stat. 814.)

§ 292 False marking

(a) Whoever, without the consent of the patentee, marks upon, or affixes to, or uses in advertising in connection with anything made, used, offered for sale, or sold by such person within the United States, or imported by the person into the United States, the name or any imitation of the name of the patentee, the patent number, or the words "patent," "patentee," or the like, with the intent of counterfeiting or imitating the mark of the patentee, or of deceiving the public and inducing them to believe that the thing was made, offered for sale, sold, or imported into the United States by or with the consent of the patentee; or

Whoever marks upon, or affixes to, or uses in advertising in connection with any unpatented article, the word "patent" or any word or number importing that the same is patented, for the purpose of deceiving the public; or

Whoever marks upon, or affixes to, or uses in advertising in connection with any article, the words "patent applied for," "patent pending," or any word importing that an application for patent has been made, when no application for patent has been made, or if made, is not pending, for the purpose of deceiving the public—

Shall be fined not more than $500 for every such offense.

(b) Any person may sue for the penalty, in which event one-half shall go to the person suing and the other to the use of the United States.

(July 19, 1952, ch. 950, §1, 66 Stat. 814; Dec. 8, 194, Pub. L. 103-465, §533, 108 Stat. 4988.)

§ 293   Nonresident patentee; service and notice

Every patentee not residing in the United States may file in the Patent and Trademark Office a written designation stating the name and address of a person residing within the United States on whom may be served process or notice of proceedings affecting the patent or rights thereunder. If the person designated cannot be found at the address given in the last designation, or if no person has been designated, the United States District Court for the District of Columbia shall have jurisdiction and summons shall be served by publication or otherwise as the court directs. The court shall have the same jurisdiction to take any action respecting the patent or rights thereunder that it would have if the patentee were personally within the jurisdiction of the court.

(July 19, 1952, ch. 950, §1, 66 Stat. 814; Jan. 2, 1975, Pub. L. 93-596, §1, 88 Stat. 1949.)

§ 294   Voluntary arbitration

(a) A contract involving a patent or any right under a patent may contain a provision requiring arbitration of any dispute relating to patent validity or infringement arising under the contract. In the absence of such a provision, the parties to an existing patent validity or infringement dispute may agree in writing to settle such dispute by arbitration. Any such provision or agreement shall be valid, irrevocable, and enforceable, except for any grounds that exist at law or in equity for revocation of a contract.

(b) Arbitration of such disputes, awards by arbitrators and confirmation of awards shall be governed by title 9, to the extent such title is not inconsistent with this section. In any such arbitration proceeding, the defenses provided for under section 282 of this title shall be considered by the arbitrator if raised by any party to the proceeding.

(c) An award by an arbitrator shall be final and binding between the parties to the arbitration but shall have no force or effect on any other person. The parties to an arbitration may agree that in the event a patent which is the subject matter of an award is subsequently determined to be invalid or unenforceable in a judgment rendered by a court of competent jurisdiction from which no appeal can or has been taken, such award may be modified by any court of competent jurisdiction upon application by any party to the arbitration. Any such modification shall govern the rights and obligations between such parties from the date of such modification.

(d) When an award is made by an arbitrator, the patentee, his assignee or licensee shall give notice thereof in writing to the Director. There shall be a separate notice prepared for each patent involved in such proceeding. Such notice shall set forth the names and addresses of the parties, the name of the inventor, and the name of the patent owner, shall designate the number of the patent, and shall contain a copy of the award. If an award is modified by a court, the party requesting such modification shall give notice of such modification to the Director. The Director shall, upon receipt of either notice, enter the same in the record of the prosecution of such patent. If the required notice is not filed with the Director, any party to the proceeding may provide such notice to the Director.

(e) The award shall be unenforceable until the notice required by subsection (d) is received by the Director.

(Aug. 27, 1982, Pub. L. 97-247, §17, 96 Stat. 322; (Nov. 2, 2002, Pub. L. 107-273, §13206, 116 Stat. 1904.)

35 U.S.C. § 294

§ 295 Presumption: Product made by patented process

In actions alleging infringement of a process patent based on the importation, sale, offer for sale, or use of a product which is made from a process patented in the United States, if the court finds—

(1) that a substantial likelihood exists that the product was made by the patented process, and

(2) that the plaintiff has made a reasonable effort to determine the process actually used in the production of the product and was unable to so determine,

the product shall be presumed to have been so made, and the burden of establishing that the product was not made by the process shall be on the party asserting that it was not so made.

(Aug. 23, 1988, Pub. L. 100-418, §9005, 102 Stat. 1566; Dec. 8, 1994, Pub. L. 103-465, §533, 108 Stat. 4988.)

§ 296 Liability of States, instrumentalities of States, and State officials for infringement of patents

(a) *In general.*—Any State, any instrumentality of a State, and any officer or employee of a State or instrumentality of a State acting in his official capacity, shall not be immune, under the eleventh amendment of the Constitution of the United States or under any other doctrine of sovereign immunity, from suit in Federal court by any person, including any governmental or nongovernmental entity, for infringement of a patent under section 271, or for any other violation under this title.

(b) *Remedies.*—In a suit described in subsection (a) for a violation described in that subsection, remedies (including remedies both at law and in equity) are available for the violation to the same extent as such remedies are available for such a violation in a suit against any private entity. Such remedies include damages, interest, costs, and treble damages under section 284, attorney fees under section 285, and the additional remedy for infringement of design patents under section 289.

(Oct. 28, 1992, Pub. L. 102-560, §2, 106 Stat. 4230.)

§ 297 Improper and deceptive invention promotion

(a) *In general.*—An invention promoter shall have a duty to disclose the following information to a customer in writing, prior to entering into a contract for invention promotion services:

(1) the total number of inventions evaluated by the invention promoter for commercial potential in the past 5 years, as well as the number of those inventions that received positive evaluations, and the number of those inventions that received negative evaluations;

(2) the total number of customers who have contracted with the invention promoter in the past 5 years, not including customers who have purchased trade show services, research, advertising, or other nonmarketing services from the invention promoter, or who have defaulted in their payment to the invention promoter;

(3) the total number of customers known by the invention promoter to have received a net financial profit as a direct result of the invention promotion services provided by such invention promoter;

(4) the total number of customers known by the invention promoter to have received license agreements for their inventions as a direct result of the invention promotion services provided by such invention promoter; and

(5) the names and addresses of all previous invention promotion companies with which the invention promoter or its officers have collectively or individually been affiliated in the previous 10 years.

(b) *Civil action.*—(1) Any customer who enters into a contract with an invention promoter and who is found by a court to have been injured by any material false or fraudulent statement or representation, or any omission of material fact, by that invention promoter (or any agent, employee, director, officer, partner, or independent contractor of such invention promoter), or by the failure of that invention promoter to disclose such information as required under subsection (a), may recover in a civil action against the invention promoter (or the officers, directors, or partners of such invention promoter), in addition to reasonable costs and attorneys' fees—

(A) the amount of actual damages incurred by the customer; or

(B) at the election of the customer at any time before final judgment is rendered, statutory damages in a sum of not more than $5,000, as the court considers just.

(2) Notwithstanding paragraph (1), in a case where the customer sustains the burden of proof, and the court finds, that the invention promoter intentionally misrepresented or omitted a material fact to such customer, or willfully failed to disclose such information as required under subsection (a), with the purpose of deceiving that customer, the court may increase damages to not more than three times the amount awarded, taking into account past complaints made against the invention promoter that resulted in regulatory sanctions or other corrective actions based on those records compiled by the Commissioner of Patents under subsection (d).

(c) *Definitions.*—For purposes of this section—

(1) a "contract for invention promotion services" means a contract by which an invention promoter undertakes invention promotion services for a customer;

(2) a "customer" is any individual who enters into a contract with an invention promoter for invention promotion services;

(3) the term "invention promoter" means any person, firm, partnership, corporation, or other entity who offers to perform or performs invention promotion services for, or on behalf of, a customer, and who holds itself out through advertising in any mass media as providing such services, but does not include—

(A) any department or agency of the Federal Government or of a State or local government;

(B) any nonprofit, charitable, scientific, or educational organization, qualified under applicable State law or described under section 170(b)(1)(A) of the Internal Revenue Code of 1986;

(C) any person or entity involved in the evaluation to determine commercial potential of, or offering to license or sell, a utility patent or a previously filed nonprovisional utility patent application;

(D) any party participating in a transaction involving the sale of the stock or assets of a business; or

(E) any party who directly engages in the business of retail sales of products or the distribution of products; and

(4) the term "invention promotion services" means the procurement or attempted procurement for a customer of a firm, corporation, or other entity to develop and market products or services that include the invention of the customer.

(d) *Records of complaints.*—

(1) *Release of complaints.*—The Commissioner of Patents shall make all complaints received by the Patent and Trademark Office involving invention promoters publicly available, together with any response of the invention promoters. The Commissioner of Patents shall notify the invention promoter of a complaint and provide a reasonable opportunity to reply prior to making such complaint publicly available.

(2) *Request for complaints.*—The Commissioner of Patents may request complaints relating to invention promotion services from any Federal or State agency and include such complaints in the records maintained under paragraph (1), together with any response of the invention promoters.

(Nov. 29, 1999, Pub. L. 106-113, §4102, 113 Stat. 1501A-552.)

CHAPTER 30—PRIOR ART CITATIONS TO OFFICE AND EX PARTE REEXAMINATION OF PATENTS

§ 301   Citation of prior art

Any person at any time may cite to the Office in writing prior art consisting of patents or printed publications which that person believes to have a bearing on the patentability of any claim of a particular patent. If the person explains in writing the pertinency and manner of applying such prior art to at least one claim of the patent, the citation of such prior art and the explanation thereof will become a part of the official file of the patent. At the written request of the person citing the prior art, his or her identity will be excluded from the patent file and kept confidential.

(Dec. 12, 1980, Pub. L. 96-517, §1, 94 Stat. 3015.)

§ 302   Request for reexamination

Any person at any time may file a request for reexamination by the Office of any claim of a patent on the basis of any prior art cited under the provisions of section 301 of this title. The request must be in writing and must be accompanied by payment of a reexamination fee established by the Director pursuant to the provisions of section 41 of this title. The request must set forth the pertinency and manner of applying cited prior art to every claim for which reexamination is requested. Unless the requesting person is the owner of the patent, the Director promptly will send a copy of the request to the owner of record of the patent.

(Dec. 12, 1980, Pub. L. 96-517, §1, 94 Stat. 3015; Nov. 29, 1999, Pub. L. 106-113, §4732, 113 Stat. 1501A-581.)

§ 303   Determination of issue by Director

(a) Within three months following the filing of a request for reexamination under the provisions of section 302 of this title, the Director will determine whether a substantial new question of patentability affecting any claim of the patent concerned is raised by the request, with or without consideration of other patents or printed publications. On his own initiative, and any time, the Director may determine whether a substantial new question of patentability is raised by patents and publications discovered by him or cited under the provisions of section 301 of this title. The existence of a substantial new question of patentability is not precluded by the fact that a patent or printed publication was previously cited by or to the Office or considered by the Office.

(b) A record of the Director's determination under subsection (a) of this section will be placed in the official file of the patent, and a copy promptly will be given or mailed to the owner of record of the patent and to the person requesting reexamination, if any.

(c) A determination by the Director pursuant to subsection (a) of this section that no substantial new question of patentability has been raised will be final and nonappealable. Upon such a determination, the Director may refund a portion of the reexamination fee required under section 302 of this title.

(Dec. 12, 1980, Pub. L. 96-517, §1, 94 Stat. 3015; Nov. 29, 1999, Pub. L. 106-113, §4732, 113 Stat. 1501A-581; Nov. 2, 2002, Pub. L. 107-273, §13105, 116 Stat. 1900.)

§ 304   Reexamination order by Director

If, in a determination made under the provisions of subsection 303(a) of this title, the Director finds that a substantial new question of patentability affecting any claim of a patent is raised, the determination will include an order for reexamination of the patent for resolution of the question. The patent owner will be given a reasonable period, not less than two months from the date a copy of the determination is given or mailed to him, within which he may file a statement on such question, including any amendment to his patent and new claim or claims he may wish to propose, for consideration in the reexamination. If the patent owner files such a statement, he promptly will serve a copy of it on the person who has requested reexamination under the provisions of section 302 of this title. Within a period of two months from the date of service, that person may file and have considered in the reexamination a reply to any statement filed by the patent owner. That person promptly will serve on the patent owner a copy of any reply filed.

(Dec. 12, 1980, Pub. L. 96-517, §1, 94 Stat. 3016.)

§ 305   Conduct of reexamination proceedings

After the times for filing the statement and reply provided for by section 304 of this title have expired, reexamination will be conducted according to the procedures established for initial examination under the provisions of sections 132 and 133 of this title. In any reexamination proceeding under this chapter, the patent owner will be permitted to propose any amendment to his patent and a new claim or claims thereto, in order to distinguish the invention as claimed from the prior art cited under the provisions of section 301 of this title, or in response to a decision adverse to the patentability of a claim of a patent. No proposed amended or new claim enlarging the scope of a claim of the patent will be permitted in a reexamination proceeding under this chapter. All reexamination proceedings under this section, including any appeal to the Board of Patent Appeals and Interferences, will be conducted with special dispatch within the Office.

(Dec. 12, 1980, Pub. L. 96-517, §1, 94 Stat. 3016; Nov. 8, 1984, Pub. L. 98-622, §204, 98 Stat. 3388.)

§ 306   Appeal

The patent owner involved in a reexamination proceeding under this chapter may appeal under the provisions of section 134 of this title, and may seek court review under the provisions of sections 141 to 145 of this title, with respect to any decision adverse to the patentability of any original or proposed amended or new claim of the patent.

(Dec. 12, 1980, Pub. L. 96-517, §1, 94 Stat. 3016.)

§ 307   Certificate of patentability, unpatentability, and claim cancellation

(a) In a reexamination proceeding under this chapter, when the time for appeal has expired or any appeal proceeding has terminated, the Director will issue and publish a certificate canceling any claim of the patent finally determined to be unpatentable, confirming any claim of the patent determined to be patentable, and incorporating in the patent any proposed amended or new claim determined to be patentable.

(b) Any proposed amended or new claim determined to be patentable and incorporated into a patent following a reexamination proceeding will have the same effect as that specified in section 252 of this title for reissued patents on the right of any person who made, purchased, or used within the United States, or imported into the United States, anything patented by such proposed amended or new claim, or who made substantial preparation for the same, prior to issuance of a certificate under the provisions of subsection (a) of this section.

(Dec. 12, 1980, Pub. L. 96-517, §1, 94 Stat. 3016; Dec. 8, 1994, Pub. L. 103-465, §533, 108 Stat. 4988.)

CHAPTER 31—OPTIONAL INTER PARTES REEXAMINATION PROCEDURES

§ 311   Request for inter partes reexamination

(a) *In general.*—Any third-party requester at any time may file a request for inter partes reexamination by the Office of a patent on the basis of any prior art cited under the provisions of section 301.

(b) *Requirements.*—The request shall—

(1) be in writing, include the identity of the real party in interest, and be accompanied by payment of an inter partes reexamination fee established by the Director under section 41; and

(2) set forth the pertinency and manner of applying cited prior art to every claim for which reexamination is requested.

(c) *Copy.*—The Director promptly shall send a copy of the request to the owner of record of the patent.

(Nov. 2, 2002, Pub. L. 107-273, §13202, 116 Stat. 1901.)

§ 312   Determination of issue by Director

(a) *Reexamination.*—Not later than 3 months after the filing of a request for inter partes reexamination under section 311, the Director shall determine whether a substantial new question of patentability affecting any claim of the patent concerned is raised by the request, with or without consideration of other patents or printed publications. The existence of a substantial new question of patentability is not precluded by the fact that a patent or printed publication was previously cited by or to the Office or considered by the Office.

(b) *Record.*—A record of the Director's determination under subsection (a) shall be placed in the official file of the patent, and a copy shall be promptly given or mailed to the owner of record of the patent and to the third-party requester.

(c) *Final decision.*—A determination by the Director under subsection (a) shall be final and non-appealable. Upon a determination that no substantial new question of patentability has been raised, the Director may refund a portion of the inter partes reexamination fee required under section 311.

(Nov. 2, 2002, Pub. L. 107-273, §§13105, 13202, 116 Stat. 1901.)

§ 313   Inter partes reexamination order by Director

If, in a determination made under section 312(a), the Director finds that a substantial new question of patentability affecting a claim of a patent is raised, the determination shall include an order for inter partes reexamination of the patent for resolution of the question. The order may be accompanied by the initial action of the Patent and Trademark Office on the merits of the inter partes reexamination conducted in accordance with section 314.

§ 314   Conduct of inter partes reexamination proceedings

(a) *In general.*—Except as otherwise provided in this section, reexamination shall be conducted according to the procedures established for initial examination under the provisions of sections 132 and 133. In any inter partes reexamination proceeding under this chapter, the patent owner shall be permitted to propose any amendment to the patent and a new claim or claims, except that no proposed amended or new claim enlarging the scope of the claims of the patent shall be permitted.

(b) *Response.*—(1) With the exception of the inter partes reexamination request, any document filed by either the patent owner or the third-party requester shall be served on the other party. In addition, the Office shall send to the third-party requester a copy of any communication sent by the Office to the patent owner concerning the patent subject to the inter partes reexamination proceeding.

(2) Each time that the patent owner files a response to an action on the merits from the Patent and Trademark Office, the third-party requester shall have one opportunity to file written comments addressing issues raised by the action of the Office or the patent owner's response thereto, if those written comments are received by the Office within 30 days after the date of service of the patent owner's response.

(c) *Special dispatch.*—Unless otherwise provided by the Director for good cause, all inter partes reexamination proceedings under this section, including any appeal to the Board of Patent Appeals and Interferences, shall be conducted with special dispatch within the Office.

(Nov. 2, 2002, Pub. L. 107-273, §13202, 116 Stat. 1901.)

§ 315   Appeal

(a) *Patent owner.*—The patent owner involved in an inter partes reexamination proceeding under this chapter—

(1) may appeal under the provisions of section 134 and may appeal under the provisions of sections 141 through 144, with respect to any decision adverse to the patentability of any original or proposed amended or new claim of the patent; and

(2) may be a party to any appeal taken by a third-party requester under subsection (b).

(b) *Third-Party Requester.* —A third-party requester—

(1) may appeal under the provisions of section 134, and may appeal under the provisions of sections 141 through 144, with respect to any final decision favorable to the patentability of any original or proposed amended or new claim of the patent; and

(2) may, subject to subsection (c), be a party to any appeal taken by the patent owner under the provisions of section 134 or sections 141 through 144.

(c) *Civil action.*—A third-party requester whose request for an inter partes reexamination results in an order under section 313 is estopped from asserting at a later time, in any civil action arising in whole or in part under section 1338 of title 28, the invalidity of any claim finally determined to be valid and patentable on any ground which the third-party requester raised or could have raised during the inter partes reexamination proceedings. This subsection does not prevent the assertion of invalidity based on newly discovered prior art unavailable to the third-party requester and the Patent and Trademark Office at the time of the inter partes reexamination proceedings.

(Nov. 2, 2002, Pub. L. 107-273, §§13106, 13202, 116 Stat. 1901.)

§ 316 Certificate of patentability, unpatentability, and claim cancellation

(a) *In general.*—In an inter partes reexamination proceeding under this chapter, when the time for appeal has expired or any appeal proceeding has terminated, the Director shall issue and publish a certificate canceling any claim of the patent finally determined to be unpatentable, confirming any claim of the patent determined to be patentable, and incorporating in the patent any proposed amended or new claim determined to be patentable.

(b) *Amended or new claim.*—Any proposed amended or new claim determined to be patentable and incorporated into a patent following an inter partes reexamination proceeding shall have the same effect as that specified in section 252 of this title for reissued patents on the right of any person who made, purchased, or used within the United States, or imported into the United States, anything patented by such proposed amended or new claim, or who made substantial preparation therefor, prior to issuance of a certificate under the provisions of subsection (a) of this section.

§ 317 Inter partes reexamination prohibited

(a) *Order for reexamination.*—Notwithstanding any provision of this chapter, once an order for inter partes reexamination of a patent has been issued under section 313, neither the third-party requester nor its privies may file a subsequent request for inter partes reexamination of the patent until an inter partes reexamination certificate is issued and published under section 316, unless authorized by the Director.

(b) *Final decision.*—Once a final decision has been entered against a party in a civil action arising in whole or in part under section 1338 of title 28, that the party has not sustained its burden of proving the invalidity of any patent claim in suit or if a final decision in an inter partes reexamination proceeding instituted by a third-party requester is favorable to the patentability of any original or proposed amended or new claim of the patent, then neither that party nor its privies may thereafter request an inter partes reexamination of any such patent claim on the basis of issues which that party or its privies raised or could have raised in such civil action or inter partes reexamination proceeding, and an inter partes reexamination requested by that party or its privies on the basis of such issues may not thereafter be maintained by the Office, notwithstanding any other provision of this chapter. This subsection does not prevent the assertion of invalidity based on newly discovered prior art unavailable to the third-party requester and the Patent and Trademark Office at the time of the inter partes reexamination proceedings.

(Nov. 2, 2002, Pub. L. 107-273, §13202, 116 Stat. 1901.)

§ 318   Stay of litigation

Once an order for inter partes reexamination of a patent has been issued under section 313, the patent owner may obtain a stay of any pending litigation which involves an issue of patentability of any claims of the patent which are the subject of the inter partes reexamination order, unless the court before which such litigation is pending determines that a stay would not serve the interests of justice.

(Nov. 29, 1999, Pub. L. 106-113, §4604, 113 Stat. 1501A-567.)

PART IV—PATENT COOPERATION TREATY

CHAPTER 35—DEFINITIONS

SEC.
  351.   Definitions.

§ 351   Definitions

When used in this part unless the context otherwise indicates—

(a) The term "treaty" means the Patent Cooperation Treaty done at Washington, on June 19, 1970.

(b) The term "Regulations", when capitalized, means the Regulations under the treaty done at Washington on the same date as the treaty. The term "regulations", when not capitalized, means the regulations established by the Director under this title.

(c) The term "international application" means an application filed under the treaty.

(d) The term "international application originating in the United States" means an international application filed in the Patent and Trademark Office when it is acting as a Receiving Office under the treaty, irrespective of whether or not the United States has been designated in that international application.

(e) The term "international application designating the United States" means an international application specifying the United States as a country in which a patent is sought, regardless where such international application is filed.

(f) The term "Receiving Office" means a national patent office or intergovernmental organization which receives and processes international applications as prescribed by the treaty and the Regulations.

(g) The terms "International Searching Authority" and "International Preliminary Examining Authority" mean a national patent office or intergovernmental organization as appointed under the treaty which processes international applications as prescribed by the treaty and the Regulations.

(h) The term "International Bureau" means the international inter-governmental organization which is recognized as the coordinating body under the treaty and the Regulations.

(i) Terms and expressions not defined in this part are to be taken in the sense indicated by the treaty and the Regulations.

(Nov. 14, 1975, Pub. L. 94-131, §1, 89 Stat. 685; Nov. 8, 1984, Pub. L. 98-622, §403, 98 Stat. 3392; Nov. 6, 1986, Pub. L. 99-616, §2, 100 Stat. 3485.)

CHAPTER 36—INTERNATIONAL STAGE

§ 361   Receiving Office

(a) The Patent and Trademark Office shall act as a Receiving Office for international applications filed by nationals or residents of the United States. In accordance with any agreement made between the United States and another country, the Patent and Trademark Office may also act as a Receiving Office for international applications filed by residents or nationals of such country who are entitled to file international applications.

(b) The Patent and Trademark Office shall perform all acts connected with the discharge of duties required of a Receiving Office, including the collection of international fees and their transmittal to the International Bureau.

(c) International applications filed in the Patent and Trademark Office shall be in the English language.

(d) The international fee, and the transmittal and search fees prescribed under section 376(a) of this part, shall either be paid on filing of an international application or within such later time as may be fixed by the Director.

(Nov. 14, 1975, Pub. L. 94-131, §1, 89 Stat. 686; Nov. 8, 1984, Pub. L. 98-622, §§401, 403, 98 Stat. 3391-92; Nov. 6, 1986, Pub. L. 99-616, §2, 100 Stat. 3485.)

§ 362 International Searching Authority and International Preliminary Examining Authority

(a) The Patent and Trademark Office may act as an International Searching Authority and International Preliminary Examining Authority with respect to international applications in accordance with the terms and conditions of an agreement which may be concluded with the International Bureau, and may discharge all duties required of such Authorities, including the collection of handling fees and their transmittal to the International Bureau.

(b) The handling fee, preliminary examination fee, and any additional fees due for international preliminary examination shall be paid within such time as may be fixed by the Director.

(Nov. 14, 1975, Pub. L. 94-131, §1, 89 Stat. 686; Nov. 8, 1984, Pub. L. 98-622, §403, 98 Stat. 3392; Nov. 6, 1986, Pub. L. 99-616, §4, 100 Stat. 3485.)

§ 363 International application designating the United States: Effect

An international application designating the United States shall have the effect, from its international filing date under article 11 of the treaty, of a national application for patent regularly filed in the Patent and Trademark Office except as otherwise provided in section 102(e) of this title.

(Nov. 14, 1975, Pub. L. 94-131, §1, 89 Stat. 686; Nov. 8, 1984, Pub. L. 98-622, §403, 98 Stat. 3392.)

§ 364 International stage: Procedure

(a) International applications shall be processed by the Patent and Trademark Office when acting as a Receiving Office, International Searching Authority, or International Preliminary Examining Authority, in accordance with the applicable provisions of the treaty, the Regulations, and this title.

(b) An applicant's failure to act within prescribed time limits in connection with requirements pertaining to a pending international application may be excused upon a showing satisfactory to the Director of unavoidable delay, to the extent not precluded by the treaty and the Regulations, and provided the conditions imposed by the treaty and the Regulations regarding the excuse of such failure to act are complied with.

(Nov. 14, 1975, Pub. L. 94-131, §1, 89 Stat. 686; Nov. 8, 1984, Pub. L. 98-622, §403, 98 Stat. 3392; Nov. 6, 1986, Pub. L. 99-616, §5, 100 Stat. 3484, 3487.)

§ 365   Right of priority; benefit of the filing date of a prior application

(a) In accordance with the conditions and requirements of subsections (a) through (d) of section 119 of this title, a national application shall be entitled to the right of priority based on a prior filed international application which designated at least one country other than the United States.

(b) In accordance with the conditions and requirement of section 119(a) of this title and the treaty and the Regulations, an international application designating the United States shall be entitled to the right of priority based on a prior foreign application, or a prior international application designating at least one country other than the United States.

(c) In accordance with the conditions and requirements of section 120 of this title, an international application designating the United States shall be entitled to the benefit of the filing date of a prior national application or a prior international application designating the United States, and a national application shall be entitled to the benefit of the filing date of a prior international application designating the United States. If any claim for the benefit of an earlier filing date is based on a prior international application which designated but did not originate in the United States, the Director may require the filing in the Patent and Trademark Office of a certified copy of such application together with a translation thereof into the English language, if it was filed in another language.

(Nov. 14, 1975, Pub. L. 94-131, §1, 89 Stat. 686; Nov. 8, 1984, Pub. L. 98-622, §403, 98 Stat. 3392; Dec. 8, 1994, Pub. L. 103-465, §532, 108 Stat. 4983.)

§ 366   Withdrawn international application

Subject to section 367 of this part, if an international application designating the United States is withdrawn or considered withdrawn, either generally or as to the United States, under the conditions of the treaty and the Regulations, before the applicant has complied with the applicable requirements prescribed by section 371(c) of this part, the designation of the United States shall have no effect after the date of withdrawal, and shall be considered as not having been made, unless a claim for the benefit of a prior filing date under section 365(c) of this part was made in a national application, or an international application designating the United States, filed before the date of such withdrawal. However, such withdrawn international application may serve as the basis for a claim of priority under section 365(a) and (b) of this part, if it designated a country other than the United States.

(Nov. 14, 1975, Pub. L. 94-131, §1, 89 Stat. 687; Nov. 8, 1984, Pub. L. 98-622, §401, 98 Stat. 3391.)

§ 367   Actions of other authorities: Review

(a) Where a Receiving Office other than the Patent and Trademark Office has refused to accord an international filing date to an international application designating the United States or where it has held such application to be withdrawn either generally or as to the United States, the applicant may request review of the matter by the Director, on compliance with the requirements of and within the time limits specified by the treaty and the Regulations. Such review may result in a determination that such application be considered as pending in the national stage.

(b) The review under subsection (a) of this section, subject to the same requirements and conditions, may also be requested in those instances where an international application designating the United States is considered withdrawn due to a finding by the International Bureau under article 12(3) of the treaty.

(Nov. 14, 1975, Pub. L. 94-131, §1, 89 Stat. 687; Nov. 8, 1984, Pub. L. 98-622, §403, 98 Stat. 3392.)

§ 368 Secrecy of certain inventions; filing international applications in foreign countries

(a) International applications filed in the Patent and Trademark Office shall be subject to the provisions of chapter 17 of this title.

(b) In accordance with article 27(8) of the treaty, the filing of an international application in a country other than the United States on the invention made in this country shall be considered to constitute the filing of an application in a foreign country within the meaning of chapter 17 of this title, whether or not the United states is designated in that international application.

(c) If a license to file in a foreign country is refused or if an international application is ordered to be kept secret and a permit refused, the Patent and Trademark Office when acting as a Receiving Office, International Searching Authority, or International Preliminary Examining Authority, may not disclose the contents of such application to anyone not authorized to receive such disclosure.

(Nov. 14, 1975, Pub. L. 94-131, §1, 89 Stat. 687; Nov. 8, 1984, Pub. L. 98-622, §403, 98 Stat. 3392; Nov. 6, 1986, Pub. L. 99-616, §6, 100 Stat. 3486.)

CHAPTER 37—NATIONAL STAGE

§ 371 National stage: Commencement

(a) Receipt from the International Bureau of copies of international applications with any amendments to the claims, international search reports, and international preliminary examination reports including any annexes thereto may be required in the case of international applications designating or electing the United States.

(b) Subject to subsection (f) of this section, the national stage shall commence with the expiration of the applicable time limit under article 22(1) or (2), or under article 39(1)(a) of the treaty.

(c) The applicant shall file in the Patent and Trademark Office—

(1) the national fee provided in section 41(a) of this title;

(2) a copy of the international application, unless not required under subsection (a) of this section or already communicated by the International Bureau, and a translation into the English language of the international application, if it was filed in another language;

(3) amendments, if any, to the claims in the international application, made under article 19 of the treaty, unless such amendments have been communicated to the Patent and Trademark Office by the International Bureau, and a translation into the English language if such amendments were made in another language;

(4) an oath or declaration of the inventor (or other person authorized under chapter 11 of this title) complying with the requirements of section 115 of this title and with regulations prescribed for oaths or declarations of applicants;

(5) a translation into the English language of any annexes to the international preliminary examination report, if such annexes were made in another language.

(d) The requirements with respect to the national fee referred to in subsection (c)(1), the translation referred to in subsection (c)(2), and the oath or declaration referred to in subsection (c)(4) of this section shall be complied with by the date of the commencement of the national stage or by such later time as may be fixed by the Director. The copy of the international application referred to in subsection (c)(2) shall be submitted by the date of the commencement of the national stage. Failure to comply with these requirements shall be regarded as abandonment of the application by the parties thereof, unless it be shown to the satisfaction of the Director that such failure to comply was unavoidable. The payment of a surcharge may be required as a condition of accepting the national fee referred to in subsection (c)(1) or the oath or declaration referred to in subsection (c)(4) of this section if these requirements are not met by the date of the commencement of the national stage. The requirements of subsection (c)(3) of this section shall be complied with by the date of the commencement of the national stage, and failure to do so shall be regarded as a cancellation of the amendments to the claims in the international application made under article 19 of the treaty. The requirement of subsection (c)(5) shall be complied with at such time as may be fixed by the Director and failure to do so shall be regarded as cancellation of the amendments made under article 34(2)(b) of the treaty.

(e) After an international application has entered the national stage, no patent may be granted or refused thereon before the expiration of the applicable time limit under article 28 or article 41 of the treaty, except with the express consent of the applicant. The applicant may present amendments to the specification, claims, and drawings of the application after the national stage has commenced.

(f) At the express request of the applicant, the national stage of processing may be commenced at any time at which the application is in order for such purpose and the applicable requirements of subsection (c) of this section have been complied with.

(Nov. 14, 1975, Pub. L. 94-131, §1, 89 Stat. 688; Nov. 8, 1984, Pub. L. 98-622, §§402-03, 98 Stat. 3391-92; Nov. 6, 1986, Pub. L. 99-616, §7, 100 Stat. 3486; Dec. 10, 1991, Pub. L. 102-204, §5, 105 Stat. 1641; (Nov. 2, 2002, Pub. L. 107-273, §13206, 116 Stat. 1904.)

§ 372   National stage: Requirements and procedure

(a) All questions of substance and, within the scope of the requirements of the treaty and Regulations, procedure in an international application designating the United States shall be determined as in the case of national applications regularly filed in the Patent and Trademark Office.

(b) In case of international applications designating but not originating in, the United States—

(1) the Director may cause to be reexamined questions relating to form and contents of the application in accordance with the requirements of the treaty and the Regulations;

(2) the Director may cause the question of unity of invention to be reexamined under section 121 of this title, within the scope of the requirements of the treaty and the Regulations; and

(3) the Director may require a verification of the translation of the international application or any other document pertaining to the application if the application or other document was filed in a language other than English.

(c) [Repealed]

(Nov. 14, 1975, Pub. L. 94-131, §1, 89 Stat. 689; Nov. 8, 1984, Pub. L. 98-622, §§402-03, 98 Stat. 3392.)

§ 373   Improper applicant

An international application designating the United States, shall not be accepted by the Patent and Trademark Office for the national stage if it was filed by anyone not qualified under chapter 11 of this title to be an applicant for the purpose of filing a national application in the United States. Such international applications shall not serve as the basis for the benefit of an earlier filing date under section 120 of this title in a subsequently filed application, but may serve as the basis for a claim of the right of priority under subsections (a) through (d) of section 119 of this title, if the United States was not the sole country designated in such international application.

(Nov. 14, 1975, Pub. L. 94-131, §1, 89 Stat. 689; Nov. 8, 1984, Pub. L. 98-622, §403, 98 Stat. 3392; Dec. 8, 1994, Pub. L. 103-465, §532, 108 Stat. 4983.)

§ 374   Publication of international application

The publication under the treaty defined in section 351(a) of this title, of an international application designating the United States shall be deemed a publication under section 122(b), except as provided in sections 102(e) and 154(d) of this title.

(Nov. 14, 1975, Pub. L. 94-131, §1, 89 Stat. 689; Nov. 29, 1999, Pub. L. 106-113, §4507, 113 Stat. 1501A-565; Nov. 2, 2002, Pub. L. 107-273, §13205, 116 Stat. 1902.)

§ 375   Patent issued on international application: Effect

(a) A patent may be issued by the Director based on an international application designating the United States, in accordance with the provisions of this title. Subject to section 102(e) of this title, such patent shall have the force and effect of a patent issued on a national application filed under the provisions of chapter 11 of this title.

(b) Where due to an incorrect translation the scope of a patent granted on an international application designating the United States, which was not originally filed in the English language, exceeds the scope of the international application in its original language, a court of competent jurisdiction may retroactively limit the scope of the patent, by declaring it unenforceable to the extent that it exceeds the scope of the international application in its original language.

(Nov. 14, 1975, Pub. L. 94-131, §1, 89 Stat. 689.)

§ 376   Fees

(a) The required payment of the international fee and the handling fee, which amounts are specified in the Regulations, shall be paid in United States currency. The Patent and Trademark Office shall charge a national fee as provided in section 41(a), and may also charge the following fees:

(1) A transmittal fee (see section 361(d)).

(2) A search fee (see section 361(d)).

(3) A supplemental search fee (to be paid when required).

(4) A preliminary examination fee and any additional fees (see section 362(b));

(5) Such other fees as established by the Director.

(b) The amounts of fees specified in subsection (a) of this section, except the international fee and the handling fee, shall be prescribed by the Director. He may refund any sum paid by mistake or in excess of the fees so specified, or if required under the treaty and the Regulations. The Director may also refund any part of the search fee, the national fee, the preliminary examination fee, and any additional fees where he determines such refund to be warranted.

(Nov. 14, 1975, Pub. L. 94-131, §1, 89 Stat. 690; amended Nov. 8, 1984, Pub. L. 98-622, §§402-03, 98 Stat. 3392; Nov. 6, 1986, Pub. L. 99-616, §8, 100 Stat. 3486; Dec. 10, 1991, Pub. L. 102-204, §5, 105 Stat. 1640; Nov. 2, 2002, Pub. L. 107-273, §13206, 116 Stat. 1904.)

Part 2

TRADEMARKS

UNITED STATES CODE
TITLE 15, CHAPTER 22—TRADEMARKS

UNITED STATES CODE

TITLE 15, CHAPTER 22—TRADEMARKS

Chapter 22—Trademarks

Subchapter I—The Principal Register

§ 1051 Registration; application; payment of fees; designation of resident for service of process and notice [Section 1]

Section 1. (a)(1) The owner of a trademark used in commerce may request registration of its trademark on the principal register hereby established by paying the prescribed fee and filing in the Patent and Trademark Office an application and a verified statement, in such form as may be prescribed by the Director*, and such number of specimens or facsimiles of the mark as used as may be required by the Director.

(2) The application shall include specification of the applicant's domicile and citizenship, the date of the applicant's first use of the mark, the date of the applicant's first use of the mark in commerce, the goods in connection with which the mark is used, and a drawing of the mark.

(3) The statement shall be verified by the applicant and specify that—

(A) the person making the verification believes that he or she, or the juristic person in whose behalf he or she makes the verification, to be the owner of the mark sought to be registered;

(B) to the best of the verifier's knowledge and belief, the facts recited in the application are accurate;

(C) the mark is in use in commerce; and

(D) to the best of the verifier's knowledge and belief, no other person has the right to use such mark in commerce either in the identical form thereof or in such near resemblance thereto as to be likely, when used on or in connection with the goods of such other person, to cause confusion, or to cause mistake, or to deceive, except that, in the case of every application claiming concurrent use, the applicant shall—

(i) state exceptions to the claim of exclusive use; and

(ii) shall specify, to the extent of the verifier's knowledge—

---

* *Ed. Note:* Pursuant to §4732(b)(1) (B) of Pub. L. 106-113, the term "Commissioner" is to be replaced with the term "Director" each place it appears in the Trademark Act of 1946,

15 U.S.C. § 1051

(I) any concurrent use by others;

(II) the goods on or in connection with which and the areas in which each concurrent use exists;

(III) the periods of each use; and

(IV) the goods and area for which the applicant desires registration.

(4) The applicant shall comply with such rules or regulations as may be prescribed by the Director. The Director shall promulgate rules prescribing the requirements for the application and for obtaining a filing date herein.

(b)(1) A person who has a bona fide intention, under circumstances showing the good faith of such person, to use a trademark in commerce may request registration of its trademark on the principal register hereby established by paying the prescribed fee and filing in the Patent and Trademark Office an application and a verified statement, in such form as may be prescribed by the Director.

(2) The application shall include specification of the applicant's domicile and citizenship, the goods in connection with which the applicant has a bona fide intention to use the mark, and a drawing of the mark.

(3) The statement shall be verified by the applicant and specify—

(A) that the person making the verification believes that he or she, or the juristic person in whose behalf he or she makes the verification, to be entitled to use the mark in commerce;

(B) the applicant's bona fide intention to use the mark in commerce;

(C) that, to the best of the verifier's knowledge and belief, the facts recited in the application are accurate; and

(D) that, to the best of the verifier's knowledge and belief, no other person has the right to use such mark in commerce either in the identical form thereof or in such near resemblance thereto as to be likely, when used on or in connection with the goods of such other person, to cause confusion, or to cause mistake, or to deceive.

15 U.S.C. § 1051

Except for applications filed pursuant to section 44, no mark shall be registered until the applicant has met the requirements of subsections (c) and (d) of this section.

(4) The applicant shall comply with such rules or regulations as may be prescribed by the Director. The Director shall promulgate rules prescribing the requirements for the application and for obtaining a filing date herein.

(c) At any time during examination of an application filed under subsection (b), an applicant who has made use of the mark in commerce may claim the benefits of such use for purposes of this Act, by amending his or her application to bring it into conformity with the requirements of subsection (a).

(d) (1) Within six months after the date on which the notice of allowance with respect to a mark is issued under section 13(b)(2) [§1063(b)(2)] to an applicant under subsection (b) of this section, the applicant shall file in the Patent and Trademark Office, together with such number of specimens or facsimiles of the mark as used in commerce as may be required by the Director and payment of the prescribed fee, a verified statement that the mark is in use in commerce and specifying the date of the applicant's first use of the mark in commerce and those goods or services specified in the notice of allowance on or in connection with which the mark is used in commerce. Subject to examination and acceptance of the statement of use, the mark shall be registered in the Patent and Trademark Office, a certificate of registration shall be issued for those goods or services recited in the statement of use for which the mark is entitled to registration, and notice of registration shall be published in the Official Gazette of the Patent and Trademark Office. Such examination may include an examination of the factors set forth in subsections (a) through (e) of section 2 [§1052]. The notice of registration shall specify the goods or services for which the mark is registered.

(2) The Director shall extend, for one additional 6-month period, the time for filing the statement of use under paragraph (1), upon written request of the applicant before the expiration of the 6-month period provided in paragraph (1). In addition to an extension under the preceding sentence, the Director may, upon a showing of good cause

by the applicant, further extend the time for filing the statement of use under paragraph (1) for periods aggregating not more than 24 months, pursuant to written request of the applicant made before the expiration of the last extension granted under this paragraph. Any request for an extension under this paragraph shall be accompanied by a verified statement that the applicant has a continued bona fide intention to use the mark in commerce and specifying those goods or services identified in the notice of allowance on or in connection with which the applicant has a continued bona fide intention to use the mark in commerce. Any request for an extension under this paragraph shall be accompanied by payment of the prescribed fee. The Director shall issue regulations setting forth guidelines for determining what constitutes good cause for purposes of this paragraph.

(3) The Director shall notify any applicant who files a statement of use of the acceptance or refusal thereof and, if the statement of use is refused, the reasons for the refusal. An applicant may amend the statement of use.

(4) The failure to timely file a verified statement of use under paragraph (1) or an extension request under paragraph (2) shall result in abandonment of the application, unless it can be shown to the satisfaction of the Director that the delay in responding was unintentional, in which case the time for filing may be extended, but for a period not to exceed the period specified in paragraphs (1) and (2) for filing a statement of use.

(e) If the applicant is not domiciled in the United States the applicant may designate, by a document filed in the United States Patent and Trademark Office, the name and address of a person resident in the United States on whom may be served notices or process in proceedings affecting the mark. Such notices or process may be served upon the person so designated by leaving with that person or mailing to that person a copy thereof at the address specified in the last designation so filed. If the person so designated cannot be found at the address given in the last designation, or if the registrant does not designate by a document filed in the United States Patent and Trademark Office the name and address of a person resident in the United States on whom may be

served notices or process in proceedings affecting the mark, such notices or process may be served on the Director.

(July 5, 1946, ch. 540, §1, 60 Stat. 427; Oct. 9, 1962, Pub. L. 87-772, §1, 76 Stat. 769;
Jan. 2, 1975, Pub. L. 93-596, §1, 88 Stat. 1949; Nov. 16, 1988, Pub. L. 100-667, §103,
102 Stat. 3935–37; Oct. 30, 1998, Pub. L. 105-330, §§103, 201, 112 Stat. 3064, 3069;
Nov. 2, 2002, Pub. L. 107-273, §13207, 116 Stat. 1906.)

§ 1052 Trademarks registrable on principal register; concurrent registration [Section 2]

No trademark by which the goods of the applicant may be distinguished from the goods of others shall be refused registration on the
principal register on account of its nature unless it—

(a) Consists of or comprises immoral, deceptive, or scandalous matter;
or matter which may disparage or falsely suggest a connection with
persons, living or dead, institutions, beliefs, or national symbols, or
bring them into contempt, or disrepute; or a geographical indication
which, when used on or in connection with wines or spirits, identifies a
place other than the origin of the goods and is first used on or in connection with wines or spirits by the applicant on or after one year after
the date on which the WTO Agreement (as defined in section 2(9) of the
Uruguay Round Agreements Act) enters into force with respect to the
United States.*

(b) Consists of or comprises the flag or coat of arms or other insignia of
the United States, or of any State or municipality, or of any foreign nation, or any simulation thereof.

(c) Consists of or comprises a name, portrait, or signature identifying a
particular living individual except by his written consent, or the name,
signature, or portrait of a deceased President of the United States during the life of his widow, if any, except by the written consent of the
widow.

(d) Consists of or comprises a mark which so resembles a mark registered in the Patent and Trademark Office, or a mark or trade name
previously used in the United States by another and not abandoned,
as to be likely, when used on or in connection with the goods of the

---

* *Ed. Note:* The WTO Agreement entered into force with respect to the United States on Jan. 1,
1995. Thus, the language after the second semicolon in §1052(a) took effect on Jan. 1, 1996.

15 U.S.C. § 1052

applicant, to cause confusion, or to cause mistake, or to deceive: *Provided*, That if the Director determines that confusion, mistake, or deception is not likely to result from the continued use by more than one person of the same or similar marks under conditions and limitations as to the mode or place of use of the marks or the goods on or in connection with which such marks are used, concurrent registrations may be issued to such persons when they have become entitled to use such marks as a result of their concurrent lawful use in commerce prior to (1) the earliest of the filing dates of the applications pending or of any registration issued under this Act; (2) July 5, 1947, in the case of registrations previously issued under the Act of March 3, 1881, or February 20, 1905, and continuing in full force and effect on that date; or (3) July 5, 1947, in the case of applications filed under the Act of February 20, 1905, and registered after July 5, 1947. Use prior to the filing date of any pending application or a registration shall not be required when the owner of such application or registration consents to the grant of a concurrent registration to the applicant. Concurrent registrations may also be issued by the Director when a court of competent jurisdiction has finally determined that more than one person is entitled to use the same or similar marks in commerce. In issuing concurrent registrations, the Director shall prescribe conditions and limitations as to the mode or place of use of the mark or the goods on or in connection with which such mark is registered to the respective persons.

(e) Consists of a mark which (1) when used on or in connection with the goods of the applicant is merely descriptive or deceptively misdescriptive of them, (2) when used on or in connection with the goods of the applicant is primarily geographically descriptive of them, except as indications of regional origin may be registrable under section 4, (3) when used on or in connection with the goods of the applicant is primarily geographically deceptively misdescriptive of them, (4) is primarily merely a surname, or (5) comprises any matter that, as a whole, is functional.

(f) Except as expressly excluded in subsections (a), (b), (c), (d), (e)(3), and (e)(5) of this section, nothing herein shall prevent the registration of a mark used by the applicant which has become distinctive of the applicant's goods in commerce. The Director may accept as prima fa-

15 U.S.C. § 1052

cie evidence that the mark has become distinctive, as used on or in connection with the applicant's goods in commerce, proof of substantially exclusive and continuous use thereof as a mark by the applicant in commerce for the five years before the date on which the claim of distinctiveness is made. Nothing in this section shall prevent the registration of a mark which, when used on or in connection with the goods of the applicant, is primarily geographically deceptively misdescriptive of them, and which became distinctive of the applicant's goods in commerce before the date of the enactment of the North American Free Trade Agreement Implementation Act.*

A mark which when used would cause dilution under section 43(c) may be refused registration only pursuant to a proceeding brought under section 13. A registration for a mark which when used would cause dilution under section 43(c) may be canceled pursuant to a proceeding brought under either section 14 or section 24.

(July 5, 1946, ch. 540, title I, §2, 60 Stat. 428; Oct. 9, 1962, Pub. L. 87-772, §2, 76 Stat. 769; Jan. 2, 1975, Pub. L. 93-596, §1, 88 Stat. 1949; Nov. 16, 1988, Pub. L. 100-667, §104, 102 Stat. 3937-38; Dec. 8, 1993, Pub. L. 103-182, §333, 107 Stat. 2114; Dec. 8, 1994, Pub. L. 103-465, §522, 108 Stat. 4982; Oct. 30, 1998, Pub. L. 105-330, §201, 112 Stat. 3069; Aug. 5, 1999, Pub. L. 106-43, §2, 113 Stat. 218.)

§ 1053   Service marks registrable [Section 3]

Subject to the provisions relating to the registration of trademarks, so far as they are applicable, service marks shall be registrable, in the same manner and with the same effect as are trademarks, and when registered they shall be entitled to the protection provided herein in the case of trademarks. Applications and procedure under this section shall conform as nearly as practicable to those prescribed for the registration of trademarks.

(July 5, 1946, ch. 540, title I, §3, 60 Stat. 429; Nov. 16, 1988, Pub. L. 100-667, §105, 102 Stat. 3938.)

---

* *Ed. Note:* The North American Free Trade Agreement Implementation Act was enacted on Dec. 8, 1993.

§ 1054   Collective marks and certification marks registrable
[Section 4]

Subject to the provisions relating to the registration of trademarks, so far as they are applicable, collective and certification marks, including indications of regional origin, shall be registrable under this act, in the same manner and with the same effect as are trademarks, by persons, and nations, States, municipalities, and the like, exercising legitimate control over the use of the marks sought to be registered, even though not possessing an industrial or commercial establishment, and when registered they shall be entitled to the protection provided herein in the case of trademarks, except in the case of certification marks when used so as to represent falsely that the owner or a user thereof makes or sells the goods or performs the services on or in connection with which such mark is used. Applications and procedure under this section shall conform as nearly as practicable to those prescribed for the registration of trademarks.

(July 5, 1946, ch. 540, title I, §4, 60 Stat. 429; Nov. 16, 1988, Pub. L. 100-667, §106, 102 Stat. 3938.)

§ 1055   Use by related companies affecting validity and registration
[Section 5]

Where a registered mark or a mark sought to be registered is or may be used legitimately by related companies, such use shall inure to the benefit of the registrant or applicant for registration, and such use shall not affect the validity of such mark or of its registration, provided such mark is not used in such manner as to deceive the public. If first use of a mark by a person is controlled by the registrant or applicant for registration of the mark with respect to the nature and quality of the goods or services, such first use shall inure to the benefit of the registrant or applicant, as the case may be.

(July 5, 1946, ch. 540, title I, §5, 60 Stat. 429; Nov. 16, 1988, Pub. L. 100-667, §107, 102 Stat. 3938.)

15 U.S.C. § 1055

§ 1056   Disclaimer of unregistrable matter [Section 6]

(a) The Director may require the applicant to disclaim an unregistrable component of a mark otherwise registrable. An applicant may voluntarily disclaim a component of a mark sought to be registered.

(b) No disclaimer, including those made under subsection (e) of section 7 [§1057] of this Act shall prejudice or affect the applicant's or registrant's rights then existing or thereafter arising in the disclaimed matter, or his right of registration on another application if the disclaimed matter be or shall have become distinctive of his goods or services.

(July 5, 1946, ch. 540, title I, §6, 60 Stat. 429; Oct. 9, 1962, Pub. L. 87-772, §3, 76 Stat. 769; Nov. 16, 1988, Pub. L. 100-667, §108, 102 Stat. 3938.)

§ 1057   Certificates of registration [Section 7]

(a) *Issuance and form.*—Certificates of registration of marks registered upon the principal register shall be issued in the name of the United States of America, under the seal of the Patent and Trademark Office, and shall be signed by the Director or have his signature placed thereon, and a record thereof shall be kept in the Patent and Trademark Office. The registration shall reproduce the mark, and state that the mark is registered on the principal register under this Act, the date of the first use of the mark, the date of the first use of the mark in commerce, the particular goods or services for which it is registered, the number and date of the registration, the term thereof, the date on which the application for registration was received in the Patent and Trademark Office, and any conditions and limitations that may be imposed in the registration.

(b) *Certificate as prima facie evidence.*—A certificate of registration of a mark upon the principal register provided by this Act shall be prima facie evidence of the validity of the registered mark and of the registration of the mark, of the registrant's ownership of the mark, and of the registrant's exclusive right to use the registered mark in commerce on or in connection with the goods or services specified in the certificate, subject to any conditions or limitations stated in the certificate.

(c) *Constructive use.*—Contingent on the registration of a mark on the principal register provided by this Act, the filing of the application to register such mark shall constitute constructive use of the mark, conferring a right of priority, nationwide in effect, on or in connection with the goods or services specified in the registration against any other person except for a person whose mark has not been abandoned and who, prior to such filing—

(1) has used the mark;

(2) has filed an application to register the mark which is pending or has resulted in registration of the mark; or

(3) has filed a foreign application to register the mark on the basis of which he or she has acquired a right of priority, and timely files an application under section 44(d) [§1126(d)] to register the mark which is pending or has resulted in registration of the mark.

(d) *Issuance to assignee.*—A certificate of registration of a mark may be issued to the assignee of the applicant, but the assignment must first be recorded in the Patent and Trademark Office. In case of change of ownership the Director shall, at the request of the owner and upon a proper showing and the payment of the prescribed fee, issue to such assignee a new certificate of registration of the said mark in the name of such assignee, and for the unexpired part of the original period.

(e) *Surrender, cancellation, or amendment by registrant.*—Upon application of the registrant the Director may permit any registration to be surrendered for cancellation, and upon cancellation appropriate entry shall be made in the records of the Patent and Trademark Office. Upon application of the registrant and payment of the prescribed fee, the Director for good cause may permit any registration to be amended or to be disclaimed in part: *Provided,* That the amendment or disclaimer does not alter materially the character of the mark. Appropriate entry shall be made in the records of the Patent and Trademark Office and upon the certificate of registration or, if said certificate is lost or destroyed, upon a certified copy thereof.

(f) *Copies of Patent and Trademark Office records as evidence.*—Copies of any records, books, papers, or drawings belonging to the Patent and Trademark Office relating to marks, and copies of registrations, when authenticated by the seal of the Patent and Trademark Office and certified by the Director, or in his name by an employee of the Office duly designated by the Director, shall be evidence in all cases wherein the

15 U.S.C. § 1057

originals would be evidence; and any person making application therefor and paying the prescribed fee shall have such copies.

(g) *Correction of Patent and Trademark Office mistake.*—Whenever a material mistake in a registration, incurred through the fault of the Patent and Trademark Office, is clearly disclosed by the records of the Office a certificate stating the fact and nature of such mistake, shall be issued without charge and recorded and a printed copy thereof shall be attached to each printed copy of the registration and such corrected registration shall thereafter have the same effect as if the same had been originally issued in such corrected form, or in the discretion of the Director a new certificate of registration may be issued without charge. All certificates of correction heretofore issued in accordance with the rules of the Patent and Trademark Office and the registrations to which they are attached shall have the same force and effect as if such certificates and their issue had been specifically authorized by statute.

(h) *Correction of applicant's mistake.*—Whenever a mistake has been made in a registration and a showing has been made that such mistake occurred in good faith through the fault of the applicant, the Director is authorized to issue a certificate of correction or, in his discretion, a new certificate upon the payment of the prescribed fee: *Provided,* That the correction does not involve such changes in the registration as to require republication of the mark.

(July 5, 1946, ch. 540, title I, §7, 60 Stat. 430; Aug 17, 1950, ch. 733, 64 Stat. 459; Oct. 9, 1962, Pub. L. 87-772, §4, 76 Stat. 769; Jan. 2, 1975, Pub. L. 93-596, §1, 88 Stat. 1949; Nov. 16, 1988, Pub. L. 100-667, §109, 102 Stat. 3938-39.)

§ 1058   Duration of registration; cancellation; affidavit of continued use; notice of Director's action [Section 8]

(a) Each registration shall remain in force for 10 years, except that the registration of any mark shall be canceled by the Director for failure to comply with the provisions of subsection (b) of this section, upon the expiration of the following time periods, as applicable:

(1) For registrations issued pursuant to the provisions of this Act, at the end of 6 years following the date of registration.

(2) For registrations published under the provisions of section 12(c), at the end of 6 years following the date of publication under such section.

(3) For all registrations, at the end of each successive 10-year period following the date of registration.

(b) During the 1-year period immediately preceding the end of the applicable time period set forth in subsection (a), the owner of the registration shall pay the prescribed fee and file in the Patent and Trademark Office—

(1) an affidavit setting forth those goods or services recited in the registration on or in connection with which the mark is in use in commerce and such number of specimens or facsimiles showing current use of the mark as may be required by the Director; or

(2) an affidavit setting forth those goods or services recited in the registration on or in connection with which the mark is not in use in commerce and showing that any such nonuse is due to special circumstances which excuse such nonuse and is not due to any intention to abandon the mark.

(c)(1) The owner of the registration may make the submissions required under this section within a grace period of 6 months after the end of the applicable time period set forth in subsection (a). Such submission is required to be accompanied by a surcharge prescribed by the Director.

(2) If any submission filed under this section is deficient, the deficiency may be corrected after the statutory time period and within the time prescribed after notification of the deficiency. Such submission is required to be accompanied by a surcharge prescribed by the Director.

(d) Special notice of the requirement for affidavits under this section shall be attached to each certificate of registration and notice of publication under section 12(c).

(e) The Director shall notify any owner who files 1 of the affidavits required by this section of the Director's acceptance or refusal thereof and, in the case of a refusal, the reasons therefor.

15 U.S.C. § 1058

(f) If the registrant is not domiciled in the United States, the registrant may designate, by a document filed in the United States Patent and Trademark Office, the name and address of a person resident in the United States on whom may be served notices or process in proceedings affecting the mark. Such notices or process may be served upon the person so designated by leaving with that person or mailing to that person a copy thereof at the address specified in the last designation so filed. If the person so designated cannot be found at the address given in the last designation, or if the registrant does not designate by a document filed in the United States Patent and Trademark Office the name and address of a person resident in the United States on whom may be served notices or process in proceedings affecting the mark, such notices or process may be served on the Director.

(July 5, 1946, ch. 540, §8, 60 Stat. 431; Jan. 2, 1975, Pub. L. 93-596, §1, 88 Stat. 1949; Aug. 27, 1982, Pub. L. 97-247, §8, 96 Stat. 320; Nov. 16, 1988, Pub. L. 100-667, §110, 102 Stat. 3939; Oct. 30, 1998, Pub. L. 105-330, §105, 112 Stat. 3066; Nov. 2, 2002, Pub. L. 107-273, §13207, 116 Stat. 1906.)

§ 1059 Renewal of registration [Section 9]

(a) Subject to the provisions of section 8, each registration may be renewed for periods of 10 years at the end of each successive 10-year period following the date of registration upon payment of the prescribed fee and the filing of a written application, in such form as may be prescribed by the Director. Such application may be made at any time within 1 year before the end of each successive 10-year period for which the registration was issued or renewed, or it may be made within a grace period of 6 months after the end of each successive 10-year period, upon payment of a fee and surcharge prescribed therefor. If any application filed under this section is deficient, the deficiency may be corrected within the time prescribed after notification of the deficiency, upon payment of a surcharge prescribed therefor.

(b) If the Director refuses to renew the registration, the Director shall notify the registrant of the Director's refusal and the reasons therefor.

(c) If the registrant is not domiciled in the United States the registrant may designate, by a document filed in the United States Patent and Trademark Office, the name and address of a person resident in the United States on whom may be served notices or process in proceedings affecting the mark. Such notices or process may be served upon the person so designated by leaving with that person or mailing to that person a copy thereof at the address specified in the last designation so filed. If the person so designated cannot be found at the address given in the last designation, or if the registrant does not designate by a document filed in the United States Patent and Trademark Office the name and address of a person resident in the United States on whom may be served notices or process in proceedings affecting the mark, such notices or process may be served on the Director.

(July 5, 1946, ch. 540, title I, §9, 60 Stat. 431; Oct. 9, 1962, Pub. L. 87-772, §5, 76 Stat. 770; Nov. 16, 1988, Pub. L. 100-667, §111, 102 Stat. 3939; Oct. 30, 1998, Pub. L. 105-330, §106, 112 Stat. 3067; Nov. 2, 2002, Pub. L. 107-273, §13207, 116 Stat. 1906.)

§ 1060   Assignment of mark; execution; recording; purchaser without notice [Section 10]

(a)(1) A registered mark or a mark for which an application to register has been filed shall be assignable with the good will of the business in which the mark is used, or with that part of the good will of the business connected with the use of and symbolized by the mark. Notwithstanding the preceding sentence, no application to register a mark under section 1(b) shall be assignable prior to the filing of an amendment under section 1(c) to bring the application into conformity with section 1(a) or the filing of the verified statement of use under section 1(d), except for an assignment to a successor to the business of the applicant, or portion thereof, to which the mark pertains, if that business is ongoing and existing.

(2) In any assignment authorized by this section, it shall not be necessary to include the good will of the business connected with the use of and symbolized by any other mark used in the business or by the name or style under which the business is conducted.

(3) Assignments shall be by instruments in writing duly executed. Acknowledgment shall be prima facie evidence of the execution of an assignment, and when the prescribed information reporting the assignment is recorded in the United States Patent and Trademark Office, the record shall be prima facie evidence of execution.

15 U.S.C. § 1060

(4) An assignment shall be void against any subsequent purchaser for valuable consideration without notice, unless the prescribed information reporting the assignment is recorded in the United States Patent and Trademark Office within 3 months after the date of the assignment or prior to the subsequent purchase.

(5) The United States Patent and Trademark Office shall maintain a record of information on assignments, in such form as may be prescribed by the Director.

(b) An assignee not domiciled in the United States may designate by a document filed in the United States Patent and Trademark Office the name and address of a person resident in the United States on whom may be served notices or process in proceedings affecting the mark. Such notices or process may be served upon the person so designated by leaving with that person or mailing to that person a copy thereof at the address specified in the last designation so filed. If the person so designated cannot be found at the address given in the last designation, or if the assignee does not designate by a document filed in the United States Patent and Trademark Office the name and address of a person resident in the United States on whom may be served notices or process in proceedings affecting the mark, such notices or process may be served upon the Director.

(July 5, 1946, ch. 540, 310, 60 Stat. 431; Oct. 9, 1962, Pub. L. 87-772, §6, 76 Stat. 770; Jan. 2, 1975, Pub. L. 93-596, §1, 88 Stat. 1949; Nov. 16, 1988, Pub. L. 100-667, §112, 102 Stat. 3939; Oct. 30, 1998, Pub. L. 105-330, §107, 112 Stat. 3068; Aug. 5, 1999, Pub. L. 106-43, §6, 113 Stat. 220; Nov. 2, 2002, Pub. L. 107-273, §13207, 116 Stat. 1906.)

§ 1061　Execution of acknowledgments and verifications [Section 11]

Acknowledgments and verifications required hereunder may be made before any person within the United States authorized by law to administer oaths, or, when made in a foreign country, before any diplomatic or consular officer of the United States or before any official authorized to administer oaths in the foreign country concerned whose authority is proved by a certificate of a diplomatic or consular officer of the United States, or apostille of an official designated by a foreign country which, by treaty or convention, accords like effect to apostilles of designated officials in the United States, and shall be valid if they comply with the laws of the state or country where made.

(July 5, 1946, ch. 540, title I, §11, 60 Stat. 432; Aug. 27, 1982, Pub. L. 97-247, §14, 96 Stat. 321.)

§ 1062   Publication; proceedings on refusal of registration; republication of marks registered under prior acts
[Section 12]

(a) Upon the filing of an application for registration and payment of the prescribed fee, the Director shall refer the application to the examiner in charge of the registration of marks, who shall cause an examination to be made and, if on such examination it shall appear that the applicant is entitled to registration, or would be entitled to registration upon the acceptance of the statement of use required by section 1(d) [§1051(d)] of this Act, the Director shall cause the mark to be published in the Official Gazette of the Patent and Trademark Office: *Provided,* That in the case of an applicant claiming concurrent use, or in the case of an application to be placed in an interference as provided for in section 16 [§1066] of this Act, the mark, if otherwise registrable, may be published subject to the determination of the rights of the parties to such proceedings.

(b) If the applicant is found not entitled to registration, the examiner shall advise the applicant thereof and of the reasons therefor. The applicant shall have a period of six months in which to reply or amend his application, which shall then be reexamined. This procedure may be repeated until (1) the examiner finally refuses registration of the mark or (2) the applicant fails for a period of six months to reply or amend or appeal, whereupon the application shall be deemed to have been abandoned, unless it can be shown to the satisfaction of the Director that the delay in responding was unintentional, whereupon such time may be extended.

(c) A registrant of a mark registered under the provisions of the Act of March 3, 1881, or the Act of February 20, 1905, may, at any time prior to the expiration of the registration thereof, upon the payment of the prescribed fee file with the Director an affidavit setting forth those goods stated in the registration on which said mark is in use in commerce and that the registrant claims the benefits of this Act for said mark. The Director shall publish notice thereof with a reproduction of said mark in the Official Gazette, and notify the registrant of such publication and of the requirement for the affidavit of use or nonuse as provided for in subsection (b) of section 8 [§1058(b)] of this Act. Marks published under this subsection shall not be subject to the provisions of section 13 [§1063] of this Act.

(July 5, 1946, ch. 540, title I, §12, 60 Stat. 432; Oct. 9, 1962, Pub. L. 87-772, §7, 76 Stat. 770; Jan. 2, 1975, Pub. L. 43-596, §1, 88 Stat. 1949; Nov. 16, 1988, Pub. L. 100-667, §113, 102 Stat. 3940; Oct. 30, 1998, Pub. L. 105-330, §104, 112 Stat. 3066.)

§ 1063   Opposition to registration [Section 13]

(a) Any person who believes that he would be damaged by the registration of a mark upon the principal register, including as a result of dilution under section 43(c), may, upon payment of the prescribed fee, file an opposition in the Patent and Trademark Office, stating the grounds therefor, within thirty days after the publication under subsection (a) of section 12 [§1062] of this Act of the mark sought to be registered. Upon written request prior to the expiration of the thirty-day period, the time for filing opposition shall be extended for an additional thirty days, and further extensions of time for filing opposition may be granted by the Director for good cause when requested prior to the expiration of an extension. The Director shall notify the applicant of each extension of the time for filing opposition. An opposition may be amended under such conditions as may be prescribed by the Director.

(b) Unless registration is successfully opposed—

(1) a mark entitled to registration on the principal register based on an application filed under section 1(a) [§1051(a)] or pursuant to section 44 [§1126] shall be registered in the Patent and Trademark Office, a certificate of registration shall be issued, and notice of the registration shall be published in the Official Gazette of the Patent and Trademark Office; or

(2) a notice of allowance shall be issued to the applicant if the applicant applied for registration under section 1(b) [§1051(b)].

(July 5, 1946, ch. 540, §13, 60 Stat. 433; Oct. 9, 1962, Pub. L. 87-772, §8, 76 Stat. 771; Jan. 2, 1975, Pub. L. 93-596, §1, 88 Stat. 1949; Jan. 2, 1975, Pub. L. 93-600, §1, 88 Stat. 1955; Aug. 27, 1982, Pub. L. 97-247, §9, 96 Stat. 320; Nov. 16, 1988, Pub. L. 100-667, §114, 102 Stat. 3940; Aug. 5, 1999, Pub. L. 106-43, §2, 113 Stat. 218.)

15 U.S.C. § 1063

§ 1064 Cancellation of registration [Section 14]

A petition to cancel a registration of a mark, stating the grounds relied upon, may, upon payment of the prescribed fee, be filed as follows by any person who believes that he is or will be damaged, including as a result of dilution under section 43(c), by the registration of a mark on the principal register established by this Act, or under the Act of March 3, 1881, or the Act of February 20, 1905:

(1) Within five years from the date of the registration of the mark under this Act.

(2) Within five years from the date of publication under section 12(c) hereof [§1062(c)] of a mark registered under the Act of March 3, 1881, or the Act of February 20, 1905.

(3) At any time if the registered mark becomes the generic name for the goods or services, or a portion thereof, for which it is registered, or is functional, or has been abandoned, or its registration was obtained fraudulently or contrary to the provisions of section 4 [§1054] or of subsection (a), (b), or (c) of section 2 [§1052] for a registration under this Act, or contrary to similar prohibitory provisions of such prior Acts for a registration under such Acts, or if the registered mark is being used by, or with the permission of, the registrant so as to misrepresent the source of the goods or services on or in connection with which the mark is used. If the registered mark becomes the generic name for less than all of the goods or services for which it is registered, a petition to cancel the registration for only those goods or services may be filed. A registered mark shall not be deemed to be the generic name of goods or services solely because such mark is also used as a name of or to identify a unique product or service. The primary significance of the registered mark to the relevant public rather than purchaser motivation shall be the test for determining whether the registered mark has become the generic name of goods or services on or in connection with which it has been used.

(4) At any time if the mark is registered under the Act of March 3, 1881, or the Act of February 20, 1905, and has not been published under the provisions of subsection (c) of section 12 [§1062] of this Act.

(5) At any time in the case of a certification mark on the ground that the registrant (A) does not control, or is not able legitimately to exer-

15 U.S.C. § 1064

cise control over, the use of such mark, or (B) engages in the production or marketing of any goods or services to which the certification mark is applied, or (C) permits the use of the certification mark for purposes other than to certify, or (D) discriminately refuses to certify or to continue to certify the goods or services of any person who maintains the standards or conditions which such mark certifies:

Provided, That the Federal Trade Commission may apply to cancel on the grounds specified in paragraphs (3) and (5) of this section any mark registered on the principal register established by this chapter, and the prescribed fee shall not be required.

Nothing in paragraph (5) shall be deemed to prohibit the registrant from using its certification mark in advertising or promoting recognition of the certification program or of the goods or services meeting the certification standards of the registrant. Such uses of the certification mark shall not be grounds for cancellation under paragraph (5), so long as the registrant does not itself produce, manufacture, or sell any of the certified goods or services to which its identical certification mark is applied.

(July 5, 1946, ch. 540, title I, §14, 60 Stat. 433; Oct. 9, 1962, Pub. L. 87-772, §9, 76 Stat. 771; Aug. 27, 1982, Pub. L. 97-247, §9(b), 96 Stat. 320; Nov. 8, 1984; Pub. L. 98-620; §102, 98 Stat. 3335; Nov. 16, 1988, Pub. L. 100-667, §115, 102 Stat. 3940-41; Oct. 30, 1998, Pub. L. 105-330, §§201, 301, 112 Stat. 3069, 3070; Aug. 5, 1999, Pub. L. 106-43, §2, 113 Stat. 218.)

§ 1065   Incontestability of right to use mark under certain conditions
[Section 15]

Except on a ground for which application to cancel may be filed at any time under paragraphs (3) and (5) of section 14 [§1064] of this Act, and except to the extent, if any, to which the use of a mark registered on the principal register infringes a valid right acquired under the law of any State or Territory by use of a mark or trade name continuing from a date prior to the date of registration under this Act of such registered mark, the right of the registrant to use such registered mark in commerce for the goods or services on or in connection with which such registered mark has been in continuous use for five consecutive years subsequent to the date of such registration and is still in use in commerce, shall be incontestable: *Provided,* That—

(1) there has been no final decision adverse to registrant's claim of ownership of such mark for such goods or services, or to registrant's right to register the same or to keep the same on the register; and

(2) there is no proceeding involving said rights pending in the Patent and Trademark Office or in a court and not finally disposed of; and

(3) an affidavit is filed with the Director within one year after the expiration of any such five-year period setting forth those goods or services stated in the registration on or in connection with which such mark has been in continuous use for such five consecutive years and is still in use in commerce, and the other matters specified in paragraphs (1) and (2) of this section; and

(4) no incontestable right shall be acquired in a mark which is the generic name for the goods or services or a portion thereof, for which it is registered.

Subject to the conditions above specified in this section, the incontestable right with reference to a mark registered under this Act shall apply to a mark registered under the Act of March 3, 1881, or the Act of February 20, 1905, upon the filing of the required affidavit with the Director within one year after the expiration of any period of five consecutive years after the date of publication of a mark under the provisions of subsection (c) of section 12 [§1062] of this Act.

The Director shall notify any registrant who files the above-prescribed affidavit of the filing thereof.

(July 5, 1946, ch. 540, §15, 60 Stat. 433; Oct. 9, 1962, Pub. L. 87-772, §10, 76 Stat. 771; Jan. 2, 1975, Pub. L. 93-596, §1, 88 Stat. 1949; Aug. 27, 1982, Pub. L. 97-247, §10, 96 Stat. 320; Nov. 16, 1988, Pub. L. 100-667, §116, 102 Stat. 3941.)

§ 1066 Interference; declaration by Director [Section 16]

Upon petition showing extraordinary circumstances, the Director may declare that an interference exists when application is made for the registration of a mark which so resembles a mark previously registered by another, or for the registration of which another has previously made application, as to be likely when used on or in connection with the goods or services of the applicant to cause confusion or mistake or to deceive. No interference shall be declared between an application and the registration of a mark the right to the use of which has become incontestable.

(July 5, 1946, ch. 540, title I, §16, 60 Stat. 434; Oct. 9, 1962, Pub. L. 87-772, §11, 76 Stat. 771; Aug. 27, 1982, Pub. L. 97-247, §11, 96 Stat. 321; Nov. 16, 1988, Pub. L. 100-667, §117, 102 Stat. 3941.)

§ 1067 Interference, opposition, and proceedings for concurrent use registration or for cancellation; notice; Trademark Trial and Appeal Board [Section 17]

(a) In every case of interference, opposition to registration, application to register as a lawful concurrent user, or application to cancel the registration of a mark, the Director shall give notice to all parties and shall direct a Trademark Trial and Appeal Board to determine and decide the respective rights of registration.

(b) The Trademark Trial and Appeal Board shall include the Director, the Deputy Commissioner,* the Commissioner for Patents, the Commissioner for Trademarks, and administrative trademark judges who are appointed by the Director.

(July 5, 1946, ch. 540, §17, 60 Stat. 434; Aug. 8, 1958, Pub. L. 85-609, §1, 72 Stat. 540; Jan. 2, 1975, Pub. L. 93-596, §1, 88 Stat. 1949; Oct. 15, 1980, Pub. L. 96-455, §1, 94 Stat. 2024; Nov. 29, 1999, Pub. L. 106-113, §4716, 113 Stat. 1501A-580; Nov. 2, 2002, Pub. L. 107-273, §13203, 116 Stat. 1902.)

§ 1068 Same; action of Director [Section 18]

In such proceedings the Director may refuse to register the opposed mark, may cancel the registration, in whole or in part, may modify the application or registration by limiting the goods or services specified therein, may otherwise restrict or rectify with respect to the register the registration of a registered mark, may refuse to register any or all of several interfering marks, or may register the mark or marks for the person or persons entitled thereto, as the rights of the parties under this chapter may be established in the proceedings: *Provided,* That in the case of the registration of any mark based on concurrent use, the Director shall determine and fix the conditions and limitations provided for in

---

* *Ed. Note:* Section 13203(a) of Pub. L. 107-273 provides for inserting "the Deputy Commissioner". Presumably, however, the term "the Deputy Director" was intended.

subsection (d) of section 2 [§1052] of this Act. However, no final judgment shall be entered in favor of an applicant under section 1(b) [§1051(b)] before the mark is registered, if such applicant cannot prevail without establishing constructive use pursuant to section 7(c) [§1057(c)].

(July 5, 1946, ch. 540, title I, §18, 60 Stat. 434; Nov. 16, 1988, Pub. L. 100-667, §118, 102 Stat. 3941.)

§ 1069 Application of equitable principles in inter partes proceedings [Section 19]

In all inter partes proceedings equitable principles of laches, estoppel, and acquiescence, where applicable may be considered and applied.

(July 5, 1946, ch. 540, §19, 60 Stat. 434; Jan. 2, 1975, Pub. L. 93-596, §1, 88 Stat. 1949; Nov. 16, 1988, Pub. L. 100-667, §119, 102 Stat. 3941.)

§ 1070 Appeals to Trademark Trial and Appeal Board from decisions of examiners [Section 20]

An appeal may be taken to the Trademark Trial and Appeal Board from any final decision of the examiner in charge of the registration of marks upon the payment of the prescribed fee.

(July 5, 1946, ch. 540, title I, §20, 60 Stat. 435; Aug. 8, 1958, Pub. L. 85-609, §1, 72 Stat. 540.)

§ 1071 Appeal to courts [Section 21]

(a) (1) An applicant for registration of a mark, party to an interference proceeding, party to an opposition proceeding, party to an application to register as a lawful concurrent user, party to a cancellation proceeding, a registrant who has filed an affidavit as provided in section 8 [§1058] of this Act, or an applicant for renewal, who is dissatisfied with the decision of the Director or Trademark Trial and Appeal Board, may appeal to the United States Court of Appeals for the Federal Circuit thereby waiving his right to proceed under subsection (b) of this section: *Provided,* That such appeal shall be dismissed if any adverse party to the proceeding, other than the Director, shall, within twenty days after the appellant has filed notice of appeal according to paragraph (2) of this subsection, files notice with the Director that he elects to have all further proceedings conducted as provided in subsection (b) of this section. Thereupon the appellant shall have thirty days thereafter within which to file a civil action under said subsection (b) of this section, in default of which the decision appealed from shall govern the further proceedings in the case.

(2) When an appeal is taken to the United States Court of Appeals for the Federal Circuit, the appellant shall file in the Patent and Trademark Office a written notice of appeal directed to the Director, within such time after the date of the decision from which the appeal is taken as the Director prescribes, but in no case less than 60 days after that date.

(3) The Director shall transmit to the United States Court of Appeals for the Federal Circuit a certified list of the documents comprising the record in the Patent and Trademark Office. The court may request that the Director forward the original or certified copies of such documents during pendency of the appeal. In an ex parte case, the Director shall submit to that court a brief explaining the grounds for the decision of the Patent and Trademark Office, addressing all the issues involved in the appeal. The court shall, before hearing an appeal, give notice of the time and place of the hearing to the Director and the parties in the appeal.

(4) The United States Court of Appeals for the Federal Circuit shall review the decision from which the appeal is taken on the record before the Patent and Trademark Office. Upon its determination the court shall issue its mandate and opinion to the Director, which shall be entered of record in the Patent and Trademark Office and shall govern the further proceedings in the case. However, no final judgment shall be entered in favor of an applicant under section 1(b) [§1051(b)] before the mark is registered, if such applicant cannot prevail without establishing constructive use pursuant to section 7(c) [§1057(c)].

(b) (1) Whenever a person authorized by subsection (a) of this section to appeal to the United States Court of Appeals for the Federal Circuit is dissatisfied with the decision of the Director or Trademark Trial and Appeal Board, said person may, unless appeal has been taken to said United States Court of Appeals for the Federal Circuit, have remedy by a civil action if commenced within such time after such decision, not less than sixty days, as the Director appoints or as provided in subsection (a) of this section. The court may adjudge that an applicant is entitled to a registration upon the application involved, that a registration involved should be canceled, or such other matter as the issues in the proceeding require, as the facts in the case may appear. Such adjudication shall authorize the Director to take any necessary action, upon compliance with the requirements of law. However, no final judgment shall be entered in favor of an applicant under section 1(b) [§1051(b)] before the mark is registered, if such applicant cannot prevail without establishing constructive use pursuant to section 7(c) [§1057(c)].

(2) The Director shall not be made a party to an inter partes proceeding under this subsection, but he shall be notified of the filing of the complaint by the clerk of the court in which it is filed and shall have the right to intervene in the action.

(3) In any case where there is no adverse party, a copy of the complaint shall be served on the Director, and, unless the court finds the expenses to be unreasonable, all the expenses of the proceeding shall be paid by the party bringing the case, whether the final decision is in favor of such party or not. In suits brought hereunder, the record in the Patent and Trademark Office shall be admitted on motion of any party, upon such terms and conditions as to costs, expenses, and the further cross-examination of the witnesses as the court imposes, without prejudice to the right of any party to take further testimony. The testimony and exhibits of the record in the Patent and Trademark Office, when admitted, shall have the same effect as if originally taken and produced in the suit.

(4) Where there is an adverse party, such suit may be instituted against the party in interest as shown by the records of the Patent and Trademark Office at the time of the decision complained of, but any party in interest may become a party to the action. If there be adverse parties residing in a plurality of districts not embraced within the same State, or an adverse party residing in a foreign country, the United States District Court for the District of Columbia shall have jurisdiction and may issue summons against the adverse parties directed to the marshal of any district in which any adverse party resides. Summons against adverse parties residing in foreign

countries may be served by publication or otherwise as the court directs.

(July 5, 1946, ch. 540, §21, 60 Stat. 435; July 19, 1952, ch. 950, §2, 66 Stat. 814; Aug. 8, 1958, Pub. L. 85-609, §1, 72 Stat. 540; Oct. 9, 1962, Pub. L. 87-772, §12, 76 Stat. 771; Jan. 2, 1975, Pub. L. 93-596, §1, 88 Stat. 1949; Jan. 2, 1975, Pub. L. 93-600, §2, 88 Stat. 1955; Apr. 2, 1982, Pub. L. 97-164, §162, 96 Stat. 49; Nov. 8, 1984, Pub. L. 98-620, §414, 98 Stat. 3363; Nov. 16, 1988, Pub. L. 100-667, §120, 102 Stat. 3942.)

§ 1072   Registration as constructive notice of claim of ownership [Section 22]

Registration of a mark on the principal register provided by this Act or under the Act of March 3, 1881, or the Act of February 20, 1905, shall be constructive notice of the registrant's claim of ownership thereof.

(July 5, 1946, ch. 540, title I, §22, 60 Stat. 435.)

SUBCHAPTER II—THE SUPPLEMENTAL REGISTER

SEC.

§ 1091   Marks registrable on supplemental register; application and proceedings for registration; nature of mark; mark used in foreign commerce [Section 23]

(a) In addition to the principal register, the Director shall keep a continuation of the register provided in paragraph (b) of section 1 of the Act of March 19, 1920, entitled "An Act to give effect to certain provisions of the convention for the protection of trademarks and commercial names, made and signed in the city of Buenos Aires, in the Argentine Republic, August 20, 1910, and for other purposes," to be called the supplemental register. All marks capable of distinguishing applicant's goods or services and not registrable on the principal register herein provided, except those declared to be unregistrable under subsections (a), (b), (c), and (d) and (e)(3) of section 2 [§1052] of this Act, which are in lawful use in commerce by the owner thereof, on or in connection with any goods or services may be registered on the supplemental register upon the payment of the prescribed fee and compliance with the provisions of subsections (a) and (e) of section 1 [§1051] so far as they are applicable. Nothing in this section shall prevent the registration on the supplemental register of a mark, capable of distinguishing the applicant's goods or services and not registrable on the principal register under this Act, that is declared to be unregistrable under section 2(e)(3), if such mark has been in lawful use in commerce by the owner thereof, on or in connection with any goods or services, since before the date of the enactment of the North American Free Trade Agreement Implementation Act.*

(b) Upon the filing of an application for registration on the supplemental register and payment of the prescribed fee the Director shall refer the application to the examiner in charge of the registration of marks, who shall cause an examination to be made and if on such examination it shall appear that the applicant is entitled to registration, the registration shall be granted. If the applicant is found not entitled to registration the provisions of subsection (b) of section 12 [§1062] of this Act shall apply.

(c) For the purposes of registration on the supplemental register, a mark may consist of any trademark, symbol, label, package, configuration of goods, name, word, slogan, phrase, surname, geographical name, numeral, device, any matter that as a whole is not functional, or any combination of any of the foregoing, but such mark must be capable of distinguishing the applicant's goods or services.

(July 5, 1946, ch. 540, title II, §23, 60 Stat. 435; Oct. 9, 1962, Pub. L. 87-772, §13, 76 Stat. 773; Nov. 16, 1988, Pub. L. 100-667, §121, 102 Stat. 3942-43; Dec. 8, 1993, Pub. L. 103-182, §333, 107 Stat. 2114; Oct. 30, 1998, Pub. L. 105-330, §201, 112 Stat. 3070; Nov. 2, 2002, Pub. L. 107-273, §13207, 116 Stat. 1906.)

---

* *Ed. Note:* The North American Free Trade Agreement Implementation Act was enacted on Dec. 8, 1993.

15 U.S.C. § 1091

§ 1092 Publication; not subject to opposition; cancellation
[Section 24]

Marks for the supplemental register shall not be published for or be subject to opposition, but shall be published on registration in the Official Gazette of the Patent and Trademark Office. Whenever any person believes that he is or will be damaged by the registration of a mark on this register, including as a result of dilution under section 43(c), he may at any time, upon payment of the prescribed fee and the filing of a petition stating the ground therefor, apply to the Director to cancel such registration. The Director shall refer such application to the Trademark Trial and Appeal Board which shall give notice thereof to the registrant. If it is found after a hearing before the Board that the registrant is not entitled to registration, or that the mark has been abandoned, the registration shall be canceled by the Director. However, no final judgment shall be entered in favor of an applicant under section 1(b) [§1051(b)] before the mark is registered, if such applicant cannot prevail without establishing constructive use pursuant to section 7(c) [§1057(c)].

(July 5, 1946, ch. 540, §24, 60 Stat. 436; Aug. 8, 1958, Pub. L. 85-609. §1, 72 Stat. 540; Oct. 9, 1962, Pub. L. 87-772, §14, 76 Stat. 773; Jan. 2, 1975, Pub. L. 93-596, §1, 88 Stat. 1949; Nov. 16, 1988, Pub. L. 100-667, §122, 102 Stat. 3943; Aug. 5, 1999, Pub. L. 106-43, §2, 113 Stat. 218.)

§ 1093 Registration certificates for marks on principal and supplemental registers to be different [Section 25]

The certificates of registration for marks registered on the supplemental register shall be conspicuously different from certificates issued for marks registered on the principal register.

(July 5, 1946, ch. 540, title II, §25, 60 Stat. 436.)

§ 1094 Provisions of chapter applicable to registrations on supplemental register [Section 26]

The provisions of this chapter shall govern so far as applicable applications for registration and registrations on the supplemental register as well as those on the principal register, but applications for and registrations on the supplemental register shall not be subject to or receive the advantages of sections 1(b), 2(e), 2(f), 7(b), 7(c), 12(a), 13 to 18, inclusive,

22, 33, and 42 of this Act [§§1051(b), 1052(e), 1052(f), 1057(b), 1057(c), 1062(a), 1063-1068, 1072, 1115, and 1124].

(July 5, 1946, ch. 540, title II, §26, 60 Stat. 436; Nov. 16, 1988, Pub. L. 100-667, §123, 102 Stat. 3943.)

§ 1095   Registration on principal register not precluded [Section 27]

Registration of a mark on the supplemental register, or under the Act of March 19, 1920, shall not preclude registration by the registrant on the principal register established by this chapter. Registration of a mark on the supplemental register shall not constitute an admission that the mark has not acquired distinctiveness.

(July 5, 1946, ch. 540, title II, §27, 60 Stat. 436; Nov. 16, 1988, Pub. L. 100-667, §124, 102 Stat. 3943.)

§ 1096   Registration on supplemental register not used to stop importations [Section 28]

Registration on the supplemental register or under the Act of March 19, 1920, shall not be filed in the Department of the Treasury or be used to stop importations.

(July 5, 1946, ch. 540, title II, §28, 60 Stat. 436.)

SUBCHAPTER III—GENERAL PROVISIONS

SEC.
1111.   Notice of registration; display with mark; recovery of profits and damages in infringement suit.
1112.   Classification of goods and services; registration in plurality of classes.
1113.   Fees.
1114.   Remedies; infringement; innocent infringement by printers and publishers.
1115.   Registration on principal register as evidence of exclusive right to use mark; defenses.
1116.   Injunctions; enforcement; notice to Director.
1117.   Recovery for violation of rights; profits, damages and costs; attorney fees.
1118.   Destruction of infringing articles.
1119.   Power of court over registration.
1120.   Civil liability for false or fraudulent registration.
1121.   Jurisdiction of Federal courts.
1122.   Liability of States, Instrumentalities of States, and State Officials.

§ 1111   Notice of registration; display with mark; recovery of profits and damages in infringement suit [Section 29]

Notwithstanding the provisions of section 22 [§1072] hereof, a registrant of a mark registered in the Patent and Trademark Office may give notice that his mark is registered by displaying with the mark the words "Registered in U.S. Patent and Trademark Office" or "Reg. U.S. Pat. & Tm. Off." or the letter R enclosed within a circle, thus ®; and in any suit for infringement under this Act by such a registrant failing to give such notice of registration, no profits and no damages shall be recovered under the provisions of this Act unless the defendant had actual notice of the registration.

(July 5, 1946, ch. 540, §29, 60 Stat. 436; Oct. 9, 1962, Pub. L. 87-772, §15, 76 Stat. 773; Jan. 2, 1975, Pub. L. 93-596, §§1 and 2, 88 Stat. 1949; Nov. 16, 1988, Pub. L. 100-667, §125, 102 Stat. 3943.)

§ 1112   Classification of goods and services; registration in plurality of classes [Section 30]

The Director may establish a classification of goods and services, for convenience of Patent and Trademark Office administration, but not to limit or extend the applicant's or registrant's rights. The applicant may apply to register a mark for any or all of the goods or services upon or in connection with which he or she is using or has a bona fide intention to use the mark in commerce: *Provided,* That if the Director by regulation permits the filing of an application for the registration of a mark for goods or services which fall within a plurality of classes, a fee equaling the sum of the fees for filing an application in each class shall be paid, and the Director may issue a single certificate of registration for such mark.

(July 5, 1946, ch. 540, §30, 60 Stat. 436; Oct. 9, 1962, Pub. L. 87-772, §16, 76 Stat. 773; Jan. 2, 1975, Pub. L. 93-596, §1, 88 Stat. 1949; Nov. 16, 1988, Pub. L. 100-667, §126, 102 Stat. 3943.)

§ 1113   Fees [Section 31]

(a) The Director shall establish fees for the filing and processing of an application for the registration of a trademark or other mark and for all other services performed by and materials furnished by the Patent and Trademark Office related to trademarks and other marks. Fees established under this subsection may be adjusted by the Director once each year to reflect, in the aggregate, any fluctuations during the preceding 12 months in the Consumer Price Index, as determined by the Secretary of Labor. Changes of less than 1 percent may be ignored. No fee established under this section shall take effect until at least 30 days after notice of the fee has been published in the Federal Register and in the Official Gazette of the Patent and Trademark Office.

(b) The Director may waive the payment of any fee for any service or material related to trademarks or other marks in connection with an occasional request made by a department or agency of the Government, or any officer thereof. The Indian Arts and Crafts Board will not be charged any fee to register Government trademarks of genuineness and quality for Indian products or for products of particular Indian tribes and groups.

(July 5, 1946, ch. 540, §31, 60 Stat. 437; Aug. 8, 1958, Pub. L. 85-609, §1, 72 Stat. 540; July 24, 1965, Pub. L. 89-83, §3, 79 Stat. 260; Jan. 2, 1975, Pub. L. 93-596, §1, 88 Stat. 1949; Dec. 12, 1980, Pub. L. 96-517, §5, 94 Stat. 3018; Aug. 27, 1982, Pub. L. 97-247, §3, 96 Stat. 319; Sept. 8, 1982, Pub. L. 97-256, §103, 96 Stat. 256; Dec. 10, 1991, Pub. L. 102-204, §5, 105 Stat. 1640.)

§ 1114   Remedies; infringement; innocent infringement by printers and publishers [Section 32]

(1) Any person who shall, without the consent of the registrant—

(a) use in commerce any reproduction, counterfeit, copy, or colorable imitation of a registered mark in connection with the sale, offering for sale, distribution, or advertising of any goods or services on or in connection with which such use is likely to cause confusion, or to cause mistake, or to deceive; or

(b) reproduce, counterfeit, copy, or colorably imitate a registered mark and apply such reproduction, counterfeit, copy, or colorable imitation to labels, signs, prints, packages, wrappers, receptacles or advertisements intended to be used in commerce upon or in connection with the sale, offering for sale, distribution, or advertising of goods or services on or in connection with which such use is likely to cause confusion, or to cause mistake, or to deceive;

shall be liable in a civil action by the registrant for the remedies hereinafter provided. Under subsection (b) hereof, the registrant shall not be entitled to recover profits or damages unless the acts have been committed with knowledge that such imitation is intended to be used to cause confusion, or to cause mistake, or to deceive.

As used in this paragraph, the term "any person" includes the United States, all agencies and instrumentalities thereof, and all individuals, firms, corporations, or other persons acting for the United States and with the authorization and consent of the United States, and any State, any instrumentality of a State, and any officer or employee of a State or instrumentality of a State acting in his or her official capacity. The United States, all agencies and instrumentalities thereof, and all individuals, firms, corporations, other persons acting for the United States and with the authorization and consent of the United States, and any State, and any such instrumentality, officer, or employee, shall be subject to the provisions of this Act in the same manner and to the same extent as any nongovernmental entity.

(2) Notwithstanding any other provision of this Act, the remedies given to the owner of a right infringed under this Act or to a person bringing an action under section 43(a) or (d) [§1125(a) or (d)] shall be limited as follows:

(A) Where an infringer or violator is engaged solely in the business of printing the mark or violating matter for others and establishes that he or she was an innocent infringer or innocent violator, the owner of the right infringed or person bringing the action under section 43(a) [§1125(a)] shall be entitled as against such infringer or violator only to an injunction against future printing.

(B) Where the infringement or violation complained of is contained in or is part of paid advertising matter in a newspaper, magazine, or other similar periodical or in an electronic communication as defined in section 2510(12) of title 18, United States Code, the remedies of the owner of the right infringed or person bringing the action under section 43(a) [§1125(a)] as against the publisher or distributor of such newspaper, magazine, or other similar periodical or electronic communication shall be limited to an injunction against the presentation of such advertising matter in future issues of such newspapers, magazines, or other similar periodicals or in future transmissions of such electronic communications. The limitations of this subparagraph shall apply only to innocent infringers and innocent violators.

(C) Injunctive relief shall not be available to the owner of the right infringed or person bringing the action under section 43(a) [§1125(a)] with respect to an issue of a newspaper, magazine, or other similar periodical or an electronic communication containing infringing matter or violating matter where restraining the dissemination of such infringing matter or violating matter in any particular issue of such periodical or in an electronic communication would delay the delivery of such issue or transmission of such electronic communication after the regular time for such delivery or transmission, and such delay would be due to the method by which publication and distribution of such periodical or transmission of such electronic communication is customarily conducted in accordance with sound business practice, and not due to any method or device adopted to evade this section or to prevent or delay the issuance of an injunction or restraining order with respect to such infringing matter or violating matter.

(D)(i)(I) A domain name registrar, a domain name registry, or other domain name registration authority that takes any action described under clause (ii) affecting a domain name shall not be liable for monetary relief or, except as provided in subclause (II), for injunctive relief, to any person for such action, regardless of whether the domain name is finally determined to infringe or dilute the mark.

(II) A domain name registrar, domain name registry, or other domain name registration authority described in subclause (I) may be subject to injunctive relief only if such registrar, registry, or other registration authority has—

(aa) not expeditiously deposited with a court, in which an action has been filed regarding the disposition of the domain name, documents sufficient for the court to establish the court's control and authority regarding the disposition of the registration and use of the domain name;

(bb) transferred, suspended, or otherwise modified the domain name during the pendency of the action, except upon order of the court; or

(cc) willfully failed to comply with any such court order.

(ii) An action referred to under clause (i)(I) is any action of refusing to register, removing from registration, transferring, temporarily disabling, or permanently canceling a domain name—

(I) in compliance with a court order under section 43(d); or

(II) in the implementation of a reasonable policy by such registrar, registry, or authority prohibiting the registration of a domain name that is identical to, confusingly similar to, or dilutive of another's mark.

(iii) A domain name registrar, a domain name registry, or other domain name registration authority shall not be liable for damages under this section for the registration or maintenance of a domain name for another absent a showing of bad faith intent to profit from such registration or maintenance of the domain name.

(iv) If a registrar, registry, or other registration authority takes an action described under clause (ii) based on a knowing and material misrepresentation by any other person that a domain name is identical to, confusingly similar to, or dilutive of a mark, the person making the knowing and material misrepresentation shall be liable for any damages, including costs and attorney's fees, incurred by the domain name registrant as a result of such action. The court may also grant injunctive relief to the domain name registrant, including the reactivation of the domain name or the transfer of the domain name to the domain name registrant.

(v) A domain name registrant whose domain name has been suspended, disabled, or transferred under a policy described under clause (ii)(II) may, upon notice to the mark owner, file a civil action to establish that the registration or use of the domain name by such registrant is not unlawful under this Act. The court may grant injunctive relief to the domain name registrant, including the reactivation of the domain name or transfer of the domain name to the domain name registrant.

(E) As used in this paragraph—

(i) the term "violator" means a person who violates section 43(a) [§1125(a)]; and

(ii) the term "violating matter" means matter that is the subject of a violation under section 43(a) [§1125(a)].

(July 5, 1946, ch. 540, title VI, §32, 60 Stat. 437; Oct. 9, 1962, Pub. L. 87-772, §17, 76 Stat. 773; Nov. 16, 1988, Pub. L. 100-667, §127, 102 Stat. 3943-44; Oct. 27, 1992, Pub. L. 102-542, §3, 106 Stat. 3567; Oct. 30, 1998, Pub. L. 105-330, §201, 112 Stat. 3070; Aug. 5, 1999, Pub. L. 106-43, §4, 113 Stat. 219; Nov. 29, 1999, Pub. L. 106-113, §3004, 113 Stat. 1501A-549.)

§ 1115 Registration on principal register as evidence of exclusive right to use mark; defenses [Section 33]

(a) Any registration issued under the Act of March 3, 1881, or the Act of February 20, 1905, or of a mark registered on the principal register provided by this Act and owned by a party to an action shall be admissible in evidence and shall be prima facie evidence of the validity of the registered mark and of the registration of the mark, of the registrant's ownership of the mark, and of the registrant's exclusive right to use the registered mark in commerce on or in connection with the goods or services specified in the registration subject to any conditions or limitations stated therein, but shall not preclude another person from proving any legal or equitable defense or defect, including those set forth in subsection (b), which might have been asserted if such mark had not been registered.

(b) To the extent that the right to use the registered mark has become incontestable under section 15 [§1065], the registration shall be conclusive evidence of the validity of the registered mark and of the registration of the mark, of the registrant's ownership of the mark, and of the registrant's exclusive right to use the registered mark in commerce. Such conclusive evidence shall relate to the exclusive right to use the mark on or in connection with the goods or services specified in the affidavit filed under the provisions of section 15 [§1065], or in the renewal application filed under the provisions of section 9 [§1059] if the goods or services specified in the renewal are fewer in number, subject to any conditions or limitations in the registration or in such affidavit or renewal application. Such conclusive evidence of the right to use the registered mark shall be subject to proof of infringement as defined in section 32 [§1114], and shall be subject to the following defenses or defects:

(1) That the registration or the incontestable right to use the mark was obtained fraudulently; or

(2) That the mark has been abandoned by the registrant; or

(3) That the registered mark is being used, by or with the permission of the registrant or a person in privity with the registrant, so as to misrepresent the source of the goods or services on or in connection with which the mark is used; or

(4) That the use of the name, term, or device charged to be an infringement is a use, otherwise than as a mark, of the party's individual name in his own business, or of the individual name of anyone in privity with such party, or of a term or device which is descriptive of and used fairly and in good faith only to describe the goods or services of such party, or their geographic origin; or

(5) That the mark whose use by a party is charged as an infringement was adopted without knowledge of the registrant's prior use and has been continuously used by such party or those in privity with him from a date prior to (A) the date of constructive use of the mark established pursuant to section 7(c) [§1057(c)], (B) the registration of the mark under this Act if the application for registration is filed before the effective date of the Trademark Law Revision Act of 1988, or (C) publication of the registered mark under subsection (c) of section 12 [§1062] of this Act: *Provided, however,* That this defense or defect shall apply only for the area in which such continuous prior use is proved; or

(6) That the mark whose use is charged as an infringement was registered and used prior to the registration under this Act or publica-

tion under subsection (c) of section 12 [§1062] of this Act of the registered mark of the registrant, and not abandoned: *Provided, however,* That this defense or defect shall apply only for the area in which the mark was used prior to such registration or such publication of the registrant's mark; or

(7) That the mark has been or is being used to violate the antitrust laws of the United States; or

(8) That the mark is functional; or

(9) That equitable principles, including laches, estoppel, and acquiescence are applicable.

(July 5, 1946, ch. 540, title VI, §33, 60 Stat. 438; Oct. 9, 1962, Pub. L. 87-772, §18, 76 Stat. 774; Nov. 16, 1988, Pub. L. 100-667, §128, 102 Stat. 3944-45; Oct. 30, 1998, Pub. L. 105-330, §201, 112 Stat. 3070; Nov. 2, 2002, Pub. L. 107-273, §13207, 116 Stat. 1906.)

§ 1116   Injunctions; enforcement; notice to Director
[Section 34]

(a) The several courts vested with jurisdiction of civil actions arising under this Act shall have power to grant injunctions, according to the principles of equity and upon such terms as the court may deem reasonable, to prevent the violation of any right of the registrant of a mark registered in the Patent and Trademark Office or to prevent a violation of subsection (a), (c), or (d) of section 43 [§1125(a), (c), or (d)]. Any such injunction may include a provision directing the defendant to file with the court and serve on the plaintiff within thirty days after the service on the defendant of such injunction, or such extended period as the court may direct, a report in writing under oath setting forth in detail the manner and form in which the defendant has complied with the injunction. Any such injunction granted upon hearing, after notice to the defendant, by any district court of the United States, may be served on the parties against whom such injunction is granted anywhere in the United States where they may be found, and shall be operative and may be enforced by proceedings to punish for contempt, or otherwise, by the court by which such injunction was granted, or by any other United States district court in whose jurisdiction the defendant may be found.

(b) The said courts shall have jurisdiction to enforce said injunction, as herein provided, as fully as if the injunction had been granted by the district court in which it is sought to be enforced. The clerk of the court or judge granting the injunction shall, when required to do so by the court before which application to enforce said injunction is made, transfer without delay to said court a certified copy of all papers on file in his office upon which said injunction was granted.

(c) It shall be the duty of the clerks of such courts within one month after the filing of any action, suit, or proceeding involving a mark registered under the provisions of this Act to give notice thereof in writing to the Director setting forth in order so far as known the names and addresses of the litigants and the designating number or numbers of the registration or registrations upon which the action, suit, or proceeding has been brought, and in the event any other registration be subsequently included in the action, suit, or proceeding by amendment, answer, or other pleading, the clerk shall give like notice thereof to the Director, and within one month after the judgment is entered or an appeal is taken the clerk of the court shall give notice thereof to the Director, and it shall be the duty of the Director on receipt of such notice forthwith to endorse the same upon the file wrapper of the said registration or registrations and to incorporate the same as a part of the contents of said file wrapper.

(d)(1) (A) In the case of a civil action arising under section 32(1)(a) of this Act (15 U.S.C. 1114) or section 220506 of title 36, United States Code, with respect to a violation that consists of using a counterfeit mark in connection with the sale, offering for sale, or distribution of goods or services, the court may, upon ex parte application, grant an order under subsection (a) of this section pursuant to this subsection providing for the seizure of goods and counterfeit marks involved in such violation and the means of making such marks, and records documenting the manufacturer, sale, or receipt of things involved in such violation.

(B) As used in this subsection the term "counterfeit mark" means—

(i) a counterfeit of a mark that is registered on the principal register in the United States Patent and Trademark Office for such goods or services sold, offered for sale, or distributed and that is in use, whether or not the person against whom relief is sought knew such mark was so registered; or

(ii) a spurious designation that is identical with, or substantially indistinguishable from, a designation as to which the remedies of this Act are made available by reason of section 220506 of title 36, United States Code;

but such term does not include any mark or designation used on or in connection with goods or services of which the manufacturer or producer was, at the time of the manufacture or production in question, authorized to use the mark or designation for the type of goods or services so manufactured or produced, by the holder of the right to use such mark or designation.

(2) The court shall not receive an application under this subsection unless the applicant has given such notice of the application as is reasonable under the circumstances to the United States attorney for the judicial district in which such order is sought. Such attorney may participate in the proceedings arising under such application if such proceedings may affect evidence of an offense against the United States. The court may deny such application if the court determines that the public interest in a potential prosecution so requires.

(3) The application for an order under this subsection shall—

(A) be based on an affidavit or the verified complaint establishing facts sufficient to support the findings of fact and conclusions of law required for such order; and

(B) contain the additional information required by paragraph (5) of this subsection to be set forth in such order.

(4) The court shall not grant such an application unless—

(A) the person obtaining an order under this subsection provides the security determined adequate by the court for the payment of such damages as any person may be entitled to recover as a result of a wrongful seizure or wrongful attempted seizure under this subsection; and

(B) the court finds that it clearly appears from specific facts that—

(i) an order other than an ex parte seizure order is not adequate to achieve the purposes of section 32 of this Act (15 U.S.C. 1114);

(ii) the applicant has not publicized the requested seizure;

(iii) the applicant is likely to succeed in showing that the person against whom seizure would be ordered used a counterfeit mark in connection with the sale, offering for sale, or distribution of goods or services;

(iv) an immediate and irreparable injury will occur if such seizure is not ordered;

(v) the matter to be seized will be located at the place identified in the application;

(vi) the harm to the applicant of denying the application outweighs the harm to the legitimate interests of the person against whom seizure would be ordered of granting the application; and

(vii) the person against whom seizure would be ordered, or persons acting in concert with such person, would destroy, move, hide, or otherwise make such matter inaccessible to the court, if the applicant were to proceed on notice to such person.

(5) An order under this subsection shall set forth—

(A) the findings of fact and conclusions of law required for the order;

(B) a particular description of the matter to be seized, and a description of each place at which such matter is to be seized;

(C) the time period, which shall end not later than seven days after the date on which such order is issued, during which the seizure is to be made;

(D) the amount of security required to be provided under this subsection; and

(E) a date for the hearing required under paragraph (10) of this subsection.

(6) The court shall take appropriate action to protect the person against whom an order under this subsection is directed from pub-

licity, by or at the behest of the plaintiff, about such order and any seizure under such order.

(7) Any materials seized under this subsection shall be taken into the custody of the court. The court shall enter an appropriate protective order with respect to discovery by the applicant of any records that have been seized. The protective order shall provide for appropriate procedures to assure that confidential information contained in such records is not improperly disclosed to the applicant.

(8) An order under this subsection, together with the supporting documents, shall be sealed until the person against whom the order is directed has an opportunity to contest such order, except that any person against whom such order is issued shall have access to such order and supporting documents after the seizure has been carried out.

(9) The court shall order that service of a copy of the order under this subsection shall be made by a Federal law enforcement officer (such as a United States marshal or an officer or agent of the United States Customs Service, Secret Service, Federal Bureau of Investigation, or Post Office) or may be made by a State or local law enforcement officer, who, upon making service, shall carry out the seizure under the order. The court shall issue orders, when appropriate, to protect the defendant from undue damage from the disclosure of trade secrets or other confidential information during the course of the seizure, including, when appropriate, orders restricting the access of the applicant (or any agent or employee of the applicant) to such secrets or information.

(10) (A) The court shall hold a hearing, unless waived by all the parties, on the date set by the court in the order of seizure. That date shall be not sooner than ten days after the order is issued and not later than fifteen days after the order is issued, unless the applicant for the order shows good cause for another date or unless the party against whom such order is directed consents to another date for such hearing. At such hearing the party obtaining the order shall have the burden to prove that the facts supporting findings of fact and conclusions of law necessary to support such order are still in effect. If that party fails to meet that bur-

den, the seizure order shall be dissolved or modified appropriately.

(B) In connection with a hearing under this paragraph, the court may make such orders modifying the time limits for discovery under the Rules of Civil Procedure as may be necessary to prevent the frustration of the purposes of such hearing.

(11) A person who suffers damage by reason of a wrongful seizure under this subsection has a cause of action against the applicant for the order under which such seizure was made, and shall be entitled to recover such relief as may be appropriate, including damages for lost profits, cost of materials, loss of good will, and punitive damages in instances where the seizure was sought in bad faith, and, unless the court finds extenuating circumstances, to recover a reasonable attorney's fee. The court in its discretion may award prejudgment interest on relief recovered under this paragraph, at an annual interest rate established under section 6621(a)(2) of the Internal Revenue Code of 1986, commencing on the date of service of the claimant's pleading setting forth the claim under this paragraph and ending on the date such recovery is granted, or for such shorter time as the court deems appropriate.

(July 5, 1946, ch. 540, title VI, §34, 60 Stat. 439; Jan. 2, 1975, Pub. L. 93-596, §1, 88 Stat. 1949; Oct. 12, 1984, Pub. L. 98-473, §1503, 98 Stat. 2179; Nov. 16, 1988, Pub. L. 100-667, §128, 102 Stat. 3944-45; July 2, 1996, Pub. L. 104-153, §6, 110 Stat. 1388; Aug. 5, 1999, Pub. L. 106-43, §3, 113 Stat. 218; Nov. 29, 1999, Pub. L. 106-113, §3003, 113 Stat. 1501A-548; Nov. 2, 2002, Pub. L. 107-273, §13207, 116 Stat. 1906.)

§ 1117   Recovery for violation of rights; profits, damages and costs; attorney fees [Section 35]

(a) When a violation of any right of the registrant of a mark registered in the Patent and Trademark Office, a violation under section 43(a) or (d) [§1125(a) or (d)], or a willful violation under section 43(c), shall have been established in any civil action arising under this Act, the plaintiff shall be entitled, subject to the provisions of sections 29 and 32 [§1111, 1114] of this Act, and subject to the principles of equity, to recover (1) defendant's profits, (2) any damages sustained by the plaintiff, and (3) the costs of the action. The court shall assess such profits and damages or cause the same to be assessed under its direction. In assessing profits the plaintiff shall be required to prove defendant's sales only; defendant must prove all elements of cost or deduction claimed. In assessing damages the court may enter judgment, according to the circumstances of the case, for any sum above the amount found as actual damages, not exceeding three times such amount. If the court shall find that the amount of the recovery based on profits is either inadequate or excessive the court may in its discretion enter judgment for such sum as the court shall find to be just, according to the circumstances of the case. Such sum in either of the above circumstances shall constitute compensation and not a penalty. The court in exceptional cases may award reasonable attorney fees to the prevailing party.

(b) In assessing damages under subsection (a), the court shall, unless the court finds extenuating circumstances, enter judgment for three times such profits or damages, whichever is greater, together with a reasonable attorney's fee, in the case of any violation of section 32(1)(a) of this Act (15 U.S.C. 1114(1)(a)) or section 220506 of title 36, United States Code, that consists of intentionally using a mark or designation, knowing such mark or designation is a counterfeit mark (as defined in section 34(d) of this Act (15 U.S.C. 1116(d)), in connection with the sale, offering for sale, or distribution of goods or services. In such cases, the court may in its discretion award prejudgment interest on such amount at an annual interest rate established under section 6621(a)(2) of the Internal Revenue Code of 1986, commencing on the date of the service of the claimant's pleadings setting forth the claim for such entry and ending on the date such entry is made, or for such shorter time as the court deems appropriate.

(c) In a case involving the use of a counterfeit mark (as defined in section 34(d) (15 U.S.C. 1116(d)) in connection with the sale, offering for sale, or distribution of goods or services, the plaintiff may elect, at any time before final judgment is rendered by the trial court, to recover, instead of actual damages and profits under subsection (a), an award of statutory damages for any such use in connection with the sale, offering for sale, or distribution of goods or services in the amount of —

(1) not less than $500 or more than $100,000 per counterfeit mark per type of goods or services sold, offered for sale, or distributed, as the court considers just; or

(2) if the court finds that the use of the counterfeit mark was willful, not more than $1,000,000 per counterfeit mark per type of goods or services sold, offered for sale, or distributed, as the court considers just.

(d) In a case involving a violation of section 43(d)(1), the plaintiff may elect, at any time before final judgment is rendered by the trial court, to recover, instead of actual damages and profits, an award of statutory damages in the amount of not less than $1,000 and not more than $100,000 per domain name, as the court considers just.

(July 5, 1946, ch. 540, title VI, §35, 60 Stat. 439; Oct. 9, 1962, Pub. L. 87-772, §19, 76 Stat. 774; Jan. 2, 1975, Pub. L. 93-596, §1, 88 Stat. 1949, Jan. 2, 1975, Pub. L. 93-600, §3, 88 Stat. 1955; Oct. 12, 1984, Pub. L. 98-473, §1503, 98 Stat. 2182; Nov. 16, 1988, Pub. L. 100-667, §129, 102 Stat. 3945; July 2, 1996, Pub. L. 104-153, §7, 110 Stat. 1388; Aug. 5, 1999, Pub. L. 106-43, §3, 113 Stat. 219 Nov. 29, 1999, Pub. L. 106-113, §3003, 113 Stat. 1501A-548; Nov. 2, 2002, Pub. L. 107-273, §13207, 116 Stat. 1906.)

§ 1118   Destruction of infringing articles [Section 36]

In any action arising under this Act, in which a violation of any right of the registrant of a mark registered in the Patent and Trademark Office, a violation under section 43(a) [§1125(a)], or a willful violation under section 43(c), shall have been established, the court may order that all labels, signs, prints, packages, wrappers, receptacles, and advertisements in the possession of the defendant, bearing the registered mark or, in the case of a violation of section 43(a) [§1125(a)] or a willful violation under section 43(c), the word, term, name, symbol, device, combination thereof, designation, description, or representation that is the subject of the violation, or any reproduction, counterfeit, copy, or colorable imitation thereof, and all plates, molds, matrices, and other means of making the same, shall be delivered up and destroyed. The party seeking an order under this section for destruction of articles seized under section 34(d) (15 U.S.C. 1116(d)) shall give ten days' notice to the United States attorney for the judicial district in which such order is sought (unless good cause is shown for lesser notice) and such United

States attorney may, if such destruction may affect evidence of an offense against the United States, seek a hearing on such destruction or participate in any hearing otherwise to be held with respect to such destruction.

(July 5, 1946, ch. 540, title VI, §36, 60 Stat 440; Jan. 2, 1975, Pub. L. 93-596, §1, 88 Stat. 1949; Oct. 12, 1984, Pub. L. 98-473, §1503, 98 Stat. 2182; Nov. 16, 1988, Pub. L. 100-667, §130, 102 Stat. 3945; Aug. 5, 1999, Pub. L. 106-43, §3, 113 Stat. 219.)

§ 1119   Power of court over registration [Section 37]

In any action involving a registered mark the court may determine the right to registration, order the cancelation of registrations, in whole or in part, restore canceled registrations, and otherwise rectify the register with respect to the registrations of any party to the action. Decrees and orders shall be certified by the court to the Director, who shall make appropriate entry upon the records of the Patent and Trademark Office, and shall be controlled thereby.

(July 5, 1946, ch. 540, title VI, §37, 60 Stat. 440; Jan. 2, 1975, Pub. L. 93-596, §1, 88 Stat. 1949.)

§ 1120   Civil liability for false or fraudulent registration [Section 38]

Any person who shall procure registration in the Patent and Trademark Office of a mark by a false or fraudulent declaration or representation, oral or in writing, or by any false means, shall be liable in a civil action by any person injured thereby for any damages sustained in consequence thereof.

(July 5, 1946, ch. 540, title VI, §38, 60 Stat. 440; Jan. 2, 1975, Pub. L. 93-596, §1, 88 Stat. 1949.)

§ 1121   Jurisdiction of Federal courts [Section 39]

(a) The district and territorial courts of the United States shall have original jurisdiction, [and] the courts of appeal of the United States (other than the United States Court of Appeals for the Federal Circuit) [and the United States Court of Appeals for the District of Columbia]* shall have appellate jurisdiction, of all actions arising under this Act,

---

* *Ed. Note:* This bracketed language is technically part of the statute, but is superfluous.

15 U.S.C. § 1121

without regard to the amount in controversy or to diversity or lack of diversity of the citizenship of the parties.

(b) No State or other jurisdiction of the United States or any political subdivision or any agency thereof may require alteration of a registered mark, or require that additional trademarks, service marks, trade names, or corporate names that may be associated with or incorporated into the registered mark be displayed in the mark in a manner differing from the display of such additional trademarks, service marks, trade names, or corporate names contemplated by the registered mark as exhibited in the certificate of registration issued by the United States Patent and Trademark Office.

(July 5, 1946, ch. 540, title VI, §39, 60 Stat. 440; June 25, 1948, ch. 646, §§1 and 32(a), 62 Stat. 870, 991; May 24, 1949, ch. 139, §127, 63 Stat. 107; Apr. 2, 1982, title I, Pub. L. 97-164, §148, 96 Stat. 46; Oct. 12, 1982, Pub. L. 97-296, 96 Stat. 1316; Nov. 16, 1988, Pub. L. 100-667, §131, 102 Stat. 3946.)

§ 1122 Liability of States, Instrumentalities of States, and State Officials [Section 40]

(a) Waiver of Sovereign Immunity by the United States— The United States, all agencies and instrumentalities thereof, and all individuals, firms, corporations, other persons acting for the United States and with the authorization and consent of the United States, shall not be immune from suit in Federal or State court by any person, including any governmental or nongovernmental entity, for any violation under this Act.

(b) Waiver of Sovereign Immunity by States— Any State, instrumentality of a State or any officer or employee of a State or instrumentality of a State acting in his or her official capacity, shall not be immune, under the eleventh amendment of the Constitution of the United States or under any other doctrine of sovereign immunity, from suit in Federal court by any person, including any governmental or nongovernmental entity for any violation under this Act.

(c) In a suit described in subsection (a) or (b) for a violation described therein, remedies (including remedies both at law and in equity) are available for the violation to the same extent as such remedies are available for such a violation in a suit against any person other than the United States or any agency or instrumentality thereof, or any individual, firm, corporation, or other person acting for the United States and with authorization and consent of the United States, or a State, instrumentality of a State, or officer or employee of a State or instrumentality of a State acting in his or her official capacity. Such remedies include injunctive relief under section 34 [§1116], actual damages, profits, costs and attorney's fees under section 35 [§1117], destruction of infringing articles under section 36 [§1118], the remedies provided for under sections 32, 37, 38, 42, and 43 [§§1114, 1119, 1120, 1124, and 1125] and for any other remedies provided under this Act.

(Added Oct. 27, 1992, Pub. L. 102-542, §3, 106 Stat. 3567-3568; Aug. 5, 1999, Pub. L. 106-43, §4, 113 Stat. 219.)

§ 1123   Rules and regulations for conduct of proceedings in Patent and Trademark Office [Section 41]

The Director shall make rules and regulations, not inconsistent with law, for the conduct of proceedings in the Patent and Trademark Office under this Act.

(July 5, 1946, ch. 540, title VI, §41, 60 Stat. 440; Jan. 2, 1975, Pub. L. 93-596, §1, 88 Stat. 1949.)

§ 1124   Importation of goods bearing infringing marks or names forbidden [Section 42]

Except as provided in subsection (d) of section 526 of the Tariff Act of 1930 [19 USCS 1526(d)], no article of imported merchandise which shall copy or simulate the name of any domestic manufacture, or manufacturer, or trader, or of any manufacturer or trader located in any foreign country which, by treaty, convention, or law affords similar privileges to citizens of the United States, or which shall copy or simulate a trademark registered in accordance with the provisions of this Act or shall bear a name or mark calculated to induce the public to believe that the article is manufactured in the United States, or that it is manufactured in any foreign country or locality other than the country or locality in which it is in fact manufactured, shall be admitted to entry at any customhouse of the United States; and, in order to aid the officers of the customs in enforcing this prohibition, any domestic manufacturer or trader, and any foreign manufacturer or trader, who is entitled under the provisions of a treaty, conviction, declaration, or agreement between the United States and any foreign country to the advantages afforded by law to citizens of the United States in respect to trademarks and commercial names, may require his name and residence, and the name of the locality in which his goods are manufactured, and a copy of the certificate of registration of his trademark, issued in accordance with the provisions of this Act, to be recorded in books which shall be kept for this purpose in the Department of the Treasury, under such regulations as the Secretary of the Treasury shall prescribe, and may furnish to the Department facsimiles of his name, the name of the locality in which his goods are manufactured, or of his registered trademark, and thereupon the Secretary of the Treasury shall cause one or more copies of the same to be transmitted to each collector or other proper officer of customs.

(July 5, 1946, ch. 540, §42, 60 Stat. 440; Oct. 3, 1978, Pub. L. 95-410, title II, §211, 92 Stat. 903; Oct. 30, 1998, Pub. L. 105-330, §201, 112 Stat. 3070.)

§ 1125   False designations of origin, false descriptions, and dilution [Section 43]

(a) (1) Any person who, on or in connection with any goods or services, or any container for goods, uses in commerce any word, term, name, symbol, or device, or any combination thereof, or any false designation of origin, false or misleading description of fact, or false or misleading representation of fact, which—

   (A) is likely to cause confusion, or to cause mistake, or to deceive as to the affiliation, connection, or association of such person with another person, or as to the origin, sponsorship, or approval of his or her goods, services, or commercial activities by another person, or

   (B) in commercial advertising or promotion, misrepresents the nature, characteristics, qualities, or geographic origin of his or her or another person's goods, services, or commercial activities,

shall be liable in a civil action by any person who believes that he or she is or is likely to be damaged by such act.

(2) As used in this subsection, the term "any person" includes any State, instrumentality of a State or employee of a State or instrumentality of a State acting in his or her official capacity. Any State, and any such instrumentality, officer, or employee, shall be subject to the provisions of this Act in the same manner and to the same extent as any nongovernmental entity.

(3) In a civil action for trade dress infringement under this Act for trade dress not registered on the principal register, the person who asserts trade dress protection has the burden of proving that the matter sought to be protected is not functional.

(b) Any goods marked or labeled in contravention of the provisions of this section shall not be imported into the United States or admitted to entry at any customhouse of the United States. The owner, importer, or consignee of goods refused entry at any customhouse under this section may have any recourse by protest or appeal that is given under the customs revenue laws or may have the remedy given by this Act in cases involving goods refused entry or seized.

(c) (1) The owner of a famous mark shall be entitled, subject to the principles of equity and upon such terms as the court deems reasonable, to an injunction against another person's commercial use in commerce of a mark or trade name, if such use begins after the mark has become famous and causes dilution of the distinctive quality of the famous mark, and to obtain such other relief as is provided in this subsection. In determining whether a mark is distinctive and famous, a court may consider factors such as, but not limited to—

(A) the degree of inherent or acquired distinctiveness of the mark;

(B) the duration and extent of use of the mark in connection with the goods or services with which the mark is used;

(C) the duration and extent of advertising and publicity of the mark;

(D) the geographical extent of the trading area in which the mark is used;

(E) the channels of trade for the goods or services with which the mark is used;

(F) the degree of recognition of the mark in the trading areas and channels of trade of the mark's owner and the person against whom the injunction is sought;

(G) the nature and extent of use of the same or similar marks by third parties; and

(H) whether the mark was registered under the Act of March 3, 1881, or the Act of February 20, 1905, or on the principal register.

(2) In an action brought under the subsection, the owner of a famous mark shall be entitled only to injunctive relief as set forth in section 34 unless the person against whom the injunction is sought willfully intended to trade on the owner's reputation or to cause dilution of the famous mark. If such willful intent is proven, the owner of a famous mark shall also be entitled to the remedies set forth in sections 35(a) and 36, subject to the discretion of the court and the principles of equity.

(3) The ownership by a person of a valid registration under the Act of March 3, 1881, or the Act of February 20, 1905, or on the principal register shall be a complete bar to an action against that person, with respect to that mark, that is brought by another person under the common law or statute of a State and that seeks to prevent dilution of the distinctiveness of a mark, label, or form of advertisement.

(4) The following shall not be actionable under this section:

(A) Fair use of a famous mark by another person in comparative commercial advertising or promotion to identify the competing goods or services of the owner of the famous mark.

(B) Noncommercial use of a mark.

(C) All forms of news reporting and news commentary.

(d)(1)(A) A person shall be liable in a civil action by the owner of a mark, including a personal name which is protected as a mark under this section, if, without regard to the goods or services of the parties, that person—

(i) has a bad faith intent to profit from that mark, including a personal name which is protected as a mark under this section; and

(ii) registers, traffics in, or uses a domain name that—

(I) in the case of a mark that is distinctive at the time of registration of the domain name, is identical or confusingly similar to that mark;

(II) in the case of a famous mark that is famous at the time of registration of the domain name, is identical or confusingly similar to or dilutive of that mark; or

(III) is a trademark, word, or name protected by reason of section 706 of title 18, United States Code, or section 220506 of title 36, United States Code.

(B)(i) In determining whether a person has a bad faith intent described under subparagraph (A), a court may consider factors such as, but not limited to—

(I) the trademark or other intellectual property rights of the person, if any, in the domain name;

(II) the extent to which the domain name consists of the legal name of the person or a name that is otherwise commonly used to identify that person;

(III) the person's prior use, if any, of the domain name in connection with the bona fide offering of any goods or services;

(IV) the person's bona fide noncommercial or fair use of the mark in a site accessible under the domain name;

(V) the person's intent to divert consumers from the mark owner's online location to a site accessible under the domain name that could harm the goodwill represented by the mark, either for commercial gain or with the intent to tarnish or disparage the mark, by creating a likelihood of confusion as to the source, sponsorship, affiliation, or endorsement of the site;

(VI) the person's offer to transfer, sell, or otherwise assign the domain name to the mark owner or any third party for financial gain without having used, or having an intent to use, the domain name in the bona fide offering of any goods or services, or the person's prior conduct indicating a pattern of such conduct;

(VII) the person's provision of material and misleading false contact information when applying for the registration of the domain name, the person's intentional failure to maintain accurate contact information, or the person's prior conduct indicating a pattern of such conduct;

(VIII) the person's registration or acquisition of multiple domain names which the person knows are identical or confusingly similar to marks of others that are distinctive at the time of registration of such domain names, or dilutive of famous marks of others that are famous at the time of registration of such domain names, without regard to the goods or services of the parties; and

(IX) the extent to which the mark incorporated in the person's domain name registration is or is not distinctive and famous within the meaning of subsection (c)(1) of section 43.

(ii) Bad faith intent described under subparagraph (A) shall not be found in any case in which the court determines that the person believed and had reasonable grounds to believe that the use of the domain name was a fair use or otherwise lawful.

(C) In any civil action involving the registration, trafficking, or use of a domain name under this paragraph, a court may order the forfeiture or cancellation of the domain name or the transfer of the domain name to the owner of the mark.

(D) A person shall be liable for using a domain name under subparagraph (A) only if that person is the domain name registrant or that registrant's authorized licensee.

(E) As used in this paragraph, the term "traffics in" refers to transactions that include, but are not limited to, sales, purchases, loans, pledges, licenses, exchanges of currency, and any other transfer for consideration or receipt in exchange for consideration.

15 U.S.C. § 1125

(2)(A) The owner of a mark may file an in rem civil action against a domain name in the judicial district in which the domain name registrar, domain name registry, or other domain name authority that registered or assigned the domain name is located if—

(i) the domain name violates any right of the owner of a mark registered in the Patent and Trademark Office, or protected under subsection (a) or (c); and

(ii) the court finds that the owner—

(I) is not able to obtain in personam jurisdiction over a person who would have been a defendant in a civil action under paragraph (1); or

(II) through due diligence was not able to find a person who would have been a defendant in a civil action under paragraph (1) by—

(aa) sending a notice of the alleged violation and intent to proceed under this paragraph to the registrant of the domain name at the postal and e-mail address provided by the registrant to the registrar; and

(bb) publishing notice of the action as the court may direct promptly after filing the action.

(B) The actions under subparagraph (A)(ii) shall constitute service of process.

(C) In an in rem action under this paragraph, a domain name shall be deemed to have its situs in the judicial district in which—

(i) the domain name registrar, registry, or other domain name authority that registered or assigned the domain name is located; or

(ii) documents sufficient to establish control and authority regarding the disposition of the registration and use of the domain name are deposited with the court.

(D)(i) The remedies in an in rem action under this paragraph shall be limited to a court order for the forfeiture or cancellation of the domain name or the transfer of the domain name to the owner of the mark. Upon receipt of written notification of a filed, stamped copy of a complaint filed by the owner of a mark in a United States district court under this paragraph, the domain name registrar, domain name registry, or other domain name authority shall—

(I) expeditiously deposit with the court documents sufficient to establish the court's control and authority regarding the disposition of the registration and use of the domain name to the court; and

(II) not transfer, suspend, or otherwise modify the domain name during the pendency of the action, except upon order of the court.

(ii) The domain name registrar or registry or other domain name authority shall not be liable for injunctive or monetary relief under this paragraph except in the case of bad faith or reckless disregard, which includes a willful failure to comply with any such court order.

(3) The civil action established under paragraph (1) and the in rem action established under paragraph (2), and any remedy available under either such action, shall be in addition to any other civil action or remedy otherwise applicable.

(4) The in rem jurisdiction established under paragraph (2) shall be in addition to any other jurisdiction that otherwise exists, whether in rem or in personam.

(July 5, 1946, ch. 540, title VIII, §43, 60 Stat. 441; Nov. 16, 1988, Pub. L. 100-667, §132, 102 Stat. 3946; Oct. 27, 1992, Pub. L. 102-542, §3, 106 Stat. 3568; Jan. 16, 1996, Pub. L. 104-98, 109 Stat. 985; Aug. 5, 1999, Pub. L. 106-43, §3, 113 Stat. 219; Aug. 5, 1999, Pub. L. 106-43, §5, 113 Stat. 219; Nov. 29, 1999, Pub. L. 106-113, §3002, 113 Stat. 1501A-545).

§ 1126   International conventions [Section 44]

(a) *Register of marks communicated by international bureaus.*—The Director shall keep a register of all marks communicated to him by the international bureaus provided for by the conventions for the protection of industrial property, trademarks, trade and commercial names, and the repression of unfair competition to which the United States is or may become a party, and upon the payment of the fees required by such conventions and the fees required in this Act may place the marks so communicated upon such register. This register shall show a facsimile of the mark or trade or commercial name; the name, citizenship, and address of the registrant; the number, date, and place of the first registration of the mark, including the dates on which application for such registration was filed and granted and the term of such registration; a list of goods or services to which the mark is applied as shown by the registration in the country of origin, and such other data as may be useful concerning the mark. This register shall be a continuation of the register provided in section 1(a) of the Act of March 19, 1920.

(b) *Benefits of section to persons whose country of origin is party to convention or treaty.*—Any person whose country of origin is a party to any convention or treaty relating to trademarks, trade or commercial names, or the repression of unfair competition, to which the United States is also a party, or extends reciprocal rights to nationals of the United States by law, shall be entitled to the benefits of this section under the conditions expressed herein to the extent necessary to give effect to any provision of such convention, treaty or reciprocal law, in addition to the rights to which any owner of a mark is otherwise entitled by this Act.

(c) *Prior registration in country of origin; country of origin defined.*—No registration of a mark in the United States by a person described in subsection (b) of this section shall be granted until such mark has been registered in the country of origin of the applicant, unless the applicant alleges use in commerce. For the purposes of this section, the country of origin of the applicant is the country in which he has a bona fide and effective industrial or commercial establishment, or if he has not such an establishment the country in which he is domiciled, or if he has not a domicile in any of the countries described in subsection (b) of this section, the country of which he is a national.

(d) *Right of priority.*—An application for registration of a mark under sections 1, 3, 4, or 23 of this Act or under subsection (e) of this section filed by a person described in subsection (b) of this section who has previously duly filed an application for registration of the same mark in one of the countries described in subsection (b) shall be accorded the same force and effect as would be accorded to the same application if filed in the United States on the same date on which the application was first filed in such foreign country: *Provided,* that—

(1) the application in the United States is filed within six months from the date on which the application was first filed in the foreign country;

(2) the application conforms as nearly as practicable to the requirements of this Act, including a statement that the applicant has a bona fide intention to use the mark in commerce;

(3) the rights acquired by third parties before the date of the filing of the first application in the foreign country shall in no way be affected by a registration obtained on an application filed under this subsection;

(4) nothing in this subsection shall entitle the owner of a registration granted under this section to sue for acts committed prior to the date on which his mark was registered in this country unless the registration is based on use in commerce.

In like manner and subject to the same conditions and requirements, the right provided in this section may be based upon a subsequent regularly filed application in the same foreign country, instead of the first filed foreign application: *Provided,* That any foreign application filed prior to such subsequent application has been withdrawn, abandoned, or otherwise disposed of, without having been laid open to public inspection and without leaving any rights outstanding, and has not served, nor thereafter shall serve, as a basis for claiming a right of priority.

(e) *Registration on principal or supplemental register; copy of foreign registration.*—A mark duly registered in the country of origin of the foreign applicant may be registered on the principal register if eligible, otherwise on the supplemental register herein provided. Such applicant shall submit, within such time period as may be prescribed by the Director, a true copy, a photocopy, a certification, or a certified copy of the registration in the country of origin of the applicant. The application must state the applicant's bona fide intention to use the mark in commerce, but use in commerce shall not be required prior to registration.

15 U.S.C. § 1126

(f) *Domestic registration independent of foreign registration.*—The registration of a mark under the provisions of subsections (c), (d), and (e) of this section by a person described in subsection (b) shall be independent of the registration in the country of origin and the duration, validity, or transfer in the United States of such registration shall be governed by the provisions of this Act.

(g) *Trade or commercial names of foreign nationals protected without registration.*—Trade names or commercial names of persons described in subsection (b) of this section shall be protected without the obligation of filing or registration whether or not they form parts of marks.

(h) *Protection of foreign nationals against unfair competition.*—Any person designated in subsection (b) of this section as entitled to the benefits and subject to the provisions of this Act shall be entitled to effective protection against unfair competition, and the remedies provided herein for infringement of marks shall be available so far as they may be appropriate in repressing acts of unfair competition.

(i) *Citizens or residents of United States entitled to benefits of section.*—Citizens or residents of the United States shall have the same benefits as are granted by this section to persons described in subsection (b) of this section.

(July 5, 1946, ch. 540, title IX, §44, 60 Stat. 441; Oct. 3, 1961, Pub. L. 87-333, §2, 75 Stat. 748; Oct. 9, 1962, Pub. L. 87-772, §20, 76 Stat. 774; Nov. 16, 1988, Pub. L. 100-667, §133, 102 Stat. 3946; Oct. 30, 1998, Pub. L. 105-330, §108, 112 Stat. 3068; Nov. 2, 2002, Pub. L. 107-273, §13207, 116 Stat. 1906.)

§ 1127 Construction and definitions; intent of chapter [Section 45]

In the construction of this Act, unless the contrary is plainly apparent from the context—

The United States includes and embraces all territory which is under its jurisdiction and control.

The word "commerce" means all commerce which may lawfully be regulated by Congress.

The term "principal register" refers to the register provided for by sections 1 through 22 hereof [§§1051-1072], and the term "supplemental register" refers to the register provided for by sections 23 through 28 thereof [§§1091-1096].

The term "person" and any other word or term used to designate the applicant or other entitled to a benefit or privilege or rendered liable under the provisions of this Act includes a juristic person as well as a natural person. The term "juristic person" includes a firm, corporation, union, association, or other organization capable of suing and being sued in a court of law.

The term "person" also includes the United States, any agency or instrumentality thereof; or any individual, firm, or corporation acting for the United States and with the authorization and consent of the United States. The United States, any agency or instrumentality thereof, and any individual, firm, or corporation acting for the United States and with the authorization and consent of the United States, shall be subject to the provisions of this Act in the same manner and to the same extent as any nongovernmental entity.

The term "person" also includes any State, any instrumentality of a State, and any officer or employee of a State or instrumentality of a State acting in his or her official capacity. Any State, and any such instrumentality, officer, or employee, shall be subject to the provisions of this Act in the same manner and to the same extent as any nongovernmental entity.

The terms "applicant" and "registrant" embrace the legal representatives, predecessors, successors and assigns of such applicant or registrant.

The term "Director" means the Under Secretary of Commerce for Intellectual Property and Director of the United States Patent and Trademark Office.

The term "related company" means any person whose use of a mark is controlled by the owner of the mark with respect to the nature and quality of the goods or services on or in connection with which the mark is used.

The terms "trade name" and "commercial name" mean any name used by a person to identify his or her business or vocation.

The term "trademark" includes any word, name, symbol, or device, or any combination thereof—

15 U.S.C. § 1127

(1) used by a person, or

(2) which a person has a bona fide intention to use in commerce and applies to register on the principal register established by this Act,

to identify and distinguish his or her goods, including a unique product, from those manufactured or sold by others and to indicate the source of the goods, even if that source is unknown.

The term "service mark" means any word, name, symbol, or device, or any combination thereof—

(1) used by a person, or

(2) which a person has a bona fide intention to use in commerce and applies to register on the principal register established by this Act,

to identify and distinguish the services of one person, including a unique service, from the services of others and to indicate the source of the services, even if that source is unknown. Titles, character names, and other distinctive features of radio or television programs may be registered as service marks notwithstanding that they, or the programs, may advertise the goods of the sponsor.

The term "certification mark" means any word, name, symbol, or device, or any combination thereof—

(1) used by a person other than its owner, or

(2) which its owner has a bona fide intention to permit a person other than the owner to use in commerce and files an application to register on the principal register established by this Act,

to certify regional or other origin, material, mode of manufacture, quality, accuracy, or other characteristics of such person's goods or services or that the work or labor on the goods or services was performed by members of a union or other organization.

The term "collective mark" means a trademark or service mark—

(1) used by the members of a cooperative, an association, or other collective group or organization, or

(2) which such cooperative, association, or other collective group or organization has a bona fide intention to use in commerce and applies to register on the principal register established by this Act,

and includes marks indicating membership in a union, an association, or other organization.

The term "mark" includes any trademark, service mark, collective mark, or certification mark.

The term "use in commerce" means the bona fide use of a mark in the ordinary course of trade, and not made merely to reserve a right in a mark. For purposes of this Act, a mark shall be deemed to be in use in commerce—

(1) on goods when—

(A) it is placed in any manner on the goods or their containers or the displays associated therewith or on the tags or labels affixed thereto, or if the nature of the goods makes such placement impracticable, then on documents associated with the goods or their sale, and

(B) the goods are sold or transported in commerce, and

(2) on services when it is used or displayed in the sale or advertising of services and the services are rendered in commerce, or the services are rendered in more than one State or in the United States and a foreign country and the person rendering the services is engaged in commerce in connection with the services.

A mark shall be deemed to be "abandoned" when either of the following occurs:

(1) When its use has been discontinued with intent not to resume such use. Intent not to resume may be inferred from circumstances. Nonuse for 3 consecutive years shall be prima facie evidence of abandonment. "Use" of a mark means the bona fide use of that mark made in the ordinary course of trade, and not made merely to reserve a right in a mark.

(2) When any course of conduct of the owner, including acts of omission as well as commission, causes the mark to become the generic name for the goods or services on or in connection with which it is used or otherwise to lose its significance as a mark. Purchaser motivation shall not be a test for determining abandonment under this paragraph.

15 U.S.C. § 1127

The term "dilution" means the lessening of the capacity of a famous mark to identify and distinguish goods or services, regardless of the presence or absence of—

(1) competition between the owner of the famous mark and other parties, or

(2) likelihood of confusion, mistake, or deception.

The term "colorable imitation" includes any mark which so resembles a registered mark as to be likely to cause confusion or mistake or to deceive.

The term "registered mark" means a mark registered in the United States Patent and Trademark Office under this Act or under the Act of March 3, 1881, or the Act of February 20, 1905, or the Act of March 19, 1920. The phrase "marks registered in the Patent and Trademark Office" means registered marks.

The term "Act of March 3, 1881," "Act of February 20, 1905," or "Act of March 19, 1920," means the respective Act as amended.

A "counterfeit" is a spurious mark which is identical with, or substantially indistinguishable from, a registered mark.

The term "domain name" means any alphanumeric designation which is registered with or assigned by any domain name registrar, domain name registry, or other domain name registration authority as part of an electronic address on the Internet.

`The term "Internet" has the meaning given that term in section 230(f)(1) of the Communications Act of 1934 (47 U.S.C. 230(f)(1)).

Words used in the singular include the plural and vice versa.

The intent of this Act is to regulate commerce within the control of Congress by making actionable the deceptive and misleading use of marks in such commerce; to protect registered marks used in such commerce from interference by State, or territorial legislation; to protect persons engaged in such commerce against unfair competition; to prevent fraud and deception in such commerce by the use of reproductions, copies, counterfeits, or colorable imitations of registered marks; and to provide rights and remedies stipulated by treaties and conventions respecting trademarks, trade names, and unfair competition entered into between the United States and foreign nations.

15 U.S.C. § 1127

(July 5, 1946, ch. 540, title X, §45, 60 Stat. 443; Oct. 9, 1962, Pub. L. 87-772, §21, 76 Stat. 774; Jan. 2, 1975, Pub. L. 93-596, §1, 88 Stat. 1949; Nov. 8, 1984, Pub. L. 98-620, §103, 98 Stat. 3336; Nov. 16, 1988, Pub. L. 100-667, §134, 102 Stat. 3946-48; Oct. 27, 1992, Pub. L. 102-542, §3, 106 Stat. 3568; Dec. 8, 1994, Pub. L. 103-465, §521, 108 Stat. 4981; Jan. 16, 1996, Pub. L. 104-98, 109 Stat. 986; Aug. 5, 1999, Pub. L. 106-43, §4, 113 Stat. 219; Nov. 29, 1999, Pub. L. 106-113, §§3005, 4732, 113 Stat. 1501A-550, 581.)

§ 1128   National Intellectual Property Law Enforcement Coordination Council

(a) *Establishment.*—There is established the National Intellectual Property Law Enforcement Coordination Council (in this section referred to as the "Council"). The Council shall consist of the following members—

> (1) The Assistant Secretary of Commerce and Commissioner of Patents and Trademarks, who shall serve as co-chair of the Council.
>
> (2) The Assistant Attorney General, Criminal Division, who shall serve as co-chair of the Council.
>
> (3) The Under Secretary of State for Economic and Agricultural Affairs.
>
> (4) The Ambassador, Deputy United States Trade Representative.
>
> (5) The Commissioner of Customs.
>
> (6) The Under Secretary of Commerce for International Trade.

(b) *Duties.*—The Council established in subsection (a) shall coordinate domestic and international intellectual property law enforcement among federal and foreign entities.

(c) *Consultation required.*—The Council shall consult with the Register of Copyrights on law enforcement matters relating to copyright and related rights and matters.

(d) *Non-derogation.*—Nothing in this section shall derogate from the duties of the Secretary of State or from the duties of the United States Trade Representative as set forth in section 141 of the Trade Act of 1974 (19 U.S.C. 2171), or from the duties and functions of the Register of Copyrights, or otherwise alter current authorities relating to copyright matters.

(e) *Report.*—The Council shall report annually on its coordination activities to the President, and to the Committees on Appropriations and on the Judiciary of the Senate and the House of Representatives.

15 U.S.C. § 1128

(f) *Funding.*—Notwithstanding section 1346 of title 31, United States Code, or section 610 of this Act, funds made available for fiscal year 2000 and hereafter by this or any other Act shall be available for inter-agency funding of the National Intellectual Property Law Enforcement Coordination Council.

(Sept. 29, 1999, Pub. L. 106-58, §653, 113 Stat. 480.)

§ 1129   Cyberpiracy protections for individuals

(1) *In general.*—

(A) *Civil liability.*—Any person who registers a domain name that consists of the name of another living person, or a name substantially and confusingly similar thereto, without that person's consent, with the specific intent to profit from such name by selling the domain name for financial gain to that person or any third party, shall be liable in a civil action by such person.

(B) *Exception.* —A person who in good faith registers a domain name consisting of the name of another living person, or a name substantially and confusingly similar thereto, shall not be liable under this paragraph if such name is used in, affiliated with, or related to a work of authorship protected under title 17, United States Code, including a work made for hire as defined in section 101 of title 17, United States Code, and if the person registering the domain name is the copyright owner or licensee of the work, the person intends to sell the domain name in conjunction with the lawful exploitation of the work, and such registration is not prohibited by a contract between the registrant and the named person. The exception under this subparagraph shall apply only to a civil action brought under paragraph (1) and shall in no manner limit the protections afforded under the Trademark Act of 1946 (15 U.S.C. 1051 et seq.) or other provision of Federal or State law.

(2) *Remedies.*—In any civil action brought under paragraph (1), a court may award injunctive relief, including the forfeiture or cancellation of the domain name or the transfer of the domain name to the plaintiff. The court may also, in its discretion, award costs and attorneys fees to the prevailing party.

15 U.S.C. § 1129

(3) *Definition.*—In this section, the term "domain name" has the meaning given that term in section 45 of the Trademark Act of 1946 (15 U.S.C. 1127).

(4) *Effective date.*—This section shall apply to domain names registered on or after November 29, 1999.

(Nov. 29, 1999, Pub. L. 106-113, §3002(b), 113 Stat. 1536.)

UNCODIFIED LANHAM ACT PROVISIONS

§ 46(a)   Time of taking effect—Repeal of prior acts

This Act shall be in force and take effect one year from its enactment, but except as otherwise herein specifically provided shall not affect any suit, proceeding, or appeal then pending. All Acts and parts of Acts inconsistent herewith are hereby repealed effective one year from the enactment hereof, including the following Acts insofar as they are inconsistent herewith: The Act of Congress approved March 3, 1881, entitled "An Act to authorize the registration of trademarks and protect the same"; the Act approved August 5, 1882, entitled "An Act relating to the registration of trademarks"; the Act of February 20, 1905 (U.S.C., title 15, secs. 81 to 109, inclusive), entitled "An Act to authorize the registration of trademarks used in commerce with foreign nations or among the several States or with Indian tribes, and to protect the same", and the amendments thereto by the Acts of May 4, 1906 (U.S.C., title 15, secs. 131 and 132; 34 Stat. 169), March 2, 1907 (34 Stat. 1251, 1252), February 18, 1909 (35 Stat. 627, 628), February 18, 1911 (36 Stat. 918), January 8, 1913 (37 Stat. 649), June 7, 1924 (43 Stat. 647), March 4, 1925 (43 Stat. 1268, 1269), April 11, 1930 (46 Stat. 155), June 10, 1938 (Public, Numbered 586, Seventy-fifth Congress, ch. 332, third session); the Act of March 19, 1920 (U.S.C., title 15, secs. 121 to 128, inclusive), entitled "an Act to give effect to certain provisions of the convention for the protection of trademarks and commercial names made and signed in the city of Buenos Aires, in the Argentine Republic, August 20, 1910, and for other purposes", and the amendments thereto, including the Act of June 10, 1938 (Public, Numbered 586, Seventy-fifth Congress, ch. 332, third session): *Provided,* That this repeal shall not affect the validity of registrations granted or applied for under any of said Acts prior to the effective date of this Act, or rights or remedies thereunder except as provided in sections 8, 12, 14, 15, and 47 [§§1058, 1062, 1064, 1065, and 47 (§47 is uncodified; see below)] of this Act; but nothing contained in this Act shall be construed as limiting, restricting, modifying, or repealing any statute in force on the effective date of this Act which does not relate to trademarks, or as restricting or increasing the authority of any Federal departments or regulatory agency except as may be specifically provided in this Act.

(July 5, 1946, ch. 540, §§46–50, 60 Stat. 444–46.)

§ 46(b)   Existing registrations under prior acts

Acts of 1881 and 1905. Registrations now existing under the Act of March 3, 1881, or the Act of February 20, 1905, shall continue in full force and effect for the unexpired terms thereof and may be renewed under the provisions of section 9 [§1059] of this Act. Such registrations and the renewals thereof shall be subject to and shall be entitled to the benefits of the provisions of this Act to the same extent and with the same force and effect as though registered on the principal register established by this Act except as limited in sections 8, 12, 14, and 15 [§§1058, 1062, 1064, and 1065] of this Act. Marks registered under the "ten-year proviso" of section 5 [§1055] of the Act of February 20, 1905, as amended, shall be deemed to have become distinctive of the registrant's goods in commerce under paragraph (f) of section 2 of this Act and may be renewed under section 9 [§1059] hereof as marks coming within said paragraph.

Act of 1920. Registrations now existing under the Act of March 19, 1920, shall expire 5 months after the effective date of this Act, or twenty years from the dates of their registrations, whichever date is later. Such registrations shall be subject to and entitled to the benefits of the provisions of this Act relating to marks registered on the supplemental register established by this Act, and may not be renewed unless renewal is required to support foreign registrations. In that event renewal may be effected on the supplemental register under the provisions of section 9 [§1059] of this Act.

Subject to registration under this Act. Marks registered under previous Acts may, if eligible, also be registered under this Act.

(July 5, 1946, ch. 540, §§46–50, 60 Stat. 444–46.)

§ 47(a)   Applications pending on effective date of Act

All applications for registration pending in the Patent and Trademark Office at the effective date of this Act may be amended, if practicable, to bring them under the provisions of this Act. The prosecution of such applications so amended and the grant of registrations thereon shall be proceeded with in accordance with the provisions of this Act. If such amendments are not made, the prosecution of said applications shall be proceeded with and registrations thereon granted in accordance with the Acts under which said applications were filed, and said Acts are hereby continued in force to this extent and for this purpose only, notwithstanding the foregoing general repeal thereof.

(July 5, 1946, ch. 540, §§46–50, 60 Stat. 444–46.)

§ 47(b)   Appeals pending on effective date of Act

In any case in which an appeal is pending before the United States Court of Customs and Patent Appeals or any United States Circuit Court of Appeals or the United States Court of Appeals for the District of Columbia or the United States Supreme Court at the effective date of this Act, the court, if it be of the opinion that the provisions of this Act are applicable to the subject matter of the appeal, may apply such provision or may remand the case to the Director or to the district court for the taking of additional evidence or a new trial or for reconsideration of the decision on the record as made, as the appellate court may deem proper.

(July 5, 1946, ch. 540, §§46–50, 60 Stat. 444–46.)

§ 48   Prior acts not repealed

Section 4 of the Act of January 5, 1905 (U.S.C., title 36, §4), as amended, entitled "An Act to incorporate the National Red Cross", and section 7 of the Act of June 15, 1916 (U.S.C., title 36, §27), entitled "An Act to incorporate the Boy Scouts of America, and for other purposes", and the Act of June 20, 1936 (U.S.C., title 22, §248), entitled "An Act to prohibit the commercial use of the coat of arms of the Swiss Confederation", are not repealed or affected by this Act.*

(July 5, 1946, ch. 540, §§46–50, 60 Stat. 444–46.)

§ 49   Preservation of existing rights

Nothing herein shall adversely affect the rights or the enforcement of rights in marks acquired in good faith prior to the effective date of this Act.

(July 5, 1946, ch. 540, §§46–50, 60 Stat. 444–46.)

§ 50   Severability

If any provision of this Act or the application of such provision to any person or circumstance is held invalid, the remainder of the Act shall not be affected thereby.

(July 5, 1946, ch. 540, §§46–50, 60 Stat. 444–46.)

§ 51   Pending Applications

All certificates of registration based upon applications for registration pending in the Patent and Trademark Office on the effective date of the Trademark Law Revision Act of 1988 shall remain in force for a period of 10 years.

(Nov. 16, 1988, Pub. L. 100-667, §135, 102 Stat. 3948.)

---

* *Ed. Note:* The first and third of the laws referred to in this section have been repealed and replaced by sections 706 and 708, respectively, of U.S.C., Title 18, Crimes and Criminal Procedure, enacted June 25, 1948, effective September 1, 1948.

§ 60   Definitions

In this title:

(1) *Basic application.*—The term "basic application" means the application for the registration of a mark that has been filed with an Office of a Contracting Party and that constitutes the basis for an application for the international registration of that mark.

(2) *Basic registration.*—The term "basic registration" means the registration of a mark that has been granted by an Office of a Contracting Party and that constitutes the basis for an application for the international registration of that mark.

(3) *Contracting Party.*—The term "Contracting Party" means any country or inter-governmental organization that is a party to the Madrid Protocol.

(4) *Date of recordal.*—The term "date of recordal" means the date on which a request for extension of protection, filed after an international registration is granted, is recorded on the International Register.

(5) *Declaration of bona fide intention to use the mark in commerce.*—The term "declaration of bona fide intention to use the mark in commerce" means a declaration that is signed by the applicant for, or holder of, an international registration who is seeking extension of protection of a mark to the United States and that contains a statement that—

(A) the applicant or holder has a bona fide intention to use the mark in commerce;

(B) the person making the declaration believes himself or herself, or the firm, corporation, or association in whose behalf he or she makes the declaration, to be entitled to use the mark in commerce; and

(C) no other person, firm, corporation, or association, to the best of his or her knowledge and belief, has the right to use such mark in

---

* *Ed. Note:* Pursuant to section 13403 of Pub. L. 107-273, the provisions set forth below shall take effect on the later of the date on which the Madrid Protocol enters into force with respect to the United States or the date occurring one year after the date of enactment, i.e. November 2, 2003.

commerce either in the identical form of the mark or in such near resemblance to the mark as to be likely, when used on or in connection with the goods of such other person, firm, corporation, or association, to cause confusion, mistake, or deception.

(6) *Extension of protection.*—The term "extension of protection" means the protection resulting from an international registration that extends to the United States at the request of the holder of the international registration, in accordance with the Madrid Protocol.

(7) *Holder of an international registration.*—A "holder" of an international registration is the natural or juristic person in whose name the international registration is recorded on the International Register.

(8) *International application.*—The term "international application" means an application for international registration that is filed under the Madrid Protocol.

(9) *International Bureau.*—The term "International Bureau" means the International Bureau of the World Intellectual Property Organization.

(10) *International Register.*—The term "International Register" means the official collection of data concerning international registrations maintained by the International Bureau that the Madrid Protocol or its implementing regulations require or permit to be recorded.

(11) *International registration.*—The term "international registration" means the registration of a mark granted under the Madrid Protocol.

(12) *International registration date.*—The term "international registration date" means the date assigned to the international registration by the International Bureau.

(13) *Madrid Protocol.*—The term "Madrid Protocol" means the Protocol Relating to the Madrid Agreement Concerning the International Registration of Marks, adopted at Madrid, Spain, on June 27, 1989.

(14) *Notification of refusal.*—The term "notification of refusal" means the notice sent by the United States Patent and Trademark Office to the International Bureau declaring that an extension of protection cannot be granted.

(15) *Office of a Contracting Party.*—The term "Office of a Contracting Party" means—

(A) the office, or governmental entity, of a Contracting Party that is responsible for the registration of marks; or

(B) the common office, or governmental entity, of more than 1 Contracting Party that is responsible for the registration of marks and is so recognized by the International Bureau.

(16) *Office of origin.*—The term "office of origin" means the Office of a Contracting Party with which a basic application was filed or by which a basic registration was granted.

(17) *Opposition period.*—The term "opposition period" means the time allowed for filing an opposition in the United States Patent and Trademark Office, including any extension of time granted under section 13.

§ 61   International applications based on United States applications or registrations

(a) *In general.*—The owner of a basic application pending before the United States Patent and Trademark Office, or the owner of a basic registration granted by the United States Patent and Trademark Office may file an international application by submitting to the United States Patent and Trademark Office a written application in such form, together with such fees, as may be prescribed by the Director.

(b) *Qualified owners.*—A qualified owner, under subsection (a), shall—

(1) be a national of the United States;

(2) be domiciled in the United States; or

(3) have a real and effective industrial or commercial establishment in the United States.

§ 62   Certification of the international application

(a) *Certification procedure.*—Upon the filing of an application for international registration and payment of the prescribed fees, the Director shall examine the international application for the purpose of certifying that the information contained in the international application corresponds to the information contained in the basic application or basic registration at the time of the certification.

(b) *Transmittal.*—Upon examination and certification of the international application, the Director shall transmit the international application to the International Bureau.

§ 63 Restriction, abandonment, cancellation, or expiration of a basic application or basic registration

With respect to an international application transmitted to the International Bureau under section 62, the Director shall notify the International Bureau whenever the basic application or basic registration which is the basis for the international application has been restricted, abandoned, or canceled, or has expired, with respect to some or all of the goods and services listed in the international registration—

(1) within 5 years after the international registration date; or

(2) more than 5 years after the international registration date if the restriction, abandonment, or cancellation of the basic application or basic registration resulted from an action that began before the end of that 5-year period.

§ 64 Request for extension of protection subsequent to international registration

The holder of an international registration that is based upon a basic application filed with the United States Patent and Trademark Office or a basic registration granted by the Patent and Trademark Office may request an extension of protection of its international registration by filing such a request—

(1) directly with the International Bureau; or

(2) with the United States Patent and Trademark Office for transmittal to the International Bureau, if the request is in such form, and contains such transmittal fee, as may be prescribed by the Director.

§ 65 Extension of protection of an international registration to the United States under the Madrid Protocol

(a) *In general.*—Subject to the provisions of section 68, the holder of an international registration shall be entitled to the benefits of extension of protection of that international registration to the United States to the extent necessary to give effect to any provision of the Madrid Protocol.

(b) *If the United States is office of origin.*—Where the United States Patent and Trademark Office is the office of origin for a trademark application or registration, any international registration based on such application or registration cannot be used to obtain the benefits of the Madrid Protocol in the United States.

§ 66 Effect of filing a request for extension of protection of an international registration to the United States

(a) *Requirement for request for extension of protection.*—A request for extension of protection of an international registration to the United States that the International Bureau transmits to the United States Patent and Trademark Office shall be deemed to be properly filed in the United States if such request, when received by the International Bureau, has attached to it a declaration of bona fide intention to use the mark in commerce that is verified by the applicant for, or holder of, the international registration.

(b) *Effect of proper filing.*—Unless extension of protection is refused under section 68, the proper filing of the request for extension of protection under subsection (a) shall constitute constructive use of the mark, conferring the same rights as those specified in section 7(c), as of the earliest of the following:

(1) The international registration date, if the request for extension of protection was filed in the international application.

(2) The date of recordal of the request for extension of protection, if the request for extension of protection was made after the international registration date.

(3) The date of priority claimed pursuant to section 67.

§ 67 Right of priority for request for extension of protection to the United States

The holder of an international registration with a request for an extension of protection to the United States shall be entitled to claim a date of priority based on a right of priority within the meaning of Article 4 of the Paris Convention for the Protection of Industrial Property if—

(1) the request for extension of protection contains a claim of priority; and

(2) the date of international registration or the date of the recordal of the request for extension of protection to the United States is not later than 6 months after the date of the first regular national filing (within the meaning of Article 4(A)(3) of the Paris Convention for the Protection of Industrial Property) or a subsequent application (within the meaning of Article 4(C)(4) of the Paris Convention for the Protection of Industrial Property).

§ 68 Examination of and opposition to request for extension of protection; notification of refusal

(a) *Examination and opposition.*—(1) A request for extension of protection described in section 66(a) shall be examined as an application for registration on the Principal Register under this Act, and if on such examination it appears that the applicant is entitled to extension of protection under this title, the Director shall cause the mark to be published in the Official Gazette of the United States Patent and Trademark Office.

(2) Subject to the provisions of subsection (c), a request for extension of protection under this title shall be subject to opposition under section 13.

(3) Extension of protection shall not be refused on the ground that the mark has not been used in commerce.

(4) Extension of protection shall be refused to any mark not registrable on the Principal Register.

(b) *Notification of refusal.*—If, a request for extension of protection is refused under subsection (a), the Director shall declare in a notification of refusal (as provided in subsection (c)) that the extension of protection cannot be granted, together with a statement of all grounds on which the refusal was based.

(c) *Notice to International Bureau.*—(1) Within 18 months after the date on which the International Bureau transmits to the Patent and Trademark Office a notification of a request for extension of protection, the Director shall transmit to the International Bureau any of the following that applies to such request:

    (A) A notification of refusal based on an examination of the request for extension of protection.

    (B) A notification of refusal based on the filing of an opposition to the request.

    (C) A notification of the possibility that an opposition to the request may be filed after the end of that 18-month period.

(2) If the Director has sent a notification of the possibility of opposition under paragraph (1)(C), the Director shall, if applicable, transmit to the International Bureau a notification of refusal on the basis of the opposition, together with a statement of all the grounds for the opposition, within 7 months after the beginning of the opposition period or within 1 month after the end of the opposition period, whichever is earlier.

(3) If a notification of refusal of a request for extension of protection is transmitted under paragraph (1) or (2), no grounds for refusal of such request other than those set forth in such notification may be transmitted to the International Bureau by the Director after the expiration of the time periods set forth in paragraph (1) or (2), as the case may be.

(4) If a notification specified in paragraph (1) or (2) is not sent to the International Bureau within the time period set forth in such paragraph, with respect to a request for extension of protection, the request for extension of protection shall not be refused and the Director shall issue a certificate of extension of protection pursuant to the request.

(d) *Designation of agent for service of process.*—In responding to a notification of refusal with respect to a mark, the holder of the international registration of the mark may designate, by a document filed in the

United States Patent and Trademark Office, the name and address of a person residing in the United States on whom notices or process in proceedings affecting the mark may be served. Such notices or process may be served upon the person designated by leaving with that person, or mailing to that person, a copy thereof at the address specified in the last designation filed. If the person designated cannot be found at the address given in the last designation, or if the holder does not designate by a document filed in the United States Patent and Trademark Office the name and address of a person residing in the United States for service of notices or process in proceedings affecting the mark, the notice or process may be served on the Director.

§ 69   Effect of extension of protection

(a) *Issuance of extension of protection.*—Unless a request for extension of protection is refused under section 68, the Director shall issue a certificate of extension of protection pursuant to the request and shall cause notice of such certificate of extension of protection to be published in the Official Gazette of the United States Patent and Trademark Office.

(b) *Effect of extension of protection.*—From the date on which a certificate of extension of protection is issued under subsection (a)—

(1) such extension of protection shall have the same effect and validity as a registration on the Principal Register; and

(2) the holder of the international registration shall have the same rights and remedies as the owner of a registration on the Principal Register.

§ 70   Dependence of extension of protection to the United States on the underlying international registration

(a) *Effect of cancellation of international registration.*—If the International Bureau notifies the United States Patent and Trademark Office of the cancellation of an international registration with respect to some or all of the goods and services listed in the international registration, the Director shall cancel any extension of protection to the United States with respect to such goods and services as of the date on which the international registration was canceled.

(b) *Effect of failure to renew international registration.*—If the International Bureau does not renew an international registration, the corresponding extension of protection to the United States shall cease to be valid as of the date of the expiration of the international registration.

(c) *Transformation of an extension of protection into a United States Application.*—The holder of an international registration canceled in whole or in part by the International Bureau at the request of the office of origin, under article 6(4) of the Madrid Protocol, may file an application, under section 1 or 44 of this Act, for the registration of the same mark for any of the goods and services to which the cancellation applies that were covered by an extension of protection to the United States based on that international registration. Such an application shall be treated as if it had been filed on the international registration date or the date of recordal of the request for extension of protection with the International Bureau, whichever date applies, and, if the extension of protection enjoyed priority under section 67 of this title, shall enjoy the same priority. Such an application shall be entitled to the benefits conferred by this subsection only if the application is filed not later than 3 months after the date on which the international registration was canceled, in whole or in part, and only if the application complies with all the requirements of this Act which apply to any application filed pursuant to section 1 or 44.

§ 71   Affidavits and fees

(a) *Required affidavits and fees.*—An extension of protection for which a certificate of extension of protection has been issued under section 69 shall remain in force for the term of the international registration upon which it is based, except that the extension of protection of any mark shall be canceled by the Director—

> (1) at the end of the 6-year period beginning on the date on which the certificate of extension of protection was issued by the Director, unless within the 1-year period preceding the expiration of that 6-year period the holder of the international registration files in the Patent and Trademark Office an affidavit under subsection (b) together with a fee prescribed by the Director; and

(2) at the end of the 10-year period beginning on the date on which the certificate of extension of protection was issued by the Director, and at the end of each 10-year period thereafter, unless—

(A) within the 6-month period preceding the expiration of such 10-year period the holder of the international registration files in the United States Patent and Trademark Office an affidavit under subsection (b) together with a fee prescribed by the Director; or

(B) within 3 months after the expiration of such 10-year period, the holder of the international registration files in the Patent and Trademark Office an affidavit under subsection (b) together with the fee described in subparagraph (A) and the surcharge prescribed by the Director.

(b) *Contents of affidavit.*—The affidavit referred to in subsection (a) shall set forth those goods or services recited in the extension of protection on or in connection with which the mark is in use in commerce and the holder of the international registration shall attach to the affidavit a specimen or facsimile showing the current use of the mark in commerce, or shall set forth that any nonuse is due to special circumstances which excuse such nonuse and is not due to any intention to abandon the mark. Special notice of the requirement for such affidavit shall be attached to each certificate of extension of protection.

(c) *Notification.*—The Director shall notify the holder of the international registration who files 1 of the affidavits of the Director's acceptance or refusal thereof and, in case of a refusal, the reasons therefor.

(d) *Service of notice or process.*—The holder of the international registration of the mark may designate, by a document filed in the United States Patent and Trademark Office, the name and address of a person residing in the United States on whom notices or process in proceedings affecting the mark may be served. Such notices or process may be served upon the person so designated by leaving with that person, or mailing to that person, a copy thereof at the address specified in the last designation so filed. If the person designated cannot be found at the address given in the last designation, or if the holder does not designate by a document filed in the United States Patent and Trademark Office the name and address of a person residing in the United States for service of notices or process in proceedings affecting the mark, the notice or process may be served on the Director.

§ 72 Assignment of an extension of protection

An extension of protection may be assigned, together with the goodwill associated with the mark, only to a person who is a national of, is domiciled in, or has a bona fide and effective industrial or commercial establishment either in a country that is a Contracting Party or in a country that is a member of an intergovernmental organization that is a Contracting Party.

§ 73 Incontestability

The period of continuous use prescribed under section 15 for a mark covered by an extension of protection issued under this title may begin no earlier than the date on which the Director issues the certificate of the extension of protection under section 69, except as provided in section 74.

§ 74 Rights of extension of protection

When a United States registration and a subsequently issued certificate of extension of protection to the United States are owned by the same person, identify the same mark, and list the same goods or services, the extension of protection shall have the same rights that accrued to the registration prior to issuance of the certificate of extension of protection.

(Nov. 2, 2002, Pub. L. 107-273, §13402, 116 Stat. 1913.)

Part 3

TECHNOLOGY INNOVATION

UNITED STATES CODE

TITLE 15, CHAPTER 63—TECHNOLOGY INNOVATION

§ 3701   Findings

The Congress finds and declares that:

(1) Technology and industrial innovation are central to the economic, environmental, and social well-being of citizens of the United States.

(2) Technology and industrial innovation offer an improved standard of living, increased public and private sector productivity, crea-

tion of new industries and employment opportunities, improved public services and enhanced competitiveness of United States products in world markets.

(3) Many new discoveries and advances in science occur in universities and Federal laboratories, while the application of this new knowledge to commercial and useful public purposes depends largely upon actions by business and labor. Cooperation among academia, Federal laboratories, labor, and industry, in such forms as technology transfer, personnel exchange, joint research projects, and others, should be renewed, expanded, and strengthened.

(4) Small businesses have performed an important role in advancing industrial and technological innovation.

(5) Industrial and technological innovation in the United States may be lagging when compared to historical patterns and other industrialized nations.

(6) Increased industrial and technological innovation would reduce trade deficits, stabilize the dollar, increase productivity gains, increase employment, and stabilize prices.

(7) Government antitrust, economic, trade, patent, procurement, regulatory, research and development, and tax policies have significant impacts upon industrial innovation and development of technology, but there is insufficient knowledge of their effects in particular sectors of the economy.

(8) No comprehensive national policy exists to enhance technological innovation for commercial and public purposes. There is a need for such a policy, including a strong national policy supporting domestic technology transfer and utilization of the science and technology resources of the Federal Government.

(9) It is in the national interest to promote the adaptation of technological innovations to State and local government uses. Technological innovations can improve services, reduce their costs, and increase productivity in State and local governments.

(10) The Federal laboratories and other performers of federally funded research and development frequently provide scientific and technological developments of potential use to State and local gov-

ernments and private industry. These developments, which include inventions, computer software, and training technologies, should be made accessible to those governments and industry. There is a need to provide means of access and to give adequate personnel and funding support to these means.

(11) The Nation should give fuller recognition to individuals and companies which have made outstanding contributions to the promotion of technology or technological manpower for the improvement of the economic, environmental, or social well-being of the United States.

(Oct. 21, 1980, Pub. L. 96-480, §2, 94 Stat. 2311; Oct. 20, 1986, Pub. L. 99-502, §9, 100 Stat. 1797.)

§ 3702 Purpose

It is the purpose of this Act to improve the economic, environmental, and social well-being of the United States by—

(1) establishing organizations in the executive branch to study and stimulate technology;

(2) promoting technology development through the establishment of cooperative research centers;

(3) stimulating improved utilization of federally funded technology developments, including inventions, software, and training technologies, by State and local governments and the private sector;

(4) providing encouragement for the development of technology through the recognition of individuals and companies which have made outstanding contributions in technology; and

(5) encouraging the exchange of scientific and technical personnel among academia, industry, and Federal laboratories.

(Oct. 21, 1980, Pub. L. 96-480, §3, 94 Stat. 2312; Oct. 20, 1986, Pub. L. 99-502, §9, 100 Stat. 1795, 1797.)

§ 3703 Definitions

As used in this Act, unless the context otherwise requires, the term—

(1) "Office" means the Office of Technology Policy established under section 5 [§3704] of this Act.

(2) "Secretary" means the Secretary of Commerce.

15 U.S.C. § 3703

(3) "Under Secretary" means the Under Secretary of Commerce for Technology appointed under section 5(b)(1) [§3704(b)(1)].

(4) "Centers" means the Cooperative Research Centers established under section 7 or section 9 [§§3706 or 3708] of this Act.

(5) "Nonprofit institution" means an organization owned and operated exclusively for scientific or educational purposes, no part of the net earnings of which inures to the benefit of any private shareholder or individual.

(6) "Federal laboratory" means any laboratory, any federally funded research and development center, or any center established under section 7 or section 9 [§§3706 or 3708] of this Act that is owned, leased, or otherwise used by a Federal agency and funded by the Federal Government, whether operated by the Government or by a contractor.

(7) "Supporting agency" means either the Department of Commerce or the National Science Foundation, as appropriate.

(8) "Federal agency" means any executive agency as defined in section 105 of title 5, United States Code, and the military departments as defined in section 102 of such title, as well as any agency of the legislative branch of the Federal Government.

(9) "Invention" means any invention or discovery which is or may be patentable or otherwise protected under title 35, United States Code, or any novel variety of plant which is or may be protectable under the Plant Variety Protection Act (7 U.S.C. 2321 et seq.).

(10) "Made" when used in conjunction with any invention means the conception or first actual reduction to practice of such invention.

(11) "Small business firm" means a small business concern as defined in section 2 of Public Law 85-536 (15 U.S.C. 632) and implementing regulations of the Administrator of the Small Business Administration.

(12) "Training technology" means computer software and related materials which are developed by a Federal agency to train employees of such agency, including but not limited to software for computer-based instructional systems and for interactive video disc systems.

15 U.S.C. § 3703

(13) "Clearinghouse" means the Clearinghouse for State and Local Initiatives on Productivity, Technology, and Innovation established by section 6 [§3704a].

(Oct. 21, 1980, Pub. L. 96-480, §4, 94 Stat. 2312; Oct. 20, 1986, Pub. L. 99-502, §9, 100 Stat. 1795, 1796; Aug. 23, 1988, Pub. L. 100-418, §5122, 102 Stat. 1439; Oct. 24, 1988, Pub. L. 100-519, §201, 102 Stat. 2594; Feb. 14, 1992, Pub. L. 102-245, §304, 106 Stat. 20; Nov. 1, 2000, Pub. L. 106-404, §7, 114 Stat. 1745.)

§ 3704   Commerce and technological innovation

(a) *Establishment.*—There is established in the Department of Commerce a Technology Administration, which shall operate in accordance with the provisions, findings, and purposes of this Act. The Technology Administration shall include—

(1) the National Institute of Standards and Technology;

(2) the National Technical Information Service; and

(3) a policy analysis office, which shall be known as the Office of Technology Policy.

(b) *Under Secretary and Assistant Secretary.*—The President shall appoint, by and with the advice and consent of the Senate, to the extent provided for in appropriations Acts—

(1) an Under Secretary of Commerce for Technology, who shall be compensated at the rate provided for level III of the Executive Schedule in section 5314 of title 5, United States Code; and

(2) an Assistant Secretary of Commerce for Technology Policy, who shall serve as policy analyst for the Under Secretary.

(c) *Duties.*—The Secretary, through the Under Secretary, as appropriate, shall—

(1) manage the Technology Administration and supervise its agencies, programs, and activities;

(2) conduct technology policy analyses to improve United States industrial productivity, technology, and innovation, and cooperate with United States industry in the improvement of its productivity, technology, and ability to compete successfully in world markets;

(3) carry out any functions formerly assigned to the Office of Productivity, Technology, and Innovation;

(4) assist in the implementation of the Metric Conversion Act of 1975;

15 U.S.C. § 3704

(5) determine the relationships of technological developments and international technology transfers to the output, employment, productivity, and world trade performance of United States and foreign industrial sectors;

(6) determine the influence of economic, labor and other conditions, industrial structure and management, and government policies on technological developments in particular industrial sectors worldwide;

(7) identify technological needs, problems, and opportunities within and across industrial sectors that, if addressed, could make a significant contribution to the economy of the United States;

(8) assess whether the capital, technical and other resources being allocated to domestic industrial sectors which are likely to generate new technologies are adequate to meet private and social demands for goods and services and to promote productivity and economic growth;

(9) propose and support studies and policy experiments, in cooperation with other Federal agencies, to determine the effectiveness of measures with the potential of advancing United States technological innovation;

(10) provide that cooperative efforts to stimulate industrial innovation be undertaken between the Under Secretary and other officials in the Department of Commerce responsible for such areas as trade and economic assistance;

(11) encourage and assist the creation of centers and other joint initiatives by State or local governments, regional organizations, private businesses, institutions of higher education, nonprofit organizations, or Federal laboratories to encourage technology transfer, to stimulate innovation, and to promote an appropriate climate for investment in technology-related industries;

(12) propose and encourage cooperative research involving appropriate Federal entities, State or local governments, regional organizations, colleges or universities, nonprofit organizations, or private industry to promote the common use of resources, to improve training programs and curricula, to stimulate interest in high technology ca-

reers, and to encourage the effective dissemination of technology skills within the wider community;

(13) serve as a focal point for discussions among United States companies on topics of interest to industry and labor, including discussions regarding manufacturing and discussions regarding emerging technologies;

(14) consider government measures with the potential of advancing United States technological innovation and exploiting innovations of foreign origin; and

(15) publish the results of studies and policy experiments.

(d) *Japanese technical literature.—*

(1) In addition to the duties specified in subsection (c) of this section, the Secretary and the Under Secretary shall establish, and through the National Technical Information Service and with the cooperation of such other offices within the Department of Commerce as the Secretary considers appropriate, maintain a program (including an office in Japan) which shall, on a continuing basis—

(A) monitor Japanese technical activities and developments;

(B) consult with businesses, professional societies, and libraries in the United States regarding their needs for information on Japanese developments in technology and engineering;

(C) acquire and translate selected Japanese technical reports and documents that may be of value to agencies and departments of the Federal Government, and to businesses and researchers in the United States; and

(D) coordinate with other agencies and departments of the Federal Government to identify significant gaps and avoid duplication in efforts by the Federal Government to acquire, translate, index, and disseminate Japanese technical information.

Activities undertaken pursuant to subparagraph (C) of this paragraph shall only be performed on a cost-reimbursable basis. Translations referred to in such subparagraph shall be performed only to the extent that they are not otherwise available from sources within the private sector in the United States.

15 U.S.C. § 3704

(2) Beginning in 1986, the Secretary shall prepare annual reports regarding important Japanese scientific discoveries and technical innovations in such areas as computers, semiconductors, biotechnology, and robotics and manufacturing. In preparing such reports, the Secretary shall consult with professional societies and businesses in the United States. The Secretary may, to the extent provided in advance by appropriation Acts, contract with private organizations to acquire and translate Japanese scientific and technical information relevant to the preparation of such reports.

(3) The Secretary also shall encourage professional societies and private businesses in the United States to increase their efforts to acquire, screen, translate, and disseminate Japanese technical literature.

(4) In addition, the Secretary shall compile, publish, and disseminate an annual directory which lists—

(A) all programs and services in the United States that collect, abstract, translate, and distribute Japanese scientific and technical information; and

(B) all translations of Japanese technical documents performed by agencies and departments of the Federal Government in the preceding 12 months that are available to the public.

(5) The Secretary shall transmit to the Congress, within 1 year after the date of enactment of the Japanese Technical Literature Act of 1986, a report on the activities of the Federal Government to collect, abstract, translate, and distribute declassified Japanese scientific and technical information.

(e) *Report.*—The Secretary shall prepare and submit to the President and Congress, within 3 years after the date of enactment of this Act, a report on the progress, findings, and conclusions of activities conducted pursuant to sections 5, 6, 8, 11, 12, and 13 [§§3704, 3705, 3707, 3710, 3711, and 3712] of this Act (as then in effect) and recommendations for possible modifications thereof.

(f) *Experimental program to stimulate competitive technology.*—

(1) *In general.*—The Secretary, acting through the Under Secretary, shall establish for fiscal year 1999 a program to be known as the Ex-

perimental Program to Stimulate Competitive Technology (referred to in this subsection as the "program"). The purpose of the program shall be to strengthen the technological competitiveness of those States that have historically received less Federal research and development funds than those received by a majority of the States.

(2) *Arrangement.*—In carrying out the program, the Secretary, acting through the Under Secretary, shall—

(A) enter into such arrangements as may be necessary to provide for the coordination of the program through the State committees established under the Experimental Program to Stimulate Competitive Research of the National Science Foundation; and

(B) cooperate with—

(i) any State science and technology council established under the program under subparagraph (A); and

(ii) representatives of small business firms and other appropriate technology-based businesses.

(3) *Grants and cooperative agreements.*—In carrying out the program, the Secretary, acting through the Under Secretary, may make grants or enter into cooperative agreements to provide for—

(A) technology research and development;

(B) technology transfer from university research;

(C) technology deployment and diffusion; and

(D) the strengthening of technological capabilities through consortia comprised of—

(i) technology-based small business firms;

(ii) industries and emerging companies;

(iii) universities; and

(iv) State and local development agencies and entities.

(4) *Requirements for making awards.*—

(A) *In general.*—In making awards under this subsection, the Secretary, acting through the Under Secretary, shall ensure that the awards are awarded on a competitive basis that includes a review of the merits of the activities that are the subject of the award.

(B) *Matching requirement.*—The non-Federal share of the activities (other than planning activities) carried out under an award under this subsection shall be not less than 25 percent of the cost of those activities.

(5) *Criteria for states.*—The Secretary, acting through the Under Secretary, shall establish criteria for achievement by each State that participates in the program. Upon the achievement of all such criteria, a State shall cease to be eligible to participate in the program.

(6) *Coordination.*—To the extent practicable, in carrying out this subsection, the Secretary, acting through the Under Secretary, shall coordinate the program with other programs of the Department of Commerce.

(7) *Report.*—

(A) *In general.*—Not later than 90 days after the date of the enactment of the Technology Administration Act of 1998, the Under Secretary shall prepare and submit a report that meets the requirements of this paragraph to the Secretary. Upon receipt of the report, the Secretary shall transmit a copy of the report to the Committee on Commerce, Science, and Transportation of the Senate and the Committee on Science of the House of Representatives.

(B) *Requirements for report.*—The report prepared under this paragraph shall contain with respect to the program—

(i) a description of the structure and procedures of the program;

(ii) a management plan for the program;

(iii) a description of the merit-based review process to be used in the program;

(iv) milestones for the evaluation of activities to be assisted under the program in fiscal year 1999;

(v) an assessment of the eligibility of each State that participates in the Experimental Program to Stimulate Competitive

Research of the National Science Foundation to participate in the program under this subsection; and

(vi) the evaluation criteria with respect to which the overall management and effectiveness of the program will be evaluated.

(Oct. 21, 1980, Pub. L. 96-480, §5, 94 Stat. 2312; Aug. 14, 1986, Pub. L. 99-382, §2, 100 Stat. 811; Oct. 20, 1986, Pub. L. 99-502, §9, 100 Stat. 1795-97; Oct. 24, 1988, Pub. L. 100-519, §201, 102 Stat. 2593, 2594; Feb. 14, 1992, Pub. L. 102-245, §306, 106 Stat. 20; Oct. 30, 1998, Pub. L 105-309, §9, 112 Stat. 2938; Nov. 1, 2000, Pub. L. 106-404, §7, 114 Stat. 1745.)

§ 3704a   Clearinghouse for State and Local Initiatives on Productivity, Technology, and Innovation

(a) *Establishment.*—There is established within the Office of Productivity, Technology, and Innovation a Clearinghouse for State and Local Initiatives on Productivity, Technology, and Innovation. The Clearinghouse shall serve as a central repository of information on initiatives by State and local governments to enhance the competitiveness of American business through the stimulation of productivity, technology, and innovation and Federal efforts to assist State and local governments to enhance competitiveness.

(b) *Responsibilities.*—The Clearinghouse may—

(1) establish relationships with State and local governments, and regional and multistate organizations of such governments, which carry out such initiatives;

(2) collect information on the nature, extent, and effects of such initiatives, particularly information useful to the Congress, Federal agencies, State and local governments, regional and multistate organizations of such governments, businesses, and the public throughout the United States;

(3) disseminate information collected under paragraph (2) through reports, directories, handbooks, conferences, and seminars;

(4) provide technical assistance and advice to such governments with respect to such initiatives, including assistance in determining sources of assistance from Federal agencies which may be available to support such initiatives;

15 U.S.C. § 3704a

(5) study ways in which Federal agencies, including Federal laboratories, are able to use their existing policies and programs to assist State and local governments, and regional and multistate organizations of such governments, to enhance the competitiveness of American business;

(6) make periodic recommendations to the Secretary, and to other Federal agencies upon their request, concerning modifications in Federal policies and programs which would improve Federal assistance to State and local technology and business assistance programs;

(7) develop methodologies to evaluate State and local programs, and, when requested, advise State and local governments, and regional and multistate organizations of such governments, as to which programs are most effective in enhancing the competitiveness of American business through the stimulation of productivity, technology, and innovation; and

(8) make use of, and disseminate, the nationwide study of State industrial extension programs conducted by the Secretary.

(c) *Contracts.*—In carrying out subsection (b), the Secretary may enter into contracts for the purpose of collecting information on the nature, extent, and effects of initiatives.

(d) *Triennial report.*—The Secretary shall prepare and transmit to the Congress once each 3 years a report on initiatives by State and local governments to enhance the competitiveness of American businesses through the stimulation of productivity, technology, and innovation. The report shall include recommendations to the President, the Congress, and to Federal agencies on the appropriate Federal role in stimulating State and local efforts in this area. The first of these reports shall be transmitted to the Congress before January 1, 1989.

(Oct. 21, 1980, Pub. L. 96-480, §6, as added Aug. 23, 1988, Pub. L. 100-418, §5122, 102 Stat. 1438.)

§ 3704b   National Technical Information Service

(a) *Powers.*—

(1) The Secretary of Commerce, acting through the Director of the National Technical Information Service (hereafter in this subtitle referred to as the "Director") is authorized to do the following:

15 U.S.C. § 3704b

(A) Enter into such contracts, cooperative agreements, joint ventures, and other transactions, in accordance with all relevant provisions of Federal law applicable to such contracts and agreements, and under reasonable terms and conditions, as may be necessary in the conduct of the business of the National Technical Information Service (hereafter in this subtitle referred to as the "Service").

(B) In addition to the authority regarding fees contained in section 2 of the Act entitled "An Act to provide for the dissemination of technological, scientific, and engineering information to American business and industry, and for other purposes" enacted September 9, 1950 (15 U.S.C. 1152), retain and, subject to appropriations Acts, utilize its net revenues to the extent necessary to implement the plan submitted under subsection (f)(3)(D).

(C) Enter into contracts for the performance of part or all of the functions performed by the Promotion Division of the Service prior to the date of the enactment of this Act. The details of any such contract, and a statement of its effect on the operations and personnel of the Service, shall be provided to the appropriate committees of the Congress 30 days in advance of the execution of such contract.

(D) Employ such personnel as may be necessary to conduct the business of the Service.

(E) For the period of October 1, 1991 through September 30, 1992, only, retain and use all earned and unearned monies heretofore or hereafter received, including receipts, revenues, and advanced payments and deposits, to fund all obligations and expenses, including inventories and capital equipment.

An increase or decrease in the personnel of the Service shall not affect or be affected by any ceilings on the number or grade of personnel.

(2) The functions and activities of the Service specified in subsection (e)(1) through (6) are permanent Federal functions to be carried out by the Secretary through the Service and its employees, and shall not be transferred from the Service, by contract or otherwise, to the private sector on a permanent or temporary basis without express approval of the Congress. Functions or activities—

15 U.S.C. § 3704b

(A) for the procurement of supplies, materials, and equipment by the Service;

(B) referred to in paragraph (1)(C); or

(C) to be performed through joint ventures or cooperative agreements which do not result in a reduction in the Federal workforce of the affected programs of the service,

shall not be considered functions or activities for purposes of this paragraph.

(3) For the purposes of this subsection, the term "net revenues" means the excess of revenues and receipts from any source, other than royalties and other income described in section 13(a)(4) of the Stevenson-Wydler Technology Innovation Act of 1980 (15 U.S.C. 3710(c)(a)(4)), over operating expenses.

(b) *Director of the Service.*—The management of the Service shall be vested in a Director who shall report to the Under Secretary of Commerce for Technology and the Secretary of Commerce.

(c) *Advisory Board.*—

(1) There is established the Advisory Board of the National Technical Information Service, which shall be composed of a chairman and four other members appointed by the Secretary.

(2) In appointing members of the Advisory Board the Secretary shall solicit recommendations from the major users and beneficiaries of the Service's activities and shall select individuals experienced in providing or utilizing technical information.

(3) The Advisory Board shall review the general policies and operations of the Service, including policies in connection with fees and charges for its services, and shall advise the Secretary and the Director with respect thereto.

(4) The Advisory Board shall meet at the call of the Secretary, but not less often than once each six months.

(d) *Audits.*—The Secretary of Commerce shall provide for annual independent audits of the Service's financial statements beginning with fiscal year 1988, to be conducted in accordance with generally accepted accounting principles.

15 U.S.C. § 3704b

(e) *Functions.*—The Secretary of Commerce, acting through the Service, shall—

(1) establish and maintain a permanent repository of nonclassified scientific, technical, and engineering information;

(2) cooperate and coordinate its operations with other Government scientific, technical, and engineering information programs;

(3) make selected bibliographic information products available in a timely manner to depository libraries as part of the Depository Library Program of the Government Printing Office;

(4) in conjunction with the private sector as appropriate, collect, translate into English, and disseminate unclassified foreign scientific, technical, and engineering information;

(5) implement new methods or media for the dissemination of scientific, technical, and engineering information, including producing and disseminating information products in electronic format; and

(6) carry out the functions and activities of the Secretary under the act entitled "An Act to provide for the dissemination of technological, scientific, and engineering information to American business and industry, and for other purposes" enacted September 9, 1950, and the functions and activities of the Secretary performed through the National Technical Information Service as of the date of enactment of this Act under the Stevenson-Wydler Technology Innovation Act of 1980, under chapter 63 of this title.

(f) *Notification of Congress.—*

(1) The Secretary of Commerce and the Director shall keep the appropriate committees of Congress fully and currently informed about all activities related to the carrying out of the functions of the Service, including changes in fee policies.

(2) Within 90 days after the date of enactment of this Act, the Secretary of Commerce shall submit to the Congress a report on the current fee structure of the Service, including an explanation of the basis for the fees, taking into consideration all applicable costs, and the adequacy of the fees, along with reasons for the declining sales at the Service of scientific, technical, and engineering publications. Such

15 U.S.C. § 3704b

report shall explain any actions planned or taken to increase such sales at reasonable fees.

(3) The Secretary shall submit an annual report to the Congress which shall—

(A) summarize the operations of the Service during the preceding year, including financial details and staff levels broken down by major activities;

(B) detail the operating plan of the Service, including specific expense and staff needs, for the upcoming year;

(C) set forth details of modernization progress made in the preceding year;

(D) describe the long-term modernization of the Service; and

(E) include the results of the most recent annual audit carried out under subsection (d).

(4) The Secretary shall also give the Congress detailed advance notice of not less than 30 calendar days of—

(A) any proposed reduction-in-force;

(B) any joint venture or cooperative agreement which involves a financial incentive to the joint venturer or contractor; and

(C) any change in the operating plan submitted under paragraph (3)(B) which would result in a variation from such plan with respect to expense levels of more than 10 percent.

(Oct. 24, 1988, Pub. L. 100-519, §212, 102 Stat. 2594; Oct. 28, 1991, Pub. L. 102-140, §200, 105 Stat. 804; Feb. 14, 1992, Pub. L. 102-245, §506, 106 Stat. 27.)

§ 3704b-1   Operating costs

Operating costs for the National Technical Information Service associated with the acquisition, processing, storage, bibliographic control, and archiving of information and documents shall be recovered primarily through the collection of fees.

(Feb. 14, 1992, Pub. L. 102-245, §103(c), 106 Stat. 8.)

§ 3704b-2   Transfer of Federal scientific and technical information

(a) *Transfer.*—The head of each Federal executive department or agency shall transfer in a timely manner to the National Technical Information

Service unclassified scientific, technical, and engineering information which results from federally funded research and development activities for dissemination to the private sector, academia, State and local governments, and Federal agencies. Only information which would otherwise be available for public dissemination shall be transferred under this subsection. Such information shall include technical reports and information, computer software, application assessments generated pursuant to section 11(c) of the Stevenson-Wydler Technology Innovation Act of 1980 (15 U.S.C. 3710(c)), and information regarding training technology and other federally owned or originated technologies. The Secretary shall issue regulations within one year after February 14, 1992 outlining procedures for the ongoing transfer of such information to the National Technical Information Service.

(b) *Annual report to Congress.*—As part of the annual report required under section 3704b(f)(3) of this title, the Secretary shall report to Congress on the status of efforts under this section to ensure access to Federal scientific and technical information by the public. Such report shall include—

(1) an evaluation of the comprehensiveness of transfers of information by each Federal executive department or agency under subsection (a) of this section;

(2) a description of the use of Federal scientific and technical information;

(3) plans for improving public access to Federal scientific and technical information; and

(4) recommendations for legislation necessary to improve public access to Federal scientific and technical information.

(Feb. 14, 1992, Pub. L. 102-245, title I, §108, 106 Stat. 13.)

§ 3705   Cooperative Research Centers

(a) *Establishment.*—The Secretary shall provide assistance for the establishment of Cooperative Research Centers. Such Centers shall be affiliated with any university, or other nonprofit institution, or group thereof, that applies for and is awarded a grant or enters into a cooperative agreement under this section. The objective of the Centers is to enhance technological innovation through—

15 U.S.C. § 3705

(1) the participation of individuals from industry and universities in cooperative technological innovation activities;

(2) the development of the generic research base, important for technological advance and innovative activity, in which individual firms have little incentive to invest, but which may have significant economic or strategic importance, such as manufacturing technology;

(3) the education and training of individuals in the technological innovation process;

(4) the improvement of mechanisms for the dissemination of scientific, engineering, and technical information among universities and industry;

(5) the utilization of the capability and expertise, where appropriate, that exists in Federal laboratories; and

(6) the development of continuing financial support from other mission agencies, from State and local government, and from industry and universities through, among other means, fees, licenses, and royalties.

(b) *Activities.*—The activities of the Centers shall include, but need not be limited to—

(1) research supportive of technological and industrial innovation including cooperative industry-university research;

(2) assistance to individuals and small businesses in the generation, evaluation and development of technological ideas supportive of industrial innovation and new business ventures;

(3) technical assistance and advisory services to industry, particularly small businesses; and

(4) curriculum development, training, and instruction in invention, entrepreneurship, and industrial innovation.

Each Center need not undertake all of the activities under this subsection.

(c) *Requirements.*—Prior to establishing a Center, the Secretary shall find that—

(1) consideration has been given to the potential contribution of the activities proposed under the Center to productivity, employment, and economic competitiveness of the United States;

15 U.S.C. § 3705

(2) a high likelihood exists of continuing participation, advice, financial support, and other contributions from the private sector;

(3) the host university or other nonprofit institution has a plan for the management and evaluation of the activities proposed within the particular Center, including:

(A) the agreement between the parties as to the allocation of patent rights on a nonexclusive, partially exclusive, or exclusive license basis to and inventions conceived or made under the auspices of the Center; and

(B) the consideration of means to place the Center, to the maximum extent feasible, on a self-sustaining basis;

(4) suitable consideration has been given to the university's or other nonprofit institution's capabilities and geographical location; and

(5) consideration has been given to any effects upon competition of the activities proposed under the Center.

(d) *Planning grants.*—The Secretary is authorized to make available nonrenewable planning grants to universities or nonprofit institutions for the purpose of developing a plan required under subsection (c)(3).

(e) *Research and development utilization.*—In the promotion of technology from research and development efforts by Centers under this section, chapter 18 of title 35, United States Code, shall apply to the extent not inconsistent with this section.

(Oct. 21, 1980, Pub. L. 96-480, §7, formerly §6, 94 Stat. 2313; Oct. 20, 1986, Pub. L. 99-502, §9, 100 Stat. 1796; Aug. 23, 1988, Pub. L. 100-418, §5122, 102 Stat. 1438.)

§ 3706 Grants and cooperative agreements

(a) *In general.*—The Secretary may make grants and enter into cooperative agreements according to the provisions of this section in order to assist any activity consistent with this Act, including activities performed by individuals. The total amount of any such grant or cooperative agreement may not exceed 75 percent of the total cost of the program.

(b) *Eligibility and procedure.*—Any person or institution may apply to the Secretary for a grant or cooperative agreement available under this section. Application shall be made in such form and manner, and with such content and other submissions, as the Assistant Secretary shall prescribe. The Secretary shall act upon each such application within 90 days after the date on which all required information is received.

(c) *Terms and conditions.*—

(1) Any grant made, or cooperative agreement entered into, under this section shall be subject to the limitations and provisions set forth in paragraph (2) of this subsection, and to such other terms, conditions, and requirements as the Secretary deems necessary or appropriate.

(2) Any person who receives or utilizes any proceeds of any grant made or cooperative agreement entered into under this section shall keep such records as the Secretary shall by regulation prescribe as being necessary and appropriate to facilitate effective audit and evaluation, including records which fully disclose the amount and disposition by such recipient of such proceeds, the total cost of the program or project in connection with which such proceeds were used, and the amount, if any, of such costs which was provided through other sources.

(Oct. 21, 1980, Pub. L. 96-480, §8, formerly §7, 94 Stat. 2315; Aug. 23, 1988, Pub. L. 100-418, §§5115, 5122, 102 Stat. 1433, 1438.)

§3707 National Science Foundation Cooperative Research Centers

(a) *Establishment and provisions.*—The National Science Foundation shall provide assistance for the establishment of Cooperative Research Centers. Such Centers shall be affiliated with a university, or other nonprofit institution, or a group thereof. The objective of the Centers is to enhance technological innovation as provided in section 7(a) through the conduct of activities as provided in section 7(b).

(b) *Planning grants.*—The National Science Foundation is authorized to make available nonrenewable planning grants to universities or nonprofit institutions for the purpose of developing the plan, as described under section 7(c)(3) [§3706(c)(3)].

(c) *Terms and conditions.*—Grants, contracts, and cooperative agreements entered into by the National Science Foundation in execution of the powers and duties of the National Science Foundation under this Act shall be governed by the National Science Foundation Act of 1950 and other pertinent Acts.

(Oct. 21, 1980, Pub. L. 96-480, §9, formerly §8, 94 Stat. 2316; Oct. 20, 1986, Pub. L. 99-502, §9, 100 Stat. 1796, 1797; Aug. 23, 1988, Pub. L. 100-418, §5122, 102 Stat. 1438; Nov. 1, 2000, Pub. L. 106-404, §7, 114 Stat. 1745.)

§ 3708   Administrative arrangements

(a) *Coordination.*—The Secretary and the National Science Foundation shall, on a continuing basis, obtain the advice and cooperation of departments and agencies whose missions contribute to or are affected by the programs established under this Act, including the development of an agenda for research and policy experimentation. These departments and agencies shall include but not be limited to the Departments of Defense, Energy, Education, Health and Human Services, Housing and Urban Development, the Environmental Protection Agency, National Aeronautics and Space Administration, Small Business Administration, Council of Economic Advisers, Council on Environmental Quality, and Office of Science and Technology Policy.

(b) *Cooperation.*—It is the sense of the Congress that departments and agencies, including the Federal laboratories, whose missions are affected by, or could contribute to, the programs established under this Act, should, within the limits of budgetary authorizations and appropriations, support or participate in activities or projects authorized by this Act.

(c) *Administrative authorization.*—

(1) Departments and agencies described in subsection (b) are authorized to participate in, contribute to, and serve as resources for the Centers and for any other activities authorized under this Act.

(2) The Secretary and the National Science Foundation are authorized to receive moneys and to receive other forms of assistance from other departments or agencies to support activities of the Centers and any other activities authorized under this Act.

(d) *Cooperative efforts.*—The Secretary and the National Science Foundation shall, on a continuing basis, provide each other the opportunity to comment on any proposed program of activity under section 7, 9, 11, 15, 17, or 20 of this Act [§§3705, 3707, 3710, 3710d, 3711a, or 3712] before

15 U.S.C. § 3708

funds are committed to such program in order to mount complementary efforts and avoid duplication.

(Oct. 21, 1980, Pub. L. 96-480, §10, formerly §9, 94 Stat. 2316; Oct. 20, 1986, Pub. L. 99-502, §9, 100 Stat. 1797; Aug. 20, 1987, Pub. L. 100-107, §3, 101 Stat. 727; Aug. 23, 1988, Pub. L. 100-418, §5122, 102 Stat. 1438, 1439; Dec. 18, 1991, Pub. L. 102-240, §6019, 105 Stat. 2183.)

§ 3709   [Repealed] (Oct. 20, 1986, Pub. L. 99-502, §9, 100 Stat. 1795).

§ 3710   Utilization of Federal technology

(a) *Policy.*—

(1) It is the continuing responsibility of the Federal Government to ensure the full use of the results of the Nation's Federal investment in research and development. To this end the Federal Government shall strive where appropriate to transfer federally owned or originated technology to State and local governments and to the private sector.

(2) Technology transfer, consistent with mission responsibilities, is a responsibility of each laboratory science and engineering professional.

(3) Each laboratory director shall ensure that efforts to transfer technology are considered positively in laboratory job descriptions, employee promotion policies, and evaluation of the job performance of scientists and engineers in the laboratory.

(b) *Establishment of Research and Technology Applications Offices.*—Each Federal laboratory shall establish an Office of Research and Technology Applications. Laboratories having existing organizational structures which perform the functions of this section may elect to combine the Office of Research and Technology Applications within the existing organization. The staffing and funding levels for these offices shall be determined between each Federal laboratory and the Federal agency operating or directing the laboratory, except that (1) each laboratory having 200 or more full-time equivalent scientific, engineering, and related technical positions shall provide one or more full-time equivalent positions as staff for its Office of Research and Technology Applications, and (2) each Federal agency which operates or directs one or more Federal laboratories shall make available sufficient funding, either as a separate line item or from the agency's research and development budget, to support the technology transfer function at the agency and at its laboratories, including support of the Offices of Research and Technology Applications. Furthermore, individuals filling positions in an Office of Research and Technology Applications shall be included in the overall laboratory/agency management development program so as to ensure that highly competent technical managers are full participants in the technology transfer process.

(c) *Functions of Research and Technology Applications Offices.*—It shall be the function of each Office of Research and Technology Applications—

(1) to prepare application assessments for selected research and development projects in which that laboratory is engaged and which in the opinion of the laboratory may have potential commercial applications;

(2) to provide and disseminate information on federally owned or originated products, processes, and services having potential application to State and local governments and to private industry;

(3) to cooperate with and assist the National Technical Information Service, the Federal Laboratory Consortium for Technology Transfer, and other organizations which link the research and development resources of that laboratory and the Federal Government as a whole to potential users in State and local government and private industry;

(4) to provide technical assistance to State and local government officials; and

(5) to participate, where feasible, in regional, State, and local programs designed to facilitate or stimulate the transfer of technology for the benefit of the region, State, or local jurisdiction in which the Federal laboratory is located.

Agencies which have established organizational structures outside their Federal laboratories which have as their principal purpose the transfer of federally owned or originated technology to State and local government and to the private sector may elect to perform the functions of this subsection in such organizational structures. No Office of Research and Technology Applications or other organizational structures performing

15 U.S.C. § 3710

the functions of this subsection shall substantially compete with similar services available in the private sector.

(d) *Dissemination of technical information.*—The National Technical Information Service shall—

(1) serve as a central clearinghouse for the collection, dissemination and transfer of information on federally owned or originated technologies having potential application to State and local governments and to private industry;

(2) utilize the expertise and services of the National Science Foundation and the Federal Laboratory Consortium for Technology Transfer; particularly in dealing with State and local governments;

(3) receive requests for technical assistance from State and local governments, respond to such requests with published information available to the Service, and refer such requests to the Federal Laboratory Consortium for Technology Transfer to the extent that such requests require a response involving more than the published information available to the Service;

(4) provide funding at the discretion of the Secretary, for Federal laboratories to provide the assistance specified in subsection (c)(3);

(5) use appropriate technology transfer mechanisms such as personnel exchanges and computer-based systems; and

(6) maintain a permanent archival repository and clearinghouse for the collection and dissemination of nonclassified scientific, technical, and engineering information.

(e) *Establishment of Federal Laboratory Consortium for Technology Transfer.—*

(1) There is hereby established the Federal Laboratory Consortium for Technology Transfer (hereinafter referred to as the "Consortium") which, in cooperation with Federal laboratories and the private sector, shall—

(A) develop and (with the consent of the Federal laboratory concerned) administer techniques, training courses, and materials concerning technology transfer to increase the awareness of Federal laboratory employees regarding the commercial potential of laboratory technology and innovations;

(B) furnish advice and assistance requested by Federal agencies and laboratories for use in their technology transfer programs (including the planning of seminars for small business and other industry);

(C) provide a clearinghouse for requests, received at the laboratory level, for technical assistance from States and units of local governments, businesses, industrial development organizations, not-for-profit organizations including universities, Federal agencies and laboratories, and other persons, and—

(i) to the extent that such requests can be responded to with published information available to the National Technical Information Service, refer such requests to that Service, and

(ii) otherwise refer these requests to the appropriate Federal laboratories and agencies;

(D) facilitate communication and coordination between Offices of Research and Technology Applications of Federal laboratories;

(E) utilize (with the consent of the agency involved) the expertise and services of the National Science Foundation, the Department of Commerce, the National Aeronautics and Space Administration, and other Federal agencies, as necessary;

(F) with the consent of any Federal laboratory, facilitate the use by such laboratory of appropriate technology transfer mechanisms such as personnel exchanges and computer-based systems;

(G) with the consent of any Federal laboratory, assist such laboratory to establish programs using technical volunteers to provide technical assistance to communities related to such laboratory;

(H) facilitate communication and cooperation between Offices of Research and Technology Applications of Federal laboratories and regional, State, and local technology transfer organizations;

(I) when requested, assist colleges or universities, businesses, nonprofit organizations, State or local governments, or regional organizations to establish programs to stimulate research and to

15 U.S.C. § 3710

encourage technology transfer in such areas as technology program development, curriculum design, long-term research planning, personnel needs projections, and productivity assessments;

(J) seek advice in each Federal laboratory consortium region from representatives of State and local governments, large and small business, universities, and other appropriate persons on the effectiveness of the program (and any such advice shall be provided at no expense to the Government); and

(K) work with the Director of the National Institute on Disability and Rehabilitation Research to compile a compendium of current and projected Federal Laboratory technologies and projects that have or will have an intended or recognized impact on the available range of assistive technology for individuals with disabilities (as defined in section 3 of the Assistive Technology Act of 1998), including technologies and projects that incorporate the principles of universal design (as defined in section 3 of such Act), as appropriate.

(2) The membership of the Consortium shall consist of the Federal laboratories described in clause (1) of subsection (b) and such other laboratories as may choose to join the Consortium. The representatives to the Consortium shall include a senior staff member of each Federal laboratory which is a member of the Consortium and a senior representative appointed from each Federal agency with one or more member laboratories.

(3) The representatives to the Consortium shall elect a Chairman of the Consortium.

(4) The Director of the National Institute of Standards and Technology shall provide the Consortium, on a reimbursable basis, with administrative services, such as office space, personnel, and support services of the Institute, as requested by the Consortium and approved by such Director.

(5) Each Federal laboratory or agency shall transfer technology directly to users or representatives of users, and shall not transfer technology directly to the Consortium. Each Federal laboratory shall conduct and transfer technology only in accordance with the prac-

tices and policies of the Federal agency which owns, leases, or otherwise uses such Federal laboratory.

(6) Not later than one year after the date of enactment of this subsection, and every year thereafter, the Chairman of the Consortium shall submit a report to the President, to the appropriate authorization and appropriation committees of both Houses of the Congress, and to each agency with respect to which a transfer of funding is made (for the fiscal year or years involved) under paragraph (7), concerning the activities of the Consortium and the expenditures made by it under this subsection during the year for which the report is made. Such report shall include an annual independent audit of the financial statements of the Consortium, conducted in accordance with generally accepted accounting principles.

(7) (A) Subject to subparagraph (B), an amount equal to 0.008 percent of the budget of each Federal agency from any Federal source, including related overhead, that is to be utilized by or on behalf of the laboratories of such agency for a fiscal year referred to in subparagraph (B)(ii) shall be transferred by such agency to the National Institute of Standards and Technology at the beginning of the fiscal year involved. Amounts so transferred shall be provided by the Institute to the Consortium for the purpose of carrying out activities of the Consortium under this subsection.

(B) A transfer shall be made by any Federal agency under subparagraph (A), for any fiscal year, only if the amount so transferred by that agency (as determined under such subparagraph) would exceed $10,000.

(C) The heads of Federal agencies and their designees, and the directors of Federal laboratories, may provide such additional support for operations of the Consortium as they deem appropriate.

(8) [repealed].

(f) *Agency reports on utilization.*—

(1) *In general.*—Each Federal agency which operates or directs one or more Federal laboratories or which conducts activities under sections 207 and 209 of title 35, United States Code, shall report annu-

ally to the Office of Management and Budget, as part of the agency's annual budget submission, on the activities performed by that agency and its Federal laboratories under the provisions of this section and of sections 207 and 209 of title 35, United States Code.

(2) *Contents.*—The report shall include—

(A) an explanation of the agency's technology transfer program for the preceding fiscal year and the agency's plans for conducting its technology transfer function, including its plans for securing intellectual property rights in laboratory innovations with commercial promise and plans for managing its intellectual property so as to advance the agency's mission and benefit the competitiveness of United States industry; and

(B) information on technology transfer activities for the preceding fiscal year, including—

(i) the number of patent applications filed;

(ii) the number of patents received;

(iii) the number of fully-executed licenses which received royalty income in the preceding fiscal year, categorized by whether they are exclusive, partially-exclusive, or non-exclusive, and the time elapsed from the date on which the license was requested by the licensee in writing to the date the license was executed;

(iv) the total earned royalty income including such statistical information as the total earned royalty income, of the top 1 percent, 5 percent, and 20 percent of the licenses, the range of royalty income, and the median, except where disclosure of such information would reveal the amount of royalty income associated with an individual license or licensee;

(v) what disposition was made of the income described in clause (iv);

(vi) the number of licenses terminated for cause; and

(vii) any other parameters or discussion that the agency deems relevant or unique to its practice of technology transfer.

15 U.S.C. § 3710

(3) *Copy to Secretary; Attorney General; Congress.*—The agency shall transmit a copy of the report to the Secretary of Commerce and the Attorney General for inclusion in the annual report to Congress and the President required by subsection (g)(2).

(4) *Public availability.*—Each Federal agency reporting under this subsection is also strongly encouraged to make the information contained in such report available to the public through Internet sites or other electronic means.

(g) *Functions of the Secretary.*—

(1) The Secretary, through the Under Secretary, and in consultation with other Federal agencies, may—

(A) make available to interested agencies the expertise of the Department of Commerce regarding the commercial potential of inventions and methods and options for commercialization which are available to the Federal laboratories, including research and development limited partnerships;

(B) develop and disseminate to appropriate agency and laboratory personnel model provisions for use on a voluntary basis in cooperative research and development arrangements; and

(C) furnish advice and assistance, upon request, to Federal agencies concerning their cooperative research and development programs and projects.

(2) *Reports.*—

(A) *Annual report required.*—The Secretary, in consultation with the Attorney General and the Commissioner of Patents and Trademarks, shall submit each fiscal year, beginning 1 year after the enactment of the Technology Transfer Commercialization Act of 2000, a summary report to the President, the United States Trade Representative, and the Congress on the use by Federal agencies and the Secretary of the technology transfer authorities specified in this Act and in sections 207 and 209 of title 35, United States Code.

(B) *Content.*—The report shall—

(i) draw upon the reports prepared by the agencies under subsection (f);

(ii) discuss technology transfer best practices and effective approaches in the licensing and transfer of technology in the context of the agencies' missions; and

(iii) discuss the progress made toward development of additional useful measures of the outcomes of technology transfer programs of Federal agencies.

(C) *Public availability.*—The Secretary shall make the report available to the public through Internet sites or other electronic means.

(3) Not later than one year after the date of enactment of the Federal Technology Transfer Act of 1986, the Secretary shall submit to the President and the Congress a report regarding—

(A) any copyright provisions or other types of barriers which tend to restrict or limit the transfer of federally funded computer software to the private sector and to State and local governments, and agencies of such State and local governments; and

(B) the feasibility and cost of compiling and maintaining a current and comprehensive inventory of all federally funded training software.

(h) *Duplication of reporting.*—The reporting obligations imposed by this section—

(1) are not intended to impose requirements that duplicate requirements imposed by the Government Performance and Results Act of 1993 (31 U.S.C. 1101 note);

(2) are to be implemented in coordination with the implementation of that Act; and

(3) are satisfied if an agency provided the information concerning technology transfer activities described in this section in its annual submission under the Government Performance and Results Act of 1993 (31 U.S.C. 1101 note).

(i) *Research equipment.*—The Director of a laboratory, or the head of any Federal agency or department, may loan, lease, or give research equipment that is excess to the needs of the laboratory, agency, or department to an educational institution or nonprofit organization for the conduct of technical and scientific education and research activities. Title of ownership shall transfer with a gift under this section.

(Oct. 21, 1980, Pub. L. 96-480, §11, 94 Stat. 2318; Oct. 20, 1986, Pub. L. 99-502, §§3-5, 9, 100 Stat. 1787, 1789, 1791, 1797; Aug. 23, 1988, Pub. L. 100-418, §§5115, 5122, 5162, 5163, 102 Stat. 1433, 1438, 1450-51; Oct. 24, 1988, Pub. L. 100-519, §§201, 212, 102 Stat. 2594-95; Nov. 29, 1989, Pub. L. 101-189, §3133, 103 Stat. 1679; Feb. 14, 1992, Pub. L. 102-245, §§301, 303, 106 Stat. 20; Mar. 7, 1996, Pub. L. 104-113, §9, 110 Stat. 775; Nov. 13, 1998, Pub. L. 105-394, §212(d), 112 Stat. 3655; Nov. 1, 2000, Pub. L. 106-404, §§7, 10, 114 Stat. 1745, 1747.)

§ 3710a   Cooperative research and development agreements

(a) *General authority.*—Each Federal agency may permit the director of any of its Government-operated Federal laboratories, and, to the extent provided in an agency-approved joint work statement or, if permitted by the agency, in an agency-approved annual strategic plan, the director of any of its Government-owned, contractor-operated laboratories—

(1) to enter into cooperative research and development agreements on behalf of such agency (subject to subsection (c) of this section) with other Federal agencies; units of State or local government; industrial organizations (including corporations, partnerships, and limited partnerships, and industrial development organizations); public and private foundations; nonprofit organizations (including universities); or other persons (including licensees of inventions owned by the Federal agency); and

(2) to negotiate licensing agreements under section 207 of title 35, United States Code, or under other authorities (in the case of a Government-owned, contractor-operated laboratory, subject to subsection (c) of this section) for inventions made or other intellectual property developed at the laboratory and other inventions or other intellectual property that may be voluntarily assigned to the Government.

(b) *Enumerated authority.*—

(1) Under an agreement entered into pursuant to subsection (a)(1), the laboratory may grant, or agree to grant in advance, to a collaborating party patent licenses or assignments, or options thereto, in

15 U.S.C. § 3710a

any invention made in whole or in part by a laboratory employee under the agreement, for reasonable compensation when appropriate. The laboratory shall ensure, through such agreement, that the collaborating party has the option to choose an exclusive license for a pre-negotiated field of use for any such invention under the agreement or, subject to section 209 of title 35, United States Code, may grant a license to an invention which is federally owned, for which a patent application was filed before the signing of the agreement, and directly within the scope of the work under the agreement, or, if there is more than one collaborating party, that the collaborating parties are offered the option to hold licensing rights that collectively encompass the rights that would be held under such an exclusive license by one party. In consideration for the Government's contribution under the agreement, grants under this paragraph shall be subject to the following explicit conditions:

(A) A nonexclusive, nontransferable, irrevocable, paid-up license from the collaborating party to the laboratory to practice the invention or have the invention practiced throughout the world by or on behalf of the Government. In the exercise of such license, the Government shall not publicly disclose trade secrets or commercial or financial information that is privileged or confidential within the meaning of section 552(b)(4) of title 5, United States Code, or which would be considered as such if it had been obtained from a non-Federal party.

(B) If a laboratory assigns title or grants an exclusive license to such an invention, the Government shall retain the right—

(i) to require the collaborating party to grant to a responsible applicant a nonexclusive, partially exclusive, or exclusive license to use the invention in the applicant's licensed field of use, on terms that are reasonable under the circumstances; or

(ii) if the collaborating party fails to grant such a license, to grant the license itself.

(C) The Government may exercise its right retained under subparagraph (B) only in exceptional circumstances and only if the Government determines that—

(i) the action is necessary to meet health or safety needs that are not reasonably satisfied by the collaborating party;

(ii) the action is necessary to meet requirements for public use specified by Federal regulations, and such requirements are not reasonably satisfied by the collaborating party; or

(iii) the collaborating party has failed to comply with an agreement containing provisions described in subsection (c)(4)(B).

This determination is subject to administrative appeal and judicial review under section 203(2) of title 35, United States Code.

(2) Under agreements entered into pursuant to subsection (a)(1), the laboratory shall ensure that a collaborating party may retain title to any invention made solely by its employee in exchange for normally granting the Government a nonexclusive, nontransferable, irrevocable, paid-up license to practice the invention or have the invention practiced throughout the world by or on behalf of the Government for research or other Government purposes.

(3) Under an agreement entered into pursuant to subsection (a)(1), a laboratory may—

(A) accept, retain, and use funds, personnel, services, and property from a collaborating party and provide personnel, services, and property to a collaborating party;

(B) use funds received from a collaborating party in accordance with subparagraph (A) to hire personnel to carry out the agreement who will not be subject to full-time-equivalent restrictions of the agency;

(C) to the extent consistent with any applicable agency requirements or standards of conduct, permit an employee or former employee of the laboratory to participate in an effort to commercialize an invention made by the employee or former employee while in the employment or service of the Government; and

(D) waive, subject to reservation by the Government of a nonexclusive, irrevocable, paid-up license to practice the invention or have the invention practiced throughout the world by or on behalf of the Government, in advance, in whole or in part, any right

15 U.S.C. § 3710a

of ownership which the Federal Government may have to any subject invention made under the agreement by a collaborating party or employee of a collaborating party.

(4) A collaborating party in an exclusive license in any invention made under an agreement entered into pursuant to subsection (a)(1) shall have the right of enforcement under chapter 29 of title 35, United States Code.

(5) A Government-owned, contractor-operated laboratory that enters into a cooperative research and development agreement pursuant to subsection (a)(1) may use or obligate royalties or other income accruing to the laboratory under such agreement with respect to any invention only—

(A) for payments to inventors;

(B) for purposes described in clauses (i), (ii), (iii), and (iv) of section 14(a)(1)(B); and

(C) for scientific research and development consistent with the research and development missions and objectives of the laboratory.

(6) (A) In the case of a laboratory that is part of the National Nuclear Security Administration, a designated official of that Administration may waive any license retained by the Government under paragraph (1)(A), (2), or (3)(D), in whole or in part and according to negotiated terms and conditions, if the designated official finds that the retention of the license by the Government would substantially inhibit the commercialization of an invention that would otherwise serve an important national security mission.

(B) The authority to grant a waiver under subparagraph (A) shall expire on the date that is five years after the date of the enactment of the Floyd D. Spence National Defense Authorization Act for Fiscal Year 2001. The expiration under the preceding sentence of authority to grant a waiver under subparagraph (A) shall not affect any waiver granted under that subparagraph before the expiration of such authority.

(C) Not later than February 15 of each year, the Administrator for Nuclear Security shall submit to Congress a report on any

15 U.S.C. § 3710a

waivers granted under this paragraph during the preceding year.

(c) *Contract considerations.*—

(1) A Federal agency may issue regulations on suitable procedures for implementing the provisions of this section; however, implementation of this section shall not be delayed until issuance of such regulations.

(2) The agency in permitting a Federal laboratory to enter into agreements under this section shall be guided by the purposes of this Act.

(3) (A) Any agency using the authority given it under subsection (a) shall review standards of conduct for its employees for resolving potential conflicts of interest to make sure they adequately establish guidelines for situations likely to arise through the use of this authority, including but not limited to cases where present or former employees or their partners negotiate licenses or assignments of titles to inventions or negotiate cooperative research and development agreements with Federal agencies (including the agency with which the employee involved is or was formerly employed).

(B) If, in implementing subparagraph (A), an agency is unable to resolve potential conflicts of interest within its current statutory framework, it shall propose necessary statutory changes to be forwarded to its authorizing committees in Congress.

(4) The laboratory director in deciding what cooperative research and development agreements to enter into shall—

(A) give special consideration to small business firms, and consortia involving small business firms; and

(B) give preference to business units located in the United States which agree that products embodying inventions made under the cooperative research and development agreement or produced through the use of such inventions will be manufactured substantially in the United States and, in the case of any industrial organization or other person subject to the control of a foreign company or government, as appropriate, take into consideration

15 U.S.C. § 3710a

whether or not such foreign government permits United States agencies, organizations, or other persons to enter into cooperative research and development agreements and licensing agreements.

(5) (A) If the head of the agency or his designee desires an opportunity to disapprove or require the modification of any such agreement presented by the director of a Government-operated laboratory, the agreement shall provide a 30-day period within which such action must be taken beginning on the date the agreement is presented to him or her by the head of the laboratory concerned.

(B) In any case in which the head of an agency or his designee disapproves or requires the modification of an agreement presented by the director of a Government-operated laboratory under this section, the head of the agency or such designee shall transmit a written explanation of such disapproval or modification to the head of the laboratory concerned.

(C) (i) Any non-Federal entity that operates a laboratory pursuant to a contract with a Federal agency shall submit to the agency any cooperative research and development agreement that the entity proposes to enter into and the joint work statement if required with respect to that agreement.

(ii) A Federal agency that receives a proposed agreement and joint work statement under clause (i) shall review and approve, request specific modifications to, or disapprove the proposed agreement and joint work statement within 30 days after such submission. No agreement may be entered into by a Government-owned, contractor-operated laboratory under this section before both approval of the agreement and approval of a joint work statement under this clause.

(iii) In any case in which an agency which has contracted with an entity referred to in clause (i) disapproves or requests the modification of a cooperative research and development agreement or joint work statement submitted under that clause, the agency shall transmit a written explanation of such disapproval or modification to the head of the laboratory concerned.

(iv) Any agency that has contracted with a non-Federal entity to operate a laboratory may develop and provide to such laboratory one or more model cooperative research and development agreements for purposes of standardizing practices and procedures, resolving common legal issues, and enabling review of cooperative research and development agreements to be carried out in a routine and prompt manner.

(v) A Federal agency may waive the requirements of clause (i) or (ii) under such circumstances as the agency considers appropriate.

(6) Each agency shall maintain a record of all agreements entered into under this section.

(7) (A) No trade secrets or commercial or financial information that is privileged or confidential, under the meaning of section 552(b)(4) of title 5, United States Code, which is obtained in the conduct of research or as a result of activities under this Act from a non-Federal party participating in a cooperative research and development agreement shall be disclosed.

(B) The director, or in the case of a contractor-operated laboratory, the agency, for a period of up to 5 years after development of information that results from research and development activities conducted under this Act and that would be a trade secret or commercial or financial information that is privileged or confidential if the information had been obtained from a non-Federal party participating in a cooperative research and development agreement, may provide appropriate protections against the dissemination of such information, including exemption from subchapter II of chapter 5 of title 5, United States Code.

(d) *Definitions.*—As used in this section—

(1) the term "cooperative research and development agreement" means any agreement between one or more Federal laboratories and one or more non-Federal parties under which the Government, through its laboratories, provides personnel, services, facilities, equipment, intellectual property, or other resources with or without reimbursement (but not funds to non-Federal parties) and the non-Federal

15 U.S.C. § 3710a

parties provide funds, personnel, services, facilities, equipment, intellectual property, or other resources toward the conduct of specified research or development efforts which are consistent with the missions of the laboratory; except that such term does not include a procurement contract or cooperative agreement as those terms are used in sections 6303, 6304, and 6305 of title 31, United States Code;

(2) the term "laboratory" means—

(A) a facility or group of facilities owned, leased, or otherwise used by a Federal agency, a substantial purpose of which is the performance of research, development, or engineering by employees of the Federal Government;

(B) a group of Government-owned, contractor-operated facilities under a common contract, when a substantial purpose of the contract is the performance of research and development for the Federal Government; and

(C) a Government-owned, contractor-operated facility that is not under a common contract described in subparagraph (B), and the primary purpose of which is the performance of research and development for the Federal Government,

but such term does not include any facility covered by Executive Order No. 12344, dated February 1, 1982, pertaining to the naval nuclear propulsion program; and

(3) the term "joint work statement" means a proposal prepared for a Federal agency by the director of a Government-owned, contractor-operated laboratory describing the purpose and scope of a proposed cooperative research and development agreement, and assigning rights and responsibilities among the agency, the laboratory, and any other party or parties to the proposed agreement.

(e) *Determination of laboratory missions.*—

For purposes of this section, an agency shall make separate determinations of the mission or missions of each of its laboratories.

(f) *Relationship to other laws.*—

Nothing in this section is intended to limit or diminish existing authorities of any agency.

15 U.S.C. § 3710a

(g) *Principles.*—In implementing this section, each agency which has contracted with a non-Federal entity to operate a laboratory shall be guided by the following principles:

(1) The implementation shall advance program missions at the laboratory, including any national security mission.

(2) Classified information and unclassified sensitive information protected by law, regulation, or Executive order shall be appropriately safeguarded.

(Oct. 21, 1980, Pub. L. 96-480, §12, as added Oct. 20, 1986, Pub. L. 99-502, §§2, 9, 100 Stat. 1785, 1797; Aug. 23, 1988, Pub. L. 100-418, §5122, 102 Stat. 1438; Oct. 24, 1980, Pub. L. 100-519, §301, 102 Stat. 2597; Nov. 29, 1989, Pub. L. 101-189, §3133, 103 Stat. 1675; April 6, 1991, Pub. L. 102-25, §705, 105 Stat. 121; Feb. 14, 1992, Pub. L. 102-245, §302, 106 Stat. 20; Oct. 23, 1992, Pub. L. 102-484, §3135, 106 Stat. 2640-41; Mar. 7, 1996, Pub. L. 104-113, §4, 110 Stat. 775; Oct. 30, 2000, Pub. L. 106-398, §3196, 114 Stat. 1654A-481-2; Nov. 1, 2000, Pub. L. 106-404, §3, 114 Stat. 1742.)

§ 3710b   Rewards for scientific, engineering, and technical personnel of Federal agencies

The head of each Federal agency that is making expenditures at a rate of more than $50,000,000 per fiscal year for research and development in its Government-operated laboratories shall use the appropriate statutory authority to develop and implement a cash awards program to reward its scientific, engineering, and technical personnel for—

(1) inventions, innovations, computer software, or other outstanding scientific or technological contributions of value to the United States due to commercial application or due to contributions to missions of the Federal agency or the Federal government or

(2) exemplary activities that promote the domestic transfer of science and technology development within the Federal Government and result in utilization of such science and technology by American industry or business, universities, State or local governments, or other non-Federal parties.

(Oct. 21, 1980, Pub. L. 96-480, §13, as added Oct. 20, 1986, Pub. L. 99-502, §§6, 9, 100 Stat. 1792, 1797; Aug. 23, 1988, Pub. L. 100-418, §5122, 102 Stat. 1438; Oct. 24, 1988, Pub. L. 100-519, §302, 102 Stat. 2597.)

15 U.S.C. § 3710b

§ 3710c   Distribution of royalties received by Federal agencies

(a) *In general.*—

(1) Except as provided in paragraphs (2) and (4), any royalties or other payments received by a Federal agency from the licensing and assignment of inventions under agreements entered into by Federal laboratories under section 12, and from the licensing of inventions of Federal laboratories under section 207 of title 35, United States Code, or under any other provision of law, shall be retained by the laboratory which produced the invention and shall be disposed of as follows:

(A) (i) The head of the agency or laboratory, or such individual's designee, shall pay each year the first $2,000, and thereafter at least 15 percent, of the royalties or other payments, other than payments of patent costs as delineated by a license or assignment agreement, to the inventor or coinventors, if the inventor's or coinventor's rights are assigned to the United States.

(ii) An agency or laboratory may provide appropriate incentives, from royalties, or other payments, to laboratory employees who are not an inventor of such inventions but who substantially increased the technical value of such inventions.

(iii) The agency or laboratory shall retain the royalties and other payments received from an invention until the agency or laboratory makes payments to employees of a laboratory under clause (i) or (ii).

(B) The balance of the royalties or other payments shall be transferred by the agency to its laboratories, with the majority share of the royalties or other payments from any invention going to the laboratory where the invention occurred. The royalties or other payments so transferred to any laboratory may be used or obligated by that laboratory during the fiscal year in which they are received or during the 2 succeeding fiscal years—

(i) to reward scientific, engineering, and technical employees of the laboratory, including developers of sensitive or classified technology, regardless of whether the technology has commercial applications;

(ii) to further scientific exchange among the laboratories of the agency;

(iii) for education and training of employees consistent with the research and development missions and objectives of the agency or laboratory, and for other activities that increase the potential for transfer of the technology of the laboratories of the agency;

(iv) for payment of expenses incidental to the administration and licensing of intellectual property by the agency or laboratory with respect to inventions made at that laboratory, including the fees or other costs for the services of other agencies, persons, or organizations for intellectual property management and licensing services; or

(v) for scientific research and development consistent with the research and development missions and objectives of the laboratory.

(C) All royalties or other payments retained by the agency or laboratory after payments have been made pursuant to subparagraphs (A) and (B) that is unobligated and unexpended at the end of the second fiscal year succeeding the fiscal year in which the royalties and other payments were received shall be paid into the Treasury.

(2) If, after payments to inventors under paragraph (1), the royalties or other payments received by an agency in any fiscal year exceed 5 percent of the budget of the agency for that year, 75 percent of such excess shall be paid to the Treasury of the United States and the remaining 25 percent may be used or obligated under paragraph (1)(B). Any funds not so used or obligated shall be paid into the Treasury of the United States.

(3) Any payment made to an employee under this section shall be in addition to the regular pay of the employee and to any other awards made to the employee, and shall not affect the entitlement of the employee to any regular pay, annuity, or award to which he is otherwise entitled or for which he is otherwise eligible or limit the amount thereof. Any payment made to an inventor as such shall continue after the inventor leaves the laboratory or agency. Pay-

ments made under this section shall not exceed $150,000 per year to any one person, unless the President approves a larger award (with the excess over $150,000 being treated as a Presidential award under section 4504 of title 5, United States Code).

(4) A Federal agency receiving royalties or other payments as a result of invention management services performed for another Federal agency or laboratory under section 207 of title 35, United States Code, may retain such royalties or payments to the extent required to offset payments to inventors under clause (i) of paragraph (1)(A), costs and expenses incurred under clause (iv) of paragraph (1)(B), and the cost of foreign patenting and maintenance for any invention of the other agency. All royalties and other payments remaining after offsetting the payments to inventors, costs, and expenses described in the preceding sentence shall be transferred to the agency for which the services were performed, for distribution in accordance with paragraph (1)(B).

(b) *Certain assignments.*—If the invention involved was one assigned to the Federal agency—

(1) by a contractor, grantee, or participant, or an employee of a contractor, grantee, or participant, in an agreement or other arrangement with the agency, or

(2) by an employee of the agency who was not working in the laboratory at the time the invention was made,

the agency unit that was involved in such assignment shall be considered to be a laboratory for purposes of this section.

(c) *Reports.*— The Comptroller General shall transmit a report to the appropriate committees of the Senate and House of Representatives on the effectiveness of Federal technology transfer programs, including findings, conclusions, and recommendations for improvements in such programs. The report shall be integrated with, and submitted at the same time as, the report required by section 202(b)(3) of title 35, United States Code.

(Oct. 21, 1980, Pub. L. 96-480, §14, as added Oct. 20, 1986, Pub. L. 99-502, §§7, 9, 100 Stat. 1792, 1797; Aug. 23, 1988, Pub. L. 100-418, §§5122, 5162, 102 Stat. 1438, 1450; Oct. 24, 1988, Pub. L. 100-519, §303, 102 Stat. 2597; Nov. 29, 1989, Pub. L. 101-189, §3133, 103 Stat. 1677; Mar. 7, 1996, Pub. L. 104-113, §5, 110 Stat. 777; Nov. 1, 2000, Pub. L. 106-404, §§7, 10, 114 Stat. 1745, 1747.)

15 U.S.C. § 3710c

§ 3710d   Employee activities

(a) *In general.*—If a Federal agency which has ownership of or the right of ownership to an invention made by a Federal employee does not intend to file for a patent application or otherwise to promote commercialization of such invention, the agency shall allow the inventor, if the inventor is a Government employee or former employee who made the invention during the course of employment with the Government, to obtain or retain title to the invention (subject to reservation by the Government of a nonexclusive, nontransferrable, irrevocable, paid-up license to practice the invention or have the invention practiced throughout the world by or on behalf of the Government). In addition, the agency may condition the inventor's right to title on the timely filing of a patent application in cases when the Government determines that it has or may have a need to practice the invention.

(b) *"Special Government employees" defined.*—For purposes of this section, Federal employees include "special Government employees" as defined in section 202 of title 18, United States Code.

(c) *Relationship to other laws.*—Nothing in this section is intended to limit or diminish existing authorities of any agency.

(Oct. 21, 1980, Pub. L. 96-480, §15, as added Oct. 20, 1986, Pub. L. 99-502, §§8, 9, 100 Stat. 1794, 1797; Aug. 23, 1988, Pub. L. 100-418, §5122, 102 Stat. 1438; Mar. 7, 1996, Pub. L. 104-113, §6, 110 Stat. 779.)

§ 3711   National Technology Medal

(a) *Establishment.*—There is hereby established a National Technology Medal, which shall be of such design and materials and bear such inscriptions as the President, on the basis of recommendations submitted by the Office of Science and Technology Policy, may prescribe.

(b) *Award.*—The President shall periodically award the medal, on the basis of recommendations received from the Secretary or on the basis of such other information and evidence as he deems appropriate, to individuals or companies, which in his judgment are deserving of special recognition by reason of their outstanding contributions to the promotion of technology or technological manpower for the improvement of the economic, environmental, or social well-being of the United States.

(c) *Presentation.*—The presentation of the award shall be made by the President with such ceremonies as he may deem proper.

(Oct. 21, 1980, Pub. L. 96-480, §16, 94 Stat. 2319; Oct. 20, 1986, Pub. L. 99-502, §§2, 9, 100 Stat. 1785, 1797; Aug. 23, 1988, Pub. L. 100-418, §5122, 102 Stat. 1438.)

§ 3711a   Malcolm Baldrige National Quality Award

(a) *Establishment.*—There is hereby established the Malcolm Baldrige National Quality Award, which shall be evidenced by a medal bearing the inscriptions "Malcolm Baldrige National Quality Award" and "The Quest for Excellence". The medal shall be of such design and materials and bear such additional inscriptions as the Secretary may prescribe.

(b) *Making and presentation of award.*—

(1) The President (on the basis of recommendations received from the Secretary), or the Secretary, shall periodically make the award to companies and other organizations which in the judgment of the President or the Secretary have substantially benefited the economic or social well-being of the United States through improvements in the quality of their goods or services resulting from the effective practice of quality management, and which as a consequence are deserving of special recognition.

(2) The presentation of the award shall be made by the President or the Secretary with such ceremonies as the President or the Secretary may deem proper.

(3) An organization to which an award is made under this section, and which agrees to help other American organizations improve their quality management, may publicize its receipt of such award and use the award in its advertising, but it shall be ineligible to receive another such award in the same category for a period of 5 years.

(c) *Categories in which award may be given.*—

(1) Subject to paragraph (2), separate awards shall be made to qualifying organizations in each of the following categories—

(A) Small businesses.

(B) Companies or their subsidiaries.

(C) Companies which primarily provide services.

(D) Health care providers.

(E) Education providers.

(2) The Secretary may at any time expand, subdivide, or otherwise modify the list of categories within which awards may be made as initially in effect under paragraph (1), and may establish separate awards for other organizations including units of government, upon a determination that the objectives of this section would be better served thereby; except that any such expansion, subdivision, modification, or establishment shall not be effective unless and until the Secretary has submitted a detailed description thereof to the Congress and a period of 30 days has elapsed since that submission.

(3) Not more than two awards may be made within any subcategory in any year, unless the Secretary determines that a third award is merited and can be given at no additional cost to the Federal Government (and no award shall be made within any category or subcategory if there are no qualifying enterprises in that category or subcategory).

(d) *Criteria for qualification.—*

(1) An organization may qualify for an award under this section only if it—

(A) applies to the Director of the National Institute of Standards and Technology in writing, for the award,

(B) permits a rigorous evaluation of the way in which its business and other operations have contributed to improvements in the quality of goods and services, and

(C) meets such requirements and specifications as the Secretary, after receiving recommendations from the Board of Overseers established under paragraph (2)(B) and the Director of the National Institute of Standards and Technology determines to be appropriate to achieve the objectives of this section.

In applying the provisions of subparagraph (C) with respect to any organization, the Director of the National Institute of Standards and Technology shall rely upon an intensive evaluation by a competent board of examiners which shall review the evidence submitted by the organization and, through a site visit, verify the accuracy of the quality improvements claimed. The examination should encompass all aspects of the organization's current practice of quality management, as well as the organization's provision for quality management in its future goals. The award shall be given only to organizations which have made outstanding improvements in the quality of their goods or services (or both) and which demonstrate effective quality management through the training and involvement of all levels of personnel in quality improvement.

(2) (A) The Director of the National Institute of Standards and Technology shall, under appropriate contractual arrangements, carry out the Director's responsibilities under subparagraphs (A) and (B) of paragraph (1) through one or more broad-based nonprofit entities which are leaders in the field of quality management and which have a history of service to society.

(B) The Secretary shall appoint a board of overseers for the award, consisting of at least five persons selected for their pre-eminence in the field of quality management. This board shall meet annually to review the work of the contractor or contractors and make such suggestions for the improvement of the award process as they deem necessary. The board shall report the results of the award activities to the Director of the National Institute of Standards and Technology each year, along with its recommendations for improvement of the process.

(e) *Information and technology transfer program.*—The Director of the National Institute of Standards and Technology shall ensure that all program participants receive the complete results of their audits as well as detailed explanations of all suggestions for improvements. The Director shall also provide information about the awards and the successful quality improvement strategies and programs of the award-winning participants to all participants and other appropriate groups.

(f) *Funding.*—The Secretary is authorized to seek and accept gifts from public and private sources to carry out the program under this section. If additional sums are needed to cover the full cost of the program, the Secretary shall impose fees upon the organizations applying for the award in amounts sufficient to provide such additional sums. The Director is authorized to use appropriated funds to carry out responsibilities under this Act.

(g) *Report.*—The Secretary shall prepare and submit to the President and the Congress, within 3 years after the date of the enactment of this section, a report on the progress, findings, and conclusions of activities conducted pursuant to this section along with recommendations for possible modifications thereof.

(Oct. 21, 1980, Pub. L. 96-480, §17, as added Aug. 20, 1987, Pub. L. 100-107, §3, 101 Stat. 725; Aug. 23, 1988, Pub. L. 100-418, §§5115, 5122, 102 Stat. 1433, 1438; Feb. 14, 1992, Pub. L. 102-245, §305, 106 Stat. 20; Oct. 30, 1998, Pub. L. 105-309, §3, 112 Stat. 2935.)

§ 3711b Conference on advanced automotive technologies

Not later than 180 days after the date of the enactment of this section, the Secretary of Commerce, through the Under Secretary of Commerce for Technology, in consultation with other appropriate officials, shall convene a conference of domestic motor vehicle manufacturers, parts suppliers, Federal laboratories, and motor vehicle users to explore ways in which cooperatively they can improve the competitiveness of the United States motor vehicle industry by developing new technologies which will enhance the safety and energy savings, and lessen the environmental impact of domestic motor vehicles, and the results of such conference shall be published and then submitted to the President and to the Committees on Science, Space, and Technology and Public Works and Transportation of the House of Representatives and the Committee on Commerce, Science, and Transportation of the Senate.

(Oct. 21, 1980, Pub. L. 96-480, §18, as added Dec. 18, 1991, Pub. L. 102-240, §6019, 105 Stat. 2183.)

§ 3711c Advanced motor vehicle research award

(a) *Establishment.*—There is established a National Award for the Advancement of Motor Vehicle Research and Development. The award shall consist of a medal, and a cash prize if funding is available for the prize under subsection (c). The medal shall be of such design and materials and bear inscriptions as is determined by the Secretary of Transportation.

(b) *Making and presenting award.*—The Secretary of Transportation shall periodically make and present the award to domestic motor vehicle manufacturers, suppliers, or Federal laboratory personnel who, in the opinion of the Secretary of Transportation, have substantially improved domestic motor vehicle research and development in safety, energy savings, or environmental impact. No person may receive the award more than once every 5 years.

15 U.S.C. § 3711c

(c) *Funding for award.*—The Secretary of Transportation may seek and accept gifts of money from private sources for the purpose of making cash prize awards under this section. Such money may be used only for that purpose, and only such money may be used for that purpose.

(Added Dec. 18, 1991, Pub. L. 102-240, §6019, 105 Stat. 2183–84.)

(Oct. 21, 1980, Pub. L. 96-480, §19, as added Dec. 18, 1991, Pub. L. 102-240, §6019, 105 Stat. 2183.)

§ 3712   Personnel exchanges

The Secretary and the National Science Foundation, jointly, shall establish a program to foster the exchange of scientific and technical personnel among academia, industry, and Federal laboratories. Such program shall include both (1) federally supported exchanges and (2) efforts to stimulate exchanges without Federal funding.

(Oct. 21, 1980, Pub. L. 96-480, §20, 94 Stat. 2319; Oct. 20, 1986, Pub. L. 99-502, §§2, 9, 100 Stat. 1785, 1797; Aug. 20, 1987, Pub. L. 100-107, §3, 101 Stat. 725; Aug. 23, 1988, Pub. L. 100-418, §5122, 102 Stat. 1438; Dec. 18, 1991, Pub. L. 102-240, §6019, 105 Stat. 2183.)

§ 3713   Authorization of appropriations

(a) (1) There is authorized to be appropriated to the Secretary for the purposes of carrying out sections 5, 11(g), and 16 of this Act [§§3704, 3710(g), and 3711] not to exceed $3,400,000 for the fiscal year ending September 30, 1988.

(2) Of the amount authorized under paragraph (1) of this subsection, $2,400,000 is authorized only for the Office of Productivity, Technology, and Innovation; $500,000 is authorized only for the purpose of carrying out the requirements of the Japanese technical literature program established under section 5(d) of this Act [§3704(d)]; and $500,000 is authorized only for the patent licensing activities of the National Technical Information Service.

(b) In addition to the authorization of appropriations provided under subsection (a) of this section, there is authorized to be appropriated to the Secretary for the purposes of carrying out section 6 of this Act [§3704a] not to exceed $500,000 for the fiscal year ending September 30, 1988, $1,000,000 for the fiscal year ending September 30, 1989, and $1,500,000 for the fiscal year ending September 30, 1990.

(c) Such sums as may be appropriated under subsections (a) and (b) shall remain available until expended.

(d) To enable the National Science Foundation to carry out its powers and duties under this Act only such sums may be appropriated as the Congress may authorize by law.

(Oct. 21, 1980, Pub. L. 96-480, §21, 94 Stat. 2319; Oct. 20, 1986, Pub. L. 99-502, §§2, 9, 100 Stat. 1785, 1797; Aug. 20, 1987, Pub. L. 100-107, §3, 101 Stat. 725; Aug. 23, 1988, Pub. L. 100-418, §§5122, 5152, 102 Stat. 1438, 1449; Dec. 18, 1991, Pub. L. 102-240, §6019, 105 Stat. 2183.)

§ 3714   Spending authority

No payments shall be made or contracts shall be entered into pursuant to the provisions of this Act (other than sections 12, 13, and 14) except to such extent or in such amounts as are provided in advance in appropriation Acts.

(Oct. 21, 1980, Pub. L. 96-480, §22, 94 Stat. 2319; Oct. 20, 1986, Pub. L. 99-502, §§2, 9, 100 Stat. 1785, 1796-97; Aug. 20, 1987, Pub. L. 100-107, §3, 101 Stat. 725; Aug. 23, 1988, Pub. L. 100-418, §5122, 102 Stat. 1438; Dec. 18, 1991, Pub. L. 102-240, §6019, 105 Stat. 2183; Nov. 1, 2000, Pub. L. 106-404, §7, 114 Stat. 1745.)

§ 3715   Use of partnership intermediaries

(a) *Authority.*—Subject to the approval of the Secretary or head of the affected department or agency, the Director of a Federal laboratory, or in the case of a federally funded research and development center that is not a laboratory (as defined in section 12(d)(2) [§3710a(d)(2)]), the Federal employee who is the contract officer, may—

(1) enter into a contract or memorandum of understanding with a partnership intermediary that provides for the partnership intermediary to perform services for the Federal laboratory that increase the likelihood of success in the conduct of cooperative or joint activities of such Federal laboratory with small business firms, institutions of higher education as defined in section 1201(a) of the Higher Education Act of 1965 (20 U.S.C. 1141(a)), or educational institutions within the meaning of section 2194 of title 10, United States Code; and

(2) pay the Federal costs of such contract or memorandum of understanding out of funds available for the support of the technology transfer function pursuant to section 11(b) of this Act [§3710(b)].

15 U.S.C. § 3715

(b) *Partnership progress reports.*—The Secretary shall include in each triennial report required under section 6(d) [§3704a(d)] of this Act a discussion and evaluation of the activities carried out pursuant to this section during the period covered by the report.

(c) *Definition.*—For purposes of this section, the term "partnership intermediary" means an agency of a State or local government, or a nonprofit entity owned in whole or in part by, chartered by, funded in whole or in part by, or operated in whole or in part by or on behalf of a State or local government, that assists, counsels, advises, evaluates, or otherwise cooperates with small business firms, institutions of higher education as defined in section 1201(a) of the Higher Education Act of 1965 (20 U.S.C. 1141(a)), or educational institutions within the meaning of section 2194 of title 10, United States Code, that need or can make demonstrably productive use of technology-related assistance from a Federal laboratory, including State programs receiving funds under cooperative agreements entered into under section 5121(b) of the Omnibus Trade and Competitiveness Act of 1988 (15 U.S.C. 2781 note).

(Oct. 21, 1980, Pub. L. 96-480, §23, as added Nov. 5, 1990, Pub. L. 101-510, §827, 104 Stat. 1606; Dec. 5, 1991, Pub. L. 102-190, §836, 105 Stat. 1448; Dec. 18, 1991, Pub. L. 102-240, §6019, 105 Stat. 2183; Nov. 1, 2000, Pub. L. 106-404, §9, 114 Stat. 1747.)

§ 3716   Critical industries

(a) *Identification of industries and development of plan.*—The Secretary shall—

(1) identify those civilian industries in the United States that are necessary to support a robust manufacturing infrastructure and critical to the economic security of the United States; and

(2) list the major research and development initiatives being undertaken, and the substantial investments being made, by the Federal Government, including its research laboratories, in each of the critical industries identified under paragraph (1).

(b) *Initial report.*—The Secretary shall submit a report to the Congress within 1 year after February 14, 1992, on the actions taken under subsection (a) of this section.

(c) *Annual updates.*—The Secretary shall annually submit to the Congress an update of the report submitted under subsection (b) of this section. Each such update shall—

(1) describe the status of each identified critical industry, including the advances and declines occurring since the most recent report; and

(2) identify any industries that should be added to the list of critical industries.

(Feb. 14, 1992, Pub. L. 102-245, §504, 106 Stat. 24.)

§ 3717   National Quality Council

(a) *Establishment and functions.*—There is established a National Quality Council (hereafter in this section referred to as the "Council"). The functions of the Council shall be—

(1) to establish national goals and priorities for Quality performance in business, education, government, and all other sectors of the Nation;

(2) to encourage and support the voluntary adoption of these goals and priorities by companies, unions, professional and business associations, coalition groups, and units of government, as well as private and nonprofit organizations;

(3) to arouse and maintain the interest of the people of the United States in Quality performance, and to encourage the adoption and institution of Quality performance methods by all corporations, government agencies, and other organizations; and

(4) to conduct a White House Conference on Quality Performance in the American Workplace that would bring together in a single forum national leaders in business, labor, education, professional societies, the media, government, and politics to address Quality performance as a means of improving United States competitiveness.

(b) *Membership.*—The Council shall consist of not less than 17 or more than 20 members, appointed by the Secretary. Members shall include—

(1) at least 2 but not more than 3 representatives from manufacturing industry;

(2) at least 2 but not more than 3 representatives from service industry;

(3) at least 2 but not more than 3 representatives from national Quality not-for-profit organizations;

(4) two representatives from education, one with expertise in elementary and secondary education, and one with expertise in post-secondary education;

(5) one representative from labor;

(6) one representative from professional societies;

(7) one representative from local and State government;

(8) one representative from the Federal Quality Institute;

(9) one representative from the National Institute of Standards and Technology;

(10) one representative from the Department of Defense;

(11) one representative from a civilian Federal agency not otherwise represented on the Council, to be rotated among such agencies every 2 years; and

(12) one representative from the Foundation for the Malcolm Baldrige National Quality Award.

(c) *Terms.*—The term of office of each member of the Council appointed under paragraphs (1) through (7) of subsection (b) of this section shall be 2 years, except that when making the initial appointments under such paragraphs; the Secretary shall appoint not more than 50 percent of the members to 1 year terms. No member appointed under such paragraphs shall serve on the Council for more than 2 consecutive terms.

(d) *Chairman and Vice Chairman.*—The Secretary shall designate one of the members initially appointed to the Council as Chairman. Thereafter, the members of the Council shall annually elect one of their number as Chairman. The members of the Council shall also annually elect one of their members as Vice Chairman. No individual shall serve as Chairman or Vice Chairman for more than 2 consecutive years.

(e) *Executive Director and employees.*—The Council shall appoint and fix the compensation of an Executive Director, who shall hire and fix the compensation of such additional employees as may be necessary to assist the Council in carrying out its functions. In hiring such additional employees, the Executive Director shall ensure than no individual hired has a conflict of interest with the responsibilities of the Council.

(f) *Funding.*—There is established in the Treasury of the United States a National Quality Performance Trust Fund, into which all funds received by the Council, through private donations or otherwise, shall be deposited. Amounts in such Trust Fund shall be available to the Council, to the extent provided in advance in appropriations Acts, for the purpose of carrying out the functions of the Council under this Act.

(g) *Contributions.*—The Council may not accept private donations from a single source in excess of $25,000 per year. Private donations from a single source in excess of $10,000 per year may be accepted by the Council only on approval of two-thirds of the Council.

(h) *Annual report.*—The Council shall annually submit to the President and the Congress a comprehensive and detailed report on—

(1) the progress in meeting the goals and priorities established by the Council;

(2) the Council's operations, activities, and financial condition;

(3) contributions to the Council from non-Federal sources;

(4) plans for the Council's operations and activities for the future; and

(5) any other information or recommendations the Council considers appropriate.

(Feb. 14, 1992, Pub. L. 102-245, §507, 106 Stat. 27.)

15 U.S.C. § 3717

Part 4

COPYRIGHTS

UNITED STATES CODE

TITLE 17—COPYRIGHTS

UNITED STATES CODE

TITLE 17—COPYRIGHTS

CHAPTER 1—SUBJECT MATTER AND SCOPE OF COPYRIGHT

§ 101   Definitions

As used in this title, the following terms and their variant forms mean the following:

An "anonymous work" is a work on the copies or phonorecords of which no natural person is identified as author.

An "architectural work" is the design of a building as embodied in any tangible medium of expression, including a building, architectural plans, or drawings. The work includes the overall form as well as the arrangement and composition of spaces and elements in the design, but does not include individual standard features.

"Audiovisual works" are works that consist of a series of related images which are intrinsically intended to be shown by the use of machines or devices such as projectors, viewers, or electronic equipment, together with accompanying sounds, if any, regardless of the nature of the material objects, such as films or tapes, in which the works are embodied.

The "Berne Convention" is the Convention for the Protection of Literary and Artistic Works, signed at Berne, Switzerland, on September 9, 1886, and all acts, protocols, and revisions thereto.

The "best edition" of a work is the edition, published in the United States at any time before the date of deposit, that the Library of Congress determines to be most suitable for its purposes.

A person's "children" are that person's immediate offspring, whether legitimate or not, and any children legally adopted by that person.

A "collective work" is a work, such as a periodical issue, anthology, or encyclopedia, in which a number of contributions, constituting separate and independent works in themselves, are assembled into a collective whole.

A "compilation" is a work formed by the collection and assembling of preexisting materials or of data that are selected, coordinated, or arranged in such a way that the resulting work as a whole constitutes an original work of authorship. The term "compilation" includes collective works.

A "computer program" is a set of statements or instructions to be used directly or indirectly in a computer in order to bring about a certain result.

"Copies" are material objects, other than phonorecords, in which a work is fixed by any method now known or later developed, and from which the work can be perceived, reproduced, or otherwise communicated, either directly or with the aid of a machine or device. The term "copies" includes the material object, other than a phonorecord, in which the work is first fixed.

"Copyright owner", with respect to any one of the exclusive rights comprised in a copyright, refers to the owner of that particular right.

A work is "created" when it is fixed in a copy or phonorecord for the first time; where a work is prepared over a period of time, the portion of it that has been fixed at any particular time constitutes the work as of that time, and where the work has been prepared in different versions, each version constitutes a separate work.

A "derivative work" is a work based upon one or more preexisting works, such as a translation, musical arrangement, dramatization, fictionalization, motion picture version, sound recording, art reproduction, abridgment, condensation, or any other form in which a work may be recast, transformed, or adapted. A work consisting of editorial revisions, annotations, elaborations, or other modifications which, as a whole, represent an original work of authorship, is a "derivative work".

A "device", "machine", or "process" is one now known or later developed.

A "digital transmission" is a transmission in whole or in part in a digital or other non-analog format.

To "display" a work means to show a copy of it, either directly or by means of a film, slide, television image, or any other device or process or, in the case of a motion picture or other audiovisual work, to show individual images nonsequentially.

An "establishment" is a store, shop, or any similar place of business open to the general public for the primary purpose of selling goods or services in which the majority of the gross square feet of space that is

17 U.S.C. § 101

nonresidential is used for that purpose, and in which nondramatic musical works are performed publicly.

A "food service or drinking establishment" is a restaurant, inn, bar, tavern, or any other similar place of business in which the public or patrons assemble for the primary purpose of being served food or drink, in which the majority of the gross square feet of space that is nonresidential is used for that purpose, and in which nondramatic musical works are performed publicly.

The term "financial gain" includes receipt, or expectation of receipt, of anything of value, including the receipt of other copyrighted works.

A work is "fixed" in a tangible medium of expression when its embodiment in a copy or phonorecord, by or under the authority of the author, is sufficiently permanent or stable to permit it to be perceived, reproduced, or otherwise communicated for a period of more than transitory duration. A work consisting of sounds, images, or both, that are being transmitted, is "fixed" for purposes of this title if a fixation of the work is being made simultaneously with its transmission.

The "Geneva Phonograms Convention" is the Convention for the Protection of Producers of Phonograms Against Unauthorized Duplication of Their Phonograms, concluded at Geneva, Switzerland, on October 29, 1971.

The "gross square feet of space" of an establishment means the entire interior space of that establishment, and any adjoining outdoor space used to serve patrons, whether on a seasonal basis or otherwise.

The terms "including" and "such as" are illustrative and not limitative.

An "international agreement" is—

(1) the Universal Copyright Convention;

(2) the Geneva Phonograms Convention;

(3) the Berne Convention;

(4) the WTO Agreement;

(5) the WIPO Copyright Treaty;

(6) the WIPO Performances and Phonograms Treaty; and

(7) any other copyright treaty to which the United States is a party.

17 U.S.C. § 101

A "joint work" is a work prepared by two or more authors with the intention that their contributions be merged into inseparable or interdependent parts of a unitary whole.

"Literary works" are works, other than audiovisual works, expressed in words, numbers, or other verbal or numerical symbols or indicia, regardless of the nature of the material objects, such as books, periodicals, manuscripts, phonorecords, film, tapes, disks, or cards, in which they are embodied.

"Motion pictures" are audiovisual works consisting of a series of related images which, when shown in succession, impart an impression of motion, together with accompanying sounds, if any.

To "perform" a work means to recite, render, play, dance, or act it, either directly or by means of any device or process or, in the case of a motion picture or other audiovisual work, to show its images in any sequence or to make the sounds accompanying it audible.

A "performing rights society" is an association, corporation, or other entity that licenses the public performance of nondramatic musical works on behalf of copyright owners of such works, such as the American Society of Composers, Authors and Publishers (ASCAP), Broadcast Music, Inc. (BMI), and SESAC, Inc.

"Phonorecords" are material objects in which sounds, other than those accompanying a motion picture or other audiovisual work, are fixed by any method now known or later developed, and from which the sounds can be perceived, reproduced, or otherwise communicated, either directly or with the aid of a machine or device. The term "phonorecords" includes the material object in which the sounds are first fixed.

"Pictorial, graphic, and sculptural works" include two-dimensional and three-dimensional works of fine, graphic, and applied art, photographs, prints and art reproductions, maps, globes, charts, diagrams, models, and technical drawings, including architectural plans. Such works shall include works of artistic craftsmanship insofar as their form but not their mechanical or utilitarian aspects are concerned; the design of a useful article, as defined in this section, shall be considered a pictorial, graphic, or sculptural work only if, and only to the extent that, such design incorporates pictorial, graphic, or sculptural features that can be

17 U.S.C. § 101

identified separately from, and are capable of existing independently of, the utilitarian aspects of the article.

For purposes of section 513, a "proprietor" is an individual, corporation, partnership, or other entity, as the case may be, that owns an establishment or a food service or drinking establishment, except that no owner or operator of a radio or television station licensed by the Federal Communications Commission, cable system or satellite carrier, cable or satellite carrier service or programmer, provider of online services or network access or the operator of facilities therefor, telecommunications company, or any other such audio or audiovisual service or programmer now known or as may be developed in the future, commercial subscription music service, or owner or operator of any other transmission service, shall under any circumstances be deemed to be a proprietor.

A "pseudonymous work" is a work on the copies or phonorecords of which the author is identified under a fictitious name.

"Publication" is the distribution of copies or phonorecords of a work to the public by sale or other transfer of ownership, or by rental, lease, or lending. The offering to distribute copies or phonorecords to a group of persons for purposes of further distribution, public performance, or public display, constitutes publication. A public performance or display of a work does not of itself constitute publication.

To perform or display a work "publicly" means—

(1) to perform or display it at a place open to the public or at any place where a substantial number of persons outside of a normal circle of a family and its social acquaintances is gathered; or

(2) to transmit or otherwise communicate a performance or display of the work to a place specified by clause (1) or to the public, by means of any device or process, whether the members of the public capable of receiving the performance or display receive it in the same place or in separate places and at the same time or at different times.

"Registration", for purposes of sections 205(c)(2), 405, 406, 410(d), 411, 412, and 506(e), means a registration of a claim in the original or renewed and extended term of copyright.

"Sound recordings" are works that result from the fixation of a series of musical, spoken, or other sounds, but not including the sounds accompanying a motion picture or other audiovisual work, regardless of the nature of the material objects, such as disks, tapes, or other phonorecords, in which they are embodied.

"State" includes the District of Columbia and the Commonwealth of Puerto Rico, and any territories to which this title is made applicable by an Act of Congress.

A "transfer of copyright ownership" is an assignment, mortgage, exclusive license, or any other conveyance, alienation, or hypothecation of a copyright or of any of the exclusive rights comprised in a copyright, whether or not it is limited in time or place of effect, but not including a nonexclusive license.

A "transmission program" is a body of material that, as an aggregate, has been produced for the sole purpose of transmission to the public in sequence and as a unit.

To "transmit" a performance or display is to communicate it by any device or process whereby images or sounds are received beyond the place from which they are sent.

A "treaty party" is a country or intergovernmental organization other than the United States that is a party to an international agreement.

The "United States", when used in a geographical sense, comprises the several States, the District of Columbia and the Commonwealth of Puerto Rico, and the organized territories under the jurisdiction of the United States Government.

For purposes of section 411, a work is a "United States work" only if—

(1) in the case of a published work, the work is first published—

(A) in the United States;

(B) simultaneously in the United States and another treaty party or parties, whose law grants a term of copyright protection that is the same as or longer than the term provided in the United States;

(C) simultaneously in the United States and a foreign nation that is not a treaty party; or

17 U.S.C. § 101

(D) in a foreign nation that is not a treaty party, and all of the authors of the work are nationals, domiciliaries, or habitual residents of, or in the case of an audiovisual work legal entities with headquarters in, the United States;

(2) in the case of an unpublished work, all the authors of the work are nationals, domiciliaries, or habitual residents of the United States, or, in the case of an unpublished audiovisual work, all the authors are legal entities with headquarters in the United States; or

(3) in the case of a pictorial, graphic, or sculptural work incorporated in a building or structure, the building or structure is located in the United States.

A "useful article" is an article having an intrinsic utilitarian function that is not merely to portray the appearance of the article or to convey information. An article that is normally a part of a useful article is considered a "useful article".

The author's "widow" or "widower" is the author's surviving spouse under the law of the author's domicile at the time of his or her death, whether or not the spouse has later remarried.

The "WIPO Copyright Treaty" is the WIPO Copyright Treaty concluded at Geneva, Switzerland, on December 20, 1996.

The "WIPO Performances and Phonograms Treaty" is the WIPO Performances and Phonograms Treaty concluded at Geneva, Switzerland, on December 20, 1996.

A "work of visual art" is—

(1) a painting, drawing, print, or sculpture, existing in a single copy, in a limited edition of 200 copies or fewer that are signed and consecutively numbered by the author, or, in the case of a sculpture, in multiple cast, carved, or fabricated sculptures of 200 or fewer that are consecutively numbered by the author and bear the signature or other identifying mark of the author; or

(2) a still photographic image produced for exhibition purposes only, existing in a single copy that is signed by the author, or in a limited edition of 200 copies or fewer that are signed and consecutively numbered by the author.

A work of visual art does not include—

17 U.S.C. § 101

(A) (i) any poster, map, globe, chart, technical drawing, diagram, model, applied art, motion picture or other audiovisual work, book, magazine, newspaper, periodical, data base, electronic information service, electronic publication, or similar publication;

(ii) any merchandising item or advertising, promotional, descriptive, covering, or packaging material or container;

(iii) any portion or part of any item described in clause (i) or (ii);

(B) any work made for hire; or

(C) any work not subject to copyright protection under this title.

A "work of the United States Government" is a work prepared by an officer or employee of the United States Government as part of that person's official duties.

A "work made for hire" is—

(1) a work prepared by an employee within the scope of his or her employment; or

(2) a work specially ordered or commissioned for use as a contribution to a collective work, as a part of a motion picture or other audiovisual work, as a translation, as a supplementary work, as a compilation, as an instructional text, as a test, as answer material for a test, or as an atlas, if the parties expressly agree in a written instrument signed by them that the work shall be considered a work made for hire. For the purpose of the foregoing sentence, a "supplementary work" is a work prepared for publication as a secondary adjunct to a work by another author for the purpose of introducing, concluding, illustrating, explaining, revising, commenting upon, or assisting in the use of the other work, such as forewords, afterwords, pictorial illustrations, maps, charts, tables, editorial notes, musical arrangements, answer material for tests, bibliographies, appendixes, and indexes, and an "instructional text" is a literary, pictorial, or graphic work prepared for publication and with the purpose of use in systematic instructional activities.

In determining whether any work is eligible to be considered a work made for hire under paragraph (2), neither the amendment contained in section 1011(d) of the Intellectual Property and Communications Omnibus Reform Act of 1999, as enacted by section 1000(a)(9) of Public Law 106-113, nor the deletion of the words added by that amendment—

(A) shall be considered or otherwise given any legal significance, or

(B) shall be interpreted to indicate congressional approval or disapproval of, or acquiescence in, any judicial determination,

by the courts or the Copyright Office. Paragraph (2) shall be interpreted as if both section 2(a)(1) of the Work Made For Hire and Copyright Corrections Act of 2000 and section 1011(d) of the Intellectual Property and Communications Omnibus Reform Act of 1999, as enacted by section 1000(a)(9) of Public Law 106-113, were never enacted, and without regard to any inaction or awareness by the Congress at any time of any judicial determinations.

The terms "WTO Agreement" and "WTO member country" have the meanings given those terms in paragraphs (9) and (10), respectively, of section 2 of the Uruguay Round Agreements Act.

(Oct. 19, 1976, Pub. L. 94-553, §101, 90 Stat. 2541; Dec. 12, 1980, Pub. L. 96-517, §10, 94 Stat. 3028; Oct. 31, 1988, Pub. L. 100-568, §4, 102 Stat. 2854; Dec. 1, 1990, Pub. L. 101-650, §602 and 702, 104 Stat. 5128, 5133; June 26, 1992, Pub. L. 102-307, §102(b), 106 Stat. 266; Nov. 1. 1995, Pub. L. 104-39, §5(a), 109 Stat. 348; Nov. 13, 1997, Pub. L. 105-80, §12, 111 Stat. 1534; Dec. 16, 1997, Pub. L. 105-147, §2(a), 111 Stat. 2678; Oct. 28, 1998; Pub. L. 105-304; §102(a), 112 Stat. 2861; Aug. 5, 1999, Pub. L. 106-44, §1(g), 113 Stat. 222; Nov. 29, 1999, Pub. L. 106-113, §1011, 113 Stat. 1501A-543; Oct. 27, 2000, Pub. L. 106-379, §2, 114 Stat. 1444; Nov. 2, 2002, Pub. L. 107-273, §13210, 116 Stat. 1909.)

§ 102   Subject matter of copyright: In general

(a) Copyright protection subsists, in accordance with this title, in original works of authorship fixed in any tangible medium of expression, now known or later developed, from which they can be perceived, reproduced, or otherwise communicated, either directly or with the aid of a machine or device. Works of authorship include the following categories:

(1) literary works;

(2) musical works, including any accompanying words;

(3) dramatic works, including any accompanying music;

(4) pantomimes and choreographic works;

(5) pictorial, graphic, and sculptural works;

(6) motion pictures and other audiovisual works;

(7) sound recordings; and

(8) architectural works.

(b) In no case does copyright protection for an original work of authorship extend to any idea, procedure, process, system, method of operation, concept, principle, or discovery, regardless of the form in which it is described, explained, illustrated, or embodied in such work.

(Oct. 19, 1976, Pub. L. 94-553, §101, 90 Stat. 2544; Dec. 1, 1990, Pub. L. 101-650, §703, 104 Stat. 5133.)

§ 103   Subject matter of copyright: Compilations and derivative works

(a) The subject matter of copyright as specified by section 102 includes compilations and derivative works, but protection for a work employing preexisting material in which copyright subsists does not extend to any part of the work in which such material has been used unlawfully.

(b) The copyright in a compilation or derivative work extends only to the material contributed by the author of such work, as distinguished from the preexisting material employed in the work, and does not imply any exclusive right in the preexisting material. The copyright in such work is independent of, and does not affect or enlarge the scope, duration, ownership, or subsistence of, any copyright protection in the preexisting material.

(Oct. 19, 1976, Pub. L. 94-553, §101, 90 Stat. 2545.)

§ 104   Subject matter of copyright: National origin

(a) *Unpublished Works*

The works specified by sections 102 and 103, while unpublished, are subject to protection under this title without regard to the nationality or domicile of the author.

(b) *Published Works*

The works specified by sections 102 and 103, when published, are subject to protection under this title if—

(1) on the date of first publication, one or more of the authors is a national or domiciliary of the United States, or is a national, domiciliary, or sovereign authority of a treaty party, or is a stateless person, wherever that person may be domiciled; or

(2) the work is first published in the United States or in a foreign nation that, on the date of first publication, is a treaty party; or

(3) the work is a sound recording that was first fixed in a treaty party; or

(4) the work is a pictorial, graphic, or sculptural work that is incorporated in a building or other structure, or an architectural work that is embodied in a building and the building or structure is located in the United States or a treaty party; or

(5) the work is first published by the United Nations or any of its specialized agencies, or by the Organization of American States; or

(6) the work comes within the scope of a Presidential proclamation. Whenever the President finds that a particular foreign nation extends, to works by authors who are nationals or domiciliaries of the United States or to works that are first published in the United States, copyright protection on substantially the same basis as that on which the foreign nation extends protection to works of its own nationals and domiciliaries and works first published in that nation, the President may by proclamation extend protection under this title to works of which one or more of the authors is, on the date of first publication, a national, domiciliary, or sovereign authority of that nation, or which was first published in that nation. The President may revise, suspend, or revoke any such proclamation or impose any conditions or limitations on protection under a proclamation.

For purposes of paragraph (2), a work that is published in the United States or a treaty party within 30 days after publication in a foreign nation that is not a treaty party shall be considered to be first published in the United States or such treaty party, as the case may be.

(c) *Effect of Berne Convention.*—No right or interest in a work eligible for protection under this title may be claimed by virtue of, or in reliance upon, the provisions of the Berne Convention, or the adherence of the United States thereto. Any rights in a work eligible for protection under this title that derive from this title, other Federal or State statutes, or the common law, shall not be expanded or reduced by virtue of, or in reliance upon, the provisions of the Berne Convention, or the adherence of the United States thereto.

(d) *Effect of phonograms treaties.*—Notwithstanding the provisions of subsection (b), no works other than sound recordings shall be eligible for protection under this title solely by virtue of the adherence of the United States to the Geneva Phonograms Convention or the WIPO Performances and Phonograms Treaty.

(Oct. 19, 1976, Pub. L. 94-553, §101, 90 Stat. 2545; Oct. 31, 1988, Pub. L. 100-568, §4, 102 Stat. 2855; Oct. 28, 1998, Pub. L. 105-304, §102(b), 112 Stat. 2862.)

§ 104A Copyright in restored works

(a) *Automatic protection and term.—*

> (1) *Term.—*

>> (A) Copyright subsists, in accordance with this section, in restored works, and vests automatically on the date of restoration.

>> (B) Any work in which copyright is restored under this section shall subsist for the remainder of the term of copyright that the work would have otherwise been granted in the United States if the work never entered the public domain in the United States.

> (2) *Exception.*—Any work in which the copyright was ever owned or administered by the Alien Property Custodian and in which the restored copyright would be owned by a government or instrumentality thereof, is not a restored work.

(b) *Ownership of restored copyright.*—A restored work vests initially in the author or initial rightholder of the work as determined by the law of the source country of the work.

(c) *Filing of notice of intent to enforce restored copyright against reliance parties.*—On or after the date of restoration, any person who owns a copyright in a restored work or an exclusive right therein may file with the Copyright Office a notice of intent to enforce that person's copyright or exclusive right or may serve such a notice directly on a reliance party. Acceptance of a notice by the Copyright Office is effective as to any reliance parties but shall not create a presumption of the validity of any of the facts stated therein. Service on a reliance party is effective as to that reliance party and any other reliance parties with actual knowledge of such service and of the contents of that notice.

(d) *Remedies for infringement of restored copyrights.*—

(1) *Enforcement of copyright in restored works in the absence of a reliance party.*—As against any party who is not a reliance party, the remedies provided in chapter 5 of this title shall be available on or after the date of restoration of a restored copyright with respect to an act of infringement of the restored copyright that is commenced on or after the date of restoration.

(2) *Enforcement of copyright in restored works as against reliance parties.*— As against a reliance party, except to the extent provided in paragraphs (3) and (4), the remedies provided in chapter 5 of this title shall be available, with respect to an act of infringement of a restored copyright, on or after the date of restoration of the restored copyright if the requirements of either of the following subparagraphs are met:

(A) (i) The owner of the restored copyright (or such owner's agent) or the owner of an exclusive right therein (or such owner's agent) files with the Copyright Office, during the 24-month period beginning on the date of restoration, a notice of intent to enforce the restored copyright; and

(ii) (I) the act of infringement commenced after the end of the 12-month period beginning on the date of publication of the notice in the Federal Register;

(II) the act of infringement commenced before the end of the 12-month period described in subclause (I) and continued after the end of that 12-month period, in which case remedies shall be available only for infringement occurring after the end of that 12-month period; or

(III) copies or phonorecords of a work in which copyright has been restored under this section are made after publication of the notice of intent in the Federal Register.

(B) (i) The owner of the restored copyright (or such owner's agent) or the owner of an exclusive right therein (or such owner's agent) serves upon a reliance party a notice of intent to enforce a restored copyright; and

(ii) (I) the act of infringement commenced after the end of the 12-month period beginning on the date the notice of intent is received;

(II) the act of infringement commenced before the end of the 12-month period described in subclause (I) and continued after the end of that 12-month period, in which case remedies shall be available only for the infringement occurring after the end of that 12-month period; or

(III) copies or phonorecords of a work in which copyright has been restored under this section are made after receipt of the notice of intent.

In the event that notice is provided under both subparagraphs (A) and (B), the 12-month period referred to in such subparagraphs shall run from the earlier of publication or service of notice.

(3) *Existing derivative works.*—

(A) In the case of a derivative work that is based upon a restored work and is created —

(i) before the date of the enactment of the Uruguay Round Agreements Act, if the source country of the restored work is an eligible country on such date, or work is an eligible country on such date, or

(ii) before the date on which the source country of the restored work becomes an eligible country, if that country is not an eligible country on such date of enactment,

a reliance party may continue to exploit that derivative work for the duration of the restored copyright if the reliance party pays to the owner of the restored copyright reasonable compensation for conduct which would be subject to a remedy for infringement but for the provisions of this paragraph.

(B) In the absence of an agreement between the parties, the amount of such compensation shall be determined by an action in United States district court, and shall reflect any harm to the actual or potential market for or value of the restored work from the reliance party's continued exploitation of the work, as well as compensation for the relative contributions of expression of the author of the restored work and the reliance party to the derivative work.

(4) *Commencement of infringement for reliance parties.*—For purposes of section 412, in the case of reliance parties, infringement shall be deemed to have commenced before registration when acts which would have constituted infringement had the restored work been subject to copyright were commenced before the date of restoration.

(e) *Notices of intent to enforce a restored copyright.*—

(1) *Notices of intent filed with the Copyright Office.*—

(A) (i) A notice of intent filed with the Copyright Office to enforce a restored copyright shall be signed by the owner of the restored copyright or the owner of an exclusive right therein, who files the notice under subsection (d)(2)(A)(i) (hereafter in this paragraph referred to as the "owner"), or by the owner's agent, shall identify the title of the restored work, and shall include an English translation of the title and any other alternative titles known to the owner by which the restored work may be identified, and an address and telephone number at which the owner may be contacted. If the notice is signed by an agent, the agency relationship must have been constituted in a writing signed by the owner before the filing of the notice. The Copyright Office may specifically require in regulations other information to be included in the notice, but failure to provide such other information shall not invalidate the notice or be a basis for refusal to list the restored work in the Federal Register.

(ii) If a work in which copyright is restored has no formal title, it shall be described in the notice of intent in detail sufficient to identify it.

(iii) Minor errors or omissions may be corrected by further notice at any time after the notice of intent is filed. Notices of corrections for such minor errors or omissions shall be accepted after the period established in subsection (d)(2)(A)(i). Notices shall be published in the Federal Register pursuant to subparagraph (B).

(B) (i) The Register of Copyrights shall publish in the Federal Register, commencing not later than 4 months after the date of restoration for a particular nation and every 4 months thereafter for a period of 2 years, lists identifying restored works and the ownership thereof if a notice of intent to enforce a restored copyright has been filed.

(ii) Not less than 1 list containing all notices of intent to enforce shall be maintained in the Public Information Office of the Copyright Office and shall be available for public inspection and copying during regular business hours pursuant to sections 705 and 708.

(C) The Register of Copyrights is authorized to fix reasonable fees based on the costs of receipt, processing, recording, and publication of notices of intent to enforce a restored copyright and corrections thereto.

(D) (i) Not later than 90 days before the date the Agreement on Trade-Related Aspects of Intellectual Property referred to in section 101(d)(15) of the Uruguay Round Agreements Act enters into force with respect to the United States,* the Copyright Office shall issue and publish in the Federal Register regulations governing the filing under this subsection of notices of intent to enforce a restored copyright.

(ii) Such regulations shall permit owners of restored copyrights to file simultaneously for registration of the restored copyright.

(2) *Notices of intent served on a reliance party.—*

(A) Notices of intent to enforce a restored copyright may be served on a reliance party at any time after the date of restoration of the restored copyright.

(B) Notices of intent to enforce a restored copyright served on a reliance party shall be signed by the owner or the owner's agent, shall identify the restored work and the work in which the restored work is used, if any, in detail sufficient to identify them, and shall include an English translation of the title, any other al-

---

* *Ed. Note:* The TRIPs Agreement entered into force with respect to the U.S. on Jan. 1, 1996.

17 U.S.C. § 104A

ternative titles known to the owner by which the work may be identified, the use or uses to which the owner objects, and an address and telephone number at which the reliance party may contact the owner. If the notice is signed by an agent, the agency relationship must have been constituted in writing and signed by the owner before service of the notice.

(3) *Effect of material false statements.*—Any material false statement knowingly made with respect to any restored copyright identified in any notice of intent shall make void all claims and assertions made with respect to such restored copyright.

(f) *Immunity from warranty and related liability.*—

(1) *In general.*—Any person who warrants, promises, or guarantees that a work does not violate an exclusive right granted in section 106 shall not be liable for legal, equitable, arbitral, or administrative relief if the warranty, promise, or guarantee is breached by virtue of the restoration of copyright under this section, if such warranty, promise, or guarantee is made before January 1, 1995.

(2) *Performances.*—No person shall be required to perform any act if such performance is made infringing by virtue of the restoration of copyright under the provisions of this section, if the obligation to perform was undertaken before January 1, 1995.

(g) *Proclamation of copyright restoration.*—Whenever the President finds that a particular foreign nation extends, to works by authors who are nationals or domiciliaries of the United States, restored copyright protection on substantially the same basis as provided under this section, the President may by proclamation extend restored protection provided under this section to any work—

(1) of which one or more of the authors is, on the date of first publication, a national, domiciliary, or sovereign authority of that nation; or

(2) which was first published in that nation. The President may revise, suspend, or revoke any such proclamation or impose any conditions or limitations on protection under such a proclamation.

(h) *Definitions.*—For purposes of this section and section 109(a):

17 U.S.C. § 104A

(1) The term "date of adherence or proclamation" means the earlier of the date on which a foreign nation which, as of the date the WTO Agreement enters into force with respect to the United States, is not a nation adhering to the Berne Convention or a WTO member country, becomes—

(A) a nation adhering to the Berne Convention;

(B) a WTO member country;

(C) a nation adhering to the WIPO Copyright Treaty;

(D) a nation adhering to the WIPO Performances and Phonograms Treaty; or

(E) subject to a Presidential proclamation under subsection (g).

(2) The "date of restoration" of a restored copyright is the later of—

(A) January 1, 1996, if the source country of the restored work is a nation adhering to the Berne Convention or a WTO member country on such date; or

(B) the date of adherence or proclamation, in the case of any other source country of the restored work.

(3) The term "eligible country" means a nation, other than the United States, that —

(A) becomes a WTO member country after the date of the enactment of the Uruguay Round Agreements Act;

(B) on such date of enactment is, or after such date of enactment becomes, a nation adhering to the Berne Convention;

(C) a nation adhering to the WIPO Copyright Treaty;

(D) a nation adhering to the WIPO Performances and Phonograms Treaty; or

(E) after such date of enactment becomes subject to a proclamation under subsection (g).

For purposes of this section, a nation that is a member of the Berne Convention on the date of the enactment of the Uruguay Round Agreements Act shall be construed to become an eligible country on such date of enactment.

17 U.S.C. § 104A

(4) The term "reliance party" means any person who—

(A) with respect to a particular work, engages in acts, before the source country of that work becomes an eligible country, which would have violated section 106 if the restored work had been subject to copyright protection, and who, after the source country becomes an eligible country, continues to engage in such acts;

(B) before the source country of a particular work becomes an eligible country, makes or acquires 1 or more copies or phonorecords of that work; or

(C) as the result of the sale or other disposition of a derivative work covered under subsection (d)(3), or significant assets of a person described in subparagraph (A) or (B), is a successor, assignee, or licensee of that person.

(5) The term "restored copyright" means copyright in a restored work under this section.

(6) The term "restored work" means an original work of authorship that—

(A) is protected under subsection (a);

(B) is not in the public domain in its source country through expiration of term of protection;

(C) is in the public domain in the United States due to—

(i) noncompliance with formalities imposed at any time by United States copyright law, including failure of renewal, lack of proper notice, or failure to comply with any manufacturing requirements;

(ii) lack of subject matter protection in the case of sound recordings fixed before February 15, 1972; or

(iii) lack of national eligibility;

(D) has at least one author or rightholder who was, at the time the work was created, a national or domiciliary of an eligible country, and if published, was first published in an eligible country and not published in the United States during the 30-day period following publication in such eligible country; and

(E) if the source country for the work is an eligible country solely by virtue of its adherence to the WIPO Performances and Phonograms Treaty, is a sound recording.

(7) The term "rightholder" means the person—

(A) who, with respect to a sound recording, first fixes a sound recording with authorization, or

(B) who has acquired rights from the person described in subparagraph (A) by means of any conveyance or by operation of law.

(8) The "source country" of a restored work is—

(A) a nation other than the United States;

(B) in the case of an unpublished work—

(i) the eligible country in which the author or rightholder is a national or domiciliary, or, if a restored work has more than 1 author or rightholder, of which the majority of foreign authors or rightholders are nationals or domiciliaries; or

(ii) if the majority of authors or rightholders are not foreign, the nation other than the United States which has the most significant contacts with the work; and

(C) in the case of a published work—

(i) the eligible country in which the work is first published, or

(ii) if the restored work is published on the same day in 2 or more eligible countries, the eligible country which has the most significant contacts with the work.

(Dec. 8, 1994; Pub. L. 103-465, §514, 108 Stat. 4976; Oct. 11, 1996, Pub. L. 104-295, Title V(2), 110 Stat. 3529; Nov. 13, 1997, Pub. L. 105-80, §2, 111 Stat. 1530-31; Oct. 28, 1998; Pub. L. 105-304; §102(c), 112 Stat. 2862.)

§ 105   Subject matter of copyright: United States Government works

Copyright protection under this title is not available for any work of the United States Government, but the United States Government is not precluded from receiving and holding copyrights transferred to it by assignment, bequest, or otherwise.

(Oct. 19, 1976, Pub. L. 94-553, §101, 90 Stat. 2546.)

§ 106 Exclusive rights in copyrighted works

Subject to sections 107 through 122, the owner of copyright under this title has the exclusive rights to do and to authorize any of the following:

(1) to reproduce the copyrighted work in copies or phonorecords;

(2) to prepare derivative works based upon the copyrighted work;

(3) to distribute copies or phonorecords of the copyrighted work to the public by sale or other transfer of ownership, or by rental, lease, or lending;

(4) in the case of literary, musical, dramatic, and choreographic works, pantomimes, and motion pictures and other audiovisual works, to perform the copyrighted work publicly;

(5) in the case of literary, musical, dramatic, and choreographic works, pantomimes, and pictorial, graphic, or sculptural works, including the individual images of a motion picture or other audiovisual work, to display the copyrighted work publicly; and

(6) in the case of sound recordings, to perform the copyrighted work publicly by means of a digital audio transmission.

(Oct. 19, 1976, Pub. L. 94-553, §101, 90 Stat. 2546; July 3, 1990, Pub. L. 101-318, §3, 104 Stat. 288; Dec. 1, 1990, Pub. L. 101-650, §704, 104 Stat. 5134; Nov. 1, 1995, Pub. L. 104-39, §2, 109 Stat. 336; Aug. 5, 1999, Pub. L. 106-44, §1(g), 113 Stat. 222; Nov. 2, 2002, Pub. L. 107-273, §13210, 116 Stat. 1909.)

§ 106A Rights of certain authors to attribution and integrity

(a) *Rights of attribution and integrity.*—Subject to section 107 and independent of the exclusive rights provided in section 106, the author of a work of visual art—

(1) shall have the right—

(A) to claim authorship of that work, and

(B) to prevent the use of his or her name as the author of any work of visual art which he or she did not create;

(2) shall have the right to prevent the use of his or her name as the author of the work of visual art in the event of a distortion, mutilation, or other modification of the work which would be prejudicial to his or her honor or reputation; and

(3) subject to the limitations set forth in section 113(d), shall have the right—

(A) to prevent any intentional distortion, mutilation, or other modification of that work which would be prejudicial to his or her honor or reputation, and any intentional distortion, mutilation, or modification of that work is a violation of that right, and

(B) to prevent any destruction of a work of recognized stature, and any intentional or grossly negligent destruction of that work is a violation of that right.

(b) *Scope and exercise of rights.*—Only the author of a work of visual art has the rights conferred by subsection (a) in that work, whether or not the author is the copyright owner. The authors of a joint work of visual art are coowners of the rights conferred by subsection (a) in that work.

(c) *Exceptions.*—

(1) The modification of a work of visual art which is a result of the passage of time or the inherent nature of the materials is not a distortion, mutilation, or other modification described in subsection (a)(3)(A).

(2) The modification of a work of visual art which is the result of conservation, or of the public presentation, including lighting and placement, of the work is not a destruction, distortion, mutilation, or other modification described in subsection (a)(3) unless the modification is caused by gross negligence.

(3) The rights described in paragraphs (1) and (2) of subsection (a) shall not apply to any reproduction, depiction, portrayal, or other use of a work in, upon, or in any connection with any item described in subparagraph (A) or (B) of the definition of "work of visual art" in section 101, and any such reproduction, depiction, portrayal, or other use of a work is not a destruction, distortion, mutilation, or other modification described in paragraph (3) of subsection (a).

(d) *Duration of rights.*—

(1) With respect to works of visual art created on or after the effective date set forth in section 610(a) of the Visual Artists Rights Act of 1990, the rights conferred by subsection (a) shall endure for a term consisting of the life of the author.

17 U.S.C. § 106A

(2) With respect to works of visual art created before the effective date set forth in section 610(a) of the Visual Artists Rights Act of 1990, but title to which has not, as of such effective date, been transferred from the author, the rights conferred by subsection (a) shall be coextensive with, and shall expire at the same time as, the rights conferred by section 106.

(3) In the case of a joint work prepared by two or more authors, the rights conferred by subsection (a) shall endure for a term consisting of the life of the last surviving author.

(4) All terms of the rights conferred by subsection (a) run to the end of the calendar year in which they would otherwise expire.

(e) *Transfer and waiver.*—

(1) The rights conferred by subsection (a) may not be transferred, but those rights may be waived if the author expressly agrees to such waiver in a written instrument signed by the author. Such instrument shall specifically identify the work, and uses of that work, to which the waiver applies, and the waiver shall apply only to the work and uses so identified. In the case of a joint work prepared by two or more authors, a waiver of rights under this paragraph made by one such author waives such rights for all such authors.

(2) Ownership of the rights conferred by subsection (a) with respect to a work of visual art is distinct from ownership of any copy of that work, or of a copyright or any exclusive right under a copyright in that work. Transfer of ownership of any copy of a work of visual art, or of a copyright or any exclusive right under a copyright, shall not constitute a waiver of the rights conferred by subsection (a). Except as may otherwise be agreed by the author in a written instrument signed by the author, a waiver of the rights conferred by subsection (a) with respect to a work of visual art shall not constitute a transfer of ownership of any copy of that work, or of ownership of a copyright or of any exclusive right under a copyright in that work.

(Dec. 1, 1990, Pub. L. 101-650, §603, 104 Stat. 5128.)

§ 107   Limitations on exclusive rights: Fair use

Notwithstanding the provisions of sections 106 and 106A, the fair use of a copyrighted work, including such use by reproduction in copies or phonorecords or by any other means specified by that section, for purposes such as criticism, comment, news reporting, teaching (including multiple copies for classroom use), scholarship, or research, is not an infringement of copyright. In determining whether the use made of a work in any particular case is a fair use the factors to be considered shall include—

(1) the purpose and character of the use, including whether such use is of a commercial nature or is for nonprofit educational purposes;

(2) the nature of the copyrighted work;

(3) the amount and substantiality of the portion used in relation to the copyrighted work as a whole; and

(4) the effect of the use upon the potential market for or value of the copyrighted work.

The fact that a work is unpublished shall not itself bar a finding of fair use if such finding is made upon consideration of all the above factors.

(Oct. 19, 1976, Pub. L. 94-533, §101, 90 Stat. 2546; Dec. 1, 1990, Pub. L. 101-650, §607, 104 Stat. 5132; Oct. 24, 1992, Pub. L. 102-492, 106 Stat. 3145.)

§ 108   Limitations on exclusive rights: Reproduction by libraries and archives

(a) Except as otherwise provided in this title and notwithstanding the provisions of section 106, it is not an infringement of copyright for a library or archives, or any of its employees acting within the scope of their employment, to reproduce no more than one copy or phonorecord of a work, except as provided in subsections (b) and (c), or to distribute such copy or phonorecord, under the conditions specified by this section, if—

(1) the reproduction or distribution is made without any purpose of direct or indirect commercial advantage;

(2) the collections of the library or archives are (i) open to the public, or (ii) available not only to researchers affiliated with the library or archives or with the institution of which it is a part, but also to other persons doing research in a specialized field; and

(3) the reproduction or distribution of the work includes a notice of copyright that appears on the copy or phonorecord that is reproduced under the provisions of this section, or includes a legend stat-

ing that the work may be protected by copyright if no such notice can be found on the copy or phonorecord that is reproduced under the provisions of this section.

(b) The rights of reproduction and distribution under this section apply to three copies or phonorecords of an unpublished work duplicated solely for purposes of preservation and security or for deposit for research use in another library or archives of the type described by clause (2) of subsection (a), if—

(1) the copy or phonorecord reproduced is currently in the collections of the library or archives; and

(2) any such copy or phonorecord that is reproduced in digital format is not otherwise distributed in that format and is not made available to the public in that format outside the premises of the library or archives.

(c) The right of reproduction under this section applies to three copies or phonorecords of a published work duplicated solely for the purpose of replacement of a copy or phonorecord that is damaged, deteriorating, lost, or stolen, or if the existing format in which the work is stored has become obsolete, if —

(1) the library or archives has, after a reasonable effort, determined that an unused replacement cannot be obtained at a fair price; and

(2) any such copy or phonorecord that is reproduced in digital format is not made available to the public in that format outside the premises of the library or archives in lawful possession of such copy.

For purposes of this subsection, a format shall be considered obsolete if the machine or device necessary to render perceptible a work stored in that format is no longer manufactured or is no longer reasonably available in the commercial marketplace.

(d) The rights of reproduction and distribution under this section apply to a copy, made from the collection of a library or archives where the user makes his or her request or from that of another library or archives, of no more than one article or other contribution to a copyrighted collection or periodical issue, or to a copy or phonorecord of a small part of any other copyrighted work, if—

(1) the copy or phonorecord becomes the property of the user, and the library or archives has had no notice that the copy or phonorecord would be used for any purpose other than private study, scholarship, or research; and

(2) the library or archives displays prominently, at the place where orders are accepted, and includes on its order form, a warning of copyright in accordance with requirements that the Register of Copyrights shall prescribe by regulation.

(e) The rights of reproduction and distribution under this section apply to the entire work, or to a substantial part of it, made from the collection of a library or archives where the user makes his or her request or from that of another library or archives, if the library or archives has first determined, on the basis of a reasonable investigation, that a copy or phonorecord of the copyrighted work cannot be obtained at a fair price, if—

(1) the copy or phonorecord becomes the property of the user, and the library or archives has had no notice that the copy or phonorecord would be used for any purpose other than private study, scholarship, or research; and

(2) the library or archives displays prominently, at the place where orders are accepted, and includes on its order form, a warning of copyright in accordance with requirements that the Register of Copyrights shall prescribe by regulation.

(f) Nothing in this section—

(1) shall be construed to impose liability for copyright infringement upon a library or archives or its employees for the unsupervised use of reproducing equipment located on its premises: *Provided,* That such equipment displays a notice that the making of a copy may be subject to the copyright law;

(2) excuses a person who uses such reproducing equipment or who requests a copy or phonorecord under subsection (d) from liability for copyright infringement for any such act, or for any later use of such copy or phonorecord, if it exceeds fair use as provided by section 107;

(3) shall be construed to limit the reproduction and distribution by lending of a limited number of copies and excerpts by a library or

archives of an audiovisual news program, subject to clauses (1), (2), and (3) of subsection (a); or

(4) in any way affects the right of fair use as provided by section 107, or any contractual obligations assumed at any time by the library or archives when it obtained a copy or phonorecord of a work in its collections.

(g) The rights of reproduction and distribution under this section extend to the isolated and unrelated reproduction or distribution of a single copy or phonorecord of the same material on separate occasions, but do not extend to cases where the library or archives, or its employee—

(1) is aware or has substantial reason to believe that it is engaging in the related or concerted reproduction or distribution of multiple copies or phonorecords of the same material, whether made on one occasion or over a period of time, and whether intended for aggregate use by one or more individuals or for separate use by the individual members of a group; or

(2) engages in the systematic reproduction or distribution of single or multiple copies or phonorecords of material described in subsection (d): *Provided,* That nothing in this clause prevents a library or archives from participating in interlibrary arrangements that do not have, as their purpose or effect, that the library or archives receiving such copies or phonorecords for distribution does so in such aggregate quantities as to substitute for a subscription to or purchase of such work.

(h)(1) For purposes of this section, during the last 20 years of any term of copyright of a published work, a library or archives, including a nonprofit educational institution that functions as such, may reproduce, distribute, display, or perform in facsimile or digital form a copy or phonorecord of such work, or portions thereof, for purposes of preservation, scholarship, or research, if such library or archives has first determined, on the basis of a reasonable investigation, that none of the conditions set forth in subparagraphs (A), (B), and (C) of paragraph (2) apply.

(2) No reproduction, distribution, display, or performance is authorized under this subsection if—

(A) the work is subject to normal commercial exploitation;

(B) a copy or phonorecord of the work can be obtained at a reasonable price; or

(C) the copyright owner or its agent provides notice pursuant to regulations promulgated by the Register of Copyrights that either of the conditions set forth in subparagraphs (A) and (B) applies.

(3) The exemption provided in this subsection does not apply to any subsequent uses by users other than such library or archives.

(i) The rights of reproduction and distribution under this section do not apply to a musical work, a pictorial, graphic or sculptural work, or a motion picture or other audiovisual work other than an audiovisual work dealing with news, except that no such limitation shall apply with respect to rights granted by subsections (b) and (c), or with respect to pictorial or graphic works published as illustrations, diagrams, or similar adjuncts to works of which copies are reproduced or distributed in accordance with subsections (d) and (e).

(Oct. 19, 1976, Pub. L. 94-553, §101, 90 Stat. 2546; June 26, 1992, Pub. L. 102-307, §301, 106 Stat. 272; Nov. 13, 1997, Pub. L. 105-80, §12, 111 Stat. 1534; Oct. 27, 1998, Pub, L, 105-298, §104, 112 Stat. 2829; Oct. 28, 1998, Pub. L. 105-304, §404, 112 Stat. 2889.)

§ 109 Limitations on exclusive rights: Effect of transfer of particular copy or phonorecord

(a) Notwithstanding the provisions of section 106(3), the owner of a particular copy or phonorecord lawfully made under this title, or any person authorized by such owner, is entitled, without the authority of the copyright owner, to sell or otherwise dispose of the possession of that copy or phonorecord. Notwithstanding the preceding sentence, copies or phonorecords of works subject to restored copyright under section 104A that are manufactured before the date of restoration of copyright or, with respect to reliance parties, before publication or service of notice under section 104A(e), may be sold or otherwise disposed of without the authorization of the owner of the restored copyright for purposes of direct or indirect commercial advantage only during the 12-month period beginning on—

(1) the date of the publication in the Federal Register of the notice of intent filed with the Copyright Office under section 104A(d)(2)(A), or

(2) the date of the receipt of actual notice served under section 104A(d)(2)(B),

whichever occurs first.

(b) (1) (A) Notwithstanding the provisions of subsection (a), unless authorized by the owners of copyright in the sound recording or the owner of copyright in a computer program (including any tape, disk, or other medium embodying such program), and in the case of a sound recording in the musical works embodied therein, neither the owner of a particular phonorecord nor any person in possession of a particular copy of a computer program (including any tape, disk, or other medium embodying such program), may, for the purposes of direct or indirect commercial advantage, dispose of, or authorize the disposal of, the possession of that phonorecord or computer program (including any tape, disk, or other medium embodying such program) by rental, lease, or lending, or by any other act or practice in the nature of rental, lease, or lending. Nothing in the preceding sentence shall apply to the rental, lease, or lending of a phonorecord for nonprofit purposes by a nonprofit library or nonprofit educational institution. The transfer of possession of a lawfully made copy of a computer program by a nonprofit educational institution to another nonprofit educational institution or to faculty, staff, and students does not constitute rental, lease, or lending for direct or indirect commercial purposes under this subsection.

(B) This subsection does not apply to—

(i) a computer program which is embodied in a machine or product and which cannot be copied during the ordinary operation or use of the machine or product; or

(ii) a computer program embodied in or used in conjunction with a limited purpose computer that is designed for playing video games and may be designed for other purposes.

(C) Nothing in this subsection affects any provision of chapter 9 of this title.

(2) (A) Nothing in this subsection shall apply to the lending of a computer program for nonprofit purposes by a nonprofit library, if each copy of a computer program which is lent by such library has affixed to the packaging containing the program a warning of copyright in accordance with requirements that the Register of Copyrights shall prescribe by regulation.

(B) Not later than three years after the date of the enactment of the Computer Software Rental Amendments Act of 1990, and at such times thereafter as the Register of Copyrights considers appropriate, the Register of Copyrights, after consultation with representatives of copyright owners and librarians, shall submit to the Congress a report stating whether this paragraph has achieved its intended purpose of maintaining the integrity of the copyright system while providing nonprofit libraries the capability to fulfill their function. Such report shall advise the Congress as to any information or recommendations that the Register of Copyrights considers necessary to carry out the purposes of this subsection.

(3) Nothing in this subsection shall affect any provision of the antitrust laws. For purposes of the preceding sentence, "antitrust laws" has the meaning given that term in the first section of the Clayton Act and includes section 5 of the Federal Trade Commission Act to the extent that section relates to unfair methods of competition.

(4) Any person who distributes a phonorecord or a copy of a computer program (including any tape, disk, or other medium embodying such program) in violation of paragraph (1) is an infringer of copyright under section 501 of this title and is subject to the remedies set forth in sections 502, 503, 504, 505, and 509. Such violation shall not be a criminal offense under section 506 or cause such person to be subject to the criminal penalties set forth in section 2319 of title 18.

(c) Notwithstanding the provisions of section 106(5), the owner of a particular copy lawfully made under this title, or any person authorized by such owner, is entitled, without the authority of the copyright owner, to display that copy publicly, either directly or by the projection of no more than one image at a time, to viewers present at the place where the copy is located.

(d) The privileges prescribed by subsections (a) and (c) do not, unless authorized by the copyright owner, extend to any person who has acquired possession of the copy or phonorecord from the copyright owner, by rental, lease, loan, or otherwise, without acquiring ownership of it.

(e) Notwithstanding the provisions of sections 106(4) and 106(5), in the case of an electronic audiovisual game intended for use in coin-operated equipment, the owner of a particular copy of such a game lawfully made under this title, is entitled, without the authority of the copyright owner of the game, to publicly perform or display that game in coin-operated equipment, except that this subsection shall not apply to any work of authorship embodied in the audiovisual game if the copyright owner of the electronic audiovisual game is not also the copyright owner of the work of authorship.*

(Oct. 19, 1976, Pub. L. 94-553, §101, 90 Stat. 2548; Oct. 4, 1984, Pub. L. 98-450, §2, 98 Stat. 1727; Nov. 5, 1988, Pub. L. 100-617, §2, 102 Stat. 3194; Dec. 1, 1990, Pub. L. 101-650, §802-03, 104 Stat. 5134-35; Dec. 8, 1994, Pub. L. 103-465, §514, 108 Stat. 4976; Nov. 13, 1997, Pub. L. 105-80, §12, 111 Stat. 1534.)

§ 110 Limitations on exclusive rights: Exemption of certain performances and displays

Notwithstanding the provisions of section 106, the following are not infringements of copyright:

(1) performance or display of a work by instructors or pupils in the course of face-to-face teaching activities of a nonprofit educational institution, in a classroom or similar place devoted to instruction, unless, in the case of a motion picture or other audiovisual work, the performance, or the display of individual images, is given by means of a copy that was not lawfully made under this title, and that the person responsible for the performance knew or had reason to believe was not lawfully made;

---

* Ed. Note: Pursuant to section 804 of Public Law 101-650, the amendment made by section 803 took effect one year from date of enactment, which was December 1, 1990. The amendments made by section 803 (enacting §(e)) do not apply to public performances or displays that occur on or after October 1, 1995.

17 U.S.C. § 110

(2) except with respect to a work produced or marketed primarily for performance or display as part of mediated instructional activities transmitted via digital networks, or a performance or display that is given by means of a copy or phonorecord that is not lawfully made and acquired under this title, and the transmitting government body or accredited nonprofit educational institution knew or had reason to believe was not lawfully made and acquired, the performance of a nondramatic literary or musical work or reasonable and limited portions of any other work, or display of a work in an amount comparable to that which is typically displayed in the course of a live classroom session, by or in the course of a transmission, if—

(A) the performance or display is made by, at the direction of, or under the actual supervision of an instructor as an integral part of a class session offered as a regular part of the systematic mediated instructional activities of a governmental body or an accredited nonprofit educational institution;

(B) the performance or display is directly related and of material assistance to the teaching content of the transmission;

(C) the transmission is made solely for, and, to the extent technologically feasible, the reception of such transmission is limited to—

(i) students officially enrolled in the course for which the transmission is made; or

(ii) officers or employees of governmental bodies as a part of their official duties or employment; and

(D) the transmitting body or institution—

(i) institutes policies regarding copyright, provides informational materials to faculty, students, and relevant staff members that accurately describe, and promote compliance with, the laws of the United States relating to copyright, and provides notice to students that materials used in connection with the course may be subject to copyright protection; and

(ii) in the case of digital transmissions—

(I) applies technological measures that reasonably prevent—

(aa) retention of the work in accessible form by recipients of the transmission from the transmitting body or institution for longer than the class session; and

(bb) unauthorized further dissemination of the work in accessible form by such recipients to others; and

(II) does not engage in conduct that could reasonably be expected to interfere with technological measures used by copyright owners to prevent such retention or unauthorized further dissemination;

(3) performance of a nondramatic literary or musical work or of a dramatico-musical work of a religious nature, or display of a work, in the course of services at a place of worship or other religious assembly;

(4) performance of a nondramatic literary or musical work otherwise than in a transmission to the public, without any purpose of direct or indirect commercial advantage and without payment of any fee or other compensation for the performance to any of its performers, promoters, or organizers, if—

(A) there is no direct or indirect admission charge; or

(B) the proceeds, after deducting the reasonable costs of producing the performance, are used exclusively for educational, religious, or charitable purposes and not for private financial gain, except where the copyright owner has served notice of objection to the performance under the following conditions:

(i) the notice shall be in writing and signed by the copyright owner or such owner's duly authorized agent; and

(ii) the notice shall be served on the person responsible for the performance at least seven days before the date of the performance, and shall state the reasons for the objection; and

(iii) the notice shall comply, in form, content, and manner of service, with requirements that the Register of Copyrights shall prescribe by regulation;

(5)(A) except as provided in subparagraph (B), communication of a transmission embodying a performance or display of a work by the public reception of the transmission on a single receiving apparatus of a kind commonly used in private homes, unless—

(i) a direct charge is made to see or hear the transmission; or

(ii) the transmission thus received is further transmitted to the public;

(B) communication by an establishment of a transmission or retransmission embodying a performance or display of a nondramatic musical work intended to be received by the general public, originated by a radio or television broadcast station licensed as such by the Federal Communications Commission, or, if an audiovisual transmission, by a cable system or satellite carrier, if—

(i) in the case of an establishment other than a food service or drinking establishment, either the establishment in which the communication occurs has less than 2,000 gross square feet of space (excluding space used for customer parking and for no other purpose), or the establishment in which the communication occurs has 2,000 or more gross square feet of space (excluding space used for customer parking and for no other purpose) and—

(I) if the performance is by audio means only, the performance is communicated by means of a total of not more than 6 loudspeakers, of which not more than 4 loudspeakers are located in any 1 room or adjoining outdoor space; or

(II) if the performance or display is by audiovisual means, any visual portion of the performance or display is communicated by means of a total of not more than 4 audiovisual devices, of which not more than 1 audiovisual device is located in any 1 room, and no such audiovisual device has a diagonal screen size greater than 55 inches, and any audio portion of the performance or display is communicated by means of a total of not more than 6 loudspeakers, of which not more than 4 loudspeakers are located in any 1 room or adjoining outdoor space;

(ii) in the case of a food service or drinking establishment, either the establishment in which the communication occurs has less than 3,750 gross square feet of space (excluding space used for customer parking and for no other purpose), or the establishment in which the communication occurs has 3,750 gross square feet of space or more (excluding space used for customer parking and for no other purpose) and—

(I) if the performance is by audio means only, the performance is communicated by means of a total of not more than 6 loudspeakers, of which not more than 4 loudspeakers are located in any 1 room or adjoining outdoor space; or

(II) if the performance or display is by audiovisual means, any visual portion of the performance or display is communicated by means of a total of not more than 4 audiovisual devices, of which not more than one audiovisual device is located in any 1 room, and no such audiovisual device has a diagonal screen size greater than 55 inches, and any audio portion of the performance or display is communicated by means of a total of not more than 6 loudspeakers, of which not more than 4 loudspeakers are located in any 1 room or adjoining outdoor space;

(iii) no direct charge is made to see or hear the transmission or retransmission;

(iv) the transmission or retransmission is not further transmitted beyond the establishment where it is received; and

(v) the transmission or retransmission is licensed by the copyright owner of the work so publicly performed or displayed;

(6) performance of a nondramatic musical work by a governmental body or a nonprofit agricultural or horticultural organization, in the course of an annual agricultural or horticultural fair or exhibition

conducted by such body or organization; the exemption provided by this clause shall extend to any liability for copyright infringement that would otherwise be imposed on such body or organization, under doctrines of vicarious liability or related infringement, for a performance by a concessionnaire, business establishment, or other person at such fair or exhibition, but shall not excuse any such person from liability for the performance;

(7) performance of a nondramatic musical work by a vending establishment open to the public at large without any direct or indirect admission charge, where the sole purpose of the performance is to promote the retail sale of copies or phonorecords of the work, or of the audiovisual or other devices utilized in such performance, and the performance is not transmitted beyond the place where the establishment is located and is within the immediate area where the sale is occurring;

(8) performance of a nondramatic literary work, by or in the course of a transmission specifically designed for and primarily directed to blind or other handicapped persons who are unable to read normal printed material as a result of their handicap, or deaf or other handicapped persons who are unable to hear the aural signals accompanying a transmission of visual signals, if the performance is made without any purpose of direct or indirect commercial advantage and its transmission is made through the facilities of: (i) a governmental body; or (ii) a noncommercial educational broadcast station (as defined in section 397 of title 47); or (iii) a radio subcarrier authorization (as defined in 47 CFR 73.293-73.295 and 73.593-73.595); or (iv) a cable system (as defined in section 111(f)).

(9) performance on a single occasion of a dramatic literary work published at least ten years before the date of the performance, by or in the course of a transmission specifically designed for and primarily directed to blind or other handicapped persons who are unable to read normal printed material as a result of their handicap, if the performance is made without any purpose of direct or indirect commercial advantage and its transmission is made through the facilities of a radio subcarrier authorization referred to in clause (8)(iii), *Provided,* That the provisions of this clause shall not be applicable to more

than one performance of the same work by the same performers or under the auspices of the same organization; and

(10) notwithstanding paragraph (4), the following is not an infringement of copyright: performance of a nondramatic literary or musical work in the course of a social function which is organized and promoted by a nonprofit veterans' organization or a nonprofit fraternal organization to which the general public is not invited, but not including the invitees of the organizations, if the proceeds from the performance, after deducting the reasonable costs of producing the performance, are used exclusively for charitable purposes and not for financial gain. For purposes of this section the social functions of any college or university fraternity or sorority shall not be included unless the social function is held solely to raise funds for a specific charitable purpose.

The exemptions provided under paragraph (5) shall not be taken into account in any administrative, judicial, or other governmental proceeding to set or adjust the royalties payable to copyright owners for the public performance or display of their works. Royalties payable to copyright owners for any public performance or display of their works other than such performances or displays as are exempted under paragraph (5) shall not be diminished in any respect as a result of such exemption.

In paragraph (2), the term "mediated instructional activities" with respect to the performance or display of a work by digital transmission under this section refers to activities that use such work as an integral part of the class experience, controlled by or under the actual supervision of the instructor and analogous to the type of performance or display that would take place in a live classroom setting. The term does not refer to activities that use, in 1 or more class sessions of a single course, such works as textbooks, course packs, or other material in any media, copies or phonorecords of which are typically purchased or acquired by the students in higher education for their independent use and retention or are typically purchased or acquired for elementary and secondary students for their possession and independent use.

For purposes of paragraph (2), accreditation—

(A) with respect to an institution providing post-secondary education, shall be as determined by a regional or national accrediting agency recognized by the Council on Higher Education Accreditation or the United States Department of Education; and

(B) with respect to an institution providing elementary or secondary education, shall be as recognized by the applicable state certification or licensing procedures.

For purposes of paragraph (2), no governmental body or accredited nonprofit educational institution shall be liable for infringement by reason of the transient or temporary storage of material carried out through the automatic technical process of a digital transmission of the performance or display of that material as authorized under paragraph (2). No such material stored on the system or network controlled or operated by the transmitting body or institution under this paragraph shall be maintained on such system or network in a manner ordinarily accessible to anyone other than anticipated recipients. No such copy shall be maintained on the system or network in a manner ordinarily accessible to such anticipated recipients for a longer period than is reasonably necessary to facilitate the transmissions for which it was made.

(Oct. 19, 1976, Pub. L. 94-553, §101, 90 Stat. 2549; Oct. 15, 1982, Pub. L. 97-366, §3, 96 Stat. 1759; Nov. 13, 1997, Pub. L. 105-80, §12, 111 Stat. 1534; Oct. 27, 1998, Pub. L. 105-298, §202(a), (b) , 112 Stat. 2830, 2831; Aug. 5, 1999, Pub. L. 106-44, §1(a), 113 Stat. 221; Nov. 2, 2002, Pub. L. 107-273, §§13210, 13301, 116 Stat. 1910.)

§ 111 Limitations on exclusive rights: Secondary transmissions

(a) *Certain secondary transmissions exempted.*—The secondary transmission of a performance or display of a work embodied in a primary transmission is not an infringement of copyright if—

(1) the secondary transmission is not made by a cable system, and consists entirely of the relaying, by the management of a hotel, apartment house, or similar establishment, of signals transmitted by a broadcast station licensed by the Federal Communications Commission, within the local service area of such station, to the private lodgings of guests or residents of such establishment, and no direct charge is made to see or hear the secondary transmission; or

(2) the secondary transmission is made solely for the purpose and under the conditions specified by clause (2) of section 110; or

(3) the secondary transmission is made by any carrier who has no direct or indirect control over the content or selection of the primary transmission or over the particular recipients of the secondary transmission, and whose activities with respect to the secondary transmission consist solely of providing wires, cables, or other communications channels for the use of others: *Provided,* That the provisions of this clause extend only to the activities of said carrier with respect to secondary transmissions and do not exempt from liability the activities of others with respect to their own primary or secondary transmissions;

(4) the secondary transmission is made by a satellite carrier for private home viewing pursuant to a statutory license under section 119; or

(5) the secondary transmission is not made by a cable system but is made by a governmental body, or other nonprofit organization, without any purpose of direct or indirect commercial advantage, and without charge to the recipients of the secondary transmission other than assessments necessary to defray the actual and reasonable costs of maintaining and operating the secondary transmission service.

(b) *Secondary transmission of primary transmission to controlled group.*— Notwithstanding the provisions of subsections (a) and (c), the secondary transmission to the public of a performance or display of a work embodied in a primary transmission is actionable as an act of infringement under section 501, and is fully subject to the remedies provided by sections 502 through 506 and 509, if the primary transmission is not made for reception by the public at large but is controlled and limited to reception by particular members of the public: *Provided,* however, That such secondary transmission is not actionable as an act of infringement if—

(1) the primary transmission is made by a broadcast station licensed by the Federal Communications Commission; and

(2) the carriage of the signals comprising the secondary transmission is required under the rules, regulations, or authorizations of the Federal Communications Commission; and

(3) the signal of the primary transmitter is not altered or changed in any way by the secondary transmitter.

17 U.S.C. § 111

(c) *Secondary transmissions by cable systems.—*

(1) Subject to the provisions of clauses (2), (3), and (4) of this subsection and section 114(d), secondary transmissions to the public by a cable system of a performance or display of a work embodied in a primary transmission made by a broadcast station licensed by the Federal Communications Commission or by an appropriate governmental authority of Canada or Mexico shall be subject to statutory licensing upon compliance with the requirements of subsection (d) where the carriage of the signals comprising the secondary transmission is permissible under the rules, regulations, or authorizations of the Federal Communications Commission.

(2) Notwithstanding the provisions of clause (1) of this subsection, the willful or repeated secondary transmission to the public by a cable system of a primary transmission made by a broadcast station licensed by the Federal Communications Commission or by an appropriate governmental authority of Canada or Mexico and embodying a performance or display of a work is actionable as an act of infringement under section 501, and is fully subject to the remedies provided by sections 502 through 506 and 509, in the following cases:

> (A) where the carriage of the signals comprising the secondary transmission is not permissible under the rules, regulations, or authorizations of the Federal Communications Commission; or

> (B) where the cable system has not deposited the statement of account and royalty fee required by subsection (d).

(3) Notwithstanding the provisions of clause (1) of this subsection and subject to the provisions of subsection (e) of this section, the secondary transmission to the public by a cable system of a performance or display of a work embodied in a primary transmission made by a broadcast station licensed by the Federal Communications Commission or by an appropriate governmental authority of Canada or Mexico is actionable as an act of infringement under section 501, and is fully subject to the remedies provided by sections 502 through 506 and sections 509 and 510, if the content of the particular program in which the performance or display is embodied, or any commercial advertising or station announcements transmitted by

17 U.S.C. § 111

the primary transmitter during, or immediately before or after, the transmission of such program, is in any way willfully altered by the cable system through changes, deletions, or additions, except for the alteration, deletion, or substitution of commercial advertisements performed by those engaged in television commercial advertising market research: *Provided,* That the research company has obtained the prior consent of the advertiser who has purchased the original commercial advertisement, the television station broadcasting that commercial advertisement, and the cable system performing the secondary transmission: *And provided further,* That such commercial alteration, deletion, or substitution is not performed for the purpose of deriving income from the sale of that commercial time.

(4) Notwithstanding the provisions of clause (1) of this subsection, the secondary transmission to the public by a cable system of a primary transmission made by a broadcast station licensed by an appropriate governmental authority of Canada or Mexico and embodying a performance or display of a work is actionable as an act of infringement under section 501, and is fully subject to the remedies provided by sections 502 through 506 and section 509, if (A) with respect to Canadian signals, the community of the cable system is located more than 150 miles from the United States-Canadian border and is also located south of the forty-second parallel of latitude, or (B) with respect to Mexican signals, the secondary transmission is made by a cable system which received the primary transmission by means other than direct interception of a free space radio wave emitted by such broadcast television station, unless prior to April 15, 1976, such cable system was actually carrying, or was specifically authorized to carry, the signal of such foreign station on the system pursuant to the rules, regulations, or authorizations of the Federal Communications Commission.

(d) *Statutory license for secondary transmissions by cable systems.**—

(1) A cable system whose secondary transmissions have been subject to statutory licensing under subsection (c) shall, on a semiannual ba-

---

* *Ed. Note:* Cable statutory license fees are revised pursuant 17 U.S.C. §§801–03.

17 U.S.C. § 111

sis, deposit with the Register of Copyrights, in accordance with requirements that the Register shall prescribe by regulation—

(A) a statement of account, covering the six months next preceding, specifying the number of channels on which the cable system made secondary transmissions to its subscribers, the names and locations of all primary transmitters whose transmissions were further transmitted by the cable system, the total number of subscribers, the gross amounts paid to the cable system for the basic service of providing secondary transmissions of primary broadcast transmitters, and such other data as the Register of Copyrights may from time to time prescribe by regulation. In determining the total number of subscribers and the gross amounts paid to the cable system for the basic service of providing secondary transmissions of primary broadcast transmitters, the system shall not include subscribers and amounts collected from subscribers receiving secondary transmissions for private home viewing pursuant to section 119. Such statement shall also include a special statement of account covering any nonnetwork television programming that was carried by the cable system in whole or in part beyond the local service area of the primary transmitter, under rules, regulations, or authorizations of the Federal Communications Commission permitting the substitution or addition of signals under certain circumstances, together with logs showing the times, dates, stations, and programs involved in such substituted or added carriage; and

(B) except in the case of a cable system whose royalty is specified in subclause (C) or (D), a total royalty fee for the period covered by the statement, computed on the basis of specified percentages of the gross receipts from subscribers to the cable service during said period for the basic service of providing secondary transmissions of primary broadcast transmitters, as follows:

(i) 0.675 of 1 per centum of such gross receipts for the privilege of further transmitting any nonnetwork programming of a primary transmitter in whole or in part beyond the local service area of such primary transmitter, such amount to be applied against the fee, if any, payable pursuant to paragraphs (ii) through (iv);

(ii) 0.675 of 1 per centum of such gross receipts for the first distant signal equivalent;

(iii) 0.425 of 1 per centum of such gross receipts for each of the second, third, and fourth distant signal equivalents;

(iv) 0.2 of 1 per centum of such gross receipts for the fifth distant signal equivalent and each additional distant signal equivalent thereafter; and

in computing the amounts payable under paragraphs (ii) through (iv), above, any fraction of a distant signal equivalent shall be computed at its fractional value and, in the case of any cable system located partly within and partly without the local service area of a primary transmitter, gross receipts shall be limited to those gross receipts derived from subscribers located without the local service area of such primary transmitter; and

(C) if the actual gross receipts paid by subscribers to a cable system for the period covered by the statement for the basic service of providing secondary transmissions of primary broadcast transmitters total $80,000 or less, gross receipts of the cable system for the purpose of this subclause shall be computed by subtracting from such actual gross receipts the amount by which $80,000 exceeds such actual gross receipts, except that in no case shall a cable system's gross receipts be reduced to less than $3,000. The royalty fee payable under this subclause shall be 0.5 of 1 per centum, regardless of the number of distant signal equivalents, if any; and

(D) if the actual gross receipts paid by subscribers to a cable system for the period covered by the statement, for the basic service of providing secondary transmissions of primary broadcast transmitters, are more than $80,000 but less than $160,000, the royalty fee payable under this subclause shall be (i) 0.5 of 1 per centum of any gross receipts up to $80,000; and (ii) 1 per centum of any gross receipts in excess of $80,000 but less than $160,000, regardless of the number of distant signal equivalents, if any.

(2) The Register of Copyrights shall receive all fees deposited under this section and, after deducting the reasonable costs incurred by the Copyright Office under this section, shall deposit the balance in the Treasury of the United States, in such manner as the Secretary of the Treasury directs. All funds held by the Secretary of the Treasury shall be invested in interest-bearing United States securities for later distribution with interest by the Librarian of Congress in the event no controversy over distribution exists, or by a copyright arbitration royalty panel in the event a controversy over such distribution exists.

(3) The royalty fees thus deposited shall, in accordance with the procedures provided by clause (4), be distributed to those among the following copyright owners who claim that their works were the subject of secondary transmissions by cable systems during the relevant semiannual period:

(A) any such owner whose work was included in a secondary transmission made by a cable system of a nonnetwork television program in whole or in part beyond the local service area of the primary transmitter; and

(B) any such owner whose work was included in a secondary transmission identified in a special statement of account deposited under clause (1)(A); and

(C) any such owner whose work was included in nonnetwork programming consisting exclusively of aural signals carried by a cable system in whole or in part beyond the local service area of the primary transmitter of such programs.

(4) The royalty fees thus deposited shall be distributed in accordance with the following procedures:

(A) During the month of July in each year, every person claiming to be entitled to statutory license fees for secondary transmissions shall file a claim with the Librarian of Congress, in accordance with requirements that the Librarian of Congress shall prescribe by regulation. Notwithstanding any provisions of the antitrust laws, for purposes of this clause any claimants may agree among themselves as to the proportionate division of statutory licensing fees among them, may lump their claims to-

17 U.S.C. § 111

gether and file them jointly or as a single claim, or may designate a common agent to receive payment on their behalf.

(B) After the first day of August of each year, the Librarian of Congress shall, upon the recommendation of the Register of Copyrights, determine whether there exists a controversy concerning the distribution of royalty fees. If the Librarian determines that no such controversy exists, the Librarian shall, after deducting reasonable administrative costs under this section, distribute such fees to the copyright owners entitled to such fees, or to their designated agents. If the Librarian finds the existence of a controversy, the Librarian shall, pursuant to chapter 8 of this title, convene a copyright arbitration royalty panel to determine the distribution of royalty fees.

(C) During the pendency of any proceeding under this subsection, the Librarian of Congress shall withhold from distribution an amount sufficient to satisfy all claims with respect to which a controversy exists, but shall have discretion to proceed to distribute any amounts that are not in controversy.

(e) *Nonsimultaneous secondary transmissions by cable systems.*—

(1) Notwithstanding those provisions of the second paragraph of subsection (f) relating to nonsimultaneous secondary transmissions by a cable system, any such transmissions are actionable as an act of infringement under section 501, and are fully subject to the remedies provided by sections 502 through 506 and sections 509 and 510, unless—

(A) the program on the videotape is transmitted no more than one time to the cable system's subscribers; and

(B) the copyrighted program, episode, or motion picture videotape, including the commercials contained within such program, episode, or picture, is transmitted without deletion or editing; and

(C) an owner or officer of the cable system (i) prevents the duplication of the videotape while in the possession of the system, (ii) prevents unauthorized duplication while in the possession of the facility making the videotape for the system if the system owns or controls the facility, or takes reasonable precautions to prevent such duplication if it does not own or control the facility, (iii) takes adequate precautions to prevent duplication while the tape is being transported, and (iv) subject to clause (2), erases or destroys, or causes the erasure or destruction of, the videotape; and

(D) within forty-five days after the end of each calendar quarter, an owner or officer of the cable system executes an affidavit attesting (i) to the steps and precautions taken to prevent duplication of the videotape, and (ii) subject to clause (2), to the erasure or destruction of all videotapes made or used during such quarter; and

(E) such owner or officer places or causes each such affidavit, and affidavits received pursuant to clause (2)(C), to be placed in a file, open to public inspection, at such system's main office in the community where the transmission is made or in the nearest community where such system maintains an office; and

(F) the nonsimultaneous transmission is one that the cable system would be authorized to transmit under the rules, regulations, and authorizations of the Federal Communications Commission in effect at the time of the nonsimultaneous transmission if the transmission had been made simultaneously, except that this subclause shall not apply to inadvertent or accidental transmissions.

(2) If a cable system transfers to any person a videotape of a program nonsimultaneously transmitted by it, such transfer is actionable as an act of infringement under section 501, and is fully subject to the remedies provided by sections 502 through 506 and 509, except that, pursuant to a written, nonprofit contract providing for the equitable sharing of the costs of such videotape and its transfer, a videotape nonsimultaneously transmitted by it, in accordance with clause (1), may be transferred by one cable system in Alaska to another system in Alaska, by one cable system in Hawaii permitted to make such nonsimultaneous transmissions to another such cable system in Hawaii, or by one cable system in Guam, the Northern Mariana Islands, or the Trust Territory of the Pacific Islands, to another cable system in any of those three territories, if—

(A) each such contract is available for public inspection in the offices of the cable systems involved, and a copy of such contract is filed, within thirty days after such contract is entered into, with the Copyright Office (which Office shall make each such contract available for public inspection); and

(B) the cable system to which the videotape is transferred complies with clause (1)(A), (B), (C)(i), (iii), and (iv), and (D) through (F); and

(C) such system provides a copy of the affidavit required to be made in accordance with clause (1)(D) to each cable system making a previous nonsimultaneous transmission of the same videotape.

(3) This subsection shall not be construed to supersede the exclusivity protection provisions of any existing agreement, or any such agreement hereafter entered into, between a cable system and a television broadcast station in the area in which the cable system is located, or a network with which such station is affiliated.

(4) As used in this subsection, the term "videotape", and each of its variant forms, means the reproduction of the images and sounds of a program or programs broadcast by a television broadcast station licensed by the Federal Communications Commission, regardless of the nature of the material objects, such as tapes or films, in which the reproduction is embodied.

(f) *Definitions.*—As used in this section, the following terms and their variant forms mean the following:

A "primary transmission" is a transmission made to the public by the transmitting facility whose signals are being received and further transmitted by the secondary transmission service, regardless of where or when the performance or display was first transmitted.

A "secondary transmission" is the further transmitting of a primary transmission simultaneously with the primary transmission, or nonsimultaneously with the primary transmission if by a "cable system" not located in whole or in part within the boundary of the forty-eight contiguous States, Hawaii, or Puerto Rico: *Provided, however,* That a nonsimultaneous further transmission by a cable system located in Hawaii of a primary transmission shall be deemed to be a secondary transmission if the carriage of the television broadcast signal comprising such further transmission is permissible under the rules, regulations, or authorizations of the Federal Communications Commission.

A "cable system" is a facility, located in any State, Territory, Trust Territory, or Possession, that in whole or in part receives signals transmitted or programs broadcast by one or more television broadcast stations licensed by the Federal Communications Commission, and makes secondary transmissions of such signals or programs by wires, cables, microwave, or other communications channels to subscribing members of the public who pay for such service. For purposes of determining the royalty fee under subsection (d)(1), two or more cable systems in contiguous communities under common ownership or control or operating from one headend shall be considered as one system.

The "local service area of a primary transmitter", in the case of a television broadcast station, comprises the area in which such station is entitled to insist upon its signal being retransmitted by a cable system pursuant to the rules, regulations, and authorizations of the Federal Communications Commission in effect on April 15, 1976, or such station's television market as defined in section 76.55(e) of title 47, Code of Federal Regulations (as in effect on September 18, 1993), or any modifications to such television market made, on or after September 18, 1993, pursuant to section 76.55(e) or 76.59 of title 47 of the Code of Federal Regulations, or in the case of a television broadcast station licensed by an appropriate governmental authority of Canada or Mexico, the area in which it would be entitled to insist upon its signal being retransmitted if it were a television broadcast station subject to such rules, regulations, and authorizations. In the case of a low power television station, as defined by the rules and regulations of the Federal Communications Commission, the "local service area of a primary transmitter" comprises the area within 35 miles of the transmitter site, except that in the case of such a station located in a standard metropolitan statistical area which has one of the 50 largest populations of all standard metropolitan statistical areas (based on the 1980 decennial census of population taken by the Secretary of Commerce), the number of miles shall be 20 miles. The "local service area

17 U.S.C. § 111

of a primary transmitter", in the case of a radio broadcast station, comprises the primary service area of such station, pursuant to the rules and regulations of the Federal Communications Commission.

A "distant signal equivalent" is the value assigned to the secondary transmission of any nonnetwork television programming carried by a cable system in whole or in part beyond the local service area of the primary transmitter of such programming. It is computed by assigning a value of one to each independent station and a value of one-quarter to each network station and noncommercial educational station for the nonnetwork programming so carried pursuant to the rules, regulations, and authorizations of the Federal Communications Commission. The foregoing values for independent, network, and noncommercial educational stations are subject, however, to the following exceptions and limitations. Where the rules and regulations of the Federal Communications Commission require a cable system to omit the further transmission of a particular program and such rules and regulations also permit the substitution of another program embodying a performance or display of a work in place of the omitted transmission, or where such rules and regulations in effect on the date of enactment of this Act permit a cable system, at its election, to effect such deletion and substitution of a nonlive program or to carry additional programs not transmitted by primary transmitters within whose local service area the cable system is located, no value shall be assigned for the substituted or additional program; where the rules, regulations, or authorizations of the Federal Communications Commission in effect on the date of enactment of this Act permit a cable system, at its election, to omit the further transmission of a particular program and such rules, regulations, or authorizations also permit the substitution of another program embodying a performance or display of a work in place of the omitted transmission, the value assigned for the substituted or additional program shall be, in the case of a live program, the value of one full distant signal equivalent multiplied by a fraction that has as its numerator the number of days in the year in which such substitution occurs and as its denominator the number of days in the year. In the case of a station carried pursuant to the late-night or specialty programming rules of the Federal Communications Commission, or a station carried on a part-time basis where full-time carriage is not possible because the cable system lacks the activated channel capacity to retransmit on a full-time basis all signals which it is authorized to carry, the values for independent, network, and noncommercial educational stations set forth above, as the case may be, shall be multiplied by a fraction which is equal to the ratio of the broadcast hours of such station carried by the cable system to the total broadcast hours of the station.

A "network station" is a television broadcast station that is owned or operated by, or affiliated with, one or more of the television networks in the United States providing nationwide transmissions, and that transmits a substantial part of the programming supplied by such networks for a substantial part of that station's typical broadcast day.

An "independent station" is a commercial television broadcast station other than a network station.

A "noncommercial educational station" is a television station that is a noncommercial educational broadcast station as defined in section 397 of title 47.

(Oct. 19, 1976, Pub. L. 94-553, §101, 90 Stat. 2550; Aug. 27, 1986, Pub. L. 99-397, §1 and 2, 100 Stat. 848; Nov. 16, 1988, Pub. L. 100-667, §202, 102 Stat. 3949; July 3, 1990, Pub. L. 101-318, §3, 104 Stat. 288; Dec. 17, 1993, Pub. L. 103-198, §6(a), 107 Stat. 2311; Oct. 18, 1994, Pub. L. 103-369, §2, 108 Stat. 3481; Nov. 1, 1995, Pub. L. 104-39, §5(b), 109 Stat. 348; Nov. 29, 1999, Pub. L. 106-113, §1011, 113 Stat. 1501A-543.)

§ 112   Limitations on exclusive rights: Ephemeral recordings

(a)(1) Notwithstanding the provisions of section 106, and except in the case of a motion picture or other audiovisual work, it is not an infringement of copyright for a transmitting organization entitled to transmit to the public a performance or display of a work, under a license, including a statutory license under section 114(f), or transfer of the copyright or under the limitations on exclusive rights in sound recordings specified by section 114(a), or for a transmitting organization that is a broadcast radio or television station licensed as such by the Federal Communications Commission and that makes a broadcast transmission of a performance of a sound recording in a digital format on a nonsubscription basis, to make no more than one copy or phonorecord of a particular transmission program embodying the performance or display, if—

(A) the copy or phonorecord is retained and used solely by the transmitting organization that made it, and no further copies or phonorecords are reproduced from it; and

(B) the copy or phonorecord is used solely for the transmitting organization's own transmissions within its local service area, or for purposes of archival preservation or security; and

(C) unless preserved exclusively for archival purposes, the copy or phonorecord is destroyed within six months from the date the transmission program was first transmitted to the public.

(2) In a case in which a transmitting organization entitled to make a copy or phonorecord under paragraph (1) in connection with the transmission to the public of a performance or display of a work is prevented from making such copy or phonorecord by reason of the application by the copyright owner of technical measures that prevent the reproduction of the work, the copyright owner shall make available to the transmitting organization the necessary means for permitting the making of such copy or phonorecord as permitted under that paragraph, if it is technologically feasible and economically reasonable for the copyright owner to do so. If the copyright owner fails to do so in a timely manner in light of the transmitting organization's reasonable business requirements, the transmitting organization shall not be liable for a violation of section 1201(a)(1) of this title for engaging in such activities as are necessary to make such copies or phonorecords as permitted under paragraph (1) of this subsection.

(b) Notwithstanding the provisions of section 106, it is not an infringement of copyright for a governmental body or other nonprofit organization entitled to transmit a performance or display of a work, under section 110(2) or under the limitations on exclusive rights in sound recordings specified by section 114(a), to make no more than thirty copies or phonorecords of a particular transmission program embodying the performance or display, if—

(1) no further copies or phonorecords are reproduced from the copies or phonorecords made under this clause; and

(2) except for one copy or phonorecord that may be preserved exclusively for archival purposes, the copies or phonorecords are destroyed within seven years from the date the transmission program was first transmitted to the public.

(c) Notwithstanding the provisions of section 106, it is not an infringement of copyright for a governmental body or other nonprofit organization to make for distribution no more than one copy or phonorecord, for each transmitting organization specified in clause (2) of this subsection, of a particular transmission program embodying a performance of a nondramatic musical work of a religious nature, or of a sound recording of such a musical work, if—

(1) there is no direct or indirect charge for making or distributing any such copies or phonorecords; and

(2) none of such copies or phonorecords is used for any performance other than a single transmission to the public by a transmitting organization entitled to transmit to the public a performance of the work under a license or transfer of the copyright; and

(3) except for one copy or phonorecord that may be preserved exclusively for archival purposes, the copies or phonorecords are all destroyed within one year from the date the transmission program was first transmitted to the public.

(d) Notwithstanding the provisions of section 106, it is not an infringement of copyright for a governmental body or other nonprofit organization entitled to transmit a performance of a work under section 110(8) to make no more than ten copies or phonorecords embodying the performance, or to permit the use of any such copy or phonorecord by any governmental body or nonprofit organization entitled to transmit a performance of a work under section 110(8), if—

(1) any such copy or phonorecord is retained and used solely by the organization that made it, or by a governmental body or nonprofit organization entitled to transmit a performance of a work under section 110(8), and no further copies or phonorecords are reproduced from it; and

17 U.S.C. § 112

(2) any such copy or phonorecord is used solely for transmissions authorized under section 110(8), or for purposes of archival preservation or security; and

(3) the governmental body or nonprofit organization permitting any use of any such copy or phonorecord by any governmental body or nonprofit organization under this subsection does not make any charge for such use.

(e) Statutory license—(1) A transmitting organization entitled to transmit to the public a performance of a sound recording under the limitation on exclusive rights specified by section 114(d)(1)(C)(iv) or under a statutory license in accordance with section 114(f) is entitled to a statutory license, under the conditions specified by this subsection, to make no more than 1 phonorecord of the sound recording (unless the terms and conditions of the statutory license allow for more), if the following conditions are satisfied:

(A) The phonorecord is retained and used solely by the transmitting organization that made it, and no further phonorecords are reproduced from it.

(B) The phonorecord is used solely for the transmitting organization's own transmissions originating in the United States under a statutory license in accordance with section 114(f) or the limitation on exclusive rights specified by section 114(d)(1)(C)(iv).

(C) Unless preserved exclusively for purposes of archival preservation, the phonorecord is destroyed within 6 months from the date the sound recording was first transmitted to the public using the phonorecord.

(D) Phonorecords of the sound recording have been distributed to the public under the authority of the copyright owner or the copyright owner authorizes the transmitting entity to transmit the sound recording, and the transmitting entity makes the phonorecord under this subsection from a phonorecord lawfully made and acquired under the authority of the copyright owner.

(2) Notwithstanding any provision of the antitrust laws, any copyright owners of sound recordings and any transmitting organizations entitled to a statutory license under this subsection may nego-

tiate and agree upon royalty rates and license terms and conditions for making phonorecords of such sound recordings under this section and the proportionate division of fees paid among copyright owners, and may designate common agents to negotiate, agree to, pay, or receive such royalty payments.

(3) No later than 30 days after the date of the enactment of the Digital Millennium Copyright Act, the Librarian of Congress shall cause notice to be published in the Federal Register of the initiation of voluntary negotiation proceedings for the purpose of determining reasonable terms and rates of royalty payments for the activities specified by paragraph (1) of this subsection during the period beginning on the date of the enactment of such Act and ending on December 31, 2000, or such other date as the parties may agree. Such rates shall include a minimum fee for each type of service offered by transmitting organizations. Any copyright owners of sound recordings or any transmitting organizations entitled to a statutory license under this subsection may submit to the Librarian of Congress licenses covering such activities with respect to such sound recordings. The parties to each negotiation proceeding shall bear their own costs.

(4) In the absence of license agreements negotiated under paragraph (2), during the 60-day period commencing 6 months after publication of the notice specified in paragraph (3), and upon the filing of a petition in accordance with section 803(a)(1), the Librarian of Congress shall, pursuant to chapter 8, convene a copyright arbitration royalty panel to determine and publish in the Federal Register a schedule of reasonable rates and terms which, subject to paragraph (5), shall be binding on all copyright owners of sound recordings and transmitting organizations entitled to a statutory license under this subsection during the period beginning on the date of the enactment of the Digital Millennium Copyright Act and ending on December 31, 2000, or such other date as the parties may agree. Such rates shall include a minimum fee for each type of service offered by transmitting organizations. The copyright arbitration royalty panel shall establish rates that most clearly represent the fees that would have been negotiated in the marketplace between a willing buyer and a willing seller. In determining such rates and terms, the copyright arbitration royalty panel shall base its decision on economic,

competitive, and programming information presented by the parties, including—

(A) whether use of the service may substitute for or may promote the sales of phonorecords or otherwise interferes with or enhances the copyright owner's traditional streams of revenue; and

(B) the relative roles of the copyright owner and the transmitting organization in the copyrighted work and the service made available to the public with respect to relative creative contribution, technological contribution, capital investment, cost, and risk.

In establishing such rates and terms, the copyright arbitration royalty panel may consider the rates and terms under voluntary license agreements negotiated as provided in paragraphs (2) and (3). The Librarian of Congress shall also establish requirements by which copyright owners may receive reasonable notice of the use of their sound recordings under this section, and under which records of such use shall be kept and made available by transmitting organizations entitled to obtain a statutory license under this subsection.

(5) License agreements voluntarily negotiated at any time between 1 or more copyright owners of sound recordings and 1 or more transmitting organizations entitled to obtain a statutory license under this subsection shall be given effect in lieu of any determination by a copyright arbitration royalty panel or decision by the Librarian of Congress.

(6) Publication of a notice of the initiation of voluntary negotiation proceedings as specified in paragraph (3) shall be repeated, in accordance with regulations that the Librarian of Congress shall prescribe, in the first week of January 2000, and at 2-year intervals thereafter, except to the extent that different years for the repeating of such proceedings may be determined in accordance with paragraph (3). The procedures specified in paragraph (4) shall be repeated, in accordance with regulations that the Librarian of Congress shall prescribe, upon filing of a petition in accordance with section 803(a)(1), during a 60-day period commencing on July 1, 2000, and at 2-year intervals thereafter, except to the extent that different years for the repeating

of such proceedings may be determined in accordance with paragraph (3). The procedures specified in paragraph (4) shall be concluded in accordance with section 802.

(7) (A) Any person who wishes to make a phonorecord of a sound recording under a statutory license in accordance with this subsection may do so without infringing the exclusive right of the copyright owner of the sound recording under section 106(1)—

(i) by complying with such notice requirements as the Librarian of Congress shall prescribe by regulation and by paying royalty fees in accordance with this subsection; or

(ii) if such royalty fees have not been set, by agreeing to pay such royalty fees as shall be determined in accordance with this subsection.

(B) Any royalty payments in arrears shall be made on or before the 20th day of the month next succeeding the month in which the royalty fees are set.

(8) If a transmitting organization entitled to make a phonorecord under this subsection is prevented from making such phonorecord by reason of the application by the copyright owner of technical measures that prevent the reproduction of the sound recording, the copyright owner shall make available to the transmitting organization the necessary means for permitting the making of such phonorecord as permitted under this subsection, if it is technologically feasible and economically reasonable for the copyright owner to do so. If the copyright owner fails to do so in a timely manner in light of the transmitting organization's reasonable business requirements, the transmitting organization shall not be liable for a violation of section 1201(a)(1) of this title for engaging in such activities as are necessary to make such phonorecords as permitted under this subsection.

(9) Nothing in this subsection annuls, limits, impairs, or otherwise affects in any way the existence or value of any of the exclusive rights of the copyright owners in a sound recording, except as otherwise provided in this subsection, or in a musical work, including the exclusive rights to reproduce and distribute a sound recording or musical work, including by means of a digital phonorecord delivery,

17 U.S.C. § 112

under sections 106(1), 106(3), and 115, and the right to perform publicly a sound recording or musical work, including by means of a digital audio transmission, under sections 106(4) and 106(6).

(f) (1) Notwithstanding the provisions of section 106, and without limiting the application of subsection (b), it is not an infringement of copyright for a governmental body or other nonprofit educational institution entitled under section 110(2) to transmit a performance or display to make copies or phonorecords of a work that is in digital form and, solely to the extent permitted in paragraph (2), of a work that is in analog form, embodying the performance or display to be used for making transmissions authorized under section 110(2), if—

(A) such copies or phonorecords are retained and used solely by the body or institution that made them, and no further copies or phonorecords are reproduced from them, except as authorized under section 110(2); and

(B) such copies or phonorecords are used solely for transmissions authorized under section 110(2).

(2) This subsection does not authorize the conversion of print or other   analog versions of works into digital formats, except that such conversion is permitted hereunder, only with respect to the amount of such works authorized to be performed or displayed under section 110(2), if—

(A) no digital version of the work is available to the institution; or

(B) the digital version of the work that is available to the institution is subject to technological protection measures that prevent its use for section 110(2).

(g) The transmission program embodied in a copy or phonorecord made under this section is not subject to protection as a derivative work under this title except with the express consent of the owners of copyright in the preexisting works employed in the program.

(Oct. 19, 1976, Pub. L. 94-553, §101, 90 Stat. 2558; Oct. 28, 1998, Pub. L. 105-304, §§402, 405(b), 112 Stat. 2888, 2899; Aug. 5, 1999, Pub. L. 106-44, §1(b), 113 Stat. 221; Nov. 2, 2002, Pub. L. 107-273, §13301, 116 Stat. 1910.)

§ 113   Scope of exclusive rights in pictorial, graphic, and sculptural works

(a) Subject to the provisions of subsections (b) and (c) of this section, the exclusive right to reproduce a copyrighted pictorial, graphic, or sculptural work in copies under section 106 includes the right to reproduce the work in or on any kind of article, whether useful or otherwise.

(b) This title does not afford, to the owner of copyright in a work that portrays a useful article as such, any greater or lesser rights with respect to the making, distribution, or display of the useful article so portrayed than those afforded to such works under the law, whether title 17 or the common law or statutes of a State, in effect on December 31, 1977, as held applicable and construed by a court in an action brought under this title.

(c) In the case of a work lawfully reproduced in useful articles that have been offered for sale or other distribution to the public, copyright does not include any right to prevent the making, distribution, or display of pictures or photographs of such articles in connection with advertisements or commentaries related to the distribution or display of such articles, or in connection with news reports.

(d) (1) In a case in which—

    (A) a work of visual art has been incorporated in or made part of a building in such a way that removing the work from the building will cause the destruction, distortion, mutilation, or other modification of the work as described in section 106A(a)(3), and

    (B) the author consented to the installation of the work in the building either before the effective date set forth in section 610(a) of the Visual Artists Rights Act of 1990, or in a written instrument executed on or after such effective date that is signed by the owner of the building and the author and that specifies that installation of the work may subject the work to destruction, distortion, mutilation, or other modification, by reason of its removal,

then the rights conferred by paragraphs (2) and (3) of section 106(A(a) shall not apply.

(2) If the owner of a building wishes to remove a work of visual art which is a part of such building and which can be removed from the

building without the destruction, distortion, mutilation, or other modification of the work as described in section 106A(a)(3), the author's rights under paragraphs (2) and (3) of section 106A(a) shall apply unless—

(A) the owner has made a diligent, good faith attempt without success to notify the author of the owner's intended action affecting the work of visual art, or

(B) the owner did provide such notice in writing and the person so notified failed, within 90 days after receiving such notice, either to remove the work or to pay its removal.

For purposes of subparagraph (A), an owner shall be presumed to have made a diligent, good faith attempt to send notice if the owner sent such notice by registered mail to the author at the most recent address of the author that was recorded with the Register of Copyrights pursuant to paragraph (3). If the work is removed at the expense of the author, title to that copy of the work shall be deemed to be in the author.

(3) The Register of Copyrights shall establish a system of records whereby any author of a work of visual art that has been incorporated in or made part of a building, may record his or her identity and address with the Copyright Office. The Register shall also establish procedures under which any such author may update the information so recorded, and procedures under which owners of buildings may record with the Copyright Office evidence of their efforts to comply with this subsection.

(Oct. 19, 1976, Pub. L. 94-553, §101, 90 Stat. 2560; Dec. 1, 1990, Pub. L. 101-650, §604, 104 Stat. 5130.)

§ 114   Scope of exclusive rights in sound recordings

(a) The exclusive rights of the owner of copyright in a sound recording are limited to the rights specified by clauses (1), (2), (3) and (6) of section 106, and do not include any right of performance under section 106(4).

(b) The exclusive right of the owner of copyright in a sound recording under clause (1) of section 106 is limited to the right to duplicate the sound recording in the form of phonorecords or copies that directly or indirectly recapture the actual sounds fixed in the recording. The exclusive right of the owner of copyright in a sound recording under clause (2) of section 106 is limited to the right to prepare a derivative work in which the actual sounds fixed in the sound recording are rearranged, remixed, or otherwise altered in sequence or quality. The exclusive rights of the owner of copyright in a sound recording under clauses (1) and (2) of section 106 do not extend to the making or duplication of another sound recording that consists entirely of an independent fixation of other sounds, even though such sounds imitate or simulate those in the copyrighted sound recording. The exclusive rights of the owner of copyright in a sound recording under clauses (1), (2), and (3) of section 106 do not apply to sound recordings included in educational television and radio programs (as defined in section 397 of title 47) distributed or transmitted by or through public broadcasting entities (as defined by section 118(g)): *Provided*, That copies or phonorecords of said programs are not commercially distributed by or through public broadcasting entities to the general public.

(c) This section does not limit or impair the exclusive right to perform publicly, by means of a phonorecord, any of the works specified by section 106(4).

(d) *Limitations on exclusive right.*—Notwithstanding the provisions of section 106(6)—

(1) *Exempt transmissions and retransmissions.*—The performance of a sound recording publicly by means of a digital audio transmission, other than as a part of an interactive service, is not an infringement of section 106(6) if the performance is part of—

(A) a nonsubscription broadcast transmission;

(B) a retransmission of a nonsubscription broadcast transmission: *Provided*, That, in the case of a retransmission of a radio station's broadcast transmission—

(i) the radio station's broadcast transmission is not willfully or repeatedly retransmitted more than a radius of 150 miles from the site of the radio broadcast transmitter, however—

(I) the 150 mile limitation under this clause shall not apply when a nonsubscription broadcast transmission by a radio station licensed by the Federal Communications Commission is retransmitted on a nonsubscription basis by a terrestrial broadcast station, terrestrial translator, or terrestrial repeater licensed by the Federal Communications Commission; and

(II) in the case of a subscription retransmission of a nonsubscription broadcast retransmission covered by subclause (I), the 150 mile radius shall be measured from the transmitter site of such broadcast retransmitter;

(ii) the retransmission is of radio station broadcast transmissions that are—

(I) obtained by the retransmitter over the air;

(II) not electronically processed by the retransmitter to deliver separate and discrete signals; and

(III) retransmitted only within the local communities served by the retransmitter;

(iii) the radio station's broadcast transmission was being retransmitted to cable systems (as defined in section 111(f)) by a satellite carrier on January 1, 1995, and that retransmission was being retransmitted by cable systems as a separate and discrete signal, and the satellite carrier obtains the radio station's broadcast transmission in an analog format: *Provided,* That the broadcast transmission being retransmitted may embody the programming of no more than one radio station; or

(iv) the radio station's broadcast transmission is made by a noncommercial educational broadcast station funded on or after January 1, 1995, under section 396(k) of the Communications Act of 1934 (47 U.S.C. 396(k)), consists solely of noncommercial educational and cultural radio programs, and the retransmission, whether or not simultaneous, is a nonsubscription terrestrial broadcast retransmission; or

(C) a transmission that comes within any of the following categories—

(i) a prior or simultaneous transmission incidental to an exempt transmission, such as a feed received by and then retransmitted by an exempt transmitter: *Provided*, That such incidental transmissions do not include any subscription transmission directly for reception by members of the public;

(ii) a transmission within a business establishment, confined to its premises or the immediately surrounding vicinity;

(iii) a retransmission by any retransmitter, including a multichannel video programming distributor as defined in section 602(12) of the Communications Act of 1934 (47 U.S.C. 522(12)), of a transmission by a transmitter licensed to publicly perform the sound recording as a part of that transmission, if the retransmission is simultaneous with the licensed transmission and authorized by the transmitter; or

(iv) a transmission to a business establishment for use in the ordinary course of its business: *Provided*, That the business recipient does not retransmit the transmission outside of its premises or the immediately surrounding vicinity, and that the transmission does not exceed the sound recording performance complement. Nothing in this clause shall limit the scope of the exemption in clause (ii).

(2) *Statutory licensing of certain transmissions*—The performance of a sound recording publicly by means of a subscription digital audio transmission not exempt under paragraph (1), an eligible nonsubscription transmission, or a transmission not exempt under paragraph (1) that is made by a preexisting satellite digital audio radio service shall be subject to statutory licensing, in accordance with subsection (f) if—

(A)(i) the transmission is not part of an interactive service;

(ii) except in the case of a transmission to a business establishment, the transmitting entity does not automatically and intentionally cause any device receiving the transmission to switch from one program channel to another; and

(iii) except as provided in section 1002(e), the transmission of the sound recording is accompanied, if technically feasible, by the information encoded in that sound recording, if any, by or under the authority of the copyright owner of that

17 U.S.C. § 114

sound recording, that identifies the title of the sound recording, the featured recording artist who performs on the sound recording, and related information, including information concerning the underlying musical work and its writer;

(B) in the case of a subscription transmission not exempt under paragraph (1) that is made by a preexisting subscription service in the same transmission medium used by such service on July 31, 1998, or in the case of a transmission not exempt under paragraph (1) that is made by a preexisting satellite digital audio radio service—

(i) the transmission does not exceed the sound recording performance complement; and

(ii) the transmitting entity does not cause to be published by means of an advance program schedule or prior announcement the titles of the specific sound recordings or phonorecords embodying such sound recordings to be transmitted; and

(C) in the case of an eligible nonsubscription transmission or a subscription transmission not exempt under paragraph (1) that is made by a new subscription service or by a preexisting subscription service other than in the same transmission medium used by such service on July 31, 1998—

(i) the transmission does not exceed the sound recording performance complement, except that this requirement shall not apply in the case of a retransmission of a broadcast transmission if the retransmission is made by a transmitting entity that does not have the right or ability to control the programming of the broadcast station making the broadcast transmission, unless—

(I) the broadcast station makes broadcast transmissions—

(aa) in digital format that regularly exceed the sound recording performance complement; or (bb) in analog format, a substantial portion of which, on a weekly basis, exceed the sound recording performance complement; and

(II) the sound recording copyright owner or its representative has notified the transmitting entity in writing that broadcast transmissions of the copyright owner's sound recordings exceed the sound recording performance complement as provided in this clause;

(ii) the transmitting entity does not cause to be published, or induce or facilitate the publication, by means of an advance program schedule or prior announcement, the titles of the specific sound recordings to be transmitted, the phonorecords embodying such sound recordings, or, other than for illustrative purposes, the names of the featured recording artists, except that this clause does not disqualify a transmitting entity that makes a prior announcement that a particular artist will be featured within an unspecified future time period, and in the case of a retransmission of a broadcast transmission by a transmitting entity that does not have the right or ability to control the programming of the broadcast transmission, the requirement of this clause shall not apply to a prior oral announcement by the broadcast station, or to an advance program schedule published, induced, or facilitated by the broadcast station, if the transmitting entity does not have actual knowledge and has not received written notice from the copyright owner or its representative that the broadcast station publishes or induces or facilitates the publication of such advance program schedule, or if such advance program schedule is a schedule of classical music programming published by the broadcast station in the same manner as published by that broadcast station on or before September 30, 1998;

(iii) the transmission—

(I) is not part of an archived program of less than 5 hours duration

(II) is not part of an archived program of 5 hours or greater in duration that is made available for a period exceeding 2 weeks;

(III) is not part of a continuous program which is of less than 3 hours duration; or

(IV) is not part of an identifiable program in which performances of sound recordings are rendered in a predetermined order, other than an archived or continuous program, that is transmitted at—

(aa) more than 3 times in any 2-week period that have been publicly announced in advance, in the case of a program of less than 1 hour in duration, or

(bb) more than 4 times in any 2-week period that have been publicly announced in advance, in the case of a program of 1 hour or more in duration,

except that the requirement of this subclause shall not apply in the case of a retransmission of a broadcast transmission by a transmitting entity that does not have the right or ability to control the programming of the broadcast transmission, unless the transmitting entity is given notice in writing by the copyright owner of the sound recording that the broadcast station makes broadcast transmissions that regularly violate such requirement;

(iv) the transmitting entity does not knowingly perform the sound recording, as part of a service that offers transmissions of visual images contemporaneously with transmissions of sound recordings, in a manner that is likely to cause confusion, to cause mistake, or to deceive, as to the affiliation, connection, or association of the copyright owner or featured recording artist with the transmitting entity or a particular product or service advertised by the transmitting entity, or as to the origin, sponsorship, or approval by the copyright owner or featured recording artist of the activities of the transmitting entity other than the performance of the sound recording itself;

(v) the transmitting entity cooperates to prevent, to the extent feasible without imposing substantial costs or burdens, a transmission recipient or any other person or entity from automatically scanning the transmitting entity's transmissions alone or together with transmissions by other transmitting entities in order to select a particular sound recording to be transmitted to the transmission recipient, except that the requirement of this clause shall not apply to a satellite digital audio service that is in operation, or that is licensed by the Federal Communications Commission, on or before July 31, 1998;

(vi) the transmitting entity takes no affirmative steps to cause or induce the making of a phonorecord by the transmission recipient, and if the technology used by the transmitting entity enables the transmitting entity to limit the making by the transmission recipient of phonorecords of the transmission directly in a digital format, the transmitting entity sets such technology to limit such making of phonorecords to the extent permitted by such technology;

(vii) phonorecords of the sound recording have been distributed to the public under the authority of the copyright owner or the copyright owner authorizes the transmitting entity to transmit the sound recording, and the transmitting entity makes the transmission from a phonorecord lawfully made under the authority of the copyright owner, except that the requirement of this clause shall not apply to a retransmission of a broadcast transmission by a transmitting entity that does not have the right or ability to control the programming of the broadcast transmission, unless the transmitting entity is given notice in writing by the copyright owner of the sound recording that the broadcast station makes broadcast transmissions that regularly violate such requirement;

(viii) the transmitting entity accommodates and does not interfere with the transmission of technical measures that are widely used by sound recording copyright owners to identify or protect copyrighted works, and that are technically feasible of being transmitted by the transmitting entity without imposing substantial costs on the transmitting entity or resulting in perceptible aural or visual degradation of the digital signal, except that the requirement of this clause shall not apply to a satellite digital audio service that is in operation, or that is licensed under the authority of the Federal Communications Commission, on or before July 31, 1998, to the extent that such service has designed, developed, or made commitments to procure equipment or technology that is not compatible with such technical measures before such technical measures are widely adopted by sound recording copyright owners; and

(ix) the transmitting entity identifies in textual data the sound recording during, but not before, the time it is performed, including the title of the sound recording, the title of the phonorecord embodying such sound recording, if any, and the featured recording artist, in a manner to permit it to be displayed to the transmission recipient by the device or technology intended for receiving the service provided by the transmitting entity, except that the obligation in this clause shall not take effect until 1 year after the date of the enactment of the Digital Millennium Copyright Act and shall not apply in the case of a retransmission of a broadcast transmission by a transmitting entity that does not have the right or ability to control the programming of the broadcast transmission, or in the case in which devices or technology intended for receiving the service provided by the transmitting entity that have the capability to display such textual data are not common in the marketplace.

(3) *Licenses for transmissions by interactive services.*—

(A) No interactive service shall be granted an exclusive license under section 106(6) for the performance of a sound recording publicly by means of digital audio transmission for a period in excess of 12 months, except that with respect to an exclusive license granted to an interactive service by a licensor that holds the copyright to 1,000 or fewer sound recordings, the period of such license shall not exceed 24 months: *Provided, however,* That the grantee of such exclusive license shall be ineligible to receive another exclusive license for the performance of that sound recording for a period of 13 months from the expiration of the prior exclusive license.

(B) The limitation set forth in subparagraph (A) of this paragraph shall not apply if—

(i) the licensor has granted and there remain in effect licenses under section 106(6) for the public performance of sound recordings by means of digital audio transmission by at least 5 different interactive services: *Provided, however,* That each such license must be for a minimum of 10 percent of the copyrighted sound recordings owned by the licensor that have been licensed to interactive services, but in no event less than 50 sound recordings; or

(ii) the exclusive license is granted to perform publicly up to 45 seconds of a sound recording and the sole purpose of the performance is to promote the distribution or performance of that sound recording.

(C) Notwithstanding the grant of an exclusive or nonexclusive license of the right of public performance under section 106(6), an interactive service may not publicly perform a sound recording unless a license has been granted for the public performance of any copyrighted musical work contained in the sound recording: *Provided,* That such license to publicly perform the copyrighted musical work may be granted either by a performing rights society representing the copyright owner or by the copyright owner.

(D) The performance of a sound recording by means of a retransmission of a digital audio transmission is not an infringement of section 106(6) if—

(i) the retransmission is of a transmission by an interactive service licensed to publicly perform the sound recording to a particular member of the public as part of that transmission; and

(ii) the retransmission is simultaneous with the licensed transmission, authorized by the transmitter, and limited to that particular member of the public intended by the interactive service to be the recipient of the transmission.

(E) For the purposes of this paragraph—

(i) a "licensor" shall include the licensing entity and any other entity under any material degree of common ownership, management, or control that owns copyrights in sound recordings; and

(ii) a "performing rights society" is an association or corporation that licenses the public performance of nondramatic musical works on behalf of the copyright owner, such as the American Society of Composers, Authors and Publishers, Broadcast Music, Inc., and SESAC, Inc.

(4) *Rights not otherwise limited.*—

(A) Except as expressly provided in this section, this section does not limit or impair the exclusive right to perform a sound recording publicly by means of a digital audio transmission under section 106(6).

(B) Nothing in this section annuls or limits in any way—

(i) the exclusive right to publicly perform a musical work, including by means of a digital audio transmission, under section 106(4);

(ii) the exclusive rights in a sound recording or the musical work embodied therein under sections 106(1), 106(2) and 106(3); or

(iii) any other rights under any other clause of section 106, or remedies available under this title, as such rights or remedies exist either before or after the date of enactment of the Digital Performance Right in Sound Recordings Act of 1995.

(C) Any limitations in this section on the exclusive right under section 106(6) apply only to the exclusive right under section 106(6) and not to any other exclusive rights under section 106. Nothing in this section shall be construed to annul, limit, impair or otherwise affect in any way the ability of the owner of a copyright in a sound recording to exercise the rights under sections 106(1), 106(2) and 106(3), or to obtain the remedies available under this title pursuant to such rights, as such rights and remedies exist either before or after the date of enactment of the Digital Performance Right in Sound Recordings Act of 1995.

(e) *Authority for negotiations.*—

(1) Notwithstanding any provision of the antitrust laws, in negotiating statutory licenses in accordance with subsection (f), any copyright owners of sound recordings and any entities performing sound recordings affected by this section may negotiate and agree upon the royalty rates and license terms and conditions for the performance of such sound recordings and the proportionate division of fees paid among copyright owners, and may designate common agents on a nonexclusive basis to negotiate, agree to, pay, or receive payments.

(2) For licenses granted under section 106(6), other than statutory licenses, such as for performances by interactive services or performances that exceed the sound recording performance complement—

(A) copyright owners of sound recordings affected by this section may designate common agents to act on their behalf to grant licenses and receive and remit royalty payments: *Provided,* That each copyright owner shall establish the royalty rates and material license terms and conditions unilaterally, that is, not in agreement, combination, or concert with other copyright owners of sound recordings; and

(B) entities performing sound recordings affected by this section may designate common agents to act on their behalf to obtain licenses and collect and pay royalty fees: *Provided,* That each entity performing sound recordings shall determine the royalty rates and material license terms and conditions unilaterally, that is, not in agreement, combination, or concert with other entities performing sound recordings.

(f) *Licenses for certain nonexempt transmissions.*—

(1)(A) No later than 30 days after the enactment of the Digital Performance Right in Sound Recordings Act of 1995, the Librarian of Congress shall cause notice to be published in the Federal Register of the initiation of voluntary negotiation proceedings for the purpose of determining reasonable terms and rates of royalty

17 U.S.C. § 114

payments for subscription transmissions by preexisting subscription services and transmissions by preexisting satellite digital audio radio services specified by subsection (d)(2) of this section during the period beginning on the effective date of such Act and ending on December 31, 2001, or, if a copyright arbitration royalty panel is convened, ending 30 days after the Librarian issues and publishes in the Federal Register an order adopting the determination of the copyright arbitration royalty panel or an order setting the terms and rates (if the Librarian rejects the panel's determination). Such terms and rates shall distinguish among the different types of digital audio transmission services then in operation. Any copyright owners of sound recordings, preexisting subscription services, or preexisting satellite digital audio radio services may submit to the Librarian of Congress licenses covering such subscription transmissions with respect to such sound recordings. The parties to each negotiation proceeding shall bear their own costs.

(B) In the absence of license agreements negotiated under subparagraph (A), during the 60-day period commencing 6 months after publication of the notice specified in subparagraph (A), and upon the filing of a petition in accordance with section 803(a)(1), the Librarian of Congress shall, pursuant to chapter 8, convene a copyright arbitration royalty panel to determine and publish in the Federal Register a schedule of rates and terms which, subject to paragraph (3), shall be binding on all copyright owners of sound recordings and entities performing sound recordings affected by this paragraph. In establishing rates and terms for preexisting subscription services and preexisting satellite digital audio radio services, in addition to the objectives set forth in section 801(b)(1), the copyright arbitration royalty panel may consider the rates and terms for comparable types of subscription digital audio transmission services and comparable circumstances under voluntary license agreements negotiated as provided in subparagraph (A).

(C)(i) Publication of a notice of the initiation of voluntary negotiation proceedings as specified in subparagraph (A) shall be repeated, in accordance with regulations that the Librarian of Congress shall prescribe—

(I) no later than 30 days after a petition is filed by any copyright owners of sound recordings, any preexisting subscription services, or any preexisting satellite digital audio radio services indicating that a new type of subscription digital audio transmission service on which sound recordings are performed is or is about to become operational; and

(II) in the first week of January 2001, and at 5-year intervals thereafter.

(ii) The procedures specified in subparagraph (B) shall be repeated, in accordance with regulations that the Librarian of Congress shall prescribe, upon filing of a petition in accordance with section 803(a)(1) during a 60-day period commencing—

(I) 6 months after publication of a notice of the initiation of voluntary negotiation proceedings under subparagraph (A) pursuant to a petition under clause (i)(I) of this subparagraph; or

(II) on July 1, 2001, and at 5-year intervals thereafter.

(iii) The procedures specified in subparagraph (B) shall be concluded in accordance with section 802.

(2)(A) No later than 30 days after the date of the enactment of the Digital Millennium Copyright Act, the Librarian of Congress shall cause notice to be published in the Federal Register of the initiation of voluntary negotiation proceedings for the purpose of determining reasonable terms and rates of royalty payments for public performances of sound recordings by means of eligible nonsubscription transmissions and transmissions by new subscription services specified by subsection (d)(2) during the period beginning on the date of the enactment of such Act and ending on December 31, 2000, or such other date as the parties may agree. Such rates and terms shall distinguish among the different types of eligible nonsubscription transmission services and new subscription services then in operation and shall include a minimum fee for each such type of service. Any copyright owners of sound recordings or any entities performing sound recordings affected by this paragraph may submit to the Librarian of Congress licenses covering such eligible nonsubscription transmissions and new subscription services with respect to such sound recordings. The parties to each negotiation proceeding shall bear their own costs.

(B) In the absence of license agreements negotiated under subparagraph (A), during the 60-day period commencing 6 months after publication of the notice specified in subparagraph (A), and upon the filing of a petition in accordance with section 803(a)(1), the Librarian of Congress shall, pursuant to chapter 8, convene a copyright arbitration royalty panel to determine and publish in the Federal Register a schedule of rates and terms which, subject to paragraph (3), shall be binding on all copyright owners of sound recordings and entities performing sound recordings affected by this paragraph during the period beginning on the date of the enactment of the Digital Millennium Copyright Act and ending on December 31, 2000, or such other date as the parties may agree. Such rates and terms shall distinguish among the different types of eligible nonsubscription transmission services then in operation and shall include a minimum fee for each such type of service, such differences to be based on criteria including, but not limited to, the quantity and nature of the use of sound recordings and the degree to which use of the service may substitute for or may promote the purchase of phonorecords by consumers. In establishing rates and terms for transmissions by eligible nonsubscription services and new subscription services, the copyright arbitration royalty panel shall establish rates and terms that most clearly represent the rates and terms that would have been negotiated in the marketplace between a willing buyer and a willing seller. In determining such rates and terms, the copyright arbitration royalty panel shall base its decision on economic, competitive and programming information presented by the parties, including—

(i) whether use of the service may substitute for or may promote the sales of phonorecords or otherwise may interfere with or may enhance the sound recording copyright owner's other streams of revenue from its sound recordings; and

(ii) the relative roles of the copyright owner and the transmitting entity in the copyrighted work and the service made available to the public with respect to relative creative contribution, technological contribution, capital investment, cost, and risk.

In establishing such rates and terms, the copyright arbitration royalty panel may consider the rates and terms for comparable types of digital audio transmission services and comparable circumstances under voluntary license agreements negotiated under subparagraph (A).

(C)(i) Publication of a notice of the initiation of voluntary negotiation proceedings as specified in subparagraph (A) shall be repeated in accordance with regulations that the Librarian of Congress shall prescribe—

(I) no later than 30 days after a petition is filed by any copyright owners of sound recordings or any eligible nonsubscription service or new subscription service indicating that a new type of eligible nonsubscription service or new subscription service on which sound recordings are performed is or is about to become operational; and

(II) in the first week of January 2000, and at 2-year intervals thereafter, except to the extent that different years for the repeating of such proceedings may be determined in accordance with subparagraph (A).

(ii) The procedures specified in subparagraph (B) shall be repeated, in accordance with regulations that the Librarian of Congress shall prescribe, upon filing of a petition in accordance with section 803(a)(1) during a 60-day period commencing—

(I) 6 months after publication of a notice of the initiation of voluntary negotiation proceedings under subparagraph (A) pursuant to a petition under clause (i)(I); or

(II) on July 1, 2000, and at 2-year intervals thereafter, except to the extent that different years for the repeating of such proceedings may be determined in accordance with subparagraph (A).

(iii) The procedures specified in subparagraph (B) shall be concluded in accordance with section 802.

(3) License agreements voluntarily negotiated at any time between 1 or more copyright owners of sound recordings and 1 or more entities performing sound recordings shall be given effect in lieu of any determination by a copyright arbitration royalty panel or decision by the Librarian of Congress.

(4)(A) The Librarian of Congress shall also establish requirements by which copyright owners may receive reasonable notice of the use of their sound recordings under this section, and under which records of such use shall be kept and made available by entities performing sound recordings.

(B) Any person who wishes to perform a sound recording publicly by means of a transmission eligible for statutory licensing under this subsection may do so without infringing the exclusive right of the copyright owner of the sound recording—

(i) by complying with such notice requirements as the Librarian of Congress shall prescribe by regulation and by paying royalty fees in accordance with this subsection; or

(ii) if such royalty fees have not been set, by agreeing to pay such royalty fees as shall be determined in accordance with this subsection.

(C) Any royalty payments in arrears shall be made on or before the twentieth day of the month next succeeding the month in which the royalty fees are set.

(5) (A) Notwithstanding section 112(e) and the other provisions of this subsection, the receiving agent may enter into agreements for the reproduction and performance of sound recordings under

section 112(e) and this section by any 1 or more small commercial webcasters or noncommercial webcasters during the period beginning on October 28, 1998, and ending on December 31, 2004, that, once published in the Federal Register pursuant to subparagraph (B), shall be binding on all copyright owners of sound recordings and other persons entitled to payment under this section, in lieu of any determination by a copyright arbitration royalty panel or decision by the Librarian of Congress. Any such agreement for small commercial webcasters shall include provisions for payment of royalties on the basis of a percentage of revenue or expenses, or both, and include a minimum fee. Any such agreement may include other terms and conditions, including requirements by which copyright owners may receive notice of the use of their sound recordings and under which records of such use shall be kept and made available by small commercial webcasters or noncommercial webcasters. The receiving agent shall be under no obligation to negotiate any such agreement. The receiving agent shall have no obligation to any copyright owner of sound recordings or any other person entitled to payment under this section in negotiating any such agreement, and no liability to any copyright owner of sound recordings or any other person entitled to payment under this section for having entered into such agreement.

(B) The Copyright Office shall cause to be published in the Federal Register any agreement entered into pursuant to subparagraph (A). Such publication shall include a statement containing the substance of subparagraph (C). Such agreements shall not be included in the Code of Federal Regulations. Thereafter, the terms of such agreement shall be available, as an option, to any small commercial webcaster or noncommercial webcaster meeting the eligibility conditions of such agreement.

(C) Neither subparagraph (A) nor any provisions of any agreement entered into pursuant to subparagraph (A), including any rate structure, fees, terms, conditions, or notice and recordkeeping requirements set forth therein, shall be admissible as evidence or otherwise taken into account in any administrative, judicial, or other government proceeding involving the setting or

17 U.S.C. § 114

368 • Patent, Trademark, and Copyright Laws, 2003 Edition

adjustment of the royalties payable for the public performance or reproduction in ephemeral phonorecords or copies of sound recordings, the determination of terms or conditions related thereto, or the establishment of notice or recordkeeping requirements by the Librarian of Congress under paragraph (4) or section 112(e)(4). It is the intent of Congress that any royalty rates, rate structure, definitions, terms, conditions, or notice and recordkeeping requirements, included in such agreements shall be considered as a compromise motivated by the unique business, economic and political circumstances of small webcasters, copyright owners, and performers rather than as matters that would have been negotiated in the marketplace between a willing buyer and a willing seller, or otherwise meet the objectives set forth in section 801(b).

(D) Nothing in the Small Webcaster Settlement Act of 2002 or any agreement entered into pursuant to subparagraph (A) shall be taken into account by the United States Court of Appeals for the District of Columbia Circuit in its review of the determination by the Librarian of Congress of July 8, 2002, of rates and terms for the digital performance of sound recordings and ephemeral recordings, pursuant to sections 112 and 114.

(E) As used in this paragraph—

(i) the term "noncommercial webcaster" means a webcaster that—

(I) is exempt from taxation under section 501 of the Internal Revenue Code of 1986 (26 U.S.C. 501);

(II) has applied in good faith to the Internal Revenue Service for exemption from taxation under section 501 of the Internal Revenue Code and has a commercially reasonable expectation that such exemption shall be granted; or

(III) is operated by a State or possession or any governmental entity or subordinate thereof, or by the United States or District of Columbia, for exclusively public purposes;

(ii) the term "receiving agent" shall have the meaning given that term in section 261.2 of title 37, Code of Federal Regulations, as published in the Federal Register on July 8, 2002; and

(iii) the term "webcaster" means a person or entity that has obtained a compulsory license under section 112 or 114 and the implementing regulations therefor to make eligible nonsubscription transmissions and ephemeral recordings.

(F) The authority to make settlements pursuant to subparagraph (A) shall expire December 15, 2002, except with respect to noncommercial webcasters for whom the authority shall expire May 31, 2003.

(g) *Proceeds from licensing of transmissions.—*

(1) Except in the case of a transmission licensed under a statutory license in accordance with subsection (f) of this section—

(A) a featured recording artist who performs on a sound recording that has been licensed for a transmission shall be entitled to receive payments from the copyright owner of the sound recording in accordance with the terms of the artist's contract; and

(B) a nonfeatured recording artist who performs on a sound recording that has been licensed for a transmission shall be entitled to receive payments from the copyright owner of the sound recording in accordance with the terms of the nonfeatured recording artist's applicable contract or other applicable agreement.

(2) An agent designated to distribute receipts from the licensing of transmissions in accordance with subsection (f) shall distribute such receipts as follows:

(A) 50 percent of the receipts shall be paid to the copyright owner of the exclusive right under section 106(6) of this title to publicly perform a sound recording by means of a digital audio transmission.

(B) 2 1/2 percent of the receipts shall be deposited in an escrow account managed by an independent administrator jointly appointed by copyright owners of sound recordings and the

American Federation of Musicians (or any successor entity) to be distributed to nonfeatured musicians (whether or not members of the American Federation of Musicians) who have performed on sound recordings.

(C) 2 1/2 percent of the receipts shall be deposited in an escrow account managed by an independent administrator jointly appointed by copyright owners of sound recordings and the American Federation of Television and Radio Artists (or any successor entity) to be distributed to nonfeatured vocalists (whether or not members of the American Federation of Television and Radio Artists) who have performed on sound recordings.

(D) 45 percent of the receipts shall be paid, on a per sound recording basis, to the recording artist or artists featured on such sound recording (or the persons conveying rights in the artists' performance in the sound recordings).

(3) A nonprofit agent designated to distribute receipts from the licensing of transmissions in accordance with subsection (f) may deduct from any of its receipts, prior to the distribution of such receipts to any person or entity entitled thereto other than copyright owners and performers who have elected to receive royalties from another designated agent and have notified such nonprofit agent in writing of such election, the reasonable costs of such agent incurred after November 1, 1995, in—

(A) the administration of the collection, distribution, and calculation of the royalties;

(B) the settlement of disputes relating to the collection and calculation of the royalties; and

(C) the licensing and enforcement of rights with respect to the making of ephemeral recordings and performances subject to licensing under section 112 and this section, including those incurred in participating in negotiations or arbitration proceedings under section 112 and this section, except that all costs incurred relating to the section 112 ephemeral recordings right may only be deducted from the royalties received pursuant to section 112.

(4) Notwithstanding paragraph (3), any designated agent designated to distribute receipts from the licensing of transmissions in accordance with subsection (f) may deduct from any of its receipts, prior to the distribution of such receipts, the reasonable costs identified in paragraph (3) of such agent incurred after November 1, 1995, with respect to such copyright owners and performers who have entered with such agent a contractual relationship that specifies that such costs may be deducted from such royalty receipts.

(h) *Licensing to affiliates.—*

(1) If the copyright owner of a sound recording licenses an affiliated entity the right to publicly perform a sound recording by means of a digital audio transmission under section 106(6), the copyright owner shall make the licensed sound recording available under section 106(6) on no less favorable terms and conditions to all bona fide entities that offer similar services, except that, if there are material differences in the scope of the requested license with respect to the type of service, the particular sound recordings licensed, the frequency of use, the number of subscribers served, or the duration, then the copyright owner may establish different terms and conditions for such other services.

(2) The limitation set forth in paragraph (1) of this subsection shall not apply in the case where the copyright owner of a sound recording licenses—

(A) an interactive service; or

(B) an entity to perform publicly up to 45 seconds of the sound recording and the sole purpose of the performance is to promote the distribution or performance of that sound recording.

(i) *No effect on royalties for underlying works.*—License fees payable for the public performance of sound recordings under section 106(6) shall not be taken into account in any administrative, judicial, or other governmental proceeding to set or adjust the royalties payable to copyright owners of musical works for the public performance of their works. It is the intent of Congress that royalties payable to copyright owners of musical works for the public performance of their works shall not be diminished in any respect as a result of the rights granted by section 106(6).

17 U.S.C. § 114

(j) *Definitions.*—As used in this section, the following terms have the following meanings:

(1) An "affiliated entity" is an entity engaging in digital audio transmissions covered by section 106(6), other than an interactive service, in which the licensor has any direct or indirect partnership or any ownership interest amounting to 5 percent or more of the outstanding voting or non-voting stock.

(2) An "archived program" is a predetermined program that is available repeatedly on the demand of the transmission recipient and that is performed in the same order from the beginning, except that an archived program shall not include a recorded event or broadcast transmission that makes no more than an incidental use of sound recordings, as long as such recorded event or broadcast transmission does not contain an entire sound recording or feature a particular sound recording.

(3) A "broadcast" transmission is a transmission made by a terrestrial broadcast station licensed as such by the Federal Communications Commission.

(4) A "continuous program" is a predetermined program that is continuously performed in the same order and that is accessed at a point in the program that is beyond the control of the transmission recipient.

(5) A "digital audio transmission" is a digital transmission as defined in section 101, that embodies the transmission of a sound recording. This term does not include the transmission of any audiovisual work.

(6) An "eligible nonsubscription transmission" is a noninteractive nonsubscription digital audio transmission not exempt under subsection (d)(1) that is made as part of a service that provides audio programming consisting, in whole or in part, of performances of sound recordings, including retransmissions of broadcast transmissions, if the primary purpose of the service is to provide to the public such audio or other entertainment programming, and the primary purpose of the service is not to sell, advertise, or promote particular products or services other than sound recordings, live concerts, or other music-related events.

(7) An "interactive service" is one that enables a member of the public to receive a transmission of a program specially created for the recipient, or on request, a transmission of a particular sound recording, whether or not as part of a program, which is selected by or on behalf of the recipient. The ability of individuals to request that particular sound recordings be performed for reception by the public at large, or in the case of a subscription service, by all subscribers of the service, does not make a service interactive, if the programming on each channel of the service does not substantially consist of sound recordings that are performed within 1 hour of the request or at a time designated by either the transmitting entity or the individual making such request. If an entity offers both interactive and noninteractive services (either concurrently or at different times), the noninteractive component shall not be treated as part of an interactive service.

(8) A "new subscription service" is a service that performs sound recordings by means of noninteractive subscription digital audio transmissions and that is not a preexisting subscription service or a preexisting satellite digital audio radio service.

(9) A "nonsubscription" transmission is any transmission that is not a subscription transmission.

(10) A "preexisting satellite digital audio radio service" is a subscription satellite digital audio radio service provided pursuant to a satellite digital audio radio service license issued by the Federal Communications Commission on or before July 31, 1998, and any renewal of such license to the extent of the scope of the original license, and may include a limited number of sample channels representative of the subscription service that are made available on a nonsubscription basis in order to promote the subscription service.

(11) A "preexisting subscription service" is a service that performs sound recordings by means of noninteractive audio-only subscription digital audio transmissions, which was in existence and was making such transmissions to the public for a fee on or before July 31, 1998, and may include a limited number of sample channels representative of the subscription service that are made available on a nonsubscription basis in order to promote the subscription service.

17 U.S.C. § 114

(12) A "retransmission" is a further transmission of an initial transmission, and includes any further retransmission of the same transmission. Except as provided in this section, a transmission qualifies as a "retransmission" only if it is simultaneous with the initial transmission. Nothing in this definition shall be construed to exempt a transmission that fails to satisfy a separate element required to qualify for an exemption under section 114(d)(1).

(13) The "sound recording performance complement" is the transmission during any 3-hour period, on a particular channel used by a transmitting entity, of no more than—

(A) 3 different selections of sound recordings from any one phonorecord lawfully distributed for public performance or sale in the United States, if no more than 2 such selections are transmitted consecutively; or

(B) 4 different selections of sound recordings—

(i) by the same featured recording artist; or

(ii) from any set or compilation of phonorecords lawfully distributed together as a unit for public performance or sale in the United States,

if no more than three such selections are transmitted consecutively:

Provided, That the transmission of selections in excess of the numerical limits provided for in clauses (A) and (B) from multiple phonorecords shall nonetheless qualify as a sound recording performance complement if the programming of the multiple phonorecords was not willfully intended to avoid the numerical limitations prescribed in such clauses.

(14) A "subscription" transmission is a transmission that is controlled and limited to particular recipients, and for which consideration is required to be paid or otherwise given by or on behalf of the recipient to receive the transmission or a package of transmissions including the transmission.

(15) A "transmission" is either an initial transmission or a retransmission.

(Oct. 19, 1976, Pub. L. 94-553, §101, 90 Stat. 2560; Nov. 1, 1995, Pub. L. 104-39, §3, 109 Stat. 336; Nov. 13, 1997, Pub. L. 105-80, §3, 111 Stat. 1531; Oct. 28, 1998, Pub. L. 105-304, §405(a), 112 Stat. 2890; Dec. 4, 2002, Pub. L. 107-321, §§4, 5, 116 Stat. 2780.)

§ 115 Scope of exclusive rights in nondramatic musical works: Compulsory license for making and distributing phonorecords

In the case of nondramatic musical works, the exclusive rights provided by clauses (1) and (3) of section 106, to make and to distribute phonorecords of such works, are subject to compulsory licensing under the conditions specified by this section.

(a) *Availability and scope of compulsory license.*—

(1) When phonorecords of a nondramatic musical work have been distributed to the public in the United States under the authority of the copyright owner, any other person, including those who make phonorecords or digital phonorecord deliveries, may, by complying with the provisions of this section, obtain a compulsory license to make and distribute phonorecords of the work. A person may obtain a compulsory license only if his or her primary purpose in making phonorecords is to distribute them to the public for private use, including by means of a digital phonorecord delivery. A person may not obtain a compulsory license for use of the work in the making of phonorecords duplicating a sound recording fixed by another, unless: (i) such sound recording was fixed lawfully; and (ii) the making of the phonorecords was authorized by the owner of copyright in the sound recording or, if the sound recording was fixed before February 15, 1972, by any person who fixed the sound recording pursuant to an express license from the owner of the copyright in the musical work or pursuant to a valid compulsory license for use of such work in a sound recording.

(2) A compulsory license includes the privilege of making a musical arrangement of the work to the extent necessary to conform it to the style or manner of interpretation of the performance involved, but the arrangement shall not change the basic melody or fundamental character of the work, and shall not be subject to protection as a derivative work under this title, except with the express consent of the copyright owner.

17 U.S.C. § 115

(b) *Notice of intention to obtain compulsory license.—*

(1) Any person who wishes to obtain a compulsory license under this section shall, before or within thirty days after making, and before distributing any phonorecords of the work, serve notice of intention to do so on the copyright owner. If the registration or other public records of the Copyright Office do not identify the copyright owner and include an address at which notice can be served, it shall be sufficient to file the notice of intention in the Copyright Office. The notice shall comply, in form, content, and manner of service, with requirements that the Register of Copyrights shall prescribe by regulation.

(2) Failure to serve or file the notice required by clause (1) forecloses the possibility of a compulsory license and, in the absence of a negotiated license, renders the making and distribution of phonorecords actionable as acts of infringement under section 501 and fully subject to the remedies provided by sections 502 through 506 and 509.

(c) *Royalty payable under compulsory license.**

(1) To be entitled to receive royalties under a compulsory license, the copyright owner must be identified in the registration or other public records of the Copyright Office. The owner is entitled to royalties for phonorecords made and distributed after being so identified, but is not entitled to recover for any phonorecords previously made and distributed.

(2) Except as provided by clause (1), the royalty under a compulsory license shall be payable for every phonorecord made and distributed in accordance with the license. For this purpose, and other than as provided in paragraph (3), a phonorecord is considered "distributed" if the person exercising the compulsory license has voluntarily and permanently parted with its possession. With respect to each work embodied in the phonorecord, the royalty shall be either two and three-fourths cents,* or one-half of one cent* per minute of playing time or fraction thereof, whichever amount is larger.

---

* *Ed. Note:* Rates are readjusted pursuant to statute. *See* 17 U.S.C. §§801-03.

17 U.S.C. § 115

(3) (A) A compulsory license under this section includes the right of the compulsory licensee to distribute or authorize the distribution of a phonorecord of a nondramatic musical work by means of a digital transmission which constitutes a digital phonorecord delivery, regardless of whether the digital transmission is also a public performance of the sound recording under section 106(6) of this title or of any nondramatic musical work embodied therein under section 106(4) of this title. For every digital phonorecord delivery by or under the authority of the compulsory licensee—

(i) on or before December 31, 1997, the royalty payable by the compulsory licensee shall be the royalty prescribed under paragraph (2) and chapter 8 of this title; and

(ii) on or after January 1, 1998, the royalty payable by the compulsory licensee shall be the royalty prescribed under subparagraphs (B) through (F) and chapter 8 of this title.

(B) Notwithstanding any provision of the antitrust laws, any copyright owners of nondramatic musical works and any persons entitled to obtain a compulsory license under subsection (a)(1) may negotiate and agree upon the terms and rates of royalty payments under this paragraph and the proportionate division of fees paid among copyright owners, and may designate common agents to negotiate, agree to, pay or receive such royalty payments. Such authority to negotiate the terms and rates of royalty payments includes, but is not limited to, the authority to negotiate the year during which the royalty rates prescribed under subparagraphs (B) through (F) and chapter 8 of this title shall next be determined.

(C) During the period of June 30, 1996, through December 31, 1996, the Librarian of Congress shall cause notice to be published in the Federal Register of the initiation of voluntary negotiation proceedings for the purpose of determining reasonable terms and rates of royalty payments for the activities specified by subparagraph (A) during the period beginning January 1, 1998, and ending on the effective date of any new terms and rates established pursuant to subparagraph (C), (D) or (F), or such other date (regarding digital phonorecord deliveries) as the parties may agree. Such terms and rates shall distinguish between (i) digital phonorecord deliveries where the reproduction or distribution of a phonorecord is incidental to the transmission which constitutes the digital phonorecord delivery, and (ii) digital phonorecord deliveries in general. Any copyright owners of nondramatic musical works and any persons entitled to obtain a compulsory license under subsection (a)(1) may submit to the Librarian of Congress licenses covering such activities. The parties to each negotiation proceeding shall bear their own costs.

(D) In the absence of license agreements negotiated under subparagraphs (B) and (C), upon the filing of a petition in accordance with section 803(a)(1), the Librarian of Congress shall, pursuant to chapter 8, convene a copyright arbitration royalty panel to determine and publish in the Federal Register a schedule of rates and terms which, subject to subparagraph (E), shall be binding on all copyright owners of nondramatic musical works and persons entitled to obtain a compulsory license under subsection (a)(1) during the period beginning January 1, 1998, and ending on the effective date of any new terms and rates established pursuant to subparagraph (C), (D) or (F), or such other date (regarding digital phonorecord deliveries) as may be determined pursuant to subparagraphs (B) and (C). Such terms and rates shall distinguish between (i) digital phonorecord deliveries where the reproduction or distribution of a phonorecord is incidental to the transmission which constitutes the digital phonorecord delivery, and (ii) digital phonorecord deliveries in general. In addition to the objectives set forth in section 801(b)(1), in establishing such rates and terms, the copyright arbitration royalty panel may consider rates and terms under voluntary license agreements negotiated as provided in subparagraphs (B) and (C). The royalty rates payable for a compulsory license for a digital phonorecord delivery under this section shall be established de novo and no precedential effect shall be given to the amount of the royalty payable by a compulsory licensee for digital phonorecord deliveries on or before December 31, 1997. The Librarian of Congress shall also establish requirements by which copyright owners may receive reasonable notice of the use of their works under this section, and under which records of such use shall be kept and made available by persons making digital phonorecord deliveries.

(E) (i) License agreements voluntarily negotiated at any time between one or more copyright owners of nondramatic musical works and one or more persons entitled to obtain a compulsory license under subsection (a)(1) shall be given effect in lieu of any determination by the Librarian of Congress. Subject to clause (ii), the royalty rates determined pursuant to subparagraph (C), (D) or (F) shall be given effect in lieu of any contrary royalty rates specified in a contract pursuant to which a recording artist who is the author of a nondramatic musical work grants a license under that person's exclusive rights in the musical work under paragraphs (1) and (3) of section 106 or commits another person to grant a license in that musical work under paragraphs (1) and (3) of section 106, to a person desiring to fix in a tangible medium of expression a sound recording embodying the musical work.

(ii) The second sentence of clause (i) shall not apply to—

(I) a contract entered into on or before June 22, 1995, and not modified thereafter for the purpose of reducing the royalty rates determined pursuant to subparagraph (C), (D) or (F) or of increasing the number of musical works within the scope of the contract covered by the reduced rates, except if a contract entered into on or before June 22, 1995, is modified thereafter for the purpose of increasing the number of musical works within the scope of the contract, any contrary royalty rates specified in the contract shall be given effect in lieu of royalty rates determined pursuant to subparagraph (C), (D) or (F) for the number of musical works within the scope of the contract as of June 22, 1995; and

(II) a contract entered into after the date that the sound recording is fixed in a tangible medium of expression substantially in a form intended for commercial release, if at the time the contract is entered into, the recording artist retains the right to grant licenses as to the musical work under paragraphs (1) and (3) of section 106.

(F) The procedures specified in subparagraphs (C) and (D) shall be repeated and concluded, in accordance with regulations that the Librarian of Congress shall prescribe, in each fifth calendar year after 1997, except to the extent that different years for the repeating and concluding of such proceedings may be determined in accordance with subparagraphs (B) and (C).

(G) Except as provided in section 1002(e) of this title, a digital phonorecord delivery licensed under this paragraph shall be accompanied by the information encoded in the sound recording, if any, by or under the authority of the copyright owner of that sound recording, that identifies the title of the sound recording, the featured recording artist who performs on the sound recording, and related information, including information concerning the underlying musical work and its writer.

(H) (i) A digital phonorecord delivery of a sound recording is actionable as an act of infringement under section 501, and is fully subject to the remedies provided by sections 502 through 506 and section 509, unless—

(I) the digital phonorecord delivery has been authorized by the copyright owner of the sound recording; and

(II) the owner of the copyright in the sound recording or the entity making the digital phonorecord delivery has obtained a compulsory license under this section or has otherwise been authorized by the copyright owner of the musical work to distribute or authorize the distribution, by means of a digital phonorecord delivery, of each musical work embodied in the sound recording.

(ii) Any cause of action under this subparagraph shall be in addition to those available to the owner of the copyright in the nondramatic musical work under subsection (c)(6) and section 106(4) and the owner of the copyright in the sound recording under section 106(6).

(I) The liability of the copyright owner of a sound recording for infringement of the copyright in a nondramatic musical work embodied in the sound recording shall be determined in accordance with applicable law, except that the owner of a copyright in a sound recording shall not be liable for a digital phonorecord delivery by a third party if the owner of the copyright in the sound recording does not license the distribution of a phonorecord of the nondramatic musical work.

(J) Nothing in section 1008 shall be construed to prevent the exercise of the rights and remedies allowed by this paragraph, paragraph (6), and chapter 5 in the event of a digital phonorecord delivery, except that no action alleging infringement of copyright may be brought under this title against a manufacturer, importer or distributor of a digital audio recording device, a digital audio recording medium, an analog recording device, or an analog recording medium, or against a consumer, based on the actions described in such section.

(K) Nothing in this section annuls or limits (i) the exclusive right to publicly perform a sound recording or the musical work embodied therein, including by means of a digital transmission, under sections 106(4) and 106(6), (ii) except for compulsory licensing under the conditions specified by this section, the exclusive rights to reproduce and distribute the sound recording and the musical work embodied therein under sections 106(1) and 106(3), including by means of a digital phonorecord delivery, or (iii) any other rights under any other provision of section 106, or remedies available under this title, as such rights or remedies exist either before or after the date of enactment of the Digital Performance Right in Sound Recordings Act of 1995.

(L) The provisions of this section concerning digital phonorecord deliveries shall not apply to any exempt transmissions or retransmissions under section 114(d)(1). The exemptions created in section 114(d)(1) do not expand or reduce the rights of copyright owners under section 106 (1) through (5) with respect to such transmissions and retransmissions.

(4) A compulsory license under this section includes the right of the maker of a phonorecord of a nondramatic musical work under subsection (a)(1) to distribute or authorize distribution of such phonorecord by rental, lease, or lending (or by acts or practices in the nature of rental, lease, or lending). In addition to any royalty payable under clause (2) and chapter 8 of this title, a royalty shall be payable by the compulsory licensee for every act of distribution of a phonorecord by or in the nature of rental, lease, or lending, by or under the authority of the compulsory licensee. With respect to each nondramatic musical work embodied in the phonorecord, the royalty shall be a proportion of the revenue received by the compulsory licensee from every such act of distribution of the phonorecord under this clause equal to the proportion of the revenue received by the compulsory licensee from distribution of the phonorecord under clause (2) that is payable by a compulsory licensee under that clause and under chapter 8. The Register of Copyrights shall issue regulations to carry out the purpose of this clause.

(5) Royalty payments shall be made on or before the twentieth day of each month and shall include all royalties for the month next preceding. Each monthly payment shall be made under oath and shall comply with requirements that the Register of Copyrights shall prescribe by regulation. The Register shall also prescribe regulations under which detailed cumulative annual statements of account, certified by a certified public accountant, shall be filed for every compulsory license under this section. The regulations covering both the monthly and the annual statements of account shall prescribe the form, content, and manner of certification with respect to the number of records made and the number of records distributed.

(6) If the copyright owner does not receive the monthly payment and the monthly and annual statements of account when due, the owner may give written notice to the licensee that, unless the default is remedied within thirty days from the date of the notice, the compulsory license will be automatically terminated. Such termination renders either the making or the distribution, or both, of all phonorecords for which the royalty has not been paid, actionable as acts

of infringement under section 501 and fully subject to the remedies provided by sections 502 through 506 and 509.

(d) *Definition.*—As used in this section, the following term has the following meaning: A "digital phonorecord delivery" is each individual delivery of a phonorecord by digital transmission of a sound recording which results in a specifically identifiable reproduction by or for any transmission recipient of a phonorecord of that sound recording, regardless of whether the digital transmission is also a public performance of the sound recording or any nondramatic musical work embodied therein. A digital phonorecord delivery does not result from a real-time, non-interactive subscription transmission of a sound recording where no reproduction of the sound recording or the musical work embodied therein is made from the inception of the transmission through to its receipt by the transmission recipient in order to make the sound recording audible.

(Oct. 19, 1976, Pub. L. 94-553, §101, 90 Stat. 2561; Oct. 4, 1984, Pub. L. 98-450, §3, 98 Stat. 1727; Nov. 1. 1995, Pub. L. 104-39, §4, 109 Stat. 344; Nov. 13, 1997, Pub. L. 105-80, §§4, 12, 111 Stat. 1531, 1534-5.)

§ 116 Negotiated licenses for public performances by means of coin-operated phonorecord players

(a) *Applicability of section.*—This section applies to any nondramatic musical work embodied in a phonorecord.

(b) *Negotiated licenses.*—

(1) *Authority for negotiations.*—Any owners of copyright in works to which this section applies and any operators of coin-operated phonorecord players may negotiate and agree upon the terms and rates of royalty payments for the performance of such works and the proportionate division of fees paid among copyright owners, and may designate common agents to negotiate, agree to, pay, or receive such royalty payments.

(2) *Arbitration.*—Parties not subject to such a negotiation may determine, by arbitration in accordance with the provisions of chapter 8, the terms and rates and the division of fees described in paragraph (1).

(c) *License agreements superior to Copyright Arbitration Royalty Panel determinations.*—License agreements between one or more copyright owners and one or more operators of coin-operated phonorecord players, which are negotiated in accordance with subsection (b), shall be given effect in lieu of any otherwise applicable determination by a copyright arbitration royalty panel.

(d) *Definitions.*—As used in this section, the following terms mean the following:

(1) A 'coin-operated phonorecord player' is a machine or device that—

(A) is employed solely for the performance of nondramatic musical works by means of phonorecords upon being activated by the insertion of coins, currency, tokens, or other monetary units or their equivalent;

(B) is located in an establishment making no direct or indirect charge for admission;

(C) is accompanied by a list which is comprised of the titles of all the musical works available for performance on it, and is affixed to the phonorecord player or posted in the establishment in a prominent position where it can readily be examined by the public; and

(D) affords a choice of works available for performance and permits the choice to be made by the patrons of the establishment in which it is located.

(2) An 'operator' is any person who, alone or jointly with others—

(A) owns a coin-operated phonorecord player;

(B) has the power to make a coin-operated phonorecord player available for placement in an establishment for purposes of public performance; or

(C) has the power to exercise primary control over the selection of the musical works made available for public performance on a coin-operated phonorecord player.

(Oct. 31, 1988, Pub. L. 100-568, §4, 102 Stat. 2855; Dec. 17, 1993, Pub. L. 103-198, §3(b), 107 Stat. 2309; Nov. 13, 1997, Pub. L. 105-80, §5, 111 Stat. 1531.)

§ 117 Limitations on exclusive rights: Computer programs

(a) *Making of additional copy or adaptation by owner of copy.*— Notwithstanding the provisions of section 106, it is not an infringement for the owner of a copy of a computer program to make or authorize the making of another copy or adaptation of that computer program provided:

(1) that such a new copy or adaptation is created as an essential step in the utilization of the computer program in conjunction with a machine and that it is used in no other manner, or

(2) that such new copy or adaptation is for archival purposes only and that all archival copies are destroyed in the event that continued possession of the computer program should cease to be rightful.

(b) *Lease, sale, or other transfer of additional copy or adaptation.*—Any exact copies prepared in accordance with the provisions of this section may be leased, sold, or otherwise transferred, along with the copy from which such copies were prepared, only as part of the lease, sale, or other transfer of all rights in the program. Adaptations so prepared may be transferred only with the authorization of the copyright owner.

(c) *Machine maintenance or repair.*—Notwithstanding the provisions of section 106, it is not an infringement for the owner or lessee of a machine to make or authorize the making of a copy of a computer program if such copy is made solely by virtue of the activation of a machine that lawfully contains an authorized copy of the computer program, for purposes only of maintenance or repair of that machine, if—

(1) such new copy is used in no other manner and is destroyed immediately after the maintenance or repair is completed; and

(2) with respect to any computer program or part thereof that is not necessary for that machine to be activated, such program or part thereof is not accessed or used other than to make such new copy by virtue of the activation of the machine.

(d) *Definitions.*—For purposes of this section—

(1) the "maintenance" of a machine is the servicing of the machine in order to make it work in accordance with its original specifications and any changes to those specifications authorized for that machine; and

(2) the "repair" of a machine is the restoring of the machine to the state of working in accordance with its original specifications and any changes to those specifications authorized for that machine.

(Oct. 19, 1976, Pub. L. 94-553, §101, 90 Stat. 2565; Dec. 12, 1980, Pub. L. 96—517, §10, 94 Stat. 3028; Oct. 28, 1998, Pub. L. 105-304, §302, 112 Stat. 2887.)

§ 118 Scope of exclusive rights: Use of certain works in connection with noncommercial broadcasting

(a) The exclusive rights provided by section 106 shall, with respect to the works specified by subsection (b) and the activities specified by subsection (d), be subject to the conditions and limitations prescribed by this section.

(b) Notwithstanding any provision of the antitrust laws, any owners of copyright in published nondramatic musical works and published pictoral, graphic, and sculptural works and any public broadcasting entities, respectively, may negotiate and agree upon the terms and rates of royalty payments and the proportionate division of fees paid among various copyright owners, and may designate common agents to negotiate, agree to, pay, or receive payments.

(1) Any owner of copyright in a work specified in this subsection or any public broadcasting entity may submit to the Librarian of Congress proposed licenses covering such activities with respect to such works. The Librarian of Congress shall proceed on the basis of the proposals submitted as well as any other relevant information. The Librarian of Congress shall permit any interested party to submit information relevant to such proceedings.

(2) License agreements, voluntarily negotiated at any time between one or more copyright owners and one or more public broadcasting entities shall be given effect in lieu of any determination by the Librarian of Congress: *Provided*, That copies of such agreements are filed in the Copyright Office within thirty days of execution in accordance with regulations that the Register of Copyrights shall prescribe.

(3) In the absence of license agreements negotiated under paragraph (2), the Librarian of Congress shall, pursuant to chapter 8, convene a copyright arbitration royalty panel to determine and publish in the Federal Register a schedule of rates and terms which, subject to paragraph (2), shall be binding on all owners of copyright in works specified by this subsection and public broadcasting entities, regard-

less of whether such copyright owners have submitted proposals to the Librarian of Congress. In establishing such rates and terms the copyright arbitration royalty panel may consider the rates for comparable circumstances under voluntary license agreements negotiated as provided in paragraph 2. The Librarian of Congress shall also establish requirements by which copyright owners may receive reasonable notice of the use of their works under this section, and under which records of such use shall be kept by public broadcasting entities.

(c) The initial procedure specified in subsection (b) shall be repeated and concluded between June 30 and December 31, 1997, and at five-year intervals thereafter, in accordance with regulations that the Librarian of Congress shall prescribe.

(d) Subject to the terms of any voluntary license agreements that have been negotiated as provided by subsection (b)(2), a public broadcasting entity may, upon compliance with the provisions of this section, including the rates and terms established by a copyright arbitration royalty panel under subsection (b)(3), engage in the following activities with respect to published nondramatic musical works and published pictorial, graphic, and sculptural works:

(1) performance or display of a work by or in the course of a transmission made by a noncommercial educational broadcast station referred to in subsection (g); and

(2) production of a transmission program, reproduction of copies or phonorecords of such a transmission program, and distribution of such copies or phonorecords, where such production, reproduction, or distribution is made by a nonprofit institution or organization solely for the purpose of transmissions specified in paragraph (1); and

(3) the making of reproductions by a governmental body or a nonprofit institution of a transmission program simultaneously with its transmission as specified in paragraph (1), and the performance or display of the contents of such program under the conditions specified by paragraph (1) of section 110, but only if the reproductions are used for performances or displays for a period of no more than seven days from the date of the transmission specified in paragraph (1), and are destroyed before or at the end of such period. No person

supplying, in accordance with paragraph (2), a reproduction of a transmission program to governmental bodies or nonprofit institutions under this clause shall have any liability as a result of failure of such body or institution to destroy such reproduction: *Provided*, That it shall have notified such body or institution of the requirement for such destruction pursuant to this clause: *And provided further*, That if such body or institution itself fails to destroy such reproduction it shall be deemed to have infringed.

(e) Except as expressly provided in this subsection, this section shall have no applicability to works other than those specified in subsection (b). Owners of copyright in nondramatic literary works and public broadcasting entities may, during the course of voluntary negotiations, agree among themselves, respectively, as to the terms and rates of royalty payments without liability under the antitrust laws. Any such terms and rates of royalty payments shall be effective upon filing in the Copyright Office, in accordance with regulations that the Register of Copyrights shall prescribe.

(f) Nothing in this section shall be construed to permit, beyond the limits of fair use as provided by section 107, the unauthorized dramatization of a nondramatic musical work, the production of a transmission program drawn to any substantial extent from a published compilation of pictorial, graphic, or sculptural works, or the unauthorized use of any portion of an audiovisual work.

(g) As used in this section, the term "public broadcasting entity" means a noncommercial educational broadcast station as defined in section 397 of title 47 and any nonprofit institution or organization engaged in the activities described in paragraph (2) of subsection (d).

(Oct. 19, 1976, Pub. L. 94-553, §101, 90 Stat. 2565; Dec. 17, 1993, Pub. L. 103-198, §4, 107 Stat. 2309; Aug. 5, 1999, Pub. L. 106-44, §1(g), 113 Stat. 222; Nov. 2, 2002, Pub. L. 107-273, §13210, 116 Stat. 1909.)

§ 119   Limitations on exclusive rights: Secondary transmissions of superstations and network stations for private home viewing*

(a) *Secondary transmissions by satellite carriers.—*

(1) *Superstations and PBS satellite feed.—*Subject to the provisions of paragraphs (3), (4), and (6) of this subsection and section 114(d), secondary transmissions of a performance or display of a work embodied in a primary transmission made by a superstation or by the Public Broadcasting Service satellite feed shall be subject to statutory licensing under this section if the secondary transmission is made by a satellite carrier to the public for private home viewing, with regard to secondary transmissions the satellite carrier is in compliance with the rules, regulations, or authorizations of the Federal Communications Commission governing the carriage of television broadcast station signals, and the carrier makes a direct or indirect charge for each retransmission service to each household receiving the secondary transmission or to a distributor that has contracted with the carrier for direct or indirect delivery of the secondary transmission to the public for private home viewing. In the case of the Public Broadcasting Service satellite feed, the statutory license shall be effective until January 1, 2002.

(2) *Network stations.—*

(A) *In general.—*Subject to the provisions of subparagraphs (B) and (C) of this paragraph and paragraphs (3), (4), (5), and (6) of this subsection and section 114(d), secondary transmissions of a performance or display of a work embodied in a primary transmission made by a network station shall be subject to statutory licensing under this section if the secondary transmission is made by a satellite carrier to the public for private home viewing, with regard to secondary transmissions the satellite carrier is in compliance with the rules, regulations, or authorizations of the Federal Communications Commission governing the carriage of television broadcast station signals, and the carrier makes a direct or indirect charge for such retransmission service to each subscriber receiving the secondary transmission.

---

* *Ed. Note:* Section 1003 of Pub. L. 106-113 provides that 17 U.S.C. §119 ceases to be effective on Dec. 31, 2004.

17 U.S.C. § 119

(B) *Secondary transmissions to unserved households.—*

(i) *In general.*—The statutory license provided for in subparagraph (A) shall be limited to secondary transmissions of the signals of no more than two network stations in a single day for each television network to persons who reside in unserved households.

(ii) *Accurate determinations of eligibility.—*

(I) *Accurate predictive model.*—In determining presumptively whether a person resides in an unserved household under subsection (d)(10)(A), a court shall rely on the Individual Location Longley-Rice model set forth by the Federal Communications Commission in Docket No. 98-201, as that model may be amended by the Commission over time under section 339(c)(3) of the Communications Act of 1934 to increase the accuracy of that model.

(II) *Accurate measurements.*—For purposes of site measurements to determine whether a person resides in an unserved household under subsection (d)(10)(A), a court shall rely on section 339(c)(4) of the Communications Act of 1934.

(iii) *C-band exemption to unserved households.—*

(I) *In general.*—The limitations of clause (i) shall not apply to any secondary transmissions by C-band services of network stations that a subscriber to C-band service received before any termination of such secondary transmissions before October 31, 1999.

(II) *Definition.*—In this clause the term "C-band service" means a service that is licensed by the Federal Communications Commission and operates in the Fixed Satellite Service under part 25 of title 47 of the Code of Federal Regulations.

(C) *Submission of subscriber lists to networks.*—A satellite carrier that makes secondary transmissions of a primary transmission made by a network station pursuant to subparagraph (A) shall,

90 days after commencing such secondary transmissions, submit to the network that owns or is affiliated with the network station a list identifying (by name and street address, including county and zip code) all subscribers to which the satellite carrier makes secondary transmissions of that primary transmission. Thereafter, on the 15th of each month, the satellite carrier shall submit to the network a list identifying (by name and street address, including county and zip code) any persons who have been added or dropped as such subscribers since the last submission under this subparagraph. Such subscriber information submitted by a satellite carrier may be used only for purposes of monitoring compliance by the satellite carrier with this subsection. The submission requirements of this subparagraph shall apply to a satellite carrier only if the network to whom the submissions are to be made places on file with the Register of Copyrights a document identifying the name and address of the person to whom such submissions are to be made. The Register shall maintain for public inspection a file of all such documents.

(3) *Noncompliance with reporting and payment requirements.*— Notwithstanding the provisions of paragraphs (1) and (2), the willful or repeated secondary transmission to the public by a satellite carrier of a primary transmission made by a superstation or a network station and embodying a performance or display of a work is actionable as an act of infringement under section 501, and is fully subject to the remedies provided by sections 502 through 506 and 509, where the satellite carrier has not deposited the statement of account and royalty fee required by subsection (b), or has failed to make the submissions to networks required by paragraph (2)(C).

(4) *Willful alterations.*—Notwithstanding the provisions of paragraphs (1) and (2), the secondary transmission to the public by a satellite carrier of a performance or display of a work embodied in a primary transmission made by a superstation or a network station is actionable as an act of infringement under section 501, and is fully subject to the remedies provided by sections 502 through 506 and sections 509 and 510, if the content of the particular program in which the performance or display is embodied, or any commercial advertising or station announcement transmitted by the primary

17 U.S.C. § 119

transmitter during, or immediately before or after, the transmission of such program, is in any way willfully altered by the satellite carrier through changes, deletions, or additions, or is combined with programming from any other broadcast signal.

(5) *Violation of territorial restrictions on statutory license for network stations.—*

(A) *Individual violations.*—The willful or repeated secondary transmission by a satellite carrier of a primary transmission made by a network station and embodying a performance or display of a work to a subscriber who does not reside in an unserved household is actionable as an act of infringement under section 501 and is fully subject to the remedies provided by sections 502 through 506 and 509, except that—

(i) no damages shall be awarded for such act of infringement if the satellite carrier took corrective action by promptly withdrawing service from the ineligible subscriber, and

(ii) any statutory damages shall not exceed $5 for such subscriber for each month during which the violation occurred.

(B) *Pattern of violations.*—If a satellite carrier engages in a willful or repeated pattern or practice of delivering a primary transmission made by a network station and embodying a performance or display of a work to subscribers who do not reside in unserved households, then in addition to the remedies set forth in subparagraph (A)—

(i) if the pattern or practice has been carried out on a substantially nationwide basis, the court shall order a permanent injunction barring the secondary transmission by the satellite carrier, for private home viewing, of the primary transmissions of any primary network station affiliated with the same network, and the court may order statutory damages of not to exceed $250,000 for each 6-month period during which the pattern or practice was carried out; and

(ii) if the pattern or practice has been carried out on a local or regional basis, the court shall order a permanent injunction barring the secondary transmission, for private home viewing in that locality or region, by the satellite carrier of the primary transmissions of any primary network station affiliated with the same network, and the court may order statutory damages of not to exceed $250,000 for each 6-month period during which the pattern or practice was carried out.

(C) *Previous subscribers excluded.*—Subparagraphs (A) and (B) do not apply to secondary transmissions by a satellite carrier to persons who subscribed to receive such secondary transmissions from the satellite carrier or a distributor before November 16, 1988.

(D) *Burden of proof.*—In any action brought under this paragraph, the satellite carrier shall have the burden of proving that its secondary transmission of a primary transmission by a network station is for private home viewing to an unserved household.*

(E) *Exception*— The secondary transmission by a satellite carrier of a performance or display of a work embodied in a primary transmission made by a network station to subscribers who do not reside in unserved households shall not be an act of infringement if—

(i) the station on May 1, 1991, was retransmitted by a satellite carrier and was not on that date owned or operated by or affiliated with a television network that offered interconnected program service on a regular basis for 15 or more hours per week to at least 25 affiliated television licensees in 10 or more States;

(ii) as of July 1, 1998, such station was retransmitted by a satellite carrier under the statutory license of this section; and

(iii) the station is not owned or operated by or affiliated with a television network that, as of January 1, 1995, offered interconnected program service on a regular basis for 15 or more

---

* *Ed. Note:* Pursuant to Section 6(b) of Pub. L. 103-369, the provisions of §119(a)(5)(D) took effect on Jan. 1, 1997, with respect to civil matters relating to the eligibility of subscribers who subscribed to service as an unserved household before Oct. 18, 1994.

17 U.S.C. § 119

hours per week to at least 25 affiliated television licensees in 10 or more States.

(6) *Discrimination by a satellite carrier.*—Notwithstanding the provisions of paragraph (1), the willful or repeated secondary transmission to the public by a satellite carrier of a performance or display of a work embodied in a primary transmission made by a superstation or a network station is actionable as an act of infringement under section 501, and is fully subject to the remedies provided by sections 502 through 506 and 509, if the satellite carrier unlawfully discriminates against a distributor.

(7) *Geographic limitation on secondary transmissions.*—The statutory license created by this section shall apply only to secondary transmissions to households located in the United States.

(8) *Transitional signal intensity measurement procedures.*—

(A) *In general.*—Subject to subparagraph (C), upon a challenge by a network station regarding whether a subscriber is an unserved household within the predicted Grade B Contour of the station, the satellite carrier shall, within 60 days after the receipt of the challenge—

(i) terminate service to that household of the signal that is the subject of the challenge, and within 30 days thereafter notify the network station that made the challenge that service to that household has been terminated; or

(ii) conduct a measurement of the signal intensity of the subscriber's household to determine whether the household is an unserved household after giving reasonable notice to the network station of the satellite carrier's intent to conduct the measurement.

(B) *Effect of measurement.*—If the satellite carrier conducts a signal intensity measurement under subparagraph (A) and the measurement indicates that—

(i) the household is not an unserved household, the satellite carrier shall, within 60 days after the measurement is conducted, terminate the service to that household of the signal that is the subject of the challenge, and within 30 days thereafter notify the network station that made the challenge that service to that household has been terminated; or

(ii) the household is an unserved household, the station challenging the service shall reimburse the satellite carrier for the costs of the signal measurement within 60 days after receipt of the measurement results and a statement of the costs of the measurement.

(C) *Limitation on measurements.—*

(i) Notwithstanding subparagraph (A), a satellite carrier may not be required to conduct signal intensity measurements during any calendar year in excess of 5 percent of the number of subscribers within the network station's local market that have subscribed to the service as of the effective date of the Satellite Home Viewer Act of 1994.

(ii) If a network station challenges whether a subscriber is an unserved household in excess of 5 percent of the subscribers within the network station's local market within a calendar year, subparagraph (A) shall not apply to challenges in excess of such 5 percent, but the station may conduct its own signal intensity measurement of the subscriber's household after giving reasonable notice to the satellite carrier of the network station's intent to conduct the measurement. If such measurement indicates that the household is not an unserved household, the carrier shall, within 60 days after receipt of the measurement, terminate service to the household of the signal that is the subject of the challenge and within 30 days thereafter notify the network station that made the challenge that service has been terminated. The carrier shall also, within 60 days after receipt of the measurement and a statement of the costs of the measurement, reimburse the network station for the cost it incurred in conducting the measurement.

(D) *Outside the predicted Grade B Contour.—*

(i) If a network station challenges whether a subscriber is an unserved household outside the predicted Grade B Contour of the station, the station may conduct a measurement of the signal intensity of the subscriber's household to determine whether the household is an unserved household after giving reasonable notice to the satellite carrier of the network station's intent to conduct the measurement.

(ii) If the network station conducts a signal intensity measurement under clause (i) and the measurement indicates that—

(I) the household is not an unserved household, the station shall forward the results to the satellite carrier who shall, within 60 days after receipt of the measurement, terminate the service to the household of the signal that is the subject of the challenge, and shall reimburse the station for the costs of the measurement within 60 days after receipt of the measurement results and a statement of such costs; or

(II) the household is an unserved household, the station shall pay the costs of the measurement.

(9) *Loser pays for signal intensity measurement; recovery of measurement costs in a civil action.*—In any civil action filed relating to the eligibility of subscribing households as unserved households—

(A) a network station challenging such eligibility shall, within 60 days after receipt of the measurement results and a statement of such costs, reimburse the satellite carrier for any signal intensity measurement that is conducted by that carrier in response to a challenge by the network station and that establishes the household is an unserved household; and

(B) a satellite carrier shall, within 60 days after receipt of the measurement results and a statement of such costs, reimburse the network station challenging such eligibility for any signal intensity measurement that is conducted by that station and that establishes the household is not an unserved household.

(10) *Inability to conduct measurement.*—If a network station makes a reasonable attempt to conduct a site measurement of its signal at a subscriber's household and is denied access for the purpose of conducting the measurement, and is otherwise unable to conduct a

measurement, the satellite carrier shall within 60 days notice thereof, terminate service of the station's network to that household.

(11) *Service to recreational vehicles and commercial trucks.—*

(A) Exemption—

(i) *In general.—*For purposes of this subsection, and subject to clauses (ii) and (iii), the term "unserved household" shall include—

(I) recreational vehicles as defined in regulations of the Secretary of Housing and Urban Development under section 3282.8 of title 24 of the Code of Federal Regulations; and

(II) commercial trucks that qualify as commercial motor vehicles under regulations of the Secretary of Transportation under section 383.5 of title 49 of the Code of Federal Regulations.

(ii) *Limitation.—*Clause (i) shall apply only to a recreational vehicle or commercial truck if any satellite carrier that proposes to make a secondary transmission of a network station to the operator of such a recreational vehicle or commercial truck complies with the documentation requirements under subparagraphs (B) and (C).

(iii) *Exclusion.—*For purposes of this subparagraph, the terms "recreational vehicle" and "commercial truck" shall not include any fixed dwelling, whether a mobile home or otherwise.

(B) *Documentation requirements.—*A recreational vehicle or commercial truck shall be deemed to be an unserved household beginning 10 days after the relevant satellite carrier provides to the network that owns or is affiliated with the network station that will be secondarily transmitted to the recreational vehicle or commercial truck the following documents:

(i) *Declaration.—*A signed declaration by the operator of the recreational vehicle or commercial truck that the satellite dish is permanently attached to the recreational vehicle or commercial truck, and will not be used to receive satellite programming at any fixed dwelling.

(ii) *Registration.*—In the case of a recreational vehicle, a copy of the current State vehicle registration for the recreational vehicle.

(iii) *Registration and license.*—In the case of a commercial truck, a copy of—

(I) the current State vehicle registration for the truck; and

(II) a copy of a valid, current commercial driver's license, as defined in regulations of the Secretary of Transportation under section 383 of title 49 of the Code of Federal Regulations, issued to the operator.

(C) *Updated documentation requirements.*—If a satellite carrier wishes to continue to make secondary transmissions to a recreational vehicle or commercial truck for more than a 2-year period, that carrier shall provide each network, upon request, with updated documentation in the form described under subparagraph (B) during the 90 days before expiration of that 2-year period.

(12) *Statutory license contingent on compliance with FCC rules and remedial steps.*—Notwithstanding any other provision of this section, the willful or repeated secondary transmission to the public by a satellite carrier of a primary transmission embodying a performance or display of a work made by a broadcast station licensed by the Federal Communications Commission is actionable as an act of infringement under section 501, and is fully subject to the remedies provided by sections 502 through 506 and 509, if, at the time of such transmission, the satellite carrier is not in compliance with the rules, regulations, and authorizations of the Federal Communications Commission concerning the carriage of television broadcast station signals.

(b) *Statutory license for secondary transmissions for private home viewing.*—

(1) *Deposits with the Register of Copyrights.*—A satellite carrier whose secondary transmissions are subject to statutory licensing under subsection (a) shall, on a semiannual basis, deposit with the Register of Copyrights, in accordance with requirements that the Register shall prescribe by regulation—

(A) a statement of account, covering the preceding 6-month period, specifying the names and locations of all superstations and network stations whose signals were retransmitted, at any time during that period, to subscribers for private home viewing as described in subsections (a)(1) and (a)(2), the total number of subscribers that received such retransmissions, and such other data as the Register of Copyrights may from time to time prescribe by regulation; and

(B) a royalty fee for that 6-month period, computed by—

(i) multiplying the total number of subscribers receiving each secondary transmission of a superstation during each calendar month by 17.5 cents per subscriber in the case of superstations that as retransmitted by the satellite carrier include any program which, if delivered by any cable system in the United States, would be subject to the syndicated exclusivity rules of the Federal Communications Commission, and 14 cents per subscriber in the case of superstations that are syndex-proof as defined in section 258.2 of title 37, Code of Federal Regulations;

(ii) multiplying the number of subscribers receiving each secondary transmission of a network station or the Public Broadcasting Service satellite feed during each calendar month by 6 cents; and

(iii) adding together the totals computed under clauses (i) and (ii).

(2) *Investment of fees.*—The Register of Copyrights shall receive all fees deposited under this section and, after deducting the reasonable costs incurred by the Copyright Office under this section (other than the costs deducted under paragraph (4)), shall deposit the balance in the Treasury of the United States, in such manner as the Secretary of the Treasury directs. All funds held by the Secretary of the Treasury shall be invested in interest-bearing securities of the United States for later distribution with interest by the Librarian of Congress as provided by this title.

(3) *Persons to whom fees are distributed.*—The royalty fees deposited under paragraph (2) shall, in accordance with the procedures pro-

17 U.S.C. § 119

vided by paragraph (4), be distributed to those copyright owners whose works were included in a secondary transmission for private home viewing made by a satellite carrier during the applicable 6-month accounting period and who file a claim with the Librarian of Congress under paragraph (4).

(4) *Procedures for distribution.*—The royalty fees deposited under paragraph (2) shall be distributed in accordance with the following procedures:

(A) *Filing of claims for fees.*—During the month of July in each year, each person claiming to be entitled to statutory license fees for secondary transmissions for private home viewing shall file a claim with the Librarian of Congress, in accordance with requirements that the Librarian of Congress shall prescribe by regulation. For purposes of this paragraph, any claimants may agree among themselves as to the proportionate division of statutory license fees among them, may lump their claims together and file them jointly or as a single claim, or may designate a common agent to receive payment on their behalf.

(B) *Determination of controversy; distributions.*—After the first day of August of each year, the Librarian of Congress shall determine whether there exists a controversy concerning the distribution of royalty fees. If the Librarian of Congress determines that no such controversy exists, the Librarian of Congress shall, after deducting reasonable administrative costs under this paragraph, distribute such fees to the copyright owners entitled to receive them, or to their designated agents. If the Librarian of Congress finds the existence of a controversy, the Librarian of Congress shall, pursuant to chapter 8 of this title, convene a copyright arbitration royalty panel to determine the distribution of royalty fees.

(C) *Withholding of fees during controversy.*—During the pendency of any proceeding under this subsection, the Librarian of Congress shall withhold from distribution an amount sufficient to satisfy all claims with respect to which a controversy exists, but shall have discretion to proceed to distribute any amounts that are not in controversy.

(c) *Determination of royalty fees.*—

17 U.S.C. § 119

(1) *Applicability and adjustment of royalty fees.*—The rate of the royalty fee payable under subsection (b)(1)(B) shall be effective unless a royalty fee is established under paragraph (2) or (3) of this subsection.

(2) *Fee set by voluntary negotiation.*—

(A) *Notice of initiation of proceedings.*—On or before July 1, 1996, the Librarian of Congress shall cause notice to be published in the Federal Register of the initiation of voluntary negotiation proceedings for the purpose of determining the royalty fee to be paid by satellite carriers under subsection (b)(1)(B).

(B) *Negotiations.*—Satellite carriers, distributors, and copyright owners entitled to royalty fees under this section shall negotiate in good faith in an effort to reach a voluntary agreement or voluntary agreements for the payment of royalty fees. Any such satellite carriers, distributors, and copyright owners may at any time negotiate and agree to the royalty fee, and may designate common agents to negotiate, agree to, or pay such fees. If the parties fail to identify common agents, the Librarian of Congress shall do so, after requesting recommendations from the parties to the negotiation proceeding. The parties to each negotiation proceeding shall bear the entire cost thereof.

(C) *Agreements binding on parties; filing of agreements.*—Voluntary agreements negotiated at any time in accordance with this paragraph shall be binding upon all satellite carriers, distributors, and copyright owners that are parties thereto. Copies of such agreements shall be filed with the Copyright Office within 30 days after execution in accordance with regulations that the Register of Copyrights shall prescribe.

(D) *Period agreement is in effect.*—The obligation to pay the royalty fees established under a voluntary agreement which has been filed with the Copyright Office in accordance with this paragraph shall become effective on the date specified in the agreement, and shall remain in effect until December 31, 1999, or in accordance with the terms of the agreement, whichever is later.

(3) *Fee set by compulsory arbitration.*—

(A) *Notice of initiation of proceedings.*—On or before January 1, 1997, the Librarian of Congress shall cause notice to be published in the Federal Register of the initiation of arbitration proceedings for the purpose of determining a reasonable royalty fee to be paid under subsection (b)(1)(B) by satellite carriers who are not parties to a voluntary agreement filed with the Copyright Office in accordance with paragraph (2). Such proceeding shall be conducted under chapter 8.

(B) *Establishment of Royalty Fees.*—In determining royalty fees under this paragraph, the copyright arbitration royalty panel appointed under chapter 8 shall establish fees for the retransmission of network stations and superstations that most clearly represent the fair market value of secondary transmissions. In determining the fair market value, the panel shall base its decision on economic, competitive, and programming information presented by the parties, including—

(i) the competitive environment in which such programming is distributed, the cost of similar signals in similar private and compulsory license marketplaces, and any special features and conditions of the retransmission marketplace;

(ii) the economic impact of such fees on copyright owners and satellite carriers; and

(iii) the impact on the continued availability of secondary transmissions to the public.

(C) *Period during which decision of Arbitration Panel or order of Librarian effective.*—The obligation to pay the royalty fee established under a determination which—

(i) is made by a copyright arbitration royalty panel in an arbitration proceeding under this paragraph and is adopted by the Librarian of Congress under section 802(f), or

(ii) is established by the Librarian of Congress under section 802(f),

shall become effective as provided in section 802(g) or July 1, 1997, whichever is later.

(D) *Establishment of Royalty Fees.*—In determining royalty fees under this paragraph, the Copyright Arbitration Panel shall establish fees for the retransmission of network stations and superstations that most clearly represent the fair market value of secondary transmissions. In determining the fair market value, the Panel shall base its decision on economic, competitive, and programming information presented by the parties, including—

(i) the competitive environment in which such programming is distributed, the cost for similar signals in similar private and compulsory license marketplaces, and any special features and conditions of the transmission marketplace;

(ii) the economic impact of such fees on copyright owners and satellite carriers; and

(iii) the impact on the continued availability of secondary transmissions to the public.

(4) *Reduction.*—

(A) *Superstation.*—The rate of the royalty fee in effect on January 1, 1998, payable in each case under subsection (b)(1)(B)(i) shall be reduced by 30 percent.

(B) *Network and Public Broadcasting satellite feed.*—The rate of the royalty fee in effect on January 1, 1998, payable under subsection (b)(1)(B)(ii) shall be reduced by 45 percent.

(5) *Public Broadcasting Service as agent.*—For purposes of section 802, with respect to royalty fees paid by satellite carriers for retransmitting the Public Broadcasting Service satellite feed, the Public Broadcasting Service shall be the agent for all public television copyright claimants and all Public Broadcasting Service member stations.

(d) *Definitions.*—As used in this section—

(1) *Distributor.*—The term "distributor" means an entity which contracts to distribute secondary transmissions from a satellite carrier and, either as a single channel or in a package with other programming, provides the secondary transmission either directly to individual subscribers for private home viewing or indirectly through other program distribution entities.

(2) *Network station.*—The term "network station" means—

17 U.S.C. § 119

(A) a television broadcast station, including any translator station or terrestrial satellite station that rebroadcasts all or substantially all of the programming broadcast by a network station, that is owned or operated by, or affiliated with, one or more of the television networks in the United States which offer an interconnected program service on a regular basis for 15 or more hours per week to at least 25 of its affiliated television licensees in 10 or more States; or

(B) a noncommercial educational broadcast station (as defined in section 397 of the Communications Act of 1934);

except that the term does not include the signal of the Alaska Rural Communications Service, or any successor entity to that service.

(3) *Primary network station.*—The term "primary network station" means a network station that broadcasts or rebroadcasts the basic programming service of a particular national network.

(4) *Primary transmission.*—The term "primary transmission" has the meaning given that term in section 111(f) of this title.

(5) *Private home viewing.*—The term "private home viewing" means the viewing, for private use in a household by means of satellite reception equipment which is operated by an individual in that household and which serves only such household, of a secondary transmission delivered by a satellite carrier of a primary transmission of a television station licensed by the Federal Communications Commission.

(6) *Satellite carrier.*—The term "satellite carrier" means an entity that uses the facilities of a satellite or satellite service licensed by the Federal Communications Commission and operates in the Fixed-Satellite Service under part 25 of title 47 of the Code of Federal Regulations or the Direct Broadcast Satellite Service under part 100 of title 47 of the Code of Federal Regulations, to establish and operate a channel of communications for point-to-multipoint distribution of television station signals, and that owns or leases a capacity or service on a satellite in order to provide such point-to-multipoint distribution, except to the extent that such entity provides such distribu-

tion pursuant to tariff under the Communications Act of 1934, other than for private home viewing.

(7) *Secondary transmission.*—The term "secondary transmission" has the meaning given that term in section 111(f) of this title.

(8) *Subscriber.*—The term "subscriber" means an individual who receives a secondary transmission service for private home viewing by means of a secondary transmission from a satellite carrier and pays a fee for the service, directly or indirectly, to the satellite carrier or to a distributor.

(9) *Superstation.*—The term "superstation" —

(A) means a television broadcast station, other than a network station, licensed by the Federal Communications Commission that is secondarily transmitted by a satellite carrier; and

(B) except for purposes of computing the royalty fee, includes the Public Broadcasting Service satellite feed.

(10) *Unserved household.*—The term "unserved household", with respect to a particular television network, means a household that—

(A) cannot receive, through the use of a conventional, stationary, outdoor rooftop receiving antenna, an over-the-air signal of a primary network station affiliated with that network of Grade B intensity as defined by the Federal Communications Commission under section 73.683(a) of title 47 of the Code of Federal Regulations, as in effect on January 1, 1999;

(B) is subject to a waiver granted under regulations established under section 339(c)(2) of the Communications Act of 1934;

(C) is a subscriber to whom subsection (e) applies;

(D) is a subscriber to whom subsection (a)(11) applies; or

(E) is a subscriber to whom the exemption under subsection (a)(2)(B)(iii) applies.

(11) *Local market.*—The term "local market" has the meaning given such term under section 122(j).

(12) *Public Broadcasting Service satellite feed.*—The term "Public Broadcasting Service satellite feed" means the national satellite feed distributed and designated for purposes of this section by the Public

Broadcasting Service consisting of educational and informational programming intended for private home viewing, to which the Public Broadcasting Service holds national terrestrial broadcast rights.

(e) *Moratorium on copyright liability.*—Until December 31, 2004, a subscriber who does not receive a signal of Grade A intensity (as defined in the regulations of the Federal Communications Commission under section 73.683(a) of title 47 of the Code of Federal Regulations, as in effect on January 1, 1999, or predicted by the Federal Communications Commission using the Individual Location Longley-Rice methodology described by the Federal Communications Commission in Docket No. 98-201) of a local network television broadcast station shall remain eligible to receive signals of network stations affiliated with the same network, if that subscriber had satellite service of such network signal terminated after July 11, 1998, and before October 31, 1999, as required by this section, or received such service on October 31, 1999.

(Nov. 16, 1988, Pub. L. 100-667, §202, 102 Stat. 3949; Dec. 17, 1993, Pub. L. 103-198, §5, 107 Stat. 2310; Oct. 18, 1994, Pub. L. 103-369, §2, 108 Stat. 3477 Nov. 1. 1995, Pub. L. 104-39, §5(c), 109 Stat. 348; Nov. 13, 1997, Pub. L. 105-80, §§2, 12, 111 Stat.1529-30, 1535; Aug. 5, 1999, Pub. L. 106-44, §1(g), 113 Stat. 222; Nov. 29, 1999, Pub. L. 106-113, §§1004, 1005- 1008, 1011, 113 Stat. 1501A-527, 527-31, 543; Nov. 2, 2002, Pub. L. 107-273, §§13209, 13210, 116 Stat. 1909.)

§ 120   Scope of exclusive rights in architectural works

(a) *Pictorial representations permitted.*—The copyright in an architectural work that has been constructed does not include the right to prevent the making, distributing, or public display of pictures, paintings, photographs, or other pictorial representations of the work, if the building in which the work is embodied is located in or ordinarily visible from a public place.

(b) *Alterations to and destruction of buildings.*—Notwithstanding the provisions of section 106(2), the owners of a building embodying an architectural work may, without the consent of the author or copyright owner of the architectural work, make or authorize the making of alterations to such building, and destroy or authorize the destruction of such building.

(Dec. 1, 1990, Pub. L. 101-650, §704, 104 Stat. 5133.)

§ 121   Limitations on exclusive rights: Reproduction for blind or other people with disabilities

(a) Notwithstanding the provisions of section 106, it is not an infringement of copyright for an authorized entity to reproduce or to distribute copies or phonorecords of a previously published, nondramatic literary work if such copies or phonorecords are reproduced or distributed in specialized formats exclusively for use by blind or other persons with disabilities.

(b) (1) Copies or phonorecords to which this section applies shall—

(A) not be reproduced or distributed in a format other than a specialized format exclusively for use by blind or other persons with disabilities;

(B) bear a notice that any further reproduction or distribution in a format other than a specialized format is an infringement; and

(C) include a copyright notice identifying the copyright owner and the date of the original publication.

(2) The provisions of this subsection shall not apply to standardized, secure, or norm-referenced tests and related testing material, or to computer programs, except the portions thereof that are in conventional human language (including descriptions of pictorial works) and displayed to users in the ordinary course of using the computer programs.

(c) For purposes of this section, the term—

(1) 'authorized entity' means a nonprofit organization or a governmental agency that has a primary mission to provide specialized services relating to training, education, or adaptive reading or information access needs of blind or other persons with disabilities;

(2) 'blind or other persons with disabilities' means individuals who are eligible or who may qualify in accordance with the Act entitled "An Act to provide books for the adult blind", approved March 3, 1931 (2 U.S.C. 135a; 46 Stat. 1487) to receive books and other publications produced in specialized formats; and

(3) 'specialized formats' means braille, audio, or digital text which is exclusively for use by blind or other persons with disabilities.

(Sept. 16, 1996, Pub. L. 104-197, §316, 110 Stat. 2416; Oct. 27, 2000, Pub. L. 106-379, §3(b), 114 Stat. 1445; Nov. 2, 2002, Pub. L. 107-273, §13210, 116 Stat. 1909.)

§ 122   Limitations on exclusive rights: Secondary transmissions by satellite carriers within local markets

(a) *Secondary transmissions of television broadcast stations by satellite carriers.*—A secondary transmission of a performance or display of a work embodied in a primary transmission of a television broadcast station into the station's local market shall be subject to statutory licensing under this section if—

(1) the secondary transmission is made by a satellite carrier to the public;

(2) with regard to secondary transmissions, the satellite carrier is in compliance with the rules, regulations, or authorizations of the Federal Communications Commission governing the carriage of television broadcast station signals; and

(3) the satellite carrier makes a direct or indirect charge for the secondary transmission to—

(A) each subscriber receiving the secondary transmission; or

(B) a distributor that has contracted with the satellite carrier for direct or indirect delivery of the secondary transmission to the public.

(b) *Reporting requirements.*—

(1) *Initial lists.*—A satellite carrier that makes secondary transmissions of a primary transmission made by a network station under subsection (a) shall, within 90 days after commencing such secondary transmissions, submit to the network that owns or is affiliated with the network station a list identifying (by name in alphabetical order and street address, including county and zip code) all subscribers to which the satellite carrier makes secondary transmissions of that primary transmission under subsection (a).

(2) *Subsequent lists.*—After the list is submitted under paragraph (1), the satellite carrier shall, on the 15th of each month, submit to the network a list identifying (by name in alphabetical order and street address, including county and zip code) any subscribers who have

been added or dropped as subscribers since the last submission under this subsection.

(3) *Use of subscriber information.*—Subscriber information submitted by a satellite carrier under this subsection may be used only for the purposes of monitoring compliance by the satellite carrier with this section.

(4) *Requirements of networks.*—The submission requirements of this subsection shall apply to a satellite carrier only if the network to which the submissions are to be made places on file with the Register of Copyrights a document identifying the name and address of the person to whom such submissions are to be made. The Register of Copyrights shall maintain for public inspection a file of all such documents.

(c) *No royalty fee required.*—A satellite carrier whose secondary transmissions are subject to statutory licensing under subsection (a) shall have no royalty obligation for such secondary transmissions.

(d) *Noncompliance with reporting and regulatory requirements.*—Notwithstanding subsection (a), the willful or repeated secondary transmission to the public by a satellite carrier into the local market of a television broadcast station of a primary transmission embodying a performance or display of a work made by that television broadcast station is actionable as an act of infringement under section 501, and is fully subject to the remedies provided under sections 502 through 506 and 509, if the satellite carrier has not complied with the reporting requirements of subsection (b) or with the rules, regulations, and authorizations of the Federal Communications Commission concerning the carriage of television broadcast signals.

(e) *Willful alterations.*—Notwithstanding subsection (a), the secondary transmission to the public by a satellite carrier into the local market of a television broadcast station of a performance or display of a work embodied in a primary transmission made by that television broadcast station is actionable as an act of infringement under section 501, and is fully subject to the remedies provided by sections 502 through 506 and sections 509 and 510, if the content of the particular program in which the performance or display is embodied, or any commercial advertising or station announcement transmitted by the primary transmitter during, or immediately before or after, the transmission of such program, is in any way willfully altered by the satellite carrier through changes, deletions, or additions, or is combined with programming from any other broadcast signal.

(f) *Violation of territorial restrictions on statutory license for television broadcast stations.*—

(1) *Individual violations.*—The willful or repeated secondary transmission to the public by a satellite carrier of a primary transmission embodying a performance or display of a work made by a television broadcast station to a subscriber who does not reside in that station's local market, and is not subject to statutory licensing under section 119 or a private licensing agreement, is actionable as an act of infringement under section 501 and is fully subject to the remedies provided by sections 502 through 506 and 509, except that—

(A) no damages shall be awarded for such act of infringement if the satellite carrier took corrective action by promptly withdrawing service from the ineligible subscriber; and

(B) any statutory damages shall not exceed $5 for such subscriber for each month during which the violation occurred.

(2) *Pattern of violations.*—If a satellite carrier engages in a willful or repeated pattern or practice of secondarily transmitting to the public a primary transmission embodying a performance or display of a work made by a television broadcast station to subscribers who do not reside in that station's local market, and are not subject to statutory licensing under section 119 or a private licensing agreement, then in addition to the remedies under paragraph (1)—

(A) if the pattern or practice has been carried out on a substantially nationwide basis, the court—

(i) shall order a permanent injunction barring the secondary transmission by the satellite carrier of the primary transmissions of that television broadcast station (and if such television broadcast station is a network station, all other television broadcast stations affiliated with such network); and

(ii) may order statutory damages not exceeding $250,000 for each 6-month period during which the pattern or practice was carried out; and

(B) if the pattern or practice has been carried out on a local or regional basis with respect to more than one television broadcast station, the court—

(i) shall order a permanent injunction barring the secondary transmission in that locality or region by the satellite carrier of the primary transmissions of any television broadcast station; and

(ii) may order statutory damages not exceeding $250,000 for each 6-month period during which the pattern or practice was carried out.

(g) *Burden of proof.*—In any action brought under subsection (f), the satellite carrier shall have the burden of proving that its secondary transmission of a primary transmission by a television broadcast station is made only to subscribers located within that station's local market or subscribers being served in compliance with section 119 or a private licensing agreement.

(h) *Geographic limitations on secondary transmissions.*—The statutory license created by this section shall apply to secondary transmissions to locations in the United States.

(i) *Exclusivity with respect to secondary transmissions of broadcast stations by satellite to members of the public.*—No provision of section 111 or any other law (other than this section and section 119) shall be construed to contain any authorization, exemption, or license through which secondary transmissions by satellite carriers of programming contained in a primary transmission made by a television broadcast station may be made without obtaining the consent of the copyright owner.

(j) *Definitions.*—In this section—

(1) *Distributor.*—The term "distributor" means an entity which contracts to distribute secondary transmissions from a satellite carrier and, either as a single channel or in a package with other programming, provides the secondary transmission either directly to indi-

vidual subscribers or indirectly through other program distribution entities.

(2) *Local market.*—

(A) *In general.*— The term "local market", in the case of both commercial and noncommercial television broadcast stations, means the designated market area in which a station is located, and—

(i) in the case of a commercial television broadcast station, all commercial television broadcast stations licensed to a community within the same designated market area are within the same local market; and

(ii) in the case of a noncommercial educational television broadcast station, the market includes any station that is licensed to a community within the same designated market area as the noncommercial educational television broadcast station.

(B) *County of license.*—In addition to the area described in subparagraph (A), a station's local market includes the county in which the station's community of license is located.

(C) *Designated market area.*—For purposes of subparagraph (A), the term "designated market area" means a designated market area, as determined by Nielsen Media Research and published in the 1999-2000 Nielsen Station Index Directory and Nielsen Station Index United States Television Household Estimates or any successor publication.

(3) *Network station; satellite carrier; secondary transmission.*—The terms "network station", "satellite carrier", and "secondary transmission" have the meanings given such terms under section 119(d).

(4) *Subscriber.*—The term "subscriber" means a person who receives a secondary transmission service from a satellite carrier and pays a fee for the service, directly or indirectly, to the satellite carrier or to a distributor.

(5) *Television broadcast station.*—The term "television broadcast station"—

(A) means an over-the-air, commercial or noncommercial television broadcast station licensed by the Federal Communications Commission under subpart E of part 73 of title 47, Code of Federal Regulations, except that such term does not include a low-power or translator television station; and

(B) includes a television broadcast station licensed by an appropriate governmental authority of Canada or Mexico if the station broadcasts primarily in the English language and is a network station as defined in section 119(d)(2)(A).

(Nov. 29, 1999, Pub. L. 106-113, §1002, 113 Stat. 1501A-523; Nov. 2, 2002, Pub. L. 107-273, §13210, 116 Stat. 1909.)

§ 201   Ownership of copyright

(a) *Initial ownership.*—Copyright in a work protected under this title vests initially in the author or authors of the work. The authors of a joint work are coowners of copyright in the work.

(b) *Works made for hire.*—In the case of a work made for hire, the employer or other person for whom the work was prepared is considered the author for purposes of this title, and, unless the parties have expressly agreed otherwise in a written instrument signed by them, owns all of the rights comprised in the copyright.

(c) *Contributions to collective works.*—Copyright in each separate contribution to a collective work is distinct from copyright in the collective work as a whole, and vests initially in the author of the contribution. In the absence of an express transfer of the copyright or of any rights under it, the owner of copyright in the collective work is presumed to have acquired only the privilege of reproducing and distributing the contribution as part of that particular collective work, any revision of that collective work, and any later collective work in the same series.

(d) *Transfer of ownership.*—

(1) The ownership of a copyright may be transferred in whole or in part by any means of conveyance or by operation of law, and may be bequeathed by will or pass as personal property by the applicable laws of intestate succession.

(2) Any of the exclusive rights comprised in a copyright, including any subdivision of any of the rights specified by section 106, may be transferred as provided by clause (1) and owned separately. The owner of any particular exclusive right is entitled, to the extent of that right, to all of the protection and remedies accorded to the copyright owner by this title.

(e) *Involuntary transfer.*—When an individual author's ownership of a copyright, or of any of the exclusive rights under a copyright, has not previously been transferred voluntarily by that individual author, no action by any governmental body or other official or organization purporting to seize, expropriate, transfer, or exercise rights of ownership with respect to the copyright, or any of the exclusive rights under a copyright, shall be given effect under this title, except as provided under title 11.

(Oct. 16, 1976, Pub. L. 94-553, §101, 90 Stat. 2568; Nov. 6, 1978, Pub. L. 95-598, §313, 92 Stat. 2676.)

§ 202 Ownership of copyright as distinct from ownership of material object

Ownership of a copyright, or of any of the exclusive rights under a copyright, is distinct from ownership of any material object in which the work is embodied. Transfer of ownership of any material object, including the copy or phonorecord in which the work is first fixed, does not of itself convey any rights in the copyrighted work embodied in the object; nor, in the absence of an agreement, does transfer of ownership of a copyright or of any exclusive rights under a copyright convey property rights in any material object.

(Oct. 19, 1976, Pub. L. 94-553, §101, 90 Stat. 2568.)

§ 203 Termination of transfers and licenses granted by the author

(a) *Conditions for termination.*—In the case of any work other than a work made for hire, the exclusive or nonexclusive grant of a transfer or license of copyright or of any right under a copyright, executed by the author on or after January 1, 1978, otherwise than by will, is subject to termination under the following conditions:

> (1) In the case of a grant executed by one author, termination of the grant may be effected by that author or, if the author is dead, by the person or persons who, under clause (2) of this subsection, own and are entitled to exercise a total of more than one-half of that author's termination interest. In the case of a grant executed by two or more authors of a joint work, termination of the grant may be effected by a majority of the authors who executed it; if any of such authors is dead, the termination interest of any such author may be exercised

as a unit by the person or persons who, under clause (2) of this subsection, own and are entitled to exercise a total of more than one-half of that author's interest.

(2) Where an author is dead, his or her termination interest is owned, and may be exercised, as follows:

(A) The widow or widower owns the author's entire termination interest unless there are any surviving children or grandchildren of the author, in which case the widow or widower owns one-half of the author's interest.

(B) The author's surviving children, and the surviving children of any dead child of the author, own the author's entire termination interest unless there is a widow or widower, in which case the ownership of one-half of the author's interest is divided among them.

(C) The rights of the author's children and grandchildren are in all cases divided among them and exercised on a per stirpes basis according to the number of such author's children represented; the share of the children of a dead child in a termination interest can be exercised only by the action of a majority of them.

(D) in the event that the author's widow or widower, children, and grandchildren are not living, the author's executor, administrator, personal representative, or trustee shall own the author's entire termination interest.

(3) Termination of the grant may be effected at any time during a period of five years beginning at the end of thirty-five years from the date of execution of the grant; or, if the grant covers the right of publication of the work, the period begins at the end of thirty-five years from the date of publication of the work under the grant or at the end of forty years from the date of execution of the grant, whichever term ends earlier.

(4) The termination shall be effected by serving an advance notice in writing, signed by the number and proportion of owners of termination interests required under clauses (1) and (2) of this subsection, or by their duly authorized agents, upon the grantee or the grantee's successor in title.

(A) The notice shall state the effective date of the termination, which shall fall within the five-year period specified by clause (3) of this subsection, and the notice shall be served not less than two or more than ten years before that date. A copy of the notice shall be recorded in the Copyright Office before the effective date of termination, as a condition to its taking effect.

(B) The notice shall comply, in form, content, and manner of service, with requirements that the Register of Copyrights shall prescribe by regulation.

(5) Termination of the grant may be effected notwithstanding any agreement to the contrary, including an agreement to make a will or to make any future grant.

(b) *Effect of termination.*—Upon the effective date of termination, all rights under this title that were covered by the terminated grants revert to the author, authors, and other persons owning termination interests under clauses (1) and (2) of subsection (a), including those owners who did not join in signing the notice of termination under clause (4) of subsection (a), but with the following limitations:

(1) A derivative work prepared under authority of the grant before its termination may continue to be utilized under the terms of the grant after its termination, but this privilege does not extend to the preparation after the termination of other derivative works based upon the copyrighted work covered by the terminated grant.

(2) The future rights that will revert upon termination of the grant become vested on the date the notice of termination has been served as provided by clause (4) of subsection (a). The rights vest in the author, authors, and other persons named in, and in the proportionate shares provided by, clauses (1) and (2) of subsection (a).

(3) Subject to the provisions of clause (4) of this subsection, a further grant, or agreement to make a further grant, of any right covered by a terminated grant is valid only if it is signed by the same number and proportion of the owners, in whom the right has vested under clause (2) of this subsection, as are required to terminate the grant under clauses (1) and (2) of subsection (a). Such further grant or agreement is effective with respect to all of the persons in whom the right it covers has vested under clause (2) of this subsection, includ-

ing those who did not join in signing it. If any person dies after rights under a terminated grant have vested in him or her, that person's legal representatives, legatees, or heirs at law represent him or her for purposes of this clause.

(4) A further grant, or agreement to make a further grant, of any right covered by a terminated grant is valid only if it is made after the effective date of the termination. As an exception, however, an agreement for such a further grant may be made between the persons provided by clause (3) of this subsection and the original grantee or such grantee's successor in title, after the notice of termination has been served as provided by clause (4) of subsection (a).

(5) Termination of a grant under this section affects only those rights covered by the grants that arise under this title, and in no way affects rights arising under any other Federal, State, or foreign laws.

(6) Unless and until termination is effected under this section, the grant, if it does not provide otherwise, continues in effect for the term of copyright provided by this title.

(Oct. 19, 1976, Pub. L. 94-553, §101, 90 Stat. 2569; Oct. 27 1998, Pub. L. 105-298, §103, 112 Stat. 2829; Nov. 2, 2002, Pub. L. 107-273, §13210, 116 Stat. 1909.)

§ 204   Execution of transfers of copyright ownership

(a) A transfer of copyright ownership, other than by operation of law, is not valid unless an instrument of conveyance, or a note or memorandum of the transfer, is in writing and signed by the owner of the rights conveyed or such owner's duly authorized agent.

(b) A certificate of acknowledgement is not required for the validity of a transfer, but is prima facie evidence of the execution of the transfer if—

(1) in the case of a transfer executed in the United States, the certificate is issued by a person authorized to administer oaths within the United States; or

(2) in the case of a transfer executed in a foreign country, the certificate is issued by a diplomatic or consular officer of the United States, or by a person authorized to administer oaths whose authority is proved by a certificate of such an officer.

(Oct. 19, 1976, Pub. L. 94-553, §101, 90 Stat. 2570.)

§ 205   Recordation of transfers and other documents

(a) *Conditions for recordation.*—Any transfer of copyright ownership or other document pertaining to a copyright may be recorded in the Copyright Office if the document filed for recordation bears the actual signature of the person who executed it, or if it is accompanied by a sworn or official certification that it is a true copy of the original, signed document.

(b) *Certificate of recordation.*—The Register of Copyrights shall, upon receipt of a document as provided by subsection (a) and of the fee provided by section 708, record the document and return it with a certificate of recordation.

(c) *Recordation as constructive notice.*—Recordation of a document in the Copyright Office gives all persons constructive notice of the facts stated in the recorded document, but only if—

(1) the document, or material attached to it, specifically identifies the work to which it pertains so that, after the document is indexed by the Register of Copyrights, it would be revealed by a reasonable search under the title or registration number of the work; and

(2) registration has been made for the work.

(d) *Priority between conflicting transfers.*—As between two conflicting transfers, the one executed first prevails if it is recorded, in the manner required to give constructive notice under subsection (c), within one month after its execution in the United States or within two months after its execution outside the United States, or at any time before recordation in such manner of the later transfer. Otherwise the later transfer prevails if recorded first in such manner, and if taken in good faith, for valuable consideration or on the basis of a binding promise to pay royalties, and without notice of the earlier transfer.

(e) *Priority between conflicting transfer of ownership and nonexclusive license.*—A nonexclusive license, whether recorded or not, prevails over a conflicting transfer of copyright ownership if the license is evidenced by a written instrument signed by the owner of the rights licensed or such owner's duly authorized agent, and if—

(1) the license was taken before execution of the transfer; or

(2) the license was taken in good faith before recordation of the transfer and without notice of it.

17 U.S.C. § 205

(Oct. 19, 1976, Pub. L. 94-553, §101, 90 Stat. 2571; Oct. 31, 1988, Pub. L. 100-568, §5, 102 Stat. 2857.)

CHAPTER 3—DURATION OF COPYRIGHT

§ 301   Preemption with respect to other laws

(a) On and after January 1, 1978, all legal or equitable rights that are equivalent to any of the exclusive rights within the general scope of copyright as specified by section 106 in works of authorship that are fixed in a tangible medium of expression and come within the subject matter of copyright as specified by sections 102 and 103, whether created before or after that date and whether published or unpublished, are governed exclusively by this title. Thereafter, no person is entitled to any such right or equivalent right in any such work under the common law or statutes of any State.

(b) Nothing in this title annuls or limits any rights or remedies under the common law or statutes of any State with respect to—

(1) subject matter that does not come within the subject matter of copyright as specified by sections 102 and 103, including works of authorship not fixed in any tangible medium of expression; or

(2) any cause of action arising from undertakings commenced before January 1, 1978;

(3) activities violating legal or equitable rights that are not equivalent to any of the exclusive rights within the general scope of copyright as specified by section 106; or

(4) State and local landmarks, historic preservation, zoning, or building codes, relating to architectural works protected under section 102(a)(8).

17 U.S.C. § 301

(c) With respect to sound recordings fixed before February 15, 1972, any rights or remedies under the common law or statutes of any State shall not be annulled or limited by this title until February 15, 2067. The preemptive provisions of subsection (a) shall apply to any such rights and remedies pertaining to any cause of action arising from undertakings commenced on and after February 15, 2067. Notwithstanding the provisions of section 303, no sound recording fixed before February 15, 1972, shall be subject to copyright under this title before, on, or after February 15, 2067.

(d) Nothing in this title annuls or limits any rights or remedies under any other Federal statute.

(e) The scope of Federal preemption under this section is not affected by the adherence of the United States to the Berne Convention or the satisfaction of obligations of the United States thereunder.

(f) (1) On or after the effective date set forth in section 610(a) of the Visual Artists Rights Act of 1990, all legal or equitable rights that are equivalent to any of the rights conferred by section 106A with respect to works of visual art to which the rights conferred by section 106A apply are governed exclusively by section 106A and section 113(d) and the provisions of this title relating to such sections. Thereafter, no person is entitled to any such right or equivalent right in any work of visual art under the common law or statutes of any State.

(2) Nothing in paragraph (1) annuls or limits any rights or remedies under the common law or statutes of any State with respect to—

(A) any cause of action from undertakings commenced before the effective date set forth in section 610(a) of the Visual Artists Rights Act of 1990;

(B) activities violating legal or equitable rights that are not equivalent to any of the rights conferred by section 106A with respect to works of visual art; or

(C) activities violating legal or equitable rights which extend beyond the life of the author.

(Oct. 19, 1976, Pub. L. 94-553, §101, 90 Stat. 2572; Oct. 31, 1988, Pub. L. 100-568, §6, 102 Stat. 2857; Dec. 1, 1990, Pub. L. 101-650, §605, §705, 104 Stat. 5131, 5134; Oct. 27, 1998, Pub. L. 105-298, §102(a), 112 Stat. 2827.)

17 U.S.C. § 301

§ 302   Duration of copyright: Works created on or after January 1, 1978

(a) *In general.*—Copyright in a work created on or after January 1, 1978, subsists from its creation and, except as provided by the following sub-sections, endures for a term consisting of the life of the author and 70 years after the author's death.

(b) *Joint works.*—In the case of a joint work prepared by two or more authors who did not work for hire, the copyright endures for a term consisting of the life of the last surviving author and 70 years after such last surviving author's death.

(c) *Anonymous works, pseudonymous works, and works made for hire.*—In the case of an anonymous work, a pseudonymous work, or a work made for hire, the copyright endures for a term of 95 years from the year of its first publication, or a term of 120 years from the year of its creation, which-ever expires first. If, before the end of such term, the identity of one or more of the authors of an anonymous or pseudonymous work is re-vealed in the records of a registration made for that work under subsec-tions (a) or (d) of section 408, or in the records provided by this subsec-tion, the copyright in the work endures for the term specified by subsec-tion (a) or (b), based on the life of the author or authors whose identity has been revealed. Any person having an interest in the copyright in an anonymous or pseudonymous work may at any time record, in records to be maintained by the Copyright Office for that purpose, a statement identifying one or more authors of the work; the statement shall also identify the person filing it, the nature of that person's interest, the source of the information recorded, and the particular work affected, and shall comply in form and content with requirements that the Regis-ter of Copyrights shall prescribe by regulation.

(d) *Records relating to death of authors.*—Any person having an interest in a copyright may at any time record in the Copyright Office a statement of the date of death of the author of the copyrighted work, or a state-ment that the author is still living on a particular date. The statement shall identify the person filing it, the nature of that person's interest, and the source of the information recorded, and shall comply in form and content with requirements that the Register of Copyrights shall prescribe by regulation. The Register shall maintain current records of

17 U.S.C. § 302

information relating to the death of authors of copyrighted works, based on such recorded statements and, to the extent the Register considers practicable, on data contained in any of the records of the Copyright Office or in other reference sources.

(e) *Presumption as to author's death.*—After a period of 95 years from the year of first publication of a work, or a period of 120 years from the year of its creation, whichever expires first, any person who obtains from the Copyright Office a certified report that the records provided by subsection (d) disclose nothing to indicate that the author of the work is living, or died less than 70 years before, is entitled to the benefits of a presumption that the author has been dead for at least 70 years. Reliance in good faith upon this presumption shall be a complete defense to any action for infringement under this title.

(Oct. 19, 1976, Pub. L. 94-553, §101, 90 Stat. 2572; Oct. 27, 1998, Pub. L. 105-298, §102(b), 112 Stat. 2827.)

§ 303   Duration of copyright: Works created but not published or copyrighted before January 1, 1978

(a) Copyright in a work created before January 1, 1978, but not theretofore in the public domain or copyrighted, subsists from January 1, 1978, and endures for the term provided by section 302. In no case, however, shall the term of copyright in such a work expire before December 31, 2002; and, if the work is published on or before December 31, 2002, the term of copyright shall not expire before December 31, 2047.

(b) The distribution before January 1, 1978, of a phonorecord shall not for any purpose constitute a publication of the musical work embodied therein.

(Oct. 19, 1976, Pub. L. 94-553, §101, 90 Stat. 2573; Nov. 13, 1997, Pub. L. 105-80, §11, 111 Stat. 1534; Oct. 27, 1998, Pub. L. 105-298, §102(c), 112 Stat. 2827.)

§ 304   Duration of copyright: Subsisting copyrights

(a) *Copyrights in their first term on January 1, 1978.*—

(1) (A) Any copyright, the first term of which is subsisting on January 1, 1978, shall endure for 28 years from the date it was originally secured.

(B) In the case of—

(i) any posthumous work or of any periodical, cyclopedic, or other composite work upon which the copyright was originally secured by the proprietor thereof, or

(ii) any work copyrighted by a corporate body (otherwise than as assignee or licensee of the individual author) or by an employer for whom such work is made for hire,

the proprietor of such copyright shall be entitled to a renewal and extension of the copyright in such work for the further term of 67 years.

(C) In the case of any other copyrighted work, including a contribution by an individual author to a periodical or to a cyclopedic or other composite work—

(i) the author of such work, if the author is still living,

(ii) the widow, widower, or children of the author, if the author is not living,

(iii) the author's executors, if such author, widow, widower, or children are not living, or

(iv) the author's next of kin, in the absence of a will of the author,

shall be entitled to a renewal and extension of the copyright in such work for a further term of 67 years.

(2) (A) At the expiration of the original term of copyright in a work specified in paragraph (1)(B) of this subsection, the copyright shall endure for a renewed and extended further term of 67 years, which—

(i) if an application to register a claim to such further term has been made to the Copyright Office within 1 year before the expiration of the original term of copyright, and the claim is registered, shall vest, upon the beginning of such further term, in the proprietor of the copyright who is entitled to claim the renewal of copyright at the time the application is made; or

(ii) if no such application is made or the claim pursuant to such application is not registered, shall vest, upon the beginning of such further term, in the person or entity that was the proprietor of the copyright as of the last day of the original term of copyright.

(B) At the expiration of the original term of copyright in a work specified in paragraph (1)(C) of this subsection, the copyright shall endure for a renewed and extended further term of 67 years, which—

(i) if an application to register a claim to such further term has been made to the Copyright Office within 1 year before the expiration of the original term of copyright, and the claim is registered, shall vest, upon the beginning of such further term, in any person who is entitled under paragraph (1)(C) to the renewal and extension of the copyright at the time the application is made; or

(ii) if no such application is made or the claim pursuant to such application is not registered, shall vest, upon the beginning of such further term, in any person entitled under paragraph (1)(C), as of the last day of the original term of copyright, to the renewal and extension of the copyright.

(3) (A) An application to register a claim to the renewed and extended term of copyright in a work may be made to the Copyright Office—

(i) within 1 year before the expiration of the original term of copyright by any person entitled under paragraph (1) (B) or (C) to such further term of 67 years; and

(ii) at any time during the renewed and extended term by any person in whom such further term vested, under paragraph (2) (A) or (B), or by any successor or assign of such person, if the application is made in the name of such person.

(B) Such an application is not a condition of the renewal and extension of the copyright in a work for a further term of 67 years.

(4) (A) If an application to register a claim to the renewed and extended term of copyright in a work is not made within 1 year before the expiration of the original term of copyright in a work, or if the claim pursuant to such application is not registered, then a derivative work prepared under authority of a grant of a transfer or license of the copyright that is made before the expiration of the original term of copyright may continue to be used under the

17 U.S.C. § 304

terms of the grant during the renewed and extended term of copyright without infringing the copyright, except that such use does not extend to the preparation during such renewed and extended term of other derivative works based upon the copyrighted work covered by such grant.

(B) If an application to register a claim to the renewed and extended term of copyright in a work is made within 1 year before its expiration, and the claim is registered, the certificate of such registration shall constitute prima facie evidence as to the validity of the copyright during its renewed and extended term and of the facts stated in the certificate. The evidentiary weight to be accorded the certificates of a registration of a renewed and extended term of copyright made after the end of that 1-year period shall be within the discretion of the court.

(b) *Copyrights in their renewal term at the time of the effective date of the Sonny Bono Copyright Term Extension Act.*—Any copyright still in its renewal term at the time that the Sonny Bono Copyright Term Extension Act becomes effective shall have a copyright term of 95 years from the date copyright was originally secured.

(c) *Termination of transfers and licenses covering extended renewal term.*—In the case of any copyright subsisting in either its first or renewal term on January 1, 1978, other than a copyright in a work made for hire, the exclusive or nonexclusive grant of a transfer or license of the renewal copyright or any right under it, executed before January 1, 1978, by any of the persons designated by subsection (a)(1)(C) of this section, otherwise than by will, is subject to termination under the following conditions:

(1) In the case of a grant executed by a person or persons other than the author, termination of the grant may be effected by the surviving person or persons who executed it. In the case of a grant executed by one or more of the authors of the work, termination of the grant may be effected, to the extent of a particular author's share in the ownership of the renewal copyright, by the author who executed it or, if such author is dead, by the person or persons who, under clause (2) of this subsection, own and are entitled to exercise a total of more than one-half of that author's termination interest.

17 U.S.C. § 304

(2) Where an author is dead, his or her termination interest is owned, and may be exercised, as follows:

(A) The widow or widower owns the author's entire termination interest unless there are any surviving children or grandchildren of the author, in which case the widow or widower owns one-half of the author's interest.

(B) The author's surviving children, and the surviving children of any dead child of the author, own the author's entire termination interest unless there is a widow or widower, in which case the ownership of one-half of the author's interest is divided among them.

(C) The rights of the author's children and grandchildren are in all cases divided among them and exercised on a per stirpes basis according to the number of such author's children represented; the share of the children of a dead child in a termination interest can be exercised only by the action of a majority of them.

(D) in the event that the author's widow or widower, children, and grandchildren are not living, the author's executor, administrator, personal representative, or trustee shall own the author's entire termination interest.

(3) Termination of the grant may be effected at any time during a period of five years beginning at the end of fifty-six years from the date copyright was originally secured, or beginning on January 1, 1978, whichever is later.

(4) The termination shall be effected by serving an advance notice in writing upon the grantee or the grantee's successor in title. In the case of a grant executed by a person or persons other than the author, the notice shall be signed by all of those entitled to terminate the grant under clause (1) of this subsection, or by their duly authorized agents. In the case of a grant executed by one or more of the authors of the work, the notice as to any one author's share shall be signed by that author or his or her duly authorized agent or, if that author is dead, by the number and proportion of the owners of his or her termination interest required under clauses (1) and (2) of this subsection, or by their duly authorized agents.

17 U.S.C. § 304

(A) The notice shall state the effective date of the termination, which shall fall within the five-year period specified by clause (3) of this subsection, or, in the case of a termination under subsection (d), within the five-year period specified by subsection (d)(2), and the notice shall be served not less than two or more than ten years before that date. A copy of the notice shall be recorded in the Copyright Office before the effective date of termination, as a condition to its taking effect.

(B) The notice shall comply, in form, content, and manner of service, with requirements that the Register of Copyrights shall prescribe by regulation.

(5) Termination of the grant may be effected notwithstanding any agreement to the contrary, including an agreement to make a will or to make any future grant.

(6) In the case of a grant executed by a person or persons other than the author, all rights under this title that were covered by the terminated grant revert, upon the effective date of termination, to all of those entitled to terminate the grant under clause (1) of this subsection. In the case of a grant executed by one or more of the authors of the work, all of a particular author's rights under this title that were covered by the terminated grant revert, upon the effective date of termination, to that author or, if that author is dead, to the persons owning his or her termination interest under clause (2) of this subsection, including those owners who did not join in signing the notice of termination under clause (4) of this subsection. In all cases the reversion of rights is subject to the following limitations:

(A) A derivative work prepared under authority of the grant before its termination may continue to be utilized under the terms of the grant after its termination, but this privilege does not extend to the preparation after the termination of other derivative works based upon the copyrighted work covered by the terminated grant.

(B) The future rights that will revert upon termination of the grant become vested on the date the notice of termination has been served as provided by clause (4) of this subsection.

(C) Where the author's rights revert to two or more persons under clause (2) of this subsection, they shall vest in those persons in the proportionate shares provided by that clause. In such a case, and subject to the provisions of subclause (D) of this clause, a further grant, or agreement to make a further grant, of a particular author's share with respect to any right covered by a terminated grant is valid only if it is signed by the same number and proportion of the owners, in whom the right has vested under this clause, as are required to terminate the grant under clause (2) of this subsection. Such further grant or agreement is effective with respect to all of the persons in whom the right it covers has vested under this subclause, including those who did not join in signing it. If any person dies after rights under a terminated grant have vested in him or her, that person's legal representatives, legatees, or heirs at law represent him or her for purposes of this subclause.

(D) A further grant, or agreement to make a further grant, of any right covered by a terminated grant is valid only if it is made after the effective date of the termination. As an exception, however, an agreement for such a further grant may be made between the author or any of the persons provided by the first sentence of clause (6) of this subsection, or between the persons provided by subclause (C) of this clause, and the original grantee or such grantee's successor in title, after the notice of termination has been served as provided by clause (4) of this subsection.

(E) Termination of a grant under this subsection affects only those rights covered by the grant that arise under this title, and in no way affects rights arising under any other Federal, State, or foreign laws.

(F) Unless and until termination is effected under this subsection, the grant, if it does not provide otherwise, continues in effect for the remainder of the extended renewal term.

(d) *Termination rights provided in subsection (c) which have expired on or before the effective date of the Sonny Bono Copyright Term Extension Act.*—In the case of any copyright other than a work made for hire, subsisting in its renewal term on the effective date of the Sonny Bono Copyright Term Extension Act for which the termination right provided in subsection (c) has expired by such date, where the author or owner of the termination right has not previously exercised such termination right, the exclusive or nonexclusive grant of a transfer or license of the renewal copyright or any right under it, executed before January 1, 1978, by any of the persons designated in subsection (a)(1)(C) of this section, other than by will, is subject to termination under the following conditions:

(1) The conditions specified in subsections (c) (1), (2), (4), (5), and (6) of this section apply to terminations of the last 20 years of copyright term as provided by the amendments made by the Sonny Bono Copyright Term Extension Act.

(2) Termination of the grant may be effected at any time during a period of 5 years beginning at the end of 75 years from the date copyright was originally secured.

(Oct. 19, 1976, Pub. L. 94-553, §101, 90 Stat. 2573; June 26, 1992, Pub. L. 102-307, §102(a) and (d), 106 Stat. 264-66; Nov. 13, 1997, Pub. L. 105-80, §12, 111 Stat. 1535; Oct. 27, 1998, Pub. L. 105-298, §§102(d), 103, 112 Stat. 2827, 2829; Nov. 2, 2002, Pub. L. 107-273, §13210, 116 Stat. 1909.)

§ 305 Duration of copyright: Terminal date

All terms of copyright provided by sections 302 through 304 run to the end of the calendar year in which they would otherwise expire.

(Oct. 19, 1976, Pub. L. 94-553, §101, 90 Stat. 2576.)

CHAPTER 4—COPYRIGHT NOTICE, DEPOSIT, AND REGISTRATION

§ 401   Notice of copyright: Visually perceptible copies

(a) *General provisions.*—Whenever a work protected under this title is published in the United States or elsewhere by authority of the copyright owner, a notice of copyright as provided by this section may be placed on publicly distributed copies from which the work can be visually perceived, either directly or with the aid of a machine or device.

(b) *Form of notice.*—If a notice appears on the copies, it shall consist of the following three elements:

> (1) the symbol © (the letter C in a circle), or the word "Copyright", or the abbreviation "Copr."; and

> (2) the year of first publication of the work; in the case of compilations, or derivative works incorporating previously published material, the year date of first publication of the compilation or derivative work is sufficient. The year date may be omitted where a pictorial, graphic, or sculptural work, with accompanying text matter, if any, is reproduced in or on greeting cards, postcards, stationery, jewelry, dolls, toys, or any useful articles; and

> (3) the name of the owner of copyright in the work, or an abbreviation by which the name can be recognized, or a generally known alternative designation of the owner.

(c) *Position of notice.*—The notice shall be affixed to the copies in such manner and location as to give reasonable notice of the claim of copyright. The Register of Copyrights shall prescribe by regulation, as examples, specific methods of affixation and positions of the notice on various types of works that will satisfy this requirement, but these specifications shall not be considered exhaustive.

(d) *Evidentiary weight of notice.*—If a notice of copyright in the form and position specified by this section appears on the published copy or copies to which a defendant in a copyright infringement suit had access, then no weight shall be given to such a defendant's interposition of a defense based on innocent infringement in mitigation of actual or statutory damages, except as provided in the last sentence of section 504(c)(2).

(Oct. 19, 1976, Pub. L. 94-553, §101, 90 Stat. 2576; Oct. 31, 1988, Pub. L. 100-568, §7, 102 Stat. 2857.)

17 U.S.C. § 401

§ 402   Notice of copyright: Phonorecords of sound recordings

(a) *General provisions.*—Whenever a sound recording protected under this title is published in the United States or elsewhere by authority of the copyright owner, a notice of copyright as provided by this section may be placed on publicly distributed phonorecords of the sound recording.

(b) *Form of notice.*—If a notice appears on the phonorecords, it shall consist of the following three elements:

(1) the symbol Ⓟ (the letter P in a circle); and

(2) the year of first publication of the sound recording; and

(3) the name of the owner of copyright in the sound recording, or an abbreviation by which the name can be recognized, or a generally known alternative designation of the owner; if the producer of the sound recording is named on the phonorecord labels or containers, and if no other name appears in conjunction with the notice, the producer's name shall be considered a part of the notice.

(c) *Position of notice.*—The notice shall be placed on the surface of the phonorecord, or on the phonorecord label or container, in such manner and location as to give reasonable notice of the claim of copyright.

(d) *Evidentiary weight of notice.*—If a notice of copyright in the form and position specified by this section appears on the published phonorecord or phonorecords to which a defendant in a copyright infringement suit had access, then no weight shall be given to such a defendant's interpretation of a defense based on innocent infringement in mitigation of actual or statutory damages, except as provided in the last sentence of section 504(c)(2).

(Oct. 19, 1976, Pub. L. 94-553, §101, 90 Stat. 2577; Oct. 31, 1988, Pub. L. 100-568, §7, 102 Stat. 2857.)

§ 403   Notice of copyright: Publications incorporating United States Government works

Section 401(d) and 402(d) shall not apply to a work published in copies or phonorecords consisting predominantly of one or more works of the United States Government unless the notice of copyright appearing on the published copies or phonorecords to which a defendant in the copyright infringement suit had access includes a statement identifying, either affirmatively or negatively, those portions of the copies or phonorecords embodying any work or works protected under this title.

(Oct. 19, 1976, Pub. L. 94-553, §101, 90 Stat. 2577; Oct. 31, 1988, Pub. L. 100-568, §7, 102 Stat. 2858.)

§ 404   Notice of copyright: Contributions to collective works

(a) A separate contribution to a collective work may bear its own notice of copyright, as provided by section 401 through 403. However, a single notice applicable to the collective work as a whole is sufficient to invoke the provisions of section 401(d) or 402(d), as applicable with respect to the separate contributions it contains (not including advertisements inserted on behalf of persons other than the owner of copyright in the collective work), regardless of the ownership of copyright in the contributions and whether or not they have been previously published.

(b) With respect to copies and phonorecords publicly distributed by authority of the copyright owner before the effective date of the Berne Convention Implementation Act of 1988, where the person named in a single notice applicable to a collective work as a whole is not the owner of copyright in a separate contribution that does not bear its own notice, the case is governed by the provisions of section 406(a).

(Oct. 19, 1976, Pub. L. 94-553, §101, 90 Stat. 2577; Oct. 31, 1988, Pub. L. 100-568, §7, 102 Stat. 2858.)

§ 405   Notice of copyright: Omission of notice

(a) *Effect of omission on copyright.*—With respect to copies and phonorecords publicly distributed by authority of the copyright owner before the effective date of the Berne Convention Implementation Act of 1988, the omission of the copyright notice described in sections 401 through 403 from copies or phonorecords publicly distributed by authority of the copyright owner does not invalidate the copyright in a work if—

(1) the notice has been omitted from no more than a relatively small number of copies or phonorecords distributed to the public; or

(2) registration for the work has been made before or is made within five years after the publication without notice, and a reasonable effort is made to add notice to all copies of phonorecords that are dis-

tributed to the public in the United States after the omission has been discovered; or

(3) the notice has been omitted in violation of an express requirement in writing that, as a condition of the copyright owner's authorization of the public distribution of copies or phonorecords, they bear the prescribed notice.

(b) *Effect of omission on innocent infringers.*—Any person who innocently infringes a copyright, in reliance upon an authorized copy or phonorecord from which the copyright notice has been omitted and which was publicly distributed by authority of the copyright owner before the effective date of the Berne Convention Implementation Act of 1988, incurs no liability for actual or statutory damages under section 504 for any infringing act committed before receiving actual notice that registration for the work has been made under section 408, if such person proves that he or she was misled by the omission of notice. In a suit for infringement in such a case the court may allow or disallow recovery of any of the infringer's profits attributable to the infringement, and may enjoin the continuation of the infringing undertaking or may require, as a condition for permitting the continuation of the infringing undertaking, that the infringer pay the copyright owner a reasonable license fee in an amount and on terms fixed by the court.

(c) *Removal of notice.*—Protection under this title is not affected by the removal, destruction, or obliteration of the notice, without the authorization of the copyright owner, from any publicly distributed copies or phonorecords.

(Oct. 19, 1976, Pub. L. 94-553, §101, 90 Stat. 2578; Oct. 31, 1988, Pub. L. 100-568, §7, 102 Stat. 2858; Nov. 13, 1997, Pub. L. 105-80, §12, 111 Stat. 1535.)

§ 406 Notice of copyright: Error in name or date

(a) *Error in name.*—With respect to copies and phonorecords publicly distributed by authority of the copyright owner before the effective date of the Berne Convention Implementation Act of 1988, where the person named in the copyright notice on copies or phonorecords publicly distributed by authority of the copyright owner is not the owner of copyright, the validity and ownership of the copyright are not affected. In such a case, however, any person who innocently begins an undertaking that infringes the copyright has a complete defense to any action for such infringement if such person proves that he or she was misled by the notice and began the undertaking in good faith under a purported transfer or license from the person named therein, unless before the undertaking was begun—

(1) registration for the work had been made in the name of the owner of copyright; or

(2) a document executed by the person named in the notice and showing the ownership of the copyright had been recorded.

(b) *Error in date.*—When the year date in the notice on copies or phonorecords distributed before the effective date of the Berne Convention Implementation Act of 1988 by authority of the copyright owner is earlier than the year in which publication first occurred, any period computed from the year of first publication under section 302 is to be computed from the year in the notice. Where the year date is more than one year later than the year in which publication first occurred, the work is considered to have been published without any notice and is governed by the provisions of section 405.

(c) *Omission of name or date.*—Where copies or phonorecords publicly distributed before the effective date of the Berne Convention Implementation Act of 1988 by authority of the copyright owner contain no name or no date that could reasonably be considered a part of the notice, the work is considered to have been published without any notice and is governed by the provision of section 405 as in effect on the day before the effective date of the Berne Convention Implementation Act of 1988.

(Oct. 19, 1976, Pub. L. 94-553, §101, 90 Stat. 2578; Oct. 31, 1988, Pub. L. 100-568, §7, 102 Stat. 2858.)

§ 407 Deposit of copies or phonorecords for Library of Congress

(a) Except as provided by subsection (c), and subject to the provisions of subsection (e), the owner of copyright or of the exclusive right of publication in a work published in the United States shall deposit, within three months after the date of such publication—

(1) two complete copies of the best edition; or

(2) if the work is a sound recording, two complete phonorecords of the best edition, together with any printed or other visually perceptible material published with such phonorecords.

Neither the deposit requirements of this subsection nor the acquisition provisions of subsection (e) are conditions of copyright protection.

(b) The required copies or phonorecords shall be deposited in the Copyright Office for the use or disposition of the Library of Congress. The Register of Copyrights shall, when requested by the depositor and upon payment of the fee prescribed by section 708, issue a receipt for the deposit.

(c) The Register of Copyrights may by regulation exempt any categories of material from the deposit requirements of this section, or require deposit of only one copy or phonorecord with respect to any categories. Such regulations shall provide either for complete exemption from the deposit requirements of this section, or for alternative forms of deposit aimed at providing a satisfactory archival record of a work without imposing practical or financial hardships on the depositor, where the individual author is the owner of copyright in a pictorial, graphic, or sculptural work and (i) less than five copies of the work have been published, or (ii) the work has been published in a limited edition consisting of numbered copies, the monetary value of which would make the mandatory deposit of two copies of the best edition of the work burdensome, unfair, or unreasonable.

(d) At any time after publication of a work as provided by subsection (a), the Register of Copyrights may make written demand for the required deposit on any of the persons obligated to make the deposit under subsection (a). Unless deposit is made within three months after the demand is received, the person or persons on whom the demand was made are liable—

(1) to a fine of not more than $250 for each work; and

(2) to pay into a specially designated fund in the Library of Congress the total retail price of the copies or phonorecords demanded, or, if no retail price has been fixed, the reasonable cost to the Library of Congress of acquiring them; and

(3) to pay a fine of $2,500, in addition to any fine or liability imposed under clauses (1) and (2), if such person willfully or repeatedly fails or refuses to comply with such a demand.

(e) With respect to transmission programs that have been fixed and transmitted to the public in the United States but have not been published, the Register of Copyrights shall, after consulting with the Librarian of Congress and other interested organizations and officials, establish regulations governing the acquisition, through deposit or otherwise, of copies or phonorecords of such programs for the collections of the Library of Congress.

(1) The Librarian of Congress shall be permitted, under the standards and conditions set forth in such regulations, to make a fixation of a transmission program directly from a transmission to the public, and to reproduce one copy or phonorecord from such fixation for archival purposes.

(2) Such regulations shall also provide standards and procedures by which the Register of Copyrights may make written demand, upon the owner of the right of transmission in the United States, for the deposit of a copy or phonorecord of a specific transmission program. Such deposit may, at the option of the owner of the right of transmission in the United States, be accomplished by gift, by loan for purposes of reproduction, or by sale at a price not to exceed the cost of reproducing and supplying the copy or phonorecord. The regulations established under this clause shall provide reasonable periods of not less than three months for compliance with a demand, and shall allow for extensions of such periods and adjustments in the scope of the demand or the methods for fulfilling it, as reasonably warranted by the circumstances. Willful failure or refusal to comply with the conditions prescribed by such regulations shall subject the owner of the right of transmission in the United States to liability for an amount, not to exceed the cost of reproducing and supplying the copy or phonorecord in question, to be paid into a specially designated fund in the Library of Congress.

(3) Nothing in this subsection shall be construed to require the making or retention, for purposes of deposit, of any copy or phonorecord of an unpublished transmission program, the transmission of which

17 U.S.C. § 407

occurs before the receipt of a specific written demand as provided by clause (2).

(4) No activity undertaken in compliance with regulations prescribed under clauses (1) or (2) of this subsection shall result in liability if intended solely to assist in the acquisition of copies or phonorecords under this subsection.

(Oct. 19, 1976, Pub. L. 94-553, §101, 90 Stat. 2579; Oct. 31, 1988, Pub. L. 100-568, §8, 102 Stat. 2859. Nov. 13, 1977, Pub. L. 105-80, §12, 111 Stat. 1535.)

§ 408   Copyright registration in general

(a) *Registration permissive.*—At any time during the subsistence of the first term of copyright in any published or unpublished work in which the copyright was secured before January 1, 1978, and during the subsistence of any copyright secured on or after that date, the owner of copyright or of any exclusive right in the work may obtain registration of the copyright claim by delivering to the Copyright Office the deposit specified by this section, together with the application and fee specified by sections 409 and 708. Such registration is not a condition of copyright protection.

(b) *Deposit for copyright registration.*—Except as provided by subsection (c), the material deposited for registration shall include—

(1) in the case of an unpublished work, one complete copy or phonorecord;

(2) in the case of a published work, two complete copies or phonorecords of the best edition;

(3) in the case of a work first published outside the United States, one complete copy or phonorecord as so published;

(4) in the case of a contribution to a collective work, one complete copy or phonorecord of the best edition of the collective work.

Copies or phonorecords deposited for the Library of Congress under section 407 may be used to satisfy the deposit provisions of this section, if they are accompanied by the prescribed application and fee, and by any additional identifying material that the Register may, by regulation, require. The Register shall also prescribe regulations establishing requirements under which copies or phonorecords acquired for the Library of Congress under subsection (e) of section 407, otherwise than by deposit, may be used to satisfy the deposit provisions of this section.

(c) *Administrative classification and optional deposit.*—

(1) The Register of Copyrights is authorized to specify by regulation the administrative classes into which works are to be placed for purposes of deposit and registration, and the nature of the copies or phonorecords to be deposited in the various classes specified. The regulations may require or permit, for particular classes, the deposit of identifying material instead of copies or phonorecords, the deposit of only one copy or phonorecord where two would normally be required, or a single registration for a group of related works. This administrative classification of works has no significance with respect to the subject matter of copyright or the exclusive rights provided by this title.

(2) Without prejudice to the general authority provided under clause (1), the Register of Copyrights shall establish regulations specifically permitting a single registration for a group of works by the same individual author, all first published as contributions to periodicals, including newspapers, within a twelve-month period, on the basis of a single deposit, application, and registration fee, under the following conditions:

(A) if the deposit consists of one copy of the entire issue of the periodical, or of the entire section in the case of a newspaper, in which each contribution was first published; and

(B) if the application identifies each work separately, including the periodical containing it and its date of first publication.

(3) As an alternative to separate renewal registrations under subsection (a) of section 304, a single renewal registration may be made for a group of works by the same individual author, all first published as contributions to periodicals, including newspapers, upon the filing of a single application and fee, under all of the following conditions:

(A) the renewal claimant or claimants, and the basis of claim or claims under section 304(a), is the same for each of the works; and

(B) the works were all copyrighted upon their first publication, either through separate copyright notice and registration or by

17 U.S.C. § 408

virtue of a general copyright notice in the periodical issue as a whole; and

(C) the renewal application and fee are received not more than twenty-eight or less than twenty-seven years after the thirty-first day of December of the calendar year in which all of the works were first published; and

(D) the renewal application identifies each work separately, including the periodical containing it and its date of first publication.

(d) *Corrections and amplifications.*—The Register may also establish, by regulation, formal procedures for the filing of an application for supplementary registration, to correct an error in a copyright registration or to amplify the information given in a registration. Such application shall be accompanied by the fee provided by section 708, and shall clearly identify the registration to be corrected or amplified. The information contained in a supplementary registration augments but does not supersede that contained in the earlier registration.

(e) *Published edition of previously registered work.*—Registration for the first published edition of a work previously registered in unpublished form may be made even though the work as published is substantially the same as the unpublished version.

(Oct. 19, 1976, Pub. L. 94-553, §101, 90 Stat. 2580; Oct. 31, 1988, Pub. L. 100-568, §9, 102 Stat. 2859; June 26, 1992, Pub. L. 102-307, §102, 106 Stat. 266.)

§ 409   Application for copyright registration

The application for copyright registration shall be made on a form prescribed by the Register of Copyrights and shall include—

(1) the name and address of the copyright claimant;

(2) in the case of a work other than an anonymous or pseudonymous work, the name and nationality or domicile of the author or authors, and, if one or more of the authors is dead, the dates of their deaths;

(3) if the work is anonymous or pseudonymous, the nationality or domicile of the author or authors;

(4) in the case of a work made for hire, a statement to this effect;

(5) if the copyright claimant is not the author, a brief statement of how the claimant obtained ownership of the copyright;

(6) the title of the work, together with any previous or alternative titles under which the work can be identified;

(7) the year in which creation of the work was completed;

(8) if the work has been published, the date and nation of its first publication;

(9) in the case of a compilation or derivative work, an identification of any preexisting work or works that it is based on or incorporates, and a brief, general statement of the additional material covered by the copyright claim being registered;

(10) in the case of a published work containing material of which copies are required by section 601 to be manufactured in the United States, the names of the persons or organizations who performed the processes specified by subsection (c) of section 601 with respect to that material, and the places where those processes were performed; and

(11) any other information regarded by the Register of Copyrights as bearing upon the preparation or identification of the work or the existence, ownership, or duration of the copyright.

If an application is submitted for the renewed and extended term provided for in section 304(a)(3)(A) and an original term registration has not been made, the Register may request information with respect to the existence, ownership, or duration of the copyright for the original term.

(Oct. 19, 1976, Pub. L. 94-553, §101, 90 Stat. 2582; June 26, 1992, Pub. L. 102-307, §102(b), 106 Stat. 266.)

§ 410   Registration of claim and issuance of certificate

(a) When, after examination, the Register of Copyrights determines that, in accordance with the provisions of this title, the material deposited constitutes copyrightable subject matter and that the other legal and formal requirements of this title have been met, the Register shall register the claim and issue to the applicant a certificate of registration under the seal of the Copyright Office. The certificate shall contain the information given in the application, together with the number and effective date of the registration.

(b) In any case in which the Register of Copyrights determines that, in accordance with the provisions of this title, the material deposited does not constitute copyrightable subject matter or that the claim is invalid for any other reason, the Register shall refuse registration and shall notify the applicant in writing of the reasons for such refusal.

(c) In any judicial proceedings the certificate of a registration made before or within five years after first publication of the work shall constitute prima facie evidence of the validity of the copyright and of the facts stated in the certificate. The evidentiary weight to be accorded the certificate of a registration made thereafter shall be within the discretion of the court.

(d) The effective date of a copyright registration is the day on which an application, deposit, and fee, which are later determined by the Register of Copyrights or by a court of competent jurisdiction to be acceptable for registration, have all been received in the Copyright Office.

(Oct. 19, 1976, Pub. L. 94-553, §101, 90 Stat. 2582.)

§ 411   Registration and infringement actions

(a) Except for an action brought for a violation of the rights of the author under section 106A(a), and subject to the provisions of subsection (b), no action for infringement of the copyright in any United States work shall be instituted until registration of the copyright claim has been made in accordance with this title. In any case, however, where the deposit, application, and fee required for registration have been delivered to the Copyright Office in proper form and registration has been refused, the applicant is entitled to institute an action for infringement if notice thereof, with a copy of the complaint, is served on the Register of Copyrights. The Register may, at his or her option, become a party to the action with respect to the issue of registrability of the copyright claim by entering an appearance within sixty days after such service, but the Register's failure to become a party shall not deprive the court of jurisdiction to determine that issue.

(b) In the case of a work consisting of sounds, images, or both, the first fixation of which is made simultaneously with its transmission, the copyright owner may, either before or after such fixation takes place, institute an action for infringement under section 501, fully subject to the remedies provided by sections 502 through 506 and sections 509 and 510, if, in accordance with requirements that the Register of Copyrights shall prescribe by regulation, the copyright owner—

(1) serves notice upon the infringer, not less than 48 hours before such fixation, identifying the work and the specific time and source of its first transmission, and declaring an intention to secure copyright in the work; and

(2) makes registration for the work, if required by subsection (a), within three months after its first transmission.

(Oct. 19, 1976, Pub. L. 94-553, §101, 90 Stat. 2583; Oct. 31, 1988, Pub. L. 100-568, §9, 102 Stat. 2859; Dec. 1, 1990, Pub. L. 101-650, §606, 104 Stat. 5131; Nov. 13, 1997, Pub. L. 105-80, §6, 111 Stat. 1532; Oct. 28, 1998, Pub. L. 105-304, §102(d), 112 Stat. 2863.)

§ 412 Registration as prerequisite to certain remedies for infringement

In any action under this title, other than an action brought for a violation of the rights of the author under section 106A(a) or an action instituted under section 411(b), no award of statutory damages or of attorney's fees, as provided by sections 504 and 505, shall be made for—

(1) any infringement of copyright in an unpublished work commenced before the effective date of its registration; or

(2) any infringement of copyright commenced after first publication of the work and before the effective date of its registration, unless such registration is made within three months after the first publication of the work.

(Oct. 19, 1976, Pub. L. 94-553, §101, 90 Stat. 2583; Dec. 1, 1990, Pub. L. 101-650, §606, 104 Stat. 5131.)

CHAPTER 5—COPYRIGHT INFRINGEMENT AND REMEDIES

§ 501   Infringement of copyright

(a) Anyone who violates any of the exclusive rights of the copyright owner as provided by sections 106 through 122, or of the author as provided in section 106A(a), or who imports copies or phonorecords into the United States in violation of section 602, is an infringer of the copyright or right of the author, as the case may be. For purposes of this chapter (other than Section 506), any reference to copyright shall be deemed to include the rights conferred by Section 106A(a). As used in this subsection, the term "anyone" includes any State, any instrumentality of a State, and any officer or employee of a State or instrumentality of a State acting in his or her official capacity. Any State, and any such instrumentality, officer, or employee, shall be subject to the provisions of this title in the same manner and to the same extent as any nongovernmental entity.

(b) The legal or beneficial owner of an exclusive right under a copyright is entitled, subject to the requirements of section 411, to institute an action for any infringement of that particular right committed while he or she is the owner of it. The court may require such owner to serve written notice of the action with a copy of the complaint upon any person shown, by the records of the Copyright Office or otherwise, to have or claim an interest in the copyright, and shall require that such notice be served upon any person whose interest is likely to be affected by a decision in the case. The court may require the joinder, and shall permit the intervention, of any person having or claiming an interest in the copyright.

(c) For any secondary transmission by a cable system that embodies a performance or a display of a work which is actionable as an act of infringement under subsection (c) of section 111, a television broadcast station holding a copyright or other license to transmit or perform the same version of that work shall, for purposes of subsection (b) of this section, be treated as a legal or beneficial owner if such secondary transmission occurs within the local service area of that television station.

(d) For any secondary transmission by a cable system that is actionable as an act of infringement pursuant to section 111(c)(3), the following shall also have standing to sue: (i) the primary transmitter whose transmission has been altered by the cable system; and (ii) any broadcast station within whose local service area the secondary transmission occurs.

(e) With respect to any secondary transmission that is made by a satellite carrier of a performance or display of a work embodied in a primary transmission and is actionable as an act of infringement under section 119(a)(5), a network station holding a copyright or other license to transmit or perform the same version of that work shall, for purposes of subsection (b) of this section, be treated as a legal or beneficial owner if such secondary transmission occurs within the local service area of that station.

(f)(1) With respect to any secondary transmission that is made by a satellite carrier of a performance or display of a work embodied in a primary transmission and is actionable as an act of infringement under section 122, a television broadcast station holding a copyright or other license to transmit or perform the same version of that work shall, for purposes of subsection (b) of this section, be treated as a legal or beneficial owner if such secondary transmission occurs within the local market of that station.

(2) A television broadcast station may file a civil action against any satellite carrier that has refused to carry television broadcast signals, as required under section 122(a)(2), to enforce that television broadcast station's rights under section 338(a) of the Communications Act of 1934.

(Oct. 19, 1976, Pub. L. 94-553, §101, 90 Stat. 2584; Oct. 31, 1988, Pub. L. 100-568, §10, 102 Stat. 2860; Nov. 16, 1988, Pub. L. 100-667, §202, 102 Stat. 3957; Nov. 15, 1990, Pub. L. 101-553, §2, 104 Stat. 2749; Dec. 1, 1990, Pub. L. 101-650, §606, 104 Stat. 5131; Aug. 5, 1999, Pub. L. 106-44, §1(g), 113 Stat. 222; Nov. 29, 1999, Pub. L. 106-113, §§1002, 1011, 113 Stat. 1501A-523, 543; Nov. 2, 2002, Pub. L. 107-273, §13210, 116 Stat. 1909.)

17 U.S.C. § 501

§ 502   Remedies for infringement: Injunctions

(a) Any court having jurisdiction of a civil action arising under this title may, subject to the provisions of section 1498 of title 28, grant temporary and final injunctions on such terms as it may deem reasonable to prevent or restrain infringement of a copyright.

(b) Any such injunction may be served anywhere in the United States on the person enjoined; it shall be operative throughout the United States and shall be enforceable, by proceedings in contempt or otherwise, by any United States court having jurisdiction of that person. The clerk of the court granting the injunction shall, when requested by any other court in which enforcement of the injunction is sought, transmit promptly to the other court a certified copy of all the papers in the case on file in such clerk's office.

(Oct. 19, 1976, Pub. L. 94-553, §101, 90 Stat. 2584.)

§ 503   Remedies for infringement: Impounding and disposition of infringing articles

(a) At any time while an action under this title is pending, the court may order the impounding, on such terms as it may deem reasonable, of all copies or phonorecords claimed to have been made or used in violation of the copyright owner's exclusive rights, and of all plates, molds, matrices, masters, tapes, film negatives, or other articles by means of which such copies or phonorecords may be reproduced.

(b) As part of a final judgment or decree, the court may order the destruction or other reasonable disposition of all copies or phonorecords found to have been made or used in violation of the copyright owner's exclusive rights, and of all plates, molds, matrices, masters, tapes, film negatives, or other articles by means of which such copies or phonorecords may be reproduced.

(Oct. 19, 1976, Pub. L. 94-553, §101, 90 Stat. 2585.)

§ 504   Remedies for infringement: Damages and profits

(a) *In general.*—Except as otherwise provided by this title, an infringer of copyright is liable for either—

(1) the copyright owner's actual damages and any additional profits of the infringer, as provided by subsection (b); or

17 U.S.C. § 502

(2) statutory damages, as provided by subsection (c).

(b) *Actual damages and profits.*—The copyright owner is entitled to recover the actual damages suffered by him or her as a result of the infringement, and any profits of the infringer that are attributable to the infringement and are not taken into account in computing the actual damages. In establishing the infringer's profits, the copyright owner is required to present proof only of the infringer's gross revenue, and the infringer is required to prove his or her deductible expenses and the elements of profit attributable to factors other than the copyrighted work.

(c) *Statutory damages.*—

(1) Except as provided by clause (2) of this subsection, the copyright owner may elect, at any time before final judgment is rendered, to recover, instead of actual damages and profits, an award of statutory damages for all infringements involved in the action, with respect to any one work, for which any one infringer is liable individually, or for which any two or more infringers are liable jointly and severally, in a sum of not less than $750 or more than $30,000 as the court considers just. For the purposes of this subsection, all the parts of a compilation or derivative work constitute one work.

(2) In a case where the copyright owner sustains the burden of proving, and the court finds, that infringement was committed willfully, the court in its discretion may increase the award of statutory damages to a sum of not more than $150,000. In a case where the infringer sustains the burden of proving, and the court finds, that such infringer was not aware and had no reason to believe that his or her acts constituted an infringement of copyright, the court in its discretion may reduce the award of statutory damages to a sum of not less than $200. The court shall remit statutory damages in any case where an infringer believed and had reasonable grounds for believing that his or her use of the copyrighted work was a fair use under section 107, if the infringer was: (i) an employee or agent of a nonprofit educational institution, library, or archives acting within the scope of his or her employment who, or such institution, library, or archives itself, which infringed by reproducing the work in copies or phonorecords; or (ii) a public broadcasting entity which or a person who, as a regular part of the nonprofit activities of a public broadcasting entity

(as defined in subsection (g) of section 118) infringed by performing a published nondramatic literary work or by reproducing a transmission program embodying a performance of such a work.

(d) *Additional damages in certain cases.*— In any case in which the court finds that a defendant proprietor of an establishment who claims as a defense that its activities were exempt under section 110(5) did not have reasonable grounds to believe that its use of a copyrighted work was exempt under such section, the plaintiff shall be entitled to, in addition to any award of damages under this section, an additional award of two times the amount of the license fee that the proprietor of the establishment concerned should have paid the plaintiff for such use during the preceding period of up to 3 years.

(Oct. 19, 1976, Pub. L. 94-553, §101, 90 Stat. 2585; Oct. 31, 1988, Pub. L. 100-568, §10, 102 Stat. 2860; Nov. 13, 1997, Pub. L. 105-80, §12, 111 Stat. 1535; Oct. 27, 1998, Pub. L. 105-298, §204, 112 Stat. 2833; Dec. 9. 1999, Pub. L. 106-160, §2, 113 Stat. 1774 .)

§ 505 Remedies for infringement: Costs and attorney's fees

In any civil action under this title, the court in its discretion may allow the recovery of full costs by or against any party other than the United States or an officer thereof. Except as otherwise provided by this title, the court may also award a reasonable attorney's fee to the prevailing party as part of the costs.

(Oct. 19, 1976, Pub. L. 94-553, §101, 90 Stat. 2586.)

§ 506 Criminal offenses

(a) *Criminal infringement.*—Any person who infringes a copyright willfully either—

(1) for purposes of commercial advantage or private financial gain, or

(2) by the reproduction or distribution, including by electronic means, during any 180-day period, of 1 or more copies or phonorecords of 1 or more copyrighted works, which have a total retail value of more than $1,000,

shall be punished as provided under section 2319 of title 18, United States Code. For purposes of this subsection, evidence of reproduction or distribution of a copyrighted work, by itself, shall not be sufficient to establish willful infringement.

17 U.S.C. § 505

(b) *Forfeiture and destruction.*—When any person is convicted of any violation of subsection (a), the court in its judgment of conviction shall, in addition to the penalty therein prescribed, order the forfeiture and destruction or other disposition of all infringing copies or phonorecords and all implements, devices, or equipment used in the manufacture of such infringing copies or phonorecords.

(c) *Fraudulent copyright notice.*—Any person who, with fraudulent intent, places on any article a notice of copyright or words of the same purport that such person knows to be false, or who, with fraudulent intent, publicly distributes or imports for public distribution any article bearing such notice or words that such person knows to be false, shall be fined not more than $2,500.

(d) *Fraudulent removal of copyright notice.*—Any person who, with fraudulent intent, removes or alters any notice of copyright appearing on a copy of a copyrighted work shall be fined not more than $2,500.

(e) *False representation.*—Any person who knowingly makes a false representation of a material fact in the application for copyright registration provided for by section 409, or in any written statement filed in connection with the application, shall be fined not more than $2,500.

(f) *Rights of attribution and integrity.*—Nothing in this section applies to infringement of the rights conferred by Section 106A(a).

(Oct. 19, 1976, Pub. L. 94-553, §101, 90 Stat. 2586; May 24, 1982, Pub. L. 97-180, §5, 96 Stat. 93; Dec. 1, 1990, Pub. L. 101-650, §606, 104 Stat. 5131; Dec. 16, 1997, Pub. L. 105-147, §2(b), 111 Stat. 2678.)

§ 507 Limitations on actions

(a) *Criminal proceedings.*—Except as expressly provided otherwise in this title, no criminal proceeding shall be maintained under the provisions of this title unless it is commenced within 5 years after the cause of action arose.

(b) *Civil actions.*—No civil action shall be maintained under the provisions of this title unless it is commenced within three years after the claim accrued.

(Oct. 19, 1976, Pub. L. 94-553, §101, 90 Stat. 2586; Dec. 16, 1997, Pub. L. 105-147, §2(c), 111 Stat. 2678; Oct. 28, 1998, Pub. L. 105-304, §102(e), 112 Stat. 2863.)

§ 508   Notification of filing and determination of actions

(a) Within one month after the filing of any action under this title, the clerks of the courts of the United States shall send written notification to the Register of Copyrights setting forth, as far as is shown by the papers filed in the court, the names and addresses of the parties and the title, author, and registration number of each work involved in the action. If any other copyrighted work is later included in the action by amendment, answer, or other pleading, the clerk shall also send a notification concerning it to the Register within one month after the pleading is filed.

(b) Within one month after any final order or judgment is issued in the case, the clerk of the court shall notify the Register of it, sending with the notification a copy of the order or judgment together with the written opinion, if any, of the court.

(c) Upon receiving the notifications specified in this section, the Register shall make them a part of the public records of the Copyright Office.

(Oct. 19, 1976, Pub. L. 94-553, §101, 90 Stat. 2586.)

§ 509   Seizure and forfeiture

(a) All copies or phonorecords manufactured, reproduced, distributed, sold, or otherwise used, intended for use, or possessed with intent to use in violation of section 506(a), and all plates, molds, matrices, masters, tapes, film negatives, or other articles by means of which such copies or phonorecords may be reproduced, and all electronic, mechanical, or other devices for manufacturing, reproducing, or assembling such copies or phonorecords may be seized and forfeited to the United States.

(b) The applicable procedures relating to (i) the seizure, summary and judicial forfeiture, and condemnation of vessels, vehicles, merchandise, and baggage for violations of the customs laws contained in title 19, (ii) the disposition of such vessels, vehicles, merchandise, and baggage or the proceeds from the sale thereof, (iii) the remission or mitigation of such forfeiture, (iv) the compromise of claims, and (v) the award of compensation to informers in respect of such forfeitures, shall apply to seizures and forfeitures incurred, or alleged to have been incurred, under the provisions of this section, insofar as applicable and not inconsistent with the provisions of this section; except that such duties as are imposed upon any officer or employee of the Treasury Department or any other person with respect to the seizure and forfeiture of vessels, vehicles, merchandise, and baggage under the provisions of the customs laws contained in title 19 shall be performed with respect to seizure and forfeiture of all articles described in subsection (a) by such officers, agents, or other persons as may be authorized or designated for that purpose by the Attorney General.

(Oct. 19, 1976, Pub. L. 94-553, §101, 90 Stat. 2587; Nov. 13, 1997, Pub. L. 105-80, §12, 111 Stat. 1535.)

§ 510 Remedies for alteration of programming by cable systems

(a) In any action filed pursuant to section 111(c)(3), the following remedies shall be available:

(1) Where an action is brought by a party identified in subsections (b) or (c) of section 501, the remedies provided by sections 502 through 505, and the remedy provided by subsection (b) of this section; and

(2) When an action is brought by a party identified in subsection (d) of section 501, the remedies provided by sections 502 and 505, together with any actual damages suffered by such party as a result of the infringement, and the remedy provided by subsection (b) of this section.

(b) In any action filed pursuant to section 111(c)(3), the court may decree that, for a period not to exceed thirty days, the cable system shall be deprived of the benefit of a statutory license for one or more distant signals carried by such cable system.

(Oct. 19, 1976, Pub. L. 94-553, §101, 90 Stat. 2587; Nov. 29, 1999, Pub. L. 106-113, §1011, 113 Stat. 1501A-543.)

§ 511 Liability of States, instrumentalities of States, and State officials for infringement of copyright

(a) *In general.*—Any State, any instrumentality of a State, and any officer or employee of a State or instrumentality of a State acting in his or her official capacity, shall not be immune, under the Eleventh Amendment of the Constitution of the United States or under any other doctrine of sovereign immunity, from suit in Federal court by any person, including any governmental or nongovernmental entity, for a violation of any of the exclusive rights of a copyright owner provided by sections 106 through 122, for importing copies of phonorecords in violation of section 602, or for any other violation under this title.

(b) *Remedies.*—In a suit described in subsection (a) for a violation described in that subsection, remedies (including remedies both at law and in equity) are available for the violation to the same extent as such remedies are available for such a violation in a suit against any public or private entity other than a State, instrumentality of a State, or officer or employee of a State acting in his or her official capacity. Such remedies include impounding and disposition of infringing articles under section 503, actual damages and profits and statutory damages under section 504, costs and attorney's fees under section 505, and the remedies provided in section 510.

(Added Nov. 15, 1990, Pub. L. 101-553, §2, 104 Stat. 2749-50; Aug. 5, 1999, Pub. L. 106-44, §1(g), 113 Stat. 222; Nov. 2, 2002, Pub. L. 107-273, §13210, 116 Stat. 1909.)

§ 512   Limitations on liability relating to material online

(a) *Transitory digital network communications.*— A service provider shall not be liable for monetary relief, or, except as provided in subsection (j), for injunctive or other equitable relief, for infringement of copyright by reason of the provider's transmitting, routing, or providing connections for, material through a system or network controlled or operated by or for the service provider, or by reason of the intermediate and transient storage of that material in the course of such transmitting, routing, or providing connections, if—

(1) the transmission of the material was initiated by or at the direction of a person other than the service provider;

(2) the transmission, routing, provision of connections, or storage is carried out through an automatic technical process without selection of the material by the service provider;

(3) the service provider does not select the recipients of the material except as an automatic response to the request of another person;

(4) no copy of the material made by the service provider in the course of such intermediate or transient storage is maintained on the system or network in a manner ordinarily accessible to anyone other

than anticipated recipients, and no such copy is maintained on the system or network in a manner ordinarily accessible to such anticipated recipients for a longer period than is reasonably necessary for the transmission, routing, or provision of connections; and

(5) the material is transmitted through the system or network without modification of its content.

(b) *System caching.*—

(1) *Limitation on liability.*—A service provider shall not be liable for monetary relief, or, except as provided in subsection (j), for injunctive or other equitable relief, for infringement of copyright by reason of the intermediate and temporary storage of material on a system or network controlled or operated by or for the service provider in a case in which—

(A) the material is made available online by a person other than the service provider;

(B) the material is transmitted from the person described in subparagraph (A) through the system or network to a person other than the person described in subparagraph (A) at the direction of that other person; and

(C) the storage is carried out through an automatic technical process for the purpose of making the material available to users of the system or network who, after the material is transmitted as described in subparagraph (B), request access to the material from the person described in subparagraph (A),

if the conditions set forth in paragraph (2) are met.

(2) *Conditions.*—The conditions referred to in paragraph (1) are that—

(A) the material described in paragraph (1) is transmitted to the subsequent users described in paragraph (1)(C) without modification to its content from the manner in which the material was transmitted from the person described in paragraph (1)(A);

(B) the service provider described in paragraph (1) complies with rules concerning the refreshing, reloading, or other updating of the material when specified by the person making the material

17 U.S.C. § 512

available online in accordance with a generally accepted industry standard data communications protocol for the system or network through which that person makes the material available, except that this subparagraph applies only if those rules are not used by the person described in paragraph (1)(A) to prevent or unreasonably impair the intermediate storage to which this subsection applies;

(C) the service provider does not interfere with the ability of technology associated with the material to return to the person described in paragraph (1)(A) the information that would have been available to that person if the material had been obtained by the subsequent users described in paragraph (1)(C) directly from that person, except that this subparagraph applies only if that technology—

(i) does not significantly interfere with the performance of the provider's system or network or with the intermediate storage of the material;

(ii) is consistent with generally accepted industry standard communications protocols; and

(iii) does not extract information from the provider's system or network other than the information that would have been available to the person described in paragraph (1)(A) if the subsequent users had gained access to the material directly from that person;

(D) if the person described in paragraph (1)(A) has in effect a condition that a person must meet prior to having access to the material, such as a condition based on payment of a fee or provision of a password or other information, the service provider permits access to the stored material in significant part only to users of its system or network that have met those conditions and only in accordance with those conditions; and

(E) if the person described in paragraph (1)(A) makes that material available online without the authorization of the copyright owner of the material, the service provider responds expeditiously to remove, or disable access to, the material that is claimed to be infringing upon notification of claimed infringement as described in subsection (c)(3), except that this subparagraph applies only if—

(i) the material has previously been removed from the originating site or access to it has been disabled, or a court has ordered that the material be removed from the originating site or that access to the material on the originating site be disabled; and

(ii) the party giving the notification includes in the notification a statement confirming that the material has been removed from the originating site or access to it has been disabled or that a court has ordered that the material be removed from the originating site or that access to the material on the originating site be disabled.

(c) *Information residing on systems or networks at director of users.*—

(1) *In general.*—A service provider shall not be liable for monetary relief, or, except as provided in subsection (j), for injunctive or other equitable relief, for infringement of copyright by reason of the storage at the direction of a user of material that resides on a system or network controlled or operated by or for the service provider, if the service provider—

(A)(i) does not have actual knowledge that the material or an activity using the material on the system or network is infringing;

(ii) in the absence of such actual knowledge, is not aware of facts or circumstances from which infringing activity is apparent; or

(iii) upon obtaining such knowledge or awareness, acts expeditiously to remove, or disable access to, the material;

(B) does not receive a financial benefit directly attributable to the infringing activity, in a case in which the service provider has the right and ability to control such activity; and

(C) upon notification of claimed infringement as described in paragraph (3), responds expeditiously to remove, or disable access to, the material that is claimed to be infringing or to be the subject of infringing activity.

(2) *Designated agent.*—The limitations on liability established in this subsection apply to a service provider only if the service provider has designated an agent to receive notifications of claimed infringement described in paragraph (3), by making available through its service, including on its website in a location accessible to the public, and by providing to the Copyright Office, substantially the following information:

(A) the name, address, phone number, and electronic mail address of the agent.

(B) other contact information which the Register of Copyrights may deem appropriate.

The Register of Copyrights shall maintain a current directory of agents available to the public for inspection, including through the Internet, in both electronic and hard copy formats, and may require payment of a fee by service providers to cover the costs of maintaining the directory.

(3) *Elements of notification.*—

(A) To be effective under this subsection, a notification of claimed infringement must be a written communication provided to the designated agent of a service provider that includes substantially the following:

(i) A physical or electronic signature of a person authorized to act on behalf of the owner of an exclusive right that is allegedly infringed.

(ii) Identification of the copyrighted work claimed to have been infringed, or, if multiple copyrighted works at a single online site are covered by a single notification, a representative list of such works at that site.

(iii) Identification of the material that is claimed to be infringing or to be the subject of infringing activity and that is to be removed or access to which is to be disabled, and information reasonably sufficient to permit the service provider to locate the material.

(iv) Information reasonably sufficient to permit the service provider to contact the complaining party, such as an address, telephone number, and, if available, an electronic mail address at which the complaining party may be contacted.

(v) A statement that the complaining party has a good faith belief that use of the material in the manner complained of is not authorized by the copyright owner, its agent, or the law.

(vi) A statement that the information in the notification is accurate, and under penalty of perjury, that the complaining party is authorized to act on behalf of the owner of an exclusive right that is allegedly infringed.

(B)(i) Subject to clause (ii), a notification from a copyright owner or from a person authorized to act on behalf of the copyright owner that fails to comply substantially with the provisions of subparagraph (A) shall not be considered under paragraph (1)(A) in determining whether a service provider has actual knowledge or is aware of facts or circumstances from which infringing activity is apparent.

(ii) In a case in which the notification that is provided to the service provider's designated agent fails to comply substantially with all the provisions of subparagraph (A) but substantially complies with clauses (ii), (iii), and (iv) of subparagraph (A), clause (i) of this subparagraph applies only if the service provider promptly attempts to contact the person making the notification or takes other reasonable steps to assist in the receipt of notification that substantially complies with all the provisions of subparagraph (A).

(d) *Information location tools.*—A service provider shall not be liable for monetary relief, or, except as provided in subsection (j), for injunctive or other equitable relief, for infringement of copyright by reason of the provider referring or linking users to an online location containing infringing material or infringing activity, by using information location tools, including a directory, index, reference, pointer, or hypertext link, if the service provider—

(1)(A) does not have actual knowledge that the material or activity is infringing;

(B) in the absence of such actual knowledge, is not aware of facts or circumstances from which infringing activity is apparent; or

(C) upon obtaining such knowledge or awareness, acts expeditiously to remove, or disable access to, the material;

(2) does not receive a financial benefit directly attributable to the infringing activity, in a case in which the service provider has the right and ability to control such activity; and

(3) upon notification of claimed infringement as described in subsection (c)(3), responds expeditiously to remove, or disable access to, the material that is claimed to be infringing or to be the subject of infringing activity, except that, for purposes of this paragraph, the information described in subsection (c)(3)(A)(iii) shall be identification of the reference or link, to material or activity claimed to be infringing, that is to be removed or access to which is to be disabled, and information reasonably sufficient to permit the service provider to locate that reference or link.

(e) *Limitation on liability of nonprofit educational institutions.*—(1) When a public or other nonprofit institution of higher education is a service provider, and when a faculty member or graduate student who is an employee of such institution is performing a teaching or research function, for the purposes of subsections (a) and (b) such faculty member or graduate student shall be considered to be a person other than the institution, and for the purposes of subsections (c) and (d) such faculty member's or graduate student's knowledge or awareness of his or her infringing activities shall not be attributed to the institution, if—

(A) such faculty member's or graduate student's infringing activities do not involve the provision of online access to instructional materials that are or were required or recommended, within the preceding 3-year period, for a course taught at the institution by such faculty member or graduate student;

(B) the institution has not, within the preceding 3-year period, received more than two notifications described in subsection (c)(3) of claimed infringement by such faculty member or graduate student, and such notifications of claimed infringement were not actionable under subsection (f); and

(C) the institution provides to all users of its system or network informational materials that accurately describe, and promote compliance with, the laws of the United States relating to copyright.

(2) For the purposes of this subsection, the limitations on injunctive relief contained in subsections (j)(2) and (j)(3), but not those in (j)(1), shall apply.

(f) *Misrepresentations.*—Any person who knowingly materially misrepresents under this section—

(1) that material or activity is infringing, or

(2) that material or activity was removed or disabled by mistake or misidentification,

shall be liable for any damages, including costs and attorneys' fees, incurred by the alleged infringer, by any copyright owner or copyright owner's authorized licensee, or by a service provider, who is injured by such misrepresentation, as the result of the service provider relying upon such misrepresentation in removing or disabling access to the material or activity claimed to be infringing, or in replacing the removed material or ceasing to disable access to it.

(g) *Replacement of removed or disabled material and limitation on other liability.*—

(1) *No liability for taking down generally.*—Subject to paragraph (2), a service provider shall not be liable to any person for any claim based on the service provider's good faith disabling of access to, or removal of, material or activity claimed to be infringing or based on facts or circumstances from which infringing activity is apparent, regardless of whether the material or activity is ultimately determined to be infringing.

(2) *Exception.*—Paragraph (1) shall not apply with respect to material residing at the direction of a subscriber of the service provider on a system or network controlled or operated by or for the service provider that is removed, or to which access is disabled by the service provider, pursuant to a notice provided under subsection (c)(1)(C), unless the service provider—

17 U.S.C. § 512

(A) takes reasonable steps promptly to notify the subscriber that it has removed or disabled access to the material;

(B) upon receipt of a counter notification described in paragraph (3), promptly provides the person who provided the notification under subsection (c)(1)(C) with a copy of the counter notification, and informs that person that it will replace the removed material or cease disabling access to it in 10 business days; and

(C) replaces the removed material and ceases disabling access to it not less than 10, nor more than 14, business days following receipt of the counter notice, unless its designated agent first receives notice from the person who submitted the notification under subsection (c)(1)(C) that such person has filed an action seeking a court order to restrain the subscriber from engaging in infringing activity relating to the material on the service provider's system or network.

(3) *Contents of counter notification.*—To be effective under this subsection, a counter notification must be a written communication provided to the service provider's designated agent that includes substantially the following:

(A) A physical or electronic signature of the subscriber.

(B) Identification of the material that has been removed or to which access has been disabled and the location at which the material appeared before it was removed or access to it was disabled.

(C) A statement under penalty of perjury that the subscriber has a good faith belief that the material was removed or disabled as a result of mistake or misidentification of the material to be removed or disabled.

(D) The subscriber's name, address, and telephone number, and a statement that the subscriber consents to the jurisdiction of Federal District Court for the judicial district in which the address is located, or if the subscriber's address is outside of the United States, for any judicial district in which the service provider may be found, and that the subscriber will accept service of process from the person who provided notification under sub-section (c)(1)(C) or an agent of such person.

(4) *Limitation on other liability.*—A service provider's compliance with paragraph (2) shall not subject the service provider to liability for copyright infringement with respect to the material identified in the notice provided under subsection (c)(1)(C).

(h) *Subpoena to identify infringer.*—

(1) *Request.*—A copyright owner or a person authorized to act on the owner's behalf may request the clerk of any United States district court to issue a subpoena to a service provider for identification of an alleged infringer in accordance with this subsection.

(2) *Contents of request.*—The request may be made by filing with the clerk—

(A) a copy of a notification described in subsection (c)(3)(A);

(B) a proposed subpoena; and

(C) a sworn declaration to the effect that the purpose for which the subpoena is sought is to obtain the identity of an alleged in-fringer and that such information will only be used for the pur-pose of protecting rights under this title.

(3) *Contents of subpoena.*—The subpoena shall authorize and order the service provider receiving the notification and the subpoena to expeditiously disclose to the copyright owner or person authorized by the copyright owner information sufficient to identify the alleged infringer of the material described in the notification to the extent such information is available to the service provider.

(4) *Basis for granting subpoena.*—If the notification filed satisfies the provisions of subsection (c)(3)(A), the proposed subpoena is in proper form, and the accompanying declaration is properly exe-cuted, the clerk shall expeditiously issue and sign the proposed sub-poena and return it to the requester for delivery to the service pro-vider.

(5) *Actions of service provider receiving subpoena.*—Upon receipt of the issued subpoena, either accompanying or subsequent to the receipt of a notification described in subsection (c)(3)(A), the service pro-

17 U.S.C. § 512

vider shall expeditiously disclose to the copyright owner or person authorized by the copyright owner the information required by the subpoena, notwithstanding any other provision of law and regardless of whether the service provider responds to the notification.

(6) *Rules applicable to subpoena.*—Unless otherwise provided by this section or by applicable rules of the court, the procedure for issuance and delivery of the subpoena, and the remedies for noncompliance with the subpoena, shall be governed to the greatest extent practicable by those provisions of the Federal Rules of Civil Procedure governing the issuance, service, and enforcement of a subpoena duces tecum.

(i) *Conditions for eligibility.*—

(1) *Accommodation of technology.*—The limitations on liability established by this section shall apply to a service provider only if the service provider—

(A) has adopted and reasonably implemented, and informs subscribers and account holders of the service provider's system or network of, a policy that provides for the termination in appropriate circumstances of subscribers and account holders of the service provider's system or network who are repeat infringers; and

(B) accommodates and does not interfere with standard technical measures.

(2) *Definition.*—As used in this subsection, the term "standard technical measures" means technical measures that are used by copyright owners to identify or protect copyrighted works and—

(A) have been developed pursuant to a broad consensus of copyright owners and service providers in an open, fair, voluntary, multi-industry standards process;

(B) are available to any person on reasonable and nondiscriminatory terms; and

(C) do not impose substantial costs on service providers or substantial burdens on their systems or networks.

(j) *Injunctions.*—The following rules shall apply in the case of any application for an injunction under section 502 against a service provider that is not subject to monetary remedies under this section:

    (1) *Scope of relief.*—(A) With respect to conduct other than that which qualifies for the limitation on remedies set forth in subsection (a), the court may grant injunctive relief with respect to a service provider only in one or more of the following forms:

        (i) An order restraining the service provider from providing access to infringing material or activity residing at a particular online site on the provider's system or network.

        (ii) An order restraining the service provider from providing access to a subscriber or account holder of the service provider's system or network who is engaging in infringing activity and is identified in the order, by terminating the accounts of the subscriber or account holder that are specified in the order.

        (iii) Such other injunctive relief as the court may consider necessary to prevent or restrain infringement of copyrighted material specified in the order of the court at a particular online location, if such relief is the least burdensome to the service provider among the forms of relief comparably effective for that purpose.

    (B) If the service provider qualifies for the limitation on remedies described in subsection (a), the court may only grant injunctive relief in one or both of the following forms:

        (i) An order restraining the service provider from providing access to a subscriber or account holder of the service provider's system or network who is using the provider's service to engage in infringing activity and is identified in the order, by terminating the accounts of the subscriber or account holder that are specified in the order.

        (ii) An order restraining the service provider from providing access, by taking reasonable steps specified in the order to block access, to a specific, identified, online location outside the United States.

17 U.S.C. § 512

(2) *Considerations.*—The court, in considering the relevant criteria for injunctive relief under applicable law, shall consider—

(A) whether such an injunction, either alone or in combination with other such injunctions issued against the same service provider under this subsection, would significantly burden either the provider or the operation of the provider's system or network;

(B) the magnitude of the harm likely to be suffered by the copyright owner in the digital network environment if steps are not taken to prevent or restrain the infringement;

(C) whether implementation of such an injunction would be technically feasible and effective, and would not interfere with access to noninfringing material at other online locations; and

(D) whether other less burdensome and comparably effective means of preventing or restraining access to the infringing material are available.

(3) *Notice and ex parte orders.*—Injunctive relief under this subsection shall be available only after notice to the service provider and an opportunity for the service provider to appear are provided, except for orders ensuring the preservation of evidence or other orders having no material adverse effect on the operation of the service provider's communications network.

(k) *Definitions.*—

(1) *Service provider.*—(A) As used in subsection (a), the term "service provider" means an entity offering the transmission, routing, or providing of connections for digital online communications, between or among points specified by a user, of material of the user's choosing, without modification to the content of the material as sent or received.

(B) As used in this section, other than subsection (a), the term "service provider" means a provider of online services or network access, or the operator of facilities therefor, and includes an entity described in subparagraph (A).

(2) *Monetary relief.*—As used in this section, the term "monetary relief" means damages, costs, attorneys' fees, and any other form of monetary payment.

(l) *Other defenses not affected.*—The failure of a service provider's conduct to qualify for limitation of liability under this section shall not bear adversely upon the consideration of a defense by the service provider that the service provider's conduct is not infringing under this title or any other defense.

(m) *Protection of privacy.*—Nothing in this section shall be construed to condition the applicability of subsections (a) through (d) on—

(1) a service provider monitoring its service or affirmatively seeking facts indicating infringing activity, except to the extent consistent with a standard technical measure complying with the provisions of subsection (i); or

(2) a service provider gaining access to, removing, or disabling access to material in cases in which such conduct is prohibited by law.

(n) *Construction.*—Subsections (a), (b), (c), and (d) describe separate and distinct functions for purposes of applying this section. Whether a service provider qualifies for the limitation on liability in any one of those subsections shall be based solely on the criteria in that subsection, and shall not affect a determination of whether that service provider qualifies for the limitations on liability under any other such subsection.

(Oct. 28, 1998, Pub. L. 105-304, §202, 112 Stat. 2877; Aug. 5, 1999, Pub. L. 106-44, §1(d), 113 Stat. 222.)

§ 513 Determination of reasonable license fees for individual proprietors

In the case of any performing rights society subject to a consent decree which provides for the determination of reasonable license rates or fees to be charged by the performing rights society, notwithstanding the provisions of that consent decree, an individual proprietor who owns or operates fewer than 7 non-publicly traded establishments in which nondramatic musical works are performed publicly and who claims that any license agreement offered by that performing rights society is unreasonable in its license rate or fee as to that individual proprietor, shall be entitled to determination of a reasonable license rate or fee as follows:

(1) The individual proprietor may commence such proceeding for determination of a reasonable license rate or fee by filing an application in the applicable district court under paragraph (2) that a rate disagreement exists and by serving a copy of the application on the performing rights society. Such proceeding shall commence in the applicable district court within 90 days after the service of such copy, except that such 90-day requirement shall be subject to the administrative requirements of the court.

(2) The proceeding under paragraph (1) shall be held, at the individual proprietor's election, in the judicial district of the district court with jurisdiction over the applicable consent decree or in that place of holding court of a district court that is the seat of the Federal circuit (other than the Court of Appeals for the Federal Circuit) in which the proprietor's establishment is located.

(3) Such proceeding shall be held before the judge of the court with jurisdiction over the consent decree governing the performing rights society. At the discretion of the court, the proceeding shall be held before a special master or magistrate judge appointed by such judge. Should that consent decree provide for the appointment of an advisor or advisors to the court for any purpose, any such advisor shall be the special master so named by the court.

(4) In any such proceeding, the industry rate shall be presumed to have been reasonable at the time it was agreed to or determined by the court. Such presumption shall in no way affect a determination of whether the rate is being correctly applied to the individual proprietor.

(5) Pending the completion of such proceeding, the individual proprietor shall have the right to perform publicly the copyrighted musical compositions in the repertoire of the performing rights society by paying an interim license rate or fee into an interest bearing escrow account with the clerk of the court, subject to retroactive adjustment when a final rate or fee has been determined, in an amount equal to the industry rate, or, in the absence of an industry rate, the amount of the most recent license rate or fee agreed to by the parties.

17 U.S.C. § 513

(6) Any decision rendered in such proceeding by a special master or magistrate judge named under paragraph (3) shall be reviewed by the judge of the court with jurisdiction over the consent decree governing the performing rights society. Such proceeding, including such review, shall be concluded within 6 months after its commencement.

(7) Any such final determination shall be binding only as to the individual proprietor commencing the proceeding, and shall not be applicable to any other proprietor or any other performing rights society, and the performing rights society shall be relieved of any obligation of nondiscrimination among similarly situated music users that may be imposed by the consent decree governing its operations.

(8) An individual proprietor may not bring more than one proceeding provided for in this section for the determination of a reasonable license rate or fee under any license agreement with respect to any one performing rights society.

(9) For purposes of this section, the term "industry rate" means the license fee a performing rights society has agreed to with, or which has been determined by the court for, a significant segment of the music user industry to which the individual proprietor belongs.

(Added Oct. 27, 1998, Pub. L. 105-298, §203, 112 Stat. 2831; Aug. 5, 1999, Pub. L. 106-44, §1(c), 113 Stat. 221.)

CHAPTER 6—MANUFACTURING REQUIREMENTS AND IMPORTATION

SEC.

§ 601 Manufacture, importation, and public distribution of certain copies

(a) Prior to July 1, 1986, and except as provided by subsection (b), the importation into or public distribution in the United States of copies of a work consisting preponderantly of nondramatic literary material that is in the English language and is protected under this title is prohibited unless the portions consisting of such material have been manufactured in the United States or Canada.

(b) The provisions of subsection (a) do not apply—

(1) where, on the date when importation is sought or public distribution in the United States is made, the author of any substantial part of such material is neither a national nor a domiciliary of the United States or, if such author is a national of the United States, he or she has been domiciled outside the United States for a continuous period of at least one year immediately preceding that date; in the case of a work made for hire, the exemption provided by this clause does not apply unless a substantial part of the work was prepared for an employer or other person who is not a national or domiciliary of the United States or a domestic corporation or enterprise;

(2) where the United States Customs Service is presented with an import statement issued under the seal of the Copyright Office, in which case a total of no more than two thousand copies of any one such work shall be allowed entry; the import statement shall be issued upon request to the copyright owner or to a person designated by such owner at the time of registration for the work under section 408 or at any time thereafter;

(3) where importation is sought under the authority or for the use, other than in schools, of the Government of the United States or of any State or political subdivision of a State;

(4) where importation, for use and not for sale, is sought—

(A) by any person with respect to no more than one copy of any work at any one time;

(B) by any person arriving from outside the United States, with respect to copies forming part of such person's personal baggage; or

(C) by an organization operated for scholarly, educational, or religious purposes and not for private gain, with respect to copies intended to form a part of its library;

(5) where the copies are reproduced in raised characters for the use of the blind; or

(6) where, in addition to copies imported under clauses (3) and (4) of this subsection, no more than two thousand copies of any one such work, which have not been manufactured in the United States or Canada, are publicly distributed in the United States; or

(7) where, on the date when importation is sought or public distribution in the United States is made—

(A) the author of any substantial part of such material is an individual and receives compensation for the transfer or license of the right to distribute the work in the United States; and

(B) the first publication of the work has previously taken place outside the United States under a transfer or license granted by such author to a transferee or licensee who was not a national or domiciliary of the United States or a domestic corporation or enterprise; and

(C) there has been no publication of an authorized edition of the work of which the copies were manufactured in the United States; and

(D) the copies were reproduced under a transfer or license granted by such author or by the transferee or licensee of the right of first publication as mentioned in subclause (B), and the transferee or the licensee of the right of reproduction was not a national or domiciliary of the United States or a domestic corporation or enterprise.

(c) The requirement of this section that copies be manufactured in the United States or Canada is satisfied if—

(1) in the case where the copies are printed directly from type that has been set, or directly from plates made from such type, the setting of the type and the making of the plates have been performed in the United States or Canada; or

(2) in the case where the making of plates by a lithographic or photoengraving process is a final or intermediate step preceding the printing of the copies, the making of the plates has been performed in the United States or Canada; and

(3) in any case, the printing or other final process of producing multiple copies and any binding of the copies have been performed in the United States or Canada.

(d) Importation or public distribution of copies in violation of this section does not invalidate protection for a work under this title. However, in any civil action or criminal proceeding for infringement of the exclusive rights to reproduce and distribute copies of the work, the infringer has a complete defense with respect to all of the nondramatic literary material comprised in the work and any other parts of the work in which the exclusive rights to reproduce and distribute copies are owned by the same person who owns such exclusive rights in the nondramatic literary material, if the infringer proves—

(1) that copies of the work have been imported into or publicly distributed in the United States in violation of this section by or with the authority of the owner of such exclusive rights; and

(2) that the infringing copies were manufactured in the United States or Canada in accordance with the provisions of subsection (c); and

(3) that the infringement was commenced before the effective date of registration for an authorized edition of the work, the copies of which have been manufactured in the United States or Canada in accordance with the provisions of subsection (c).

(e) In any action for infringement of the exclusive rights to reproduce and distribute copies of a work containing material required by this section to be manufactured in the United States or Canada, the copyright owner shall set forth in the complaint the names of the persons or organizations who performed the processes specified by subsection (c) with respect to that material, and the places where those processes were performed.

(Oct. 19, 1976, Pub. L. 94-553, §101, 90 Stat. 2588; July 13, 1982, Pub. L. 97-215, 96 Stat. 178; Nov. 13, 1997, Pub. L. 105-80, §12, 111 Stat. 1535.)

§ 602   Infringing importation of copies or phonorecords

(a) Importation into the United States, without the authority of the owner of copyright under this title, of copies or phonorecords of a work that have been acquired outside the United States is an infringement of the exclusive right to distribute copies or phonorecords under section 106, actionable under section 501. This subsection does not apply to—

(1) importation of copies or phonorecords under the authority or for the use of the Government of the United States or of any State or political subdivision of a State, but not including copies or phonorecords for use in schools, or copies of any audiovisual work imported for purposes other than archival use;

(2) importation, for the private use of the importer and not for distribution, by any person with respect to no more than one copy or phonorecord of any one work at any one time, or by any person arriving from outside the United States with respect to copies or phonorecords forming part of such person's personal baggage; or

(3) importation by or for an organization operated for scholarly, educational, or religious purposes and not for private gain, with respect to no more than one copy of an audiovisual work solely for its archival purposes, and no more than five copies or phonorecords of any other work for its library lending or archival purposes, unless the importation of such copies or phonorecords is part of an activity consisting of systematic reproduction or distribution, engaged in by such organization in violation of the provisions of section 108(g)(2).

(b) In a case where the making of the copies or phonorecords would have constituted an infringement of copyright if this title had been applicable, their importation is prohibited. In a case where the copies or phonorecords were lawfully made, the United States Customs Service has no authority to prevent their importation unless the provisions of section 601 are applicable. In either case, the Secretary of the Treasury is authorized to prescribe, by regulation, a procedure under which any person claiming an interest in the copyright in a particular work may, upon payment of a specified fee, be entitled to notification by the Customs Service of the importation of articles that appear to be copies or phonorecords of the work.

(Oct. 19, 1976, Pub. L. 94-553, §101, 90 Stat. 2589.)

§ 603   Importation prohibitions: Enforcement and disposition of excluded articles

(a) The Secretary of the Treasury and the United States Postal Service shall separately or jointly make regulations for the enforcement of the provisions of this title prohibiting importation.

(b) These regulations may require, as a condition for the exclusion of articles under section 602—

(1) that the person seeking exclusion obtain a court order enjoining importation of the articles; or

(2) that the person seeking exclusion furnish proof, of a specified nature and in accordance with prescribed procedures, that the copyright in which such person claims an interest is valid and that the importation would violate the prohibition in section 602; the person seeking exclusion may also be required to post a surety bond for any injury that may result if the detention or exclusion of the articles proves to be unjustified.

(c) Articles imported in violation of the importation prohibitions of this title are subject to seizure and forfeiture in the same manner as property imported in violation of the customs revenue laws. Forfeited articles shall be destroyed as directed by the Secretary of the Treasury or the court, as the case may be.

(Oct. 19, 1976, Pub. L. 94-553, §101, 90 Stat. 2590; July 2, 1996, Pub. L. 104-153, §8, 110 Stat. 1388.)

CHAPTER 7—COPYRIGHT OFFICE

§ 701 The Copyright Office: General responsibilities and organization

(a) All administrative functions and duties under this title, except as otherwise specified, are the responsibility of the Register of Copyrights as director of the Copyright Office of the Library of Congress. The Register of Copyrights, together with the subordinate officers and employees of the Copyright Office, shall be appointed by the Librarian of Congress, and shall act under the Librarian's general direction and supervision.

(b) In addition to the functions and duties set out elsewhere in this chapter, the Register of Copyrights shall perform the following functions:

(1) Advise Congress on national and international issues relating to copyright, other matters arising under this title, and related matters.

(2) Provide information and assistance to Federal departments and agencies and the Judiciary on national and international issues relating to copyright, other matters arising under this title, and related matters.

(3) Participate in meetings of international intergovernmental organizations and meetings with foreign government officials relating to copyright, other matters arising under this title, and related matters, including as a member of United States delegations as authorized by the appropriate Executive branch authority.

(4) Conduct studies and programs regarding copyright, other matters arising under this title, and related matters, the administration of the Copyright Office, or any function vested in the Copyright Office by law, including educational programs conducted cooperatively with foreign intellectual property offices and international intergovernmental organizations.

(5) Perform such other functions as Congress may direct, or as may be appropriate in furtherance of the functions and duties specifically set forth in this title.

(c) The Register of Copyrights shall adopt a seal to be used on and after January 1, 1978, to authenticate all certified documents issued by the Copyright Office.

(d) The Register of Copyrights shall make an annual report to the Librarian of Congress of the work and accomplishments of the Copyright Office during the previous fiscal year. The annual report of the Register of Copyrights shall be published separately and as a part of the annual report of the Librarian of Congress.

(e) Except as provided by section 706(b) and the regulations issued thereunder, all actions taken by the Register of Copyrights under this title are subject to the provisions of the Administrative Procedure Act of June 11, 1946, as amended (c. 324, 60 Stat. 237, title 5, United States Code, Chapter 5, Subchapter II and Chapter 7).

(f) The Register of Copyrights shall be compensated at the rate of pay in effect for level III of the Executive Schedule under section 5314 of title 5. The Librarian of Congress shall establish not more than four positions for Associate Registers of Copyrights, in accordance with the recommendations of the Register of Copyrights. The Librarian shall make appointments to such positions after consultation with the Register of Copyrights. Each Associate Register of Copyrights shall be paid at a rate not to exceed the maximum annual rate of basic pay payable for GS-18 of the General Schedule under section 5332 of title 5.

(Oct. 19, 1976, Pub. L. 94-553, §101, 90 Stat. 2591; July 3, 1990, Pub. L. 101-319, §2, 104 Stat. 290; Oct. 28, 1998, Pub. L. 105-304, §401, 112 Stat. 2887.)

§ 702   Copyright Office regulations

The Register of Copyrights is authorized to establish regulations not inconsistent with law for the administration of the functions and duties made the responsibility of the Register under this title. All regulations established by the Register under this title are subject to the approval of the Librarian of Congress.

(Oct. 19, 1976, Pub. L. 94-553, §101, 90 Stat. 2591.)

§ 703   Effective date of actions in Copyright Office

In any case in which time limits are prescribed under this title for the performance of an action in the Copyright Office, and in which the last day of the prescribed period falls on a Saturday, Sunday, holiday, or other nonbusiness day within the District of Columbia or the Federal Government, the action may be taken on the next succeeding business day, and is effective as of the date when the period expired.

(Oct. 19, 1976, Pub. L. 94-553, §101, 90 Stat. 2591.)

§ 704   Retention and disposition of articles deposited in Copyright Office

(a) Upon their deposit in the Copyright Office under sections 407 and 408, all copies, phonorecords, and identifying material, including those deposited in connection with claims that have been refused registration, are the property of the United States Government.

(b) In the case of published works, all copies, phonorecords, and identifying material deposited are available to the Library of Congress for its collections, or for exchange or transfer to any other library. In the case of unpublished works, the Library is entitled, under regulations that the Register of Copyrights shall prescribe, to select any deposits for its collections or for transfer to the National Archives of the United States or to a Federal records center, as defined in section 2901 of title 44.

(c) The Register of Copyrights is authorized, for specific or general categories of works, to make a facsimile reproduction of all or any part of the material deposited under section 408, and to make such reproduction a part of the Copyright Office records of the registration, before transferring such material to the Library of Congress as provided by subsection (b), or before destroying or otherwise disposing of such material as provided by subsection (d).

(d) Deposits not selected by the Library under subsection (b), or identifying portions or reproductions of them, shall be retained under the control of the Copyright Office, including retention in Government storage facilities, for the longest period considered practicable and desirable by the Register of Copyrights and the Librarian of Congress. After that period it is within the joint discretion of the Register and the Librarian to order their destruction or other disposition; but, in the case of unpublished works, no deposit shall be knowingly or intentionally destroyed or otherwise disposed of during its term of copyright unless a facsimile reproduction of the entire deposit has been made a part of the Copyright Office records as provided by subsection (c).

(e) The depositor of copies, phonorecords, or identifying material under section 408, or the copyright owner of record, may request retention, under the control of the Copyright Office, of one or more of such articles for the full term of copyright in the work. The Register of Copyrights shall prescribe, by regulation, the conditions under which such requests are to be made and granted, and shall fix the fee to be charged under section 708(a)(10) if the request is granted.

(Oct. 19, 1976, Pub. L. 94-553, §101, 90 Stat. 2591; July 3, 1990, Pub. L. 101-318, §2, 104 Stat. 288.)

§ 705 Copyright Office records: Preparation, maintenance, public inspection, and searching

(a) The Register of Copyrights shall ensure that records of deposits, registrations, recordations, and other actions taken under this title are maintained, and that indexes of such records are prepared.

(b) Such records and indexes, as well as the articles deposited in connection with completed copyright registrations and retained under the control of the Copyright Office, shall be open to public inspection.

(c) Upon request and payment of the fee specified by section 708, the Copyright Office shall make a search of its public records, indexes, and deposits, and shall furnish a report of the information they disclose with respect to any particular deposits, registrations, or recorded documents.

(Oct. 19, 1976, Pub. L. 94-553, §101, 90 Stat. 2592; Oct. 27, 2000, Pub. L. 106-379, §3(a), 114 Stat. 1445.)

§ 706 Copies of Copyright Office records

(a) Copies may be made of any public records or indexes of the Copyright Office; additional certificates of copyright registration and copies of any public records or indexes may be furnished upon request and payment of the fees specified by section 708.

(b) Copies or reproductions of deposited articles retained under the control of the Copyright Office shall be authorized or furnished only under the conditions specified by the Copyright Office regulations.

(Oct. 19, 1976, Pub. L. 94-553, §101, 90 Stat. 2592.)

§ 707   Copyright Office forms and publications

(a) *Catalog of copyright entries.*—The Register of Copyrights shall compile and publish at periodic intervals catalogs of all copyright registrations. These catalogs shall be divided into parts in accordance with the various classes of works, and the Register has discretion to determine, on the basis of practicability and usefulness, the form and frequency of publication of each particular part.

(b) *Other publications.*—The Register shall furnish, free of charge upon request, application forms for copyright registration and general informational material in connection with the functions of the Copyright Office. The Register also has the authority to publish compilations of information, bibliographies, and other material he or she considers to be of value to the public.

(c) *Distribution of publications.*—All publications of the Copyright Office shall be furnished to depository libraries as specified under section 1905 of title 44, and, aside from those furnished free of charge, shall be offered for sale to the public at prices based on the cost of reproduction and distribution.

(Oct. 19, 1976, Pub. L. 94-553, §101, 90 Stat. 2592.)

§ 708   Copyright Office fees

(a) *Fees.*—Fees shall be paid to the Register of Copyrights—

(1) on filing each application under section 408 for registration of a copyright claim or for a supplementary registration, including the issuance of a certificate of registration if registration is made;

(2) on filing each application for registration of a claim for renewal of a subsisting copyright under section 304(a), including the issuance of a certificate of registration if registration is made;

(3) for the issuance of a receipt for a deposit under section 407;

(4) for the recordation, as provided by section 205, of a transfer of copyright ownership or other document;

(5) for the filing, under section 115(b), of a notice of intention to obtain a compulsory license;

(6) for the recordation, under section 302(c), of a statement revealing the identity of an author of an anonymous or pseudonymous work, or for the recordation, under section 302(d), of a statement relating to the death of an author;

(7) for the issuance, under section 706, of an additional certificate of registration;

(8) for the issuance of any other certification; and

(9) for the making and reporting of a search as provided by section 705, and for any related services.

The Register is authorized to fix fees for other services, including the cost of preparing copies of Copyright Office records, whether or not such copies are certified, based on the cost of providing the service.

(b) *Adjustment of Fees.*—The Register of Copyrights may, by regulation, adjust the fees for the services specified in paragraphs (1) through (9) of subsection (a) in the following manner:

(1) The Register shall conduct a study of the costs incurred by the Copyright Office for the registration of claims, the recordation of documents, and the provision of services. The study shall also consider the timing of any adjustment in fees and the authority to use such fees consistent with the budget.

(2) The Register may, on the basis of the study under paragraph (1), and subject to paragraph (5), adjust fees to not more than that necessary to cover the reasonable costs incurred by the Copyright Office for the services described in paragraph (1), plus a reasonable inflation adjustment to account for any estimated increase in costs.

(3) Any fee established under paragraph (2) shall be rounded off to the nearest dollar, or for a fee less than $12, rounded off to the nearest 50 cents.

(4) Fees established under this subsection shall be fair and equitable and give due consideration to the objectives of the copyright system.

(5) If the Register determines under paragraph (2) that fees should be adjusted, the Register shall prepare a proposed fee schedule and submit the schedule with the accompanying economic analysis to the Congress. The fees proposed by the Register may be instituted

after the end of 120 days after the schedule is submitted to the Congress unless, within that 120-day period, a law is enacted stating in substance that the Congress does not approve the schedule.

(c) The fees prescribed by or under this section are applicable to the United States Government and any of its agencies, employees, or officers, but the Register of Copyrights has discretion to waive the requirement of this subsection in occasional or isolated cases involving relatively small amounts.

(d) (1) Except as provided in paragraph (2), all fees received under this section shall be deposited by the Register of Copyrights in the Treasury of the United States and shall be credited to the appropriations for necessary expenses of the Copyright Office. Such fees that are collected shall remain available until expended. The Register may, in accordance with regulations that he or she shall prescribe, refund any sum paid by mistake or in excess of the fee required by this section.

(2) In the case of fees deposited against future services, the Register of Copyrights shall request the Secretary of the Treasury to invest in interest-bearing securities in the United States Treasury any portion of the fees that, as determined by the Register, is not required to meet current deposit account demands. Funds from such portion of fees shall be invested in securities that permit funds to be available to the Copyright Office at all times if they are determined to be necessary to meet current deposit account demands. Such investments shall be in public debt securities with maturities suitable to the needs of the Copyright Office, as determined by the Register of Copyrights, and bearing interest at rates determined by the Secretary of the Treasury, taking into consideration current market yields on outstanding marketable obligations of the United States of comparable maturities.

(3) The income on such investments shall be deposited in the Treasury of the United States and shall be credited to the appropriations for necessary expenses of the Copyright Office.

(Oct. 19, 1976, Pub. L. 94-553, §101, 90 Stat. 2593; Aug. 5, 1977, Pub. L. 95-94, §406, 91 Stat. 682; Oct. 15, 1982, Pub. L. 97-366, §1, 96 Stat. 1759; July 3, 1990, Pub. L. 101-318, §2, 104 Stat. 287-88; June 26, 1992, Pub. L. 102-307, §102(f), 106 Stat. 266; Nov. 13, 1997, Pub. L. 105-80 §7, 111 Stat. 1532-33; Oct. 27, 2000, Pub. L. 106-379, §3(a), 114 Stat. 1445.)

§ 709   Delay in delivery caused by disruption of postal or other services

In any case in which the Register of Copyrights determines, on the basis of such evidence as the Register may by regulation require, that a deposit, application, fee, or any other material to be delivered to the Copyright Office by a particular date, would have been received in the Copyright Office in due time except for a general disruption or suspension of postal or other transportation or communications services, the actual receipt of such material in the Copyright Office within one month after the date on which the Register determines that the disruption or suspension of such services has terminated, shall be considered timely.

(Oct. 19, 1976, Pub. L. 94-553, §101, 90 Stat. 2594.)

§ 710   [Repealed]

(Oct. 19, 1976, Pub. L. 94-553, §101, 90 Stat. 2594; Oct. 27, 2000, Pub. L. 106-379, §3(a), 114 Stat. 1445.)

Chapter 8—Copyright Arbitration Royalty Panels

Sec.
- 801.   Copyright arbitration royalty panels: Establishment and purpose.
- 802.   Membership and proceedings of copyright arbitration royalty panels.
- 803.   Institution and conclusion of proceedings.

§ 801   Copyright arbitration royalty panels: Establishment and purpose

(a) *Establishment.*—The Librarian of Congress, upon the recommendation of the Register of Copyrights, is authorized to appoint and convene copyright arbitration royalty panels.

(b) *Purposes.*—Subject to the provisions of this chapter, the purposes of the copyright arbitration royalty panels shall be as follows:

(1) To make determinations concerning the adjustment of reasonable copyright royalty rates as provided in sections 114, 115, 116, and 119 and to make determinations as to reasonable terms and rates of royalty payments as provided in section 118. The rates applicable under sections 114(f)(1)(B), 115, and 116 shall be calculated to achieve the following objectives:

(A) To maximize the availability of creative works to the public;

(B) To afford the copyright owner a fair return for his creative work and the copyright user a fair income under existing economic conditions;

(C) To reflect the relative roles of the copyright owner and the copyright user in the product made available to the public with respect to relative creative contribution, technological contribution, capital investment, cost, risk, and contribution to the opening of new markets for creative expression and media for their communication;

(D) To minimize any disruptive impact on the structure of the industries involved and on generally prevailing industry practices.

(2) To make determinations concerning the adjustment of the copyright royalty rates in section 111 solely in accordance with the following provisions:

(A) The rates established by section 111(d)(1)(B) may be adjusted to reflect (i) national monetary inflation or deflation or (ii) changes in the average rates charged cable subscribers for the basic service of providing secondary transmissions to maintain the real constant dollar level of the royalty fee per subscriber which existed as of the date of enactment of this Act: *Provided,* That if the average rates charged cable system subscribers for the basic service of providing secondary transmissions are changed so that the average rates exceed national monetary inflation, no change in the rates established by section 111(d)(1)(B) shall be permitted: *And provided further,* That no increase in the royalty fee shall be permitted based on any reduction in the average number of distant signal equivalents per subscriber. The copyright arbitration royalty panels may consider all factors relating to the maintenance of such level of payments including, as an extenuating factor, whether the cable industry has been restrained by subscriber rate regulating authorities from increasing the rates for the basic service of providing secondary transmissions.

(B) In the event that the rules and regulations of the Federal Communications Commission are amended at any time after

17 U.S.C. § 801

April 15, 1976, to permit the carriage by cable systems of additional television broadcast signals beyond the local service area of the primary transmitters of such signals, the royalty rates established by section 111(d)(1)(B) may be adjusted to insure that the rates for the additional distant signal equivalents resulting from such carriage are reasonable in the light of the changes effected by the amendment to such rules and regulations. In determining the reasonableness of rates proposed following an amendment of Federal Communications Commission rules and regulations, the copyright arbitration royalty panels shall consider, among other factors, the economic impact on copyright owners and users: *Provided,* That no adjustment in royalty rates shall be made under this subclause with respect to any distant signal equivalent or fraction thereof represented by (i) carriage of any signal permitted under the rules and regulations of the Federal Communications Commission in effect on April 15, 1976, or the carriage of a signal of the same type (that is, independent, network, or noncommercial educational) substituted for such permitted signal, or (ii) a television broadcast signal first carried after April 15, 1976, pursuant to an individual waiver of the rules and regulations of the Federal Communications Commission, as such rules and regulations were in effect on April 15, 1976.

(C) In the event of any change in the rules and regulations of the Federal Communications Commission with respect to syndicated and sports program exclusivity after April 15, 1976, the rates established by section 111(d)(1)(B) may be adjusted to assure that such rates are reasonable in light of the changes to such rules and regulations, but any such adjustment shall apply only to the affected television broadcast signals carried on those systems affected by the change.

(D) The gross receipts limitations established by section 111(d)(1)(C) and (D) shall be adjusted to reflect national monetary inflation or deflation or changes in the average rates charged cable system subscribers for the basic service of providing secondary transmissions to maintain the real constant dollar value of the exemption provided by such section; and the royalty rate specified therein shall not be subject to adjustment.

(3) To distribute royalty fees deposited with the Register of Copyrights under sections 111, 116, 119(b), and 1003, and to determine, in cases where controversy exists, the distribution of such fees.

(c) *Rulings.*—The Librarian of Congress, upon the recommendation of the Register of Copyrights, may, before a copyright arbitration royalty panel is convened, make any necessary procedural or evidentiary rulings that would apply to the proceedings conducted by such panel, including—

(1) authorizing the distribution of those royalty fees collected under sections 111, 119, and 1005 that the Librarian has found are not subject to controversy; and

(2) accepting or rejecting royalty claims filed under sections 111, 119, and 1007 on the basis of timeliness or the failure to establish the basis for a claim.

(d) *Support and Reimbursement of Arbitration Panels.*—The Librarian of Congress, upon the recommendation of the Register of Copyrights, shall provide the copyright arbitration royalty panels with the necessary administrative services related to proceedings under this chapter, and shall reimburse the arbitrators presiding in distribution proceedings at such intervals and in such manner as the Librarian shall provide by regulation. Each such arbitrator is an independent contractor acting on behalf of the United States, and shall be hired pursuant to a signed agreement between the Library of Congress and the arbitrator. Payments to the arbitrators shall be considered reasonable costs incurred by the Library of Congress and the Copyright Office for purposes of section 802(h)(1).

(Oct. 19, 1976, Pub. L. 94-553, §101, 90 Stat. 2594; Aug. 27, 1986, Pub. L. 99-397, §2(c) and (d), 100 Stat. 848; Oct. 31, 1988, Pub. L. 100-568, §11, 102 Stat. 2860; Nov. 16, 1988, Pub. L. 100-667, §202, 102 Stat. 3958; July 3, 1990, Pub. L. 101-318, §3, 104 Stat. 288; Oct. 29, 1992, Pub. L. 102-563, §3, 106 Stat. 4247-48; Dec. 17, 1993, Pub. L. 103-198, §2, 107 Stat. 2304; Nov. 13, 1997, Pub. L. 105-80, §§ 8(a), 12, 111 Stat. 1533, 1535; Oct. 28, 1998, Pub. L. 105-304, §405(e), 112 Stat. 2902.)

17 U.S.C. § 801

§ 802 Membership and proceedings of copyright arbitration royalty panels

(a) *Composition of copyright arbitration royalty panels.*—A copyright arbitration royalty panel shall consist of 3 arbitrators selected by the Librarian of Congress pursuant to subsection (b).

(b) *Selection of arbitration panel.*—Not later than 10 days after publication of a notice in the Federal Register initiating an arbitration proceeding under section 803, and in accordance with procedures specified by the Register of Copyrights, the Librarian of Congress shall, upon the recommendation of the Register of Copyrights, select 2 arbitrators from lists provided by professional arbitration associations. Qualifications of the arbitrators shall include experience in conducting arbitration proceedings and facilitating the resolution and settlement of disputes, and any qualifications which the Librarian of Congress, upon the recommendation of the Register of Copyrights, shall adopt by regulation. The 2 arbitrators so selected shall, within 10 days after their selection, choose a third arbitrator from the same lists, who shall serve as the chairperson of the arbitrators. If such 2 arbitrators fail to agree upon the selection of a third arbitrator, the Librarian of Congress shall promptly select the third arbitrator. The Librarian of Congress, upon the recommendation of the Register of Copyrights, shall adopt regulations regarding standards of conduct which shall govern arbitrators and the proceedings under this chapter.

(c) *Arbitration proceedings.*—Copyright arbitration royalty panels shall conduct arbitration proceedings, subject to subchapter II of chapter 5 of title 5, for the purpose of making their determinations in carrying out the purposes set forth in section 801. The arbitration panels shall act on the basis of a fully documented written record, prior decisions of the Copyright Royalty Tribunal, prior copyright arbitration panel determinations, and rulings by the Librarian of Congress under section 801(c). Any copyright owner who claims to be entitled to royalties under section 111, 112, 114, 116, or 119, any transmitting organization entitled to a statutory license under section 112(g), any person entitled to a statutory license under section 114(d), any person entitled to a compulsory license under section 115, or any interested copyright party who claims to be entitled to royalties under section 1006, may submit relevant information and proposals to the arbitration panels in proceedings applicable to such copyright owner or interested copyright party, and any other person participating in arbitration proceedings may submit such relevant information and proposals to the arbitration panel conducting the proceedings. In ratemaking proceedings, the parties to the proceedings shall bear the entire cost thereof in such manner and proportion as the arbitration panels shall direct. In distribution proceedings, the parties shall bear the cost in direct proportion to their share of the distribution.

(d) *Procedures.*—Effective on the date of the enactment of the Copyright Royalty Tribunal Reform Act of 1993, the Librarian of Congress shall adopt the rules and regulations set forth in chapter 3 of title 37 of the Code of Federal Regulations to govern proceedings under this chapter. Such rules and regulations shall remain in effect unless and until the Librarian, upon the recommendation of the Register of Copyrights, adopts supplemental or superseding regulations under subchapter II of chapter 5 of title 5.

(e) *Report to Librarian of Congress.*—Not later than 180 days after publication of the notice in the Federal Register initiating an arbitration proceeding, the copyright arbitration royalty panel conducting the proceeding shall report to the Librarian of Congress its determination concerning the royalty fee or distribution of royalty fees, as the case may be. Such report shall be accompanied by the written record, and shall set forth the facts that the arbitration panel found relevant to its determination.

(f) *Action by Librarian of Congress.*—Within 90 days after receiving the report of a copyright arbitration royalty panel under subsection (e), the Librarian of Congress, upon the recommendation of the Register of Copyrights, shall adopt or reject the determination of the arbitration panel. The Librarian shall adopt the determination of the arbitration panel unless the Librarian finds that the determination is arbitrary or contrary to the applicable provisions of this title. If the Librarian rejects the determination of the arbitration panel, the Librarian shall, before the end of an additional 30-day period, and after full examination of the record created in the arbitration proceeding, issue an order setting the royalty fee or distribution of fees, as the case may be. The Librarian shall cause to be published in the Federal Register the determination of the arbitration panel, and the decision of the Librarian (including an order

17 U.S.C. § 802

issued under the preceding sentence). The Librarian shall also publicize such determination and decision in such other manner as the Librarian considers appropriate. The Librarian shall also make the report of the arbitration panel and the accompanying record available for public inspection and copying.

(g) *Judicial review.*—Any decision of the Librarian of Congress under subsection (f) with respect to a determination of an arbitration panel may be appealed, by any aggrieved party who would be bound by the determination, to the United States Court of Appeals for the District of Columbia Circuit, within 30 days after the publication of the decision in the Federal Register. If no appeal is brought within such 30-day period, the decision of the Librarian is final, and the royalty fee or determination with respect to the distribution of fees, as the case may be, shall take effect as set forth in the decision. When this title provides that the royalty rates or terms that were previously in effect are to expire on a specified date, any adjustment by the Librarian of those rates or terms shall be effective as of the day following the date of expiration of the rates or terms that were previously in effect, even if the Librarian's decision is rendered on a later date. The pendency of an appeal under this paragraph shall not relieve persons obligated to make royalty payments under sections 111, 112, 114, 115, 116, 118, 119, or 1003 who would be affected by the determination on appeal to deposit the statement of account and royalty fees specified in those sections. The court shall have jurisdiction to modify or vacate a decision of the Librarian only if it finds, on the basis of the record before the Librarian, that the Librarian acted in an arbitrary manner. If the court modifies the decision of the Librarian, the court shall have jurisdiction to enter its own determination with respect to the amount or distribution of royalty fees and costs, to order the repayment of any excess fees, and to order the payment of any underpaid fees, and the interest pertaining respectively thereto, in accordance with its final judgment. The court may further vacate the decision of the arbitration panel and remand the case to the Librarian for arbitration proceedings in accordance with subsection (c).

(h) *Administrative matters.*—

(1) *Deduction of costs of Library of Congress and Copyright Office from royalty fees.*—The Librarian of Congress and the Register of Copy-

rights may, to the extent not otherwise provided under this title, deduct from royalty fees deposited or collected under this title the reasonable costs incurred by the Library of Congress and the Copyright Office under this chapter. Such deduction may be made before the fees are distributed to any copyright claimants. In addition, all funds made available by an appropriations Act as offsetting collections and available for deductions under this subsection shall remain available until expended. In ratemaking proceedings, the reasonable costs of the Librarian of Congress and the Copyright Office shall be borne by the parties to the proceedings as directed by the arbitration panels under subsection (c).

(2) *Positions required for administration of compulsory licensing.*—Section 307 of the Legislative Branch Appropriations Act, 1994, shall not apply to employee positions in the Library of Congress that are required to be filled in order to carry out section 111, 112 114, 115, 116, 118, or 199 or chapter 10.

(Oct. 19, 1976, Pub. L. 94-553, §101, 90 Stat. 2596; July 3, 1990, Pub. L. 101-319, §2, 104 Stat. 290; Dec. 17, 1993, Pub. L. 103-198, §2, 107 Stat. 2305; Nov. 13, 1997, Pub. L. 105-80, §8(b), 111 Stat. 1533; ; Oct. 28, 1998, Pub. L. 105-304, §405(d), (e), 112 Stat. 2902; Nov. 2, 2002, Pub. L. 107-273, §13301, 116 Stat. 1910.)

§ 803   Institution and conclusion of proceedings

(a) (1) With respect to proceedings under section 801(b)(1) concerning the adjustment of royalty rates as provided in sections 112, 114, 115 and 116, and with respect to proceedings under subparagraphs (A) and (D) of section 801(b)(2), during the calendar years specified in the schedule set forth in paragraphs (2), (3), (4) and (5) any owner or user of a copyrighted work whose royalty rates are specified by this title, established by the Copyright Royalty Tribunal before the date of enactment of the Copyright Royalty Tribunal Reform Act of 1993, or established by a copyright arbitration royalty panel after such date of enactment, may file a petition with the Librarian of Congress declaring that the petitioner requests an adjustment of the rate. The Librarian of Congress shall, upon the recommendation of the Register of Copyrights, make a determination as to whether the petitioner has such a significant interest in the royalty rate in which an adjustment is requested. If the Librarian determines that the petitioner has such a significant interest, the Librarian shall cause notice of this determination, with the reasons therefor, to be published in the Federal Register, together with the notice of commencement of proceedings under this chapter.

(2) In proceedings under section 801(b)(2)(A) and (D), a petition described in paragraph (1) may be filed during 1995 and in each subsequent fifth calendar year.

(3) In proceedings under section 801(b)(1) concerning the adjustment of royalty rates as provided in section 115, a petition described in paragraph (1) may be filed in 1997 and in each subsequent tenth calendar year or as prescribed in section 115(c)(3)(D).

(4) (A) In proceedings under section 801(b)(1) concerning the adjustment of royalty rates as provided in section 116, a petition described in paragraph (1) may be filed at any time within 1 year after negotiated licenses authorized by section 116 are terminated or expire and are not replaced by subsequent agreements.

(B) If a negotiated license authorized by section 116 is terminated or expires and is not replaced by another such license agreement which provides permission to use a quantity of musical works not substantially smaller than the quantity of such works performed on coin-operated phonorecord players during the 1-year period ending March 1, 1989, the Librarian of Congress shall, upon petition filed under paragraph (1) within 1 year after such termination or expiration, convene a copyright arbitration royalty panel. The arbitration panel shall promptly establish an interim royalty rate or rates for the public performance by means of a coin-operated phonorecord player of non-dramatic musical works embodied in phonorecords which had been subject to the terminated or expired negotiated license agreement. Such rate or rates shall be the same as the last such rate or rates and shall remain in force until the conclusion of proceedings by the arbitration panel, in accordance with section 802, to adjust the royalty rates applicable to such works, or until superseded by a new negotiated license agreement, as provided in section 116(b).

(5) With respect to proceedings under section 801(b)(1) concerning the determination of reasonable terms and rates of royalty payments

as provided in section 112 or 114, the Librarian of Congress shall proceed when and as provided by those sections.

(b) With respect to proceedings under subparagraph (B) or (C) of section 801(b)(2), following an event described in either of those subsections, any owner or user of a copyrighted work whose royalty rates are specified by section 111, or by a rate established by the Copyright Royalty Tribunal or the Librarian of Congress may, within twelve months, file a petition with the Librarian declaring that the petitioner requests an adjustment of the rate. In this event the Librarian shall proceed as in subsection (a) of this section. Any change in royalty rates made by the Copyright Royalty Tribunal or the Librarian of Congress pursuant to this subsection may be reconsidered in 1980, 1985, and each fifth calendar year thereafter, in accordance with the provisions in section 801(b)(2)(B) or (C), as the case may be.

(c) With respect to proceedings under section 801(b)(1), concerning the determination of reasonable terms and rates of royalty payments as provided in section 118, the Librarian of Congress shall proceed when and as provided by that section.

(d) With respect to proceedings under section 801(b)(3) or (4), concerning the distribution of royalty fees in certain circumstances under section 111, 116, 119, or 1007, the Librarian of Congress shall, upon a determination that a controversy exists concerning such distribution, cause to be published in the Federal Register notice of commencement of proceedings under this chapter.

(Oct. 19, 1976, Pub. L. 94-553, §101, 90 Stat. 2597; Oct. 31, 1988, Pub. L. 100-568, §11, 102 Stat. 2860; Nov. 16, 1988, Pub. L. 100-667, §202, 102 Stat. 3958; July 3, 1990, Pub. L. 101-318, §3, 104 Stat. 288; Oct. 29, 1992, Pub. L. 102-563, §3, 106 Stat. 4248; Dec. 17, 1993, Pub. L. 103-198, §2(d), 107 Stat. 2307; Nov. 1. 1995, Pub. L. 104-39, §5(d), 109 Stat. 348; Nov. 13, 1997, Pub. L. 105-80, §12, 111 Stat. 1535; Oct. 28, 1998, Pub. L. 105-304, §405(e), 112 Stat. 2902.)

CHAPTER 9—PROTECTION OF SEMICONDUCTOR CHIP PRODUCTS

Sec.

§ 901   Definitions

(a) As used in this chapter—

(1) a "semiconductor chip product" is the final or intermediate form of any product—

(A) having two or more layers of metallic, insulating, or semiconductor material, deposited or otherwise placed on, or etched away or otherwise removed from, a piece of semiconductor material in accordance with a predetermined pattern; and

(B) intended to perform electronic circuitry functions;

(2) a "mask work" is a series of related images, however fixed or encoded—

(A) having or representing the predetermined, three-dimensional pattern of metallic, insulating, or semiconductor material present or removed from the layers of a semiconductor chip product; and

(B) in which series the relation of the images to one another is that each image has the pattern of the surface of one form of the semiconductor chip product;

(3) a mask work is "fixed" in a semiconductor chip product when its embodiment in the product is sufficiently permanent or stable to permit the mask work to be perceived or reproduced from the product for a period of more than transitory duration;

(4) to "distribute" means to sell, or to lease, bail, or otherwise transfer, or to offer to sell, lease, bail, or otherwise transfer;

(5) to "commercially exploit" a mask work is to distribute to the public for commercial purposes a semiconductor chip product embodying the mask work; except that such term includes an offer to sell or transfer a semiconductor chip product only when the offer is in writ-

ing and occurs after the mask work is fixed in the semiconductor chip product;

(6) the "owner" of a mask work is the person who created the mask work, the legal representative of that person if that person is deceased or under a legal incapacity, or a party to whom all the rights under this chapter of such person or representative are transferred in accordance with section 903(b); except that, in the case of a work made within the scope of a person's employment, the owner is the employer for whom the person created the mask work or a party to whom all the rights under this chapter of the employer are transferred in accordance with section 903(b);

(7) an "innocent purchaser" is a person who purchases a semiconductor chip product in good faith and without having notice of protection with respect to the semiconductor chip product;

(8) having "notice of protection" means having actual knowledge that, or reasonable grounds to believe that, a mask work is protected under this chapter; and

(9) an "infringing semiconductor chip product" is a semiconductor chip product which is made, imported, or distributed in violation of the exclusive rights of the owner of a mask work under this chapter.

(b) For purposes of this chapter, the distribution or importation of a product incorporating a semiconductor chip product as a part thereof is a distribution or importation of that semiconductor chip product.

(Added Nov. 8, 1984, Pub. L. 98-620, §302, 98 Stat. 3347.)

§ 902   Subject matter of protection

(a) (1) Subject to the provisions of subsection (b), a mask work fixed in a semiconductor chip product, by or under the authority of the owner of the mask work, is eligible for protection under this chapter if—

(A) on the date on which the mask work is registered under section 908, or is first commercially exploited anywhere in the world, whichever occurs first, the owner of the mask work is (i) a national or domiciliary of the United States, (ii) a national, domiciliary, or sovereign authority of a foreign nation that is a party to a treaty affording protection to mask works to which the

United States is also a party, or (iii) a stateless person, wherever that person may be domiciled;

(B) the mask work is first commercially exploited in the United States; or

(C) the mask work comes within the scope of a Presidential proclamation issued under paragraph (2).

(2) Whenever the President finds that a foreign nation extends, to mask works of owners who are nationals or domiciliaries of the United States protection (A) on substantially the same basis as that on which the foreign nation extends protection to mask works of its own nationals and domiciliaries and mask works first commercially exploited in that nation, or (B) on substantially the same basis as provided in this chapter, the President may by proclamation extend protection under this chapter to mask works (i) of owners who are, on the date on which the mask works are registered under section 908, or the date on which the mask works are first commercially exploited anywhere in the world, whichever occurs first, nationals, domiciliaries, or sovereign authorities of that nation, or (ii) which are first commercially exploited in that nation. The President may revise, suspend, or revoke any such proclamation or impose any conditions or limitations on protection extended under any such proclamation.

(b) Protection under this chapter shall not be available for a mask work that—

(1) is not original; or

(2) consists of designs that are staple, commonplace, or familiar in the semiconductor industry, or variations of such designs, combined in a way that, considered as a whole, is not original.

(c) In no case does protection under this chapter for a mask work extend to any idea, procedure, process, system, method of operation, concept, principle, or discovery, regardless of the form in which it is described, explained, illustrated, or embodied in such work.

(Nov. 8, 1984, Pub. L. 98-620, §302, 98 Stat. 3348; Nov. 9, 1987, Pub. L. 100-159, §3, 101 Stat. 900.)

§ 903   Ownership, transfer, licensing, and recordation

(a) The exclusive rights in a mask work subject to protection under this chapter belong to the owner of the mask work.

(b) The owner of the exclusive rights in a mask work may transfer all of those rights, or license all or less than all of those rights, by any written instrument signed by such owner or a duly authorized agent of the owner. Such rights may be transferred or licensed by operation of law, may be bequeathed by will, and may pass as personal property by the applicable laws of intestate succession.

(c) (1) Any document pertaining to a mask work may be recorded in the Copyright Office if the document filed for recordation bears the actual signature of the person who executed it, or if it is accompanied by a sworn or official certification that it is a true copy of the original, signed document. The Register of Copyrights shall, upon receipt of the document and the fee specified pursuant to section 908(d), record the document and return it with a certificate of recordation. The recordation of any transfer or license under this paragraph gives all persons constructive notice of the facts stated in the recorded document concerning the transfer or license.

(2) In any case in which conflicting transfers of the exclusive rights in a mask work are made, the transfer first executed shall be void as against a subsequent transfer which is made for a valuable consideration and without notice of the first transfer, unless the first transfer is recorded in accordance with paragraph (1) within three months after the date on which it is executed, but in no case later than the day before the date of such subsequent transfer.

(d) Mask works prepared by an officer or employee of the United States Government as part of that person's official duties are not protected under this chapter, but the United States Government is not precluded from receiving and holding exclusive rights in mask works transferred to the Government under subsection (b).

(Added Nov. 8, 1984, Pub. L. 98-620, §302, 98 Stat. 3349; Nov. 2, 2002, Pub. L. 107-273, §13210, 116 Stat. 1909.)

§ 904   Duration of protection

(a) The protection provided for a mask work under this chapter shall commence on the date on which the mask work is registered under section 908, or the date on which the mask work is first commercially exploited anywhere in the world, whichever occurs first.

(b) Subject to subsection (c) and the provisions of this chapter, the protection provided under this chapter to a mask work shall end ten years after the date on which such protection commences under subsection (a).

(c) All terms of protection provided in this section shall run to the end of the calendar year in which they would otherwise expire.

(Nov. 8, 1984, Pub. L. 98-620, §302, 98 Stat. 3349.)

§ 905   Exclusive rights in mask works

The owner of a mask work provided protection under this chapter has the exclusive rights to do and to authorize any of the following:

> (1) to reproduce the mask work by optical, electronic, or any other means;

> (2) to import or distribute a semiconductor chip product in which the mask work is embodied; and

> (3) to induce or knowingly to cause another person to do any of the acts described in paragraphs (1) and (2).

(Nov. 8, 1984, Pub. L. 98-620, §302, 98 Stat. 3350.)

§ 906   Limitation on exclusive rights: reverse engineering; first sale

(a) Notwithstanding the provisions of section 905, it is not an infringement of the exclusive rights of the owner of a mask work for—

> (1) a person to reproduce the mask work solely for the purpose of teaching, analyzing, or evaluating the concepts or techniques embodied in the mask work or the circuitry, logic flow, or organization of components used in the mask work; or

> (2) a person who performs the analysis or evaluation described in paragraph (1) to incorporate the results of such conduct in an original mask work which is made to be distributed.

(b) Notwithstanding the provisions of section 905(2), the owner of a particular semiconductor chip product made by the owner of the mask work, or by any person authorized by the owner of the mask work, may import, distribute, or otherwise dispose of or use, but not reproduce, that particular semiconductor chip product without the authority of the owner of the mask work.

(Nov. 8, 1984, Pub. L. 98-620, §302, 98 Stat. 3350.)

§ 907   Limitation on exclusive rights: innocent infringement

(a) Notwithstanding any other provision of this chapter, an innocent purchaser of an infringing semiconductor chip product—

> (1) shall incur no liability under this chapter with respect to the importation or distribution of units of the infringing semiconductor chip product that occurs before the innocent purchaser has notice of protection with respect to the mask work embodied in the semiconductor chip product; and

> (2) shall be liable only for a reasonable royalty on each unit of the infringing semiconductor chip product that the innocent purchaser imports or distributes after having notice of protection with respect to the mask work embodied in the semiconductor chip product.

(b) The amount of the royalty referred to in subsection (a)(2) shall be determined by the court in a civil action for infringement unless the parties resolve the issue by voluntary negotiation, mediation, or binding arbitration.

(c) The immunity of an innocent purchaser from liability referred to in subsection (a)(1) and the limitation of remedies with respect to an innocent purchaser referred to in subsection (a)(2) shall extend to any person who directly or indirectly purchases an infringing semiconductor chip product from an innocent purchaser.

(d) The provisions of subsections (a), (b), and (c) apply only with respect to those units of an infringing semiconductor chip product that an innocent purchaser purchased before having notice of protection with respect to the mask work embodied in the semiconductor chip product.

(Nov. 8, 1984, Pub. L. 98-620, §302, 98 Stat. 3350.)

§ 908   Registration of claims of protection

(a) The owner of a mask work may apply to the Register of Copyrights for registration of a claim of protection in a mask work. Protection of a mask work under this chapter shall terminate if application for registration of a claim of protection in the mask work is not made as provided in this chapter within two years after the date on which the mask work is first commercially exploited anywhere in the world.

(b) The Register of Copyrights shall be responsible for all administrative functions and duties under this chapter. Except for section 708, the provisions of chapter 7 of this title relating to the general responsibilities, organization, regulatory authority, actions, records, and publications of the Copyright Office shall apply to this chapter, except that the Register of Copyrights may make such changes as may be necessary in applying those provisions to this chapter.

(c) The application for registration of a mask work shall be made on a form prescribed by the Register of Copyrights. Such form may require any information regarded by the Register as bearing upon the preparation or identification of the mask work, the existence or duration of protection of the mask work under this chapter, or ownership of the mask work. The application shall be accompanied by the fee set pursuant to subsection (d) and the identifying material specified pursuant to such subsection.

(d) The Register of Copyrights shall by regulation set reasonable fees for the filing of applications to register claims of protection in mask works under this chapter, and for other services relating to the administration of this chapter or the rights under this chapter, taking into consideration the cost of providing those services, the benefits of a public record, and statutory fee schedules under this title. The Register shall also specify the identifying material to be deposited in connection with the claim for registration.

(e) If the Register of Copyrights, after examining an application for registration, determines, in accordance with the provisions of this chapter, that the application relates to a mask work which is entitled to protection under this chapter, then the Register shall register the claim of protection and issue to the applicant a certificate of registration of the claim of protection under the seal of the Copyright Office. The effective date of registration of a claim of protection shall be the date on which an application, deposit of identifying material, and fee, which are determined by the Register of Copyrights or by a court of competent jurisdiction to be acceptable for registration of the claim, have all been received in the Copyright Office.

(f) In any action for infringement under this chapter, the certificate of registration of a mask work shall constitute prima facie evidence (1) of the facts stated in the certificate, and (2) that the applicant issued the certificate has met the requirements of this chapter, and the regulations issued under this chapter, with respect to the registration of claims.

(g) Any applicant for registration under this section who is dissatisfied with the refusal of the Register of Copyrights to issue a certificate of registration under this section may seek judicial review of that refusal by bringing an action for such review in an appropriate United States district court not later than sixty days after the refusal. The provisions of chapter 7 of title 5 shall apply to such judicial review. The failure of the Register of Copyrights to issue a certificate of registration within four months after an application for registration is filed shall be deemed to be a refusal to issue a certificate of registration for purposes of this subsection and section 910(b)(2), except that, upon a showing of good cause, the district court may shorten such four-month period.

(Nov. 8, 1984, Pub. L. 98-620, §302, 98 Stat. 3351.)

§ 909   Mask work notice

(a) The owner of a mask work provided protection under this chapter may affix notice to the mask work, and to masks and semiconductor chip products embodying the mask work, in such manner and location as to give reasonable notice of such protection. The Register of Copyrights shall prescribe by regulation, as examples, specific methods of affixation and positions of notice for purposes of this section, but these specifications shall not be considered exhaustive. The affixation of such notice is not a condition of protection under this chapter, but shall constitute prima facie evidence of notice of protection.

(b) The notice referred to in subsection (a) shall consist of—

(1) the words ["mask work,"]* the symbol *M*, or the symbol Ⓜ (the letter M in a circle); and

(2) the name of the owner or owners of the mask work or an abbreviation by which the name is recognized or is generally known. (Nov. 8, 1984, Pub. L. 98-620, §302, 98 Stat. 3352.)

§ 910 Enforcement of exclusive rights

(a) Except as otherwise provided in this chapter, any person who violates any of the exclusive rights of the owner of a mask work under this chapter, by conduct in or affecting commerce, shall be liable as an infringer of such rights. As used in this subsection, the term "any person" includes any State, any instrumentality of a State, and any officer or employee of a State or instrumentality of a State acting in his or her official capacity. Any State, and any such instrumentality, officer, or employee, shall be subject to the provisions of this chapter in the same manner and to the same extent as any nongovernmental entity.

(b) (1) The owner of a mask work protected under this chapter, or the exclusive licensee of all rights under this chapter with respect to the mask work, shall, after a certificate of registration of a claim of protection in that mask work has been issued under section 908, be entitled to institute a civil action for any infringement with respect to the mask work which is committed after the commencement of protection of the mask work under section 904(a).

(2) In any case in which an application for registration of a claim of protection in a mask work and the required deposit of identifying material and fee have been received in the Copyright Office in proper form and registration of the mask work has been refused, the applicant is entitled to institute a civil action for infringement under this chapter with respect to the mask work if notice of the action, together with a copy of the complaint, is served on the Register of Copyrights, in accordance with the Federal Rules of Civil Procedure. The Register may, at his or her option, become a party to the action with respect to the issue of whether the claim of protection is eligible for registration by entering an appearance within sixty days after

---

* *Ed. Note:* Statute uses "mask force." Probably should be "mask work."

such service, but the failure of the Register to become a party to the action shall not deprive the court of jurisdiction to determine that issue.

(c) (1) The Secretary of the Treasury and the United States Postal Service shall separately or jointly issue regulations for the enforcement of the rights set forth in section 905 with respect to importation. These regulations may require, as a condition for the exclusion of articles from the United States, that the person seeking exclusion take any one or more of the following actions:

(A) Obtain a court order enjoining, or an order of the International Trade Commission under section 337 of the Tariff Act of 1930 excluding, importation of the articles.

(B) Furnish proof that the mask work involved is protected under this chapter and that the importation of the articles would infringe the rights in the mask work under this chapter.

(C) Post a surety bond for any injury that may result if the detention or exclusion of the articles proves to be unjustified.

(2) Articles imported in violation of the rights set forth in section 905 are subject to seizure and forfeiture in the same manner as property imported in violation of the customs laws. Any such forfeited articles shall be destroyed as directed by the Secretary of the Treasury or the court, as the case may be, except that the articles may be returned to the country of export whenever it is shown to the satisfaction of the Secretary of the Treasury that the importer had no reasonable grounds for believing that his or her acts constituted a violation of the law.

(Nov. 8, 1984, Pub. L. 98-620, §302, 98 Stat. 3352; Nov. 15, 1990, Pub. L. 101-553, §2, 104 Stat. 2750.)

§ 911   Civil actions

(a) Any court having jurisdiction of a civil action arising under this chapter may grant temporary restraining orders, preliminary injunctions, and permanent injunctions on such terms as the court may deem reasonable to prevent or restrain infringement of the exclusive rights in a mask work under this chapter.

(b) Upon finding an infringer liable, to a person entitled under section 910(b)(1) to institute a civil action, for an infringement of any exclusive right under this chapter, the court shall award such person actual damages suffered by the person as a result of the infringement. The court shall also award such person the infringer's profits that are attributable to the infringement and are not taken into account in computing the award of actual damages. In establishing the infringer's profits, such person is required to present proof only of the infringer's gross revenue, and the infringer is required to prove his or her deductible expenses and the elements of profit attributable to factors other than the mask work.

(c) At any time before final judgment is rendered, a person entitled to institute a civil action for infringement may elect, instead of actual damages and profits as provided by subsection (b), an award of statutory damages for all infringements involved in the action, with respect to any one mask work for which any one infringer is liable individually, or for which any two or more infringers are liable jointly and severally, in an amount not more than $250,000 as the court considers just.

(d) An action for infringement under this chapter shall be barred unless the action is commenced within three years after the claim accrues.

(e) (1) At any time while an action for infringement of the exclusive rights in a mask work under this chapter is pending, the court may order the impounding, on such terms as it may deem reasonable, of all semiconductor chip products, and any drawings, tapes, masks, or other products by means of which such products may be reproduced, that are claimed to have been made, imported, or used in violation of those exclusive rights. Insofar as practicable, applications for orders under this paragraph shall be heard and determined in the same manner as an application for a temporary restraining order or preliminary injunction.

(2) As part of a final judgment or decree, the court may order the destruction or other disposition of any infringing semiconductor chip products, and any masks, tapes, or other articles by means of which such products may be reproduced.

(f) In any civil action arising under this chapter, the court in its discretion may allow the recovery of full costs, including reasonable attorneys' fees, to the prevailing party.

(g) (1) Any State, any instrumentality of a State, and any officer or employee of a State or instrumentality of a State acting in his or her official capacity, shall not be immune, under the Eleventh Amendment of the Constitution of the United States or under any other doctrine of sovereign immunity, from suit in Federal court by any person, including any governmental or nongovernmental entity, for a violation of any of the exclusive rights of the owner of a mask work under this chapter, or for any other violation under this chapter.

(2) In a suit described in paragraph (1) for a violation described in that paragraph, remedies (including remedies both at law and in equity) are available for the violation to the same extent as such remedies are available for such a violation in a suit against any public or private entity other than a State, instrumentality of a State, or officer or employee of a State acting in his or her official capacity. Such remedies include actual damages and profits under subsection (b), statutory damages under subsection (c), impounding and disposition of infringing articles under subsection (e), and costs and attorney's fees under subsection (f).

(Nov. 8, 1984, Pub. L. 98-620, §302, 98 Stat. 3353; Nov. 15, 1990, Pub. L. 101-553, §2, 104 Stat. 2750.)

§ 912   Relation to other laws

(a) Nothing in this chapter shall affect any right or remedy held by any person under chapters 1 through 8 or 10 of this title, or under title 35.

(b) Except as provided in section 908(b) of this title, references to "this title" or "title 17" in chapters 1 through 8 or 10 of this title shall be deemed not to apply to this chapter.

(c) The provisions of this chapter shall preempt the laws of any State to the extent those laws provide any rights or remedies with respect to a mask work which are equivalent to those rights or remedies provided by this chapter, except that such preemption shall be effective only with respect to actions filed on or after January 1, 1986.

(d) Notwithstanding subsection (c), nothing in this chapter shall detract from any rights of a mask work owner, whether under Federal law (exclusive of this chapter) or under the common law or the statutes of a State, heretofore or hereafter declared or enacted, with respect to any mask work first commercially exploited before July 1, 1983.

(Nov. 8, 1984, Pub. L. 98-620, §302, 98 Stat. 3354; Nov. 19, 1988, Pub. L. 100-702, §1020, 102 Stat. 4672; Oct. 29, 1992, Pub. L. 102-563, §3, 106 Stat. 4248.)

§ 913 Transitional provisions

(a) No application for registration under section 908 may be filed, and no civil action under section 910 or other enforcement proceeding under this chapter may be instituted, until sixty days after the date of the enactment of this chapter.

(b) No monetary relief under section 911 may be granted with respect to any conduct that occurred before the date of the enactment of this chapter, except as provided in subsection (d).

(c) Subject to subsection (a), the provisions of this chapter apply to all mask works that are first commercially exploited or are registered under this chapter, or both, on or after the date of the enactment of this chapter.

(d) (1) Subject to subsection (a), protection is available under this chapter to any mask work that was first commercially exploited on or after July 1, 1983, and before the date of the enactment of this chapter, if a claim of protection in the mask work is registered in the Copyright Office before July 1, 1985, under section 908.

(2) In the case of any mask work described in paragraph (1) that is provided protection under this chapter, infringing semiconductor chip product units manufactured before the date of the enactment of this chapter may, without liability under sections 910 and 911, be imported into or distributed in the United States, or both, until two years after the date of registration of the mask work under section 908, but only if the importer or distributor, as the case may be, first pays or offers to pay the reasonable royalty referred to in section 907(a)(2) to the mask work owner, on all such units imported or distributed, or both, after the date of the enactment of this chapter.

(3) In the event that a person imports or distributes infringing semi-conductor chip product units described in paragraph (2) of this subsection without first paying or offering to pay the reasonable royalty specified in such paragraph, or if the person refuses or fails to make such payment, the mask work owner shall be entitled to the relief provided in sections 910 and 911.

(Nov. 8, 1984, Pub. L. 98-620, §302, 98 Stat. 3354.)

§ 914 International transitional provisions

(a) Notwithstanding the conditions set forth in subparagraphs (A) and (C) of section 902(a)(1) with respect to the availability of protection under this chapter to nationals, domiciliaries, and sovereign authorities of a foreign nation, the Secretary of Commerce may, upon the petition of any person, or upon the Secretary's own motion, issue an order extending protection under this chapter to such foreign nationals, domiciliaries, and sovereign authorities if the Secretary finds—

(1) that the foreign nation is making good faith efforts and reasonable progress toward—

(A) entering into a treaty described in section 902(a)(1)(A); or

(B) enacting or implementing legislation that would be in compliance with subparagraph (A) or (B) of section 902(a)(2); and

(2) that the nationals, domiciliaries, and sovereign authorities of the foreign nation, and persons controlled by them, are not engaged in the misappropriation, or unauthorized distribution or commercial exploitation, of mask works; and

(3) that issuing the order would promote the purposes of this chapter and international comity with respect to the protection of mask works.

(b) While an order under subsection (a) is in effect with respect to a foreign nation, no application for registration of a claim for protection in a mask work under this chapter may be denied solely because the owner of the mask work is a national, domiciliary, or sovereign authority of that foreign nation, or solely because the mask work was first commercially exploited in that foreign nation.

17 U.S.C. § 914

(c) Any order issued by the Secretary of Commerce under subsection (a) shall be effective for such period as the Secretary designates in the order, except that no such order may be effective after the date on which the authority of the Secretary of Commerce terminates under subsection (e). The effective date of any such order shall also be designated in the order. In the case of an order issued upon the petition of a person, such effective date may be no earlier than the date on which the Secretary receives such petition.

(d) (1) Any order issued under this section shall terminate if—

> (A) the Secretary of Commerce finds that any of the conditions set forth in paragraphs (1), (2), and (3) of subsection (a) no longer exist; or

> (B) mask works of nationals, domiciliaries, and sovereign authorities of that foreign nation or mask works first commercially exploited in that foreign nation become eligible for protection under subparagraph (A) or (C) of section 902(a)(1).

(2) Upon the termination or expiration of an order issued under this section, registrations of claims of protection in mask works made pursuant to that order shall remain valid for the period specified in section 904.

(e) The authority of the Secretary of Commerce under this section shall commence on the date of the enactment of this chapter, and shall terminate on July 1, 1995.

(f) (1) The Secretary of Commerce shall promptly notify the Register of Copyrights and the Committees on the Judiciary of the Senate and the House of Representatives of the issuance or termination of any order under this section, together with a statement of the reasons for such action. The Secretary shall also publish such notification and statement of reasons in the Federal Register.

(2) Two years after the date of the enactment of this chapter, the Secretary of Commerce, in consultation with the Register of Copyrights, shall transmit to the Committees on the Judiciary of the Senate and the House of Representatives a report on the actions taken under this section and on the current status of international recognition of mask work protection. The report shall include such recommendations for modifications of the protection accorded under this chapter to mask

works owned by nationals, domiciliaries, or sovereign authorities of foreign nations as the Secretary, in consultation with the Register of Copyrights, considers would promote the purposes of this chapter and international comity with respect to mask work protection. Not later than July 1, 1994, the Secretary of Commerce, in consultation with the Register of Copyrights, shall transmit to the Committees on the Judiciary of the Senate and the House of Representatives a report updating the matters contained in the report transmitted under the preceding sentence.

(Nov. 8, 1984, Pub. L. 98-620, §302, 98 Stat. 3355; Nov. 9, 1987, Pub. L. 100-159, §2, 4, 101 Stat. 899, 900; June 28, 1991, Pub. L. 102-64, §3, 4, 105 Stat. 320, 321.)

CHAPTER 10—DIGITAL AUDIO RECORDING DEVICES AND MEDIA

SUBCHAPTER A—DEFINITIONS

§ 1001   Definitions

As used in this chapter, the following terms have the following meanings:

(1) A "digital audio copied recording" is a reproduction in a digital recording format of a digital musical recording, whether that reproduction is made directly from another digital musical recording or indirectly from a transmission.

(2) A "digital audio interface device" is any machine or device that is designed specifically to communicate digital audio information and related interface data to a digital audio recording device through a nonprofessional interface.

(3) A "digital audio recording device" is any machine or device of a type commonly distributed to individuals for use by individuals, whether or not included with or as part of some other machine or device, the digital recording function of which is designed or marketed for the primary purpose of, and that is capable of, making a digital audio copied recording for private use, except for—

(A) professional model products, and

(B) dictation machines, answering machines, and other audio recording equipment that is designed and marketed primarily for the creation of sound recordings resulting from the fixation of nonmusical sounds.

(4) (A) A "digital audio recording medium" is any material object in a form commonly distributed for use by individuals, that is primarily marketed or most commonly used by consumers for the purpose of making digital audio copied recordings by use of a digital audio recording device.

(B) Such term does not include any material object—

(i) that embodies a sound recording at the time it is first distributed by the importer or manufacturer; or

(ii) that is primarily marketed and most commonly used by consumers either for the purpose of making copies of motion pictures or other audiovisual works or for the purpose of making copies of nonmusical literary works, including computer programs or data bases.

(5) (A) A "digital musical recording" is a material object—

(i) in which are fixed, in a digital recording format, only sounds, and material, statements, or instructions incidental to those fixed sounds, if any, and

(ii) from which the sounds and material can be perceived, reproduced, or otherwise communicated, either directly or with the aid of a machine or device.

(B) A "digital musical recording" does not include a material object—

(i) in which the fixed sounds consist entirely of spoken word recordings, or

(ii) in which one or more computer programs are fixed, except that a digital musical recording may contain statements or instructions constituting the fixed sounds and incidental material, and statements or instructions to be used directly or indirectly in order to bring about the perception, reproduction, or communication of the fixed sounds and incidental material.

(C) For purposes of this paragraph—

(i) a "spoken word recording" is a sound recording in which are fixed only a series of spoken words, except that the spoken words may be accompanied by incidental musical or other sounds, and

(ii) the term "incidental" means related to and relatively minor by comparison.

(6) "Distribute" means to sell, lease, or assign a product to consumers in the United States, or to sell, lease, or assign a product in the United States for ultimate transfer to consumers in the United States.

(7) An "interested copyright party" is—

(A) the owner of the exclusive right under section 106(1) of this title to reproduce a sound recording of a musical work that has been embodied in a digital musical recording or analog musical recording lawfully made under this title that has been distributed;

(B) the legal or beneficial owner of, or the person that controls, the right to reproduce in a digital musical recording or analog musical recording a musical work that has been embodied in a digital musical recording or analog musical recording lawfully made under this title that has been distributed;

(C) a featured recording artist who performs on a sound recording that has been distributed; or

(D) any association or other organization—

(i) representing persons specified in subparagraph (A), (B), or (C), or

(ii) engaged in licensing rights in musical works to music users on behalf of writers and publishers.

(8) To "manufacture" means to produce or assemble a product in the United States. A "manufacturer" is a person who manufactures.

(9) A "music publisher" is a person that is authorized to license the reproduction of a particular musical work in a sound recording.

(10) A "professional model product' is an audio recording device that is designed, manufactured, marketed, and intended for use by recording professionals in the ordinary course of a lawful business, in accordance with such requirements as the Secretary of Commerce shall establish by regulation.

(11) The term "serial copying" means the duplication in a digital format of a copyrighted musical work or sound recording from a digital reproduction of a digital musical recording. The term "digital reproduction of a digital musical recording" does not include a digital musical recording as distributed, by authority of the copyright owner, for ultimate sale to consumers.

(12) The "transfer price" of a digital audio recording device or a digital audio recording medium—

(A) is, subject to subparagraph (B)—

(i) in the case of an imported product, the actual entered value at United States Customs (exclusive of any freight, insurance, and applicable duty), and

(ii) in the case of a domestic product, the manufacturer's transfer price (FOB the manufacturer, and exclusive of any direct sales taxes or excise taxes incurred in connection with the sale); and

(B) shall, in a case in which the transferor and transferee are related entities or within a single entity, not be less than a reasonable arms-length price under the principles of the regulations adopted pursuant to section 482 of the Internal Revenue Code of 1986, or any successor provision to such section.

(13) A "writer" is the composer or lyricist of a particular musical work.

(Oct. 28, 1992, Pub. L. 102-563, §2, 106 Stat. 4237-39.)

SUBCHAPTER B—COPYING CONTROLS

§ 1002   Incorporation of copying controls

(a) *Prohibition on importation, manufacture, and distribution.*—No person shall import, manufacture, or distribute any digital audio recording device or digital audio interface device that does not conform to—

(1) the Serial Copy Management System;

(2) a system that has the same functional characteristics as the Serial Copy Management System and requires that copyright and generation status information be accurately sent, received, and acted upon between devices using the system's method of serial copying regulation and devices using the Serial Copy Management System; or

(3) any other system certified by the Secretary of Commerce as prohibiting unauthorized serial copying.

(b) *Development of verification procedure.*—The Secretary of Commerce shall establish a procedure to verify, upon the petition of an interested party, that a system meets the standards set forth in subsection (a)(2).

(c) *Prohibition on circumvention of the system.*—No person shall import, manufacture, or distribute any device, or offer or perform any service, the primary purpose or effect of which is to avoid, bypass, remove, deactivate, or otherwise circumvent any program or circuit which implements, in whole or in part, a system described in subsection (a).

17 U.S.C. § 1002

(d) *Encoding of information on digital musical recordings.*—

(1) *Prohibition on encoding inaccurate information.*—No person shall encode a digital musical recording of a sound recording with inaccurate information relating to the category code, copyright status, or generation status of the source material for the recording.

(2) *Encoding of copyright status not required.*—Nothing in this chapter requires any person engaged in the importation or manufacture of digital musical recordings to encode any such digital musical recording with respect to its copyright status.

(e) *Information accompanying transmissions in digital format.*—Any person who transmits or otherwise communicates to the public any sound recording in digital format is not required under this chapter to transmit or otherwise communicate the information relating to the copyright status of the sound recording. Any such person who does transmit or otherwise communicate such copyright status information shall transmit or communicate such information accurately.

(Oct. 28, 1992, Pub. L. 102-563, §2, 106 Stat. 4240.)

Subchapter C—Royalty Payments

§ 1003   Obligation to make royalty payments

(a) *Prohibition on importation and manufacture.*—No person shall import into and distribute, or manufacture and distribute, any digital audio recording device or digital audio recording medium unless such person records the notice specified by this section and subsequently deposits the statements of account and applicable royalty payments for such device or medium specified in section 1004.

(b) *Filing of notice.*—The importer or manufacturer of any digital audio recording device or digital audio recording medium, within a product category or utilizing a technology with respect to which such manufacturer or importer has not previously filed a notice under this subsection, shall file with the Register of Copyrights a notice with respect to such device or medium, in such form and content as the Register shall prescribe by regulation.

(c) *Filing of quarterly and annual statements of account.*—

(1) *Generally.*—Any importer or manufacturer that distributes any digital audio recording device or digital audio recording medium that it manufactured or imported shall file with the Register of Copyrights, in such form and content as the Register shall prescribe by regulation, such quarterly and annual statements of account with respect to such distribution as the Register shall prescribe by regulation.

(2) *Certification, verification, and confidentiality.*—Each such statement shall be certified as accurate by an authorized officer or principal of the importer or manufacturer. The Register shall issue regulations to provide for the verification and audit of such statements and to protect the confidentiality of the information contained in such statements. Such regulations shall provide for the disclosure, in confidence, of such statements to interested copyright parties.

(3) *Royalty payments.*—Each such statement shall be accompanied by the royalty payments specified in section 1004.

(Oct. 28, 1992, Pub. L. 102-563, §2, 106 Stat. 4240-41.)

§ 1004   Royalty payments

(a) *Digital audio recording devices.*—

(1) *Amount of payment.*—The royalty payment due under section 1003 for each digital audio recording device imported into and distributed in the United States, or manufactured and distributed in the United States, shall be 2 percent of the transfer price. Only the first person to manufacture and distribute or import and distribute such device shall be required to pay the royalty with respect to such device.

(2) *Calculation for devices distributed with other devices.*—With respect to a digital audio recording device first distributed in combination with one or more devices, either as a physically integrated unit or as separate components, the royalty payment shall be calculated as follows:

(A) If the digital audio recording device and such other devices are part of a physically integrated unit, the royalty payment shall be based on the transfer price of the unit, but shall be reduced by any royalty payment made on any digital audio recording device included within the unit that was not first distributed in combination with the unit.

17 U.S.C. § 1004

(B) If the digital audio recording device is not part of a physically integrated unit and substantially similar devices have been distributed separately at any time during the preceding 4 calendar quarters, the royalty payment shall be based on the average transfer price of such devices during those 4 quarters.

(C) If the digital audio recording device is not part of a physically integrated unit and substantially similar devices have not been distributed separately at any time during the preceding 4 calendar quarters, the royalty payment shall be based on a constructed price reflecting the proportional value of such device to the combination as a whole.

(3) *Limits on royalties.*—Notwithstanding paragraph (1) or (2), the amount of the royalty payment for each digital audio recording device shall not be less than $1 nor more than the royalty maximum. The royalty maximum shall be $8 per device, except that in the case of a physically integrated unit containing more than 1 digital audio recording device, the royalty maximum for such unit shall be $12. During the 6th year after the effective date of this chapter, and not more than once each year thereafter, any interested copyright party may petition the Librarian of Congress to increase the royalty maximum and, if more than 20 percent of the royalty payments are at the relevant royalty maximum, the Librarian of Congress shall prospectively increase such royalty maximum with the goal of having no more than 10 percent of such payments at the new royalty maximum; however the amount of any such increase as a percentage of the royalty maximum shall in no event exceed the percentage increase in the Consumer Price Index during the period under review.

(b) *Digital audio recording media.*—The royalty payment due under section 1003 for each digital audio recording medium imported into and distributed in the United States, or manufactured and distributed in the United States, shall be 3 percent of the transfer price. Only the first person to manufacture and distribute or import and distribute such medium shall be required to pay the royalty with respect to such medium.

(Oct. 28, 1992, Pub. L. 102-563, §2, 106 Stat. 4241-42.)

17 U.S.C. § 1004

§ 1005 Deposit of royalty payments and deduction of expenses

The Register of Copyrights shall receive all royalty payments deposited under this chapter and, after deducting the reasonable costs incurred by the Copyright Office under this chapter, shall deposit the balance in the Treasury of the United States as offsetting receipts, in such manner as the Secretary of the Treasury directs. All funds held by the Secretary of the Treasury shall be invested in interest-bearing United States securities for later distribution with interest under section 1007. The Register may, in the Register's discretion, 4 years after the close of any calendar year, close out the royalty payments account for that calendar year, and may treat any funds remaining in such account and any subsequent deposits that would otherwise be attributable to that calendar year as attributable to the succeeding calendar year.

(Oct. 28, 1992, Pub. L. 102-563, §2, 106 Stat. 4242; Dec. 17, 1993, Pub. L. 103-198, §6(b), 107 Stat. 2312.)

§ 1006 Entitlement to royalty payments

(a) *Interested copyright parties.*—The royalty payments deposited pursuant to section 1005 shall, in accordance with the procedures specified in section 1007, be distributed to any interested copyright party—

> (1) whose musical work or sound recording has been—
>
>> (A) embodied in a digital musical recording or an analog musical recording lawfully made under this title that has been distributed, and
>>
>> (B) distributed in the form of digital musical recordings or analog musical recordings or disseminated to the public in transmissions, during the period to which such payments pertain; and
>
> (2) who has filed a claim under section 1007.

(b) *Allocation of royalty payments to groups.*—The royalty payments shall be divided into 2 funds as follows:

> (1) *The sound recordings fund.*—66⅔ percent of the royalty payments shall be allocated to the Sound Recordings Fund. 2⅝ percent of the royalty payments allocated to the Sound Recordings Fund shall be placed in an escrow account managed by an independent administrator jointly appointed by the interested copyright parties described

17 U.S.C. § 1006

in section 1001(7)(A) and the American Federation of Musicians (or any successor entity) to be distributed to nonfeatured musicians (whether or not members of the American Federation of Musicians or any successor entity) who have performed on sound recordings distributed in the United States. 1⅜ percent of the royalty payments allocated to the Sound Recordings Fund shall be placed in an escrow account managed by an independent administrator jointly appointed by the interested copyright parties described in section 1001(7)(A) and the American Federation of Television and Radio Artists (or any successor entity) to be distributed to nonfeatured vocalists (whether or not members of the American Federation [of] Television and Radio Artists or any successor entity) who have performed on sound recordings distributed in the United States. 40 percent of the remaining royalty payments in the Sound Recordings Fund shall be distributed to the interested copyright parties described in section 1001(7)(C), and 60 percent of such remaining royalty payments shall be distributed to the interested copyright parties described in section 1001(7)(A).

(2) *The musical works fund.—*

(A) 33 percent of the royalty payments shall be allocated to the Musical Works Fund for distribution to interested copyright parties described in section 1001(7)(B).

(B) (i) Music publishers shall be entitled to 50 percent of the royalty payments allocated to the Musical Works Fund.

(ii) Writers shall be entitled to the other 50 percent of the royalty payments allocated to the Musical Works Fund.

(c) *Allocation of royalty payments within groups.—*If all interested copyright parties within a group specified in subsection (b) do not agree on a voluntary proposal for the distribution of the royalty payments within each group, the Librarian of Congress shall convene a copyright arbitration royalty panel which shall, pursuant to the procedures specified under section 1007(c), allocate royalty payments under this section based on the extent to which, during the relevant period—

(1) for the Sound Recordings Fund, each sound recording was distributed in the form of digital musical recordings or analog musical recordings; and

(2) for the Musical Works Fund, each musical work was distributed in the form of digital musical recordings or analog musical recordings or disseminated to the public in transmissions.

(Oct. 28, 1992, Pub. L. 102-563, §2, 106 Stat. 4242-44; Dec. 17, 1993, Pub. L. 103-198, §6(b), 107 Stat. 2312.)

§ 1007 Procedures for distributing royalty payments

(a) *Filing of claims and negotiations.*—

(1) *Filing of claims.*—During the first 2 months of each calendar year after calendar year 1992, every interested copyright party seeking to receive royalty payments to which such party is entitled under section 1006 shall file with the Librarian of Congress a claim for payments collected during the preceding year in such form and manner as the Librarian of Congress shall prescribe by regulation.

(2) *Negotiations.*—Notwithstanding any provision of the antitrust laws, for purposes of this section interested copyright parties within each group specified in section 1006(b) may agree among themselves to the proportionate division of royalty payments, may lump their claims together and file them jointly or as a single claim, or may designate a common agent, including any organization described in section 1001(7)(D), to negotiate or receive payment on their behalf; except that no agreement under this subsection may modify the allocation of royalties specified in section 1006(b).

(b) *Distribution of payments in the absence of a dispute.*—After the period established for the filing of claims under subsection (a), in each year after 1992, the Librarian of Congress shall determine whether there exists a controversy concerning the distribution of royalty payments under section 1006(c). If the Librarian of Congress determines that no such controversy exists, the Librarian of Congress shall, within 30 days after such determination, authorize the distribution of the royalty payments as set forth in the agreements regarding the distribution of royalty payments entered into pursuant to subsection (a), after deducting its reasonable administrative costs under this section.

(c) *Resolution of disputes.*—If the Librarian of Congress finds the existence of a controversy, the Librarian shall, pursuant to chapter 8 of this title, convene a copyright arbitration royalty panel to determine the distribution of royalty payments. During the pendency of such a proceeding, the Librarian of Congress shall withhold from distribution an amount sufficient to satisfy all claims with respect to which a controversy exists, but shall, to the extent feasible, authorize the distribution of any amounts that are not in controversy. The Librarian of Congress shall, before authorizing the distribution of such royalty payments, deduct the reasonable administrative costs incurred by the Librarian under this section.

(Oct. 28, 1992, Pub. L. 102-563, §2, 106 Stat. 4244; Dec. 17, 1993, Pub. L. 103-198, §6(b), 107 Stat. 2312; Nov. 13, 1997, Pub. L. 105-80, §9, 12, 111 Stat. 1534, 1536.)

SUBCHAPTER D—PROHIBITION ON CERTAIN INFRINGEMENT ACTIONS, REMEDIES, AND ARBITRATION

§ 1008   Prohibition on certain infringement actions

No action may be brought under this title alleging infringement of copyright based on the manufacture, importation, or distribution of a digital audio recording device, a digital audio recording medium, an analog recording device, or an analog recording medium, or based on the noncommercial use by a consumer of such a device or medium for making digital musical recordings or analog musical recordings.

(Oct. 28, 1992, Pub. L. 102-563, §2, 106 Stat. 4244.)

§ 1009   Civil remedies

(a) *Civil actions.*—Any interested copyright party injured by a violation of section 1002 or 1003 may bring a civil action in an appropriate United States district court against any person for such violation.

(b) *Other civil actions.*—Any person injured by a violation of this chapter may bring a civil action in an appropriate United States district court for actual damages incurred as a result of such violation.

(c) *Powers of the court.*—In an action brought under subsection (a), the court—

(1) may grant temporary and permanent injunctions on such terms as it deems reasonable to prevent or restrain such violation;

(2) in the case of a violation of section 1002, or in the case of an injury resulting from a failure to make royalty payments required by section 1003, shall award damages under subsection (d);

(3) in its discretion may allow the recovery of costs by or against any party other than the United States or an officer thereof; and

(4) in its discretion may award a reasonable attorney's fee to the prevailing party.

(d) *Award of damages.—*

    (1) *Damages for section 1002 or 1003 violations.—*

        (A) *Actual damages.—*

            (i) In an action brought under subsection (a), if the court finds that a violation of section 1002 or 1003 has occurred, the court shall award to the complaining party its actual damages if the complaining party elects such damages at any time before final judgment is entered.

            (ii) In the case of section 1003, actual damages shall constitute the royalty payments that should have been paid under section 1004 and deposited under section 1005. In such a case, the court, in its discretion, may award an additional amount of not to exceed 50 percent of the actual damages.

        (B) *Statutory damages for section 1002 violations.—*

            (i) *Device.*—A complaining party may recover an award of statutory damages for each violation of section 1002 (a) or (c) in the sum of not more than $2,500 per device involved in such violation or per device on which a service prohibited by section 1002(c) has been performed, as the court considers just.

            (ii) *Digital musical recording.*—A complaining party may recover an award of statutory damages for each violation of section 1002(d) in the sum of not more than $25 per digital musical recording involved in such violation, as the court considers just.

            (iii) *Transmission.*—A complaining party may recover an award of damages for each transmission or communication that violates section 1002(e) in the sum of not more than $10,000, as the court considers just.

(2) *Repeated violations.*—In any case in which the court finds that a person has violated section 1002 or 1003 within 3 years after a final judgment against that person for another such violation was entered, the court may increase the award of damages to not more than double the amounts that would otherwise be awarded under paragraph (1), as the court considers just.

(3) *Innocent violations of section 1002.*—The court in its discretion may reduce the total award of damages against a person violating section 1002 to a sum of not less than $250 in any case in which the court finds that the violator was not aware and had no reason to believe that its acts constituted a violation of section 1002.

(e) *Payment of damages.*—Any award of damages under subsection (d) shall be deposited with the Register pursuant to section 1005 for distribution to interested copyright parties as though such funds were royalty payments made pursuant to section 1003.

(f) *Impounding of articles.*—At any time while an action under subsection (a) is pending, the court may order the impounding, on such terms as it deems reasonable, of any digital audio recording device, digital musical recording, or device specified in section 1002(c) that is in the custody or control of the alleged violator and that the court has reasonable cause to believe does not comply with, or was involved in a violation of, section 1002.

(g) *Remedial modification and destruction of articles.*—In an action brought under subsection (a), the court may, as part of a final judgment or decree finding a violation of section 1002, order the remedial modification or the destruction of any digital audio recording device, digital musical recording, or device specified in section 1002(c) that—

(1) does not comply with, or was involved in a violation of, section 1002, and

(2) is in the custody or control of the violator or has been impounded under subsection (f).

(Oct. 28, 1992, Pub. L. 102-563, §2, 106 Stat. 4245-46.)

17 U.S.C. § 1009

§ 1010   Arbitration of certain disputes

(a) *Scope of arbitration.*—Before the date of first distribution in the United States of a digital audio recording device or a digital audio interface device, any party manufacturing, importing, or distributing such device, and any interested copyright party may mutually agree to binding arbitration for the purpose of determining whether such device is subject to section 1002, or the basis on which royalty payments for such device are to be made under section 1003.

(b) *Initiation of arbitration proceedings.*—Parties agreeing to such arbitration shall file a petition with the Librarian of Congress requesting the commencement of an arbitration proceeding. The petition may include the names and qualifications of potential arbitrators. Within 2 weeks after receiving such a petition, the Librarian of Congress shall cause notice to be published in the Federal Register of the initiation of an arbitration proceeding. Such notice shall include the names and qualifications of 3 arbitrators chosen by the Librarian of Congress from a list of available arbitrators obtained from the American Arbitration Association or such similar organization as the Librarian of Congress shall select, and from potential arbitrators listed in the parties' petition. The arbitrators selected under this subsection shall constitute an Arbitration Panel.

(c) *Stay of judicial proceedings.*—Any civil action brought under section 1009 against a party to arbitration under this section shall, on application of one of the parties to the arbitration, be stayed until completion of the arbitration proceeding.

(d) *Arbitration proceeding.*—The Arbitration Panel shall conduct an arbitration proceeding with respect to the matter concerned, in accordance with such procedures as it may adopt. The Panel shall act on the basis of a fully documented written record. Any party to the arbitration may submit relevant information and proposals to the Panel. The parties to the proceeding shall bear the entire cost thereof in such manner and proportion as the Panel shall direct.

(e) *Report to Librarian of Congress.*—Not later than 60 days after publication of the notice under subsection (b) of the initiation of an arbitration proceeding, the Arbitration Panel shall report to the Librarian of Congress its determination concerning whether the device concerned is subject to section 1002, or the basis on which royalty payments for the device are to be made under section 1003. Such report shall be accompanied by the written record, and shall set forth the facts that the Panel found relevant to its determination.

(f) *Action by the Librarian of Congress.*—Within 60 days after receiving the report of the Arbitration Panel under subsection (e), the Librarian of Congress shall adopt or reject the determination of the Panel. The Librarian of Congress shall adopt the determination of the Panel unless the Librarian of Congress finds that the determination is clearly erroneous. If the Librarian of Congress rejects the determination of the Panel, the Librarian of Congress shall, before the end of that 60-day period, and after full examination of the record created in the arbitration proceeding, issue an order setting forth the Librarian's decision and the reasons therefor. The Librarian of Congress shall cause to be published in the Federal Register the determination of the Panel and the decision of the Librarian of Congress under this subsection with respect to the determination (including any order issued under the preceding sentence).

(g) *Judicial review.*—Any decision of the Librarian of Congress under subsection (f) with respect to a determination of the Arbitration Panel may be appealed, by a party to the arbitration, to the United States Court of Appeals for the District of Columbia Circuit, within 30 days after the publication of the decision in the Federal Register. The pendency of an appeal under this subsection shall not stay the decision of the Librarian of Congress. The court shall have jurisdiction to modify or vacate a decision of the Librarian of Congress only if it finds, on the basis of the record before the Librarian of Congress, that the Arbitration Panel or the Librarian of Congress acted in an arbitrary manner. If the court modifies the decision of the Librarian of Congress, the court shall have jurisdiction to enter its own decision in accordance with its final judgment. The court may further vacate the decision of the Librarian of Congress and remand the case for arbitration proceedings as provided in this section.

(Oct. 28, 1992, Pub. L. 102-563, §2, 106 Stat. 4246-47; Dec. 17, 1993, Pub. L. 103-198, §6(b), 107 Stat. 2312.)

17 U.S.C. § 1010

CHAPTER 11—SOUND RECORDINGS AND MUSIC VIDEOS

SEC.

1101.   Unauthorized fixation and trafficking in sound recordings and music videos.

§ 1101   Unauthorized fixation and trafficking in sound recordings and music videos

(a) *Unauthorized acts.*—Anyone who, without the consent of the performer or performers involved—

   (1) fixes the sounds or sounds and images of a live musical performance in a copy or phonorecord, or reproduces copies or phonorecords of such a performance from an unauthorized fixation,

   (2) transmits or otherwise communicates to the public the sounds or sounds and images of a live musical performance, or

   (3) distributes or offers to distribute, sells or offers to sell, rents or offers to rent, or traffics in any copy or phonorecord fixed as described in paragraph (1), regardless of whether the fixations occurred in the United States,

shall be subject to the remedies provided in sections 502 through 505, to the same extent as an infringer of copyright.

(b) *Definition.*—As used in this section, the term "traffic in" means transport, transfer, or otherwise dispose of, to another, as consideration for anything of value, or make or obtain control of with intent to transport, transfer, or dispose of.

(c) *Applicability.*—This section shall apply to any act or acts that occur on or after the date of the enactment of the Uruguay Round Agreements Act [Dec. 8, 1994].

(d) *State law not preempted.*—Nothing in this section may be construed to annul or limit any rights or remedies under the common law or statutes of any State.

(Dec. 8, 1994, Pub. L. 103-465, §512, 108 Stat. 4974.)

§ 1201   Circumvention of copyright protection systems

(a) Violations regarding circumvention of technological measures-

(1) (A) No person shall circumvent a technological measure that effectively controls access to a work protected under this title. The prohibition contained in the preceding sentence shall take effect at the end of the 2-year period beginning on the date of the enactment of this chapter.

(B) The prohibition contained in subparagraph (A) shall not apply to persons who are users of a copyrighted work which is in a particular class of works, if such persons are, or are likely to be in the succeeding 3-year period, adversely affected by virtue of such prohibition in their ability to make noninfringing uses of that particular class of works under this title, as determined under subparagraph (C).

(C) During the 2-year period described in subparagraph (A), and during each succeeding 3-year period, the Librarian of Congress, upon the recommendation of the Register of Copyrights, who shall consult with the Assistant Secretary for Communications and Information of the Department of Commerce and report and comment on his or her views in making such recommendation, shall make the determination in a rulemaking proceeding for purposes of subparagraph (B) of whether persons who are users of a copyrighted work are, or are likely to be in the succeeding 3-year period, adversely affected by the prohibition under subparagraph (A) in their ability to make noninfringing uses under this title of a particular class of copyrighted works. In conducting such rulemaking, the Librarian shall examine—

(i) the availability for use of copyrighted works;

(ii) the availability for use of works for nonprofit archival, preservation, and educational purposes;

(iii) the impact that the prohibition on the circumvention of technological measures applied to copyrighted works has on criticism, comment, news reporting, teaching, scholarship, or research;

(iv) the effect of circumvention of technological measures on the market for or value of copyrighted works; and

(v) such other factors as the Librarian considers appropriate.

(D) The Librarian shall publish any class of copyrighted works for which the Librarian has determined, pursuant to the rule-making conducted under subparagraph (C), that noninfringing uses by persons who are users of a copyrighted work are, or are likely to be, adversely affected, and the prohibition contained in subparagraph (A shall not apply to such users with respect to such class of works for the ensuing 3-year period.

(E) Neither the exception under subparagraph (B) from the applicability of the prohibition contained in subparagraph (A), nor any determination made in a rulemaking conducted under subparagraph (C), may be used as a defense in any action to enforce any provision of this title other than this paragraph.

(2) No person shall manufacture, import, offer to the public, provide, or otherwise traffic in any technology, product, service, device, component, or part thereof, that—

(A) is primarily designed or produced for the purpose of circumventing a technological measure that effectively controls access to a work protected under this title;

(B) has only limited commercially significant purpose or use other than to circumvent a technological measure that effectively controls access to a work protected under this title; or

(C) is marketed by that person or another acting in concert with that person with that person's knowledge for use in circumventing a technological measure that effectively controls access to a work protected under this title.

17 U.S.C. § 1201

(3) As used in this subsection—

(A) to "circumvent a technological measure" means to descramble a scrambled work, to decrypt an encrypted work, or otherwise to avoid, bypass, remove, deactivate, or impair a technological measure, without the authority of the copyright owner; and

(B) a technological measure "effectively controls access to a work" if the measure, in the ordinary course of its operation, requires the application of information, or a process or a treatment, with the authority of the copyright owner, to gain access to the work.

(b) *Additional violations.*—(1) No person shall manufacture, import, offer to the public, provide, or otherwise traffic in any technology, product, service, device, component, or part thereof, that—

(A) is primarily designed or produced for the purpose of circumventing protection afforded by a technological measure that effectively protects a right of a copyright owner under this title in a work or a portion thereof;

(B) has only limited commercially significant purpose or use other than to circumvent protection afforded by a technological measure that effectively protects a right of a copyright owner under this title in a work or a portion thereof; or

(C) is marketed by that person or another acting in concert with that person with that person's knowledge for use in circumventing protection afforded by a technological measure that effectively protects a right of a copyright owner under this title in a work or a portion thereof.

(2) As used in this subsection—

(A) to "circumvent protection afforded by a technological measure" means avoiding, bypassing, removing, deactivating, or otherwise impairing a technological measure; and

(B) a technological measure "effectively protects a right of a copyright owner under this title" if the measure, in the ordinary course of its operation, prevents, restricts, or otherwise limits the exercise of a right of a copyright owner under this title.

(c) *Other rights, etc., not affected.*—(1) Nothing in this section shall affect rights, remedies, limitations, or defenses to copyright infringement, including fair use, under this title.

(2) Nothing in this section shall enlarge or diminish vicarious or contributory liability for copyright infringement in connection with any technology, product, service, device, component, or part thereof.

(3) Nothing in this section shall require that the design of, or design and selection of parts and components for, a consumer electronics, telecommunications, or computing product provide for a response to any particular technological measure, so long as such part or component, or the product in which such part or component is integrated, does not otherwise fall within the prohibitions of subsection (a)(2) or (b)(1).

(4) Nothing in this section shall enlarge or diminish any rights of free speech or the press for activities using consumer electronics, telecommunications, or computing products.

(d) *Exemption for nonprofit libraries, archives, and educational institutions.*—(1) A nonprofit library, archives, or educational institution which gains access to a commercially exploited copyrighted work solely in order to make a good faith determination of whether to acquire a copy of that work for the sole purpose of engaging in conduct permitted under this title shall not be in violation of subsection (a)(1)(A). A copy of a work to which access has been gained under this paragraph—

(A) may not be retained longer than necessary to make such good faith determination; and

(B) may not be used for any other purpose.

(2) The exemption made available under paragraph (1) shall only apply with respect to a work when an identical copy of that work is not reasonably available in another form.

(3) A nonprofit library, archives, or educational institution that willfully for the purpose of commercial advantage or financial gain violates paragraph (1)—

(A) shall, for the first offense, be subject to the civil remedies under section 1203; and

17 U.S.C. § 1201

(B) shall, for repeated or subsequent offenses, in addition to the civil remedies under section 1203, forfeit the exemption provided under paragraph (1).

(4) This subsection may not be used as a defense to a claim under subsection (a)(2) or (b), nor may this subsection permit a nonprofit library, archives, or educational institution to manufacture, import, offer to the public, provide, or otherwise traffic in any technology, product, service, component, or part thereof, which circumvents a technological measure.

(5) In order for a library or archives to qualify for the exemption under this subsection, the collections of that library or archives shall be—

(A) open to the public; or

(B) available not only to researchers affiliated with the library or archives or with the institution of which it is a part, but also to other persons doing research in a specialized field.

(e) *Law enforcement, intelligence, and other government activities.*—This section does not prohibit any lawfully authorized investigative, protective, information security, or intelligence activity of an officer, agent, or employee of the United States, a State, or a political subdivision of a State, or a person acting pursuant to a contract with the United States, a State, or a political subdivision of a State. For purposes of this subsection, the term "information security" means activities carried out in order to identify and address the vulnerabilities of a government computer, computer system, or computer network.

(f) *Reverse engineering.*—(1) Notwithstanding the provisions of subsection (a)(1)(A), a person who has lawfully obtained the right to use a copy of a computer program may circumvent a technological measure that effectively controls access to a particular portion of that program for the sole purpose of identifying and analyzing those elements of the program that are necessary to achieve interoperability of an independently created computer program with other programs, and that have not previously been readily available to the person engaging in the circumvention, to the extent any such acts of identification and analysis do not constitute infringement under this title.

17 U.S.C. § 1201

(2) Notwithstanding the provisions of subsections (a)(2) and (b), a person may develop and employ technological means to circumvent a technological measure, or to circumvent protection afforded by a technological measure, in order to enable the identification and analysis under paragraph (1), or for the purpose of enabling interoperability of an independently created computer program with other programs, if such means are necessary to achieve such interoperability, to the extent that doing so does not constitute infringement under this title.

(3) The information acquired through the acts permitted under paragraph (1), and the means permitted under paragraph (2), may be made available to others if the person referred to in paragraph (1) or (2), as the case may be, provides such information or means solely for the purpose of enabling interoperability of an independently created computer program with other programs, and to the extent that doing so does not constitute infringement under this title or violate applicable law other than this section.

(4) For purposes of this subsection, the term "interoperability" means the ability of computer programs to exchange information, and of such programs mutually to use the information which has been exchanged.

(g) *Encryption research.*—

(1) *Definitions.*—For purposes of this subsection—

(A) the term "encryption research" means activities necessary to identify and analyze flaws and vulnerabilities of encryption technologies applied to copyrighted works, if these activities are conducted to advance the state of knowledge in the field of encryption technology or to assist in the development of encryption products; and

(B) the term "encryption technology" means the scrambling and descrambling of information using mathematical formulas or algorithms.

(2) *Permissible acts of encryption research.*—Notwithstanding the provisions of subsection (a)(1)(A), it is not a violation of that subsection for a person to circumvent a technological measure as applied to a

copy, phonorecord, performance, or display of a published work in the course of an act of good faith encryption research if—

(A) the person lawfully obtained the encrypted copy, phonorecord, performance, or display of the published work;

(B) such act is necessary to conduct such encryption research;

(C) the person made a good faith effort to obtain authorization before the circumvention; and

(D) such act does not constitute infringement under this title or a violation of applicable law other than this section, including section 1030 of title 18 and those provisions of title 18 amended by the Computer Fraud and Abuse Act of 1986.

(3) *Factors in determining exemption.*—In determining whether a person qualifies for the exemption under paragraph (2), the factors to be considered shall include—

(A) whether the information derived from the encryption research was disseminated, and if so, whether it was disseminated in a manner reasonably calculated to advance the state of knowledge or development of encryption technology, versus whether it was disseminated in a manner that facilitates infringement under this title or a violation of applicable law other than this section, including a violation of privacy or breach of security;

(B) whether the person is engaged in a legitimate course of study, is employed, or is appropriately trained or experienced, in the field of encryption technology; and

(C) whether the person provides the copyright owner of the work to which the technological measure is applied with notice of the findings and documentation of the research, and the time when such notice is provided.

(4) *Use of technological means for research activities.*—Notwithstanding the provisions of subsection (a)(2), it is not a violation of that subsection for a person to—

(A) develop and employ technological means to circumvent a technological measure for the sole purpose of that person performing the acts of good faith encryption research described in paragraph (2); and

(B) provide the technological means to another person with whom he or she is working collaboratively for the purpose of conducting the acts of good faith encryption research described in paragraph (2) or for the purpose of having that other person verify his or her acts of good faith encryption research described in paragraph (2).

(5) *Report to Congress.*—Not later than 1 year after the date of the enactment of this chapter, the Register of Copyrights and the Assistant Secretary for Communications and Information of the Department of Commerce shall jointly report to the Congress on the effect this subsection has had on—

(A) encryption research and the development of encryption technology;

(B) the adequacy and effectiveness of technological measures designed to protect copyrighted works; and

(C) protection of copyright owners against the unauthorized access to their encrypted copyrighted works.

The report shall include legislative recommendations, if any.

(h) *Exceptions regarding minors.*—In applying subsection (a) to a component or part, the court may consider the necessity for its intended and actual incorporation in a technology, product, service, or device, which—

(1) does not itself violate the provisions of this title; and

(2) has the sole purpose to prevent the access of minors to material on the Internet.

(i) *Protection of personally identifying information.*—

(1) *Circumvention permitted.*—Notwithstanding the provisions of subsection (a)(1)(A), it is not a violation of that subsection for a person to circumvent a technological measure that effectively controls access to a work protected under this title, if—

(A) the technological measure, or the work it protects, contains the capability of collecting or disseminating personally identify-

17 U.S.C. § 1201

ing information reflecting the online activities of a natural person who seeks to gain access to the work protected;

(B) in the normal course of its operation, the technological measure, or the work it protects, collects or disseminates personally identifying information about the person who seeks to gain access to the work protected, without providing conspicuous notice of such collection or dissemination to such person, and without providing such person with the capability to prevent or restrict such collection or dissemination;

(C) the act of circumvention has the sole effect of identifying and disabling the capability described in subparagraph (A), and has no other effect on the ability of any person to gain access to any work; and

(D) the act of circumvention is carried out solely for the purpose of preventing the collection or dissemination of personally identifying information about a natural person who seeks to gain access to the work protected, and is not in violation of any other law.

(2) *Inapplicability to certain technological measures.*—This subsection does not apply to a technological measure, or a work it protects, that does not collect or disseminate personally identifying information and that is disclosed to a user as not having or using such capability.

(j) *Security testing.*—

(1) *Definition.*—For purposes of this subsection, the term "security testing" means accessing a computer, computer system, or computer network, solely for the purpose of good faith testing, investigating, or correcting, a security flaw or vulnerability, with the authorization of the owner or operator of such computer, computer system, or computer network.

(2) *Permissible acts of security testing.*—Notwithstanding the provisions of subsection (a)(1)(A), it is not a violation of that subsection for a person to engage in an act of security testing, if such act does not constitute infringement under this title or a violation of applicable law other than this section, including section 1030 of title 18 and

those provisions of title 18 amended by the Computer Fraud and Abuse Act of 1986.

(3) *Factors in determining exemption.*—In determining whether a person qualifies for the exemption under paragraph (2), the factors to be considered shall include—

(A) whether the information derived from the security testing was used solely to promote the security of the owner or operator of such computer, computer system or computer network, or shared directly with the developer of such computer, computer system, or computer network; and

(B) whether the information derived from the security testing was used or maintained in a manner that does not facilitate infringement under this title or a violation of applicable law other than this section, including a violation of privacy or breach of security.

(4) *Use of technological means for security testing.*—Notwithstanding the provisions of subsection (a)(2), it is not a violation of that subsection for a person to develop, produce, distribute or employ technological means for the sole purpose of performing the acts of security testing described in subsection (2), provided such technological means does not otherwise violate section (a)(2).

(k) *Certain analog devices and certain technological measures.*—

(1) *Certain analog devices.*—

(A) Effective 18 months after the date of the enactment of this chapter, no person shall manufacture, import, offer to the public, provide or otherwise traffic in any—

(i) VHS format analog video cassette recorder unless such recorder conforms to the automatic gain control copy control technology;

(ii) 8mm format analog video cassette camcorder unless such camcorder conforms to the automatic gain control technology;

(iii) Beta format analog video cassette recorder, unless such recorder conforms to the automatic gain control copy control technology, except that this requirement shall not apply until there are 1,000 Beta format analog video cassette recorders sold in the United States in any one calendar year after the date of the enactment of this chapter;

(iv) 8mm format analog video cassette recorder that is not an analog video cassette camcorder, unless such recorder conforms to the automatic gain control copy control technology, except that this requirement shall not apply until there are 20,000 such recorders sold in the United States in any one calendar year after the date of the enactment of this chapter; or

(v) analog video cassette recorder that records using an NTSC format video input and that is not otherwise covered under clauses (i) through (iv), unless such device conforms to the automatic gain control copy control technology.

(B) Effective on the date of the enactment of this chapter, no person shall manufacture, import, offer to the public, provide or otherwise traffic in—

(i) any VHS format analog video cassette recorder or any 8mm format analog video cassette recorder if the design of the model of such recorder has been modified after such date of enactment so that a model of recorder that previously conformed to the automatic gain control copy control technology no longer conforms to such technology; or

(ii) any VHS format analog video cassette recorder, or any 8mm format analog video cassette recorder that is not an 8mm analog video cassette camcorder, if the design of the model of such recorder has been modified after such date of enactment so that a model of recorder that previously conformed to the four-line colorstripe copy control technology no longer conforms to such technology.

Manufacturers that have not previously manufactured or sold a VHS format analog video cassette recorder, or an 8mm format analog cassette recorder, shall be required to conform to the four-line colorstripe copy control technology in the initial model of any such recorder manufactured after the date of the enactment of this chapter, and thereafter to continue conforming to the four-line colorstripe copy control technology. For purposes of this subparagraph, an analog video cassette recorder "conforms to" the four-line colorstripe copy control technology if it records a signal that, when played back by the playback function of that recorder in the normal viewing mode, exhibits, on a reference display device, a display containing distracting visible lines through portions of the viewable picture.

(2) *Certain encoding restrictions.*—No person shall apply the automatic gain control copy control technology or colorstripe copy control technology to prevent or limit consumer copying except such copying—

(A) of a single transmission, or specified group of transmissions, of live events or of audiovisual works for which a member of the public has exercised choice in selecting the transmissions, including the content of the transmissions or the time of receipt of such transmissions, or both, and as to which such member is charged a separate fee for each such transmission or specified group of transmissions;

(B) from a copy of a transmission of a live event or an audiovisual work if such transmission is provided by a channel or service where payment is made by a member of the public for such channel or service in the form of a subscription fee that entitles the member of the public to receive all of the programming contained in such channel or service;

(C) from a physical medium containing one or more prerecorded audiovisual works; or

(D) from a copy of a transmission described in subparagraph (A) or from a copy made from a physical medium described in subparagraph (C).

In the event that a transmission meets both the conditions set forth in subparagraph (A) and those set forth in subparagraph (B), the transmission shall be treated as a transmission described in subparagraph (A).

(3) *Inapplicability.*—This subsection shall not—

(A) require any analog video cassette camcorder to conform to the automatic gain control copy control technology with respect to any video signal received through a camera lens;

(B) apply to the manufacture, importation, offer for sale, provision of, or other trafficking in, any professional analog video cassette recorder; or

(C) apply to the offer for sale or provision of, or other trafficking in, any previously owned analog video cassette recorder, if such recorder was legally manufactured and sold when new and not subsequently modified in violation of paragraph (1)(B).

(4) *Definitions.*—For purposes of this subsection:

(A) An "analog video cassette recorder" means a device that records, or a device that includes a function that records, on electromagnetic tape in an analog format the electronic impulses produced by the video and audio portions of a television program, motion picture, or other form of audiovisual work.

(B) An "analog video cassette camcorder" means an analog video cassette recorder that contains a recording function that operates through a camera lens and through a video input that may be connected with a television or other video playback device.

(C) An analog video cassette recorder "conforms" to the automatic gain control copy control technology if it—

(i) detects one or more of the elements of such technology and does not record the motion picture or transmission protected by such technology; or

(ii) records a signal that, when played back, exhibits a meaningfully distorted or degraded display.

(D) The term "professional analog video cassette recorder" means an analog video cassette recorder that is designed, manufactured, marketed, and intended for use by a person who regularly employs such a device for a lawful business or industrial use, including making, performing, displaying, distributing, or transmitting copies of motion pictures on a commercial scale.

(E) The terms "VHS format" "8mm format", "Beta format", "automatic gain control copy control technology", "colorstripe copy control technology", "four-line version of the colorstripe copy control technology", and "NTSC" have the meanings that are commonly understood in the consumer electronics and motion picture industries as of the date of the enactment of this chapter.

(5) *Violations.*—Any violation of paragraph (1) of this subsection shall be treated as a violation of subsection (b)(1) of this section. Any violation of paragraph (2) of this subsection shall be deemed an "act of circumvention" for the purposes of section 1203(c)(3)(A) of this chapter.

(Oct. 28, 1998, Pub. L. 105-304, §103, 112 Stat. 2863; Nov. 29, 1999, Pub. L. 106-113, §5006, 113 Stat. 1501A-594.)

§ 1202   Integrity of copyright management information

(a) *False copyright management information.*—No person shall knowingly and with the intent to induce, enable, facilitate, or conceal infringement—

(1) provide copyright management information that is false, or

(2) distribute or import for distribution copyright management information that is false.

(b) *Removal or alteration of copyright management information.*—No person shall, without the authority of the copyright owner or the law—

(1) intentionally remove or alter any copyright management information,

(2) distribute or import for distribution copyright management information knowing that the copyright management information has been removed or altered without authority of the copyright owner or the law, or

(3) distribute, import for distribution, or publicly perform works, copies of works, or phonorecords, knowing that copyright management information has been removed or altered without authority of the copyright owner or the law,

knowing, or, with respect to civil remedies under section 1203, having reasonable grounds to know, that it will induce, enable, facilitate, or conceal an infringement of any right under this title.

(c) *Definition.*—As used in this section, the term "copyright management information" means any of the following information conveyed in connection with copies or phonorecords of a work or performances or displays of a work, including in digital form, except that such term does not include any personally identifying information about a user of a work or of a copy, phonorecord, performance, or display of a work:

(1) The title and other information identifying the work, including the information set forth on a notice of copyright.

(2) The name of, and other identifying information about, the author of a work.

(3) The name of, and other identifying information about, the copyright owner of the work, including the information set forth in a notice of copyright.

(4) With the exception of public performances of works by radio and television broadcast stations, the name of, and other identifying information about, a performer whose performance is fixed in a work other than an audiovisual work.

(5) With the exception of public performances of works by radio and television broadcast stations, in the case of an audiovisual work, the name of, and other identifying information about, a writer, performer, or director who is credited in the audiovisual work.

(6) Terms and conditions for use of the work.

(7) Identifying numbers or symbols referring to such information or links to such information.

(8) Such other information as the Register of Copyrights may prescribe by regulation, except that the Register of Copyrights may not require the provision of any information concerning the user of a copyrighted work.

(d) *Law enforcement, intelligence, and other government activities.*—This section does not prohibit any lawfully authorized investigative, protective, information security, or intelligence activity of an officer, agent, or employee of the United States, a State, or a political subdivision of a State, or a person acting pursuant to a contract with the United States, a State, or a political subdivision of a State. For purposes of this subsection, the term "information security" means activities carried out in order to identify and address the vulnerabilities of a government computer, computer system, or computer network.

(e) *Limitations on liability.*—

(1) *Analog transmissions.*—In the case of an analog transmission, a person who is making transmissions in its capacity as a broadcast station, or as a cable system, or someone who provides programming to such station or system, shall not be liable for a violation of subsection (b) if—

(A) avoiding the activity that constitutes such violation is not technically feasible or would create an undue financial hardship on such person; and

(B) such person did not intend, by engaging in such activity, to induce, enable, facilitate, or conceal infringement of a right under this title.

(2) *Digital transmissions.*—

(A) If a digital transmission standard for the placement of copyright management information for a category of works is set in a voluntary, consensus standard-setting process involving a representative cross-section of broadcast stations or cable systems and copyright owners of a category of works that are intended for public performance by such stations or systems, a person identified in paragraph (1) shall not be liable for a violation of subsection (b) with respect to the particular copyright management information addressed by such standard if—

(i) the placement of such information by someone other than such person is not in accordance with such standard; and

(ii) the activity that constitutes such violation is not intended to induce, enable, facilitate, or conceal infringement of a right under this title.

(B) Until a digital transmission standard has been set pursuant to subparagraph (A) with respect to the placement of copyright

17 U.S.C. § 1202

management information for a category of works, a person identified in paragraph (1) shall not be liable for a violation of subsection (b) with respect to such copyright management information, if the activity that constitutes such violation is not intended to induce, enable, facilitate, or conceal infringement of a right under this title, and if—

(i) the transmission of such information by such person would result in a perceptible visual or aural degradation of the digital signal; or

(ii) the transmission of such information by such person would conflict with—

(I) an applicable government regulation relating to transmission of information in a digital signal;

(II) an applicable industry-wide standard relating to the transmission of information in a digital signal that was adopted by a voluntary consensus standards body prior to the effective date of this chapter; or

(III) an applicable industry-wide standard relating to the transmission of information in a digital signal that was adopted in a voluntary, consensus standards-setting process open to participation by a representative cross-section of broadcast stations or cable systems and copyright owners of a category of works that are intended for public performance by such stations or systems.

(3) *Definitions.*—As used in this subsection—

(A) the term "broadcast station" has the meaning given that term in section 3 of the Communications Act of 1934 (47 U.S.C. 153); and

(B) the term "cable system" has the meaning given that term in section 602 of the Communications Act of 1934 (47 U.S.C. 522).

(Oct. 28, 1998, Pub. L. 105-304, §103, 112 Stat. 2863; Aug. 5, 1999, Pub. L. 106-44, §1(e), 113 Stat. 222.)

17 U.S.C. § 1202

§ 1203   Civil remedies

(a) *Civil actions.*—Any person injured by a violation of section 1201 or 1202 may bring a civil action in an appropriate United States district court for such violation.

(b) *Powers of the court.*—In an action brought under subsection (a), the court—

(1) may grant temporary and permanent injunctions on such terms as it deems reasonable to prevent or restrain a violation, but in no event shall impose a prior restraint on free speech or the press protected under the 1st amendment to the Constitution;

(2) at any time while an action is pending, may order the impounding, on such terms as it deems reasonable, of any device or product that is in the custody or control of the alleged violator and that the court has reasonable cause to believe was involved in a violation;

(3) may award damages under subsection (c);

(4) in its discretion may allow the recovery of costs by or against any party other than the United States or an officer thereof;

(5) in its discretion may award reasonable attorney's fees to the prevailing party; and

(6) may, as part of a final judgment or decree finding a violation, order the remedial modification or the destruction of any device or product involved in the violation that is in the custody or control of the violator or has been impounded under paragraph (2).

(c) *Award of damages.*—

(1) *In general.*—Except as otherwise provided in this title, a person committing a violation of section 1201 or 1202 is liable for either—

(A) the actual damages and any additional profits of the violator, as provided in paragraph (2), or

(B) statutory damages, as provided in paragraph (3).

(2) *Actual damages.*—The court shall award to the complaining party the actual damages suffered by the party as a result of the violation, and any profits of the violator that are attributable to the violation and are not taken into account in computing the actual damages, if

17 U.S.C. § 1203

the complaining party elects such damages at any time before final judgment is entered.

(3) *Statutory damages.*—(A) At any time before final judgment is entered, a complaining party may elect to recover an award of statutory damages for each violation of section 1201 in the sum of not less than $200 or more than $2,500 per act of circumvention, device, product, component, offer, or performance of service, as the court considers just.

(B) At any time before final judgment is entered, a complaining party may elect to recover an award of statutory damages for each violation of section 1202 in the sum of not less than $2,500 or more than $25,000.

(4) *Repeated violations.*—In any case in which the injured party sustains the burden of proving, and the court finds, that a person has violated section 1201 or 1202 within 3 years after a final judgment was entered against the person for another such violation, the court may increase the award of damages up to triple the amount that would otherwise be awarded, as the court considers just.

(5) *Innocent violations.*—

(A) *In general.*—The court in its discretion may reduce or remit the total award of damages in any case in which the violator sustains the burden of proving, and the court finds, that the violator was not aware and had no reason to believe that its acts constituted a violation.

(B) *Nonprofit library, archives, educational institutions, or public broadcasting entities.*—

(i) *Definition.*—In this subparagraph, the term "public broadcasting entity" has the meaning given such term under section 118(g).

(ii) *In general.*—In the case of a nonprofit library, archives, educational institution, or public broadcasting entity, the court shall remit damages in any case in which the library, archives, educational institution, or public broadcasting entity sustains the burden of proving, and the court finds, that the library, archives, educational institution, or public broadcasting entity was not aware and had no reason to believe that its acts constituted a violation.

(Oct. 28, 1998, Pub. L. 105-304, §103, 112 Stat. 2863; Nov. 29, 1999, Pub. L. 106-113, §5004, 113 Stat. 1501A-593.)

§ 1204   Criminal offenses and penalties

(a) *In general.*—Any person who violates section 1201 or 1202 willfully and for purposes of commercial advantage or private financial gain—

(1) shall be fined not more than $500,000 or imprisoned for not more than 5 years, or both, for the first offense; and

(2) shall be fined not more than $1,000,000 or imprisoned for not more than 10 years, or both, for any subsequent offense.

(b) *Limitation for nonprofit library, archives, educational institution, or public broadcasting entity.*—Subsection (a) shall not apply to a nonprofit library, archives, educational institution, or public broadcasting entity (as defined under section 118(g)).

(c) *Statute of limitations.*—No criminal proceeding shall be brought under this section unless such proceeding is commenced within 5 years after the cause of action arose.

(Oct. 28, 1998, Pub. L. 105-304, §103, 112 Stat. 2863; Nov. 29, 1999, Pub. L. 106-113, §5004, 113 Stat. 1501A-593.)

§ 1205   Savings clause

Nothing in this chapter abrogates, diminishes, or weakens the provisions of, nor provides any defense or element of mitigation in a criminal prosecution or civil action under, any Federal or State law that prevents the violation of the privacy of an individual in connection with the individual's use of the Internet.

(Oct. 28, 1998, Pub. L. 105-304, §103, 112 Stat. 2863.)

CHAPTER 13—PROTECTION OF ORIGINAL DESIGNS

§ 1301   Designs Protected

(a) *Designs protected.*—

(1) *In general.*—The designer or other owner of an original design of a useful article which makes the article attractive or distinctive in appearance to the purchasing or using public may secure the protection provided by this chapter upon complying with and subject to this chapter.

(2) *Vessel hulls.*—The design of a vessel hull, including a plug or mold, is subject to protection under this chapter, notwithstanding section 1302(4).

(b) *Definitions.*—For the purpose of this chapter, the following terms have the following meanings:

17 U.S.C. § 1301

(1) A design is "original" if it is the result of the designer's creative endeavor that provides a distinguishable variation over prior work pertaining to similar articles which is more than merely trivial and has not been copied from another source.

(2) A "useful article" is a vessel hull, including a plug or mold, which in normal use has an intrinsic utilitarian function that is not merely to portray the appearance of the article or to convey information. An article which normally is part of a useful article shall be deemed to be a useful article.

(3) A "vessel" is a craft—

(A) that is designed and capable of independently steering a course on or through water through its own means of propulsion; and

(B) that is designed and capable of carrying and transporting one or more passengers.

(4) A "hull" is the frame or body of a vessel, including the deck of a vessel, exclusive of masts, sails, yards, and rigging.

(5) A "plug" means a device or model used to make a mold for the purpose of exact duplication, regardless of whether the device or model has an intrinsic utilitarian function that is not only to portray the appearance of the product or to convey information.

(6) A "mold" means a matrix or form in which a substance for material is used, regardless of whether the matrix or form has an intrinsic utilitarian function that is not only to portray the appearance of the product or to convey information.

(Oct. 28, 1998, Pub. L. 105-304, §502, 112 Stat. 2905; Nov. 29, 1999, Pub. L. 106-113, §5005, 113 Stat. 1501A-593.)

§ 1302 Designs not subject to protection

Protection under this chapter shall not be available for a design that is—

(1) not original;

(2) staple or commonplace, such as a standard geometric figure, a familiar symbol, an emblem, or a motif, or another shape, pattern, or configuration which has become standard, common, prevalent, or ordinary;

(3) different from a design excluded by paragraph (2) only in insignificant details or in elements which are variants commonly used in the relevant trades;

(4) dictated solely by a utilitarian function of the article that embodies it; or

(5) embodied in a useful article that was made public by the designer or owner in the United States or a foreign country more than 2 years before the date of the application for registration under this chapter.

(Oct. 28, 1998, Pub. L. 105-304, §502, 112 Stat. 2905; Aug. 5, 1999, Pub. L. 106-44, §1(f), 113 Stat. 222.)

§ 1303   Revisions, adaptations, and rearrangements

Protection for a design under this chapter shall be available notwithstanding the employment in the design of subject matter excluded from protection under section 1302 if the design is a substantial revision, adaptation, or rearrangement of such subject matter. Such protection shall be independent of any subsisting protection in subject matter employed in the design, and shall not be construed as securing any right to subject matter excluded from protection under this chapter or as extending any subsisting protection under this chapter.

(Oct. 28, 1998, Pub. L. 105-304, §502, 112 Stat. 2905.)

§ 1304   Commencement of protection

The protection provided for a design under this chapter shall commence upon the earlier of the date of publication of the registration under section 1313(a) or the date the design is first made public as defined by section 1310(b).

(Oct. 28, 1998, Pub. L. 105-304, §502, 112 Stat. 2905.)

§ 1305   Term of protection

(a) *In general.*—Subject to subsection (b), the protection provided under this chapter for a design shall continue for a term of 10 years beginning on the date of the commencement of protection under section 1304.

(b) *Expiration.*—All terms of protection provided in this section shall run to the end of the calendar year in which they would otherwise expire.

(c) *Termination of rights.*—Upon expiration or termination of protection in a particular design under this chapter, all rights under this chapter in the design shall terminate, regardless of the number of different articles in which the design may have been used during the term of its protection.

(Oct. 28, 1998, Pub. L. 105-304, §502, 112 Stat. 2905.)

§ 1306   Design notice

(a) *Contents of design notice.*—(1) Whenever any design for which protection is sought under this chapter is made public under section 1310(b), the owner of the design shall, subject to the provisions of section 1307, mark it or have it marked legibly with a design notice consisting of—

> (A) the words "Protected Design", the abbreviation "Prot'd Des.", or the letter "D" with a circle, or the symbol *D*;

> (B) the year of the date on which protection for the design commenced; and

> (C) the name of the owner, an abbreviation by which the name can be recognized, or a generally accepted alternative designation of the owner.

Any distinctive identification of the owner may be used for purposes of subparagraph (C) if it has been recorded by the Administrator before the design marked with such identification is registered.

> (2) After registration, the registration number may be used instead of the elements specified in subparagraphs (B) and (C) of paragraph (1).

(b) *Location of notice.*—The design notice shall be so located and applied as to give reasonable notice of design protection while the useful article embodying the design is passing through its normal channels of commerce.

(c) *Subsequent removal of notice.*—When the owner of a design has complied with the provisions of this section, protection under this chapter shall not be affected by the removal, destruction, or obliteration by others of the design notice on an article.

(Oct. 28, 1998, Pub. L. 105-304, §502, 112 Stat. 2905.)

§ 1307   Effect of omission of notice

(a) *Actions with notice.*—Except as provided in subsection (b), the omission of the notice prescribed in section 1306 shall not cause loss of the protection under this chapter or prevent recovery for infringement under this chapter against any person who, after receiving written notice of the design protection, begins an undertaking leading to infringement under this chapter.

(b) *Actions without notice.*—The omission of the notice prescribed in section 1306 shall prevent any recovery under section 1323 against a person who began an undertaking leading to infringement under this chapter before receiving written notice of the design protection. No injunction shall be issued under this chapter with respect to such undertaking unless the owner of the design reimburses that person for any reasonable expenditure or contractual obligation in connection with such undertaking that was incurred before receiving written notice of the design protection, as the court in its discretion directs. The burden of providing written notice of design protection shall be on the owner of the design.

(Oct. 28, 1998, Pub. L. 105-304, §502, 112 Stat. 2905.)

§ 1308   Exclusive rights

The owner of a design protected under this chapter has the exclusive right to--

(1) make, have made, or import, for sale or for use in trade, any useful article embodying that design; and

(2) sell or distribute for sale or for use in trade any useful article embodying that design.

(Oct. 28, 1998, Pub. L. 105-304, §502, 112 Stat. 2905.)

§ 1309   Infringement

(a) *Acts of infringement.*—Except as provided in subsection (b), it shall be infringement of the exclusive rights in a design protected under this chapter for any person, without the consent of the owner of the design, within the United States and during the term of such protection, to—

(1) make, have made, or import, for sale or for use in trade, any infringing article as defined in subsection (e); or

(2) sell or distribute for sale or for use in trade any such infringing article.

(b) *Acts of sellers and distributors.*—A seller or distributor of an infringing article who did not make or import the article shall be deemed to have infringed on a design protected under this chapter only if that person—

(1) induced or acted in collusion with a manufacturer to make, or an importer to import such article, except that merely purchasing or giving an order to purchase such article in the ordinary course of business shall not of itself constitute such inducement or collusion; or

(2) refused or failed, upon the request of the owner of the design, to make a prompt and full disclosure of that person's source of such article, and that person orders or reorders such article after receiving notice by registered or certified mail of the protection subsisting in the design.

(c) *Acts without knowledge.*—It shall not be infringement under this section to make, have made, import, sell, or distribute, any article embodying a design which was created without knowledge that a design was protected under this chapter and was copied from such protected design.

(d) *Acts in ordinary course of business.*—A person who incorporates into that person's product of manufacture an infringing article acquired from others in the ordinary course of business, or who, without knowledge of the protected design embodied in an infringing article, makes or processes the infringing article for the account of another person in the ordinary course of business, shall not be deemed to have infringed the rights in that design under this chapter except under a condition contained in paragraph (1) or (2) of subsection (b). Accepting an order or reorder from the source of the infringing article shall be deemed ordering or reordering within the meaning of subsection (b)(2).

(e) *Infringing article defined.*—As used in this section, an "infringing article" is any article the design of which has been copied from a design

17 U.S.C. § 1309

protected under this chapter, without the consent of the owner of the protected design. An infringing article is not an illustration or picture of a protected design in an advertisement, book, periodical, newspaper, photograph, broadcast, motion picture, or similar medium. A design shall not be deemed to have been copied from a protected design if it is original and not substantially similar in appearance to a protected design.

(f) *Establishing originality.*—The party to any action or proceeding under this chapter who alleges rights under this chapter in a design shall have the burden of establishing the design's originality whenever the opposing party introduces an earlier work which is identical to such design, or so similar as to make prima facie showing that such design was copied from such work.

(g) *Reproduction for teaching or analysis.*—It is not an infringement of the exclusive rights of a design owner for a person to reproduce the design in a useful article or in any other form solely for the purpose of teaching, analyzing, or evaluating the appearance, concepts, or techniques embodied in the design, or the function of the useful article embodying the design.

(Oct. 28, 1998, Pub. L. 105-304, §502, 112 Stat. 2905.)

§ 1310   Application for registration

(a) *Time limit for application for registration.*—Protection under this chapter shall be lost if application for registration of the design is not made within 2 years after the date on which the design is first made public.

(b) *When design is made public.*—A design is made public when an existing useful article embodying the design is anywhere publicly exhibited, publicly distributed, or offered for sale or sold to the public by the owner of the design or with the owner's consent.

(c) *Application by owner of design.*—Application for registration may be made by the owner of the design.

(d) *Contents of application.*—The application for registration shall be made to the Administrator and shall state—

   (1) the name and address of the designer or designers of the design;

(2) the name and address of the owner if different from the designer;

(3) the specific name of the useful article embodying the design;

(4) the date, if any, that the design was first made public, if such date was earlier than the date of the application;

(5) affirmation that the design has been fixed in a useful article; and

(6) such other information as may be required by the Administrator.

The application for registration may include a description setting forth the salient features of the design, but the absence of such a description shall not prevent registration under this chapter.

(e) *Sworn statement.*—The application for registration shall be accompanied by a statement under oath by the applicant or the applicant's duly authorized agent or representative, setting forth, to the best of the applicant's knowledge and belief—

(1) that the design is original and was created by the designer or designers named in the application;

(2) that the design has not previously been registered on behalf of the applicant or the applicant's predecessor in title; and

(3) that the applicant is the person entitled to protection and to registration under this chapter.

If the design has been made public with the design notice prescribed in section 1306, the statement shall also describe the exact form and position of the design notice.

(f) *Effect of errors.*—(1) Error in any statement or assertion as to the utility of the useful article named in the application under this section, the design of which is sought to be registered, shall not affect the protection secured under this chapter.

(2) Errors in omitting a joint designer or in naming an alleged joint designer shall not affect the validity of the registration, or the actual ownership or the protection of the design, unless it is shown that the error occurred with deceptive intent.

(g) *Design made in scope of employment.*—In a case in which the design was made within the regular scope of the designer's employment and individual authorship of the design is difficult or impossible to ascribe and the application so states, the name and address of the employer for whom the design was made may be stated instead of that of the individual designer.

(h) *Pictorial representation of design.*—The application for registration shall be accompanied by two copies of a drawing or other pictorial representation of the useful article embodying the design, having one or more views, adequate to show the design, in a form and style suitable for reproduction, which shall be deemed a part of the application.

(i) *Design in more than one useful article.*—If the distinguishing elements of a design are in substantially the same form in different useful articles, the design shall be protected as to all such useful articles when protected as to one of them, but not more than one registration shall be required for the design.

(j) *Application for more than one design.*—More than one design may be included in the same application under such conditions as may be prescribed by the Administrator. For each design included in an application the fee prescribed for a single design shall be paid.

(Oct. 28, 1998, Pub. L. 105-304, §502, 112 Stat. 2905.)

§ 1311   Benefit of earlier filing date in foreign country

An application for registration of a design filed in the United States by any person who has, or whose legal representative or predecessor or successor in title has, previously filed an application for registration of the same design in a foreign country which extends to designs of owners who are citizens of the United States, or to applications filed under this chapter, similar protection to that provided under this chapter shall have that same effect as if filed in the United States on the date on which the application was first filed in such foreign country, if the application in the United States is filed within 6 months after the earliest date on which any such foreign application was filed.

(Oct. 28, 1998, Pub. L. 105-304, §502, 112 Stat. 2905.)

§ 1312   Oaths and acknowledgments

(a) *In general.*—Oaths and acknowledgments required by this chapter—

   (1) may be made—

(A) before any person in the United States authorized by law to administer oaths; or

(B) when made in a foreign country, before any diplomatic or consular officer of the United States authorized to administer oaths, or before any official authorized to administer oaths in the foreign country concerned, whose authority shall be proved by a certificate of a diplomatic or consular officer of the United States; and

(2) shall be valid if they comply with the laws of the State or country where made.

(b) *Written declaration in lieu of oath.*—(1) The Administrator may by rule prescribe that any document which is to be filed under this chapter in the Office of the Administrator and which is required by any law, rule, or other regulation to be under oath, may be subscribed to by a written declaration in such form as the Administrator may prescribe, and such declaration shall be in lieu of the oath otherwise required.

(2) Whenever a written declaration under paragraph (1) is used, the document containing the declaration shall state that willful false statements are punishable by fine or imprisonment, or both, pursuant to section 1001 of title 18, and may jeopardize the validity of the application or document or a registration resulting therefrom.

(Oct. 28, 1998, Pub. L. 105-304, §502, 112 Stat. 2905.)

§ 1313   Examination of application and issue or refusal of registration

(a) *Determination of registrability of design; registration.*—Upon the filing of an application for registration in proper form under section 1310, and upon payment of the fee prescribed under section 1316, the Administrator shall determine whether or not the application relates to a design which on its face appears to be subject to protection under this chapter, and, if so, the Register shall register the design. Registration under this subsection shall be announced by publication. The date of registration shall be the date of publication.

(b) *Refusal to register; reconsideration.*—If, in the judgment of the Administrator, the application for registration relates to a design which on its face is not subject to protection under this chapter, the Administrator shall send to the applicant a notice of refusal to register and the grounds for the refusal. Within 3 months after the date on which the notice of refusal is sent, the applicant may, by written request, seek reconsideration of the application. After consideration of such a request, the Administrator shall either register the design or send to the applicant a notice of final refusal to register.

(c) *Application to cancel registration.*—Any person who believes he or she is or will be damaged by a registration under this chapter may, upon payment of the prescribed fee, apply to the Administrator at any time to cancel the registration on the ground that the design is not subject to protection under this chapter, stating the reasons for the request. Upon receipt of an application for cancellation, the Administrator shall send to the owner of the design, as shown in the records of the Office of the Administrator, a notice of the application, and the owner shall have a period of 3 months after the date on which such notice is mailed in which to present arguments to the Administrator for support of the validity of the registration. The Administrator shall also have the authority to establish, by regulation, conditions under which the opposing parties may appear and be heard in support of their arguments. If, after the periods provided for the presentation of arguments have expired, the Administrator determines that the applicant for cancellation has established that the design is not subject to protection under this chapter, the Administrator shall order the registration stricken from the record. Cancellation under this subsection shall be announced by publication, and notice of the Administrator's final determination with respect to any application for cancellation shall be sent to the applicant and to the owner of record. Costs of the cancellation procedure under this subsection shall be borne by the nonprevailing party or parties, and the Administrator shall have the authority to assess and collect such costs.

(Oct. 28, 1998, Pub. L. 105-304, §502, 112 Stat. 2905; Nov. 29, 1999, Pub. L. 106-113, §5005, 113 Stat. 1501A-593.)

§ 1314   Certification of registration

Certificates of registration shall be issued in the name of the United States under the seal of the Office of the Administrator and shall be recorded in the official records of the Office. The certificate shall state the name of the useful article, the date of filing of the application, the date of registration, and the date the design was made public, if earlier than the date of filing of the application, and shall contain a reproduction of the drawing or other pictorial representation of the design. If a description of the salient features of the design appears in the application, the description shall also appear in the certificate. A certificate of registration shall be admitted in any court as prima facie evidence of the facts stated in the certificate.

(Oct. 28, 1998, Pub. L. 105-304, §502, 112 Stat. 2905.)

§ 1315   Publication of announcements and indexes

(a) *Publications of the administrator.*—The Administrator shall publish lists and indexes of registered designs and cancellations of designs and may also publish the drawings or other pictorial representations of registered designs for sale or other distribution.

(b) *File of representatives of registered designs.*—The Administrator shall establish and maintain a file of the drawings or other pictorial representations of registered designs. The file shall be available for use by the public under such conditions as the Administrator may prescribe.

(Oct. 28, 1998, Pub. L. 105-304, §502, 112 Stat. 2905.)

§ 1316   Fees

The Administrator shall by regulation set reasonable fees for the filing of applications to register designs under this chapter and for other services relating to the administration of this chapter, taking into consideration the cost of providing these services and the benefit of a public record.

(Oct. 28, 1998, Pub. L. 105-304, §502, 112 Stat. 2905.)

§ 1317   Regulations

The Administrator may establish regulations for the administration of this chapter.

(Oct. 28, 1998, Pub. L. 105-304, §502, 112 Stat. 2905.)

§ 1318   Copies of records

Upon payment of the prescribed fee, any person may obtain a certified copy of any official record of the Office of the Administrator that relates to this chapter. That copy shall be admissible in evidence with the same effect as the original.

(Oct. 28, 1998, Pub. L. 105-304, §502, 112 Stat. 2905.)

§ 1319   Correction of errors in certificates

The Administrator may, by a certificate of correction under seal, correct any error in a registration incurred through the fault of the Office, or, upon payment of the required fee, any error of a clerical or typographical nature occurring in good faith but not through the fault of the Office. Such registration, together with the certificate, shall thereafter have the same effect as if it had been originally issued in such corrected form.

(Oct. 28, 1998, Pub. L. 105-304, §502, 112 Stat. 2905.)

§ 1320   Ownership and transfer

(a) *Property right in design.*—The property right in a design subject to protection under this chapter shall vest in the designer, the legal representatives of a deceased designer or of one under legal incapacity, the employer for whom the designer created the design in the case of a design made within the regular scope of the designer's employment, or a person to whom the rights of the designer or of such employer have been transferred. The person in whom the property right is vested shall be considered the owner of the design.

(b) *Transfer of property right.*—The property right in a registered design, or a design for which an application for registration has been or may be filed, may be assigned, granted, conveyed, or mortgaged by an instrument in writing, signed by the owner, or may be bequeathed by will.

(c) *Oath or acknowledgment of transfer.*—An oath or acknowledgment under section 1312 shall be prima facie evidence of the execution of an assignment, grant, conveyance, or mortgage under subsection (b).

(d) *Recordation of transfer.*—An assignment, grant, conveyance, or mortgage under subsection (b) shall be void as against any subsequent purchaser or mortgagee for a valuable consideration, unless it is recorded in the Office of the Administrator within 3 months after its date of execution or before the date of such subsequent purchase or mortgage.

(Oct. 28, 1998, Pub. L. 105-304, §502, 112 Stat. 2905; Aug. 5, 1999, Pub. L. 106-44, §1(f), 113 Stat. 222.)

§ 1321 Remedy for infringement

(a) *In general.*—The owner of a design is entitled, after issuance of a certificate of registration of the design under this chapter, to institute an action for any infringement of the design.

(b) *Review of refusal to register.*— (1) Subject to paragraph (2), the owner of a design may seek judicial review of a final refusal of the Administrator to register the design under this chapter by bringing a civil action, and may in the same action, if the court adjudges the design subject to protection under this chapter, enforce the rights in that design under this chapter.

(2) The owner of a design may seek judicial review under this section if—

(A) the owner has previously duly filed and prosecuted to final refusal an application in proper form for registration of the design;

(B) the owner causes a copy of the complaint in the action to be delivered to the Administrator within 10 days after the commencement of the action; and

(C) the defendant has committed acts in respect to the design which would constitute infringement with respect to a design protected under this chapter.

(c) *Administrator as party to action.*—The Administrator may, at the Administrator's option, become a party to the action with respect to the issue of registrability of the design claim by entering an appearance within 60 days after being served with the complaint, but the failure of the Administrator to become a party shall not deprive the court of jurisdiction to determine that issue.

(d) *Use of arbitration to resolve dispute.*—The parties to an infringement dispute under this chapter, within such time as may be specified by the Administrator by regulation, may determine the dispute, or any aspect of the dispute, by arbitration. Arbitration shall be governed by title 9. The parties shall give notice of any arbitration award to the Administrator, and such award shall, as between the parties to the arbitration, be dispositive of the issues to which it relates. The arbitration award shall be unenforceable until such notice is given. Nothing in this subsection shall preclude the Administrator from determining whether a design is subject to registration in a cancellation proceeding under section 1313(c).

(Oct. 28, 1998, Pub. L. 105-304, §502, 112 Stat. 2905.)

§ 1322   Injunctions

(a) *In general.*—A court having jurisdiction over actions under this chapter may grant injunctions in accordance with the principles of equity to prevent infringement of a design under this chapter, including, in its discretion, prompt relief by temporary restraining orders and preliminary injunctions.

(b) *Damages for injunctive relief wrongfully obtained.*—A seller or distributor who suffers damage by reason of injunctive relief wrongfully obtained under this section has a cause of action against the applicant for such injunctive relief and may recover such relief as may be appropriate, including damages for lost profits, cost of materials, loss of good will, and punitive damages in instances where the injunctive relief was sought in bad faith, and, unless the court finds extenuating circumstances, reasonable attorney's fees.

(Oct. 28, 1998, Pub. L. 105-304, §502, 112 Stat. 2905.)

§ 1323   Recovery for infringement

(a) *Damages.*—Upon a finding for the claimant in an action for infringement under this chapter, the court shall award the claimant damages adequate to compensate for the infringement. In addition, the court may increase the damages to such amount, not exceeding $50,000 or $1 per copy, whichever is greater, as the court determines to be just. The damages awarded shall constitute compensation and not a penalty. The court may receive expert testimony as an aid to the determination of damages.

(b) *Infringer's profits.*—As an alternative to the remedies provided in subsection (a), the court may award the claimant the infringer's profits resulting from the sale of the copies if the court finds that the infringer's sales are reasonably related to the use of the claimant's design. In such a case, the claimant shall be required to prove only the amount of the infringer's sales and the infringer shall be required to prove its expenses against such sales.

(c) *Statute of limitations.*—No recovery under subsection (a) or (b) shall be had for any infringement committed more than 3 years before the date on which the complaint is filed.

(d) *Attorney's fees.*—In an action for infringement under this chapter, the court may award reasonable attorney's fees to the prevailing party.

(e) *Disposition of infringing and other articles.*—The court may order that all infringing articles, and any plates, molds, patterns, models, or other means specifically adapted for making the articles, be delivered up for destruction or other disposition as the court may direct.

(Oct. 28, 1998, Pub. L. 105-304, §502, 112 Stat. 2905.)

§ 1324   Power of court over registration

In any action involving the protection of a design under this chapter, the court, when appropriate, may order registration of a design under this chapter or the cancellation of such a registration. Any such order shall be certified by the court to the Administrator, who shall make an appropriate entry upon the record.

(Oct. 28, 1998, Pub. L. 105-304, §502, 112 Stat. 2905.)

§ 1325   Liability for action on registration fraudulently obtained

Any person who brings an action for infringement knowing that registration of the design was obtained by a false or fraudulent representation materially affecting the rights under this chapter, shall be liable in the sum of $10,000, or such part of that amount as the court may determine. That amount shall be to compensate the defendant and shall be charged against the plaintiff and paid to the defendant, in addition to such costs and attorney's fees of the defendant as may be assessed by the court.

(Oct. 28, 1998, Pub. L. 105-304, §502, 112 Stat. 2905.)

17 U.S.C. § 1325

§ 1326   Penalty for false marking

(a) *In general.*—Whoever, for the purpose of deceiving the public, marks upon, applies to, or uses in advertising in connection with an article made, used, distributed, or sold, a design which is not protected under this chapter, a design notice specified in section 1306, or any other words or symbols importing that the design is protected under this chapter, knowing that the design is not so protected, shall pay a civil fine of not more than $500 for each such offense.

(b) *Suit by private persons.*—Any person may sue for the penalty established by subsection (a), in which event one-half of the penalty shall be awarded to the person suing and the remainder shall be awarded to the United States.

(Oct. 28, 1998, Pub. L. 105-304, §502, 112 Stat. 2905.)

§ 1327   Penalty for false representation

Whoever knowingly makes a false representation materially affecting the rights obtainable under this chapter for the purpose of obtaining registration of a design under this chapter shall pay a penalty of not less than $500 and not more than $1,000, and any rights or privileges that individual may have in the design under this chapter shall be forfeited.

(Oct. 28, 1998, Pub. L. 105-304, §502, 112 Stat. 2905.)

§ 1328   Enforcement by Treasury and Postal Service

(a) *Regulations.*—The Secretary of the Treasury and the United States Postal Service shall separately or jointly issue regulations for the enforcement of the rights set forth in section 1308 with respect to importation. Such regulations may require, as a condition for the exclusion of articles from the United States, that the person seeking exclusion take any one or more of the following actions:

(1) Obtain a court order enjoining, or an order of the International Trade Commission under section 337 of the Tariff Act of 1930 excluding, importation of the articles.

(2) Furnish proof that the design involved is protected under this chapter and that the importation of the articles would infringe the rights in the design under this chapter.

(3) Post a surety bond for any injury that may result if the detention or exclusion of the articles proves to be unjustified.

(b) Seizure and forfeiture—Articles imported in violation of the rights set forth in section 1308 are subject to seizure and forfeiture in the same manner as property imported in violation of the customs laws. Any such forfeited articles shall be destroyed as directed by the Secretary of the Treasury or the court, as the case may be, except that the articles may be returned to the country of export whenever it is shown to the satisfaction of the Secretary of the Treasury that the importer had no reasonable grounds for believing that his or her acts constituted a violation of the law.

(Oct. 28, 1998, Pub. L. 105-304, §502, 112 Stat. 2905.)

§ 1329   Relation to design patent law

The issuance of a design patent under title 35, United States Code, for an original design for an article of manufacture shall terminate any protection of the original design under this chapter.

(Oct. 28, 1998, Pub. L. 105-304, §502, 112 Stat. 2905.)

§ 1330   Common law and other rights unaffected Designs Protected

Nothing in this chapter shall annul or limit—

(1) common law or other rights or remedies, if any, available to or held by any person with respect to a design which has not been registered under this chapter; or

(2) any right under the trademark laws or any right protected against unfair competition.

(Oct. 28, 1998, Pub. L. 105-304, §502, 112 Stat. 2905.)

§ 1331   Administrator; Office of the Administrator

In this chapter, the "Administrator" is the Register of Copyrights, and the "Office of the Administrator" and the "Office" refer to the Copyright Office of the Library of Congress.

(Oct. 28, 1998, Pub. L. 105-304, §502, 112 Stat. 2905.)

17 U.S.C. § 1331

§ 1332   No retroactive effect

Protection under this chapter shall not be available for any design that has been made public under section 1310(b) before the effective date of this chapter.

(Oct. 28, 1998, Pub. L. 105-304, §502, 112 Stat. 2905.)

Part 5

OTHER STATUTES

OTHER STATUTES

Note.—Some sections, or portions of sections, of other titles of the United States Code and of the District of Columbia Code relating to patents, trademarks, copyrights, trade secrets, or to the Patent and Trademark Office and the Copyright Office, are reprinted or noted here for convenience. This collection does not purport to be complete.

I. REMEDIES FOR INFRINGEMENT OF PATENTS AND TRADEMARKS AND OTHER ACTIONS

A. Federal District Courts—Jurisdiction, Venue and Service of Process; ITC-Related Provisions

28 U.S.C. § 1338 **Patents, plant variety protection, copyrights, mask works, designs, trademarks, and unfair competition**

(a) The district courts shall have original jurisdiction of any civil action arising under any Act of Congress relating to patents, plant variety protection, copyrights and trademarks. Such jurisdiction shall be exclusive of the courts of the states in patent, plant variety protection and copyright cases.

(b) The district courts shall have original jurisdiction of any civil action asserting a claim of unfair competition when joined with a substantial and related claim under the copyright, patent, plant variety protection or trademark laws.

(c) Subsections (a) and (b) apply to exclusive rights in mask works under chapter 9 of title 17, and to exclusive rights in designs under chapter 13 of title 17, to the same extent as such subsections apply to copyrights.

(June 25, 1948, ch. 646, §1, 62 Stat. 931; Dec. 24, 1970, Pub. L. 91-577, §143, 84 Stat. 1559; Nov. 19, 1988, Pub. L. 100-702, §1020, 102 Stat. 4671, Oct. 28, 1998, Pub. L. 105-304, §503(b), 112 Stat. 2917; Nov. 29, 1999, Pub. L. 106-113, §3009, 113 Stat. 1501A-551.)

28 U.S.C. § 1368 **Counterclaims in unfair practices in international trade**

The district courts shall have original jurisdiction of any civil action based on a counterclaim raised pursuant to section 337(c) of the Tariff Act of 1930, to the extent that it arises out of the transaction or occurrence that is the subject mater of the opposing party's claim in the proceeding under section 337(a) of that Act.

(Dec. 8, 1994, Pub. L. 103-465, §321, 108 Stat. 4943.)

28 U.S.C. § 1391 Venue generally

(a) A civil action wherein jurisdiction is founded only on diversity of citizenship may, except as otherwise provided by law, be brought only in (1) a judicial district where any defendant resides, if all defendants reside in the same State, (2) a judicial district in which a substantial part of the events or omissions giving rise to the claim occurred, or a substantial part of property that is the subject of the action is situated, or (3) a judicial district in which any defendant is subject to personal jurisdiction at the time the action is commenced, if there is no district in which the action may otherwise be brought.

(b) A civil action wherein jurisdiction is not founded solely on diversity of citizenship may, except as otherwise provided by law, be brought only in (1) a judicial district where any defendant resides, if all defendants reside in the same State, (2) a judicial district in which a substantial part of the events or omissions giving rise to the claim occurred, or a substantial part of property that is the subject of the action is situated, or (3) a judicial district in which any defendant may be found, if there is no district in which the action may otherwise be brought.

(c) For purposes of venue under this chapter, a defendant that is a corporation shall be deemed to reside in any judicial district in which it is subject to personal jurisdiction at the time the action is commenced. In a State which has more than one judicial district and in which a defendant that is a corporation is subject to personal jurisdiction at the time an action is commenced, such corporation shall be deemed to reside in any district in that State within which its contacts would be sufficient to subject it to personal jurisdiction if that district were a separate State, and, if there is no such district, the corporation shall be deemed to reside in the district within which it has the most significant contacts.

(d) An alien may be sued in any district.

* * *

(June 25, 1948, ch. 646, §1, 62 Stat. 935; Oct. 5, 1962, Pub. L. 87-748, §2, 76 Stat. 744; Dec. 23, 1963, Pub. L. 88-234, 77 Stat. 473; Nov. 2, 1966, Pub. L. 89-714, §§1, 2, 80 Stat. 1111; Oct. 21, 1976, Pub. L. 94-583, §§3, 5, 90 Stat. 2721, 2897; Nov. 19, 1988, Pub. L. 100-702, §1013, 102 Stat. 4669; Dec. 1, 1990, Pub. L. 101-650, §311, 104 Stat. 5114; Dec. 9, 1991, Pub. L. 102-198, §3, 105 Stat. 1623; Oct. 29, 1992, Pub. L. 102-572, §902(a), 106 Stat. 4516; Oct. 3, 1995, Pub. L. 104-34, §1, 109 Stat. 293.)

28 U.S.C. § 1400   Patents and copyrights, mask works, and designs

(a) Civil actions, suits, or proceedings arising under any Act of Congress relating to copyrights or exclusive rights in mask works or designs may be instituted in the district in which the defendant or his agent resides or may be found.

(b) Any civil action for patent infringement may be brought in the judicial district where the defendant resides, or where the defendant has committed acts of infringement and has a regular and established place of business.

(June 25, 1948, ch. 646, §1, 62 Stat. 936; Nov. 19, 1988, Pub. L. 100-702, §1020, 102 Stat. 4671; Oct. 28, 1998, Pub. L. 105-304, §503(c), 112 Stat. 2917.)

28 U.S.C. § 1446   Procedure for removal

* * *

(f) With respect to any counterclaim removed to a district court pursuant to section 337(c) of the Tariff Act of 1930, the district court shall resolve such counterclaim in the same manner as an original complaint under the Federal Rules of Civil Procedure, except that the payment of a filing fee shall not be required in such cases and the counterclaim shall relate back to the date of the original complaint in the proceeding before the International Trade Commission under section 337 of that Act.

(Dec. 8, 1994, Pub. L. 103-465, §321, 108 Stat. 4943.)

28 U.S.C. § 1498   Patent and copyright cases

(a) Whenever an invention described in and covered by a patent of the United States is used or manufactured by or for the United States without license of the owner thereof or lawful right to use or manufacture the same, the owner's remedy shall be by action against the United States in the United States Court of Federal Claims for the recovery of his reasonable and entire compensation for such use and manufacture. Reasonable and entire compensation shall include the owner's reasonable costs, including reasonable fees for expert witnesses and attorneys, in pursuing the action if the owner is an independent inventor, a nonprofit organization, or an entity that had no more than 500 employees at any time during the 5-year period preceding the use or manufacture of the patented invention by or for the United States. Notwithstanding the preceding sentences, unless the action has been pending for more than 10 years from the time of filing to the time that the owner applies for such costs and fees, reasonable and entire compensation shall not include such costs and fees if the court finds that the position of the United States was substantially justified or that special circumstances make an award unjust.*

For the purposes of this section, the use or manufacture of an invention described in and covered by a patent of the United States by a contractor, a subcontractor, or any person, firm, or corporation for the Government and with the authorization or consent of the Government, shall be construed as use or manufacture for the United States.

The court shall not award compensation under this section if the claim is based on the use or manufacture by or for the United States of any article owned, leased, used by, or in the possession of the United States prior to July 1, 1918.

A Government employee shall have the right to bring suit against the Government under this section except where he was in a position to order, influence, or induce use of the invention by the Government. This section shall not confer a right of action on any patentee or any assignee of such patentee with respect to any invention discovered or invented by a person while in the employment or service of the United States, where the invention was related to the official functions of the employee, in cases in which such functions included research and development, or in the making of which Government time, materials or facilities were used.

(b) Hereafter, whenever the copyright in any work protected under the copyright laws of the United States shall be infringed by the United States, by a corporation owned or controlled by the United States, or by a contractor, subcontractor, or any person, firm, or corporation acting for the Government and with the authorization or consent of the Government, the exclusive action which may be brought for such infringement shall be an action by the copyright owner

---

* *Ed. Note.* Pursuant to section 1(b) of Public Law 104-308, the amendment made by section 1(a) applies to actions under section 1498(a) of title 28, United States Code, that are pending on, or brought on or after, the date of the enactment, which was October 19, 1996.

28 U.S.C. § 1498

against the United States in the Court of Federal Claims for the recovery of his reasonable and entire compensation as damages for such infringement, including the minimum statutory damages as set forth in section 504(c) of title 17, United States Code: *Provided,* That a Government employee shall have a right of action against the Government under this subsection except where he was in a position to order, influence, or induce use of the copyrighted work by the Government. *Provided, however,* That this subsection shall not confer a right of action on any copyright owner or any assignee of such owner with respect to any copyrighted work prepared by a person while in the employment or service of the United States, where the copyrighted work was prepared as a part of the official functions of the employee, or in the preparation of which Government time, material, or facilities were used: *And provided further,* That before such action against the United States has been instituted the appropriate corporation owned or controlled by the United States or the head of the appropriate department or agency of the Government, as the case may be, is authorized to enter into an agreement with the copyright owner in full settlement and compromise for the damages accruing to him by reason of such infringement and to settle the claim administratively out of available appropriations.

Except as otherwise provided by law, no recovery shall be had for any infringement of a copyright covered by this subsection committed more than three years prior to the filing of the complaint or counterclaim for infringement in the action, except that the period between the date of receipt of a written claim for compensation by the department or agency of the Government or corporation owned or controlled by the United States, as the case may be, having authority to settle such claim and the date of mailing by the Government of a notice to the claimant that his claim has been denied shall not be counted as a part of the three years, unless suit is brought before the last-mentioned date.

(c) The provisions of this section shall not apply to any claim arising in a foreign country.

*   *   *

28 U.S.C. § 1498

(e) Subsections (b) and (c) of this section apply to exclusive rights in mask works under chapter 9 of title 17, and to exclusive rights in designs under chapter 13 of title 17, to the same extent as such subsections apply to copyrights.

(June 25, 1948, ch. 646, §1, 62 Stat. 941; May 24, 1949, ch. 139, §87, 63 Stat. 102; Oct. 31, 1951, ch. 655, §50, 65 Stat. 727; July 17, 1952, ch. 930, 66 Stat. 757; Sept. 8, 1960, Pub. L. 86-726, §§1, 4, 74 Stat. 855, 856; Oct. 19, 1976, Pub. L. 94-553, §105, 90 Stat. 2599; Apr. 2, 1982, Pub. L. 97-164, §133, 96 Stat. 40; Nov. 19, 1988, Pub. L. 100-702, §1020, 102 Stat. 4671; Oct. 29, 1992, Pub. L. 102-572, §902(a), 106 Stat. 4516; Oct. 19, 1996, Pub. L. 104-308 §1(a), 110 Stat. 3814; Dec. 16, 1997, Pub. L. 105-147, §3, 111 Stat. 2680; Oct. 28, 1998, Pub. L. 105-304, §503(d), 112 Stat. 2917.)

28 U.S.C. § 1659　Stay of certain actions pending disposition of related proceedings before the United States International Trade Commission

(a) *Stay.*—In a civil action involving parties that are also parties to a proceeding before the United States International Trade Commission under section 337 of the Tariff Act of 1930, at the request of a party to the civil action that is also a respondent in the proceeding before the Commission, the district court shall stay, until the determination of the Commission becomes final, proceedings in the civil action with respect to any claim that involves the same issues involved in the proceeding before the Commission, but only if such request is made within—

(1) 30 days after the party is named as a respondent in the proceeding before the Commission, or

(2) 30 days after the district court action is filed,

whichever is later.

(b) *Use of Commission record.*—Notwithstanding section 337(n)(l) of the Tariff Act of 1930, after dissolution of a stay under subsection (a), the record of the proceeding before the United States International Trade Commission shall be transmitted to the district court and shall be admissible in the civil action, subject to such protective order as the district court determines necessary, to the extent permitted under the Federal Rules of Evidence and the Federal Rules of Civil Procedure.

(Dec. 8, 1994, Pub. L. 103-465, §321, 108 Stat. 4943.)

28 U.S.C. § 1694   Patent infringement action

In a patent infringement action commenced in a district where the defendant is not a resident but has a regular and established place of business, service of process, summons or subpoena upon such defendant may be made upon his agent or agents conducting such business.

(June 25, 1948, ch. 646, §1, 62 Stat. 945.)

28 U.S.C. § 1928   Patent infringement actions; disclaimer not filed

Whenever a judgment is rendered for the plaintiff in any patent infringement action involving a part of a patent and it appears that the patentee, in his specifications, claimed to be, but was not, the original and first inventor or discoverer of any material or substantial part of the thing patented, no costs shall be included in such judgment, unless the proper disclaimer has been filed in the United States Patent and Trademark Office prior to the commencement of the action.

(June 25, 1948, ch. 646, §1, 62 Stat. 957; Nov. 29, 1999, Pub. L. 106-113, §4732, 113 Stat. 1501A-581.)

B. COURTS OF APPEAL—JURISDICTION—U.S. COURT OF APPEALS FOR THE FEDERAL CIRCUIT

28 U.S.C. § 44   Appointment, tenure, residence and salary of circuit judges

(a) The President shall appoint, by and with the advice and consent of the Senate, circuit judges for the several circuits as follows:

Circuits	Number of judges
District of Columbia	12
First	6
Second	13
Third	14
Fourth	15
Fifth	17

* * *

(Apr. 2, 1982, Pub. L. 97-164, §102, 96 Stat. 25; Dec. 1, 1990, Pub. L. 101-650, §201, 104 Stat. 5099.)

Pub. L. 97-164   (Related Provisions)

Ed. Note: Sections 165, 166, and 168 of Pub. L. 97-164 contain miscellaneous provisions regarding the membership of the United States Court of Appeals for the Federal Circuit, as follows:

§165. Continued Service of Current Judges.—The judges of the United States Court of Claims and of the United States Court of Customs and Patent Appeals in regular active service on the effective date of this Act shall continue in office as judges of the United States Court of Appeals for the Federal Circuit. Senior judges of the United States Court of Claims and of the United States Court of Customs and Patent Appeals on the effective date of this Act shall continue in office as senior judges of the United States Court of Appeals for the Federal Circuit.

§166. Appointment of Chief Judge of Court of Appeals for the Federal Circuit.— Notwithstanding the provisions of section 45(a) of title 28, United States Code, the first chief judge of the United States Court of Appeals for the Federal Circuit shall be the Chief Judge of the United States Court of Claims or the Chief Judge of the United States Court of Customs and Patent Appeals, whoever has served longer as chief judge of his court. Notwithstanding section 45 of title 28, United States Code, whichever of the two chief judges does not become the first chief judge of the United States Court of Appeals for the Federal Circuit under the preceding sentence shall, while in active service, have precedence and be deemed senior in commission over all the circuit judges of the United States Court of Appeals for the Federal Circuit (other than the first chief judge of that circuit). When the person who serves as chief judge of the United States Court of Appeals for the Federal Circuit vacates that position, the position shall be filled

in accordance with section 45(a) of title 28, United States Code, as modified by the preceding sentence of this section.

§168. *Appointment of Judges by the President.*—The Congress—

(1) takes notice of the fact that the quality of the Federal judiciary is determined by the competence and experience of its judges; and

(2) suggests that the President, in nominating individuals to judgeships on the United States Court of Appeals for the Federal Circuit and the United States Claims Court [now the U.S. Court of Federal Claims—ed.], select from a broad range of qualified individuals.

(Apr. 2, 1982, Pub. L. 97-164, §§165, 166, & 168, 96 Stat. 51.)

28 U.S.C. § 46   Assignment of judges; divisions; hearings; quorum

(a) Circuit judges shall sit on the court and its panel in such order and at such times as the court directs.

(b) In each circuit the court may authorize the hearing and determination of cases and controversies by separate panels, each consisting of three judges, at least a majority of whom shall be judges of that court, unless such judges cannot sit because recused or disqualified, or unless the chief judge of that court certifies that there is an emergency including, but not limited to, the unavailability of a judge of the court because of illness. Such panels shall sit at the times and places and hear the cases and controversies assigned as the court directs. The United States Court of Appeals for the Federal Circuit shall determine by rule a procedure for the rotation of judges from panel to panel to ensure that all of the judges sit on a representative cross section of the cases heard and, notwithstanding the first sentence of this subsection, may determine by rule the number of judges, not less than three, who constitute a panel.

(c) Cases and controversies shall be heard and determined by a court or panel of not more than three judges (except that the United States Court of Appeals for the Federal Circuit may sit in panels of more than three judges if its rules so provide), unless a hearing or rehearing before the court in banc is ordered by a majority of the circuit judges of the circuit who are in regular active service. A court in banc shall consist of all circuit judges in regular active service, or such number of judges as may be prescribed in accordance with section 6 of Public Law 95-486 (92 Stat. 1633), except that any senior circuit judge of the circuit shall be eligible

(1) to participate, at his election and upon designation and assignment pursuant to section 294(c) of this title and the rules of the circuit, as a member of an in banc court reviewing a decision of a panel of which such judge was a member, or (2) to continue to participate in the decision of a case or controversy that was heard or reheard by the court in banc at a time when such judge was in regular active service.

(d) A majority of the number of judges authorized to constitute a court or panel thereof, as provided in paragraph (c), shall constitute a quorum.

(June 25, 1948, ch. 646, §1, 62 Stat. 871; Nov. 13, 1963, Pub. L. 88-176, §1, 77 Stat. 331; Oct. 20, 1978, Pub. L. 95-486, §5, 92 Stat. 1633; Apr. 2, 1982, Pub. L. 97-164, §§103, 205, 96 Stat. 25, 53; Aug. 6, 1996, Pub. L. 104-175, §1, 110 Stat. 1556.)

28 U.S.C. § 1291   Final decisions of district courts

The courts of appeals (other than the United States Court of Appeals for the Federal Circuit) shall have jurisdiction of appeals from all final decisions of the district courts of the United States, the United States District Court for the District of the Canal Zone, the District Court of Guam, and the District Court of the Virgin Islands, except where a direct review may be had in the Supreme Court. The jurisdiction of the United States Court of Appeals for the Federal Circuit shall be limited to the jurisdiction described in sections 1292(c) and (d) and 1295 of this title.

(June 25, 1948, ch. 646, §1, 62 Stat. 929; Oct. 31, 1951, ch. 655, §48, 65 Stat. 726; July 7, 1958, Pub. L. 85-508, §12, 72 Stat. 348; Apr. 2, 1982, Pub. L. 97-164, §124, 96 Stat. 36.)

28 U.S.C. § 1292   Interlocutory decisions

(a) Except as provided in subsections (c) and (d) of this section, the courts of appeals shall have jurisdiction of appeals from:

(1) Interlocutory orders of the district courts of the United States, the United States District Court for the District of the Canal Zone, the District Court of Guam, and the District Court of the Virgin Islands, or of the judges thereof, granting, continuing, modifying, refusing or dissolving injunctions, or refusing to dissolve or modify injunctions, except where a direct review may be had in the Supreme Court.

(2) Interlocutory orders appointing receivers, or refusing orders to wind up receiverships or to take steps to accomplish the purposes thereof, such as directing sales or other disposals of property;

(3) Interlocutory decrees of such district courts or the judges thereof determining the rights and liabilities of the parties to admiralty cases in which appeals from final decrees are allowed.

(b) When a district judge, in making in a civil action an order not otherwise appealable under this section, shall be of the opinion that such order involves a controlling question of law as to which there is substantial ground for difference of opinion and that an immediate appeal from the order may materially advance the ultimate termination of the litigation, he shall so state in writing in such order. The Court of Appeals which would have jurisdiction of an appeal of such action may thereupon, in its discretion, permit an appeal to be taken from such order, if application is made to it within ten days after the entry of the order: *Provided, however*, That application for an appeal hereunder shall not stay proceedings in the district court unless the district judge or the Court of Appeals or a judge thereof shall so order.

(c) The United States Court of Appeals for the Federal Circuit shall have exclusive jurisdiction—

(1) of an appeal from an interlocutory order or decree described in subsection (a) or (b) of this section in any case over which the court would have jurisdiction of an appeal under section 1295 of this title; and

(2) of an appeal from a judgment in a civil action for patent infringement which would otherwise be appealable to the United States Court of Appeals for the Federal Circuit and is final except for an accounting.

(d)(1) When the chief judge of the Court of International Trade issues an order under the provisions of section 256(b) of this title, or when any judge of the Court of International Trade, in issuing any other interlocutory order, includes in the order a statement that a controlling question of law is involved with respect to which there is a substantial ground for difference of opinion and that an immediate appeal from that order may materially advance the ultimate termination of the litigation, the United States Court of Appeals for the Federal Circuit may, in its discretion, permit an appeal to be taken from such order, if application is made to that Court within ten days after the entry of such order.

28 U.S.C. § 1292

(2) When any judge of the United States Claims Court,* in issuing an interlocutory order, includes in the order a statement that a controlling question of law is involved with respect to which there is a substantial ground for difference of opinion and that an immediate appeal from that order may materially advance the ultimate termination of the litigation, the United States Court of Appeals for the Federal Circuit may, in its discretion, permit an appeal to be taken from such order, if application is made to that Court within ten days after the entry of such order.

(3) Neither the application for nor the granting of an appeal under this subsection shall stay proceedings in the Court of International Trade or in the Claims Court, as the case may be, unless a stay is ordered by a judge of the Court of International Trade or of the Claims Court or by the United States Court of Appeals for the Federal Circuit or a judge of that court.

(4) (A) The United States Court of Appeals for the Federal Circuit shall have exclusive jurisdiction of an appeal from an interlocutory order of a district court of the United States, the District Court of Guam, the District Court of the Virgin Islands, or the District Court for the Northern Mariana Islands, granting or denying, in whole or in part, a motion to transfer an action to the United States Claims Court under section 1631 of this title.

(B) When a motion to transfer an action to the Claims Court is filed in a district court, no further proceedings shall be taken in the district court until 60 days after the court has ruled upon the motion. If an appeal is taken from the district court's grant or denial of the motion, proceedings shall be further stayed until the appeal has been decided by the Court of Appeals for the Federal Circuit. The stay of proceedings in the district court shall not bar the granting of preliminary or injunctive relief, where appropriate and where expedition is reasonably necessary. However, during the period in which proceedings are stayed as provided in this subparagraph, no transfer to the Claims Court pursuant to the motion shall be carried out.

---

* *Ed. Note:* Pursuant to the Court of Federal Claims Technical and Procedural Improvements Act of 1992, §902(b)(2), Pub. L. 102-572, 106 Stat. 4516, statutory references to the U.S. Claims Court are deemed to refer to the U.S. Court of Federal Claims.

28 U.S.C. § 1292

(e) The Supreme Court may prescribe rules, in accordance with section 2072 of this title, to provide for an appeal of an interlocutory decision to the courts of appeals that is not otherwise provided for under subsection (a), (b), (c), or (d).

(June 25, 1948, ch. 646, §1, 62 Stat. 929; Oct. 31, 1951, ch. 655, §49, 65 Stat. 726; July 7, 1958, Pub. L. 85-508, §12(e), 72 Stat. 348; Sept. 2, 1958, Pub. L. 85-919, 72 Stat. 1770; Apr. 2, 1982, Pub. L. 97-164, §125, 96 Stat. 36; Nov. 8, 1984, Pub. L. 98-620, §412, 98 Stat. 3362; Nov. 19, 1988, Pub. L. 100-702, §501, 102 Stat. 4652; Oct. 29, 1992, Pub. L. 102-572, §101, 106 Stat. 4516.)

28 U.S.C. § 1294 Circuits in which decisions reviewable

Except as provided in sections 1292(c), 1292(d), and 1295 of this title, appeals from reviewable decisions of the district and territorial courts shall be taken to the courts of appeals as follows:

(1) From a district court of the United States to the court of appeals for the circuit embracing the district;

(2) From the United States District Court for the District of the Canal Zone, to the Court of Appeals for the Fifth Circuit;

(3) From the District Court of the Virgin Islands, to the Court of Appeals for the Third Circuit;

(4) From the District Court of Guam, to the Court of Appeals for the Ninth Circuit.

(June 25, 1948, ch. 646, 62 Stat. 930; Oct. 31, 1951, ch. 655, §50, 65 Stat. 727; July 7, 1958, Pub. L. 85-508, §12, 72 Stat. 348; Mar. 18, 1959, Pub. L. 86-3, §14, 73 Stat. 10; Aug. 30, 1961, Pub. L. 87-189, §5, 75 Stat. 417; Nov. 6, 1978, Pub. L. 95-598, §237, 92 Stat. 2667; Apr. 2, 1982, Pub. L. 97-164, §126, 96 Stat. 37.)

28 U.S.C. § 1295 Jurisdiction of the United States Court of Appeals for the Federal Circuit

(a) The United States Court of Appeals for the Federal Circuit shall have exclusive jurisdiction—

(1) of an appeal from a final decision of a district court of the United States, the United States District Court for the District of the Canal Zone, the District Court of Guam, the District Court of the Virgin Islands, or the District Court for the Northern Mariana Islands, if the jurisdiction of that court was based, in whole or in part, on section 1338 of this title, except that a case involving a claim arising under

28 U.S.C. § 1295

any Act of Congress relating to copyrights, exclusive rights in mask works, or trademarks and no other claims under section 1338(a) shall be governed by sections 1291, 1292, and 1294 of this title;

(2) of an appeal from a final decision of a district court of the United States, the United States District Court for the District of the Canal Zone, the District Court of Guam, the District Court of the Virgin Islands, or the District Court for the Northern Mariana Islands, if the jurisdiction of that court was based, in whole or in part, on section 1346 of this title, except that jurisdiction of an appeal in a case brought in a district court under section 1346(a)(1), 1346(b), 1346(e), or 1346(f) of this title or under section 1346(a)(2) when the claim is founded upon an Act of Congress or a regulation of an executive department providing for internal revenue shall be governed by sections 1291, 1292, and 1294 of this title;

(3) of an appeal from a final decision of the United States Claims Court;*

(4) of an appeal from a decision of—

(A) the Board of Patent Appeals and Interferences of the United States Patent and Trademark Office with respect to patent applications and interferences, at the instance of an applicant for a patent or any party to a patent interference, and any such appeal shall waive the right of such applicant or party to proceed under section 145 or 146 of title 35;

(B) the Under Secretary of Commerce for Intellectual Property and Director of the United States Patent and Trademark Office or the Trademark Trial and Appeal Board with respect to applications for registration of marks and other proceedings as provided in section 21 of the Trademark Act of 1946 (15 U.S.C. 1071); or

(C) a district court to which a case was directed pursuant to section 145, 146, or 154(b) of title 35;

---

* *Ed. Note:* Pursuant to the Court of Federal Claims Technical and Procedural Improvements Act of 1992, §902(b)(2), Pub. L. 102-572, 106 Stat. 4516, statutory references to the U.S. Claims Court are deemed to refer to the U.S. Court of Federal Claims.

28 U.S.C. § 1295

(5) of an appeal from a final decision of the United States Court of International Trade;

(6) to review the final determinations of the United States International Trade Commission relating to unfair practices in import trade, made under section 337 of the Tariff Act of 1930 (19 U.S.C. 1337);

(7) to review, by appeal on questions of law only, findings of the Secretary of Commerce under U.S. note 6 to subchapter X of chapter 98 of the Harmonized Tariff Schedule of the United States (relating to importation of instruments or apparatus);

(8) of an appeal under section 71 of the Plant Variety Protection Act (7 U.S.C. 2461);

(9) of an appeal from a final order or final decision of the Merit Systems Protection Board, pursuant to sections 7703(b)(1) and 7703(d) of title 5;

(10) of an appeal from a final decision of an agency board of contract appeals pursuant to section 8(g)(1) of the Contract Disputes Act of 1978 (41 U.S.C. 607(g)(1));

(11) of an appeal under section 211 of the Economic Stabilization Act of 1970;

(12) of an appeal under section 5 of the Emergency Petroleum Allocation Act of 1973;

(13) of an appeal under section 506(c) of the Natural Gas Policy Act of 1978; and

(14) of an appeal under section 523 of the Energy Policy and Conservation Act.

(b) The head of any executive department or agency may, with the approval of the Attorney General, refer to the Court of Appeals for the Federal Circuit for judicial review any final decision rendered by a board of contract appeals pursuant to the terms of any contract with the United States awarded by that department or agency which the head of such department or agency has concluded is not entitled to finality pursuant to the review standards specified in section 10(b) of the Contract Disputes Act of 1978 (41 U.S.C. 609(b)). The head of each executive department or agency shall make any referral under this section within one hundred and twenty days after the receipt of a copy of the final appeal decision.

(c) The Court of Appeals for the Federal Circuit shall review the matter referred in accordance with the standards specified in section 10(b) of the Contract Disputes Act of 1978. The court shall proceed with judicial review on the administrative record made before the board of contract appeals on matters so referred as in other cases pending in such court, shall determine the issue of finality of the appeal decision, and shall, if appropriate, render judgment thereon, or remand the matter to any administrative or executive body or official with such direction as it may deem proper and just.

(Apr. 2, 1982, Pub. L. 97-164, §127, 96 Stat. 37; Nov. 8, 1984, Pub. L. 98-622, §205, 98 Stat. 3388; Aug. 23, 1988, Pub. L. 100-418, §1214, 102 Stat. 1156; Nov. 19, 1988, Pub. L. 100-702, §1020, 102 Stat. 4671; Oct. 29, 1992, Pub. L. 102-572, §102(c), 106 Stat. 4506; Nov. 29, 1999, Pub. L. 106-113, §§4402, 4732, 113 Stat. 1501A-557, 581.)

C. INTELLECTUAL PROPERTY AND INTERNATIONAL TRADE

19 U.S.C. § 1337   Unfair practices in import trade

(a) *Unlawful activities; covered industries; definitions.—*

(1) Subject to paragraph (2), the following are unlawful, and when found by the Commission to exist shall be dealt with, in addition to any other provision of law, as provided in this section:

(A) Unfair methods of competition and unfair acts in the importation of articles (other than articles provided for in subparagraphs (B), (C), (D), and (E)) into the United States, or in the sale of such articles by the owner, importer, or consignee, the threat or effect of which is—

(i) to destroy or substantially injure an industry, in the United States;

(ii) to prevent the establishment of such an industry; or

(iii) to restrain or monopolize trade and commerce in the United States.

(B) The importation into the United States, the sale for importation, or the sale within the United States after importation by the owner, importer, or consignee, of articles that—

(i) infringe a valid and enforceable United States patent or a valid and enforceable United States copyright registered under title 17, United States Code; or

(ii) are made, produced, processed, or mined under, or by means of, a process covered by the claims of a valid and enforceable United States patent.

(C) The importation into the United States, the sale for importation, or the sale within the United States after importation by the owner, importer, or consignee, of articles that infringe a valid and enforceable United States trademark registered under the Trademark Act of 1946.

(D) The importation into the United States, the sale for importation, or the sale within the Untied States after importation by the owner, importer, or consignee, of a semiconductor chip product in a manner that constitutes infringement of a mask work registered under chapter 9 of title 17, United States Code.

(E) The importation into the United States, the sale for importation, or the sale within the United States after importation by the owner, importer, or consigner, of an article that constitutes infringement of the exclusive rights in a design protected under chapter 13 of title 17, United States Code.

(2) Subparagraphs (B), (C), and (D) of paragraph (1) apply only if an industry in the United States, relating to the articles protected by the patent, copyright, trademark, mask work, or design concerned, exists or is in the process of being established.

(3) For purposes of paragraph (2), an industry in the United States shall be considered to exist if there is in the United States, with respect to the articles protected by the patent, copyright, trademark, mask work, or design concerned—

(A) significant investment in plant and equipment;

19 U.S.C. § 1337

(B) significant employment of labor or capital; or

(C) substantial investment in its exploitation, including engineering, research and development, or licensing.

(4) For the purposes of this section, the phrase "owner, importer, or consignee" includes any agent of the owner, importer, or consignee.

(b) *Investigation of violations by Commission.*—

(1) The Commission shall investigate any alleged violation of this section on complaint under oath or upon its initiative. Upon commencing any such investigation, the Commission shall publish notice thereof in the Federal Register. The Commission shall conclude any such investigation and make its determination under this section at the earliest practicable time after the date of publication of notice of such investigation. To promote expeditious adjudication, the Commission shall, within 45 days after an investigation is initiated, establish a target date for its final determination.

(2) During the course of each investigation under this section, the Commission shall consult with, and seek advice and information from, the Department of Health and Human Services, the Department of Justice, the Federal Trade Commission, and such other departments and agencies as it considers appropriate.

(3) Whenever, in the course of an investigation under this section, the Commission has reason to believe, based on information before it, that a matter, in whole or in part, may come within the purview of this Act or of part II of subtitle IV of this chapter, it shall promptly notify the Secretary of Commerce so that such action may be taken as is otherwise authorized by such subtitle. If the Commission has reason to believe that the matter before it (A) is based solely on alleged acts and effects which are within the purview of section 303, 671, or 673 [§1303, 1671, or 1673], or (B) relates to an alleged copyright infringement with respect to which action is prohibited by section 1008 of title 17, United States Code, the Commission shall terminate, or not institute, any investigation into the matter. If the Commission has reason to believe the matter before it is based in part on alleged acts and effects which are within the purview of section 1303, 1671, or 1673 of this title, and in part on alleged acts and effects which may, independently from or in conjunction with those

within the purview of such section, establish a basis for relief under this section, then it may institute or continue an investigation into the matter. If the Commission notifies the Secretary or the administering authority (as defined in section 1677(1) of this title) with respect to a matter under this paragraph, the Commission may suspend its investigation during the time the matter is before the Secretary or administering authority for final decision. Any final decision of the Secretary under section 1303 of this title or by the administering authority under section 1671 or 1673 of this title with respect to the matter within such section 1303, 1671, or 1673 of this title of which the Commission has notified the Secretary or administering authority shall be conclusive upon the Commission with respect to the issue of less-than-fair-value sales or subsidization and the matters necessary for such decision.

(c) *Determinations; review.*—The Commission shall determine, with respect to each investigation conducted by it under this section, whether or not there is a violation of this section, except that the Commission may, by issuing a consent order or on the basis of an agreement between the private parties to the investigation, including an agreement to present the matter for arbitration, terminate any such investigation, in whole or in part, without making such a determination. Each determination under subsection (d) or (e) of this section shall be made on the record after notice and opportunity for a hearing in conformity with the provisions of subchapter II of chapter 5 of title 5. All legal and equitable defenses may be presented in all cases. A respondent may raise any counterclaim in a manner prescribed by the Commission. Immediately after a counterclaim is received by the Commission, the respondent raising such counterclaim shall file a notice of removal with a United States district court in which venue for any of the counterclaims raised by the party would exist under section 1391 of title 28, United States Code. Any counterclaim raised pursuant to this section shall relate back to the date of the original complaint in the proceeding before the Commission. Action on such counterclaim shall not delay or affect the proceeding under this section, including the legal and equitable defenses that may be raised under this subsection. Any person adversely affected by a final determination of the Commission under subsection (d), (e), (f), or (g), of this section may appeal such determination within 60 days after the determination becomes final, to the United States Court of Appeals for the Federal Circuit for review in accordance with chapter 7 of title 5. Notwithstanding the foregoing provisions of this subsection, Commission determinations under subsections (d), (e), (f), or (g), of this section with respect to its findings on the public health and welfare, competitive conditions in the United States economy, the production of like or directly competitive articles in the United States, and United States consumers, the amount and nature of bond, or the appropriate remedy shall be reviewable in accordance with section 706 of title 5. Determinations by the Commission under subsections (e), (f), and (j) with respect to forfeiture of bonds and under subsection (h) with respect to the imposition of sanctions for abuse of discovery or abuse of process shall also be reviewable in accordance with section 706 of title 5, United States Code.

(d) *Exclusion of articles from entry.—*

(1) If the Commission determines, as a result of an investigation under this section, that there is a violation of this section, it shall direct that the articles concerned, imported by any person violating the provision of this section, be excluded from entry into the United States, unless, after considering the effect of such exclusion upon the public health and welfare, competitive conditions in the United States economy, the production of like or directly competitive articles in the United States, and United States consumers, it finds that such articles should not be excluded from entry. The Commission shall notify the Secretary of the Treasury of its action under this subsection directing such exclusion from entry, and upon receipt of such notice, the Secretary shall, through the proper officers, refuse such entry.

(2) The authority of the Commission to order an exclusion from entry of articles shall be limited to persons determined by the Commission to be violating this section unless the Commission determines that—

(A) a general exclusion from entry of articles is necessary to prevent circumvention of an exclusion order limited to products of named persons; or

(B) there is a pattern of violation of this section and it is difficult to identify the source of infringing products.

(e) *Exclusion of articles from entry during investigation except under bond.*—

(1) If, during the course of an investigation under this section, the Commission determines that there is reason to believe that there is a violation of this section, it may direct that the articles concerned, imported by any person with respect to whom there is reason to believe that such person is violating this section, be excluded from entry into the United States, unless, after considering the effect of such exclusion upon the public health and welfare, competitive conditions in the United States economy, the production of like or directly competitive articles in the United States, and United States consumers, it finds that such articles should not be excluded from entry. The Commission shall notify the Secretary of the Treasury of its action under this subsection directing such exclusion from entry, and upon receipt of such notice, the Secretary shall, through the proper officers, refuse such entry, except that such articles shall be entitled to entry under bond prescribed by the Secretary in an amount determined by the Commission to be sufficient to protect the complainant from any injury. If the Commission later determines that the respondent has violated the provisions of this section, the bond may be forfeited to the complainant.

(2) A complainant may petition the Commission for the issuance of an order under this subsection. The Commission shall make a determination with regard to such petition by not later than the 90th day after the date on which the Commission's notice of investigation is published in the Federal Register. The Commission may extend the 90-day period for an additional 60 days in a case it designates as a more complicated case. The Commission shall publish in the Federal Register its reasons why it designated the case as being more complicated. The Commission may require the complainant to post a bond as a prerequisite to the issuance of an order under this subsection. If the Commission later determines that the respondent has not violated the provisions of this section, the bond may be forfeited to the respondent.

19 U.S.C. § 1337

(3) The Commission may grant preliminary relief under this subsection or subsection (f) of this section to the same extent as preliminary injunctions and temporary restraining orders may be granted under the Federal Rules of Civil Procedure.

(4) The Commission shall prescribe the terms and conditions under which bonds may be forfeited under paragraphs (1) and (2).

(f) *Cease and desist orders; civil penalty for violation of orders.*—

(1) In addition to, or in lieu of, taking action under subsection (d) or (e), the Commission may issue and cause to be served on any person violating this section, or believed to be violating this section, as the case may be, an order directing such person to cease and desist from engaging in the unfair methods or acts involved, unless after considering the effect of such order upon the public health and welfare, competitive conditions in the United States economy, the production of like or directly competitive articles in the United States, and United States consumers, it finds that such order should not be issued. The Commission may at any time, upon such notice and in such manner as it deems proper, modify or revoke any such order, and, in the case of a revocation, may take action under subsection (d) or (e) of this section, as the case may be. If a temporary cease and desist order is issued in addition to, or in lieu of, an exclusion order under subsection (e), the Commission may require the complainant to post a bond, in an amount determined by the Commission to be sufficient to protect the respondent from any injury, as a prerequisite to the issuance of an order under this subsection. If the Commission later determines that the respondent has not violated the provisions of this section, the bond may be forfeited to the respondent. The Commission shall prescribe the terms and conditions under which the bonds may be forfeited under this paragraph.

(2) Any person who violates an order issued by the Commission under paragraph (1) after it has become final shall forfeit and pay to the United States a civil penalty for each day on which an importation of articles, or their sale, occurs in violation of the order of not more than the greater of $100,000 or twice the domestic value of the articles entered or sold on such day in violation of the order. Such penalty shall accrue to the United States and may be recovered for the

United States in a civil action brought by the Commission in the Federal District Court for the District of Columbia or for the district in which the violation occurs. In such actions, the United States district courts may issue mandatory injunctions incorporating the relief sought by the Commission as they deem appropriate in the enforcement of such final orders of the Commission.

(g) *Exclusion from entry or cease and desist order; conditions and procedures applicable.*—

(1) If—

(A) a complaint is filed against a person under this section;

(B) the complaint and a notice of investigation are served on the person;

(C) the person fails to respond to the complaint and notice or otherwise fails to appear to answer the complaint and notice;

(D) the person fails to show good cause why the person should not be found in default; and

(E) the complainant seeks relief limited solely to that person;

the Commission shall presume the facts alleged in the complaint to be true and shall, upon request, issue an exclusion from entry or a cease and desist order, or both, limited to that person unless, after considering the effect of such exclusion or order upon the public health and welfare, competitive conditions in the United States economy, the production of like or directly competitive articles in the United States, and United States consumers, the Commission finds that such exclusion or order should not be issued.

(2) In addition to the authority of the Commission to issue a general exclusion from entry of articles when a respondent appears to contest an investigation concerning a violation of the provisions of this section, a general exclusion from entry of articles, regardless of the source or importer of the articles, may be issued if—

(A) no person appears to contest an investigation concerning a violation of the provisions of this section,

(B) such a violation is established by substantial, reliable, and probative evidence, and

(C) the requirements of subsection (d)(2) are met.

(h) Sanctions for abuse of discovery and abuse of process.—The Commission may by rule prescribe sanctions for abuse of discovery and abuse of process to the extent authorized by Rule 11 and Rule 37 of the Federal Rules of Civil Procedure.

(i) *Forfeiture.*—

(1) In addition to taking action under subsection (d), the Commission may issue an order providing that any article imported in violation of the provisions of this section be seized and forfeited to the United States if—

(A) the owner, importer, or consignee of the article previously attempted to import the article into the United States;

(B) the article was previously denied entry into the United States by reason of an order issued under subsection (d); and

(C) upon such previous denial of entry, the Secretary of the Treasury provided the owner, importer, or consignee of the article written notice of—

(i) such order, and

(ii) the seizure and forfeiture that would result from any further attempt to import the article into the United States.

(2) The Commission shall notify the Secretary of the Treasury of any order issued under this subsection and, upon receipt of such notice, the Secretary of the Treasury shall enforce such order in accordance with the provisions of this section.

(3) Upon the attempted entry of articles subject to an order issued under this subsection, the Secretary of the Treasury shall immediately notify all ports of entry of the attempted importation and shall identify the persons notified under paragraph (1)(C).

(4) The Secretary of the Treasury shall provide—

(A) the written notice described in paragraph (1)(C) to the owner, importer, or consignee of any article that is denied entry into the United States by reason of an order issued under subsection (d); and

(B) a copy of such written notice to the Commission.

19 U.S.C. § 1337

(j) *Referral to President.*—

(1) If the Commission determines that there is a violation of this section, or that, for purposes of subsection (e), there is reason to believe that there is such a violation, it shall—

(A) publish such determination in the Federal Register, and

(B) transmit to the President a copy of such determination and the action taken under subsection (d), (e), (f), (g), or (i), with respect thereto, together with the record upon which such determination is based.

(2) If, before the close of the 60-day period beginning on the day after the day on which he receives a copy of such determination, the President, for policy reasons, disapproves such determination and notifies the Commission of his disapproval, then, effective on the date of such notice, such determination and the action taken under subsection (d), (e), (f), (g), or (i) with respect thereto shall have no force or effect.

(3) Subject to the provisions of paragraph (2), such determination shall, except for purposes of subsection (c), be effective upon publication thereof in the Federal Register, and the action taken under subsection (d), (e), (f), (g), or (i), with respect thereto shall be effective as provided in such subsections, except that articles directed to be excluded from entry under subsection (d) or subject to a cease and desist order under subsection (f) shall, until such determination becomes final, be entitled to entry under bond prescribed by the Secretary in an amount determined by the Commission to be sufficient to protect the complainant from any injury. If the determination becomes final, the bond may be forfeited to the complainant. The Commission shall prescribe the terms and conditions under which bonds may be forfeited under this paragraph.

(4) If the President does not disapprove such determination within such 60-day period, or if he notifies the Commission before the close of such period that he approves such determination, then, for purposes of paragraph (3) and subsection (c) such determination shall become final on the day after the close of such period or the day on which the President notifies the Commission of his approval, as the case may be.

19 U.S.C. § 1337

(k) *Period of effectiveness; termination of violation or modification or rescission of exclusion or order.*—

(1) Except as provided in subsections (f) and (j), any exclusion from entry or order under this section shall continue in effect until the Commission finds, and in the case of exclusion from entry notifies the Secretary of the Treasury, that the conditions which led to such exclusion from entry or order no longer exist.

(2) If any person who has previously been found by the Commission to be in violation of this section petitions the Commission for a determination that the petitioner is no longer in violation of this section or for a modification or rescission of an exclusion from entry or order under subsection (d), (e), (f), (g), or (i)—

(A) the burden of proof in any proceeding before the Commission regarding such petition shall be on the petitioner; and

(B) relief may be granted by the Commission with respect to such petition—

(i) on the basis of new evidence or evidence that could not have been presented at the prior proceeding, or

(ii) on grounds which would permit relief from a judgment or order under the Federal Rules of Civil Procedure.

(*l*) *Importation by or for United States.*—

Any exclusion from entry or order under subsection (d), (e), (f), (g), or (i), in cases based on a proceeding involving a patent, copyright, mask work, or design under subsection (a)(1), shall not apply to any articles imported by and for the use of the United States, or imported for, and to be used for, the United States with the authorization or consent of the Government. Whenever any article would have been excluded from entry or would not have been entered pursuant to the provisions of such subsections but for the operation of this subsection, an owner of the patent, copyright, mask work, or design adversely affected shall be entitled to reasonable and entire compensation in an action before the United States Court of Federal Claims pursuant to the procedures of section 1498 of title 28, United States Code.

(m) *Definition of "United States".*—

For purposes of this section and sections 1338 and 1340, the term "United States" means the customs territory of the United States as defined in general note 2 of the Harmonized Tariff Schedule of the United States.

(n) *Disclosure of confidential information.*—

(1) Information submitted to the Commission or exchanged among the parties in connection with proceedings under this section which is properly designated as confidential pursuant to Commission rules may not be disclosed (except under a protective order issued under regulations of the Commission which authorizes limited disclosure of such information) to any person (other than a person described in paragraph (2)) without the consent of the person submitting it.

(2) Notwithstanding the prohibition contained in paragraph (1), information referred to in that paragraph may be disclosed to—

(A) an officer or employee of the Commission who is directly concerned with—

(i) carrying out the investigation or related proceeding in connection with which the information is submitted,

(ii) the administration of a bond posted pursuant to subsection (e), (f), or (j),

(iii) the administration or enforcement of an exclusion order issued pursuant to subsection (d), (e), or (g), a cease and desist order issued pursuant to subsection (f), or a consent order issued pursuant to subsection (c),

(iv) proceedings for the modification or rescission of a temporary or permanent order issued under subsection (d), (e), (f), (g), or (i), or a consent order issued under this section, or

(v) maintaining the administrative record of the investigation or related proceeding,

(B) an officer or employee of the United States Government who is directly involved in the review under subsection (j), or

(C) an officer or employee of the United States Customs Service who is directly involved in administering an exclusion from entry under subsection (d), (e), or (g) resulting from the investigation in connection with which the information is submitted.

19 U.S.C. § 1337

(June 17, 1930, ch. 497, §337, 46 Stat. 703; Aug. 20, 1958, Pub. L. 85-686, §9, 72 Stat. 679; Jan. 3, 1975, Pub. L. 93-618, §341, 88 Stat. 2053; July 26, 1979, Pub. L. 96-39, §§106, 1105, 93 Stat. 193, 310; Oct. 10, 1980, Pub. L. 96-417, §604, 94 Stat. 1744; Apr. 2, 1982, Pub. L. 97-164, §§160, 163, 96 Stat. 48, 49; Nov. 8, 1984, Pub. L. 98-620, §413, 98 Stat. 3362; Aug. 23, 1988, Pub. L. 100-418, §§1214, 1342, 102 Stat. 1157, 1212-15; Nov. 10, 1988, Pub. L. 100-647, §9001, 102 Stat. 3807; Oct. 29, 1992, Pub. L. 102-563, §3, 106 Stat. 4248; Dec. 8, 1994, Pub. L. 103-465, §321, 108 Stat. 4943; Oct. 11, 1996, Pub. L. 104-295, Title II(12), 110 Stat. 3527; Nov. 29, 1999, Pub. L. 106-113, §5005, 113 Stat. 1501A-593.)

19 U.S.C. § 1526   Merchandise bearing American trademark

(a) *Importation prohibited.*—Except as provided in subsection (d) of this section, it shall be unlawful to import into the United States any merchandise of foreign manufacture if such merchandise, or the label, sign, print, package, wrapper, or receptacle, bears a trademark owned by a citizen of, or by a corporation or association created or organized within, the United States, and registered in the Patent and Trademark Office by a person domiciled in the United States, under the provisions of sections 81 to 109 of title 15, and if a copy of the certificate of registration of such trademark is filed with the Secretary of the Treasury, in the manner provided in section 106 of said title 15, unless written consent of the owner of such trademark is produced at the time of making entry.

(b) *Seizure and forfeiture.*—Any such merchandise imported into the United States in violation of the provisions of this section shall be subject to seizure and forfeiture for violation of the customs laws.

(c) *Injunction and damages.*—Any person dealing in any such merchandise may be enjoined from dealing therein within the United States or may be required to export or destroy such merchandise or to remove or obliterate such trademark and shall be liable for the same damages and profits provided for wrongful use of a trade-mark, under the provisions of sections 81 to 109 of title 15.

(d) *Exemptions; publication in Federal Register; forfeitures; rules and regulations.*—

(1) The trademark provisions of this section and section 1124 of title 15, do not apply to the importation of articles accompanying any person arriving in the United States when such articles are for his

personal use and not for sale if (A) such articles are within the limits of types and quantities determined by the Secretary pursuant to paragraph (2) of this subsection, and (B) such person has not been granted an exemption under this subsection within thirty days immediately preceding his arrival.

(2) The Secretary shall determine and publish in the Federal Register lists of the types of articles and the quantities of each which shall be entitled to the exemption provided by this subsection. In determining such quantities of particular types of trademarked articles, the Secretary shall give such consideration as he deems necessary to the numbers of such articles usually purchased at retail for personal use.

(3) If any article which has been exempted from the restrictions on importation of the trademark laws under this subsection is sold within one year after the date of importation, such article, or its value (to be recovered from the importer), is subject to forfeiture. A sale pursuant to a judicial order or in liquidation of the estate of a decedent is not subject to the provisions of this paragraph.

(4) The Secretary may prescribe such rules and regulations as may be necessary to carry out the provisions of this subsection.

(e) *Merchandise bearing counterfeit mark; seizure and forfeiture; disposition of seized goods.*—Any such merchandise bearing a counterfeit mark (within the meaning of section 1127 of title 15) imported into the United States in violation of the provisions of section 1124 of title 15, shall be seized and, in the absence of the written consent of the trademark owner, forfeited for violations of the customs laws. Upon seizure of such merchandise, the Secretary shall notify the owner of the trademark, and shall, after forfeiture, destroy the merchandise. Alternatively, if the merchandise is not unsafe or a hazard to health, and the Secretary has the consent of the trademark owner, the Secretary may obliterate the trademark where feasible and dispose of the goods seized—

(1) by delivery to such Federal, State, and local government agencies as in the opinion of the Secretary have a need for such merchandise,

(2) by gift to such eleemosynary institutions as in the opinion of the Secretary have a need for such merchandise, or

19 U.S.C. § 1526

(3) more than 90 days after the date of forfeiture, by sale by the Customs Service at public auction under such regulations as the Secretary prescribes, except that before making any such sale the Secretary shall determine that no Federal, State, or local government agency or eleemosynary institution has established a need for such merchandise under paragraph (1) or (2).

(f) *Civil Penalties.*—(1) Any person who directs, assists financially or otherwise, or aids and abets the importation of merchandise for sale or public distribution that is seized under subsection (e) shall be subject to a civil fine.

(2) For the first such seizure, the fine shall be not more than the value that the merchandise would have had if it were genuine, according to the manufacturer's suggested retail price, determined under regulations promulgated by the Secretary.

(3) For the second seizure and thereafter, the fine shall be not more than twice the value that the merchandise would have had if it were genuine, as determined under regulations promulgated by the Secretary.

(4) The imposition of a fine under this subsection shall be within the discretion of the Customs Service, and shall be in addition to any other civil or criminal penalty or other remedy authorized by law.

(June 17, 1930, ch 497, Title IV, Part III, §526, 46 Stat. 741; Oct. 3, 1978, Pub. L. 95-410, Title II, §211 (a), (c), 92 Stat. 903; Dec. 8, 1993, Pub. L. 103—182, Title VI, Subtitle C, §663, 107 Stat. 2214; July 2, 1996, Pub. L. 104-153, §§9-10, 110 Stat. 1388.)

19 U.S.C. § 2411 Actions by United States Trade Representative [Section 301]*

(a) *Mandatory action.*—

(1) If the United States Trade Representative determines under section 304(a)(1) that—

(A) the rights of the United States under any trade agreement are being denied; or

---

* *Ed. Note:* The bracketed references are to the section designations of the Trade Act of 1974.

(B) an act, policy, or practice of a foreign country—

(i) violates, or is inconsistent with, the provisions of, or otherwise denies benefits to the United States under, any trade agreement, or

(ii) is unjustifiable and burdens or restricts United States commerce;

the Trade Representative shall take action authorized in subsection (c), subject to the specific direction, if any, of the President regarding any such action, and shall take all other appropriate and feasible action within the power of the President that the President may direct the Trade Representative to take under this subsection, to enforce such rights or to obtain the elimination of such act, policy, or practice. Actions may be taken that are within the power of the President with respect to trade in any goods or services, or with respect to any other area of pertinent relations with the foreign country.

(2) The Trade Representative is not required to take action under paragraph (1) in any case in which—

(A) the Contracting Parties to the General Agreement on Tariffs and Trade have determined, a panel of experts has reported to the Contracting Parties, or a ruling issued under the formal dispute settlement proceeding provided under any other trade agreement finds, that—

(i) the rights of the United States under a trade agreement are not being denied, or

(ii) the act, policy, or practice—

(I) is not a violation of, or inconsistent with, the rights of the United States, or

(II) does not deny, nullify, or impair benefits to the United States under any trade agreement; or

(B) the Trade Representative finds that—

(i) the foreign country is taking satisfactory measures to grant the rights of the United States under a trade agreement,

(ii) the foreign country has—

19 U.S.C. § 2411

(I) agreed to eliminate or phase out the act, policy, or practice, or

(II) agreed to an imminent solution to the burden or restriction on United States commerce that is satisfactory to the Trade Representative,

(iii) it is impossible for the foreign country to achieve the results described in clause (i) or (ii), as appropriate, but the foreign country agrees to provide to the United States compensatory trade benefits that are satisfactory to the Trade Representative,

(iv) in extraordinary cases, where the taking of action under this subsection would have an adverse impact on the United States economy substantially out of proportion to the benefits of such action, taking into account the impact of not taking such action on the credibility of the provisions of this chapter, or

(v) the taking of action under this subsection would cause serious harm to the national security of the United States.

(3) Any action taken under paragraph (1) to eliminate an act, policy, or practice shall be devised so as to affect goods or services of the foreign country in an amount that is equivalent in value to the burden or restriction being imposed by that country on United States commerce.

(b) *Discretionary action.*—If the Trade Representative determines under section 304(a)(1) that—

(1) an act, policy, or practice of a foreign country is unreasonable or discriminatory and burdens or restricts United States commerce, and

(2) action by the United States is appropriate, the Trade Representative shall take all appropriate and feasible action authorized under subsection (c), subject to the specific direction, if any, of the President regarding any such action, and all other appropriate and feasible action within the power of the President that the President may direct the Trade Representative to take under this subsection, to obtain the elimination of that act, policy, or practice. Actions may be taken that are within the power of the President with respect to trade in any goods or services, or with respect to any other area of pertinent relations with the foreign country.

19 U.S.C. § 2411

(c) *Scope of authority.*—

(1) For purposes of carrying out the provisions of subsection (a) or (b), the Trade Representative is authorized to—

(A) suspend, withdraw, or prevent the application of, benefits of trade agreement concessions to carry out a trade agreement with the foreign country referred to in such subsection;

(B) impose duties or other import restrictions on the goods of, and, notwithstanding any other provision of law, fees or restrictions on the services of, such foreign country for such time as the Trade Representative determines appropriate;

(C) in a case in which the act, policy, or practice also fails to meet the eligibility criteria for receiving duty-free treatment under subsections (b) and (c) of section 502 of this Act, subsections (b) and (c) of section 212 of the Caribbean Basin Economic Recovery Act (19 U.S.C. 2702(b) and (c)), or subsections (c) and (d) of section 203 of the Andean Trade Preference Act (19 U.S.C. 3202(c) and (d)), withdraw, limit, or suspend such treatment under such provisions, notwithstanding the provisions of subsection (a)(3) of this section; or

(D) enter into binding agreements with such foreign country, that commit such foreign country to—

(i) eliminate, or phase out, the act, policy, or practice that is the subject of the action to be taken under subsection (a) or (b),

(ii) eliminate any burden or restriction on United States commerce resulting from such act, policy, or practice, or

(iii) provide the United States with compensatory trade benefits that—

(I) are satisfactory to the Trade Representative, and

(II) meet the requirements of paragraph (4).

(2) (A) Notwithstanding any other provision of law governing any service sector access authorization, and in addition to the authority conferred in paragraph (1), the Trade Representative may, for purposes of carrying out the provisions of subsection (a) or (b)—

19 U.S.C. § 2411

(i) restrict, in the manner and to the extent the Trade Representative determines appropriate, the terms and conditions of any such authorization, or

(ii) deny the issuance of any such authorization.

(B) Actions described in subparagraph (A) may only be taken under this section with respect to service sector access authorizations granted, or applications therefor pending, on or after the date on which—

(i) a petition is filed under section 302(a), or

(ii) a determination to initiate an investigation is made by the Trade Representative under section 302(b).

(C) Before the Trade Representative takes any action under this section involving the imposition of fees or other restrictions on the services of a foreign country, the Trade Representative shall, if the services involved are subject to regulation by any agency of the Federal Government or of any State, consult, as appropriate, with the head of the agency concerned.

(3) The actions the Trade Representative is authorized to take under subsection (a) or (b) may be taken against any goods or economic sector—

(A) on a nondiscriminatory basis or solely against the foreign country described in such subsection, and

(B) without regard to whether or not such goods or economic sector were involved in the act, policy, or practice that is the subject of such action.

(4) Any trade agreement described in paragraph (1)(D)(iii) shall provide compensatory trade benefits that benefit the economic sector which includes the domestic industry that would benefit from the elimination of the act, policy, or practice that is the subject of the action to be taken under subsection (a) or (b), or benefit the economic sector as closely related as possible to such economic sector, unless—

(A) the provision of such trade benefits is not feasible, or

(B) trade benefits that benefit any other economic sector would be more satisfactory than such trade benefits.

19 U.S.C. § 2411

(5) If the Trade Representative determines that actions to be taken under subsection (a) or (b) are to be in the form of import restrictions, the Trade Representative shall—

(A) give preference to the imposition of duties over the imposition of other import restrictions, and

(B) if an import restriction other than a duty is imposed, consider substituting, on an incremental basis, an equivalent duty for such other import restriction.

(6) Any action taken by the Trade Representative under this section with respect to export targeting shall, to the extent possible, reflect the full benefit level of the export targeting to the beneficiary over the period during which the action taken has an effect.

(d) *Definitions and special rules.*—For purposes of this chapter—

(1) The term "commerce" includes, but is not limited to—

(A) services (including transfers of information) associated with international trade, whether or not such services are related to specific goods, and

(B) foreign direct investment by United States persons with implications for trade in goods or services.

(2) An act, policy, or practice of a foreign country that burdens or restricts United States commerce may include the provision, directly or indirectly, by that foreign country of subsidies for the construction of vessels used in the commercial transportation by water of goods between foreign countries and the United States.

(3) (A) An act, policy, or practice is unreasonable if the act, policy, or practice, while not necessarily in violation of, or inconsistent with, the international legal rights of the United States, is otherwise unfair and inequitable.

(B) Acts, policies, and practices that are unreasonable include, but are not limited to, any act, policy, or practice, or any combination of acts, policies, or practices, which—

(i) denies fair and equitable—

(I) opportunities for the establishment of an enterprise,

19 U.S.C. § 2411

(II) provision of adequate and effective protection of intellectual property rights notwithstanding the fact that the foreign country may be in compliance with the specific obligations of the Agreement on Trade-Related Aspects of Intellectual Property Rights referred to in section 101(d)(15) of the Uruguay Round Agreements Act,

(III) nondiscriminatory market access opportunities for United States persons that rely upon intellectual property protection, or

(IV) market opportunities, including the toleration by a foreign government of systematic anticompetitive activities by enterprises or among enterprises in the foreign country that have the effect of restricting, on a basis that is inconsistent with commercial considerations, access of United States goods or services to a foreign market,

(ii) constitutes export targeting, or

(iii) constitutes a persistent pattern of conduct that—

(I) denies workers the right of association,

(II) denies workers the right to organize and bargain collectively,

(III) permits any form of forced or compulsory labor,

(IV) fails to provide a minimum age for the employment of children, or

(V) fails to provide standards for minimum wages, hours of work, and occupational safety and health of workers.

(C) (i) Acts, policies, and practices of a foreign country described in subparagraph (B)(iii) shall not be treated as being unreasonable if the Trade Representative determines that—

(I) the foreign country has taken, or is taking, actions that demonstrate a significant and tangible overall advancement in providing throughout the foreign country (including any designated zone within the foreign country) the rights and other standards described in the sub-clauses of subparagraph (B)(iii), or

(II) such acts, policies, and practices are not inconsistent with the level of economic development of the foreign country.

(ii) The Trade Representative shall publish in the Federal Register any determination made under clause (i), together with a description of the facts on which such determination is based.

(D) For purposes of determining whether any act, policy, or practice is unreasonable, reciprocal opportunities in the United States for foreign nationals and firms shall be taken into account, to the extent appropriate.

(E) The term "export targeting" means any government plan or scheme consisting of a combination of coordinated actions (whether carried out severally or jointly) that are bestowed on a specific enterprise, industry, or group thereof, the effect of which is to assist the enterprise, industry, or group to become more competitive in the export of a class or kind of merchandise.

(F) (i) For the purposes of subparagraph (B)(i)(II), adequate and effective protection of intellectual property rights includes adequate and effective means under the laws of the foreign country for persons who are not citizens or nationals of such country to secure, exercise, and enforce rights and enjoy commercial benefits relating to patents, trademarks, copyrights and related rights, mask works, trade secrets, and plant breeder's rights.

(ii) For purposes of subparagraph (B)(i)(IV), the denial of fair and equitable nondiscriminatory market access opportunities includes restrictions on market access related to the use, exploitation, or enjoyment of commercial benefits derived from exercising intellectual property rights in protected works or fixations or products embodying protected works.

(4) (A) An act, policy, or practice is unjustifiable if the act, policy, or practice is in violation of, or inconsistent with, the international legal rights of the United States.

19 U.S.C. § 2411

(B) Acts, policies, and practices that are unjustifiable include, but are not limited to, any act, policy, or practice described in subparagraph (A) which denies national or most-favored-nation treatment or the right of establishment or protection of intellectual property rights.

(5) Acts, policies, and practices that are discriminatory include, when appropriate, any act, policy, and practice which denies national or most-favored-nation treatment to United States goods, services, or investment.

(6) The term "service sector access authorization" means any license, permit, order, or other authorization, issued under the authority of Federal law, that permits a foreign supplier of services access to the United States market in a service sector concerned.

(7) The term "foreign country" includes any foreign instrumentality. Any possession or territory of a foreign country that is administered separately for customs purposes shall be treated as a separate foreign country.

(8) The term "Trade Representative" means the United States Trade Representative.

(9) The term "interested persons", only for purposes of sections 302(a)(4)(B), 304(b)(1)(A), 306(c)(2), and 307(a)(2), includes, but is not limited to, domestic firms and workers, representatives of consumer interests, United States product exporters, and any industrial user of any goods or services that may be affected by actions taken under subsection (a) or (b).

(Jan. 3, 1975, Pub. L. 93-618, §301, as added July 26, 1979, Pub. L. 96-39, §901, 93 Stat. 295; Oct. 30, 1984, Pub. L. 98-573, §304, 98 Stat. 3002, 3005; Aug. 23, 1988, Pub. L. 100-418, §1301, 102 Stat. 1164; Dec. 8, 1994, Pub. L. 103-465, §314, 108 Stat. 4939; Oct. 11, 1996, Pub. L. 104-295, Title III(4), 110 Stat. 3528.)

19 U.S.C. § 2412   Initiation of investigations [Section 302]

(a) *Petitions.—*

(1) Any interested person may file a petition with the Trade Representative requesting that action be taken under section 301 and setting forth the allegations in support of the request.

(2) The Trade Representative shall review the allegations in any petition filed under paragraph (1) and, not later than 45 days after the date on which the Trade Representative received the petition, shall determine whether to initiate an investigation.

(3) If the Trade Representative determines not to initiate an investigation with respect to a petition, the Trade Representative shall inform the petitioner of the reasons therefor and shall publish notice of the determination, together with a summary of such reasons, in the Federal Register.

(4) If the Trade Representative makes an affirmative determination under paragraph (2) with respect to a petition, the Trade Representative shall initiate an investigation regarding the issues raised in the petition. The Trade Representative shall publish a summary of the petition in the Federal Register and shall, as soon as possible, provide opportunity for the presentation of views concerning the issues, including a public hearing—

(A) within the 30-day period beginning on the date of the affirmative determination (or on a date after such period if agreed to by the petitioner) if a public hearing within such period is requested in the petition, or

(B) at such other time if a timely request therefor is made by the petitioner or by any interested person.

(b) *Initiation of investigation by means other than petition.*—

(1) (A) If the Trade Representative determines that an investigation should be initiated under this chapter with respect to any matter in order to determine whether the matter is actionable under section 301, the Trade Representative shall publish such determination in the Federal Register and shall initiate such investigation.

(B) The Trade Representative shall, before making any determination under subparagraph (A), consult with appropriate committees established pursuant to section 135.

(2) (A) By no later than the date that is 30 days after the date on which a country is identified under section 182(a)(2), the Trade Representative shall initiate an investigation under this chapter with respect to any act, policy, or practice of that country that—

19 U.S.C. § 2412

(i) was the basis for such identification, and

(ii) is not at that time the subject of any other investigation or action under this chapter.

(B) The Trade Representative is not required under subparagraph (A) to initiate an investigation under this chapter with respect to any act, policy, or practice of a foreign country if the Trade Representative determines that the initiation of the investigation would be detrimental to United States economic interests.

(C) If the Trade Representative makes a determination under subparagraph (B) not to initiate an investigation, the Trade Representative shall submit to the Congress a written report setting forth, in detail—

(i) the reasons for the determination, and

(ii) the United States economic interests that would be adversely affected by the investigation.

(D) The Trade Representative shall, from time to time, consult with the Register of Copyrights, the Under Secretary of Commerce for Intellectual Property and Director of the United States Patent and Trademark Office, and other appropriate officers of the Federal Government, during any investigation initiated under this chapter by reason of subparagraph (A).

(c) *Discretion.*—In determining whether to initiate an investigation under subsection (a) or (b) of any act, policy, or practice that is enumerated in any provision of section 301(d), the Trade Representative shall have discretion to determine whether action under section 301 would be effective in addressing such act, policy, or practice.

(Jan. 3, 1975, Pub. L. 93-618, §302, as added July 26, 1979, Pub. L. 96-39, §901, 93 Stat. 296; Oct. 30, 1984, Pub. L. 98-573, §304, 98 Stat. 3003; Aug. 23, 1988, Pub. L. 100-418, §1301, 102 Stat. 1168; Nov. 29, 1999, Pub. L. 106-113, §4732, 1113 Stat. 1501A-581.)

19 U.S.C. § 2413   Consultation upon initiation of investigation
[Section 303]

(a) *In general.*—

(1) On the date on which an investigation is initiated under section 302, the Trade Representative, on behalf of the United States, shall request consultations with the foreign country concerned regarding the issues involved in such investigation.

(2) If the investigation initiated under section 302 involves a trade agreement and a mutually acceptable resolution is not reached before the earlier of—

    (A) the close of the consultation period, if any, specified in the trade agreement, or

    (B) the 150th day after the day on which consultation was commenced,

the Trade Representative shall promptly request proceedings on the matter under the formal dispute settlement procedures provided under such agreement.

(3) The Trade Representative shall seek information and advice from the petitioner (if any) and the appropriate committees established pursuant to section 135 in preparing United States presentations for consultations and dispute settlement proceedings.

(b) *Delay of request for consultations.*—

    (1) Notwithstanding the provisions of subsection (a)—

        (A) the United States Trade Representative may, after consulting with the petitioner (if any), delay for up to 90 days any request for consultations under subsection (a) for the purpose of verifying or improving the petition to ensure an adequate basis for consultation, and

        (B) if such consultations are delayed by reason of subparagraph (A), each time limitation under section 304 shall be extended for the period of such delay.

    (2) The Trade Representative shall—

        (A) publish notice of any delay under paragraph (1) in the Federal Register, and

        (B) report to Congress on the reasons for such delay in the report required under section 309(a)(3).

19 U.S.C. § 2413

(Jan. 3, 1975, Pub. L. 93-618, §303, as added July 26, 1979, Pub. L. 96-39, §901, 93 Stat. 297; Oct. 30, 1984, Pub. L. 98-573, §§304, 306, 98 Stat. 3004-05, 3012; Aug. 23, 1988, Pub. L. 100-418, §1301, 102 Stat. 1170.)

19 U.S.C. § 2414   Determination by the Trade Representative
[Section 304]

(a) *In general.*—

(1) On the basis of the investigation initiated under section 302 and the consultations (and the proceedings, if applicable) under section 303, the Trade Representative shall—

(A) determine whether—

(i) the rights to which the United States is entitled under any trade agreement are being denied, or

(ii) any act, policy, or practice described in subsection (a)(1)(B) or (b)(1) of section 301 exists, and

(B) if the determination made under subparagraph (A) is affirmative, determine what action, if any, the Trade Representative should take under subsection (a) or (b) of section 301.

(2) The Trade Representative shall make the determinations required under paragraph (1) on or before—

(A) in the case of an investigation involving a trade agreement, the earlier of—

(i) the date that is 30 days after the date on which the dispute settlement procedure is concluded, or

(ii) the date that is 18 months after the date on which the investigation is initiated, or

(B) in all cases not described in subparagraph (A) or paragraph (3), the date that is 12 months after the date on which the investigation is initiated.

(3) (A) If an investigation is initiated under this chapter by reason of section 302(b)(2) and the Trade Representative does not consider that a trade agreement, including the Agreement on Trade-Related Aspects of Intellectual Property Rights (referred to in section 101(d)(15) of the Uruguay Round Agreements Act), is involved or does not make a determination described in subpara-

graph (B) with respect to such investigation, the Trade Representative shall make the determinations required under paragraph (1) with respect to such investigation by no later than the date that is 6 months after the date on which such investigation is initiated.

(B) If the Trade Representative determines with respect to an investigation initiated by reason of section 302(b)(2) (other than an investigation involving a trade agreement) that—

(i) complex or complicated issues are involved in the investigation that require additional time,

(ii) the foreign country involved in the investigation is making substantial progress in drafting or implementing legislative or administrative measures that will provide adequate and effective protection of intellectual property rights, or

(iii) such foreign country is undertaking enforcement measures to provide adequate and effective protection of intellectual property rights,

the Trade Representative shall publish in the Federal Register notice of such determination and shall make the determinations required under paragraph (1) with respect to such investigation by no later than the date that is 9 months after the date on which such investigation is initiated.

(4) In any case in which a dispute is not resolved before the close of the minimum dispute settlement period provided for in a trade agreement, the Trade Representative, within 15 days after the close of such dispute settlement period, shall submit a report to Congress setting forth the reasons why the dispute was not resolved within the minimum dispute settlement period, the status of the case at the close of the period, and the prospects for resolution. For purposes of this paragraph, the minimum dispute settlement period provided for under any such trade agreement is the total period of time that results if all stages of the formal dispute settlement procedures are carried out within the time limitations specified in the agreement, but computed without regard to any extension authorized under the agreement at any stage.

(b) *Consultation before determinations.*—

19 U.S.C. § 2414

(1) Before making the determinations required under subsection (a)(1), the Trade Representative, unless expeditious action is required—

(A) shall provide an opportunity (after giving not less than 30 days notice thereof) for the presentation of views by interested persons, including a public hearing if requested by any interested person,

(B) shall obtain advice from the appropriate committees established pursuant to section 135, and

(C) may request the views of the United States International Trade Commission regarding the probable impact on the economy of the United States of the taking of action with respect to any goods or service.

(2) If the Trade Representative does not comply with the requirements of subparagraphs (A) and (B) of paragraph (1) because expeditious action is required, the Trade Representative shall, after making the determinations under subsection (a)(1), comply with such subparagraphs.

(c) *Publication.*—The Trade Representative shall publish in the Federal Register any determination made under subsection (a)(1), together with a description of the facts on which such determination is based.

(Jan. 3, 1975, Pub. L. 93-618, §304, as added July 26, 1979, Pub. L. 96-39, §901, 93 Stat. 297; Oct. 30, 1984, Pub. L. 98-573, §§304, 306, 98 Stat. 3004-05, 3012; Aug. 23, 1988, Pub. L. 100-418, §1301, 102 Stat. 1170; Dec. 8, 1994, Pub. L. 103-465, §314, 108 Stat. 4939; Oct. 11, 1996, Pub. L. 104-295, Title III(6), 110 Stat. 3528.)

19 U.S.C. § 2415   Implementation of actions [Section 305]

(a) *Actions to be taken under section 301.*—

(1) Except as provided in paragraph (2), the Trade Representative shall implement the action the Trade Representative determines under section 304(a)(1)(B) to take under section 301, subject to the specific direction, if any, of the President regarding any such action, by no later than the date that is 30 days after the date on which such determination is made.

(2) (A) Except as otherwise provided in this paragraph, the Trade Representative may delay, by not more than 180 days, the implementation of any action that is to be taken under section 301—

(i) if—

(I) in the case of an investigation initiated under section 302(a), the petitioner requests a delay, or

(II) in the case of an investigation initiated under section 302(b)(1) or to which section 304(a)(3)(B) applies, a delay is requested by a majority of the representatives of the domestic industry that would benefit from the action, or

(ii) if the Trade Representative determines that substantial progress is being made, or that a delay is necessary or desirable, to obtain United States rights or a satisfactory solution with respect to the acts, policies, or practices that are the subject of the action.

(B) The Trade Representative may not delay under subparagraph (A) the implementation of any action that is to be taken under section 301 with respect to any investigation to which section 304(a)(3)(A) applies.

(C) The Trade Representative may not delay under subparagraph (A) the implementation of any action that is to be taken under section 301 with respect to any investigation to which section 304(a)(3)(B) applies by more than 90 days.

(b) *Alternative actions in certain cases of export targeting.*—

(1) If the Trade Representative makes an affirmative determination under section 304(a)(1)(A) involving export targeting by a foreign country and determines to take no action under section 301 with respect to such affirmation determination, the Trade Representative—

(A) shall establish an advisory panel to recommend measures which will promote the competitiveness of the domestic industry affected by the export targeting,

(B) on the basis of the report of such panel submitted under paragraph (2)(B) and subject to the specific direction, if any, of the President, may take any administrative actions authorized

19 U.S.C. § 2415

under any other provision of law, and, if necessary, propose legislation to implement any other actions, that would restore or improve the international competitiveness of the domestic industry affected by the export targeting, and

(C) shall, by no later than the date that is 30 days after the date on which the report of such panel is submitted under paragraph (2)(B), submit a report to the Congress on the administrative actions taken, and legislative proposals made, under subparagraph (B) with respect to the domestic industry affected by the export targeting.

(2) (A) The advisory panels established under paragraph (1)(A) shall consist of individuals appointed by the Trade Representative who—

(i) earn their livelihood in the private sector of the economy, including individuals who represent management and labor in the domestic industry affected by the export targeting that is the subject of the affirmative determination made under section 304(a)(1)(A), and

(ii) by education or experience, are qualified to serve on the advisory panel.

(B) By no later than the date that is 6 months after the date on which an advisory panel is established under paragraph (1)(A), the advisory panel shall submit to the Trade Representative and to the Congress a report on measures that the advisory panel recommends be taken by the United States to promote the competitiveness of the domestic industry affected by the export targeting that is the subject of the affirmative determination made under section 304(a)(1)(A).

(Jan. 3, 1975, Pub. L. 93-618, §305, as added July 26, 1979, Pub. L. 96-39, §901, 93 Stat. 299; Oct. 30, 1984, Pub. L. 98-573, §304, 98 Stat. 3006; Aug. 23, 1988, Pub. L. 100-418, §1301, 102 Stat. 1172.)

19 U.S.C. § 2416   Monitoring of foreign compliance [Section 306]

(a) *In general.*—The Trade Representative shall monitor the implementation of each measure undertaken, or agreement that is entered into, by a foreign country to provide a satisfactory resolution of a matter subject to investigation under this chapter or subject to dispute settlement proceedings to enforce the rights of the United States under a trade agreement providing for such proceedings.

(b) *Further action.—*

(1) *In general.*—If, on the basis of the monitoring carried out under subsection (a), the Trade Representative considers that a foreign country is not satisfactorily implementing a measure or agreement referred to in subsection (a), the Trade Representative shall determine what further action the Trade Representative shall take under section 301(a). For purposes of section 301, any such determination shall be treated as a determination made under section 304(a)(1).

(2) *WTO dispute settlement recommendations.—*

(A) *Failure to implement recommendation.*—If the measure or agreement referred to in subsection (a) concerns the implementation of a recommendation made pursuant to dispute settlement proceedings under the World Trade Organization, and the Trade Representative considers that the foreign country has failed to implement it, the Trade Representative shall make the determination in paragraph (1) no later than 30 days after the expiration of the reasonable period of time provided for such implementation under paragraph 21 of the Understanding on Rules and Procedures Governing the Settlement of Disputes that is referred to in section 101(d)(16) of the Uruguay Round Agreements Act.

(B) *Revision of retaliation list and action.—*

(i) *In general.*—Except as provided in clause (ii), in the event that the United States initiates a retaliation list or takes any other action described in section 301(c)(1)(A) or (B) against the goods of a foreign country or countries because of the failure of such country or countries to implement the recommendation made pursuant to a dispute settlement proceeding under the World Trade Organization, the Trade Representative shall periodically revise the list or action to affect other goods of the country or countries that have failed to implement the recommendation.

19 U.S.C. § 2416

(ii) *Exception.*—The Trade Representative is not required to revise the retaliation list or the action described in clause (i) with respect to a country, if—

(I) the Trade Representative determines that implementation of a recommendation made pursuant to a dispute settlement proceeding described in clause (i) by the country is imminent; or

(II) the Trade Representative together with the petitioner involved in the initial investigation under this chapter (or if no petition was filed, the affected United States industry) agree that it is unnecessary to revise the retaliation list.

(C) *Schedule for revising list or action.*—The Trade Representative shall, 120 days after the date the retaliation list or other section 301(a) action is first taken, and every 180 days thereafter, review the list or action taken and revise, in whole or in part, the list or action to affect other goods of the subject country or countries.

(D) *Standards for revising list or action.*—In revising any list or action against a country or countries under this subsection, the Trade Representative shall act in a manner that is most likely to result in the country or countries implementing the recommendations adopted in the dispute settlement proceeding or in achieving a mutually satisfactory solution to the issue that gave rise to the dispute settlement proceeding. The Trade Representative shall consult with the petitioner, if any, involved in the initial investigation under this chapter.

(E) *Retaliation list.*—The term "retaliation list" means the list of products of a foreign country or countries that have failed to comply with the report of the panel or Appellate Body of the WTO and with respect to which the Trade Representative is imposing duties above the level that would otherwise be imposed under the Harmonized Tariff Schedule of the United States.

(F) *Requirement to include reciprocal goods on retaliation list.*—The Trade Representative shall include on the retaliation list, and on any revised lists, reciprocal goods of the industries affected by the failure of the foreign country or countries to implement the recommendation made pursuant to a dispute settlement proceeding under the World Trade Organization, except in cases where existing retaliation and its corresponding preliminary retaliation list do not already meet this requirement.

(c) *Consultations.*—Before making any determination under subsection (b), the Trade Representative shall—

(1) consult with the petitioner, if any, involved in the initial investigation under this chapter and with representatives of the domestic industry concerned; and

(2) provide an opportunity for the presentation of views by interested persons.

(Jan. 3, 1975, Pub. L. 93-618, §306, as added July 26, 1979, Pub. L. 96-39, §901, 93 Stat. 299; Aug. 23, 1988, Pub. L. 100-418, §1301, 102 Stat. 1173; Dec. 8, 1994, Pub. L. 103-465, §314, 108 Stat. 4939; May. 18, 2000, Pub. L. 106-200, §407, 114 Stat. 293.)

19 U.S.C. § 2417   Modification and termination of actions
[Section 307]

(a) *In general.*—

(1) The Trade Representative may modify or terminate any action, subject to the specific direction, if any, of the President with respect to such action, that is being taken under section 301 if—

(A) any of the conditions described in section 301(a)(2) exist,

(B) the burden or restriction on United States commerce of the denial rights, or of the acts, policies, and practices, that are the subject of such action has increased or decreased, or

(C) such action is being taken under section 301(b) and is no longer appropriate.

(2) Before taking any action under paragraph (1) to modify or terminate any action taken under section 301, the Trade Representative shall consult with the petitioner, if any, and with representatives of the domestic industry concerned, and shall provide opportunity for the presentation of views by other interested persons affected by the proposed modification or termination concerning the effects of the

modification or termination and whether any modification or termination of the action is appropriate.

(b) *Notice; report to Congress.*—The Trade Representative shall promptly publish in the Federal Register notice of, and report in writing to the Congress with respect to, any modification or termination of any action taken under section 301 and the reasons therefor.

(c) *Review of necessity.*—

(1) If—

(A) a particular action has been taken under section 301 during any 4-year period, and

(B) neither the petitioner nor any representative of the domestic industry which benefits from such action has submitted to the Trade Representative during the last 60 days of such 4-year period a written request for the continuation of such action,

such action shall terminate at the close of such 4-year period.

(2) The Trade Representative shall notify by mail the petitioner and representatives of the domestic industry described in paragraph (1)(B) of any termination of action by reason of paragraph (1) at least 60 days before the date of such termination.

(3) If a request is submitted to the Trade Representative under paragraph (1)(B) to continue taking a particular action under section 301, the Trade Representative shall conduct a review of—

(A) the effectiveness in achieving the objectives of section 301 of—

(i) such action, and

(ii) other actions that could be taken (including actions against other products or services) and

(B) the effects of such actions on the United States economy, including consumers.

(Jan. 3, 1975, Pub. L. 93-618, §307, as added Aug. 23, 1988, Pub. L. 100-418, §1301, 102 Stat. 1174.)

19 U.S.C. § 2418   Request for information [Section 308]

(a) *In general.*—Under receipt of written request therefor from any person, the Trade Representative shall make available to that person information (other than that to which confidentiality applies) concerning—

(1) the nature and extent of a specific trade policy or practice of a foreign country with respect to particular goods, services, investment, or intellectual property rights, to the extent that such information is available to the Trade Representative or other Federal agencies;

(2) United States rights under any trade agreement and the remedies which may be available under that agreement and under the laws of the United States; and

(3) past and present domestic and international proceedings or actions with respect to the policy or practice concerned.

(b) *If information not available.*—If information that is requested by a person under subsection (a) is not available to the Trade Representative or other Federal agencies, the Trade Representative shall, within 30 days after receipt of the request—

(1) request the information from the foreign government; or

(2) decline to request the information and inform the person in writing of the reasons for refusal.

(c) *Certain business information not made available.*—

(1) Except as provided in paragraph (2), and notwithstanding any other provision of law (including section 552 of title 5, United States Code), no information requested and received by the Trade Representative in aid of any investigation under this chapter shall be made available to any person if—

(A) the person providing such information certifies that—

(i) such information is business confidential,

(ii) the disclosure of such information would endanger trade secrets or profitability, and

(iii) such information is not generally available;

(B) the Trade Representative determines that such certification is well-founded; and

(C) to the extent required in regulations prescribed by the Trade Representative, the person providing such information provides an adequate nonconfidential summary of such information.

(2) The Trade Representative may—

(A) use such information, or make such information available (in his own discretion) to any employee of the Federal Government for use, in any investigation under this chapter, or

(B) may make such information available to any other person in a form which cannot be associated with, or otherwise identify, the person providing the information.

(Jan. 3, 1975, Pub. L. 93-618, §308, as added Aug. 23, 1988, Pub. L. 100-418, §1301, 102 Stat. 1175.)

19 U.S.C. § 2419   Administration [Section 309]

The Trade Representative shall—

(1) issue regulations concerning the filing of petitions and the conduct of investigations and hearings under this subchapter,

(2) keep the petitioner regularly informed of all determinations and developments regarding the investigation conducted with respect to the petition under this chapter, including the reasons for any undue delays, and

(3) submit a report to the House of Representatives and the Senate semiannually describing—

(A) the petitions filed and the determinations made (and reasons therefor) under section 302,

(B) developments in, and the current status of, each investigation or proceeding under this chapter,

(C) the actions taken, or the reasons for no action, by the Trade Representative under section 301 with respect to investigations conducted under this chapter, and

(D) the commercial effects of actions taken under section 301.

(Jan. 3, 1975, Pub. L. 93-618, §309, as added Aug. 23, 1988, Pub. L. 100-418, §1301, 102 Stat. 1175-76.)

19 U.S.C. § 2242   **Identification of countries that deny adequate protection, or market access, for intellectual property rights** [Section 182]

(a) *In general.*—By no later than the date that is 30 days after the date on which the annual report is submitted to Congressional committees under section 181(b) [19 U.S.C. §2241(b)], the United States Trade Representative (hereafter in this section referred to as the "Trade Representative") shall identify—

(1) those foreign countries that—

(A) deny adequate and effective protection of intellectual property rights, or

(B) deny fair and equitable market access to United States persons that rely upon intellectual property protection, and

(2) those foreign countries identified under paragraph (1) that are determined by the Trade Representative to be priority foreign countries.

(b) *Special rules for identifications.*—

(1) In identifying priority foreign countries under subsection (a)(2), the Trade Representative shall only identify those foreign countries—

(A) that have the most onerous or egregious acts, policies, or practices that—

(i) deny adequate and effective intellectual property rights, or

(ii) deny fair and equitable market access to United States persons that rely upon intellectual property protection,

(B) whose acts, policies, or practices described in subparagraph (A) have the greatest adverse impact (actual or potential) on the relevant United States products, and

(C) that are not—

(i) entering into good faith negotiations, or

(ii) making significant progress in bilateral or multilateral negotiations, to provide adequate and effective protection of intellectual property rights.

(2) In identifying priority foreign countries under subsection (a)(2), the Trade Representative shall—

(A) consult with the Register of Copyrights, the Under Secretary of Commerce for Intellectual Property and Director of the United States Patent and Trademark Office, other appropriate officers of the Federal Government, and

(B) take into account information from such sources as may be available to the Trade Representative and such information as may be submitted to the Trade Representative by interested persons, including information contained in reports submitted under section 181(b) [19 U.S.C. §224(b)] and petitions submitted under section 302.

(3) The Trade Representative may identify a foreign country under subsection (a)(1)(B) only if the Trade Representative finds that there is a factual basis for the denial of fair and equitable market access as a result of the violation of international law or agreement, or the existence of barriers, referred to in subsection (d)(3).

(4) In identifying foreign countries under paragraphs (1) and (2) of subsection (a), the Trade Representative shall take into account—

(A) the history of intellectual property laws and practices of the foreign country, including any previous identification under subsection (a)(2), and

(B) the history of efforts of the United States, and the response of the foreign country, to achieve adequate and effective protection and enforcement of intellectual property rights.

(c) *Revocations and additional identifications.—*

(1) The Trade Representative may at any time—

(A) revoke the identification of any foreign country as a priority foreign country under this section, or

(B) identify any foreign country as a priority foreign country under this section,

if information available to the Trade Representative indicates that such action is appropriate.

19 U.S.C. § 2242

(2) The Trade Representative shall include in the semiannual report submitted to the Congress under section 309(3) a detailed explanation of the reasons for the revocation under paragraph (1) of the identification of any foreign country as a priority foreign country under this section.

(d) *Definitions.*—For purposes of this section—

(1) The term "persons that rely upon intellectual property protection" means persons involved in—

(A) the creation, production or licensing of works of authorship (within the meaning of sections 102 and 103 of title 17, United States Code) that are copyrighted, or

(B) the manufacture of products that are patented or for which there are process patents.

(2) A foreign country denies adequate and effective protection of intellectual property rights if the foreign country denies adequate and effective means under the laws of the foreign country for persons who are not citizens or nationals of such foreign country to secure, exercise, and enforce rights relating to patents, process patents, registered trademarks, copyrights and mask works.

(3) A foreign country denies fair and equitable market access if the foreign country effectively denies access to a market for a product protected by a copyright or related right, patent, trademark, mask work, trade secret, or plant breeder's right, through the use of laws, procedures, practices, or regulations which—

(A) violate provisions of international law or international agreements to which both the United States and the foreign country are parties, or

(B) constitute discriminatory nontariff trade barriers.

(4) A foreign country may be determined to deny adequate and effective protection of intellectual property rights, notwithstanding the fact that the foreign country may be in compliance with the specific obligations of the Agreement on Trade-Related Aspects of Intellectual Property Rights referred to in section 101(d)(15) of the Uruguay Round Agreements Act.

19 U.S.C. § 2242

(e) *Publication.*—The Trade Representative shall publish in the Federal Register a list of foreign countries identified under subsection (a) and shall make such revisions to the list as may be required by reason of action under subsection (c).

(f) *Special rule for actions affecting United States cultural industries.—*

(1) *In general.*—By no later than the date that is 30 days after the date on which the annual report is submitted to Congressional committees under section 2241(b) of this title, the Trade Representative shall identify any act, policy, or practice of Canada which—

(A) affects cultural industries,

(B) is adopted or expanded after December 17, 1992, and

(C) is actionable under article 2106 of the North American Free Trade Agreement.

(2) *Special rules for identifications.*—For purposes of section 2412(b)(2)(A) of this title, an act, policy, or practice identified under this subsection shall be treated as an act, policy, or practice that is the basis for identification of a country under subsection (a)(2) of this section, unless the United States has already taken action pursuant to article 2106 of the North American Free Trade Agreement in response to such act, policy, or practice. In deciding whether to identify an act, policy, or practice under paragraph (1), the Trade Representative shall—

(A) consult with and take into account the views of representatives of the relevant domestic industries, appropriate committees established pursuant to section 2155 of this title, and appropriate officers of the Federal Government, and

(B) take into account the information from such sources as may be available to the Trade Representative and such information as may be submitted to the Trade Representative by interested persons, including information contained in reports submitted under section 2241(b) of this title.

(3) *Cultural industries.*—For purposes of this subsection the term "cultural industries" means persons engaged in any of the following activities:

(A) The publication, distribution, or sale of books, magazines, periodicals, or newspapers in print or machine readable form but not including the sole activity of printing or typesetting any of the foregoing.

(B) The production, distribution, sale, or exhibition of film or video recordings.

(C) The production, distribution, sale, or exhibition of audio or video music recordings.

(D) The publication, distribution, or sale of music in print or machine readable form.

(E) Radio communications in which the transmissions are intended for direct reception by the general public, and all radio, television, and cable broadcasting undertakings and all satellite programming and broadcast network services.

(g) *Annual report.*—The Trade Representative shall, by not later than the date by which countries are identified under subsection (a), transmit to the Committee on Ways and Means of the House of Representatives and the Committee on Finance of the Senate, a report on actions taken under this section during the 12 months preceding such report, and the reasons for such actions, including a description of progress made in achieving improved intellectual property protection and market access for persons relying on intellectual property rights.

(Jan. 3, 1975, Pub. L. 93-618, §182, as added Aug. 23, 1988, Pub. L. 100-418, §1303, 102 Stat. 1179; Dec. 8, 1994, Pub. L. 103-465, §313, 108 Stat. 4938; Dec. 8, 1994, Pub. L. 103-465, §313, 108 Stat. 4938)

D. DOCUMENTARY EVIDENCE IN PATENT CASES

28 U.S.C. § 1733   Government records and papers; copies

(a) Books or records of account or minutes of proceedings of any department or agency of the United States shall be admissible to prove the act, transaction or occurrence as a memorandum of which the same were made or kept.

(b) Properly authenticated copies or transcripts of any books, records, papers or documents of any department or agency of the United States shall be admitted in evidence equally with the originals thereof.

28 U.S.C. § 1733

(c) This section does not apply to cases, actions, and proceedings to which the Federal Rules of Evidence apply.

(June 25, 1948, ch. 646, §1, 62 Stat. 946; Jan. 2, 1975, Pub. L. 93-595, §2, 88 Stat. 1949.)

28 U.S.C. § 1741   Foreign official documents

An official record or document of a foreign country may be evidenced by a copy, summary, or excerpt authenticated as provided in the Federal Rules of Civil Procedure.

(June 25, 1948, ch. 646, §1, 62 Stat. 948; May 24, 1949, ch. 139, §92, 63 Stat. 103; Oct. 3, 1964, Pub. L. 88-619, §5, 78 Stat. 996.)

28 U.S.C. § 1744   Copies of United States Patent and Trademark Office documents, generally

Copies of letters patent or of any records, books, papers, or drawings belonging to the United States Patent and Trademark Office and relating to patents, authenticated under the seal of the United States Patent and Trademark Office and certified by the Under Secretary of Commerce for Intellectual Property and Director of the United States Patent and Trademark Office, or by another officer of the United States Patent and Trademark Office authorized to do so by the Director, shall be admissible in evidence with the same effect as the originals.

Any person making application and paying the required fee may obtain such certified copies.

(June 25, 1948, ch. 646, §1, 62 Stat. 948; May 24, 1949, ch. 139, §92, 63 Stat. 103; Nov. 29, 1999, Pub. L. 106-113, §4732, 113 Stat. 1501A-581.)

28 U.S.C. § 1745   Copies of foreign patent documents

Copies of specifications and drawings of foreign letters patent, or applications for foreign letters patent, and copies of excerpts of the official journals and other official publications of foreign patent offices belonging to the United States Patent and Trademark Office, certified in the manner provided by section 1744 of this title are prima facie evidence of their contents and of the dates indicated on their face.

(June 25, 1948, ch. 646, §1, 62 Stat. 948; May 24, 1949, ch. 139, §92, 63 Stat. 103; Oct. 3, 1964, Pub. L. 88-619, §7, 78 Stat. 996; Nov. 29, 1999, Pub. L. 106-113, §4732, 113 Stat. 1501A-581.)

28 U.S.C. § 1781   Transmittal of letter rogatory or request

(a) The Department of State has power, directly, or through suitable channels—

(1) to receive a letter rogatory issued, or request made, by a foreign or international tribunal, to transmit it to the tribunal, officer, or agency in the United States to whom it is addressed, and to receive and return it after execution; and

(2) to receive a letter rogatory issued, or request made, by a tribunal in the United States, to transmit it to the foreign or international tribunal, officer, or agency to whom it is addressed, and to receive and return it after execution.

(b) This section does not preclude—

(1) the transmittal of a letter rogatory or request directly from a foreign or international tribunal to the tribunal, officer, or agency in the United States to whom it is addressed and its return in the same manner; or

(2) the transmittal of a letter rogatory or request directly from a tribunal in the United States to the foreign or international tribunal, officer, or agency to whom it is addressed and its return in the same manner.

(June 25, 1945, ch. 646, §1, 62 Stat. 949; Oct. 3, 1964, Pub. L. 88-619, §8, 78 Stat. 996.)

II. THE PATENT AND TRADEMARK OFFICE

A. ESTABLISHMENT, OFFICERS AND EMPLOYEES

15 U.S.C. § 1511   Bureaus in Department

The following named bureaus, administrations, services, offices, and programs of the public service, and all that pertains thereto, shall be under the jurisdiction and subject to the control of the Secretary of Commerce: *   *   *

(4) United States Patent and Trademark Office;*

* * *

(As amended, Jan. 2, 1975, Pub. L. 93-596, §3, 88 Stat. 1949; Aug. 6, 1981, Pub. L. 97-31, §12, 95 Stat. 154; Nov. 29, 1999, Pub. L. 106-113, §4732, 113 Stat. 1501A-581.)

5 U.S.C. § 3104   Employment of specially qualified scientific and professional personnel

(a) The Director of the Office of Personnel Management may establish, and from time to time revise, the maximum number of scientific or professional positions for carrying out research and development functions which require the services of specially qualified personnel which may be established outside of the General Schedule. Any such position may be established by action of the Director or, under such standards and procedures as the Office prescribes (including procedures under which the prior approval of the Director may be required), by agency action.

(b) The provisions of subsection (a) of this section shall not apply to any Senior Executive Service position (as defined in section 3132(a) of this title [5 USC §3132(a)]).

(c) In addition to the number of positions authorized by subsection (a) of this section, the Librarian of Congress may establish, without regard to the second sentence of subsection (a) of this section, not more than 8 scientific or professional positions to carry out the research and development functions of the Library of Congress which require the services of specially qualified personnel.

(Sept. 6, 1966, Pub. L. 89-554, §1, 80 Stat. 415; Sept. 11, 1967, Pub. L. 90-83, §1, 81 Stat. 196; Aug. 12, 1970, Pub. L. 1-375, §6, 84 Stat. 776; Oct. 13, 1978, Pub. L. 95-454, §§414, 801, 92 Stat. 1178, 1221; Aug. 22, 1986, Pub. L. 99-386, §101, 100 Stat. 821; Oct. 2, 1992, Pub. L. 102-378, §2, 106 Stat. 1346.)

---

* *Ed. Note:* By executive order, the Department of Commerce also has special responsibility in respect of patent protection abroad of inventions resulting from research financed by the government. (*See* notes to 35 U.S.C.§266 (repealed).)

5 U.S.C. § 3325   Appointments to scientific and professional positions

(a) Positions established under section 3104 of this title are in the competitive service. However, appointments to the positions are made without competitive examination on approval of the qualifications of the proposed appointee by the Office of Personnel Management or its designee for this purpose. *   *   *

(Sept. 6, 1966, Pub. L. 89-554, §1, 80 Stat. 423; Oct. 13, 1978, Pub. L. 95-454, §906, 92 Stat. 1224.)

5 U.S.C. § 5102   Definitions; application

*   *   *

(c) This chapter [5 U.S.C. §§5101 et seq. ("Classification")] does not apply to *   *   *

(23) administrative patent judges and designated administrative patent judges in the United States Patent and Trademark Office; *   *   *

(Sept. 6, 1966, Pub. L. 89-554, §1, 80 Stat. 444; Aug. 14, 1979, Pub. L. 96-54, §2, 93 Stat. 382; Nov. 29, 1999, Pub. L. 106-113, §4732, 113 Stat. 1501A-581.)

*   *   *   *   *   *   *

B. PATENT AND TRADEMARK OFFICE AUTHORIZATION

Pub. L. 107-273   Patent and Trademark Office Authorization

§ 13102.   Authorization of amounts available to the Patent and Trademark Office.

(a) *In general.*—There are authorized to be appropriated to the United States Patent and Trademark Office for salaries and necessary expenses for each of the fiscal years 2003 through 2008 an amount equal to the fees estimated by the Secretary of Commerce to be collected in each such fiscal year, respectively, under—

(1) title 35, United States Code; and

(2) the Act entitled "An Act to provide for the registration and protection of trademarks used in commerce, to carry out the provisions of certain international conventions, and for other purposes", approved July 5, 1946 (15 U.S.C. 1051 et seq.) (commonly referred to as the Trademark Act of 1946).

(b) *Estimates.*—Not later than February 15, of each fiscal year, the Undersecretary of Commerce for Intellectual Property and the Director of the Patent and Trademark Office (in this subtitle referred to as the Director) shall submit an estimate of all fees referred to under subsection (a) to be collected in the next fiscal year to the chairman and ranking member of—

(1) the Committees on Appropriations and Judiciary of the Senate; and

(2) the Committees on Appropriations and Judiciary of the House of Representatives.

§ 13103. Electronic filing and processing of patent and trademark applications.

(a) *Electronic filing and processing.*—The Director shall, beginning not later than 90 days after the date of enactment of this Act, and during the 3-year period thereafter, develop an electronic system for the filing and processing of patent and trademark applications, that—

(1) is user friendly; and

(2) includes the necessary infrastructure—

(A) to allow examiners and applicants to send all communications electronically; and

(B) to allow the Office to process, maintain, and search electronically the contents and history of each application.

(b) *Authorization of appropriations.*—Of amounts authorized under section 13102, there is authorized to be appropriated to carry out subsection (a) of this section not more than $50,000,000 for each of fiscal years 2003, 2004, and 2005. Amounts made available pursuant to this subsection shall remain available until expended.

§ 13104. Strategic plan.

(a) Development of plan.—

(1) *In general.*—The Director shall, in close consultation with the Patent Public Advisory Committee and the Trademark Public Advisory Committee, develop a strategic plan that sets forth the goals and methods by which the United States Patent and Trademark Office will, during the 5-year period beginning on January 1, 2003—

(A) enhance patent and trademark quality;

(B) reduce patent and trademark pendency; and

(C) develop and implement an effective electronic system for use by the Patent and Trademark Office and the public for all aspects of the patent and trademark processes, including, in addition to the elements set forth in section 13103, searching, examining, communicating, publishing, and making publicly available, patents and trademark registrations.

(2) *Contents and consultation.*—The strategic plan shall include milestones and objective and meaningful criteria for evaluating the progress and successful achievement of the plan. The Director shall consult with the Public Advisory Committees with respect to the development of each aspect of the strategic plan.

(b) *Report to congressional committees.*—Not later than 4 months after the date of enactment of this Act, the Director shall submit the plan developed under subsection (a) to the Committees on the Judiciary of the Senate and the House of Representatives.

(Nov. 2, 2002, Pub. L 107-273, §§13101- 13104, 116 Stat. 1899.)

III. PROCEEDINGS IN THE PATENT AND TRADEMARK OFFICE

A. HOLIDAYS

5 U.S.C. § 6103   Holidays

(a) The following are legal public holidays:

New Year's Day, January 1.

Birthday of Martin Luther King, Jr., the third Monday in January.

Washington's Birthday, the third Monday in February.

Memorial Day, the last Monday in May.

Independence Day, July 4.

Labor Day, the first Monday in September.

Columbus Day, the second Monday in October.

Veterans Day, November 11.

Thanksgiving Day, the fourth Thursday in November.

Christmas Day, December 25.

(b) For purposes of statutes relating to pay and leave of employees, with respect to a legal public holiday and any other day declared to be a holiday by Federal statute or Executive order, the following rules apply:

(1) Instead of a holiday that occurs on a Saturday, the Friday immediately before is a legal public holiday for—

(A) Employees whose basic workweek is Monday through Friday; and

(B) the purpose of section 6309 [repealed Dec. 31, 1971, Pub. L. 94-183, §2, 89 Stat. 1058.] of this title.

(2) Instead of a holiday that occurs on a regular weekly nonworkday of an employee whose basic workweek is other than Monday through Friday, except the regular weekly nonworkday administratively scheduled for the employee instead of Sunday, the workday immediately before that regular weekly nonworkday is a legal public holiday for the employee.

This subsection, except subparagraph (B) of paragraph (1), does not apply to an employee whose basic workweek is Monday through Saturday.

* * *

(Sept. 6, 1966, Pub. L. 89-554, §1, 80 Stat. 515; June 28, 1968, Pub. L. 90-363, §1, 82 Stat. 250; Sept. 18, 1975, Pub. L. 94-97, 89 Stat. 479; Nov. 2, 1983, Pub. L. 98-144, §1, 97 Stat. 917.)

5 U.S.C. § 6103

D.C. Code § 28-2701   Holidays designated—Time for performing acts extended

The following days in each year, namely, New Year's Day, January 1; Dr. Martin Luther King, Jr.'s Birthday, the third Monday in January; Washington's Birthday, the third Monday in February; Memorial Day, the last Monday in May; Independence Day, July 4; Labor Day, the first Monday in September; Columbus Day, the second Monday in October; Veteran's Day, November 11; Thanksgiving Day, the fourth Thursday in November; Christmas Day, December 25; every Saturday, after twelve o'clock noon; any day appointed by the President of the United States as a day of public feasting or thanksgiving; and the day of the inauguration of the President, in every fourth year, are holidays in the District for all purposes. When a day set apart as a legal holiday, other than the day of the inauguration of the President, falls on a Saturday, the next preceding day is a holiday. When a day set apart as a legal holiday falls on a Sunday, the next succeeding day is a holiday. In such cases, when a Sunday and a holiday or holidays fall on successive days, all commercial papers falling due on any of those days shall, for all purposes of presenting for payment or acceptance, be deemed to mature and be presentable for payment or acceptance on the next secular business day succeeding. Every Saturday is a holiday in the District for (1) every bank or banking institution having an office or banking house located within the District, (2) every Federal savings and loan association whose main office is in the District, and (3) every building association, building and loan association, or savings and loan association, incorporated or unincorporated, organized and operating under the laws of and having an office located within the District. An act which would otherwise be required, authorized, or permitted to be performed on Saturday in the District at the office or banking house of, or by, any such bank or bank institution, Federal savings and loan association, building association, building and loan association, or savings and loan association, if Saturday were not a holiday, shall or may be so performed on the next succeeding business day, and liability or loss of rights of any kind may not result from such delay.

(Aug. 30, 1964, Pub. L. 88-509, §1, 78 Stat. 671; Aug. 1, 1975, D.C. Law 1-11, §103, 22 DCR 1804; July 12, 1977, D.C. Law 2-13, §2, 24 DCR 1443; Mar. 16, 1982, D.C. Law 4-77, §2, 29 DCR 46; Mar. 14, 1985, D.C. Law 5-155, §3, 32 DCR 11.)

D.C. Code § 28-2701

* * * * * * *

IV. PRACTICE BEFORE THE PATENT AND TRADEMARK OFFICE

A. REGULATIONS FOR AGENTS AND ATTORNEYS

5 U.S.C. § 500   Administrative practice; general provisions

* * *

(b) An individual who is a member in good standing of the bar of the highest court of a State may represent a person before an agency on filing with the agency a written declaration that he is currently qualified as provided by this subsection and is authorized to represent the particular person in whose behalf he acts. *   *   *

(e) Subsections (b)–(d) of this section do not apply to practice before the United States Patent and Trademark Office with respect to patent matters that continue to be covered by chapter 3 (sections 31-33) of title 35. * * *

(Sept. 11, 1967, Pub. L. 90-83, §1, 81 Stat. 195; Nov. 29, 1999, Pub. L. 106-113, §4732, 113 Stat. 1501A-581.)

18 U.S.C. § 207   Restrictions on former officers, employees, and elected officials of the executive and legislative branches

(a) *Restrictions on all officers and employees of the executive branch and certain other agencies.—*

(1) Permanent restrictions on representation on particular matters.— Any person who is an officer or employee (including any special Government employee) of the executive branch of the United States (including any independent agency of the United States), or of the District of Columbia, and who, after the termination of his or her service or employment with the United States or the District of Columbia, knowingly makes, with the intent to influence, any communication to or appearance before any officer or employee of any department, agency, court, or court-martial of the United States or the District of Columbia, on behalf of any other person (except the United States or the District of Columbia), in connection with a particular matter—

(A) in which the United States or the District of Columbia is a party or has a direct and substantial interest,

(B) in which the person participated personally and substantially as such officer or employee, and

(C) which involved a specific party or specific parties at the time of such participation,

shall be punished as provided in section 216 of this title.

(2) *Two-year restrictions concerning particular matters under official responsibility.*—Any person subject to the restrictions contained in paragraph (1) who, within 2 years after the termination of his or her service or employment with the United States or the District of Columbia knowingly makes, with the intent to influence, any communication to or appearance before any officer or employee of any department, agency, court, or court-martial of the United States or the District of Columbia, on behalf of any other person (except the United States or the District of Columbia), in connection with a particular matter—

(A) in which the United States or the District of Columbia is a party or has a direct and substantial interest,

(B) which such person knows or reasonably should know was actually pending under his or her official responsibility as such officer or employee within a period of 1 year before the termination of his or her service or employment with the United States or the District of Columbia, and

(C) which involved a specific party or specific parties at the time it was so pending,

shall be punished as provided in section 216 of this title.

(3) *Clarification of restrictions.*—The restrictions contained in paragraphs (1) and (2) shall apply—

(A) in the case of an officer or employee of the executive branch of the United States (including any independent agency), only with respect to communications to or appearances before any officer or employee of any department, agency, court, or court-martial of the United States on behalf of any other person (except the United States), and only with respect to a matter in which the United States is a party or has a direct and substantial interest; and

18 U.S.C. § 207

(B) in the case of an officer or employee of the District of Columbia, only with respect to communications to or appearances before any officer or employee of any department, agency, or court of the District of Columbia on behalf of any other person (except the District of Columbia), and only with respect to a matter in which the District of Columbia is a party or has a direct and substantial interest.

(b) *One-year restrictions on aiding or advising.—*

(1) *In general.*—Any person who is a former officer or employee of the executive branch of the United States (including any independent agency) and is subject to the restrictions contained in subsection (a)(1), or any person who is a former officer or employee of the legislative branch or a former Member of Congress, who personally and substantially participated in any ongoing trade or treaty negotiation on behalf of the United States within the 1-year period preceding the date on which his or her service or employment with the United States terminated, and who had access to information concerning such trade or treaty negotiation which is exempt from disclosure under section 552 of title 5, which is so designated by the appropriate department or agency, and which the person knew or should have known was so designated, shall not, on the basis of that information, knowingly represent, aid, or advise any other person (except the United States) concerning such ongoing trade or treaty negotiation for a period of 1 year after his or her service or employment with the United States terminates. Any person who violates this subsection shall be punished as provided in section 216 of this title.

(2) *Definition.*—For purposes of this paragraph—

(A) the term "trade negotiation" means negotiations which the President determines to undertake to enter into a trade agreement pursuant to section 1102 of the Omnibus Trade and Competitiveness Act of 1988, and does not include any action taken before that determination is made; and

(B) the term "treaty" means an international agreement made by the President that requires the advice and consent of the Senate.

(c) *One-year restrictions on certain senior personnel of the executive branch and independent agencies.—*

(1) *Restrictions.*—In addition to the restrictions set forth in subsections (a) and (b), any person who is an officer or employee (including any special Government employee) of the executive branch of the United States (including an independent agency), who is referred to in paragraph (2), and who, within 1 year after the termination of his or her service or employment as such officer or employee, knowingly makes, with the intent to influence, any communication to or appearance before any officer or employee of the department or agency in which such person served within 1 year before such termination, on behalf of any other person (except the United States), in connection with any matter on which such person seeks official action by any officer or employee of such department or agency, shall be punished as provided in section 216 of this title.

(2) *Persons to whom restrictions apply.*—

(A) Paragraph (1) shall apply to a person (other than a person subject to the restrictions of subsection (d))—

(i) employed at a rate of pay specified in or fixed according to subchapter II of chapter 53 of title 5,

(ii) employed in a position which is not referred to in clause (i) and for which the basic rate of pay, exclusive of any locality-based pay adjustment under section 5302 of title 5 (or any comparable adjustment pursuant to interim authority of the President), is equal to or greater than the rate of basic pay payable for level 5 of the Senior Executive Service;

(iii) appointed by the President to a position under section 105(a)(2)(B) of title 3 or by the Vice President to a position under section 106(a)(1)(B) of title 3,

(iv) employed in a position which is held by an active duty commissioned officer of the uniformed services who is serving in a grade or rank for which the pay grade (as specified in section 201 of title 37) is pay grade 0-7 or above; or

(v) assigned from a private sector organization to an agency under chapter 37 of title 5.

(B) Paragraph (1) shall not apply to a special Government employee who serves less than 60 days in the 1-year period before his or her service or employment as such employee terminates.

18 U.S.C. § 207

(C) At the request of a department or agency, the Director of the Office of Government Ethics may waive the restrictions contained in paragraph (1) with respect to any position, or category of positions, referred to in clause (ii) or (iv) of subparagraph (A), in such department or agency if the Director determines that—

(i) the imposition of the restrictions with respect to such position or positions would create an undue hardship on the department or agency in obtaining qualified personnel to fill such position or positions, and

(ii) granting the waiver would not create the potential for use of undue influence or unfair advantage.

(d) *Restrictions on very senior personnel of the executive branch and independent agencies.*—

(1) *Restrictions.*—In addition to the restrictions set forth in subsections (a) and (b), any person who—

(A) serves in the position of Vice President of the United States,

(B) is employed in a position in the executive branch of the United States (including any independent agency) at a rate of pay payable for level I of the Executive Schedule, or employed in a position in the Executive Office of the President at a rate of pay payable for level II of the Executive Schedule, or

(C) is appointed by the President to a position under section 105(a)(2)(A) of title 3 or by the Vice President to a position under section 106(a)(1)(A) of title 3,

and who, within 1 year after the termination of that person's service in that position, knowingly makes, with the intent to influence, any communication to or appearance before any person described in paragraph (2), on behalf of any other person (except the United States), in connection with any matter on which such person seeks official action by any officer or employee of the executive branch of the United States, shall be punished as provided in section 216 of this title.

(2) *Persons who may not be contacted.*—The persons referred to in paragraph (1) with respect to appearances or communications by a

person in a position described in subparagraph (A), (B), or (C) of paragraph (1) are—

(A) any officer or employee of any department or agency in which such person served in such position within a period of 1 year before such person's service or employment with the United States Government terminated, and

(B) any person appointed to a position in the executive branch which is listed in section 5312, 5313, 5314, 5315, or 5316 of title 5.

* * *

(Oct. 23, 1962, Pub. L. 87-849, §1, 76 Stat. 1123; Oct. 26, 1978, Pub. L. 95-521, §501, 92 Stat. 1864; June 22, 1979, Pub. L. 96-28, 93 Stat. 76; Nov. 30, 1989, Pub. L. 101-194, §101, 103 Stat. 1716; May 4, 1990, Pub. L. 101-280, §§2, 5, 104 Stat. 149, 159; Nov. 5, 1990, Pub. L. 101-509, §529, 104 Stat. 1440; Aug. 6, 1996, Pub. L. 104-179, §6, 110 Stat. 1568; Dec. 17, 2002, Pub. L. 107-347, §209, 116 Stat. 2930.)

* * * * * * *

V. THE COPYRIGHT OFFICE

A. COPYRIGHT OFFICE APPROPRIATIONS*

Pub. L. 107-68   **Copyright Office Appropriations for Fiscal Year 2002**

For necessary expenses of the Copyright Office, $40,896,000, of which not more than $21,880,000, to remain available until expended, shall be derived from collections credited to this appropriation during fiscal year 2002 under section 708(d) of title 17, United States Code: *Provided,* That the Copyright Office may not obligate or expend any funds derived from collections under such section, in excess of the amount authorized for obligation or expenditure in appropriations Acts: *Provided further,* That not more than $5,984,000 shall be derived from collections during fiscal year 2002 under sections 111(d)(2), 119(b)(2), 802(h), and 1005 of such title: *Provided further,* That the total amount available for obligation shall be reduced by the amount by which collections are less than $27,864,000: *Provided further,* That not more than $100,000 of the

---

* *Ed. Note:* As of February 10, 2003, the Copyright Office is operating under a continuing appropriations authorization.

Pub. L. § 107-68

amount appropriated is available for the maintenance of an "International Copyright Institute" in the Copyright Office of the Library of Congress for the purpose of training nationals of developing countries in intellectual property laws and policies: *Provided further,* That not more than $4,250 may be expended, on the certification of the Librarian of Congress, in connection with official representation and reception expenses for activities of the International Copyright Institute and for copyright delegations, visitors, and seminars.

(Nov. 12, 2001, Pub. L. 107-68, 115 Stat. 585.)

* * * * * * *

VI. PLANTS

PLANT VARIETY PROTECTION ACT

Ed. Note: The "Plant Variety Protection Act," protecting novel varieties of sexually reproduced plants, comprises Chapter 57 of title 7; sections 1545 and 2353 of title 28; amendments to 7 U.S.C. 1551, 1562 (The Federal Seed Act) and sections 1338 and 1498 of title 28; and enacting provisions. (Pub. L. 91-577, Dec. 24, 1970, 84 Stat. 1542; Pub. L. 103-349, Oct. 6, 1994, 108 Stat 3136.)

The text of the Act and the Regulations and Rules of Practice of the Plant Variety Protection Office are available in pamphlet form from that Office, Room 301 National Agricultural Library, AMS, USDA, Beltsville, Md. 20705.

* * * * * * *

VII. GOVERNMENT INTERESTS IN PATENTS

A. DEPARTMENT OF ENERGY / NUCLEAR REGULATORY COMMISSION

1. INVENTIONS RELATING TO ATOMIC WEAPONS*

42 U.S.C. § 2014   Definitions

The intent of the Congress in the definitions as given in this section should be construed from the words or phrases used in the definitions. As used in this Act [Atomic Energy Act of 1954]:

* * *

(c) The term "atomic energy" means all forms of energy released in the course of nuclear fission or nuclear transformation.

(d) The term "atomic weapon" means any device utilizing atomic energy, exclusive of the means for transporting or propelling the device (where such means is a separable and divisible part of the device), the

---

* *Ed. Note:* References to the "Commission" in sections 42 U.S.C. 2014 and 2181–90 incl., no longer mean the Atomic Energy Commission, which has been abolished. See sections 42 U.S.C. 5811, 5814, 5841, and 7151, *infra*, under which its functions have been transferred to the Department of Energy and the Nuclear Regulatory Commission. Under the transitional provisions (42 U.S.C. 5871) a reference to "Commission" in any existing statute may mean either of these new agencies.

principal purpose of which is for use as, for development of, a weapon, a weapon prototype, or a weapon test device.

* * *

(u) The term "produce," when used in relation to special nuclear material, means (1) to manufacture, make, produce, or refine special nuclear material; (2) to separate special nuclear material from other substances in which such material may be contained; or (3) to make or to produce new special nuclear material.

* * *

(z) The term "source material" means (1) uranium, thorium, or any other material which is determined by the Commission pursuant to the provisions of section 61 [42 U.S.C. §2091] to be source material; or (2) ores containing one or more of the foregoing materials, in such concentration as the Commission may by regulation determine from time to time.

(aa) The term "special nuclear material" means (1) plutonium, uranium enriched in the isotope 233 or in the isotope 235, and any other material which the Commission, pursuant to the provisions of section 51 [42 U.S.C. §2071], determines to be special nuclear material, but does not include source material; or (2) any material artificially enriched by any of the foregoing, but does not include source material. * * *

(Aug. 30, 1954, c. 1073, ch. 2, §11, 68 Stat. 922; Sept. 2, 1957, Pub. L. 85-256, §3, 71 Stat. 576.)

42 U.S.C. § 2181   Inventions relating to atomic weapons, and filing of reports

(a) No patent shall hereafter be granted for any invention or discovery which is useful solely in the utilization of special nuclear material or atomic energy in an atomic weapon. Any patent granted for any such invention or discovery is hereby revoked, and just compensation shall be made therefor.

(b) No patent hereafter granted shall confer any rights with respect to any invention or discovery to the extent that such invention or discovery is used in the utilization of special nuclear material or atomic energy in atomic weapons. Any rights conferred by any patent heretofore granted for any invention or discovery are revoked to the extent that such invention or discovery is so used, and just compensation shall be made therefor.

(c) Any person who has made or hereafter makes any invention or discovery useful in the production or utilization of special nuclear material or atomic energy, shall file with the Commission a report containing a complete description thereof unless such invention or discovery is described in an application for a patent filed with the Under Secretary of Commerce for Intellectual Property and Director of the United States Patent and Trademark Office by such person within the time required for the filing of such report. The report covering any such invention or discovery shall be filed on or before the one hundred and eightieth day after such person first discovers or first has reason to believe that such invention or discovery is useful in such production or utilization.

(d) The Under Secretary of Commerce for Intellectual Property and Director of the United States Patent and Trademark Office shall notify the Commission of all applications for patents heretofore or hereafter filed which, in his opinion, disclose inventions or discoveries required to be reported under subsection (c) of this section, and shall provide the Commission access to all such applications.

(e) Reports filed pursuant to subsection (c) of this section, and applications to which access is provided under subsection (d) of this section, shall be kept in confidence by the Commission, and no information concerning the same given without authority of the inventor or owner unless necessary to carry out the provisions of any Act of Congress or in such special circumstances as may be determined by the Commission.

(Aug. 30, 1954, c. 1073, ch. 13, §151, 68 Stat. 943; Sept. 6, 1961, Pub. L. 87-206, §§7-9, 75 Stat. 477; Nov. 29, 1999, Pub. L. 106-113, §4732, 113 Stat. 1501A-581.)

42 U.S.C. § 2182 Inventions conceived during Commission contracts

Any invention or discovery, useful in the production or utilization of special nuclear material or atomic energy, made or conceived in the course of or under any contract, subcontract, or arrangement entered into with or for the benefit of the Commission, regardless of whether the contract, subcontract, or arrangement involved the expenditure of funds by the Commission, shall be vested in, and be the property of, the

Commission, except that the Commission may waive its claim to any such invention or discovery under such circumstances as the Commission may deem appropriate, consistent with the policy of this section. No patent for any invention or discovery, useful in the production or utilization of special nuclear material or atomic energy, shall be issued unless the applicant files with the application, or within thirty days after request therefor by the Under Secretary of Commerce for Intellectual Property and Director of the United States Patent and Trademark Office (unless the Commission advises the Under Secretary of Commerce for Intellectual Property and Director of the United States Patent and Trademark Office that its rights have been determined and that accordingly no statement is necessary) a statement under oath setting forth the full facts surrounding the making or conception of the invention or discovery described in the application and whether the invention or discovery was made or conceived in the course of or under any contract, subcontract, or arrangement entered into with or for the benefit of the Commission, regardless of whether the contract, subcontract, or arrangement involved the expenditure of funds by the Commission. The Under Secretary of Commerce for Intellectual Property and Director of the United States Patent and Trademark Office shall as soon as the application is otherwise in condition for allowance forward copies of the application and the statement to the Commission.

The Under Secretary of Commerce for Intellectual Property and Director of the United States Patent and Trademark Office may proceed with the application and issue the patent to the applicant (if the invention or discovery is otherwise patentable) unless the Commission, within 90 days after receipt of copies of the application and statement, directs the Under Secretary of Commerce for Intellectual Property and Director of the United States Patent and Trademark Office to issue the patent to the Commission (if the invention or discovery is otherwise patentable) to be held by the Commission as the agent of and on behalf of the United States.

If the Commission files such a direction with the Under Secretary of Commerce for Intellectual Property and Director of the United States Patent and Trademark Office, and if the applicant's statement claims, and the applicant still believes, that the invention or discovery was not made or conceived in the course of or under any contract, subcontract, or arrangement entered into with or for the benefit of the Commission entitling the Commission to the title to the application or the patent the applicant may, within 30 days after notification of the filing of such a direction, request a hearing before the Board of Patent Appeals and Interferences. The Board shall have the power to hear and determine whether the Commission was entitled to the direction filed with the Under Secretary of Commerce for Intellectual Property and Director of the United States Patent and Trademark Office. The Board shall follow the rules and procedures established for interference cases and an appeal may be taken by either the applicant or the Commission from the final order of the Board to the United States Court of Appeals for the Federal Circuit in accordance with the procedures governing the appeals from the Board of Patent Appeals and Interferences.

If the statement filed by the applicant should thereafter be found to contain false material statements any notification by the Commission that it has no objections to the issuance of a patent to the applicant shall not be deemed in any respect to constitute a waiver of the provisions of this section or of any applicable civil or criminal statute, and the Commission may have the title to the patent transferred to the Commission on the records of the Under Secretary of Commerce for Intellectual Property and Director of the United States Patent and Trademark Office in accordance with the provisions of this section. A determination of rights by the Director pursuant to a contractual provision or other arrangement prior to the request of the Under Secretary of Commerce for Intellectual Property and Director of the United States Patent and Trademark Office for the statement, shall be final in the absence of false material statements or nondisclosure of material facts by the applicant.

(Aug. 30, 1954, c. 1073, ch. 13, §152, 68 Stat. 944; Sept. 6, 1961, Pub. L. 87-206, §10, 75 Stat. 477; Aug. 29, 1962, Pub. L. 87-615, §11, 76 Stat. 411; Apr. 2, 1982, Pub. L. 97-164, §162, 96 Stat. 49; Nov. 8, 1984, Pub. L. 98-622, §205, 98 Stat. 3388; Nov. 29, 1988, Pub. L. 106-113, §4732, 113 Stat. 1501A-581.)

42 U.S.C. § 2183   Nonmilitary utilization

(a) The Commission may, after giving the patent owner an opportunity for a hearing, declare any patent to be affected with the public interest if (1) the invention or discovery covered by the patent is of primary importance in the production or utilization of special nuclear material or atomic energy; and (2) the licensing of such invention or discovery under this section is of primary importance to effectuate the policies and purposes of this Act.

(b) Whenever any patent has been declared affected with the public interest, pursuant to subsection (a) of this section—

(1) the Commission is hereby licensed to use the invention or discovery covered by such patent in performing any of its powers under this Act; and

(2) any person may apply to the Commission for a nonexclusive patent license to use the invention or discovery covered by such patent, and the Commission shall grant such patent license to the extent that it finds that the use of the invention or discovery is of primary importance to the conduct of an activity by such person authorized under this Act.

(c) Any person—

(1) who has made application to the Commission for a license under sections 2073, 2092, 2093, 2111, 2133 or 2134 of this title, or a permit or lease under section 2097 of this title;

(2) to whom such license, permit, or lease has been issued by the Commission;

(3) who is authorized to conduct such activities as such applicant is conducting or proposes to conduct under a general license issued by the Commission under sections 2092 or 2111 of this title; or

(4) whose activities or proposed activities are authorized under section 2051 of this title,

may at any time make application to the Commission for a patent license for the use of an invention or discovery useful in the production or utilization of special nuclear material or atomic energy covered by a patent. Each such application shall set forth the nature and purpose of the use which the applicant intends to make of the patent license, the steps taken by the applicant to obtain a patent license from the owner of the patent, and a statement of the effects, as estimated by the applicant, on the authorized activities which will result from failure to obtain such patent license and which will result from the granting of such patent license.

42 U.S.C. § 2183

(d) Whenever any person has made an application to the Commission for a patent license pursuant to subsection (c) of this section—

(1) the Commission, within 30 days after the filing of such application, shall make available to the owner of the patent all of the information contained in such application, and shall notify the owner of the patent of the time and place at which a hearing will be held by the Commission;

(2) the Commission shall hold a hearing within 60 days after the filing of such application at a time and place designated by the Commission; and

(3) in the event an applicant for two or more patent licenses, the Commission may, in its discretion, order the consolidation of such applications, and if the patents are owned by more than one owner, such owners may be made parties to one hearing.

(e) If, after any hearing conducted pursuant to subsection (d) of this section, the Commission finds that—

(1) the invention or discovery covered by the patent is of primary importance in the production or utilization of special nuclear material or atomic energy;

(2) the licensing of such invention or discovery is of primary importance to the conduct of the activities of the applicant;

(3) the activities to which the patent license are proposed to be applied by such applicant are of primary importance to the furtherance of policies and purposes of this Act; and

(4) such applicant cannot otherwise obtain a patent license from the owner of the patent on terms which the Commission deems to be reasonable for the intended use of the patent to be made by such applicant,

the Commission shall license the applicant to use the invention or discovery covered by the patent for the purposes stated in such application on terms deemed equitable by the Commission and generally not less fair than those granted by the patentee or by the Commission to similar licensees for comparable use.

(f) The Commission shall not grant any patent license pursuant to subsection (e) of this section for any other purpose than that stated in the

42 U.S.C. § 2183

application. Nor shall the Commission grant any patent license to any other applicant for a patent license on the same patent without an application being made by such applicant pursuant to subsection (c) of this section, and without separate notification and hearing as provided in subsection (d) of this section, and without a separate finding as provided in subsection (e) of this section.

(g) The owner of the patent affected by a declaration or a finding made by the Commission pursuant to subsection (b) or (e) of this section shall be entitled to a reasonable royalty fee from the licensee for any use of an invention or discovery licensed by this section. Such royalty fee may be agreed upon by such owner and the patent licensee, or in the absence of such agreement shall be determined for each patent license by the Commission pursuant to section 2187(c) of this title.

(h) The provisions of this section shall apply to any patent the application for which shall have been filed before September 1, 1979.

(Aug. 30, 1954, c. 1073, ch. 13, 68 Stat. 945; amended variously as to the date in (h) the latest being Aug. 17, 1974, Pub. L. 93-377, §6, 88 Stat. 475.)

42 U.S.C. § 2184   Injunctions

No court shall have jurisdiction or power to stay, restrain, or otherwise enjoin the use of any invention or discovery by a patent licensee, to the extent that such use is licensed by section 2183(b) or 2183(e) of this title. If, in any action against such patent licensee, the court shall determine that the defendant is exercising such license, the measure of damages shall be the royalty fee determined pursuant to section 2187(c) of this title, together with such costs, interest, and reasonable attorney's fees as may be fixed by the court. If no royalty fee has been determined, the court shall stay the proceeding until the royalty fee is determined pursuant to section 2187(c) of this title. If any such patent licensee shall fail to pay such royalty fee, the patentee may bring an action in any court of competent jurisdiction for such royalty fee, together with such costs, interest, and reasonable attorney's fees as may be fixed by the court.

(Aug. 30, 1954, c. 1073, ch. 13, §154, 68 Stat. 946.)

42 U.S.C. § 2185   Prior art

In connection with applications for patents covered by this subchapter, the fact that the invention or discovery was known or used before shall be a bar to the patenting of such invention or discovery even though such prior knowledge or use was under secrecy within the atomic energy program of the United States.

(Aug. 30, 1954, c. 1073, ch. 13, §155, 68 Stat. 947.)

42 U.S.C. § 2186   Commission patent licenses

The Commission shall establish standard specifications upon which it may grant a patent license to use any patent declared to be affected with the public interest pursuant to section 2183(a) of this title. Such a patent license shall not waive any of the other provisions of this Act.

(Aug. 30, 1954, c. 1073, ch. 13, 68 Stat. 947; Dec. 12, 1980, Pub. L. 96-517, §7, 94 Stat. 3027.)

42 U.S.C. § 2187   Compensation, awards, and royalties

(a) *Patent Compensation Board.*—The Commission shall designate a Patent Compensation Board to consider applications under this section. The members of the Board shall receive a per diem compensation for each day spent in meetings or conferences, and all members shall receive their necessary traveling or other expenses while engaged in the work of the Board. The members of the Board may serve as such without regard to the provisions of sections 281, 283, or 284 of Title 18 of the United States Code, except in so far as such sections may prohibit any such member from receiving compensation in respect of any particular matter which directly involves the Commission or in which the Commission is directly interested.

(b) *Eligibility.*—

　　(1) Any owner of a patent licensed under section 2188 or subsections 2183(b) or 2183(e) of this title, or any patent licensee thereunder may make application to the Commission for the determination of a reasonable royalty fee in accordance with such procedures as the Commission by regulation may establish.

　　(2) Any person seeking to obtain the just compensation provided in section 2181 of this title shall make application therefor to the Commission in accordance with such procedures as the Commission may by regulation establish.

(3) Any person making any invention or discovery useful in the production or utilization of special nuclear material or atomic energy, who is not entitled to compensation or a royalty therefor under this Act and who has complied with the provisions of section 2181(c) of this title may make application to the Commission for, and the Commission may grant, an award. The Commission may also, after consultation with the General Advisory Committee, and with the approval of the President, grant an award for any especially meritorious contribution to the development, use, or control of atomic energy.

(c) *Standards.*—

(1) In determining a reasonable royalty fee as provided for in section 2183(b) or 2183(e) of this title, the Commission shall take into consideration (A) the advice of the Patent Compensation Board; (B) any defense, general or special, that might be pleaded by a defendant in an action for infringement; (C) the extent to which, if any, such patent was developed through federally financed research; and (D) the degree of utility, novelty, and importance of the invention or discovery, and may consider the cost to the owner of the patent of developing such invention or discovery or acquiring such patent.

(2) In determining what constitutes just compensation as provided for in section 2181 of this title, or in determining the amount of any award under subsection (b)(3) of this section, the Commission shall take into account the considerations set forth in subsection (c)(1) of this subsection and the actual use of such invention or discovery. Such compensation may be paid by the Commission in periodic payments or in a lump sum.

(d) *Limitations.*—Every application under this section shall be barred unless filed within six years after the date on which first accrues the right to such reasonable royalty fee, just compensation, or award for which such application is filed.

(Aug. 30, 1954, c. 1073, ch. 13, §157, 68 Stat. 947; Sept. 6, 1961, Pub. L. 87-206, §11, 75 Stat. 478; May 10, 1974, Pub. L. 93-276, §201, 88 Stat. 119.)

Ed. Note.—The Patent Compensation Board and the General Advisory Committee, referred to above, have been transferred to the Department of Energy. See 42 U.S.C. 5814(d) and 7151, *infra.*

42 U.S.C. § 2187

42 U.S.C. § 2188   Monopolistic use of patents

Whenever the owner of any patent hereafter granted for any invention or discovery of primary use in the utilization or production of special nuclear material or atomic energy is found by a court of competent jurisdiction to have intentionally used such patent in a manner so as to violate any of the antitrust laws specified in section 2135(a) of this title, there may be included in the judgment of the court, in its discretion and in addition to any other lawful sanctions, a requirement that such owner license such patent to any other licensee of the Commission who demonstrates a need therefor. If the court, at its discretion, deems that such licensee shall pay a reasonable royalty to the owner of the patent, the reasonable royalty shall be determined in accordance with section 2187 of this title.

(Aug. 30, 1954, c. 1073, ch. 13, §158, 68 Stat. 947; Sept. 6, 1961, Pub. L. 87-206, §12, 75 Stat. 478.)

42 U.S.C. § 2189   Federally financed research

Nothing in this Act shall affect the right of the Commission to require that patents granted on inventions, made or conceived during the course of federally financed research or operations, be assigned to the United States.

(Aug. 30, 1954, c. 1073, ch. 13, §159, 68 Stat. 948.)

42 U.S.C. § 2190   Saving clause

Any patent application on which a patent was denied by the United States Patent Office under sections 11(a)(1), 11(a)(2), or 11(b) of the Atomic Energy Act of 1946, and which is not prohibited by section 2181 or 2185 of this title may be reinstated upon application to the Director of Patents within one year after enactment of this Act [August 30, 1954], and shall then be deemed to have been continuously pending since its original filing date: *Provided, however,* That no patent issued upon any patent application so reinstated shall in any way furnish a basis of claim against the Government of the United States.

(Aug. 30, 1954, c. 1073, ch. 13, §160, 68 Stat. 948.)

*   *   *   *   *   *   *

42 U.S.C. § 2190

2. GENERAL PROVISIONS

42 U.S.C. § 2201 General provisions

In the performance of its functions the Commission is authorized to

* * *

(g) acquire, purchase, lease, and hold real and personal property, including patents, as agent of and on behalf of the United States, subject to the provisions of section 2224 of this title, and to sell, lease, grant and dispose of such real and personal property as provided in this Act; * * *

(Aug. 30, 1954, c. 1073, ch. 14, §161, 68 Stat. 948.)

42 U.S.C. § 5811 Establishment of Energy Research and Development Administration

There is hereby established an independent executive agency to be known as the Energy Research and Development Administration (hereinafter in this Act referred to as the "Administration").

(Oct. 11, 1974, Pub. L. 93-438, §101, 88 Stat. 1234.)

42 U.S.C. § 5814 Abolition and transfers

(a) The Atomic Energy Commission is hereby abolished. * * *

(b) All other functions of the Commission, the Chairman and members of the Commission, and the officers and components of the Commission are hereby transferred or allowed to lapse pursuant to the provisions of this Act.

(c) There are hereby transferred to and vested in the Administrator all functions of the Atomic Energy Commission, the Chairman and members of the Commission, and the officers and components of the Commission, except as otherwise provided in this Act.

(d) The General Advisory Committee established pursuant to section 2036 of this title, the Patent Compensation Board established pursuant to section 2187 of this title * * * are transferred to the Energy Research and Development Administration and the functions of the Commission with respect thereto * * * are transferred to the Administrator.

* * *

(Oct. 11, 1974, Pub. L. 93-438, §104, 88 Stat. 1237.)

42 U.S.C. § 2201

42 U.S.C. § 5817   Powers of the Administrator [now Secretary of Energy]

(a) *Research and development.*—* * * Such functions of the Administrator under this Act as are applicable to the nuclear activities transferred pursuant to this title shall be subject to the provisions of the Atomic Energy Act of 1954, as amended, and to other authority applicable to such nuclear activities. * * *

* * *

(d) *Acquisition of copyrights and patents.*—The administrator is authorized to acquire any of the following described rights if the property acquired thereby is for the use in, or is useful to, the performance of functions vested in him:

(1) Copyrights, patents, and applications for patents, designs, processes, specifications, and data.

(2) Licenses under copyrights, patents, and applications for patents.

(3) Releases, before suit is brought, for past infringement of patents or copyrights.

* * *

(Pub. L. 93-438, Oct. 11, 1974, 88 Stat. 1240.)

42 U.S.C. § 5841   Establishment and transfers

(a) (1) There is established an independent regulatory Commission to be known as the Nuclear Regulatory Commission which shall be composed of five members * * *

* * *

(f) There are hereby transferred to the Commission all the licensing and related regulatory functions of the Atomic Energy Commission * * * which functions * * * are excepted from the transfer to the Administrator by section 5814(c) of this title. * * *

(Oct. 11, 1974, Pub. L. 93-438, §201, 88 Stat. 1242; Aug. 9, 1975, Pub. L. 94-79, §§201-03, 89 Stat. 413-14.)

42 U.S.C. § 5845   Office of Nuclear Regulatory Research

* * *

(b) Subject to the provisions of this Act, the Director of Nuclear Regulatory Research shall perform such functions as the Commission shall delegate including:

* * *

(2) Engaging in or contracting for research which the Commission deems necessary for the performance of its licensing and related regulatory functions.

* * *

(Oct. 11, 1974, Pub. L. 93-438, §205, 88 Stat. 1246.)

42 U.S.C. § 7151   General transfers

(a) Except as otherwise provided in this Act, there are hereby transferred to, and vested in, the Secretary [of Energy] all of the functions vested by law in the * * * Administrator of the Energy Research and Development Administration or the Energy Research and Development Administration * * *

(Aug. 4, 1977, Pub. L. 95-91, §301, 91 Stat. 577.)

42 U.S.C. § 7261   Acquisition of copyrights, patents etc.

The Secretary is authorized to acquire any of the following described rights if the property acquired thereby is for use by or for, or useful to, the Department:

(1) copyrights, patents, and applications for patents, designs, processes, and manufacturing data;

(2) licenses under copyrights, patents, and applications for patents; and

(3) releases, before suit is brought, for past infringement of patents or copyrights.

(Aug. 4, 1977, Pub. L. 95-91, §651, 91 Stat. 601.)

42 U.S.C. § 7261a   Protection of sensitive technical information

(a) *Property rights in inventions and discoveries.*

(1) Whenever any contractor makes an invention or discovery to which the title vests in the Department of Energy pursuant to exercise of section 202(a)(ii) or (iv) of title 35, United States Code, or pursuant to section 152 of the Atomic Energy Act of 1954 (42 U.S.C. 2182) or section 9 of the Federal Nonnuclear Energy Research and Development Act of 1974 (42 U.S.C. 5908) in the course of or under any Government contract or subcontract of the Naval Nuclear Propulsion Program or the nuclear weapons programs or other atomic energy defense activities of the Department of Energy and the contractor requests waiver of any or all of the Government's property rights, the Secretary of Energy may decide to waive the Government's rights and assign the rights in such invention or discovery.

(2) Such decision shall be made within 150 days after the date on which a complete request for waiver of such rights has been submitted to the Secretary by the contractor. For purposes of this paragraph, a complete request includes such information, in such detail and form, as the Secretary by regulation prescribes as necessary to allow the Secretary to take into consideration the matters described in subsection (b) in making the decision.

(3) If the Secretary fails to make the decision within such 150-day period, the Secretary shall submit to the Committees on Armed Services of the House of Representatives and the Senate, within 10 days after the end of the 150-day period, a report on the reasons for such failure. The submission of such report shall not relieve the Secretary of the requirement to make the decision under this section. The Secretary shall, at the end of each 30-day period after submission of the first report during which the Secretary continues to fail to make the decision required by this section, submit another report on the reasons for such failure to the committees listed in this paragraph.

(b) *Matters to be considered.*—In making a decision under this section, the Secretary shall consider, in addition to the applicable policies of section 152 of the Atomic Energy Act of 1954 (42 U.S.C. 2182) or subsections (c) and (d) of section 9 of the Federal Nonnuclear Energy Research and Development Act of 1974 (42 U.S.C. 5908)—

(1) whether national security will be compromised;

(2) whether sensitive technical information (whether classified or unclassified) under the Naval Nuclear Propulsion Program or the nuclear weapons programs or other atomic energy defense activities of the department of Energy for which dissemination is controlled under federal statutes and regulations will be released to unauthorized person;

(3) whether an organizational conflict of interest contemplated by Federal statutes and regulations will result; and

(4) whether failure to assert such a claim will adversely affect the operation of the Naval Nuclear Propulsion Program or the nuclear weapons programs or other atomic energy defense activities of the Department of Energy.

(Nov. 14, 1986, Pub. L. 99-661, §3131, 100 Stat. 4062; Dec. 4, 1987, Pub. L. 100-180, §3135, 101 Stat. 1240.)

* * * * * * *

3. Rights to Inventions Arising from Sponsored R&D

42 U.S.C. § 5908   Patents and inventions

(a) *Vesting of title to invention and issuance of patents to United States; pre-requisites.*—Whenever any invention is made or conceived in the course of or under any contract of the Secretary other than nuclear energy research, development, and demonstration pursuant to the Atomic Energy Act of 1954 (42 U.S.C. 2011 et. seq.) and the Secretary determines that—

(1) the person who made the invention was employed or assigned to perform research, development, or demonstration work and the invention is related to the work he was employed or assigned to perform, or that it was within the scope of his employment duties, whether or not it was made during working hours, or with a contribution by the Government of the use of Government facilities, equipment, materials, allocated funds, information proprietary to

the Government, or services of Government employees during working hours; or

(2) the person who made the invention was not employed or assigned to perform research, development, or demonstration work, but the invention is nevertheless related to the contract or to the work or duties he was employed or assigned to perform, and was made during working hours, or with a contribution from the Government of the sort referred to in clause (1),

title to such invention shall vest in the United States, and if patents on such invention are issued they shall be issued to the United States, unless in particular circumstances the Secretary waives all or any part of the rights of the United States to such invention in conformity with the provisions of this section.

(b) *Contract as requiring report to Secretary of inventions, etc., made in course of contract.*—Each contract entered into by the Secretary with any person shall contain effective provisions under which such person shall furnish promptly to the Secretary a written report containing full and complete technical information concerning any invention, discovery, improvement, or innovation which may be made in the course of or under such contract.

(c) *Waiver by Secretary of rights of United States: regulations prescribing procedures; record of waiver determinations; objectives.*—Under such regulations in conformity with the provisions of this section as the Secretary shall prescribe, the Secretary may waive all or any part of the rights of the United States under this section with respect to any invention or class of inventions made or which may be made by any person or class of persons in the course of or under any contract of the Secretary if he determines that the interests of the United States and the general public will best be served by such waiver. The Secretary shall maintain a publicly available, periodically updated record of waiver determinations. In making such determinations, the Secretary shall have the following objectives:

(1) Making the benefits of the energy research, development, and demonstration program widely available to the public in the shortest practicable time.

(2) Promoting the commercial utilization of such inventions.

42 U.S.C. § 5908

(3) Encouraging participation by private persons in the Secretary's energy research, development, and demonstration program.

(4) Fostering competition and preventing undue market concentration or the creation or maintenance of other situations inconsistent with the antitrust laws.

(d) *Considerations applicable at time of contracting for waiver determination by Secretary.*—In determining whether a waiver to the contractor at the time of contracting will best serve the interests of the United States and the general public, the Secretary shall specifically include as considerations—

(1) the extent to which the participation of the contractor will expedite the attainment of the purposes of the program;

(2) the extent to which a waiver of all or any part of such rights in any or all fields of technology is needed to secure the participation of the particular contractor;

(3) the extent to which the contractor's commercial position may expedite utilization of the research, development, and demonstration program results;

(4) the extent to which the Government has contributed to the field of technology to be funded under the contract;

(5) the purpose and nature of the contract, including the intended use of the results developed thereunder;

(6) the extent to which the contractor has made or will make substantial investment of financial resources or technology developed at the contractor's private expense which will directly benefit the work to be performed under the contract;

(7) the extent to which the field of technology to be funded under the contract has been developed at the contractor's private expense;

(8) the extent to which the Government intends to further develop to the point of commercial utilization the results of the contract effort;

(9) the extent to which the contract objectives are concerned with the public health, public safety, or public welfare;

(10) the likely effect of the waiver on competition and market concentration; and

42 U.S.C. § 5908

(11) in the case of a nonprofit educational institution, the extent to which such institution has a technology transfer capability and program, approved by the Secretary as being consistent with the applicable policies of this section.

(e) *Considerations applicable to identified invention for waiver determination by Secretary.*—In determining whether a waiver to the contractor or inventor of rights to an identified invention will best serve the interests of the United States and the general public, the Secretary shall specifically include as considerations paragraphs (4) through (11) of subsection (d) of this section as applied to the invention and—

(1) the extent to which such waiver is a reasonable and necessary incentive to call forth private risk capital for the development and commercialization of the invention; and

(2) the extent to which the plans, intentions, and ability of the contractor or inventor will obtain expeditious commercialization of such invention.

(f) *Rights subject to reservation where title to invention vested in United States.*—Whenever title to an invention is vested in the United States there may be reserved to the contractor or inventor—

(1) a revocable or irrevocable nonexclusive, paid-up license for the practice of the invention throughout the world; and

(2) the rights to such invention in any foreign country where the United States has elected not to secure patent rights and the contractor elects to do so, subject to the rights set forth in paragraphs (2), (3), (6), and (7) of subsection (h) of this section: *Provided*, That when specifically requested by the Secretary and three years after issuance of such a patent, the contractor shall submit the report specified in subsection (h)(1) of this section.

(g) – (i) [Repealed].

(j) *Small business status of applicant for waiver or licenses.*—The Secretary shall, in granting waivers or licenses, consider the small business status of the applicant.

(k) *Protection of invention, etc., rights by Secretary.*—The Secretary is authorized to take all suitable and necessary steps to protect any invention or discovery to which the United States holds title, and to require that

42 U.S.C. § 5908

contractors or persons who acquire rights to inventions under this section protect such inventions.

(*l*) *Department of Energy as defense agency of United States for purpose of maintaining secrecy of inventions.*—The Department of Energy shall be considered a defense agency of the United States for the purpose of chapter 17 of Title 35.

(m) *Definitions.*—As used in this section—

(1) the term "person" means any individual, partnership, corporation, association, institution, or other entity;

(2) the term "contract" means any contract, grant, agreement, understanding, or other arrangement, which includes research, development, or demonstration work, and includes any assignment, substitution of parties, or subcontract executed or entered into thereunder;

(3) the term "made," when used in relation to any invention, means the conception or first actual reduction to practice of such invention;

(4) the term "invention" means inventions or discoveries, whether patented or unpatented; and

(5) the term "contractor" means any person having a contract with or on behalf of the Administration.

(n) *Report concerning applicability of existing patent policies to energy programs; time for submission to President and appropriate congressional committees.*—Within twelve months after December 31, 1974, the Secretary with the participation of the Attorney General, the Secretary of Commerce, and other officials as the President may designate, shall submit to the President and the appropriate congressional committees a report concerning the applicability of existing patent policies affecting the programs under this chapter, along with his recommendations for amendments or additions to the statutory patent policy, including his recommendations on mandatory licensing, which he deems advisable for carrying out the purposes of this chapter.

(Dec. 31, 1974, Pub. L. 93-577, §9, 88 Stat. 1887; Aug. 4, 1977, Pub. L. 95-91, §§301, 703, 707, 91 Stat. 577, 606, 607; Dec. 12, 1980, Pub. L. 96-517, §7, 94 Stat. 3027.)

42 U.S.C. § 5908

B. National Aeronautics and Space Administration

42 U.S.C. § 2457   Property rights in inventions

(a) *Exclusive property of United States; issuance of patent.*—Whenever any invention is made in the performance of any work under any contract of the [National Aeronautics and Space] Administration, and the Administrator determines that—

(1) the person who made the invention was employed or assigned to perform research, development, or exploration work and the invention is related to the work he was employed or assigned to perform, or that it was within the scope of his employment duties, whether or not it was made during working hours, or with a contribution by the Government of the use of Government facilities, equipment, materials, allocated funds, information proprietary to the Government, or services of Government employees during working hours; or

(2) the person who made the invention was not employed or assigned to perform research, development, or exploration work, but the invention is nevertheless related to the contract, or to the work or duties he was employed or assigned to perform, and was made during working hours, or with a contribution from the Government of the sort referred to in clause (1),

such invention shall be the exclusive property of the United States, and if such invention is patentable a patent therefor shall be issued to the United States upon application made by the Administrator, unless the Administrator waives all or any part of the rights of the United States to such invention in conformity with the provisions of subsection (f) of this section.

(b) *Contract provisions.*—Each contract entered into by the Administrator with any party for the performance of any work shall contain effective provisions under which such party shall furnish promptly to the Administrator a written report containing full and complete technical information concerning any invention, discovery, improvement, or innovation which may be made in the performance of any such work.

(c) *Patent application.*—No patent may be issued to any applicant other than the Administrator for any invention which appears to the Under Secretary of Commerce for Intellectual Property and Director of the

United States Patent and Trademark Office (hereafter in this section referred to as the "Director") to have significant utility in the conduct of aeronautical and space activities unless the applicant files with the Director, with the application or within thirty days after request therefor by the Director, a written statement executed under oath setting forth the full facts concerning the circumstances under which such invention was made and stating the relationship (if any) of such invention to the performance of any work under any contract of the Administration. Copies of each such statement and the application to which it relates shall be transmitted forthwith by the Director to the Administrator.

(d) *Board of Patent Appeals and Interferences.*—Upon any application as to which any such statement has been transmitted to the Administrator, the Director may, if the invention is patentable, issue a patent to the applicant unless the Administrator, within ninety days after receipt of such application and statement, requests that such patent be issued to him on behalf of the United States. If, within such time, the Administrator files such a request with the Director, the Director shall transmit notice thereof to the applicant, and shall issue such patent to the Administrator unless the applicant within thirty days after receipt of such notice requests a hearing before the Board of Patent Appeals and Interferences on the question whether the Administrator is entitled under this section to receive such patent. The Board may hear and determine, in accordance with rules and procedures established for interference cases, the question so presented, and its determination shall be subject to appeal by the applicant or by the Administrator to the United States Court of Appeals for the Federal Circuit in accordance with procedures governing appeals from decisions of the Board of Patent Appeals and Interferences in other proceedings.

(e) *False representations.*—Whenever any patent has been issued to any applicant in conformity with subsection (d) of this section, and the Administrator thereafter has reason to believe that the statement filed by the applicant in connection therewith contained any false representation of any material fact, the Administrator within five years after the date of issuance of such patent may file with the Director request for the transfer to the Administrator of title to such patent on the records of the Director. Notice of any such request shall be transmitted by the Director to the owner of record of such patent, and title to such patent shall be so transferred to the Administrator unless within thirty days after receipt of such notice such owner of record requests a hearing before the Board of Patent Appeals and Interferences on the question whether any such false representation was contained in such statement. Such question shall be heard and determined, and determination thereof shall be subject to review, in the manner prescribed by subsection (d) of this section for questions arising thereunder. No request made by the Administrator under this subsection for the transfer of title to any patent, and no prosecution for the violation of any criminal statute, shall be barred by any failure of the Administrator to make a request under subsection (d) of this section for the issuance of such patent to him, or by any notice previously given by the Administrator stating that he had no objection to the issuance of such patent to the applicant therefor.

(f) *Waiver; Inventions and Contributions Board.*—Under such regulations in conformity with this subsection as the Administrator shall prescribe, he may waive all or any part of the rights of the United States under this section with respect to any invention or class of inventions made or which may be made by any person or class of persons in the performance of any work required by any contract of the Administration if the Administrator determines that the interests of the United States will be served thereby. Any such waiver may be made upon such terms and under such conditions as the Administrator shall determine to be required for the protection of the interests of the United States. Each such waiver made with respect to any invention shall be subject to the reservation by the Administrator of an irrevocable, nonexclusive, nontransferable, royalty-free license for the practice of such invention throughout the world by or on behalf of the United States or any foreign government pursuant to any treaty or agreement with the United States. Each proposal for any waiver under this subsection shall be referred to an Inventions and Contributions Board which shall be established by the Administrator within the Administration. Such Board shall accord to each interested party an opportunity for hearing, and shall transmit to the Administrator its findings of fact with respect to such proposal and its recommendations for action to be taken with respect thereto.

(g) [Repealed].

42 U.S.C. § 2457

(h) *Protection of title.*—The Administrator is authorized to take all suitable and necessary steps to protect any invention or discovery to which he has title, and to require that contractors or persons who retain title to inventions or discoveries under this section protect the inventions or discoveries to which the Administration has or may acquire a license of use.

(i) *Defense agency.*—The Administration shall be considered a defense agency of the United States for the purpose of chapter 17 of Title 35 of the United States Code.

(j) *Definitions.*—As used in this section—

(1) the term "person" means any individual, partnership, corporation, association, institution, or other entity;

(2) the term "contract" means any actual or proposed contract, agreement, understanding, or other arrangement, and includes any assignment, substitution of parties, subcontract executed or entered into thereunder; and

(3) the term "made," when used in relation to any invention, means the conception or first actual reduction to practice of such invention.

(k) Any object intended for launch, launched, or assembled in outer space shall be considered a vehicle for the purpose of section 272 of title 35, United States Code.

(*l*) The use or manufacture of any patented invention incorporated in a space vehicle launched by the United States Government for a person other than the United States shall not be considered to be a use or manufacture by or for the United States within the meaning of section 1498(a) of title 28, United States Code unless the Administration gives an express authorization or consent for such use or manufacture.

(July 29, 1958, Pub. L. 85-568, §305, 72 Stat. 435; Dec. 12, 1980, Pub. L. 96-517, §7, 94 Stat. 3027; Dec. 21, 1981, Pub. L. 97-96, §7, 95 Stat. 1210; Apr. 2, 1982, Pub. L. 97-164, §162, 96 Stat. 49; Nov. 8, 1984, Pub. L. 98-622, §205, 98 Stat. 3388; Nov. 29, 1999, Pub. L. 106-113, §4732, 113 Stat. 1501A-581.)

42 U.S.C. § 2458   Contributions awards

(a) Subject to the provisions of this section, the Administrator is authorized, upon his own initiative or upon application of any person, to make a monetary award, in such amount and upon such terms as he shall determine to be warranted, to any person (as defined by section 2457 of this title) for any scientific or technical contribution to the Administration which is determined by the Administrator to have significant value in the conduct of aeronautical and space activities. Each application made for any such award shall be referred to the Inventions and Contributions Board established under section 2457 of this title. Such Board shall accord to each such applicant an opportunity for hearing upon such application, and shall transmit to the Administrator its recommendation as to the terms of the award, if any, to be made to such applicant for such contribution. In determining the terms and conditions of any award the Administrator shall take into account—

(1) the value of the contribution to the United States;

(2) the aggregate amount of any sums which have been expended by the applicant for the development of such contribution;

(3) the amount of any compensation (other than salary received for services rendered as an officer or employee of the Government) previously received by the applicant for or on account of the use of such contribution by the United States; and

(4) such other factors as the Administrator shall determine to be material.

(b) If more than one applicant under subsection (a) of this section claims an interest in the same contribution, the Administrator shall ascertain and determine the respective interests of such applicants, and shall apportion any award to be made with respect to such contribution among such applicants in such proportions as he shall determine to be equitable. No award may be made under subsection (a) of this section with respect to any contribution—

(1) unless the applicant surrenders, by such means as the Administrator shall determine to be effective, all claims which such applicant may have to receive any compensation (other than the award made under this section) for the use of such contribution or any element thereof at any time by or on behalf of the United States, or by or on behalf of any foreign government pursuant to any treaty or agreement with the United States, within the United States, or at any other place;

(2) in any amount exceeding $100,000, unless the Administrator has transmitted to the appropriate committees of the Congress a full and

complete report concerning the amount and terms of, and the basis for, such proposed award, and thirty calendar days of regular session of the Congress have expired after receipt of such report by such committees.

(July 29, 1958, Pub. L. 85-568, §306, 72 Stat. 437.)

42 U.S.C. § 2473   Functions of the Administration

* * *

(c) In the performance of its functions the (National Aeronautics and Space) Administration is authorized—

* * *

(3) to acquire * * * such other real and personal property (including patents), or any interest therein, as the Administration deems necessary within and outside the continental United States; * * * to sell and otherwise dispose of real and personal property (including patents and rights thereunder) in accordance with the provision of the Federal Property and Administrative Services Act of 1949, as amended (40 U.S.C. 471 *et seq.*); * * *

(July 29, 1958, Pub. L. 85-568, §203, 72 Stat. 429; Sept. 30, 1978, Pub. L. 95-401, §6, 92 Stat. 860.)

* * * * * * * *

C. DEPARTMENT OF HEALTH AND HUMAN SERVICES

21 U.S.C. § 355   New drugs

(a) No person shall introduce or deliver for introduction into interstate commerce any new drug, unless an approval of an application filed pursuant to subsection (b) or (j) of this section is effective with respect to such drug.

(b) (1) Any person may file with the Secretary an application with respect to any drug subject to the provisions of subsection (a) of this section. Such person shall submit to the Secretary as a part of the application (A) full reports of investigations which have been made to show whether or not such drug is safe for use and whether such drug is effective in use; (B) a full list of the articles used as components of such drug; (C) a full statement of the composition of such drug; (D) a full description of the methods used in, and the facilities and controls used for, the manufacture, processing, and packing of such drug; (E) such samples of such drug and of the articles used as components thereof as the Secretary may require; and (F) specimens of the labeling proposed to be used for such drug. The applicant shall file with the application the patent number and the expiration date of any patent which claims the drug for which the applicant submitted the application or which claims a method of using such drug and with respect to which a claim of patent infringement could reasonably be asserted if a person not licensed by the owner engaged in the manufacture, use, or sale of the drug. If an application is filed under this subsection for a drug and a patent which claims such drug or a method of using such drug is issued after the filing date but before approval of the application, the applicant shall amend the application to include the information required by the preceding sentence. Upon approval of the application, the Secretary shall publish information submitted under the two preceding sentences.

(2) An application submitted under paragraph (1) for a drug for which the investigations described in clause (A) of such paragraph and relied upon by the applicant for approval of the application were not conducted by or for the applicant and for which the applicant has not obtained a right of reference or use from the person by or for whom the investigations were conducted shall also include—

> (A) a certification, in the opinion of the applicant and to the best of his knowledge, with respect to each patent which claims the drug for which such investigations were conducted or which claims a use for such drug for which the applicant is seeking approval under this subsection and for which information is required to be filed under paragraph (1) or subsection (c)—
>
> > (i) that such patent information has not been filed,
> >
> > (ii) that such patent has expired,
> >
> > (iii) of the date on which such patent will expire, or

(iv) that such patent is invalid or will not be infringed by the manufacture, use, or sale of the new drug for which the application is submitted; and

(B) if with respect to the drug for which investigations described in paragraph (1)(A) were conducted information was filed under paragraph (1) or subsection (c) for a method of use patent which does not claim a use for which the applicant is seeking approval under this subsection, a statement that the method of use patent does not claim such a use.

(3) (A) An applicant who makes a certification described in paragraph (2)(A)(iv) shall include in the application a statement that the applicant will give the notice required by subparagraph (B) to—

(i) each owner of the patent which is the subject of the certification or the representative of such owner designated to receive such notice, and

(ii) the holder of the approved application under subsection (b) for the drug which is claimed by the patent or a use of which is claimed by the patent or the representative of such holder designated to receive such notice.

(B) The notice referred to in subparagraph (A) shall state that an application has been submitted under this subsection for the drug with respect to which the certification is made to obtain approval to engage in the commercial manufacture, use, or sale of the drug before the expiration of the patent referred to in the certification. Such notice shall include a detailed statement of the factual and legal basis of the applicant's opinion that the patent is not valid or will not be infringed.

(C) If an application is amended to include a certification described in paragraph (2)(A)(iv), the notice required by subparagraph (B) shall be given when the amended application is submitted.

(4) (A) The Secretary shall issue guidance for the individuals who review applications submitted under paragraph (1) or under section 351 of the Public Health Service Act, which shall relate to

promptness in conducting the review, technical excellence, lack of bias and conflict of interest, and knowledge of regulatory and scientific standards, and which shall apply equally to all individuals who review such applications.

(B) The Secretary shall meet with a sponsor of an investigation or an applicant for approval for a drug under this subsection or section 351 of the Public Health Service Act if the sponsor or applicant makes a reasonable written request for a meeting for the purpose of reaching agreement on the design and size of clinical trials intended to form the primary basis of an effectiveness claim. The sponsor or applicant shall provide information necessary for discussion and agreement on the design and size of the clinical trials. Minutes of any such meeting shall be prepared by the Secretary and made available to the sponsor or applicant upon request.

(C) Any agreement regarding the parameters of the design and size of clinical trials of a new drug under this paragraph that is reached between the Secretary and a sponsor or applicant shall be reduced to writing and made part of the administrative record by the Secretary. Such agreement shall not be changed after the testing begins, except—

(i) with the written agreement of the sponsor or applicant; or

(ii) pursuant to a decision, made in accordance with subparagraph (D) by the director of the reviewing division, that a substantial scientific issue essential to determining the safety or effectiveness of the drug has been identified after the testing has begun.

(D) A decision under subparagraph (C)(ii) by the director shall be in writing and the Secretary shall provide to the sponsor or applicant an opportunity for a meeting at which the director and the sponsor or applicant will be present and at which the director will document the scientific issue involved.

(E) The written decisions of the reviewing division shall be binding upon, and may not directly or indirectly be changed by, the field or compliance division personnel unless such field or compliance division personnel demonstrate to the reviewing division why such decision should be modified.

(F) No action by the reviewing division may be delayed because of the unavailability of information from or action by field personnel unless the reviewing division determines that a delay is necessary to assure the marketing of a safe and effective drug.

(G) For purposes of this paragraph, the reviewing division is the division responsible for the review of an application for approval of a drug under this subsection or section 351 of the Public Health Service Act (including all scientific and medical matters, chemistry, manufacturing, and controls).

(c) (1) Within one hundred and eighty days after the filing of an application under subsection (b), or such additional period as may be agreed upon by the Secretary and the applicant, the Secretary shall either—

(A) approve the application if he then finds that none of the grounds for denying approval specified in subsection (d) of this section applies, or

(B) give the applicant notice of an opportunity for a hearing before the Secretary under subsection (d) of this section on the question whether such application is approvable. If the applicant elects to accept the opportunity for hearing by written request with thirty days after such notice, such hearing shall commence not more than ninety days after the expiration of such thirty days unless the Secretary and the applicant otherwise agree. Any such hearing shall thereafter be conducted on an expedited basis and the Secretary's order thereon shall be issued within ninety days after the date fixed by the Secretary for filing final briefs.

(2) If the patent information described in subsection (b) could not be filed with the submission of an application under subsection (b) because the application was filed before the patent information was required under subsection (b) or a patent was issued after the application was approved under such subsection, the holder of an approved application shall file with the Secretary the patent number and the expiration date of any patent which claims the drug for which the application was submitted or which claims a method of using such

drug and with respect to which a claim of patent infringement could reasonably be asserted if a person not licensed by the owner engaged in the manufacture, use, or sale of the drug. If the holder of an approved application could not file patent information under subsection (b) because it was not required at the time the application was approved, the holder shall file such information under this subsection not later than thirty days after the date of the enactment of this sentence, and if the holder of an approved application could not file patent information under subsection (b) because no patent had been issued when an application was filed or approved, the holder shall file such information under this subsection not later than thirty days after the date the patent involved is issued. Upon the submission of patent information under this subsection, the Secretary shall publish it.

(3) The approval of an application filed under subsection (b) which contains a certification required by paragraph (2) of such subsection shall be made effective on the last applicable date determined under the following:

(A) If the applicant only made a certification described in clause (i) or (ii) of subsection (b)(2)(A) or in both such clauses, the approval may be made effective immediately.

(B) If the applicant made a certification described in clause (iii) of subsection (b)(2)(A), the approval may be made effective on the date certified under clause (iii).

(C) If the applicant made a certification described in clause (iv) of subsection (b)(2)(A), the approval shall be made effective immediately unless an action is brought for infringement of a patent which is the subject of the certification before the expiration of forty-five days from the date the notice provided under paragraph (3)(B) is received. If such an action is brought before the expiration of such days, the approval may be made effective upon the expiration of the thirty-month period beginning on the date of the receipt of the notice provided under paragraph (3)(B) or such shorter or longer period as the court may order because either party to the action failed to reasonably cooperate in expediting the action, except that—

21 U.S.C. § 355

(i) if before the expiration of such period the court decides that such patent is invalid or not infringed, the approval may be made effective on the date of the court decision.

(ii) if before the expiration of such period the court decides that such patent has been infringed, the approval may be made effective on such date as the court orders under section 271(e)(4)(A) of title 35, United States Code, or

(iii) if before the expiration of such period the court grants a preliminary injunction prohibiting the applicant from engaging in the commercial manufacture or sale of the drug until the court decides the issues of patent validity and infringement and if the court decides that such patent is invalid or not infringed, the approval shall be made effective on the date of such court decision.

In such an action, each of the parties shall reasonably cooperate in expediting the action. Until the expiration of forty-five days from the date the notice made under paragraph (3)(B) is received, no action may be brought under section 2201 of title 28, United States Code, for a declaratory judgment with respect to the patent. Any action brought under such section 2201 shall be brought in the judicial district where the defendant has its principal place of business or a regular and established place of business.

(D) (i) If an application (other than an abbreviated new drug application) submitted under subsection (b) for a drug, no active ingredient (including any ester or salt of the active ingredient) of which has been approved in any other application under subsection (b), was approved during the period beginning January 1, 1982, and ending on the date of the enactment of this subsection [September 24, 1984], the Secretary may not make the approval of another application for a drug for which the investigations described in clause (A) of subsection (b)(1) and relied upon by the applicant for approval of the application were not conducted by or for the applicant and for which the applicant has not obtained a right of reference or use from the person by or for whom the investigations were conducted effective before the expiration of ten years from the date of the approval of the application previously approved under subsection (b).

(ii) If an application submitted under subsection (b) for a drug, no active ingredient (including any ester or salt of the active ingredient) of which has been approved in any other application under subsection (b), is approved after the date of the enactment of this clause [September 24, 1984], no application which refers to the drug for which the subsection (b) application was submitted and for which the investigations described in clause (A) of subsection (b)(1) and relied upon by the applicant for approval of the application was not conducted by or for the applicant and for which the applicant has not obtained a right of reference or use from the person by or for whom the investigations were conducted may be submitted under subsection (b) before the expiration of five years from the date of the approval of the application under subsection (b), except that such an application may be submitted under subsection (b) after the expiration of four years from the date of the approval of the subsection (b) application if it contains a certification of patent invalidity or noninfringement described in clause (iv) of subsection (b)(2)(A). The approval of such an application shall be made effective in accordance with this paragraph except that, if an action for patent infringement is commenced during the one-year period beginning forty-eight months after the date of the approval of the subsection (b) application, the thirty-month period referred to in subparagraph (C) shall be extended by such amount of time (if any) which is required for seven and one-half years to have elapsed from the date of approval of the subsection (b) application.

(iii) If an application submitted under subsection (b) for a drug, which includes an active ingredient (including any ester or salt of the active ingredient) that has been approved in another application approved under subsection (b), is approved after the date of the enactment of this clause and if such application contains reports of new clinical investigations (other than bioavailability studies) essential to the ap-

21 U.S.C. § 355

proval of the application and conducted or sponsored by the applicant, the Secretary may not make the approval of an application submitted under subsection (b) for the conditions of approval of such drug in the approved subsection (b) application effective before the expiration of three years from the date of the approval of the application under subsection (b) if the investigations described in clause (A) of subsection (b)(1) and relied upon by the applicant for approval of the application were not conducted by or for the applicant and if the applicant has not obtained a right of reference or use from the person by or for whom the investigations were conducted.

(iv) If a supplement to an application approved under subsection (b) is approved after the date of enactment of this clause and the supplement contains reports of new clinical investigations (other than bioavailability studies) essential to the approval of the supplement and conducted or sponsored by the person submitting the supplement, the Secretary may not make the approval of an application submitted under subsection (b) for a change approved in the supplement effective before the expiration of three years from the date of the approval of the supplement under subsection (b) if the investigations described in clause (A) of subsection (b)(1) and relied upon by the applicant for approval of the application were not conducted by or for the applicant and if the applicant has not obtained a right of reference or use from the person by or for whom the investigations were conducted.

(v) If an application (or supplement to an application) submitted under subsection (b) for a drug, which includes an active ingredient (including any ester or salt of the active ingredient) that has been approved in another application under subsection (b), was approved during the period beginning January 1, 1982, and ending on the date of the enactment of this clause, the Secretary may not make the approval of an application submitted under this subsection and for which the investigations described in clause (A) of subsection (b)(1) and relied upon by the applicant for approval of the application were not conducted by or for the applicant and for which the applicant has not obtained a right of reference or use from the person by or for whom the investigations were conducted and which refers to the drug for which the subsection (b) application was submitted effective before the expiration of two years from the date of enactment of this clause.

(4) A drug manufactured in a pilot or other small facility may be used to demonstrate the safety and effectiveness of the drug and to obtain approval for the drug prior to manufacture of the drug in a larger facility, unless the Secretary makes a determination that a full scale production facility is necessary to ensure the safety or effectiveness of the drug.

(d) If the Secretary finds, after due notice to the applicant in accordance with subsection (c) of this section and giving him an opportunity for a hearing, in accordance with said subsection, that (1) the investigations, reports of which are required to be submitted to the Secretary pursuant to subsection (b) of this section, do not include adequate tests by all methods reasonably applicable to show whether or not such drug is safe for use under the conditions prescribed, recommended, or suggested in the proposed labeling thereof; (2) the results of such tests show that such drug is unsafe for use under such conditions or do not show that such drug is safe for use under such conditions; (3) the methods used in, and the facilities and controls used for, the manufacture, processing, and packing of such drug are inadequate to preserve its identity, strength, quality, and purity; (4) upon the basis of the information submitted to him as part of the application, or upon the basis of any other information before him with respect to such drug, he has insufficient information to determine whether such drug is safe for use under such conditions; or (5) evaluated on the basis of the information submitted to him as part of the application and any other information before him with respect to such drug, there is a lack of substantial evidence that the drug will have the effect it purports or is represented to have under the conditions of use prescribed, recommended, or suggested in the proposed labeling thereof; or (6) the application failed to contain the patent information prescribed by subsection (b); or (7) based on a fair evaluation of all material facts, such labeling is false or misleading in any particular; he shall issue an order refusing to approve the application. If, after such notice and opportunity for hearing, the Secretary finds that clauses (1) through (7) do not apply, he shall issue an order approving the application. As used in this subsection and subsection (e) of this section, the term "substantial evidence" means evidence consisting of adequate and well-controlled investigations, including clinical investigations, by experts qualified by scientific training and experience to evaluate the effectiveness of the drug involved, on the basis of which it could fairly and responsibly be concluded by such experts that the drug will have the effect it purports or is represented to have under the conditions of use prescribed, recommended, or suggested in the labeling or proposed labeling thereof.

(e) The Secretary shall, after due notice and opportunity for hearing to the applicant, withdraw approval of an application with respect to any drug under this section if the Secretary finds (1) that clinical or other experience, tests, or other scientific data show that such drug is unsafe for use under the conditions of use upon the basis of which the application was approved; (2) that new evidence of clinical experience, not contained in such application or not available to the Secretary until after such application was approved, or tests by new methods, or tests by methods not deemed reasonably applicable when such application was approved, evaluated together with the evidence available to the Secretary when the application was approved, shows that such drug is not shown to be safe for use under the conditions of use upon the basis of which the application was approved; or (3) on the basis of new information before him with respect to such drug, evaluated together with the evidence available to him when the application was approved, that there is a lack of substantial evidence that the drug will have the effect it purports or is represented to have under the conditions of use prescribed, recommended, or suggested in the labeling thereof; or (4) the patent information prescribed by subsection (c) was not filed within thirty days after the receipt of written notice from the Secretary specifying the failure to file such information; or (5) that the application contains any untrue statement of a material fact: *Provided,* That if the Secretary (or in his absence the officer acting as Secretary) finds that there is an imminent hazard to the public health, he may suspend the approval of such application immediately, and give the applicant prompt notice of his action and afford the applicant the opportunity for an expedited hearing under this subsection; but the authority conferred by this proviso to suspend the approval of an application shall not be delegated. The Secretary may also, after due notice and opportunity for hearing to the applicant, withdraw the approval of an application submitted under subsection (b) or (j) with respect to any drug under this section if the Secretary finds (1) that the applicant has failed to establish a system for maintaining required records, or has repeatedly or deliberately failed to maintain such records or to make required reports, in accordance with a regulation or order under subsection (k) of this section or to comply with the notice requirements of section 360(j)(2) of this title, or the applicant has refused to permit access to, or copying or verification of, such records as required by paragraph (2) of such subsection; or (2) that on the basis of new information before him, evaluated together with the evidence before him when the application was approved, the methods used in, or the facilities and controls used for, the manufacture, processing, and packing of such drug are inadequate to assure and preserve its identity, strength, quality, and purity and were not made adequate within a reasonable time after receipt of written notice from the Secretary specifying the matter complained of; or (3) that on the basis of new information before him, evaluated together with the evidence before him when the application was approved, the labeling of such drug, based on a fair evaluation of all material facts, is false or misleading in any particular and was not corrected within a reasonable time after receipt of written notice from the Secretary specifying the matter complained of. Any order under the subsection shall state the findings upon which it is based.

(f) Whenever the Secretary finds that the facts so require, he shall revoke any previous order under subsection (d) or (e) of this section refusing, withdrawing, or suspending approval of an application and shall approve such application or reinstate such approval, as may be appropriate.

(g) Orders of the Secretary issued under this section shall be served (1) in person by any officer or employee of the Department designated by the Secretary or (2) by mailing the order by registered mail or by certi-

21 U.S.C. § 355

fied mail addressed to the applicant or respondent at his last-known address in the records of the Secretary.

(h) An appeal may be taken by the applicant from an order of the Secretary refusing or withdrawing approval of an application under this section. Such appeal shall be taken by filing in the United States court of appeals for the circuit wherein such applicant resides or has his principal place of business, or in the United States Court of Appeals for the District of Columbia Circuit, within sixty days after the entry of such order, a written petition praying that the order of the Secretary be set aside. A copy of such petition shall be forthwith transmitted by the clerk of the court to the Secretary, or any officer designated by him for that purpose, and thereupon the Secretary shall certify and file in the court the record upon which the order complained of was entered, as provided in section 2112 of title 28, United States Code. Upon the filing of such petition such court shall have exclusive jurisdiction to affirm or set aside such order, except that until the filing of the record the Secretary may modify or set aside his order. No objection to the order of the Secretary shall be considered by the court unless such objection shall have been urged before the Secretary or unless there were reasonable grounds for failure so to do. The finding of the Secretary as to the facts, if supported by substantial evidence, shall be conclusive. If any person shall apply to the court for leave to adduce additional evidence, and shall show to the satisfaction of the court that such additional evidence is material and that there were reasonable grounds for failure to adduce such evidence in the proceeding before the Secretary, the court may order such additional evidence to be taken before the Secretary and to be adduced upon the hearing in such manner and upon such terms and conditions as to the court may seem proper. The Secretary may modify his findings as to the facts by reason of the additional evidence so taken, and he shall file with the court such modified findings which, if supported by substantial evidence, shall be conclusive, and his recommendation, if any, for the setting aside of the original order. The judgment of the court affirming or setting aside any such order of the Secretary shall be final, subject to review by the Supreme Court of the United States upon certiorari or certification as provided in section 1254 of title 28 of the United States Code. The commencement of proceedings under this subsection shall not, unless specifically ordered by the court to the contrary, operate as a stay of the Secretary's order.

(i) (1) The Secretary shall promulgate regulations for exempting from the operation of the foregoing subsections of this section drugs intended solely for investigational use by experts qualified by scientific training and experience to investigate the safety and effectiveness of drugs. Such regulations may, within the discretion of the Secretary, among other conditions relating to the protection of the public health, provide for conditioning such exemption upon—

(A) the submission to the Secretary, before any clinical testing of a new drug is undertaken, of reports, by the manufacturer or the sponsor of the investigation of such drug, of preclinical tests (including tests on animals) of such drug adequate to justify the proposed clinical testing;

(B) the manufacturer or the sponsor of the investigation of a new drug proposed to be distributed to investigators for clinical testing obtaining a signed agreement from each of such investigators that patients to whom the drug is administered will be under his personal supervision, or under the supervision of investigators responsible to him, and that he will not supply such drug to any other investigator, or to clinics, for administration to human beings; and

(C) the establishment and maintenance of such records, and the making of such reports to the Secretary, by the manufacturer or the sponsor of the investigation of such drug, of data (including but not limited to analytical reports by investigators) obtained as the result of such investigational use of such drug, as the Secretary finds will enable him to evaluate the safety and effectiveness of such drug in the event of the filing of an application pursuant to subsection (b) of this section.

(2) Subject to paragraph (3), a clinical investigation of a new drug may begin 30 days after the Secretary has received from the manufacturer or sponsor of the investigation a submission containing such information about the drug and the clinical investigation, including—

(A) information on design of the investigation and adequate reports of basic information, certified by the applicant to be accurate reports, necessary to assess the safety of the drug for use in clinical investigation; and

(B) adequate information on the chemistry and manufacturing of the drug, controls available for the drug, and primary data tabulations from animal or human studies.

(3) (A) At any time, the Secretary may prohibit the sponsor of an investigation from conducting the investigation (referred to in this paragraph as a "clinical hold") if the Secretary makes a determination described in subparagraph (B). The Secretary shall specify the basis for the clinical hold, including the specific information available to the Secretary which served as the basis for such clinical hold, and confirm such determination in writing.

(B) For purposes of subparagraph (A), a determination described in this subparagraph with respect to a clinical hold is that—

(i) the drug involved represents an unreasonable risk to the safety of the persons who are the subjects of the clinical investigation, taking into account the qualifications of the clinical investigators, information about the drug, the design of the clinical investigation, the condition for which the drug is to be investigated, and the health status of the subjects involved; or

(ii) the clinical hold should be issued for such other reasons as the Secretary may by regulation establish (including reasons established by regulation before the date of the enactment of the Food and Drug Administration Modernization Act of 1997).

(C) Any written request to the Secretary from the sponsor of an investigation that a clinical hold be removed shall receive a decision, in writing and specifying the reasons therefor, within 30 days after receipt of such request. Any such request shall include sufficient information to support the removal of such clinical hold.

(4) Regulations under paragraph (1) shall provide that such exemption shall be conditioned upon the manufacturer, or the sponsor of the investigation, requiring that experts using such drugs for investigational purposes certify to such manufacturer or sponsor that they will inform any human beings to whom such drugs, or any controls used in connection therewith, are being administered, or their repre-

sentatives, that such drugs are being used for investigational purposes and will obtain the consent of such human beings or their representatives, except where it is not feasible or it is contrary to the best interests of such human beings. Nothing in this subsection shall be construed to require any clinical investigator to submit directly to the Secretary reports on the investigational use of drugs.

(j) (1) Any person may file with the Secretary an abbreviated application for the approval of a new drug.

(2) (A) An abbreviated application for a new drug shall contain—

(i) information to show that the conditions of use prescribed, recommended, or suggested in the labeling proposed for the new drug have been previously approved for a drug listed under paragraph (7) (hereinafter in this subsection referred to as a "listed drug");

(ii) (I) if the listed drug referred to in clause (i) has only one active ingredient, information to show that the active ingredient of the new drug is the same as that of the listed drug;

(II) if the listed drug referred to in clause (i) has more than one active ingredient, information to show that the active ingredients of the new drug are the same as those of the listed drug, or

(III) if the listed drug referred to in clause (i) has more than one active ingredient and if one of the active ingredients of the new drug is different and the application is filed pursuant to the approval of a petition filed under subparagraph (C), information to show that the other active ingredients of the new drug are the same as the active ingredients of the listed drug, information to show that the different active ingredient is an active ingredient of a listed drug or of a drug which does not meet the requirements of section 201(p) [21 U.S.C. §321(p)], and such other information respecting the different active ingredient with respect to which the petition was filed as the Secretary may require;

(iii) information to show that the route of administration, the dosage form, and the strength of the new drug are the same as those of the listed drug referred to in clause (i) or, if the route of administration, the dosage form, or the strength of the new drug is different and the application is filed pursuant to the approval of a petition filed under subparagraph (C), such information respecting the route of administration, dosage form, or strength with respect to which the petition was filed as the Secretary may require;

(iv) information to show that the new drug is bioequivalent to the listed drug referred to in clause (i), except that if the application is filed pursuant to the approval of a petition filed under subparagraph (C), information to show that the active ingredients of the new drug are of the same pharmacological or therapeutic class as those of the listed drug referred to in clause (i) and the new drug can be expected to have the same therapeutic effect as the listed drug when administered to patients for a condition of use referred to in clause (i);

(v) information to show that the labeling proposed for the new drug is the same as the labeling approved for the listed drug referred to in clause (i) except for changes required because of differences approved under a petition filed under subparagraph (C) or because the new drug and the listed drug are produced or distributed by different manufacturers;

(vi) the items specified in clauses (B) through (F) of subsection (b)(1);

(vii) a certification, in the opinion of the applicant and to the best of his knowledge, with respect to each patent which claims the listed drug referred to in clause (i) or which claims a use for such listed drug for which the applicant is seeking approval under this subsection and for which information is required to be filed under subsection (b) or (c)—

(I) that such patent information has not been filed,

(II) that such patent has expired,

(III) of the date on which such patent will expire, or

(IV) that such patent is invalid or will not be infringed by the manufacture, use, or sale of the new drug for which the application is submitted; and

(viii) if with respect to the listed drug referred to in clause (i) information was filed under subsection (b) or (c) for a method of use patent which does not claim a use for which the applicant is seeking approval under this subsection, a statement that the method of use patent does not claim such a use.

The Secretary may not require that an abbreviated application contain information in addition to that required by clauses (i) through (viii).

(B) (i) An applicant who makes a certification described in sub-paragraph (A)(vii)(IV) shall include in the application a statement that the applicant will give the notice required by clause (ii) to—

(I) each owner of the patent which is the subject of the certification or the representative of such owner designated to receive such notice, and

(II) the holder of the approved application under subsection (b) for the drug which is claimed by the patent or a use of which is claimed by the patent or the representative of such holder designated to receive such notice.

(ii) The notice referred to in clause (i) shall state that an application, which contains data from bioavailability or bioequivalence studies, has been submitted under this subsection for the drug with respect to which the certification is made to obtain approval to engage in the commercial manufacture, use, or sale of such drug before the expiration of the patent referred to in the certification. Such notice shall include a detailed statement of the factual and legal basis of the applicant's opinion that the patent is not valid or will not be infringed.

(iii) If an application is amended to include a certification described in subparagraph (A)(vii)(IV), the notice required by clause (ii) shall be given when the amended application is submitted.

(C) If a person wants to submit an abbreviated application for a new drug which has a different active ingredient or whose route of administration, dosage form, or strength differ from that of a listed drug, such person shall submit a petition to the Secretary seeking permission to file such an application. The Secretary shall approve or disapprove a petition submitted under this subparagraph within ninety days of the date the petition is submitted. The Secretary shall approve such a petition unless the Secretary finds—

(i) that investigations must be conducted to show the safety and effectiveness of the drug or of any of its active ingredients, the route of administration, the dosage form, or strength which differ from the listed drug; or

(ii) that any drug with a different active ingredient may not be adequately evaluated for approval as safe and effective on the basis of the information required to be submitted in an abbreviated application.

(3) (A) The Secretary shall issue guidance for the individuals who review applications submitted under paragraph (1), which shall relate to promptness in conducting the review, technical excellence, lack of bias and conflict of interest, and knowledge of regulatory and scientific standards, and which shall apply equally to all individuals who review such applications.

(B) The Secretary shall meet with a sponsor of an investigation or an applicant for approval for a drug under this subsection if the sponsor or applicant makes a reasonable written request for a meeting for the purpose of reaching agreement on the design and size of bioavailability and bioequivalence studies needed for approval of such application. The sponsor or applicant shall provide information necessary for discussion and agreement on the design and size of such studies. Minutes of any such meeting shall be prepared by the Secretary and made available to the sponsor or applicant.

(C) Any agreement regarding the parameters of design and size of bioavailability and bioequivalence studies of a drug under this paragraph that is reached between the Secretary and a sponsor or applicant shall be reduced to writing and made part of the administrative record by the Secretary. Such agreement shall not be changed after the testing begins, except—

(i) with the written agreement of the sponsor or applicant; or

(ii) pursuant to a decision, made in accordance with subparagraph (D) by the director of the reviewing division, that a substantial scientific issue essential to determining the safety or effectiveness of the drug has been identified after the testing has begun.

(D) A decision under subparagraph (C)(ii) by the director shall be in writing and the Secretary shall provide to the sponsor or applicant an opportunity for a meeting at which the director and the sponsor or applicant will be present and at which the director will document the scientific issue involved.

(E) The written decisions of the reviewing division shall be binding upon, and may not directly or indirectly be changed by, the field or compliance office personnel unless such field or compliance office personnel demonstrate to the reviewing division why such decision should be modified.

(F) No action by the reviewing division may be delayed because of the unavailability of information from or action by field personnel unless the reviewing division determines that a delay is necessary to assure the marketing of a safe and effective drug.

(G) For purposes of this paragraph, the reviewing division is the division responsible for the review of an application for approval of a drug under this subsection (including scientific matters, chemistry, manufacturing, and controls).

(4) Subject to paragraph (5), the Secretary shall approve an application for a drug unless the Secretary finds—

(A) the methods used in, or the facilities and controls used for, the manufacture, processing, and packing of the drug are inadequate to assure and preserve its identity, strength, quality, and purity;

(B) information submitted with the application is insufficient to show that each of the proposed conditions of use have been previously approved for the listed drug referred to in the application;

(C) (i) if the listed drug has only one active ingredient, information submitted with the application is insufficient to show that the active ingredient is the same as that of the listed drug;

(ii) if the listed drug has more than one active ingredient, information submitted with the application is insufficient to show that the active ingredients are the same as the active ingredients of the listed drug, or

(iii) if the listed drug has more than one active ingredient and if the application is for a drug which has an active ingredient different from the listed drug, information submitted with the application is insufficient to show—

(I) that the other active ingredients are the same as the active ingredients of the listed drug, or

(II) that the different active ingredient is an active ingredient of a listed drug or a drug which does not meet the requirements of section 201(p) [21 U.S.C. §321(p)],

or no petition to file an application for the drug with the different ingredient was approved under paragraph (2)(C);

(D) (i) if the application is for a drug whose route of administration, dosage form, or strength of the drug is the same as the route of administration, dosage form, or strength of the listed drug referred to in the application, information submitted in the application is insufficient to show that the route of administration, dosage form, or strength is the same as that of the listed drug, or

(ii) if the application is for a drug whose route of administration, dosage form, or strength of the drug is different from that of the listed drug referred to in the application, no petition to file an application for the drug with the different route of administration, dosage form, or strength was approved under paragraph (2)(C);

(E) if the application was filed pursuant to the approval of a petition under paragraph (2)(C), the application did not contain the information required by the Secretary respecting the active ingredient, route of administration, dosage form, or strength which is not the same;

(F) information submitted in the application is insufficient to show that the drug is bioequivalent to the listed drug referred to in the application or, if the application was filed pursuant to a petition approved under paragraph (2)(C), information submitted in the application is insufficient to show that the active ingredients of the new drug are of the same pharmacological or therapeutic class as those of the listed drug referred to in paragraph (2)(A)(i) and that the new drug can be expected to have the same therapeutic effect as the listed drug when administered to patients for a condition of use referred to in such paragraph;

(G) information submitted in the application is insufficient to show that the labeling proposed for the drug is the same as the labeling approved for the listed drug referred to in the application except for changes required because of differences approved under a petition filed under paragraph (2)(C) or because the drug and the listed drug are produced or distributed by different manufacturers;

(H) information submitted in the application or any other information available to the Secretary shows that (i) the inactive ingredients of the drug are unsafe for use under the conditions prescribed, recommended, or suggested in the labeling proposed for the drug, or (ii) the composition of the drug is unsafe under such conditions because of the type or quantity of inactive ingredients included or the manner in which the inactive ingredients are included;

(I) the approval under subsection (c) of the listed drug referred to in the application under this subsection has been withdrawn or suspended for grounds described in the first sentence of subsection (e), the Secretary has published a notice of opportunity for hearing to withdraw approval of the listed drug under subsection (c) for grounds described in the first sentence of subsection (e), the approval under this subsection of the listed drug referred to in the application under this subsection has been withdrawn or suspended under paragraph (6), or the Secretary has determined that the listed drug has been withdrawn from sale for safety or effectiveness reasons;

(J) the application does not meet any other requirement of paragraph (2)(A); or

(K) the application contains an untrue statement of material fact.

(5) (A) Within one hundred and eighty days of the initial receipt of an application under paragraph (2) or within such additional period as may be agreed upon by the Secretary and the applicant, the Secretary shall approve or disapprove the application.

(B) The approval of an application submitted under paragraph (2) shall be made effective on the last applicable date determined under the following:

(i) If the applicant only made a certification described in subclause (I) or (II) of paragraph (2)(A)(vii) or in both such subclauses, the approval may be made effective immediately.

(ii) If the applicant made a certification described in subclause (III) of paragraph (2)(A)(vii), the approval may be made effective on the date certified under subclause (III).

(iii) If the applicant made a certification described in subclause (IV) of paragraph (2)(A)(vii), the approval shall be made effective immediately unless an action is brought for infringement of a patent which is the subject of the certification before the expiration of forty-five days from the date the notice provided under paragraph (2)(B)(i) is received. If such an action is brought before the expiration of such days, the approval shall be made effective upon the expiration of the thirty-month period beginning on the date of the receipt of the notice provided under paragraph (2)(B)(i) or such shorter or longer period as the court may order because either party to the action failed to reasonably cooperate in expediting the action, except that—

(I) if before the expiration of such period the court decides that such patent is invalid or not infringed, the approval shall be made effective on the date of the court decision,

(II) if before the expiration of such period the court decides that such patent has been infringed, the approval shall be made effective on such date as the court orders under section 271(e)(4)(A) of title 35, United States Code, or

(III) if before the expiration of such period the court grants a preliminary injunction prohibiting the applicant from engaging in the commercial manufacture or sale of the drug until the court decides the issues of patent validity and infringement and if the court decides that such patent is invalid or not infringed, the approval shall be made effective on the date of such court decision.

In such an action, each of the parties shall reasonably cooperate in expediting the action. Until the expiration of forty-five days from the date the notice made under paragraph (2)(B)(i) is received, no action may be brought under section 2201 of title 28, United States Code, for a declaratory judgment with respect to the patent. Any action brought under section 2201 shall be brought in the judicial district where the defendant has its principal place of business or a regular and established place of business.

(iv) If the application contains a certification described in subclause (IV) of paragraph (2)(A)(vii) and is for a drug for which a previous application has been submitted under this subsection continuing such a certification, the application shall be made effective not earlier than one hundred and eighty days after—

(I) the date the Secretary receives notice from the applicant under the previous application of the first commercial marketing of the drug under the previous application, or

(II) the date of a decision of a court in an action described in clause (iii) holding the patent which is the subject of the certification to be invalid or not infringed,

21 U.S.C. § 355

whichever is earlier.

(C) If the Secretary decides to disapprove an application, the Secretary shall give the applicant notice of an opportunity for a hearing before the Secretary on the question of whether such application is approvable. If the applicant elects to accept the opportunity for hearing by written request within thirty days after such notice, such hearing shall commence not more than ninety days after the expiration of such thirty days unless the Secretary and the applicant otherwise agree. Any such hearing shall thereafter be conducted on an expedited basis and the Secretary's order thereon shall be issued within ninety days after the date fixed by the Secretary for filing final briefs.

(D) (i) If an application (other than an abbreviated new drug application) submitted under subsection (b) for a drug, no active ingredient (including any ester or salt of the active ingredient) of which has been approved in any other application under subsection (b), was approved during the period beginning January 1, 1982, and ending on the date of the enactment of this subsection [September 24, 1984], the Secretary may not make the approval of an application submitted under this subsection which refers to the drug for which the subsection (b) application was submitted effective before the expiration of ten years from the date of the approval of the application under subsection (b).

(ii) If an application submitted under subsection (b) for a drug, no active ingredient (including any ester or salt of the active ingredient) of which has been approved in any other application under subsection (b), is approved after the date of the enactment of this subsection, no application may be submitted under this subsection which refers to the drug for which the subsection (b) application was submitted before the expiration of five years from the date of the approval of the application under subsection (b), except that such an application may be submitted under this subsection after the expiration of four years from the date of the approval of the subsection (b) application if it contains a certification of patent invalidity or noninfringement described in subclause

(IV) of paragraph (2)(A)(vii). The approval of such an application shall be made effective in accordance with subparagraph (B) except that, if an action for patent infringement is commenced during the one-year period beginning forty-eight months after the date of the approval of the subsection (b) application, the thirty-month period referred to in subparagraph (B)(iii) shall be extended by such amount of time (if any) which is required for seven and one-half years to have elapsed from the date of approval of the subsection (b) application.

(iii) If an application submitted under subsection (b) for a drug, which includes an active ingredient (including any ester or salt of the active ingredient) that has been approved in another application approved under subsection (b), is approved after the date of enactment of this subsection and if such application contains reports of new clinical investigations (other than bioavailability studies) essential to the approval of the application and conducted or sponsored by the applicant, the Secretary may not make the approval of an application submitted under this subsection for the conditions of approval of such drug in the subsection (b) application effective before the expiration of three years from the date of the approval of the application under subsection (b) for such drug.

(iv) If a supplement to an application approved under subsection (b) is approved after the date of enactment of this subsection and the supplement contains reports of new clinical investigations (other than bioavailability studies) essential to the approval of the supplement and conducted or sponsored by the person submitting the supplement, the Secretary may not make the approval of an application submitted under this subsection for a change approved in the supplement effective before the expiration of three years from the date of the approval of the supplement under subsection (b).

(v) If an application (or supplement to an application) submitted under subsection (b) for a drug, which includes an active ingredient (including any ester or salt of the active ingredient) that has been approved in another application under subsection (b), was approved during the period beginning January 1, 1982, and ending on the date of the enactment of this subsection, the Secretary may not make the approval of an application submitted under this subsection which refers to the drug for which the subsection (b) application was submitted or which refers to a change approved in a supplement to the subsection (b) application effective before the expiration of two years from the date of enactment of this subsection.

(6) If a drug approved under this subsection refers in its approved application to a drug the approval of which was withdrawn or suspended for grounds described in the first sentence of subsection (e) or was withdrawn or suspended under this paragraph or which, as determined by the Secretary, has been withdrawn from sale for safety or effectiveness reasons, the approval of the drug under this subsection shall be withdrawn or suspended—

(A) for the same period as the withdrawal or suspension under subsection (e) or this paragraph, or

(B) if the listed drug has been withdrawn from sale, for the period of withdrawal from sale or, if earlier, the period ending on the date the Secretary determines that the withdrawal from sale is not for safety or effectiveness reasons.

(7) (A) (i) Within sixty days of the date of the enactment of this subsection [September 24, 1984], the Secretary shall publish and make available to the public—

(I) a list in alphabetical order of the official and proprietary name of each drug which has been approved for safety and effectiveness under subsection (c) before the date of the enactment of this subsection;

(II) the date of approval if the drug is approved after 1981 and the number of the application which was approved; and

(III) whether in vitro or in vivo bioequivalence studies, or both such studies, are required for applications filed under this subsection which will refer to the drug published.

(ii) Every thirty days after the publication of the first list under clause (i) the Secretary shall revise the list to include each drug which has been approved for safety and effectiveness under subsection (c) or approved under this subsection during the thirty-day period.

(iii) When patent information submitted under subsection (b) or (c) respecting a drug included on the list is to be published by the Secretary the Secretary shall, in revisions made under clause (ii), include such information for such drug.

(B) A drug approved for safety and effectiveness under subsection (c) or approved under this subsection shall, for purposes of this subsection, be considered to have been published under subparagraph (A) on the date of its approval or the date of enactment, whichever is later.

(C) If the approval of a drug was withdrawn or suspended for grounds described in the first sentence of subsection (e) or was withdrawn or suspended under paragraph (6) or if the Secretary determines that a drug has been withdrawn from sale for safety or effectiveness reasons, it may not be published in the list under subparagraph (A) or, if the withdrawal or suspension occurred after its publication in such list, it shall be immediately removed from such list—

(i) for the same period as the withdrawal or suspension under subsection (e) or paragraph (6), or

(ii) if the listed drug has been withdrawn from sale, for the period of withdrawal from sale or, if earlier, the period ending on the date the Secretary determines that the withdrawal from sale is not for safety or effectiveness reasons.

A notice of the removal shall be published in the Federal Register.

(8) For purposes of this subsection:

(A) The term "bioavailability" means the rate and extent to which the active ingredient or therapeutic ingredient is absorbed from a drug and becomes available at the site of drug action.

(B) A drug shall be considered to be bioequivalent to a listed drug if—

(i) the rate and extent of absorption of the drug do not show a significant difference from the rate and extent of absorption of the listed drug when administered at the same molar dose of the therapeutic ingredient under similar experimental conditions in either a single dose or multiple doses; or

(ii) the extent of absorption of the drug does not show a significant difference from the extent of absorption of the listed drug when administered at the same molar dose of the therapeutic ingredient under similar experimental conditions in either a single dose or multiple doses and the difference from the listed drug in the rate of absorption of the drug is intentional, is reflected in its proposed labeling, is not essential to the attainment of effective body drug concentrations on chronic use, and is considered medically insignificant for the drug.

(9) The Secretary shall, with respect to each application submitted under this subsection, maintain a record of—

(A) the name of the applicant,

(B) the name of the drug covered by the application,

(C) the name of each person to whom the review of the chemistry of the application was assigned and the date of such assignment, and

(D) the name of each person to whom the bioequivalence review for such application was assigned and the date of such assignment.

The information the Secretary is required to maintain under this paragraph with respect to an application submitted under this subsection shall be made available to the public after the approval of such application.

(k) (1) In the case of any drug for which an approval of an application filed under subsection (b) or (j) is in effect, the applicant shall establish and maintain such records, and make such reports to the Secretary, of data relating to clinical experience and other data or information, received or otherwise obtained by such applicant with respect to such drug, as the Secretary may by general regulation, or by order with respect to such application, prescribe on the basis of a finding that such records and reports are necessary in order to enable the Secretary to determine, or facilitate a determination, whether there is or may be ground for invoking subsection (e) of this section: *Provided, however,* That regulations and orders issued under this subsection and under subsection (i) of this section shall have due regard for the professional ethics of the medical profession and the interests of patients and shall provide, where the Secretary deems it to be appropriate, for the examination, upon request, by the persons to whom such regulations or orders are applicable, of similar information received or otherwise obtained by the Secretary.

(2) Every person required under this section to maintain records, and every person in charge or custody thereof, shall, upon request of an officer or employee designated by the Secretary, permit such officer or employee at all reasonable times to have access to and copy and verify such records.

(l) Safety and effectiveness data and information which has been submitted in an application under subsection (b) for a drug and which has not previously been disclosed to the public shall be made available to the public, upon request, unless extraordinary circumstances are shown—

(1) if no work is being or will be undertaken to have the application approved,

(2) if the Secretary has determined that the application is not approvable and all legal appeals have been exhausted,

(3) if approval of the application under subsection (c) is withdrawn and all legal appeals have been exhausted,

(4) if the Secretary has determined that such drug is not a new drug, or

(5) upon the effective date of the approval of the first application under subsection (j) which refers to such drug or upon the date upon

which the approval of an application under subsection (j) which refers to such drug could be made effective if such an application had been submitted.

(m) For purposes of this section, the term "patent" means a patent issued by the United States Patent and Trademark Office.

(n) (1) For the purpose of providing expert scientific advice and recommendations to the Secretary regarding a clinical investigation of a drug or the approval for marketing of a drug under section 505 or section 351 of the Public Health Service Act, the Secretary shall establish panels of experts or use panels of experts established before the date of enactment of the Food and Drug Administration Modernization Act of 1997, or both.

(2) The Secretary may delegate the appointment and oversight authority granted under section 904 to a director of a center or successor entity within the Food and Drug Administration.

(3) The Secretary shall make appointments to each panel established under paragraph (1) so that each panel shall consist of—

(A) members who are qualified by training and experience to evaluate the safety and effectiveness of the drugs to be referred to the panel and who, to the extent feasible, possess skill and experience in the development, manufacture, or utilization of such drugs;

(B) members with diverse expertise in such fields as clinical and administrative medicine, pharmacy, pharmacology, pharmacoeconomics, biological and physical sciences, and other related professions;

(C) a representative of consumer interests, and a representative of interests of the drug manufacturing industry not directly affected by the matter to be brought before the panel; and

(D) two or more members who are specialists or have other expertise in the particular disease or condition for which the drug under review is proposed to be indicated. Scientific, trade, and consumer organizations shall be afforded an opportunity to nominate individuals for appointment to the panels. No individual who is in the regular full-time employ of the United States and engaged in the administration of this Act may be a voting member of any panel. The Secretary shall designate one of the members of each panel to serve as chairman thereof.

(4) Each member of a panel shall publicly disclose all conflicts of interest that member may have with the work to be undertaken by the panel. No member of a panel may vote on any matter where the member or the immediate family of such member could gain financially from the advice given to the Secretary. The Secretary may grant a waiver of any conflict of interest requirement upon public disclosure of such conflict of interest if such waiver is necessary to afford the panel essential expertise, except that the Secretary may not grant a waiver for a member of a panel when the member's own scientific work is involved.

(5) The Secretary shall, as appropriate, provide education and training to each new panel member before such member participates in a panel's activities, including education regarding requirements under this Act and related regulations of the Secretary, and the administrative processes and procedures related to panel meetings.

(6) Panel members (other than officers or employees of the United States), while attending meetings or conferences of a panel or otherwise engaged in its business, shall be entitled to receive compensation for each day so engaged, including traveltime, at rates to be fixed by the Secretary, but not to exceed the daily equivalent of the rate in effect for positions classified above grade GS-15 of the General Schedule. While serving away from their homes or regular places of business, panel members may be allowed travel expenses (including per diem in lieu of subsistence) as authorized by section 5703 of title 5, United States Code, for persons in the Government service employed intermittently.

(7) The Secretary shall ensure that scientific advisory panels meet regularly and at appropriate intervals so that any matter to be reviewed by such a panel can be presented to the panel not more than 60 days after the matter is ready for such review. Meetings of the panel may be held using electronic communication to convene the meetings.

(8) Within 90 days after a scientific advisory panel makes recommendations on any matter under its review, the Food and Drug

Administration official responsible for the matter shall review the conclusions and recommendations of the panel, and notify the affected persons of the final decision on the matter, or of the reasons that no such decision has been reached. Each such final decision shall be documented including the rationale for the decision.

(June 25, 1938, ch. 675, §505, 52 Stat. 1052; June 11, 1960, Pub. L. 86-507, §1(18), 74 Stat. 201; Oct. 10, 1962, Pub. L. 87-781, §§102-04, 76 Stat. 781-85; Aug. 16, 1972, Pub. L. 92-387, §4, 86 Stat. 562; Sept. 24, 1984, Pub. L. 98-417, §§101-04, 98 Stat. 1585, 1592-93, 1597; May 13, 1992, Pub. L. 102-282, §5, 106 Stat. 161; Nov. 21, 1997, Pub. L. 105-115, §§117, 119, 120, 124, 111 Stat. 2315; Nov. 29, 1999, Pub. L. 106-113, §4732, 113 Stat. 1501A-581.)

* * * * * * *

VIII. TREATMENT OF INTELLECTUAL PROPERTY UNDER FEDERAL TAX LAW

26 U.S.C. § 197   Amortization of Goodwill and Certain Other Intangibles

(a) *General rule.*—A taxpayer shall be entitled to an amortization deduction with respect to any amortizable section 197 intangible. The amount of such deduction shall be determined by amortizing the adjusted basis (for purposes of determining gain) of such intangible ratably over the 15-year period beginning with the month in which such intangible was acquired.

(b) *No other depreciation or amortization deduction allowable.*—Except as provided in subsection (a), no depreciation or amortization deduction shall be allowable with respect to any amortizable section 197 intangible.

(c) *Amortizable Section 197 intangible.*—For purposes of this section—

(1) *In general.*—Except as otherwise provided in this section, the term "amortizable section 197 intangible" means any section 197 intangible—

(A) which is acquired by the taxpayer after the date of the enactment of this section, and

(B) which is held in connection with the conduct of a trade or business or an activity described in section 212.

(2) *Exclusion of self-created intangibles, etc.*—The term "amortizable section 197 intangible" shall not include any section 197 intangible—

(A) which is not described in subparagraph (D), (E), or (F) of subsection (d)(1), and

(B) which is created by the taxpayer.

This paragraph shall not apply if the intangible is created in connection with a transaction (or series of related transactions) involving the acquisition of assets constituting a trade or business or substantial portion thereof.

(3) *Anti-churning rules.*—For exclusion of intangibles acquired in certain transactions, see subsection (f)(9).

(d) *Section 197 intangible.*—For purposes of this section—

26 U.S.C. § 197

(1) *In general.*—Except as otherwise provided in this section, the term "section 197 intangible" means—

    (A) goodwill,

    (B) going concern value,

    (C) any of the following intangible items:

        (i) workforce in place including its composition and terms and conditions (contractual or otherwise) of its employment,

        (ii) business books and records, operating systems, or any other information base (including lists or other information with respect to current or prospective customers),

        (iii) any patent, copyright, formula, process, design, pattern, knowhow, format, or other similar item,

        (iv) any customer-based intangible,

        (v) any supplier-based intangible, and

        (vi) any other similar item,

    (D) any license, permit, or other right granted by a governmental unit or an agency or instrumentality thereof,

    (E) any covenant not to compete (or other arrangement to the extent such arrangement has substantially the same effect as a covenant not to compete) entered into in connection with an acquisition (directly or indirectly) of an interest in a trade or business or substantial portion thereof, and

    (F) any franchise, trademark, or trade name.

(2) *Customer-based intangible.*—

    (A) *In general.*—The term "customer-based intangible" means—

        (i) composition of market,

        (ii) market share, and

        (iii) any other value resulting from future provision of goods or services pursuant to relationships (contractual or otherwise) in the ordinary course of business with customers.

    (B) *Special rule for financial institutions.*—In the case of a financial institution, the term "customer-based intangible" includes deposit base and similar items.

26 U.S.C. § 197

(3) *Supplier-based intangible.*—The term "supplier-based intangible" means any value resulting from future acquisitions of goods or services pursuant to relationships (contractual or otherwise) in the ordinary course of business with suppliers of goods or services to be used or sold by the taxpayer.

(e) *Exceptions.*—For purposes of this section, the term "section 197 intangible" shall not include any of the following:

(1) *Financial interests.*—Any interest—

(A) in a corporation, partnership, trust, or estate, or

(B) under an existing futures contract, foreign currency contract, notional principal contract, or other similar financial contract.

(2) *Land.*—Any interest in land.

(3) *Computer software.*—

(A) *In general.*—Any—

(i) computer software which is readily available for purchase by the general public, is subject to a nonexclusive license, and has not been substantially modified, and

(ii) other computer software which is not acquired in a transaction (or series of related transactions) involving the acquisition of assets constituting a trade or business or substantial portion thereof.

(B) *Computer software defined.*—For purposes of subparagraph (A), the term "computer software" means any program designed to cause a computer to perform a desired function. Such term shall include any data base or similar item unless the data base or item is in the public domain and is incidental to the operation of otherwise qualifying computer software.

(4) *Certain interests or rights acquired separately.*—Any of the following not acquired in a transaction (or series of related transactions) involving the acquisition of assets constituting a trade business or substantial portion thereof:

(A) Any interest in a film, sound recording, video tape, book, or similar property.

(B) Any right to receive tangible property or services under a contract or granted by a governmental unit or agency or instrumentality thereof.

(C) Any interest in a patent or copyright.

(D) To the extent provided in regulations, any right under a contract (or granted by a governmental unit or an agency or instrumentality thereof) if such right—

(i) has a fixed duration of less than 15 years, or

(ii) is fixed as to amount and, without regard to this section, would be recoverable under a method similar to the unit-of-production method.

(5) *Interests under leases and debt instruments.*—Any interest under—

(A) an existing lease of tangible property, or

(B) except as provided in subsection (d)(2)(B), any existing indebtedness.

(6) *Treatment of sports franchises.*—A franchise to engage in professional football, basketball, baseball, or other professional sport, and any item acquired in connection with such a franchise.

(7) *Mortgage servicing.*—Any right to service indebtedness which is secured by residential real property unless such right is acquired in a transaction (or series of related transactions) involving the acquisition of assets (other than rights described in this paragraph) constituting a trade or business or substantial portion thereof.

(8) *Certain transaction costs.*—Any fees for professional services, and any transaction costs, incurred by parties to a transaction with respect to which any portion of the gain or loss is not recognized under part III of subchapter C.

(f) *Special Rules.*—

(1) *Treatment of certain dispositions, etc.*—

(A) *In general.*—If there is a disposition of any amortizable section 197 intangible acquired in a transaction or series of related transactions (or any such intangible becomes worthless) and one or more other amortizable section 197 intangibles acquired in such transaction or series of related transactions are retained—

(i) no loss shall be recognized by reason of such disposition (or such worthlessness), and

(ii) appropriate adjustments to the adjusted bases of such retained intangibles shall be made for any loss not recognized under clause (i).

(B) *Special rule for covenants not to compete.*—In the case of any section 197 intangible which is a covenant not to compete (or other arrangement) described in subsection (d)(1)(E), in no event shall such covenant or other arrangement be treated as disposed of (or becoming worthless) before the disposition of the entire interest described in such subsection in connection with such covenant (or other arrangement) was entered into.

(C) *Special rule.*—All persons treated as a single taxpayer under section 41(f)(1) shall be so treated for purposes of this paragraph.

(2) *Treatment of certain transfers.*—

(A) *In general.*—In the case of any section 197 intangible transferred in a transaction described in subparagraph (B), the transferee shall be treated as the transferor for purposes of applying this section with respect to so much of the adjusted basis in the hands of the transferee as does not exceed the adjusted basis in the hands of the transferor.

(B) *Transactions covered.*—The transactions described in this subparagraph are—

(i) any transaction described in section 332, 351, 361, 721, 731, 1031, or 1033, and

(ii) any transaction between members of the same affiliated group during any taxable year for which a consolidated return is made by such group.

(3) *Treatment of amounts paid pursuant to covenants not to compete, etc.*—Any amount paid or incurred pursuant to a covenant or arrangement referred to in subsection (d)(1)(E) shall be treated as an amount chargeable to capital account.

(4) *Treatment of franchises, etc.*—

(A) *Franchise.*—The term "franchise" has the meaning given to such term by section 1253(b)(1).

26 U.S.C. § 197

(B) *Treatment of renewals.*—Any renewal of a franchise, trademark, or trade name (or of a license, a permit, or other right referred to in subsection (d)(1)(D)) shall be treated as an acquisition. The preceding sentence shall only apply with respect to costs incurred in connection with such renewal.

(C) *Certain amounts not taken into account.*—Any amount to which section 1253(d)(1) applies shall not be taken into account under this section.

(5) *Treatment of certain reinsurance transactions.*—In the case of any amortizable section 197 intangible resulting from an assumption reinsurance transaction, the amount taken into account as the adjusted basis of such intangible under this section shall be the excess of—

(A) the amount paid or incurred by the acquirer under the assumption reinsurance transaction, over

(B) the amount required to be capitalized under section 848 in connection with such transaction.

Subsection (b) shall not apply to any amount required to be capitalized under section 848.

(6) *Treatment of certain subleases.*—For purposes of this section, a sublease shall be treated in the same manner as a lease of the underlying property involved.

(7) *Treatment as depreciable.*—For purposes of this chapter, any amortizable section 197 intangible shall be treated as property which is of a character subject to the allowance for depreciation provided in section 167.

(8) *Treatment of certain increments in value.*—This section shall not apply to any increment in value if, without regard to this section, such increment is properly taken into account in determining the cost of property which is not a section 197 intangible.

(9) *Anti-churning rules.*—For purposes of this section—

(A) *In general.*—The term "amortizable section 197 intangible" shall not include any section 197 intangible which is described in subparagraph (A) or (B) of subsection (d)(1) (or for which depreciation or amortization would not have been allowable but for this section) and which is acquired by the taxpayer after the date of the enactment of this section, if—

(i) the intangible was held or used at any time on or after July 25, 1991, and on or before such date of enactment by the taxpayer or a related person,

(ii) the intangible was acquired from a person who held such intangible at any time on or after July 25, 1991, and on or before such date of enactment, and, as part of the transaction, the user of such intangible does not change, or

(iii) the taxpayer grants the right to use such intangible to a person (or person related to such person) who held or used such intangible at any time on or after July 25, 1991, and on or before such date of enactment.

For purposes of this subparagraph, the determination of whether the user of property changes as part of a transaction shall be determined in accordance with regulations prescribed by the Secretary. For purposes of this subparagraph, deductions allowable under section 1253(d) shall be treated as deductions allowable for amortization.

(B) *Exception where gain recognized.*—If—

(i) subparagraph (A) would not apply to an intangible acquired by the taxpayer but for the last sentence of subparagraph (C)(i), and

(ii) the person from whom the taxpayer acquired the intangible elects, notwithstanding any other provision of this title—

(I) to recognize gain on the disposition of the intangible, and

(II) to pay as tax on such gain which, when added to any other income tax on such gain under this title, equals such gain multiplied by the highest rate of income applicable to such person under this title,

then subparagraph (A) shall apply to the intangible only to the extent that the taxpayer's adjusted basis in the intangible exceeds the gain recognized under clause (ii)(I).

(C) *Related person defined.*—For purposes of this paragraph—

26 U.S.C. § 197

(i) *Related person.*—A person (hereinafter in this paragraph referred to as the "related person") is related to any person if—

(I) the related person bears a relationship to such person specified in section 267(b) or section 707(b)(1), or

(II) the related person and such person are engaged in trades or businesses under common control (within the meaning of subparagraphs (A) and (B) of section 41(f)(1)).

For purposes of subclause (I), in applying section 267(b) or 707(b)(1), "20 percent" shall be substituted for "50 percent".

(ii) *Time for making determination.*—A person shall be treated as related to another person if such relationship exists immediately before or immediately after the acquisition of the intangible involved.

(D) *Acquisitions by reason of death.*—Subparagraph (A) shall not apply to the acquisition of any property by the taxpayer if the basis of the property in the hands of the taxpayer is determined under section 1014(a).

(E) *Special rule for partnerships.*—With respect to any increase in the basis of partnership property under section 732, 734, or 743, determinations under this paragraph shall be made at the partner level and each partner shall be treated as having owned and used such partner's proportionate share of the partnership assets.

(F) *Anti-abuse rules.*—The term "amortizable section 197 intangible" does not include any section 197 intangible acquired in a transaction, one of the principal purposes of which is to avoid the requirement of subsection (c)(1) that the intangible be acquired after the date of the enactment of this section or to avoid the provisions of subparagraph (A).

(g) *Regulations.*—The Secretary shall prescribe such regulations as may be appropriate to carry out the purposes of this section, including such regulations as may be appropriate to prevent avoidance of the purposes of this section through related persons or otherwise.

(Aug. 10, 1993, Pub. L. 103-66, §13261, 107 Stat. 533.)

26 U.S.C. § 197

26 U.S.C. § 543   Personal Holding Company Income

(a) *General rule.*—For purposes of this subtitle, the term "personal holding company income" means the portion of the adjusted ordinary gross income which consists of:

(1) *Dividends, etc.*—Dividends, interest, royalties (other than mineral, oil, or gas royalties or copyright royalties), and annuities. This paragraph shall not apply to—

(A) interest constituting rent (as defined in subsection (b)(3)),

(B) interest on amounts set aside in a reserve fund under section 511 or 607 of the Merchant Marine Act, 1936 (46 U.S.C. App. 1161 or 1177),

(C) active business computer software royalties (within the meaning of subsection (d)), * * *

* * *

(4) *Copyright royalties.*—Copyright royalties; except that copyright royalties shall not be included if—

(A) such royalties (exclusive of royalties received for the use of, or right to use, copyrights or interests in copyrights on works created in whole, or in part, by any shareholder) constitute 50 percent or more of the ordinary gross income,

(B) the personal holding company income for the taxable year computed—

(i) without regard to copyright royalties, other than royalties received for the use of, or right to use, copyrights or interests in copyrights in works created in whole, or in part, by any shareholder owning more than 10 percent of the total outstanding capital stock of the corporation,

(ii) without regard to dividends from any corporation in which the taxpayer owns at least 50 percent of all classes of stock entitled to vote and at least 50 percent of the total value of all classes of stock and which corporation meets the requirements of this subparagraph and subparagraphs (A) and (C), and

(iii) by including as personal holding company income the adjusted income from rents and the adjusted income from mineral, oil, and gas royalties, is not more than 10 percent of the ordinary gross income, and

(C) the sum of the deductions which are properly allocable to such royalties and which are allowable under section 162, other than—

(i) deductions for compensation for personal services rendered by the shareholders,

(ii) deductions for royalties, paid or accrued, and

(iii) deductions which are specifically allowable under sections other than section 162,

equals or exceeds 25 percent of the amount by which the ordinary gross income exceeds the sum of the royalties paid or accrued and the amounts allowable as deductions under section 167 (relating to depreciation) with respect to copyright royalties.

For purposes of this subsection, the term "copyright royalties" means compensation, however designated, for the use of, or the right to use, copyrights in works protected by copyright issued under title 17 of the United States Code and to which copyright protection is also extended by the laws of any country other than the United States of America by virtue of any international treaty, convention, or agreement, or interests in any such copyrighted works, and includes payments from any person for performing rights in any such copyrighted work and payments (other than produced film rents as defined in paragraph (5)(B)) received for the use of, or right to use, films. For purposes of this paragraph, the term "shareholder" shall include any person who owns stock within the meaning of section 544. This paragraph shall not apply to active business computer software royalties.

(5) *Produced film rents.—*

(A) Produced film rents; except that such rents shall not be included if such rents constitute 50 percent or more of the ordinary gross income.

(B) For purposes of this section, the term "produced film rents" means payments received with respect to an interest in a film for the use of, or right to use, such film, but only to the extent that such interest was acquired before substantial completion of production of such film. In the case of a producer who actively participates in the production of the film, such term includes an interest in the proceeds or profits from the film, but only to the extent such interest is attributable to such active participation.

* * *

(Aug. 16, 1954, ch. 736, 68A Stat. 186; Apr. 22, 1960, Pub. L. 86-435, §1, 74 Stat. 77; Feb. 2, 1962, Pub. L. 87-403, §3, 76 Stat. 6; Feb. 26, 1964, Pub. L. 88-272, §225, 78 Stat. 81, 93; Aug. 22, 1964, Pub. L. 88-484, §3, 78 Stat. 598; Nov. 13, 1966, Pub. L. 89-809, §§104, 206, 80 Stat. 1559, 1578-79; Oct. 4, 1976, Pub. L. 94-455, §§211, 1901, 1906, 2106, 90 Stat. 1544, 1800, 1834, 1902; Oct. 19, 1976, Pub. L. 94-553, §105, 90 Stat. 2599; Sept. 3, 1982, Pub. L. 97-248, §222, 96 Stat. 480; July 18, 1984, Pub. L. 98-369, §712, 98 Stat. 948; Oct. 22, 1986, Pub. L. 99-514, §§645, 1899, 100 Stat. 2289, 2291, 2959; Nov. 10, 1988, Pub. L. 100-647, §§1010, 6279, 102 Stat. 3454, 3754.)

26 U.S.C. § 174   Research and experimental expenditures

(a) *Treatment as expenses.*—

(1) *In general.*—A taxpayer may treat research or experimental expenditures which are paid or incurred by him during the taxable year in connection with his trade or business as expenses which are not chargeable to capital account. The expenditures so treated shall be allowed as a deduction.

(2) *When method may be adopted.*—

(A) *Without consent.*—A taxpayer may, without the consent of the Secretary, adopt the method provided in this subsection for his first taxable year—

(i) which begins after December 31, 1953, and ends after August 16, 1954, and

(ii) for which expenditures described in paragraph (1) are paid or incurred.

(B) *With consent.*—A taxpayer may, with the consent of the Secretary, adopt at any time the method provided in this subsection.

(3) *Scope.*—the method adopted under this subsection shall apply to all expenditures described in paragraph (1). The method adopted shall be adhered to in computing taxable income for the taxable year and for all subsequent taxable years unless, with the approval of the Secretary, a change to a different method is authorized with respect to part or all of such expenditures.

(b) *Amortization of certain research and experimental expenditures.*—

(1) *In general.*—At the election of the taxpayer, made in accordance with regulations prescribed by the Secretary, research or experimental expenditures which are—

(A) paid or incurred by the taxpayer, in connection with his trade or business,

(B) not treated as expenses under subsection (a), and

(C) chargeable to capital account but not chargeable to property of a character which is subject to the allowance under section 167 (relating to allowance for depreciation, etc.) or section 611 (relating to allowance for depletion),

may be treated as deferred expenses. In computing taxable income, such deferred expenses shall be allowed as a deduction ratably over such period of not less than 60 months as may be selected by the taxpayer (beginning with the month in which the taxpayer first realizes benefits from such expenditures). Such deferred expenses are expenditures properly chargeable to capital account for purposes of section 1016(a)(1) (relating to adjustments to basis of property).

(2) *Time for and scope of election.*—The election provided by paragraph (1) may be made for any taxable year beginning after December 31, 1953, but only if made not later than the time prescribed by law for filing the return for such taxable year (including extensions thereof). The method so elected, and the period selected by the taxpayer, shall be adhered to in computing taxable income for the taxable year for which the election is made and for all subsequent taxable years unless, with the approval of the Secretary, a change to a different method (or to a different period) is authorized with respect to part or all of such expenditures. The election shall not apply to any expenditure paid or incurred during any taxable year before the taxable year for which the taxpayer makes the election.

(c) *Land and other property.*—This section shall not apply to any expenditure for the acquisition or improvement of land, or for the acquisition or improvement of property to be used in connection with the research or experimentation and of a character which is subject to the allowance under section 167 (relating to allowance for depreciation, etc.) or section 611 (relating to allowance for depletion); but for purposes of this section

26 U.S.C. § 174

allowances under section 167, and allowances under section 611, shall be considered as expenditures.

(d) *Exploration expenditures.*—This section shall not apply to any expenditure paid or incurred for the purpose of ascertaining the existence, location, extent, or quality of any deposit of ore or other mineral (including oil and gas).

(e) This section shall apply to a research or experimental expenditure only to the extent that the amount thereof is reasonable under the circumstances.

* * *

(Aug. 16, 1954, ch. 736, 68A Stat. 66; Oct. 4, 1976, Pub. L. 94-455, §§1901, 1906, 90 Stat. 1769, 1834; Sept. 3, 1982, Pub. L. 97-248, §201, 96 Stat. 420; Jan. 12, 1983, Pub. L. 97-448, §306, 96 Stat. 2400; Oct. 22, 1986, Pub. L. 99-514, §701, 100 Stat. 2343; Nov. 10, 1988, Pub. L. 100-647, §1007, 102 Stat. 3435; Dec. 19, 1989, Pub. L. 101-239, §7110, 103 Stat. 2325.)

26 U.S.C. § 1235   Sale or exchange of patents.

(a) *General.*—A transfer (other than by gift, inheritance, or devise) of property consisting of all substantial rights to a patent, or an undivided interest therein which includes a part of all such rights, by any holder shall be considered the sale or exchange of a capital asset held for more than 1 year,* regardless of whether or not payments in consideration of such transfer are—

> (1) payable periodically over a period generally coterminous with the transferee's use of the patent, or

> (2) contingent on the productivity, use, or disposition of the property transferred.

(b) *"Holder" defined.*—For purposes of this section, the term "holder" means—

> (1) any individual whose efforts created such property, or

> (2) any other individual who has acquired his interest in such property in exchange for consideration in money or money's worth paid to such creator prior to actual reduction to practice of the invention covered by the patent, if such individual is neither—

---

* *Ed. Note:* Pub. L. 98-369 temporarily substituted "6 months" for "1 year" applicable to property acquired after June 22, 1984 and before January 1, 1988.

26 U.S.C. § 1235

(A) the employer of such creator, nor

(B) related to such creator (within the meaning of subsection (d)).

(c) *Effective date.*—This section shall be applicable with regard to any amounts received, or payments made, pursuant to a transfer described in subsection (a) in any taxable year to which this subtitle applies, regardless of the taxable year in which such transfer occurred.

(d) *Related persons.*—Subsection (a) shall not apply to any transfer, directly or indirectly, between persons specified within any one of the paragraphs of section 267(b) or persons described in section 707(b); except that, in applying section 267(b) and (c) and section 707(b) for purposes of this section—

(1) the phrase "25 percent or more" shall be substituted for the phrase "more than 50 percent" each place it appears in section 267(b) or 707(b), and

(2) paragraph (4) of section 267(c) shall be treated as providing that the family of an individual shall include only his spouse, ancestors, and lineal descendants.

* * *

(Aug. 16, 1954, ch. 736, 68A Stat. 329; Sept. 2, 1958, Pub. L. 85-866, §54, 72 Stat. 1644; Oct. 4, 1976, Pub. L. 94-455, §1402, 90 Stat. 1732; July 18, 1984, Pub. L. 98-369, §§174, 1001, 98 Stat. 707, 1012;.)

26 U.S.C. § 1249   Gain from certain sales or exchanges of patents etc., to foreign corporations

(a) *General rule.*—Gain from the sale or exchange after December 31, 1962, of a patent, an invention, model, or design (whether or not patented), a copyright, a secret formula or process, or any other similar property right to any foreign corporation by any United States person (as defined in section 7701(a)(30)) which controls such foreign corporation shall, if such gain would (but for the provisions of this subsection) be gain from the sale or exchange of a capital asset or of property described in section 1231, be considered as ordinary income.

(b) *Control.*—For purposes of subsection (a), control means, with respect to any foreign corporation, the ownership, directly or indirectly, of stock possessing more than 50 percent of the total combined voting power of all classes of stock entitled to vote. For purposes of this subsection, the rules for determining ownership of stock prescribed by section 958 shall apply.

(Oct. 16, 1962, Pub. L. 87-834, §16, 76 Stat. 1045; Nov. 13, 1966, Pub. L. 89-809, §104, 80 Stat. 1563; Oct. 4, 1976, Pub. L. 94-455, §1901, 90 Stat. 1793.)

26 U.S.C. § 1253   Transfers of franchises, trademarks, and trade names.

(a) *General rule.*—A transfer of a franchise, trademark, or trade name shall not be treated as a sale or exchange of a capital asset if the transferor retains any significant power, right, or continuing interest with respect to the subject matter of the franchise, trademark, or trade name.

(b) *Definitions.*—For purposes of this section—

(1) *Franchise.*—The term "franchise" includes an agreement which gives one of the parties to the agreement the right to distribute, sell, or provide goods, services, or facilities, within a specified area.

(2) *Significant power, right, or continuing interest.*—The term "significant power, right, or continuing interest" includes, but is not limited to, the following rights with respect to the interest transferred:

(A) A right to disapprove any assignment of such interest, or any part thereof.

(B) A right to terminate at will.

(C) A right to prescribe the standards of quality of products used or sold, or of services furnished, and of the equipment and facilities used to promote such products or services.

(D) A right to require that the transferee sell or advertise only products or services of the transferor.

(E) A right to require that the transferee purchase substantially all of his supplies and equipment from the transferor.

(F) A right to payments contingent on the productivity, use, or disposition of the subject matter of the interest transferred, if such payments constitute a substantial element under the transfer agreement.

(3) *Transfer.*—The term "transfer" includes the renewal of a franchise, trademark, or trade name.

(c) *Treatment of contingent payments by transferor.*—Amounts received or accrued on account of a transfer, sale, or other disposition of a franchise, trademark, or trade name which are contingent on the productivity, use, or disposition of the franchise, trademark, or trade name transferred shall be treated as amounts received or accrued from the sale or other disposition of property which is not a capital asset.

(d) *Treatment of payments by transferee.—*

(1) *Contingent serial payments.—*

(A) *In general.*—Any amount described in subparagraph (B) which is paid or incurred during the taxable year on account of a transfer, sale, or other disposition of a franchise, trademark, or trade name shall be allowed as a deduction under section 162(a) (relating to trade or business expenses).

(B) *Amounts to which paragraph applies.*—An amount is described in this subparagraph if it—

(i) is contingent on the productivity, use, or disposition of the franchise, trademark, or trade name, and

(ii) is paid as part of a series of payments—

(I) which are payable not less frequently than annually throughout the entire term of the transfer agreement, and

(II) which are substantially equal in amount (or payable under a fixed formula).

(2) *Other payments.*—Any amount paid or incurred on account of a transfer, sale, or other disposition of a franchise, trademark, or trade name to which paragraph (1) does not apply shall be treated as an amount chargeable to capital account.

(3) *Renewals, etc.*—For purposes of determining the term of a transfer agreement under this section, there shall be taken into account all renewal options (and any other period for which the parties reasonably expect the agreement to be renewed.)

* * *

(Dec. 30, 1969, Pub. L. 91-172, §516, 83 Stat. 647; Oct. 4, 1976, Pub. L. 94-455, §1906, 90 Stat. 1834; Dec. 19, 1989, Pub. L. 101-239, §7622, 103 Stat. 2377; Nov. 5, 1990, Pub. L. 101-508, §1170, 104 Stat. 1388; Aug. 10, 1993, Pub. L. 103-66, §13261(c), 107 Stat. 539.)

26 U.S.C. § 1253

IX. MISCELLANEOUS

A. INTERNATIONAL

22 U.S.C. § 269f   **International Bureau of Intellectual Property; Authorization of appropriations**

Funds appropriated to the Secretary of State for "International Organizations and Conferences" shall be available for the payment by the United States of its proportionate share of the expenses of the International Bureau for the Protection of Industrial Property for any year after 1981 as determined under article 16(4) of the Paris Convention for the Protection of Industrial Property, as revised, except that in no event shall the payment for any year exceed 6 per centum of all expenses of the Bureau apportioned among countries for that year.

(July 12, 1960, Pub. L. 86-614, 74 Stat. 381; July 19, 1963, Pub. L. 88-69, 77 Stat. 82; Oct. 20, 1972, Pub. L. 92-511, 86 Stat. 918; Nov. 22, 1983, Pub. L. 98-164, §112, 97 Stat. 1019.)

19 U.S.C. § 2435   Commercial agreements

(a) *Presidential authority.*—Subject to the provisions of subsections (b) and (c) of this section, the President may authorize the entry into force of bilateral commercial agreements providing nondiscriminatory treatment to the products of countries heretofore denied such treatment whenever he determines that such agreements with such countries will promote the purposes of this Act [ch. 12—Trade Act of 1974] and are in the national interest.

(b) *Terms of agreements.*—Any such bilateral commercial agreement shall—

*   *   *

(4) if the other party to the bilateral agreement is not a party to the Paris convention for the Protection of Industrial Property, provide rights for United States nationals with respect to patents and trademarks in such country not less than the rights specified in such convention;

*   *   *

(Jan. 3, 1975, Pub. L. 93-618, §405, 88 Stat. 2061.)

*   *   *   *   *   *   *

19 U.S.C. § 2435

B. Bankruptcy

11 U.S.C. § 365   **Executory Contracts Licensing Rights to Intellectual Property**

*   *   *

(n) (1) If the trustee rejects an executory contract under which the debtor is a licensor of a right to intellectual property, the licensee under such contract may elect—

(A) to treat such contract as terminated by such rejection if such rejection by the trustee amounts to such a breach as would entitle the licensee to treat such contract as terminated by virtue of its own terms, applicable nonbankruptcy law, or an agreement made by the licensee with another entity; or

(B) to retain its rights (including a right to enforce any exclusivity provision of such contract, but excluding any other right under applicable nonbankruptcy law to specific performance of such contract) under such contract and under any agreement supplementary to such contract, to such intellectual property (including any embodiment of such intellectual property to the extent protected by applicable nonbankruptcy law), as such rights existed immediately before the case commenced, for—

(i) the duration of such contract; and

(ii) any period for which such contract may be extended by the licensee as of right under applicable nonbankruptcy law.

(2) If the licensee elects to retain its rights, as described in paragraph (1)(B) of this subsection, under such contract—

(A) the trustee shall allow the licensee to exercise such rights;

(B) the licensee shall make all royalty payments due under such contract for the duration of such contract and for any period described in paragraph (1)(B) of this subsection for which the licensee extends such contract; and

(C) the licensee shall be deemed to waive—

(i) any right of setoff it may have with respect to such contract under this title or applicable nonbankruptcy law; and

(ii) any claim allowable under section 503(b) of this title arising from the performance of such contract.

(3) If the licensee elects to retain its rights, as described in paragraph (1)(B) of this subsection, then on the written request of the licensee the trustee shall—

(A) to the extent provided in such contract, or any agreement supplementary to such contract, provide to the licensee any intellectual property (including such embodiment) held by the trustee; and

(B) not interfere with the rights of the licensee as provided in such contract, or any agreement supplementary to such contract, to such intellectual property (including such embodiment) including any right to obtain such intellectual property (or such embodiment) from another entity.

(4) Unless and until the trustee rejects such contract, on the written request of the licensee the trustee shall—

(A) to the extent provided in such contract or any agreement supplementary to such contract—

(i) perform such contract; or

(ii) provide to the licensee such intellectual property (including any embodiment of such intellectual property to the extent protected by applicable nonbankruptcy law) held by the trustee; and

(B) not interfere with the rights of the licensee as provided in such contract, or any agreement supplementary to such contract, to such intellectual property (including such embodiment), including any right to obtain such intellectual property (or such embodiment) from another entity.

* * *

(Oct. 18, 1988, Pub. L. 100-506, §1, 102 Stat. 2538.)

11 U.S.C. § 365

C. Assumption of Certain Contractual Obligations

28 U.S.C. § 4001   **Assumption of contractual obligations related to transfers of rights in motion pictures**

(a) Assumption of obligations- (1) In the case of a transfer of copyright ownership under United States law in a motion picture (as the terms "transfer of copyright ownership" and "motion picture" are defined in section 101 of title 17) that is produced subject to 1 or more collective bargaining agreements negotiated under the laws of the United States, if the transfer is executed on or after the effective date of this chapter and is not limited to public performance rights, the transfer instrument shall be deemed to incorporate the assumption agreements applicable to the copyright ownership being transferred that are required by the applicable collective bargaining agreement, and the transferee shall be subject to the obligations under each such assumption agreement to make residual payments and provide related notices, accruing after the effective date of the transfer and applicable to the exploitation of the rights transferred, and any remedies under each such assumption agreement for breach of those obligations, as those obligations and remedies are set forth in the applicable collective bargaining agreement, if—

(A) the transferee knows or has reason to know at the time of the transfer that such collective bargaining agreement was or will be applicable to the motion picture; or

(B) in the event of a court order confirming an arbitration award against the transferor under the collective bargaining agreement, the transferor does not have the financial ability to satisfy the award within 90 days after the order is issued.

(2) For purposes of paragraph (1)(A), "knows or has reason to know" means any of the following:

(A) Actual knowledge that the collective bargaining agreement was or will be applicable to the motion picture.

(B)(i) Constructive knowledge that the collective bargaining agreement was or will be applicable to the motion picture, arising from recordation of a document pertaining to copyright in the motion picture under section 205 of title 17 or from publication, at a site available to the public on-line that is operated by the relevant union, of information that identifies the motion picture as subject to a collective bargaining agreement with that union, if the site permits commercially reasonable verification of the date on which the information was available for access.

(ii) Clause (i) applies only if the transfer referred to in subsection (a)(1) occurs—

(I) after the motion picture is completed, or

(II) before the motion picture is completed and--

(aa) within 18 months before the filing of an application for copyright registration for the motion picture under section 408 of title 17, or

(bb) if no such application is filed, within 18 months before the first publication of the motion picture in the United States.

(C) Awareness of other facts and circumstances pertaining to a particular transfer from which it is apparent that the collective bargaining agreement was or will be applicable to the motion picture.

(b) Scope of exclusion of transfers of public performance rights- For purposes of this section, the exclusion under subsection (a) of transfers of copyright ownership in a motion picture that are limited to public performance rights includes transfers to a terrestrial broadcast station, cable system, or programmer to the extent that the station, system, or programmer is functioning as an exhibitor of the motion picture, either by exhibiting the motion picture on its own network, system, service, or station, or by initiating the transmission of an exhibition that is carried on another network, system, service, or station. When a terrestrial broadcast station, cable system, or programmer, or other transferee, is also functioning otherwise as a distributor or as a producer of the motion picture, the public performance exclusion does not affect any obligations imposed on the transferee to the extent that it is engaging in such functions.

28 U.S.C. § 4001

(c) *Exclusion for grants of security interests.*—Subsection (a) shall not apply to—

(1) a transfer of copyright ownership consisting solely of a mortgage, hypothecation, or other security interest; or

(2) a subsequent transfer of the copyright ownership secured by the security interest described in paragraph (1) by or under the authority of the secured party, including a transfer through the exercise of the secured party's rights or remedies as a secured party, or by a subsequent transferee.

The exclusion under this subsection shall not affect any rights or remedies under law or contract.

(d) *Deferral pending resolution of bona fide dispute.*—A transferee on which obligations are imposed under subsection (a) by virtue of paragraph (1) of that subsection may elect to defer performance of such obligations that are subject to a bona fide dispute between a union and a prior transferor until that dispute is resolved, except that such deferral shall not stay accrual of any union claims due under an applicable collective bargaining agreement.

(e) *Scope of obligations determined by private agreement.*—Nothing in this section shall expand or diminish the rights, obligations, or remedies of any person under the collective bargaining agreements or assumption agreements referred to in this section.

(f) *Failure to notify.*—If the transferor under subsection (a) fails to notify the transferee under subsection (a) of applicable collective bargaining obligations before the execution of the transfer instrument, and subsection (a) is made applicable to the transferee solely by virtue of subsection (a)(1)(B), the transferor shall be liable to the transferee for any damages suffered by the transferee as a result of the failure to notify.

(g) *Determination of disputes and claims.*—Any dispute concerning the application of subsections (a) through (f) shall be determined by an action in United States district court, and the court in its discretion may allow the recovery of full costs by or against any party and may also award a reasonable attorney's fee to the prevailing party as part of the costs.

28 U.S.C. § 4001

(h) *Study.*—The Comptroller General, in consultation with the Register of Copyrights, shall conduct a study of the conditions in the motion picture industry that gave rise to this section, and the impact of this section on the motion picture industry. The Comptroller General shall report the findings of the study to the Congress within 2 years after the effective date of this chapter.

(Oct. 28, 1998, Pub. L. 105-304, §406, 112 Stat. 2902.)

X. COPYRIGHT AND CRIMINAL LAW

A. NATIONAL STOLEN PROPERTY ACT

18 U.S.C. § 2314   **Transportation of stolen goods, securities, moneys, fraudulent State tax stamps, or articles used in counterfeiting**

Whoever transports, transmits, or transfers in interstate or foreign commerce any goods, wares, merchandise, securities or money, of the value of $5,000 or more, knowing the same to have been stolen, converted or taken by fraud; or

Whoever, having devised or intending to devise any scheme or artifice to defraud, or for obtaining money or property by means of false or fraudulent pretenses, representations, or promises, transports or causes to be transported, or induces any person or persons to travel in, or to be transported in interstate or foreign commerce in the execution or concealment of a scheme or artifice to defraud that person or those persons of money or property having a value of $5,000 or more; or

Whoever, with unlawful or fraudulent intent, transports in interstate or foreign commerce any falsely made, forged, altered, or counterfeited securities or tax stamps, knowing the same to have been falsely made, forged, altered, or counterfeited; or

Whoever, with unlawful or fraudulent intent, transports in interstate or foreign commerce any traveler's check bearing a forged countersignature; or

Whoever, with unlawful or fraudulent intent, transports in interstate or foreign commerce, any tool, implement, or thing used or fitted to be used in falsely making, forging, altering, or counterfeiting any security or tax stamps, or any part thereof—

Shall be fined not more than $10,000 or imprisoned not more than ten years, or both.

This section shall not apply to any falsely made, forged, altered, counterfeited or spurious representation of an obligation or other security of the United States, or of an obligation, bond, certificate, security, treasury note, bill, promise to pay or bank note issued by any foreign government. This section also shall not apply to any falsely made, forged, altered, counterfeited, or spurious representation of any bank note or bill issued by a bank or corporation of any foreign country which is intended by the laws or usage of such country to circulate as money.

(June 25, 1948, ch. 645, §1, 62 Stat. 806, May 24, 1949, ch. 139, §45, 63 Stat. 96; July 9, 1956, ch. 519, 70 Stat. 507; Oct. 4, 1961, Pub. L. 87-371, §2, 75 Stat. 802; Sept. 28, 1968, Pub. L. 90-535, 82 Stat. 885; Nov. 18, 1988, Pub. L. 100-690, §§7057, 7080, 102 Stat. 4402, 4406; Nov. 29, 1990, Pub. L. 101-647, §1208, 104 Stat. 4832.)

B. PIRACY AND COUNTERFEITING AMENDMENTS OF 1982

18 U.S.C. § 2318   **Trafficking in counterfeit labels for phonorecords, copies of computer programs or computer program documentation or packaging, and copies of motion pictures or other audio visual works, and trafficking in counterfeit computer program documentation or packaging**

(a) Whoever, in any of the circumstances described in subsection (c) of this section, knowingly traffics in a counterfeit label affixed or designed to be affixed to a phonorecord, or a copy of a computer program or documentation or packaging for a computer program, or a copy of a motion picture or other audiovisual work, and whoever, in any of the circumstances described in subsection (c) of this section, knowingly traffics in counterfeit documentation or packaging for a computer program, shall be fined not more than $250,000 or imprisoned for not more than five years, or both.

(b) As used in this section—

(1) the term "counterfeit label" means an identifying label or container that appears to be genuine, but is not;

(2) the term "traffic" means to transport, transfer or otherwise dispose of, to another, as consideration for anything of value or to make or obtain control of with intent to so transport, transfer or dispose of; and

(3) the terms "copy", "phonorecord", "motion picture", "computer program", and "audiovisual work" have, respectively, the meanings given those terms in section 101 (relating to definitions) of title 17.

(c) The circumstances referred to in subsection (a) of this section are—

(1) the offense is committed within the special maritime and territorial jurisdiction of the United States; or within the special aircraft jurisdiction of the United States (as defined in section 101 of the Federal Aviation Act of 1958);

(2) the mail or a facility of interstate or foreign commerce is used or intended to be used in the commission of the offense;

(3) the counterfeit label is affixed to or encloses, or is designed to be affixed to or enclose a copy of a copyrighted computer program or copyrighted documentation or packaging for a computer program, a copyrighted motion picture or other audiovisual work, or a phonorecord of a copyrighted sound recording; or

(4) the counterfeited documentation or packaging for a computer program is copyrighted.

(d) When any person is convicted of any violation of subsection (a), the court in its judgment of conviction shall in addition to the penalty therein prescribed, order the forfeiture and destruction or other disposition of all counterfeit labels and all articles to which counterfeit labels have been affixed or which were intended to have had such labels affixed.

(e) Except to the extent they are inconsistent with the provisions of this title, all provisions of section 509, title 17, United States Code, are applicable to violations of subsection (a).

(Oct. 9, 1962, Pub. L. 87-773, §1, 76 Stat. 775; Dec. 31, 1974, Pub. L. 93-573, §103, 88 Stat. 1873; Oct. 19, 1976, Pub. L. 94-553, §111, 90 Stat. 2600; May 24, 1982, Pub. L. 97-180, §2, 96 Stat. 91; Nov. 29, 1990, Pub. L. 101-647, §3567, 104 Stat. 4928; July 2, 1996, Pub. L. 104-153, §4, 110 Stat. 1386.)

18 U.S.C. § 2318

18 U.S.C. § 2319   Criminal infringement of a copyright

(a) Whoever violates section 506(a) (relating to criminal offenses) of title 17 shall be punished as provided in subsections (b) and (c) of this section and such penalties shall be in addition to any other provisions of title 17 or any other law.

(b) Any person who commits an offense under section 506(a)(1) of title 17—

(1) shall be imprisoned not more than 5 years, or fined in the amount set forth in this title, or both, if the offense consists of the reproduction or distribution, including by electronic means, during any 180-day period, of at least 10 copies or phonorecords, of 1 or more copyrighted works, which have a total retail value of more than $2,500;

(2) shall be imprisoned not more than 10 years, or fined in the amount set forth in this title, or both, if the offense is a second or subsequent offense under paragraph (1); and

(3) shall be imprisoned not more than 1 year, or fined in the amount set forth in this title, or both, in any other case.

(c) Any person who commits an offense under section 506(a)(2) of title 17, United States Code—

(1) shall be imprisoned not more than 3 years, or fined in the amount set forth in this title, or both, if the offense consists of the reproduction or distribution of 10 or more copies or phonorecords of 1 or more copyrighted works, which have a total retail value of $2,500 or more;

(2) shall be imprisoned not more than 6 years, or fined in the amount set forth in this title, or both, if the offense is a second or subsequent offense under paragraph (1); and

(3) shall be imprisoned not more than 1 year, or fined in the amount set forth in this title, or both, if the offense consists of the reproduction or distribution of 1 or more copies or phonorecords of 1 or more copyrighted works, which have a total retail value of more than $1,000.

(d) (1) During preparation of the presentence report pursuant to Rule 32(c) of the Federal Rules of Criminal Procedure, victims of the offense shall be permitted to submit, and the probation officer shall receive, a victim impact statement that identifies the victim of the offense and the extent and scope of the injury and loss suffered by the victim, including the estimated economic impact of the offense on that victim.

(2) Persons permitted to submit victim impact statements shall include—

(A) producers and sellers of legitimate works affected by conduct involved in the offense;

(B) holders of intellectual property rights in such works; and

(C) the legal representatives of such producers, sellers, and holders.

(e) As used in this section—

(1) the terms "phonorecord" and "copies" have, respectively, the meanings set forth in section 101 (relating to definitions) of title 17; and

(2) the terms "reproduction" and "distribution" refer to the exclusive rights of a copyright owner under clauses (1) and (3) respectively of section 106 (relating to exclusive rights in copyrighted works), as limited by sections 107 through 122, of title 17.

(May 24, 1982, Pub. L. 97-180, §3, 96 Stat. 92; Oct. 28, 1992, Pub. L. 102-561, §§1-2, 106 Stat. 4233; Nov. 13, 1997, Pub. L. 105-80, §12, 111 Stat. 1536; Dec. 16, 1997, Pub. L. 105-147, §2(d), 111 Stat. 2678; Nov. 2, 2002, Pub. L. 107-273, §13211, 116 Stat. 1910.)

18 U.S.C. § 2319A   Unauthorized fixation of and trafficking in sound recordings and music videos of live musical performances

(a) *Offense.*—Whoever, without the consent of the performer or performers involved, knowingly and for purposes of commercial advantage or private financial gain—

(1) fixes the sounds or sounds and images of a live musical performance in a copy or phonorecord, or reproduces copies or phonorecords of such a performance from an unauthorized fixation;

(2) transmits or otherwise communicates to the public the sounds or sounds and images of a live musical performance; or

(3) distributes or offers to distribute, sells or offers to sell, rents or offers to rent, or traffics in any copy or phonorecord fixed as de-

scribed in paragraph (1), regardless of whether the fixations occurred in the United States;

shall be imprisoned for not more than 5 years or fined in the amount set forth in this title, or both, or if the offense is a second or subsequent offense, shall be imprisoned for not more than 10 years or fined in the amount set forth in this title, or both.

(b) *Forfeiture and Destruction.*—When a person is convicted of a violation of subsection (a), the court shall order the forfeiture and destruction of any copies or phonorecords created in violation thereof, as well as any plates, molds, matrices, masters, tapes, and film negatives by means of which such copies or phonorecords may be made. The court may also, in its discretion, order the forfeiture and destruction of any other equipment by means of which such copies or phonorecords may be reproduced, taking into account the nature, scope, and proportionality of the use of the equipment in the offense.

(c) *Seizure and Forfeiture.*—If copies or phonorecords of sounds or sounds and images of a live musical performance are fixed outside of the United States without the consent of the performer or performers involved, such copies or phonorecords are subject to seizure and forfeiture in the United States in the same manner as property imported in violation of the customs laws. The Secretary of the Treasury shall, not later than 60 days after the date of the enactment of the Uruguay Round Agreements Act, issue regulations to carry out this subsection, including regulations by which any performer may, upon payment of a specified fee, be entitled to notification by the United States Customs Service of the importation of copies or phonorecords that appear to consist of unauthorized fixations of the sounds or sounds and images of a live musical performance.

(d) *Victim Impact Statement.*—(1) During preparation of the presentence report pursuant to Rule 32(c) of the Federal Rules of Criminal Procedure, victims of the offense shall be permitted to submit, and the probation officer shall receive, a victim impact statement that identifies the victim of the offense and the extent and scope of the injury and loss suffered by the victim, including the estimated economic impact of the offense on that victim.

18 U.S.C. § 2319A

(2) Persons permitted to submit victim impact statements shall include—

(A) producers and sellers of legitimate works affected by conduct involved in the offense;

(B) holders of intellectual property rights in such works; and

(C) the legal representatives of such producers, sellers, and holders.

(e) *Definitions.*—As used in this section—

(1) the terms "copy", "fixed", "musical work", "phonorecord", "reproduce", "sound recordings", and "transmit" mean those terms within the meaning of title 17; and

(2) the term "traffic in" means transport, transfer, or otherwise dispose of, to another, as consideration for anything of value, or make or obtain control of with intent to transport, transfer, or dispose of.

(f) *Applicability.*—This section shall apply to any Act or Acts that occur on or after the date of the enactment of the Uruguay Round Agreements Act.*

(Dec. 8, 1994, Pub. L. 103-465, §513, 108 Stat. 4974; Dec. 16, 1997, Pub. L. 105-147, §2(e), 111 Stat. 2679.)

C. TRADEMARK COUNTERFEITING ACT OF 1984

18 U.S.C. § 2320   Trafficking in counterfeit goods or services

(a) Whoever intentionally traffics or attempts to traffic in goods or services and knowingly uses a counterfeit mark on or in connection with such goods or services shall, if an individual, be fined not more than $2,000,000 or imprisoned not more than 10 years, or both, and, if a person other than an individual, be fined not more than $5,000,000. In the case of an offense by a person under this section that occurs after that person is convicted of another offense under this section, the person convicted, if an individual, shall be fined not more than $5,000,000 or

---

* *Ed. Note:* The date of enactment of the Uruguay Round Agreements Act was Dec. 8, 1994.

18 U.S.C. § 2320

imprisoned not more than 20 years, or both, and if other than an individual, shall be fined not more than $15,000,000.

(b) Upon a determination by a preponderance of the evidence that any articles in the possession of a defendant in a prosecution under this section bear counterfeit marks, the United States may obtain an order for the destruction of such articles.

(c) All defenses, affirmative defenses, and limitations on remedies that would be applicable in an action under the Lanham Act shall be applicable in a prosecution under this section. In a prosecution under this section, the defendant shall have the burden of proof, by a preponderance of the evidence, of any such affirmative defense.

(d) (1) During preparation of the presentence report pursuant to Rule 32(c) of the Federal Rules of Criminal Procedure, victims of the offense shall be permitted to submit, and the probation officer shall receive, a victim impact statement that identifies the victim of the offense and the extent and scope of the injury and loss suffered by the victim, including the estimated economic impact of the offense on that victim.

(2) Persons permitted to submit victim impact statements shall include—

   (A) producers and sellers of legitimate goods or services affected by conduct involved in the offense;

   (B) holders of intellectual property rights in such goods or services; and

   (C) the legal representatives of such producers, sellers, and holders.

(e) For the purposes of this section—

   (1) the term "counterfeit mark" means—

      (A) a spurious mark—

         (i) that is used in connection with trafficking in goods or services;

         (ii) that is identical with, or substantially indistinguishable from, a mark registered for those goods or services on the principal register in the United States Patent and Trademark

Office and in use, whether or not the defendant knew such mark was so registered; and

(iii) the use of which is likely to cause confusion, to cause mistake, or to deceive; or

(B) a spurious designation that is identical with, or substantially indistinguishable from, a designation as to which the remedies of the Lanham Act are made available by reason of section 220506 of title 36;

but such term does not include any mark or designation used in connection with goods or services of which the manufacturer or producer was, at the time of the manufacture or production in question, authorized to use the mark or designation for the type of goods or services so manufactured or produced, by the holder of the right to use such mark or designation;

(2) the term "traffic" means transport, transfer, or otherwise dispose of, to another, as consideration for anything of value, or make or obtain control of with intent so to transport, transfer, or dispose of; and

(3) the term "Lanham Act" means the Act entitled "An Act to provide for the registration and protection of trademarks used in commerce, to carry out the provisions of certain international conventions, and for other purposes", approved July 5, 1946 (15 U.S.C. 1051 et seq.).

(f) (1) Beginning with the first year after the date of enactment of this subsection, the Attorney General shall include in the report of the Attorney General to Congress on the business of the Department of Justice prepared pursuant to section 522 of title 28, an accounting, on a district by district basis, of the following with respect to all actions taken by the Department of Justice that involve trafficking in counterfeit labels for phonorecords, copies of computer programs or computer program documentation or packaging, copies of motion pictures or other audiovisual works (as defined in section 2318 of this title), criminal infringement of copyrights (as defined in section 2319 of this title), unauthorized fixation of and trafficking in sound recordings and music videos of live musical performances (as defined in section 2319A of this title), or trafficking in goods or services bearing counterfeit marks (as defined in section 2320 of this title):

(A) The number of open investigations.

18 U.S.C. § 2320

(B) The number of cases referred by the United States Customs Service.

(C) The number of cases referred by other agencies or sources.

(D) The number and outcome, including settlements, sentences, recoveries, and penalties, of all prosecutions brought under sections 2318, 2319, 2319A, and 2320 of this title.

(2) (A) The report under paragraph (1), with respect to criminal infringement of copyright, shall include the following:

(i) The number of infringement cases in these categories: audiovisual (videos and films); audio (sound recordings); literary works (books and musical compositions); computer programs; video games; and, others.

(ii) The number of online infringement cases.

(iii) The number and dollar amounts of fines assessed in specific categories of dollar amounts. These categories shall be: no fines ordered; fines under $500; fines from $500 to $1,000; fines from $1,000 to $5,000; fines from $5,000 to $10,000; and fines over $10,000.

(iv) The total amount of restitution ordered in all copyright infringement cases.

(B) In this paragraph, the term "online infringement cases" as used in paragraph (2) means those cases where the infringer—

(i) advertised or publicized the infringing work on the Internet; or

(ii) made the infringing work available on the Internet for download, reproduction, performance, or distribution by other persons.

(C) The information required under subparagraph (A) shall be submitted in the report required in fiscal year 2005 and thereafter.

(Oct. 12, 1984, Pub. L. 98-473, §1502, 98 Stat. 2178; Sept. 13, 1994, Pub. L. 103-322, §320104, 108 Stat. 2110; July 2, 1996, Pub. L. 104-153, §5, 110 Stat. 1387; Dec. 16, 1997, Pub. L. 105-147, §2(f), 111 Stat. 2679; August 12, 1998, Pub. L. 105-225, §4, 112 Stat. 1499; Nov. 3, 1998, Pub. L. 105-354, §2(b), 112 Stat. 3244; Nov. 2, 2002, Pub. L. 107-273, §205(e), 116 Stat. 1778; Feb. 8, 2002, Pub. L. 107-140, §1, 116 Stat. 12.)

18 U.S.C. § 2320

D. ECONOMIC ESPIONAGE ACT OF 1996

TITLE I—PROTECTION OF TRADE SECRETS

18 U.S.C. § 1831   Economic espionage

(a) *In general.*—Whoever, intending or knowing that the offense will benefit any foreign government, foreign instrumentality, or foreign agent, knowingly—

(1) steals, or without authorization appropriates, takes, carries away, or conceals, or by fraud, artifice, or deception obtains a trade secret;

(2) without authorization copies, duplicates, sketches, draws, photographs, downloads, uploads, alters, destroys, photocopies, replicates, transmits, delivers, sends, mails, communicates, or conveys a trade secret;

(3) receives, buys, or possesses a trade secret, knowing the same to have been stolen or appropriated, obtained, or converted without authorization;

(4) attempts to commit any offense described in any of paragraphs (1) through (3); or

(5) conspires with one or more other persons to commit any offense described in any of paragraphs (1) through (3), and one or more of such persons do any act to effect the object of the conspiracy,

shall, except as provided in subsection (b), be fined not more than $500,000 or imprisoned not more than 15 years, or both.

(b) *Organizations.*—Any organization that commits any offense described in subsection (a) shall be fined not more than $10,000,000.

18 U.S.C. § 1832   Theft of trade secrets

(a) Whoever, with intent to convert a trade secret, that is related to or included in a product that is produced for or placed in interstate or foreign commerce, to the economic benefit of anyone other than the owner thereof, and intending or knowing that the offense will, injure any owner of that trade secret, knowingly—

18 U.S.C. § 1832

(1) steals, or without authorization appropriates, takes, carries away, or conceals, or by fraud, artifice, or deception obtains such information;

(2) without authorization copies, duplicates, sketches, draws, photographs, downloads, uploads, alters, destroys, photocopies, replicates, transmits, delivers, sends, mails, communicates, or conveys such information;

(3) receives, buys, or possesses such information, knowing the same to have been stolen or appropriated, obtained, or converted without authorization;

(4) attempts to commit any offense described in paragraphs (1) through (3); or

(5) conspires with one or more other persons to commit any offense described in paragraphs (1) through (3), and one or more of such persons do any act to effect the object of the conspiracy,

shall, except as provided in subsection (b), be fined under this title or imprisoned not more than 10 years, or both.

(b) Any organization that commits any offense described in subsection (a) shall be fined not more than $5,000,000.

18 U.S.C. § 1833   Exceptions to prohibitions

This chapter does not prohibit—

(1) any otherwise lawful activity conducted by a governmental entity of the United States, a State, or a political subdivision of a State; or

(2) the reporting of a suspected violation of law to any governmental entity of the United States, a State, or a political subdivision of a State, if such entity has lawful authority with respect to that violation.

18 U.S.C. § 1834   Criminal forfeiture

(a) The court, in imposing sentence on a person for a violation of this chapter, shall order, in addition to any other sentence imposed, that the person forfeit to the United States—

(1) any property constituting, or derived from, any proceeds the person obtained, directly or indirectly, as the result of such violation; and

18 U.S.C. § 1833

(2) any of the person's property used, or intended to be used, in any manner or part, to commit or facilitate the commission of such violation, if the court in its discretion so determines, taking into consideration the nature, scope, and proportionality of the use of the property in the offense.

(b) Property subject to forfeiture under this section, any seizure and disposition thereof, and any administrative or judicial proceeding in relation thereto, shall be governed by section 413 of the Comprehensive Drug Abuse Prevention and Control Act of 1970 (21 U.S.C. 853), except for subsections (d) and (j) of such section, which shall not apply to forfeitures under this section.

18 U.S.C. § 1835   Orders to preserve confidentiality

In any prosecution or other proceeding under this chapter, the court shall enter such orders and take such other action as may be necessary and appropriate to preserve the confidentiality of trade secrets, consistent with the requirements of the Federal Rules of Criminal and Civil Procedure, the Federal Rules of Evidence, and all other applicable laws. An interlocutory appeal by the United States shall lie from a decision or order of a district court authorizing or directing the disclosure of any trade secret.

18 U.S.C. § 1836   Civil proceedings to enjoin violations

(a) The Attorney General may, in a civil action, obtain appropriate injunctive relief against any violation of this chapter.

(b) The district courts of the United States shall have exclusive original jurisdiction of civil actions under this section.

18 U.S.C. § 1837   Applicability to conduct outside the United States

This chapter also applies to conduct occurring outside the United States if—

(1) the offender is a natural person who is a citizen or permanent resident alien of the United States, or an organization organized under the laws of the United States or a State or political subdivision thereof; or

(2) an act in furtherance of the offense was committed in the United States.

18 U.S.C. § 1837

18 U.S.C. § 1838   Construction with other laws

This chapter shall not be construed to preempt or displace any other remedies, whether civil or criminal, provided by United States Federal, State, commonwealth, possession, or territory law for the misappropriation of a trade secret, or to affect the otherwise lawful disclosure of information by any Government employee under section 552 of title 5 (commonly known as the Freedom of Information Act).

18 U.S.C. § 1839   Definitions

As used in this chapter—

(1) the term "foreign instrumentality" means any agency, bureau, ministry, component, institution, association, or any legal, commercial, or business organization, corporation, firm, or entity that is substantially owned, controlled, sponsored, commanded, managed, or dominated by a foreign government;

(2) the term "foreign agent" means any officer, employee, proxy, servant, delegate, or representative of a foreign government;

(3) the term "trade secret" means all forms and types of financial, business, scientific, technical, economic, or engineering information, including patterns, plans, compilations, program devices, formulas, designs, prototypes, methods, techniques, processes, procedures, programs, or codes, whether tangible or intangible, and whether or how stored, compiled, or memorialized physically, electronically, graphically, photographically, or in writing if—

(A) the owner thereof has taken reasonable measures to keep such information secret; and

(B) the information derives independent economic value, actual or potential, from not being generally known to, and not being readily ascertainable through proper means by, the public; and

(4) the term "owner", with respect to a trade secret, means the person or entity in whom or in which rightful legal or equitable title to, or license in, the trade secret is reposed.

(Oct. 11, 1996, Pub. L. 104-294, §101, 110 Stat. 3488; Nov. 2, 2002, Pub. L. 107-273, §4002(e)(9), 116 Stat. 1810.)

Part 6

INDEX

INDEX

B

D

E

F

G

M

N

O

R

S

T

U

V

W